NATIONAL GEOGRAPHIC

TRAVELER

Canada

NATIONAL GEOGRAPHIC

TRAVELER
Canada

Michael Ivory

National Geographic
Washington, D.C.

Contents

How to use this guide 6–7 About the author 8
The regions 53–338 Travelwise 339–89
Index 390–97 Credits 398–99

History & culture 9
Canada today 10–17
Native peoples today 18–19
Land & landscape 20–25
Canadian history 26–39
Building Canada 40–45
The cultural scene 46–49
What to see & how to go
  about it 50–52

The Maritimes 53
Introduction & map 54–55
Feature: Acadie & after 62–63
Drive: Saint John River Valley
  64–65
Drive: Atlantic coast 75–77
Feature: Maritime heritage
  78–79
Drive: Cape Breton Island
  & the Cabot Trail 82–83

Newfoundland 85
Introduction & map 86–87
Feature: Fish & more fish
  92–93
Feature: Norsemen in
  Newfoundland 100–101

Quebec 103
Introduction & map 104–105
Feature: New France
  106–107
Walk: In Old Montreal
  110–111
Walk: Around Old Quebec
  138–39
Drive: Île d'Orléans & the
  Beaupré shore 142–43

Ontario 155
Introduction & map 156–57
Feature: Upper Canada
  158–59
Walk: Toronto 176–77
Feature: The Great Lakes
  178–79
Feature: Canadian painting
  & the Group of Seven
  186–87
Feature: Canadian wines
  194–95
Feature: Minerals & mining
  towns 204–205

The Prairies 211
Introduction & map 212–13
Feature: Populating the
  Prairies 214–15
Feature: The Hudson's Bay
  Company & the fur trade
  220–21
Feature: Louis Riel &
  rebellion 228–29
Feature: Calgary Stampede
  238–39

The Rockies 241
Introduction & map 242–43
Drive: Icefields Parkway
  252–55
Feature: Rock, ice, & water
  256–57
Feature: Routes through
  the Rockies 262–63

West Coast 271
Introduction & map 272–73
Feature: Super-natural British
  Columbia 274–75
Walk: Around Victoria
  292–93
The Inside Passage 299–301
Feature: First Nation peoples
  of western British
  Columbia 304–305
Drive: Hope to Kamloops
  308–309

The North 313
Introduction & map 314–17
Feature: Arctic animals
  318–19
Drive: The Alaska Highway
  320–22
Feature: The Gold Rush
  326–27
Feature: The Inuit people
  330–31
Feature: The Northwest
  Passage 334–35

Travelwise 339
Planning your trip 340
Before you go 340
How to get to Canada
  341–42
Practical advice 342–46
Emergencies 346–47
Hotels & restaurants
  by region 348–74
Shopping 375–79
Entertainment &
  activities 380–89

Index 390–97
Credits 398–99

Page 1: Totem, Museum of
Anthropology, Vancouver,
British Columbia
Pages 2–3: Canoeing on
Lake Louise, Alberta
Left: Polar bear, Churchill,
Manitoba

How to use this guide

See back flap for keys to text and map symbols

The *National Geographic Traveler* brings you the best of Canada in text, pictures, and maps. Divided into three main sections, the guide begins with an overview of history and culture. Following are eight regional chapters with sites selected by the author for their particular interest and treated in depth. Each chapter opens with its own contents list for easy reference.

The regions and sites within the regions are arranged geographically. Some regions are further divided into two or three smaller areas. A map introduces each region, highlighting the featured sites.

Walks and drives, all plotted on their own maps, suggest routes for discovering an area. Features and sidebars offer details on history, culture, or contemporary life. A More Places to Visit page rounds off the regional chapters.

The final section, Travelwise, lists essential information for the traveler, such as pre-trip planning, getting around, communications, money matters, and emergencies, plus a selection of hotels, restaurants, shops, and activities.

To the best of our knowledge, site information is accurate as of the press date.

National Historic Sites Many of the attractions in this guide are National Historic Sites. Due to space restrictions this has sometimes been abbreviated to NHS.

62

Color coding
Each region is color coded for easy reference. Find the region you want on the map on the front flap, and look for the color flash at the top of the pages of the relevant chapter. Information in **Travelwise** is also color coded to each region.

CN Tower
www.cntower.ca
✉ 301 Front St. W.
☎ 416/868-6937
🚇 Subway: Union,
then CN Skywalk
💲 $$$

Visitor information
Practical information is given in the side column by each major site (see key to symbols on back flap). The map reference gives the page number where the site is mapped, followed by the grid reference. Further details include the site's address, telephone number, days closed, entrance fee in a range from $ (under $4) to $$$$$ (over $25), and the nearest metro or subway stop for Montreal and Toronto sites. Visitor information for smaller sites is provided within the text.

TRAVELWISE

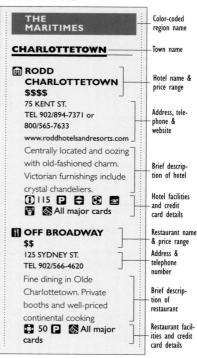

THE MARITIMES — Color-coded region name

CHARLOTTETOWN — Town name

🏨 **RODD CHARLOTTETOWN $$$$** — Hotel name & price range

75 KENT ST.
TEL 902/894-7371 or
800/565-7633
www.roddhotelsandresorts.com — Address, telephone & website

Centrally located and oozing with old-fashioned charm. Victorian furnishings include crystal chandeliers. — Brief description of hotel

🛏 115 🅿 🚻 💲 ⊠
📺 🚭 All major cards — Hotel facilities and credit card details

🍴 **OFF BROADWAY $$** — Restaurant name & price range

125 SYDNEY ST.
TEL 902/566-4620 — Address & telephone number

Fine dining in Olde Charlottetown. Private booths and well-priced continental cooking — Brief description of restaurant

🍽 50 🅿 🚭 All major cards — Restaurant facilities and credit card details

Hotel & restaurant prices
An explanation of the price ranges used in entries is given in the Hotels & Restaurants section beginning on p. 348.

REGIONAL MAPS

- A locator map accompanies each regional map and shows the location of that region in the country.
- Adjacent regions are shown, with page references.

WALKING TOURS

- An information box gives the starting and ending points, time and length of walk, and places not to miss along the route.
- Where two walks are marked on the map, the second route is shown in orange.

DRIVING TOURS

- An information box provides details including starting and finishing points, places not to miss along the route, time and length of drive, and tips on the terrain.

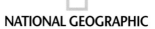

NATIONAL GEOGRAPHIC

TRAVELER
Canada

About the authors

After studying modern languages at Oxford University, Michael Ivory qualified as a landscape architect and town planner. A former Canadian resident, Ivory is now based in the United Kingdom and currently works as a freelance lecturer and travel writer. His many books have included guides to Australia, the Czech Republic, and Hungary. He is the author of *National Geographic Traveler: Germany.*

With contributions by:
Richard Sale, Arctic ecology specialist and travel writer
Amy Pataki, Travelwise compiler
Fiona Malins, journalist, travel writer, and specialist tour guide; 2nd edition update
Sean Connolly, travel writer and editor

History & culture

Canada today 10–17
Native peoples today 18–19
Land & landscape 20–25
Canadian history 26–39
Building Canada 40–45
The cultural scene 46–49
What to see & how to go
about it 50–52

**Maple leaf clipped
into a Mountie's horse**

Canada today

ASK MOST PEOPLE TO THINK OF CANADA AND A STRING OF FAMILIAR images appears: the peaks and ice fields of the Rockies, the vast expanse of the Prairies, endless forests of dark conifers, the austere and icy North … a world of untouched nature, a wilderness of almost infinite extent. Then there is another side, almost cozy by contrast, which might include the silhouette of Québec City on its rock above the broad St. Lawrence, or the Gothic towers of Ottawa's Parliament Hill guarded by smiling Mounties.

Like most clichés, these images are true, and you could spend your time in Canada confirming them. A ten-day Highlights of Canada tour could whisk you across the country from one three-star sight to another, starting perhaps with a whale-watching trip off the Newfoundland coast, going on to where Anne of Green Gables lived on Prince Edward Island, to Old Montréal, Niagara Falls, Banff National Park, and ending up with afternoon tea in Victoria's Empress Hotel. What a marathon! What marvelous pictures you could take to show family and friends! You would have enjoyed contact with wildlife, dipped into childhood memories, visited a fascinating city, marveled at a great natural wonder, had a taste of the wilderness, and rounded off the trip in Edwardian comfort.

But most—if not all—of these ingredients of a memorable journey could be enjoyed in Canada without having to travel 3,000 miles or more. Every region of the country has something of this rich mixture. Far apart from one another, provincial capitals and other cities have developed strong identities of their own. Each is proud of its history, which in the east may go back four centuries, and presents it with verve and flair in carefully restored heritage buildings and in museums that include some of the world's finest works of art.

The Frenchness of Montréal and Québec gives them a special savor, but all Canadian cities have become more vibrant in recent years, in part because of the multicultural transformation many of them have undergone. "Toronto the Good" has metamorphosed into something far more exciting, a world city of enormous ethnic variety and endless fascination.

Each city is within easy reach of countryside that may have been lived in for hundreds of years, like rural Québec, which still breathes the atmosphere of New France. There is a strong sense of the past in other rural areas too, in the outports of Newfoundland, the fishing villages of the Maritimes, and the Loyalist towns of Ontario. Equally compelling are places settled almost within living memory, like Ukrainian villages of the Prairies or mining towns in British Columbia.

Wilderness or the ocean is near at hand, too. Halifax is backed by vast forests and looks out across its Atlantic harbor, one of the finest in the world. Québec, Montréal, Ottawa, Toronto…all are within a short distance of the forests, lakes, and uplands of the Canadian Shield. The Rockies can be seen from Calgary, while incomparable Vancouver is blessed by both sea and mountains.

Areas within easy reach of cities are understandably more popular. Farther afield, you will find places shared only with others who have made the same effort to escape as you. It could be aboard ship among the icebergs off the Labrador coast, on the tundra of polar bear country around Hudson Bay, at a deserted Haida village in the far-off Queen Charlotte Islands, or at the very end of the highway at Yellowknife on the northern shore of Great Slave Lake.

CANADIANS

What is a real Canadian? The question troubles many citizens of this prosperous and decent-minded country, ranked high, even top in most surveys of people's preferences of where they would like to live in the world. A glance along the shelves of any big bookstore in Canada will reveal a clutch of titles attempting an answer, usually with the word

Spectacular views abound in Canada's Rockies, such as this one over Moraine Lake in Banff National Park.

"identity" featuring prominently.

Canada's original inhabitants were, of course, the Inuit and the several hundred thousand members of the First Nations, but the first Canadians as such were the "Canadiens"—the French-speaking subjects of the King of France who settled in the St. Lawrence Valley in the 17th and 18th centuries. Abandoned by France after 1763, they then shared their name with their new, English-speaking fellow citizens—the English, Irish, Scots, and Welsh from across the Atlantic, or Loyalists from the United States. In the 20th century, "Canadien" has given way to "Québécois" as French speakers in Québec (or francophones, to use another new term) have felt the need to affirm their own particular identity. Alongside English speakers (anglophones), French speakers form one of the country's founding nations. In the province of Québec they are the majority of the population, but there are important French-speaking minorities in other provinces, particularly Manitoba (around 50,000, about five percent of the population), New Brunswick (around 240,000, about 32 percent), and Ontario (more than 550,000, about five percent).

Canadian "mosaic"

From the early 19th century until quite recently, people of British or Irish descent formed the majority of the country's population, and for many years Canada had a distinctly "British" identity, the weakening of which was symbolized by the replacement of the Union flag with the maple leaf in 1965. Without even thinking about it, nearly all immigrants to Canada adopted English as their language and the key to opportunity in North America as a whole. These newcomers came from all over the world, but the most important sources of new Canadians were Germany, the Ukraine, Italy, the Netherlands, and Poland. More recently there has been an upsurge in immigrants from Asia, the Indian subcontinent, South and Central America, and the Caribbean. Canada is officially a multicultural country; the word "mosaic" appeared early in the 20th century to describe a pattern of population in which newcomers were not thrown into a "melting pot" but maintained many of the traditions of their countries of origin. This is most obvious in the Prairie Provinces, which were settled from the outset by cohesive ethnic communities, particularly from the Ukraine, and in Toronto, with its distinctive ethnic "villages" and public services in an extraordinary array of languages.

At the federal level, Canada is officially a bilingual country, committed to serving its citizens in either English or French across the country and even outside it. Thus your phone call to a Canadian embassy will be answered by a friendly *bonjour* as well as "hello," and the ranger in the Rockies will have a badge showing "Parc Banff." Among the provinces, New Brunswick is bilingual, but Québec, despite its large anglophone population, is officially monolingual. For many French-speaking Québécois, this is a vital question of identity. They fear that failure to assert the primacy of French would eventually result in its dilution and the loss of the francophone culture of 6 million people isolated among the nearly 300 million English-speaking North Americans.

GIANT TO THE SOUTH

But what about the distinctive culture of English-speaking Canadians? Far from being isolated, many such Canadians feel themselves to be very much, perhaps too much, involved with what goes on south of the 49th parallel. American culture is everywhere, in books, in magazines, on radio, and on TV. Every agreement on trade has increased American participation in the Canadian economy. American vacation destinations draw millions of Canadians southward every year, most famously the "snowbirds" who migrate to Florida every winter. American job opportunities and higher salaries exert a similar pull on the career-minded. And American speech patterns exercise an increasing influence on the way Canadians express themselves. Some Canadians feel closer to their near neighbors just across the border than to their fellow citizens in provinces thousands of miles away.

That Canadians were not Americans once seemed guaranteed by the British connection,

A walk through the Galleria of Toronto's BCE Place is a must for all modern architecture enthusiasts.

but as ties with the United Kingdom weakened, this no longer applied. Nevertheless, Canada has so far not followed the example of Australia in moving toward republicanism, and the image of the British monarch still appears on the coinage. Canadians like to think of themselves as good partners of the United States, but take great care to point out

Three occupants of the village of Povungnituk in the northern part of Québec.

the ways in which the two countries' views of the world differ. Early recognition of communism in Cuba and China is a case in point, a detached attitude to the United States predicament in Vietnam another—between 1965 and 1974 as many as 125,000 young Americans found sanctuary from the draft in Canada. Canadian forces fought in Korea and in the Persian Gulf, and were stationed for many years in Germany, but otherwise their service abroad has been as United Nations peacekeepers. The country has enjoyed an enviable international reputation for mediation and compromise and for support of the United Nations generally. Way down the international league in terms of wealth and population, the country makes the fourth largest contribution to the UN budget.

Canadian compromises

The ability to make creative compromises is perhaps one of the qualities that characterize the Canadian way of doing things. The Confederation of 1867 was essentially a compromise between the potentially conflicting interests of the provinces that it united, and over recent years much effort has gone into formulating a resolution that would keep Québec in Canada. Canadians are more ready to mock themselves than most, and this desire for moderation has not escaped the attention of humorists:

> Question: Why did the Canadian cross the road?
> Answer: To get to the middle.

GOVERNMENT & POLITICS

Canada's ten provinces and three territories are part of a federation, a parliamentary democracy that is a member of the British Commonwealth and whose head of state is the British monarch. The monarch's functions, almost entirely ceremonial, are carried out by a governor-general, appointed by the monarch but chosen by the prime minister and cabinet. Legislative power rests with the lower chamber of parliament, the Commons, with 308 elected M.P.s (members of parliament) representing ridings (constituencies) across the country. The timing of elections is the responsibility of the prime minister, but the maximum term between elections is five years. The upper chamber of parliament is the Senate, with 105 members appointed by the governor-general on the advice of the prime minister. The Senate's right to block legislation is little used in practice, its main role being to give bills a second hearing and clarify their content. Parliament sits in the handsome Gothic Revival buildings in Ottawa, chosen as capital in 1867.

Political roots

Political parties are organized on both provincial and national levels. Ever since Confederation in 1867, the balance of power in Ottawa has swung between the Conservatives and the Liberals. Both parties are centrist in nature; the Conservatives traditionally incline toward supporting Canadian businesses, the Liberals the rights of the individual. Both parties draw support from across the nation. The New Democratic Party also operates on the national level. A Socialist International member, it represents the interests of organized labor and is social-democrat in character. A more recent player on the national scene is the Green Party, which puts care for the environment front and center in its program. Other smaller parties represent more regional interests. Found solely in the province of Québec, for example, is the Bloc Québécois, which works for Québec independence.

In 2006, feelings of alienation in Western Canada and outrage in Québec over the gross misuse of public funds by the ruling Liberals headed by Prime Minister Paul Martin—the so-called "Sponsorship Scandal"—led to the general election and installation of a Conservative government led by an Albertan, Stephen Harper, with rather surprisingly, strong representation in Québec.

Provincial matters

In the provinces, political parties may or may not have a strong link with their counterparts at the federal level, and it is not uncommon for voters to support one party in provincial elections and another in Ottawa. Leading politicians have been known to switch their allegiance, too. In the mid-1990s, Québec's separatist party, the Parti Québécois, had as its leader Lucien Bouchard, a former member of the Progressive Conservative Party. The chief opponents of separatism in Québec are the provincial Liberals. In 2003, they were elected to power with, as their leader, Jean Charest, former chief of the federal Conservatives.

Confronting Canada's concerns

Canada faces most of the problems that confront any Western democracy. The financing of a large public sector is a constant concern and in Ontario, for example, this issue has led to confrontation between a heavily unionized teaching profession and a provincial government intent on reducing public expenditures. The country is proud of having established universal health care, but the performance of the system does not always measure up to expectations. Increasing crime is a worry, but in comparison with the United States, levels of criminal activity are very low.

Many issues in Canadian politics concern the relationship between national and provincial interests, inevitably so in such a vast country where the individual provinces differ so much from one another. The position of Québec within the federation is the greatest of these issues, but by no means the only one. With their resource-based industrial structure,

Young and old Québecers came out to help campaign for the Parti Québécois in the referendum of 1995.

the western provinces in particular often feel that their priorities are taken little notice of by a federal government far away in central Canada with its much greater population and its dynamic, diversified economy. Also, the fundamental reasons for the disastrous decline of the vital Atlantic cod fishery may never be discovered, but many in the Maritimes and Newfoundland point to the federal Department of Fisheries and Oceans as the chief culprit.

The attempts made in the 1980s and 90s to renew the fabric of the Canadian state have so far come to nothing, but have given a new twist to the perennial debate about the nature of Canadian identity. High-profile Prime Minister Pierre Elliott Trudeau put all his passion into promoting an all-Canadian

identity encompassing the two founding nations (French and British), as well as native peoples and immigrants from whatever background. The keystone of his policy was the repatriation of the Constitution; in 1982 the British North America Act of 1867 was replaced by a Constitution Act and by a Canadian Charter of Rights and Freedoms. But Québec failed to endorse the new arrangements. After several years of debate, Prime Minister Brian Mulroney and all ten

British influence is strong even in the all-French Royal 22nd Regiment, seen here in ceremonial dress at the Québec Citadelle.

provincial premiers assembled in 1987 at Meech Lake just outside Ottawa and managed to agree on a form of words that, among other things, recognized Québec's special status as a "distinct society." When some of the provinces had second thoughts, the agreement faltered. It was finally killed in

1990 by the "No" of a Cree member of the Manitoba Parliament. Undaunted, Mulroney tried again. In 1992 a deal was signed at Prince Edward Island's Charlottetown, the place where the Confederation had been agreed to in 1867. As well as satisfying the ten provincial premiers, it pleased the leaders of the territories, the First Nations, the Inuit, and the Métis. The population at large, however, was not persuaded: In the referendum that followed, the Charlottetown Accord was rejected by the electorate.

A massive upsurge of Québec separatist feeling followed the failure of the Charlottetown agreement, but when in 1995 the Parti Québécois government put the question of secession to Québec voters in another referendum, they were defeated, albeit by the narrowest of margins. These events of the 1990s seem to show that, despite their differences, Canadians from coast to coast see no real alternative to staying together. ■

Native peoples today

CANADA'S ORIGINAL INHABITANTS BELONG TO MANY DIFFERENT GROUPS who followed different ways of life, the vestiges of which remain to this day.

The people of the Arctic are perhaps the most distinctive of Canada's native people. Until recently, they were referred to as Eskimos, although the term used today is Inuit (singular, Inuk), which in their own language of Inuktitut means simply "the people." Inuit depended traditionally on the resources of the sea, especially sea mammals such as whale, seal, and walrus, all of which they exploited using advanced hunting techniques. They traveled over vast areas of tundra to maximize their use of these resources. The big change in their lives came during World War II and the Cold War, when the Arctic took on new strategic significance, and the building of airfields and radar sites across the area brought to the Inuit the full impact of outside culture, including wage employment.

Today, almost all Inuit live in settlements, many of which had their origins either in wartime or postwar military sites, or in the fur-trading posts or missions that preceded them. Although many Inuit still enjoy being on the land and will go on extended hunting, sealing, or fishing trips, their home base is now in the villages. Thanks to satellites, television, telephone service, and other forms of telecommunications, they enjoy most of the amenities of modern life, even though their community may be thousands of miles from the commer-

cial hubs. Larger towns are served by frequent jet service to outside centers. To a visitor, an Arctic Canadian community presents an odd mixture of the traditional and the modern, perhaps best exemplified by an Inuk grand-mother dressed in traditional clothes hurtling across the snow on her snowmobile.

The First Nations

Canada's other original inhabitants, the First Nations, as they are now called, consist of the people who used to be called Indians and are still, to their growing dissatisfaction, adminis-tered under the Federal Indian Act. Although they belong to many different nations, each with its own language and culture, they have now found common cause in reasserting their

This caribou-clad Inuk hunter and his dog sled present a classic image of the frozen Canadian north.

identity. Political action has often focused on wresting control of their educational systems from the federal government and establishing locally controlled schools that reflect their own languages and cultures. Reserves that were first established to segregate First Nations peoples from nonnatives have now become the basis for extensive land claims. For many First Nations people, political action is seen as the best way of redressing some of the injus-tices of the past, especially those created by a system of residential schools that forcibly removed children from what was then seen as the corrupting influence of their parents and their home community.

Constitutional issues

The Assembly of First Nations, with its elected Grand Chief, seeks to speak for all First Nations people in Canada, and its views are increasingly heard in constitutional debate. The high rates of alcoholism and substance abuse, of diseases such as diabetes, and of violence, which prevail on many of Canada's nearly 3,000 reserves, and which many First Nations spokespeople attribute directly to the abuses of the residential school system, have often acted as the lightning rod for political action by the assembly and other groups. Nevertheless, many First Nations communities can also show a record of gradual success, with many more young people than in the past going on to secondary school and to universities.

Although First Nations people often speak with a common voice on political matters, they come from widely differing cultures, many of them based on the resources of the land they occupied. These cultures are reflected in the more than 50 languages they speak and in the ways they express them-selves through the arts. Inuit soapstone carv-ings have developed to the point where fine pieces by well-known carvers command very high prices in the best galleries. From the totem poles, wood carvings, and jewelry of the West Coast Salish, Haida, Kwakiutl, and other nations, to the basketwork and extraor-dinary prints of the East Coast Mi'kmaq, First Nations communities are using art not only as a means of expressing their distinctive cultures, but as an important base for com-mercial development. ■

Land & landscape

COMPLAINING ABOUT THE SHEER SIZE OF THE YOUNG COUNTRY, PRIME Minister W. L. Mackenzie King once remarked, "If some countries have too much history, we have too much geography." Covering 3.9 million square miles, Canada is second only to Russia in area. Point Pelee on Lake Erie shares the same latitude as central Italy, while the country's northernmost point is a mere 500 miles from the North Pole. A journey from Cape Spear in the east to the Alaskan border in the west covers about 3,500 miles and crosses six time zones. Such vastness encompasses great extremes of climate, landscape, and human settlement. Canadian winters are famous, but proximity to the ocean or to the Great Lakes tempers their harshness, as well as making summers cooler. The barren land above the Arctic Circle is virtually uninhabited, the Canadian Shield covering almost half the country hardly less so. The overwhelming majority of the population of about 32 million lives along the U.S. border, most of them in towns and cities. The people of the Maritimes are closer to Europe than to their fellow-countrymen in British Columbia, and most Canadians have more neighbors along the U.S. border than in the adjoining provinces to the east or west.

CANADIAN SHIELD

This two-million-square-mile mass of ancient rock planed by glaciers is the dominant feature on the map of Canada, sweeping in a great arc around Hudson Bay from far northwest to far northeast. In the south it fringes the Great Lakes and extends to city suburbs in Ontario and Québec. Between southern Ontario and Manitoba it forms a formidable thousand-mile-wide barrier that had to be overcome before these long-settled eastern provinces could be united with the newer Canada of the west.

The rocks of the shield are among the most ancient on earth, mainly granites and gneisses formed more than two billion years ago. During the ice ages glaciers advanced and retreated over the area, scraping the surface down to its present level, hollowing out the countless lakes, and removing most of the existing soil. Along its southern rim, the shield forms uplands like the Laurentian Mountains, which reach a maximum height of 3,175 feet at Mont Tremblant. It then slopes gradually down to sea level along the shore of Hudson Bay, though in the east the Torngat range overlooks the Labrador Sea from a height of more than 5,000 feet. North of the timberline stretches the tundra, a bleak landscape of dwarf birch and willow, mosses, lichens, and a burst of small flowering plants in the short summer. This merges southward with the boreal forest, or taiga, with conifers like black-and-white spruce and jack pine together with willow and poplar, and extensive areas of muskeg, basins filled with peat moss.

Clay soils exist in a few areas on the southern fringe of the shield, but attempts to bring them into agricultural use have met with little success. Wildlife was the great resource of the shield, supporting the native population and supplying the fur trade with much of its material. Since the end of the 19th century, the area's mineral wealth has sustained both temporary and permanent settlements, and, more recently, some of its vast potential for hydroelectric power has been tapped, notably by the giant Hydro-Québec corporation. Logging has also occurred over much of the area, and the forestry industry is a backbone of the economy in many provinces.

APPALACHIAN REGION

The northernmost parts of the Appalachian range reach into eastern Québec and the Maritimes, then appear again in Newfoundland. They consist of complex folded mountains, eroded by the ice that once covered them, and smaller areas of lowland along river valleys or coastlines.

A lone rower savors the spectacular setting of Dougans Lake in British Columbia.

The mountains and uplands are generally rounded, reaching heights of more than 4,000 feet in the Gaspé Peninsula, and more than 2,500 feet in Newfoundland, but only 1,750 feet on Cape Breton Island.

The central feature of the region is the Gulf of St. Lawrence, an inland sea with outlets via the Cabot Strait between Cape Breton Island and Newfoundland, and through the Strait of Belle Isle separating Newfoundland from the Labrador mainland. The scattered human settlements of the region used to be linked to each other and to the outside world by the sea rather than by land routes. It was the sea's produce that until recently provided a living for many of its inhabitants. The extension of the continental shelf called the Grand Banks was one of the world's richest fishing grounds (see pp. 92–93). The cod may have disappeared, but the sea, with its mixing of cold and warm currents and its highly indented coastline, still forms a rich habitat for marine life, including several species of whale. Here, offshore oil has become an important resource.

Inland, most of the area is covered with mixed woodlands, once ruthlessly exploited for timber used in the shipyards that existed all along the coast.

ATLANTIC REGION

This area overlaps the Appalachian region in parts, but is largely defined by Nova Scotia, New Brunswick, and Prince Edward Island. Moderately fertile soils support agriculture in a number of areas including the Saint John River Valley and Sussex country in New Brunswick; on Prince Edward Island where a famous crop of potatoes is produced; and in the Annapolis Valley of Nova Scotia, equally well known for its orchards. Halifax is the largest city, but there is no regional metropolis; Moncton, Saint John, and Fredericton all have their own hinterland in New Brunswick, while St. John's, despite its location on the far eastern coast of Newfoundland, is the island's undisputed capital.

GREAT LAKES

More than half the population of Canada lives in the relatively benign environment along the shores of the Great Lakes and in the St. Lawrence Valley. Between Detroit's neighbor,

Primarily grown in the prairie provinces, canola is one of Canada's most important agricultural crops.

Windsor, and Québec City, about 700 miles to the northeast, the chain of urban settlements includes Canada's two greatest metropolitan cities, Toronto and Montréal.

Much of the country's earliest human history was played out in this region, leaving a visible heritage in the form of fine old towns like Ontario's Niagara-on-the-Lake and mature rural landscapes like Québec's Richelieu Valley.

Although winters are cold and summers hot, the climate is less extreme than in most of the rest of the country, allowing a wide range

of crops to be grown. The vast quantities of water held in the Great Lakes have a balancing effect on local climates, tempering both winter cold and summer heat. Many areas have fertile soils that have formed on the sedimentary rocks overlying the far older rocks of the Canadian Shield. The diversity of crops grown even includes grapes, most importantly in the Niagara area but also in other parts of Ontario and even in southern Québec. In places such as Point Pelee on Lake Erie, luxuriant remnants of natural woodland represent the northernmost extension of the Carolinian forest with southern species like tulip trees and hackberries. Elsewhere, although 90 percent of the mixed forest was cleared by pioneer farmers or logged by lumbermen, enough remains

to justify the use of the maple leaf for the national flag, delight visitors with the spectacle of autumn leaves, and provide abundant sap for maple syrup.

INTERIOR PLAINS

The interior plains are the extension of the lowlands that run northward from the Rio Grande through the United States. In Canada they stretch more than 1,500 miles between the shield and the Rocky Mountains to where the Mackenzie River discharges through its delta into the Arctic Ocean. The plains include the southern parts of Manitoba and Saskatchewan, most of Alberta and the southwestern part of the Northwest Territories. Along the boundary with the shield are great

Untracked Rockies wilderness is known as "shin tangle"—a phrase that contributed to the naming of Tangle Falls.

bodies of water such as Lake Winnipeg, Lake Athabasca, and Great Slave Lake. Boreal forest and tundra dominate the north, but in the south the fertile soils that once supported an ocean of grassland are now farmed, producing the bulk of the country's grain. Along with the prairie grasses, the countless bison that once roamed the plains have been virtually exterminated.

Cattle ranching as well as grain brought settlers to the plains, but it is the oil and gas resources beneath the surface that have determined the recent economic pace of the prairie provinces, particularly Alberta, where Edmonton and Calgary have outpaced Winnipeg, Manitoba, the original capital of the region.

CANADIAN CORDILLERA

Part of the 9,000-mile chain of mountains stretching from the Tierra del Fuego to Alaska, a series of ranges and plateaus 500 miles across make up all the Yukon and most of British Columbia, while the crest of the Rocky Mountains forms much of the border with Alberta. Here are the highest peaks and most dramatic landscapes in Canada, a challenge to explorers until late in the country's history. The highest point in the Canadian Rockies is Mount Robson (12,972 feet). Several peaks in the Yukon's Mackenzie Mountains exceed 8,000 feet, but the highest mountain in Canada and the second highest in all of North America is Mount Logan (19,550 feet) in the St. Elias Mountains of the southwest Yukon.

The mountains were formed in a complex folding process that began some 70 million years ago, but their present outline is due to the action of ice, and glaciers are still at work today, as in the great Columbia Icefield. The alpine climate yields some of the country's highest snowfall, up to 370 inches a year in Glacier National Park. By contrast, the area around the Strait of Georgia on the Pacific coast has an almost balmy local climate, with frequent rain but relatively rare frosts.

The wildlife that brought fur traders into the region is still abundant in many places. Brown and grizzly bears still inhabit the alpine forests of the east and the cool rain forest of the west, but the once plentiful salmon have experienced a severe decline in numbers. Logging remains a vitally important industry, though its operations are often contested by environmentalists.

Settlement is thinly distributed over the cordillera, mainly in old mining towns or in the fertile valleys along the U.S. border, where warm summers favor fruit and wine production. The majority of the region's population lives in an emerging, outward-looking metropolitan region based on the Strait of Georgia with Vancouver as its focal point. ∎

Canadian history

THE VAST LAND THAT LAY UNKNOWINGLY IN WAIT FOR EUROPEAN subjugation was already a complex cultural mosaic, the home of peoples as varied and distinctive as those of the continent on the far shore of the eastern Atlantic. Population densities were low; there may have been a total of some 300,000 inhabitants just before the period of European contact, but all parts of the country were occupied by people extremely well adapted to the very diverse resources of the different regions.

FIRST PEOPLES

Perhaps up to 20,000 years ago, when sea levels were much lower than today, the first human beings to live in Canada were Siberian hunters who had pursued their prey of giant bison, wooly mammoth, and hairy rhino over the Bering Strait. As they and their descendants spread throughout North and South America, they were followed by successive waves of immigrants. Among them, about 5,000 years ago, were the first Inuit people, identified as the Dorset. They were displaced by people of the Thule culture, the direct ancestors of today's Inuit. Living between the Arctic shore and the northern limit of the boreal forest, they were hunters, following the seasonal movements of the creatures (whales, seals, fish, caribou) on which they depended not only for food, but for clothing and every kind of implement, including expertly fashioned

bone harpoons. In drier areas like southern Labrador, a winter shelter might have consisted of a shallow pit and wood-frame structure with a sod roof. But the archetypal dwelling was the snowhouse or igloo, whose geometrical perfection caused one European explorer to compare it with a "Grecian temple…both are triumphs of art, inimitable in their kinds."

Woodland tribes

Within the forests to the south lived other hunters, speaking dialects of the Athapaskan and Algonquian languages, members of what have come to be called the Woodland tribes. Their mobility depended on use of that supremely functional artifact, the birchbark canoe, highly maneuverable and light enough

Paul Kane's 19th-century painting depicts First Nations' life on Lake Huron.

to carry over long portages. Where cultivable soil occurred and the climate was milder, as in the St. Lawrence Valley, the Iroquois lived a more settled life, building villages and long-houses, and growing corn, beans, and squash. Sophisticated political structures were able to develop, of which the most famous was the League of the Iroquois—comprising the Seneca, Cayuga, Oneida, Onondaga, and Mohawk. This high degree of organization enabled the Iroquois to trade with their Algonquian neighbors to the north, exchanging surplus corn for furs and game. It also seems to have encouraged their warlike tendencies. They were implacable foes of the Huron, whose society they destroyed, and came into constant conflict with the French.

People of the plains

In the endless grasslands between the Canadian Shield and the Rocky Mountains lived the Plains tribes—Cree, Assiniboine, Blackfoot, and others—often in mutual hostility despite their shared way of life. Much more than any other animal, the favorite quarry of these hunters was the bison, which roamed the plains in huge herds and which supplied them with meat from its flesh, tools from its bones, garments and tepee coverings from its hide, glue from its hooves, and even kettles from its paunch. Bison were slaughtered in large numbers, in winter by being decoyed into pounds, in summer by being driven over the cliffs known as buffalo jumps, some of which (like Alberta's famous Head-Smashed-In) were in use for thousands of years. Women were responsible for the butchering and for making pemmican, a concentrated and highly nutritious mixture of powdered meat and grease, often flavored with Saskatoon berries.

Pacific coast

In what is now British Columbia, West Coast natives such as the Gitksan and Haida did not need to go to such lengths to feed themselves. The abundance of fish, fur, and game and a benign climate created a high standard of material life. Cedar trees supplied the planks with which substantial houses were built as well as the material for superb canoes, some of them up to 70 feet long and capable of ocean journeys of several hundred miles. Trading networks were well developed: Even the fat extracted from the eulachon, or candlefish, was carried far inland along routes that came to be known as "grease trails." Perhaps the most remarkable achievement of West Coast people lay in the powerful art that graced and gave meaning to everyday life and to ritual. Tools, baskets, and clothing were all elaborately decorated, but the most impressive works of art were the great totem poles with their bold carvings of men and beasts.

FIRST EUROPEANS

Commissioned by royalty and required to report fully on their findings, John Cabot (1450–1498) and Jacques Cartier (1491–1557) have gone down in the history books as the "discoverers" of Canada. The look-out aboard Cabot's *Matthew* sighted land on June 24, 1497, although it is still a matter of speculation whether it was Newfoundland or Cape Breton Island. Cartier sailed through the Strait of Belle Isle between Newfoundland and Labrador 37 years later, in May 1534. But Europeans had been crossing the Atlantic long before these well-documented voyages.

Medieval Norse sagas told of adventurers such as Leif Eriksson (10th–11th centuries) bound from Greenland finding a land of vines and plentiful timber, and archaeologists have found evidence at L'Anse aux Meadows in northern Newfoundland of a Viking settlement dating from around the year A.D. 1000 (see pp. 100–101). In the years that followed, Viking interest diminished, but it is possible that Basque and British fishermen had discovered the cod-rich waters around Newfoundland in the years preceding Cabot's venture.

Trading contact

Neither Cabot nor Cartier had crossed the Atlantic in search of codfish, but to look for a more direct route to the silks, spices, and other riches of the Orient. Nothing of this kind could be found on the bleak coasts of eastern Canada. Nevertheless, on Cabot's return to England, Henry VII (R.1485–1509) was sufficiently impressed to reward him with a princely £10 and to finance a second voyage, in 1498. This time Cabot did not return, and no trace of him or his ships has been found.

Cartier's contact with the new continent was more prolonged. After passing through the Strait of Belle Isle, he sailed past the Magdalen Islands, landed on Prince Edward Island, and looked into the Baie des Chaleurs, where he was greeted by Mi'kmaq wanting to trade furs with him. At Gaspé he encountered Iroquois on a fishing expedition from their settlement at Stadacona, near present-day Québec City. Pleasantries were exchanged, but when Cartier erected a huge cross on shore bearing the emblem of the king of France, his hosts declared that the land was their domain and definitely not for the taking. Cartier returned the following year, sailing up the St. Lawrence as far as the Iroquois village of Hochelaga, the future site of Montréal, where he was

Massive quantities of furs were shipped to Europe from the desolate shores of Hudson Bay.

welcomed with great ceremony. Wintering close to Stadacona, he began to lose his men to scurvy until the Iroquois showed him how to treat it with a brew of cedar leaves and bark, but relations between the French and natives had already become strained. Cartier kidnapped several Iroquois and took them back to France, where they died, probably of a European disease to which they had no immunity, a harbinger of the fate many more were to suffer in the years to come. When Cartier returned once again in 1541, the Iroquois put to siege his winter encampment. He left for France for the last time, hoping that his cargo of glittering rocks contained gold. It turned out to be iron pyrites.

Fish and furs

For the next half century, European interest in Canada was confined to cod. The British, French, Basque, and Portuguese fished the Grand Banks (see pp. 92–93). They made no real attempt to found permanent settlements on the coast of Newfoundland, but annoyed the Beothuk natives by cluttering up their best fishing sites with gear and destroying the forest for firewood.

At the beginning of the 17th century, French interest in the new land gained a fresh impulse—from fur. Beaver felt was the ideal material—easily shaped, durable, and waterproof—for hats. While European beavers were on the point of extinction, the Canadian forests teemed with them. Once more, royal encouragement was given to an expedition. In 1603 the man subsequently regarded as the Father of New France, Samuel de Champlain (1567–1635), was instructed to survey the St. Lawrence. In 1605 he founded a fortified post known as the Habitation, at Port Royal on the Annapolis Basin in what is now Nova Scotia. This Habitation was soon abandoned, but in 1608 Champlain founded another. Beneath a great rock overlooking the St. Lawrence, at a place the Iroquois called Kebek, or "the narrowing of the waters," this Habitation was destined to endure and to become the capital of New France.

COLONIZATION & CONFLICT

Cartier claimed Canada for France in 1534, and in 1583 Sir Humphrey Gilbert (1539–1583) claimed Newfoundland for England. For two centuries, the English and French led an uneasy coexistence that often developed into harassment, piracy, and warfare.

French control

At the beginning, the French grip on the new land was far firmer. Towns were founded and colonists brought in to settle them and the nearby countryside. The church was a major player, establishing monasteries and sending missions far into the interior, as at Sainte-Marie among the Hurons on Georgian Bay. The basis of the fur trade was established, with natives using their traditional expertise to supply French traders with beaver pelts and other furs. From the earliest days, French strategy favored the Huron, long-standing enemies of the Iroquois who often blocked the routes leading into the interior from the colony. As early as 1609, Champlain fought an Iroquois army near the lake subsequently named after him. Caught in the open and subjected to fire from the Europeans' harquebuses, the Iroquois were routed, but remained formidable foes. In the late 1640s their attacks on Huronia led to the martyrdom of missionaries, the abandonment of Sainte-Marie among the Hurons, and the destruction of the Huron nation. In the early 1660s, the Iroquois terrorized New France, besieging Montréal and pillaging the countryside. Their attack led directly to the

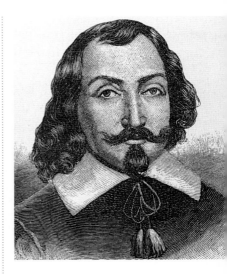

The Father of New France—Samuel de Champlain (1567–1635)

fall of the Cent-Associés, the trading association that had hitherto run the affairs of New France, and to the placing of the colony under royal control.

Far away, other Frenchmen were settling the shores of the Bay of Fundy, where Champlain had located his first two Habitations. Raiders from Virginia destroyed the Habitation at Port Royal. The Acadians developed stronger trading ties to New England than their fellow countrymen in the St. Lawrence Valley though they, too, were harrassed by the Colonies to the south. In the 1620s a British attempt was made to found a colony in their midst by Sir William Alexander. His venture failed but the name he gave to the land stuck—Nova Scotia.

British inroads

English fishermen had already settled along the coasts of Newfoundland, despite official prohibition. St. John's, on its wonderful sheltered harbor, was the largest settlement. Attempts were made to found organized colonies, by John Guy of Bristol at Conception Bay in 1610, then a decade later by Lord Baltimore at Ferryland on the Avalon Peninsula. Guy's party stayed, but after one winter Lord Baltimore left for the much milder shores of Maryland.

Despite the development of New France

Champlain's arrival in New France stimulated conflict with the Iroquois.

under the royal regime, the "French fact" in North America was very vulnerable. British sea power was constantly growing and the population along the St. Lawrence Valley was a fraction of that in the 13 Colonies. In 1670 the Hudson's Bay Company had been founded, a northern rival to the French fur trade and a portent of things to come in the west. Intermittent fighting broke out again toward the end of the 17th century. The Iroquois had been armed by the English; in 1689 they made a famous attack on Lachine near Montréal, and in 1692 another at Verchères in which they were beaten off by the 15-year-old daughter of the local seigneur. In 1690 the English adventurer Sir William Phips, fresh from attacking Port Royal, sailed up the St. Lawrence to Québec City and commanded Governor Frontenac to surrender. "I have no reply to make to your general other than from the mouths of my cannon," was Frontenac's immortal response to Phips's emissary, and Phips retired, discouraged by this show of resistance but also wary of the ice threatening to imprison his ships. In 1711 another British plan to attack Québec failed when the ships of Admiral Walker's fleet came to grief on the coast of Anticosti Island in the Gulf of St. Lawrence. The Québec church, which had been renamed Notre-Dame de la Victoire in 1690, now added an "s" to its name.

Atlantic possessions

The turn-of-the-century conflict between Britain and a now bankrupt France was brought to an end by the Treaty of Utrecht of 1713, in which France ceded Acadia/Nova Scotia, gave up claims to parts of Newfoundland, and renounced interest in Hudson Bay. But France kept Cape Breton Island, and, to protect the vulnerable approach to the St. Lawrence through the Cabot Strait, began to build the huge fortress of Louisbourg looking out over the Atlantic. This was not to New England's liking, and, when Britain and France went to war again in 1744, a force of militia supported by the British Caribbean fleet stormed the fortress and after a six-week siege deported its population to France. But in the diplomatic maneuvers that ended what had been a war partly about issues in Europe, Louisbourg was returned to France and rapidly regarrisoned. The end of the war turned out to be no more than a truce. Anglo-French rivalry in North America intensified. As a counterweight to Louisbourg, Halifax was founded in 1749, its citadel and magnificent harbor destined to watch over Britain's Atlantic interests for the next two centuries. At this time Britain preferred not to send emigrants overseas, and when the town of Lunenburg was established

down the Nova Scotia coast from Halifax, it was populated by foreign Protestants. Mostly from Germany and Switzerland, these people were thought to be more reliable subjects of His Majesty than the Catholic Acadians, whose calvary was soon to begin. As the war clouds gathered, British officialdom felt unable to trust these French speakers to maintain their neutrality in the coming conflict. The Acadians were rounded up, deported, and dispersed around the American Colonies, which were often unwilling to receive them. The rich pastures that their ancestors had laboriously reclaimed from the marshlands around the Bay of Fundy mostly fell into the hands of immigrants from New England, and the Acadians who doggedly made their way back home had to resettle elsewhere, usually on far less favorable land.

"First World War"

The year 1756 saw the outbreak of what has been called the first war fought on a global scale, the Seven Years' War. In North America there was fighting on the western frontier and on the invasion corridor between New York

and Montréal around Lake Champlain. But the decisive battle was fought in Québec. Louisbourg had been taken again, and its garrison and inhabitants sent permanently packing. It could now serve as a base for the invasion of Québec. By 1759 New France had lost all its forts on the Great Lakes and Lake Champlain. Its survival depended on French naval power, but France was preoccupied in Europe. In June the British commander, Gen. James Wolfe (1727–1759), sailed unopposed up the St. Lawrence to confront his adversary, the Marquis de Montcalm (1712–1759). The

The elevated Plains of Abraham near Québec City saw Canada's defining battle in 1759, as shown in this engraving by Bowles.

residents had rallied to the flag, and Montcalm had more men at his command than the Englishman, but, wrote Wolfe, "Montcalm is at the head of a great number of bad soldiers and I am at the head of a small number of good ones." The preliminary skirmishes at Montmorency Falls, however, showed the French militiamen and their native allies as more than a match for the British. Wolfe

The capture of the H.M.S. *Cyane* **and** *Levant* **by the U.S.S.** *Constitution* **during the War of 1812**

ranged up and down the St. Lawrence, destroying crops and property in a scorched earth campaign, and subjected Québec to a more or less continuous bombardment. As autumn approached, Wolfe sought a decisive encounter before the river began to freeze and immobilize his ships. On the night of September 12, he sent his men up a dry streambed to the heights of the Plains of Abraham, taking the French by surprise and defeating them in a 15-minute battle.

The war was not over. The French forces retreated to Montréal, and by the following spring sallied forth and gave the British a bloody nose at Sainte-Foy, only a mile or so southwest of the Plains of Abraham. Hoping for naval help from France, they subjected Québec to a second siege, but the first ships to come up the St. Lawrence were British. In the summer, three British armies advancing from Québec, Lake Champlain, and Lake Ontario delivered the coup de grâce, and Montréal surrendered.

The defeat of New France was a great bargaining chip for the British when peace negotiations began in 1763, but it was by no means inevitable that Britain would hold on to its conquest in the St. Lawrence Valley. Strong arguments were made in favor of trading

Québec for warmer and more fertile French possessions in the Caribbean, but in the end it was decided that henceforth Canada was to be British. Tears were shed in France over this, but many agreed with cynical Voltaire that these *quelques arpents de neige* (few acres of snow) had already cost the mother country far too dearly and that she was well rid of them.

French exodus

Military men and high officials in Québec had to leave for France; the citizens and habitants who had nowhere else to go were more preoccupied with putting their lives back together again after the disruption of a long war that had killed up to a tenth of the population.

There were too many of them—around 80,000—to be dealt with as the British had dealt with their cousins the Acadians, by scattering them around the Colonies. The French fact in Canada would have to stay, and even be courted, to prevent the spread of the growing restlessness in the American Colonies. In 1774 the Québec Act was passed, reassuring Canadians that their Catholic religion and civil law would not be tampered with by their new Protestant masters. The outrage felt by many New Englanders that their old foes should be so favored added to American unrest, and the feeling was shared by the Boston merchants who had flocked to Canada in the wake of victory.

American advances

In 1775 the Americans advanced along the Lake Champlain invasion route toward Montréal, while another force struggled through the forests of Maine toward Québec City. Their hope that the Canadiens would join them in defeating the British was not fulfilled, and local militiamen helped defeat the Americans. There was fierce fighting when Québec City was besieged and Montréal was occupied for several months, but in 1776 naval defeat on Lake Champlain spelled the end of the American invasion. In the east, despite the close connections many of its inhabitants had with New England, Nova Scotia resisted American blandishments and fought off raids by privateers to remain in what came to be known as British North America.

The American Revolution helped solve Britain's problem of how to colonize Canada with people of British stock. Numerous Americans who resisted independence and wished to remain British moved northward. By 1783 some 45,000 Loyalists had crossed into Canada, most settling in Nova Scotia, others in the Eastern Townships of Québec, and some in what was to become Ontario. They set a pattern of migration that other Americans were soon to follow, less for political reasons than in search of cheap land. The balance of population in what was still called Québec began to turn against French speakers, and in 1791, in an attempt to reconcile differences, two provinces came into being: Upper Canada (present-day Ontario), mostly English speaking, and Lower Canada (today's Québec), mostly French speaking.

PRESSING NORTH & WEST

During this time, the native population of what was to become Canada still outnumbered Europeans, though in the east Caucasians now predominated. Here, native numbers had declined because of disease and other pressures on traditional ways of life. In the west, European explorers pressed onward in search of alternative outlets for the fur trade. In 1789 Alexander Mackenzie (1755–1820) reached the

The confederation chamber in Charlottetown, Prince Edward Island, was the scene of Canada's creation in 1864.

Arctic and in 1793 the Pacific, the first European to cross the continent north of Mexico. He narrowly missed encountering Captain George Vancouver aboard H.M.S. *Discovery*, who was surveying the Pacific coast. In 1808 Simon Fraser made the journey down the river to be named after him and reached the Pacific near present-day Vancouver. Both he and Mackenzie were in the employ of the North West Company, soon to be merged with the Hudson's Bay Company, which still held sway over all the vast territory west and north of Lake Superior.

TOWARD A UNITED CANADA

The War of 1812 between the United States and Britain saw plenty of fighting in Canada. Many Americans assumed that their overwhelming superiority in numbers meant the end of British North America, that Canada's conquest would be, in President Thomas Jefferson's words, "a mere matter of marching." But resistance to American attack was stiffer than expected. A famous victory was won at Queenston Heights above the Niagara River. And though U.S. forces occupied and burned York (the future Toronto), British naval power

was decisive in the end, assuring the political independence of Canada from its great neighbor. Britain then built great forts such as Québec's Citadel, just in case.

Internal problems now became the main concern. Britain had initially hoped that Canada might resemble the old country, with a local aristocracy to keep the lower orders in place and to discourage contamination by democratic ideas from the south. In practice, this led to rule by an oligarchy, nicknamed "the family compact" in Upper Canada and the *château clique* in Lower Canada.

Resentment grew, fanned in York by a firebrand journalist, William Lyon Mackenzie (1795–1861), and given an extra edge in Lower Canada by French–British antagonism. In 1837–38, resentment turned to rebellion. In York, the uprising led by Mackenzie almost degenerated into farce, as his motley army of toughs was quickly routed by the local militia. In Lower Canada, the *Patriote* followers of Louis-Joseph Papineau fought valiantly against British troops, but the issue was never really in doubt, especially after nearly a hundred of them were killed at

Resolutely different, the province of Québec is proud of its heritage and not afraid to show its independent nature.

Sainte-Eustache near Montréal.

Canada needed attention. It got it from a new governor-general, John George Lambton, Earl of Durham, who soon earned the nickname "Radical Jack" by his ruthless anatomy of the Canadian problem and his willingness to think of innovative solutions. His description of French–British relations as "two nations warring in the bosom of a single state" still resonates today. But his promotion of a union of all Britain's North American colonies came a little too early, and in 1841 he had to content himself with reuniting Upper and Lower Canada in a system of "responsible government" where unelected cliques would no longer be dominant.

The country was developing rapidly as immigrants poured in from Great Britain and Ireland, although a proportion of them subsequently moved on to the even more rapidly developing United States. The Pacific coast experienced sudden growth from 1858, when tens of thousands of mostly American prospectors used Victoria on Vancouver Island as a staging post on the way to the gold strikes on the mainland. Fearful of a U.S. takeover (as had happened in California), the mainland and Vancouver Island were joined together as the new colony of British Columbia. Meanwhile, around the Red River in what was to become Manitoba, land-hungry farmers mov-

The monument to fallen Canadian soldiers at Vimy Ridge, France

ing west from Ontario were disturbing the way of life of the Métis, people of French and native descent, who lived by bison-hunting and providing the Hudson's Bay Company with pemmican and other supplies.

Dawn of the Confederation

The passions unleashed by the Civil War in the United States disturbed the inhabitants of British North America. Perhaps it was time to get together after all. In 1864 representatives from the province of Canada gate-crashed a meeting at Charlottetown that politicians from Nova Scotia, Prince Edward Island, New Brunswick, and Newfoundland had called to discuss a possible union of the Maritime colonies. In a remarkable display of synergy, a few days of debate, drinks, and dances sufficed for the idea of a confederation of all the colonies to be accepted. The Canadian Confederation was established by the British North America Act of 1867. A strong federal government was to rule from Ottawa, but the provinces retained many powers. Prince Edward Island remained outside until 1873, when it persuaded Ottawa

to take over its debts and provide a ferry service in perpetuity (replaced in 1997 by the aptly named Confederation Bridge). But Newfoundland resisted and stayed a colony of Great Britain until 1949.

In 1868 the new Confederation gave notice of its serious interest in the west by buying most of the Hudson's Bay domain, at the bargain price of 1.5 million dollars. British Columbia joined the Confederation in 1871, having been promised a railroad linking it with its new partners thousands of miles to the east.

Resistance to the smooth completion of the Confederation came from the Prairies, where the Métis' grievances led to the Red River Rebellion of 1869–1870 led by Louis Riel (see pp. 228–29). Though Riel himself was forced into exile, many of the issues he raised were dealt with when the province of Manitoba was created in 1870. The Métis' way of life was doomed to disappear, whatever government guarantees were given; the bison had almost been exterminated, and the Prairies were soon to be put under the plow or converted into grazing grounds for cattle. In 1885 the Métis, together with some natives, rebelled again, but were swiftly put down by troops. Probably the most famous photograph in Canadian history was taken later that year, as Donald Smith, president of the Canadian Pacific Railway, hammered home the last spike at Craigellachie in the Columbia Mountains (see pp. 262–63). In June the following year, the first scheduled train made its six-day, 2,891-mile journey across the continent from Montréal to Port Moody on the Pacific, a potent demonstration of the new country stretching *A mari usque ad mare* (from sea to sea)—Canada's motto.

MODERN TIMES

In the late 19th and early 20th centuries, the Prairies filled up with settlers from many parts of Europe, and the open grasslands that had stretched for a thousand miles gave way to fields, farms, and grain elevators. The provinces of Alberta and Saskatchewan were carved out of the Northwest Territories in 1905. In the years before 1914, the country boomed economically, and continued to prosper during World War I. Canada had loyally entered the war at Great Britain's side, but the pledge to raise a force of half a million men by voluntary enlistment proved impossible to fulfill. Conscription was eventually introduced, against the opposition of most French Canadians, who saw the war as a far-off struggle among European powers. British Canadians took great pride in the fighting prowess of the army in France; the fall of Vimy Ridge to Canadian troops after the failure of British and French attacks became a symbol of national valor. More than 60,000 Canadians were killed in the conflict. In gratitude, France gave Canada a square kilometer of land on Vimy Ridge, and one of the greatest memorials of the war was erected there in 1936.

Comradeship in arms could not conceal the waning of British influence in Canada. In 1922 American investment in the country surpassed the British total for the first time. Like the rest of the industrial world, Canada suffered the Great Depression that followed the Wall Street crash of 1929. The promise of the Prairies seemed negated by the dust-bowl conditions of the 1930s. Canada tried to stand aside from the worsening world crisis of the '30s, but in 1939 was once more obliged to go to war at Britain's side. Canada's war effort was immense; by 1945 a million people had put on uniform. Once again conscription threatened national unity, which was nevertheless held together by the excellent political skills of Prime Minister Mackenzie King (1874–1950).

Postwar prosperity brought a new stream of immigrants to Canada. Britons came, but were outnumbered by waves of displaced people from Central Europe, then by southern Europeans. Resistance to non-European immigration crumbled, adding Asians and Caribbean Islanders to the mosaic.

In the 1950s and 1960s the British Commonwealth was a focus of interest, but this declined as Britain turned to Europe. As a member of NATO, Canada kept troops in Europe, and sent others in support of UN missions around the world. A friendly but sometimes critical view was taken of American foreign policy.

The Québec issue

At home, Québec found a new voice and confidence as a result of the Révolution Tranquille (Quiet Revolution) of the 1960s. A cultural flowering accompanied a rejection of the Catholic Church's lead in education and social welfare and the growth of a new middle class, mainly employed in a vastly expanded public sector. The issue of Québec's role in the country had never gone away; now it steadily intensified.

The most dramatic episode came in 1970, when a terrorist group called the Front de

Canada's armed forces have served as UN peacekeepers repeatedly since World War II.

Libération du Québec kidnapped and subsequently murdered a British diplomat, then a provincial government minister. Prime Minister Pierre Trudeau declared martial law. Canadians across the country were shocked by scenes of armed troops on Montréal streets. Québécois were shocked, too, though many resented Trudeau's action, seeing it as a heavy-handed military occupation of their province.

More significant were federal attempts to give French speakers (including the hundreds of thousands outside Québec) the same status as English speakers. Canada became officially bilingual, and the government made great efforts to increase the number of francophones in the public service. But Québec refused to be placated. The nationalist Parti Québécois came to power in 1976 and pushed, if not for outright independence for the province, then for a form of "sovereignty association." Put to referendum, however, such aspirations have been defeated, roundly in 1980 and by a narrow margin in 1995. Talk of separation continues but, for the time being, Canada remains united. ■

Building Canada

THE GROWTH AND DEVELOPMENT OF CANADA—AND THE EVER EVOLVING idea of what it means to be Canadian—can be observed through the country's architecture. From the first dwellings erected by native peoples to the imperial edifices of French and British culture, and onward to the futuristic skyscrapers in most Canadian cities, architecture has been an accurate barometer of national identity and aspiration.

EARLIEST STRUCTURES

No examples remain of buildings erected in Canada before the arrival of the Europeans, but numerous reconstructions and copies give an excellent idea of the variety of ways First Nations provided shelter for themselves. People who lived a migratory existence needed portable structures, and Europeans have long marveled at the superb functionality of the tepee used by Plains people. The tepee was made of bison hides stretched over a conical framework of wooden poles, and could easily be taken apart, transported, and reerected. The wigwam used by the Algonquian groups in eastern Canada was also transportable. Its shape could be domed as well as conical, while its covering could be of bark, mats of reeds, or hides.

Leading a more settled existence, various Iroquois groups built permanent longhouses of timber, often grouped together in a palisaded village. Up to 180 feet in length, longhouses could accommodate several families and a number of separate hearths. An example of a Huron longhouse has been rebuilt at the settlement of Sainte-Marie among the Hurons in Ontario (see p. 202). The most impressive First Nations architecture, however, belongs to the Pacific coast, where groups like the Haida or Gitksan took advantage of the availability of fine timber to construct longhouses of imposing dimensions and great durability. Even in ruin, the Haida villages of the Queen Charlotte Islands are a magnificent sight.

EUROPEAN INFLUENCES

The first Europeans to build in Canada were the Vikings, who ranged along the Atlantic coast around A.D. 1000. One of the most fascinating sites in the country is the reconstructed Viking settlement at L'Anse aux Meadows (see pp. 100–101) in Newfoundland, at the northern end of the Strait of Belle Isle. Longhouses with walls and roofs of sod must have been built with permanent residence in mind, but it seems that the occupants made only a short stay before abandoning what might have become the continent's first European colony.

As whaling and fishing developed in the 16th century, Basque whalers built tryworks and simple dwellings on the coast of Labrador,

Ice skating in Nathan Philips Square is a popular pastime for many Torontonians during the long winter.

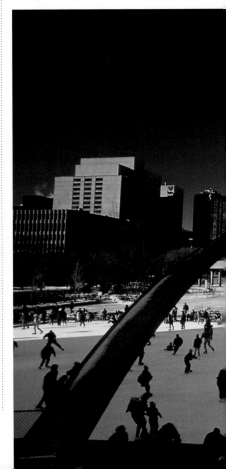

while English and French fishermen erected various structures, including the primitive shelters known as tilts, along the rugged coast of Newfoundland.

FORTIFICATION

Far more sophisticated were the Habitations, a series of compact fortified settlements built by Samuel de Champlain and his associates as they attempted to establish a French presence in the New World. While the Habitation of 1604 on Île Sainte-Croix in Passamaquoddy Bay lasted only a year, the Habitation established in 1608 at the foot of Cap Diamant grew into the city of Québec. The Habitation of 1605 at Port Royal in Nova Scotia was destroyed, but was meticulously reconstructed in the 1930s. The other Habitations were protected by a palisade, but at Port Royal the solid timber buildings are grouped around a quad-rangle and are defended by their almost windowless outer walls as well as by the cannon mounted on a protruding bastion.

Champlain's Habitations introduce a persistent theme of fortification in Canadian building. The French and British needed protection from wild beasts, and natives, but most of all from each other and later from Americans. The fur trade was conducted from fortified posts, usually consisting of a timber palisade enclosing an array of structures. A fort of the Hudson's Bay Company, like Lower Fort Garry near Winnipeg, achieved a degree of grandeur. Begun in 1830, it is surrounded by a rectangle of substantial stone walls with circular bastions at the corners. Its centerpiece, the splendid governor's residence, called the Big House, was protected by a picket fence intended to exclude all but company officers and their families.

Defensive designs

Franco-British rivalry in the early 18th century led to the strengthening of Québec City's defenses and from 1713 onward the construction of the remarkable fortified town of Louisbourg on Cape Breton Island. Louisbourg covered an area of 60 acres, and

Because it could be transported with ease, the functional tepee was the preferred dwelling of the Plains people.

for several decades flourished as a port and trading center. It was protected from the sea by a series of batteries and landward by a curtain wall with bastions that failed to save it from British attacks. This whole complex has been magnificently rebuilt from ruin.

Where Louisbourg failed, Halifax prospered. Begun in 1749 as a counterweight to the French fortress, Halifax was protected by a palisade and by a citadel. The palisade was soon absorbed into the growth of the town, but the citadel, much extended over the years, is still a dominating presence. With its star-shaped plan, bastions, ditch, and outworks, it reflects the principles on which European fortresses had been built a century before, and was obsolete before it was completed. This was true, too, of the great citadel at Québec City, built between 1820 and 1850 and complemented by a wonderful circuit of city walls unique in North America.

The layout of Québec City, and of Montréal as well, is attractively irregular. Some streets are straight, others reflect the lay of the land or, like Montréal's Rue Saint-Paul, follow the meandering alignment of old footpaths. The townscape that results recalls the ancient towns of Europe. By contrast, most towns laid out by the British conform to the gridiron plan so familiar in the rest of North America, imposed on the land with scant regard to natural features. Halifax is one example where the grid of streets has survived two and a half centuries of building and rebuilding, and there are many others, including Charlottetown and York, the ancestor of Toronto. In Nova Scotia's Lunenburg, little seems to have changed since 1753, when the surveyors traced out the rectangular street pattern stepping up the slopes overlooking the harbor. Like Québec City, this wonderfully preserved example of urban design has been designated by UNESCO as a world heritage site.

CABINS, CHURCHES, & GOVERNMENT BUILDINGS

Early settlers built themselves cabins and modest houses of timber, practically none of which have survived. By the start of the 18th century in the Québec countryside, the inhabitants of Québec began to live in fieldstone houses with steep roofs of timber or thatch, whose designs owed at least something to the vernacular building in France's Normandy, Maine, and Anjou provinces. A century later, a characteristically French-Canadian house had developed, again of fieldstone, with a more gently sloping roof with overhanging eaves and perhaps dormer windows. A seigneur's manor might be indistinguishable from the houses of his former neighbors, or simply be a larger, more ornamental version. In Québec, Montréal, and Trois-Rivières, a number of houses from the time of the French Regime survive. A distinguishing feature where buildings adjoin one another is the firewall extending above the roofline, a response to the terrible fires that periodically devastated towns built of timber.

Churches and other religious buildings dominated the countryside as well as the townscape of French Canada. Country churches were usually built in a prominent position, on a bluff overlooking a river or at a bend in a road. Many are overly simple, others elaborate, sometimes with exquisite interiors.

The central role of the Roman Catholic

Church in Québec's history is expressed by such great religious institutions as the Couvent des Ursulines in Québec City, begun in 1641, or the Vieux Séminaire de Saint-Sulpice in Montréal, begun in 1685. Montréal also has two superb 19th-century basilicas: Notre-Dame, with its twin towers and mystically lit interior, and Marie-Reine-du-Monde, modeled on St. Peter's in the Vatican. Pilgrimages played—and still play—an important part in the religious life of Québec; their setting could be simple, like the hillside Stations of the Cross at Oka outside Montréal, or truly monumental, like the great shrines of Montréal's Saint-Joseph (begun in 1924) or Sainte-Anne-de-Beaupré (completed in 1934). Saint-Joseph was partly the work of architect-monk Dom Bellot, who in the 1930s created a brilliantly successful fusion of the traditional and the modern at the monastery of Saint-Benoît-du-Lac in Québec's Eastern Townships.

British contributions

French-Canadian architectural traditions persisted in Québec long after the British Conquest, but they were soon complemented by styles that had their origin in Britain, and later New England. Like other churches in the New World, the Anglican Holy Trinity Cathedral in Québec City (begun in 1800) is closely modeled on London's St. Martin-in-the-Fields of three-quarters of a century earlier. These Georgian churches were followed in the mid-19th century by edifices in the Gothic Revival style, among them the Anglican cathedrals in Montréal and Fredericton and Toronto's tall-spired St. James'. But the greatest Gothic structure in Canada is a secular one, the government complex gracing Ottawa's Parliament Hill, built in a direct line of descent from London's Houses of Parliament and in a magnificent setting overlooking the Ottawa River.

PROGRESS IN THE PROVINCES

Almost matching the grandeur of the buildings housing the federal government are some of the provincial legislatures. Ontario's parliament in Toronto (1893) is in the neo-Romanesque style developed by the U.S. architect Henry Hobson Richardson, quite distinct from the beaux arts style favored for the

capitals of the Prairie Provinces. Winnipeg, Regina, and Edmonton all have early 20th-century legislative buildings that perfectly express the high aspirations of the more recent provincial capitals.

The railroad stations of this era were equally grandiose. Montréal's Windsor Station is an exercise in Richardsonian Romanesque,

Toronto's downtown includes a wealth of outstanding contemporary office buildings.

while the beaux arts magnificence of the Great Hall of Toronto's Union Station is unmatched elsewhere in North America. Intimately associated with the railroads were the great hotels of the era. Beginning with the Banff Springs Hotel in 1888, a "Canadian château" architectural style was developed with which luxury trans-Canada travel will always be associated. The finest of these gloriously picturesque structures is perhaps the Château Frontenac in Québec City, followed closely by Victoria's waterfront Empress Hotel.

Individuals could not hope to match the scale of these institutional buildings, but Canada has many distinguished houses. They range from the elegant Grange (1817) in Toronto, a Palladian mansion that could have come straight from the countryside of Georgian England, to Victoria's ostentatious mock-castle of Craigdarroch (1890) or the delightfully Italianate Bellevue (1841) at Kingston, early home of future Prime Minister John A. Macdonald (1815–1891). A world removed from the luxury of such edifices was

housing for the masses. In Montréal, the developers of row houses in working-class suburbs saved on construction costs by putting the staircases outside. Often attractively curved and with balconies to match, they were a real menace in icy winter weather, but have become a much loved feature of the townscape.

International themes

In the course of the 20th century, international architectural influences have tended to outweigh any specifically Canadian characteristics. There are fine examples of art deco skyscrapers in Québec City (Price Building, 1930) and in Vancouver (Marine Building, 1930).

The country even has examples of the work of that most international of all architects, Mies van der Rohe. Austere towers in black steel and glass designed by him or by his followers form the Toronto Dominion Centre (begun in 1964) and rise over Westmount Square in Montréal (1966). Since the 1970s, Canadian architects have cast aside such severity and attempted to design structures with more individuality, and occasionally with

Cabins on the shoreline of Lake O'Hara, British Columbia

greater sensitivity to their surroundings. Among more recent high buildings in Toronto is the Royal Bank Plaza (1976), whose glittering gilt skin reflects every change in the light. Vancouver's Cathedral Place (1991) pays tribute to its château-style hotel neighbor in much the same way as Montréal's Place de la Cathédrale (1988) makes friendly gestures to the adjacent Christ Church Cathedral.

But perhaps the most characteristically Canadian developments have been those that respond to the country's long winter by creating an interior, weather-proof world. Montréal has its Underground City, fully integrated with its marvelous modern Metro, while Toronto has its PATH system of pedestrian spaces threading through the city center. Winnipeg, Calgary, and Edmonton have all striven to give pedestrians the same sort of shelter in their city centers, while suburban Edmonton boasts the biggest shopping center in the country, the internationally famous West Edmonton Mall. ■

The cultural scene

CANADIAN CULTURE SINCE THE 18TH CENTURY HAS REFLECTED A GROWING sense of place, which in turn has evolved into a notion of nationhood. The two main strands—French and English—began by trying to match the standards of the "home country." Confederation in 1867 brought this sense of nationhood into focus.

A Confederation school of poetry, dealing with specifically Canadian concerns, gave it a voice, and visually this pride of place culminated in the paintings of the Group of Seven—unsentimental studies of Canada in all its diversity. This regional awareness was, in turn, reflected in novels like *Anne of Green Gables*, Lucy Maud Montgomery's tender account of life on Prince Edward Island.

In recent years Canada has earned a distinctive reputation in the arts, achieving a high profile worldwide. Perhaps its modern population is the clue to this success, as the often cited Canadian mosaic has encouraged individuality and distinctive cultural pursuits among the many peoples who now make up the Canadian nation. One of the striking aspects of culture today is not its division into British and French camps but its multiethnic face. Ballet stars with Chinese roots or writers with origins in Sri Lanka and Brazil are becoming as representative of Canada as the Stratford Festival has been for English culture and the Festival d'été for French culture.

VISUAL ARTS

For Canadian artists imbued with the sense of the modern, the Group of Seven's representational landscapes presented a stylistic straitjacket. Québec artists, their eyes fixed on Paris, were quick to pick up on movements such as cubism and surrealism. The major Québécois artist in the 1940s was Paul Emile Borduas, whose abstract paintings inspired the group known as the Automatistes. These painters saw spontaneous creation as the way forward. At the same time, the Toronto-based Painters Eleven were producing works that were at the forefront of abstract expressionism.

Since the 1970s, Canada's artistic community has exhibited an incredible richness and diversity. Michael Snow broke new ground in

Film shoots are common occurrences in Montréal.

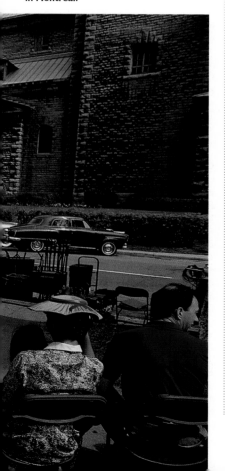

abstract painting while Inuit artists have benefited from cultural reappraisals. In the midst of these developments is the mainstay of Canadian art—the landscape—although now it is often given a new twist from Canada's foreign-born artists such as Samir Ghanem, Elena Khomoutova, and Robert Milner.

LITERATURE

Outstanding among recent Canadian novelists who have made their mark internationally is Robertson Davies, who died in 1995. His final work, *The Cunning Man* (1994), was acclaimed worldwide. In 1992, Michael Ondaatje was a joint Booker Prize winner with his novel *The English Patient*, which has also been made into a successful film. Toronto's Margaret Atwood (*Oryx and Crake*, 2003) has an international profile, as have literary curmudgeon Mordecai Richler of Montréal (*Barney's Version*, 1997), who died in 2001, and Carol Shields (*Larry's Party*, 1997).

Among writers of historical narrative, few can rival Pierre Berton with his more than 40 books on different aspects of Canada's history. Up-and-coming writers include Joy Nozomi Kogawa, Ruby Wiebe, Rohinton Mistry, Neil Bissoondath, and Thomson Highway.

Among numerous first-rate writers in French, Anne Hébert's name stands out with many titles to her credit. Her *Kamouraska* is considered a classic and was made into a film of the same name by Claude Jutra.

THEATER

The granddaddy of Canadian theater in both age and influence is the Shakespeare festival founded in 1953 in Stratford, Ontario. Featuring musicals and contemporary classics as well as Shakespeare, it is the largest classical theater company in Canada and is an important training ground for actors, directors, and stage technicians. Another important theater company performs at the Shaw Festival in Niagara-on-the-Lake, Ontario, and there are more than 90 other regional theaters across the country.

French-language theater flourishes with the works of well-established playwrights such as Michel Tremblay, who has revolutionized the scene in Québec with his works in "joual" (slang), such as *Les Belles Soeurs* and more recently *Un geste de beauté,* and Michel-Marc

Oscar Peterson's dazzling skills have thrilled jazz fans since the late '40s.

Joni Mitchell's soul-baring lyrics have inspired songwriters worldwide.

Bouchard, whose works such as *Les Muses Orphelines* are similarly popular. There are also avant-garde companies such as Gilles-Maheu's Carbon 14 dance theater, whose recent work, *l'Hiver*, was first performed in early 1998.

In a category all of its own is the Montréal-based Cirque du Soleil, a nontraditional circus with no animal acts, where trapeze artists, jugglers, and acrobats of all kinds create a fast-moving, almost magical festival of francophone culture in North America.

MUSIC
In the world of classical music, the Orchestre Symphonique de Montréal, with its conductor Kent Nagano, is world renowned. Famous Canadian performers included the late virtuoso pianist Glenn Gould. The country boasts several opera companies, notably the Toronto, with such opera singers as Maureen Forrester, Jon Vickers, and Teresa Stratas.

In the world of jazz, Montréal has a highly respected festival (Festival international de jazz), and the city was home to the brilliant and popular pianist Oscar Peterson.

Turning to popular music, the fame of several very different women has transcended Canadian borders. Singer-songwriter Joni

Mitchell is from Macleod, Alberta, pop diva Céline Dion from Montréal, country music star Shania Twayne from Timmins, Ontario, and rocker Alanis Morrissette from Ottawa. The popularity of these very talented women has reached phenomenal proportions, each scoring huge record sales worldwide.

DANCE
Canada boasts several world-class classical ballet companies, such as the Royal Winnipeg; Les Grands Ballets Canadiens, based in Montréal; and the National Ballet of Canada, with their long-time prima ballerina, Karen Kain, known as Canada's sweetheart until her 1997 retirement.

Montréal has become the Canadian capital of contemporary choreography both in dance and theater, thanks to some very avant-garde troupes, among them the Marie Chouinard Company, Ginette Laurin's company, O Vertigo Danse, and Edouard Lock's incredibly energetic and acrobatic Lalala Human Steps.

BROADCASTING & FILM
Television in Canada is dominated by the Canadian Broadcasting Corporation, which has existed since 1936. Today, it is a continent-

Novelist Margaret Atwood dissects Canadian life in her unflinching prose.

Screen actor Donald Sutherland hails from Saint John, New Brunswick.

wide network of television and radio stations broadcasting in English, French, and a number of First Nations and Inuit languages, and is a major producer of shows and series of all types.

In the realm of film, the National Film Board of Canada trains and develops filmmakers. It also produces its own features for theatrical and nontheatrical release, as well as its famous film shorts, which have won a number of Oscars, notably works by Frédéric Back ("The Man Who Planted Trees and Crack").

Important film festivals are held every year in Toronto, Vancouver, and Montréal. Among Canadian directors with an international reputation are David Cronenberg, whose horror movie *Crash* caused a sensation in 1997, Atom Egoyan *(Sweet Hereafter,* 1997), Bruce Beresford *(Black Robe,* 1991), and James Cameron, director of the enormously successful *Titanic* (1997).

Famous Canadian actors include Michael J. Fox, Donald Sutherland, Christopher Plummer, Geneviève Bujold, and Carole Laure; First Nations stars Graham Greene *(Dances with Wolves)* and Tina Keeper and Tom Jackson of CBC's series *North of '60* also have an international profile.

In French, Claude Jutra's coming-of-age classic, *Mon oncle Antoine* (1971), is considered by many to be Canada's best film ever. Other notable directors include Gilles Carle (whose *Maria Chapdelaine* starred Geneviève Bujold), Denys Arcand *(The Decline and Fall of the American Empire* and *The Barbarian Invasions),* and Jean-Claude Lauzon *(Léolo,* 1992).

In a category of his own is Québec City's Robert Lepage, an immensely talented actor, director, producer, and filmmaker *(Far Side of the Moon,* 2003), who catapulted to fame with his *Plaques tectoniques,* which had worldwide success for its unusual visual effects and music.

COMEDY

From Wayne and Schuster to Rich Little, Canadians have a distinctive, rather self-deprecatory wit. Celebrating 30 years of existence in 2003, the *Royal Canadian Air Farce,* which started life on CBC Radio, is a Friday night television tradition in most Canadian homes, closely followed by a brash crowd mainly from Newfoundland who produce *22 Minutes Live*—a satirical look at the news, also on CBC Television.

Finally, Montréal's Festival Juste pour Rire ("Just for Laughs Festival") has created a solid reputation for humor in its 20-year existence and is the world's largest comedy fest. ■

What to see
& how to go about it

INTIMIDATED BY THE SHEER SCALE OF THE COUNTRY, MANY VISITORS TO Canada find themselves at a loss to decide just what they will do. Should they try to get an "all-over" look at Canada, touching base in the Atlantic provinces and moving west through the shield, plains, Rockies, and then to the northern wilderness—or would it be more sensible to single out a city or a region? Either choice is feasible, and many visitors manage to combine bits of both approaches.

TOURING

Some Canadians consider it a rite of passage to have crossed their vast country by car, but you don't have to follow them! However, it is perfectly possible to base a car tour on part of a province or region. Provincial tourist departments have helped by naming routes, some of which have become classics, like Nova Scotia's Cabot Trail. Find out also about ferry crossings, particularly in the east, where ferries may help you devise an interesting circular route. In the west, four ferry routes link the B.C. mainland with Vancouver Island, making a number of permutations possible. This gives a taste of the Pacific coast, enough perhaps to whet the appetite for the Inside Passage, the stunning journey linking Port Hardy with Prince Rupert and Alaska's Skagway.

Canada is, of course, the home of the bush plane, which has a much more exciting rela-tionship with the earth's surface than any air-liner. Some places are only accessible by this form of transport, but even the short trip from Vancouver across the Georgia Strait is a lot of fun in a little floatplane, and far quicker than the ferry.

VIEW FROM THE TRAIN

The all-time classic train route is, of course, the crossing of the Rocky Mountains. There are in fact three routes from the Prairies to the Pacific; the first, the original line of the Canadian Pacific, links Calgary with Vancouver via Banff, while the second also has Vancouver as its destination but starts at Edmonton and enters the mountains near Jasper, converging with the first at Kamloops. The third route connects Edmonton with the far-off port of Prince Rupert via the spectacu-lar Skeena Valley. VIA Rail has abandoned the first two routes but they have been revived by Rocky Mountaineer, a private company. You can start out from either end of the route. An overnight stop in Kamloops means that you don't miss any of the scenery. You may find it worth the extra cost to sit in one of the panorama cars as you glide effortlessly through some of the world's finest mountain landscapes. Less well-known is another route in British Columbia, also run by Rocky Mountaineer, which takes its passengers north from Whistler through the grand scenery of the Fraser Valley to Jasper.

A rail trip is perhaps the easiest way to get the measure of the vastness of the Canadian Shield. The lonely port of Churchill on Hudson Bay has become a visitor destination because of its wildlife, particularly the polar bears. You can fly there, of course, but why not take the two-night train from Winnipeg, at least one way?

In central and eastern Canada, the train is more of an everyday means of transport, but the line that curls around the Gaspé Peninsula is an effortless way of getting to know this remote part of eastern Québec.

SEEING THE CITIES

Most of Canada's large cities are extremely visitor friendly and easily explored on foot. The main attractions are often close together, and when they're not, a well-developed and efficient public transportation system will usu-ally be the best way of reaching them. Traveling underground on Montréal's immaculate rubber-tired Metro is an experience in itself.

Canada's landscapes and resources are so diverse as to accommodate even the most daring hobbies.

You should have little difficulty in finding your way to places where locals and visitors hang out and which seem to encapsulate the spirit of the city. Halifax has its waterfront Historic Properties, Québec its Place Royale, Winnipeg its meeting-place around The Forks. City authorities usually position their information bureaus in these locations.

Canada's many miles of highway make touring by car an easy option for exploring the country.

GETTING OUT OF TOWN

In a country with a tourist industry as well developed as Canada's, you'll find plenty of organized bus tours, and choosing among them may be difficult. Most operations are seasonal, with less choice of destination and timing at the beginning and end of the season. Renting a car, of course, will give you more flexibility, and is possible throughout the country.

GREAT OUTDOORS

One of the best ways of finding out about nature in Canada is by visiting the national parks. The country has a total of 194 national parks and national historic sites. Parks Canada is set up on broadly similar lines to the U.S. National Park Service, and protects the finest and most representative landscapes and habitats across the country, as well as providing high quality information and appropriate access for the public. A national park visitor center will often be the best place to start your exploration, whether it is of the Saguenay Marine Park, with its whales and other wildlife, or Banff National Park, where you may pick up useful hints on how to avoid the crowds.

There are also many provincial parks, where the scenery is often no less spectacular, and where there may be more campgrounds and other facilities.

WHEN TO GO

Canada welcomes visitors at all times of the year, and it might be simpler to ask when not to go. The least attractive times of the year are the brief transition periods between fall and winter, when it is cold but winter sports haven't begun, and between winter and spring, when conditions can be wet and slushy. Otherwise, every season has its attraction, though heat and humidity might be a problem for some in high summer in the east. Canadians have long known that winter is the season for fun. It is fun in town, when the bright lights and warmth of indoors contrast with the chill outside, city streets become hockey rinks, parks are laced with cross-country ski trails, and civil servants skate to work along Ottawa's Rideau Canal. Nothing could be more fun than Québec City's winter carnival, when the populace goes wild in the streets at the sight of the Bonhomme (giant snowman), and ice castles sprout from the snow. It is fun in the countryside, too, when Canadians mix with Americans and the rest of the world in world-class ski resorts such as B.C.'s Whistler or at Mont Tremblant and Mont Sainte-Anne in Québec. ∎

Steeped in sea air, Canada's three Maritime Provinces preserve an old-fashioned atmosphere, with pretty fishing villages, towns with a Loyalist imprint, and plenty of evocative reminders of the French Acadia of long ago.

The Maritimes

Introduction & map **54–55**
New Brunswick 56–65
New Brunswick's Fundy Shore
   56–61
Acadie & after **62–63**
Saint John River Valley drive **64–65**
Prince Edward Island 66–71
Nova Scotia 72–84
Halifax **72–74**
Atlantic coast drive **75–77**
Annapolis Valley and the French
   shore **80–81**
Cape Breton Island and
   the Cabot Trail **82–83**
Louisbourg **84**
Hotels & restaurants in the
   Maritimes **349–51**

**Lobster traps
at North Rustico Harbour**

The Maritimes

THE MOSAIC OF DIVERSE LANDSCAPES that make up this sparsely populated region have one thing in common—the sea. The Maritime Provinces—New Brunswick, Prince Edward Island, and Nova Scotia—were settled from the sea, and most of their two million or so inhabitants live in coastal settlements of one kind or another. It is the timeless-seeming fishing villages and little ports that draw many of today's visitors to this long and deeply indented coastline, with its bays and coves, inlets and estuaries, cliffs and islands, and awe-inspiring Fundy tides.

The interior of the Maritimes, by contrast, seems deserted, blanketed by forest growing on the thin and hungry soils of uplands whose rocks are related to those of the Appalachians. The fertile intervals that do occur seem all the more welcoming, as in New Brunswick's Saint John River Valley, and the Annapolis Valley in Nova Scotia. Prince Edward Island (P.E.I.) is an exception: The neatly ordered farming pattern in which cultivation of the potato prevails has earned the province the name of "Million Acre Farm," or, less politely, "Spud Island."

The Maritimes have no natural focus; the sea divides and brings together. Halifax may be the biggest city, but its destiny has always been an oceanic one, with strong ties to Europe and the United States as well as with its hinterland. Well inland, genteel Fredericton, the capital of New Brunswick, shares the province's urban functions with the port city of Saint John and with Moncton, which still serves as the regional rail hub and in a newer role as a center for the Acadian population. Prince Edward Island, reluctant to join the rest of Canada at the time of Confederation, is still immersed in dreams of a separate identity, despite the construction of a great bridge linking it to its neighbors across the Northumberland Strait. Cape Breton Island, too, is quite distinct—its rust-belt industries lie cheek by jowl with the wild scenery of its Gaelic coast and Cape Breton Highlands National Park. Cape Breton is also

the site of the greatest of the Maritimes' many historic monuments—the vast, reconstructed French fortress of Louisbourg.

The Maritimes are the most ethnically homogenous of Canada's regions. The French are still present in all three provinces, despite the rigors of the Acadian deportation carried out by the British in the mid-18th century. Though their numbers are small in P.E.I. and only slightly larger in Nova Scotia, they form about a third of the population in New Brunswick, the nation's only officially bilingual province. Otherwise the vast majority of the population claim descent from

5▷ QUÉBEC p.105

Dalhe
Campbellto

17

St.-Quentin

Edmundston
★

820m
MT. CARLETON
PROVINCIAL
PARK
Nepis

St.-Léonard

2

Grand Falls
● Drummond

NEW
BRUNSWICK

Plaster
Rock

4▷

Doaktown

● Hartland

● Nashwa
Bridge

● Woodstock

Saint John

2

Fredericto
★
Oromo

King's Landing
Historical Settlement

3▷

Oromocto
Lake

7

U.S.A.

St. Croix

Saint Joh

St.Andrews

1

● Letete

Deer Island

Passamaquoddy
Bay
Campobello I.

Grand
Manan
Island

2▷

St. Mary's
Bay
Weymou
Long I.

Brier I.

Meteghan ●

Mavillette

Yarmouth ●

1▷

Wedgepor

△
A

Baie des Chaleurs
Miscou Island
Petit-Rocher
Caraquet
Bathurst
Shippagan
Village Historique Acadien
Gulf of St. Lawrence
Îles de la Madeleine (Québec)
St. Paul Island
Cape North
Bay St. Lawrence
CAPE BRETON HIGHLANDS NATIONAL PARK
Pleasant Bay
532m
Ingonish
Miramichi Bay
North Point
Tignish
Chatham
Newcastle
KOUCHIBOUGUAC
Renous NATIONAL PARK
West Point
PRINCE EDWARD ISLAND
Chéticamp
Cape Breton Island
Margaree Harbour
South Gut
St. Ann's
North Sydney
Glace Bay
Richibucto
Cavendish
PRINCE EDWARD ISLAND NATIONAL PARK
Elmira
Inverness
Baddeck
Sydney
Harcourt
Miscouche
New London
Souris
Basin Head Fisheries Museum
Port Hood
Bouctouche
Summerside
Borden
Charlottetown
Orwell
Louisbourg
Shediac
PARLEE BEACH
Port Elgin
Fort Amherst
St. George's Bay
Port Hastings
St. Peter's
Moncton
PROV. PARK
Cape Tormentine
Wood Islands
Strait
105
Bras d'Or Lake
Isle Madame
Hopewell Cape
Amherst
Pugwash
Caribou
Antigonish
Port Hawkesbury
4
Fort Beauséjour
Wentworth
6
Pictou
Mulgrave
Canso
Sussex
FUNDY NATIONAL PARK
Springhill
104
New Glasgow
104
Hampton
Glenholme
Parrsboro
Truro
St. Mary's
Minas Basin
102
Stewiacke
Wolfville
Sherbrooke
Kentville
GRANDE PRÉ NAT. HIST. PARK
Sheet Harbour
Liscomb
101
Windsor
Port Dufferin
Fort Anne
Middleton
Bridgetown
Dartmouth
Musquodoboit Harbour
Annapolis Royal
Bedford
Port Royal Nat. Hist. Park - The Habitation
Mahone Bay
HALIFAX
igby
10
Chester
Peggys Cove
KEJIMKUJIK NAT. PARK
South Brookfield
Lunenburg
hurch oint
Bridgewater
Lake Rossignol
Liverpool
Shelburne
103
Lockeport
Barrington
Shag Harbour
Cape Sable
B
C
D
E
0   100 kilometers
0   50 miles
Ottawa

British or Irish stock. Scots live all over Nova Scotia, with Highlanders and Islanders concentrated on Cape Breton Island; many Irish inhabit the cities as do American Loyalists, for whom New Brunswick in particular became a second home. Among the Loyalists were freed slaves, ancestors of Halifax's contemporary black community. Earlier, the British had settled "foreign Protestants," mostly German in origin, in the planned port town of Lunenburg, part of the strategy for consolidating their hold on a region whose colonial population was almost entirely French. It took many years, the expulsion of the Acadians (1755), and two

sieges of Louisbourg (1745 and 1758) before the Maritimes finally passed wholly into British hands, and Île-St.-Jean became St. John's Island, and, later, Prince Edward Island.

In the 19th century, the economy of the Maritimes boomed on "wood, wind, and water." Local timber was exported or used in building the region's famed sailing ships. With the advent of steel ships after 1880, a long slump began, relieved temporarily by two world wars, and, more recently, by determined modernization and encouragement of such enterprises as salmon, agriculture, and—increasingly—tourism. ∎

New Brunswick's Fundy Shore

THE BAY OF FUNDY IS A REMARKABLE BODY OF TIDAL water. Nothing else quite like it exists in the marine world. Some of the world's highest tides—as much as 50 feet—have been recorded here. Their height is caused by the bay's funnel shape—wide and deep at the entrance, narrow and shallow at the head. These impressive tides carry about 100 billion tons of water in and out of the bay every day, providing a magnificent display in the process.

Tourism New Brunswick
www.tourismnbcanada.com
☎ 800/561-0123

St. Andrews
🅰 54 A3

Visitor Information
✉ 46 Reed Ave.
☎ 506/529-3555

Fundy National Park's Bennett Lake guarantees beautiful scenery both on and off the water.

The incessant movement of the waters helps create an array of fascinating phenomena such as the sculptured rocks at Hopewell Cape, the Reversing Falls at Saint John, and the Old Sow whirlpool among the islands of Passamaquoddy Bay. It also acts as a nutrient pump to support an extraordinary variety of marine life in the broad intertidal zone and offshore. For example, off the Fundy Islands, swarms of krill attract fin and humpback whales, along with large flocks of maritime birds such as phalaropes, shearwaters, and gulls.

Visitors should be warned that the great difference between the high and low tides and the speed of the incoming tide make it essential to consult the tide table carefully before taking a walk along the beach. (Tide timetables are

available from tourist offices throughout the region.) Bear in mind that the Bay of Fundy is also renowned for its fogs.

ST. ANDREWS & ST. CROIX ISLAND

In 1604 a tiny island in the St. Croix River dividing New Brunswick from Maine was chosen by Sieur des Monts and Samuel de Champlain as their first Habitation, though their first winter caused them to abandon the site in favor of Port Royal (see p. 80) on the Nova Scotia shore. Today, St. Croix Island, visible from the riverside roads on both sides of the U.S./Canada border, is an international historic site. You will, however, need your own boat if you wish to visit it.

Passamaquoddy Bay essentially remains a summer place, a

favored vacation spot for well-to-do Americans and Canadians. Its focal point is **St. Andrews** (*Welcome Centre, tel 506/529-3556*), now primarily a fishing harbor and resort, but once a flourishing trading port. The town was founded in 1783 by Loyalists who had fled north and settled in Castine, Maine, only to discover a few years later that a redrawing of the frontier had left them stranded in the United States. Undaunted, they dismantled their newly built houses and shipped them north again, reerecting them in St. Andrews, where some of them still stand today and help to give the town its particular charm. Named for the 15 children of King George III, its tree-lined streets are fringed with elegant houses and churches. Among the most distinguished of these buildings are **Sheriff Andrews House Provincial Historic Site** (*63 King St., tel 506/529-5080*) of 1820 and the exquisitely furnished 1824 **Ross Memorial Museum.**

DEER ISLAND & CAMPOBELLO

If you have half a day to spare, an island-hopping excursion in Passamaquoddy Bay is fun. From Letete take the free ferry to **Deer Island** (*Tel 506/466-7340*); it offers lots of spray and bracing sea air. Then continue to **Campobello Island** by the rather primitive ferry, which gives you a close-up view of the **Old Sow Whirlpool**—but not too close. Take the Roosevelt–Campobello International Suspension Bridge (a very long name for a short bridge) to Lubec, Maine, and then US 1 and Maine 189 to the Canadian border. If time permits, you won't regret making a stop at the **Ganong Chocolatier Plant** in St. Stephen (*73 Milltown Blvd., tel 506/465-5600*).

SAINT JOHN

New Brunswick's biggest city straddles the rocky ground astride the mouth of the Saint John River.

Ross Memorial Museum
✉ 188 Montague St.
☎ 506/529-5124
$ Donation

Saint John
🅰 54 A3

Visitor Information
www.TourismSaintJohn.com
✉ I Market Square
☎ 506/658-2855
🕐 Open all year

Franklin D. Roosevelt & Campobello

In 1883, a land development company promoted the soft yet bracing air and fog of Campobello Island as "gentle restoratives for an over-strung race." Among those enticed were James and Sara Delano Roosevelt, parents of one-year-old Franklin D. Roosevelt (1882–1945).

In 1904, Franklin and his young wife, Eleanor, acquired their own home here. Many years later, in 1921, after fighting a forest fire for hours, he took a dip in the frigid Bay of Fundy waters and contracted the polio

An early photograph of Franklin D. Roosevelt

virus that was to cripple him for the rest of his life. Twelve years passed before he felt able to return to his "beloved island," and by that time he was President of the United States.

A visit to Campobello is a poignant return in time. Franklin and Eleanor's 34-room abode is impeccably maintained as a historic site by the governments of Canada and the U.S. part of Roosevelt–Campobello International Park (*see map pp. 54–55, tel 506/752-2922, house closed mid-Oct.–early May*). ∎

Loyalist House
- ✉ 120 Union St.
- ☎ 506/652-3590
- 🕐 Closed mid-Sept.–mid-May
- 💲 $

Barbour's General Store
- ✉ The Market Slip
- ☎ 506/658-2939
- 🕐 Closed mid-Sept.–mid-June

New Brunswick Museum
www.nbm-mnb.ca
- ✉ Market Square
- ☎ 506/643-2300
- 🕐 Closed Mon. mid-Nov.–mid-May
- 💲 $$

Home to the wealthy and powerful Irving family, who control many of the city's interests, Saint John is an important port, with a huge oil refinery (the biggest in Canada) and a mighty pulp mill. Fondly known as Fog City throughout New Brunswick, it is laid out on a series of dead-end streets that can cause frustrations for visitors.

The waterfront at Market Slip makes a good starting point for exploring the city's attractions. The centerpiece is **Barbour's General Store,** an authentic 19th-century emporium stocked with goods of the period. Old warehouses have been incorporated into Market Square, completed in 1983 as a multipurpose development. Its main feature is the **New Brunswick Museum** opening off the central atrium. Its rich collections cover much of the province's human and natural history.

Every July the waterfront is the site of an annual reenactment of the Loyalist landing, and the city center has several reminders of this period in Saint John's history. The **Loyalist House** of 1817 escaped a great fire in 1877 and has a beautifully furnished interior. King Square is laid out in the form of a British Union flag, and is bounded by the **Loyalist Burial Ground**

Salt spray has not prevented the vigorous growth of vegetation on the sandstone sea stacks at Hopewell Cape.

with many original tombstones.

The city's biggest tourist draw is just outside the city's center. A trip to see **Reversing Falls Rapids** *(lookout point off Hwy. 100, tel 506/658-2937)* is a memorable part of a visit to Saint John. At low tide the river current carries water downstream to the Bay of Fundy. At high tide the force of the Fundy tides carries water upstream. From the viewpoint you can see the water flow as it reverses over the rapids. Be warned that the smell of the pulp mill upstream can be rather strong.

THE FUNDY SHORE
Eastward from the attractive little lobster port of St. Martins stretch 25 miles of rugged coastline, one of the least accessible shorelines in eastern North America.

The coast can also be reached at the **Fundy National Park,** with its tracts of mixed hardwood and

evergreen forest as well as cliffs, coves, rock pools, and intertidal flats. **St. Mary's Point,** an important resting and feeding site for countless migratory seabirds, marks the division between Chignecto and Shepody Bays. At **Hopewell Cape** *(S of Moncton by Rte. 114)*, the scouring Fundy tides have carved the cliffs of red sandstone into improbable flowerpot shapes, capped by vigorous tree growth. The trees are all that show at high tide and the flowerpots have become a scatter of little islands.

MONCTON

Originally called The Bend because of its location on a curve of the Petitcodiac River, Moncton then became The Hub, the focus of the Maritimes' railroad network and the site of Canadian National's (CN) huge maintenance depot. CN closed the depot in 1989, but the town has partly recovered by becoming the telecommunications center of Canada. Moncton's bilingualism helped here; the town is also the informal capital of Acadia, with about 30 percent of its population descended from returning Acadians (see pp. 62–63).

The Fundy tides have a final fling as they meet the Petitcodiac. The wave that precedes the incoming tide (known as the Tidal Bore) can be viewed from **Boreview Park** *(Main & King Sts.)* in the center of town. The bore can vary from a ripple to nearly two feet in height (but is commonly a ripple), depending on the phase of the moon. What is generally much more impressive is the tremendous inrush of water that follows the bore and the rapid rise in the water level. From a small stream crossing mudflats a mile wide, the Petitcodiac River becomes a wide channel with no mud in sight.

The longest of New Brunswick's covered bridges spans the Saint John River at Hartland.

Fundy National Park
www.pc.gc.ca
55 B3
Route 114, Alma
506/887-6000
Closed mid-Oct.–mid-May
$ vehicle fee, free in winter

Moncton visitor information
www.gomoncton.com
55 B3
City Hall, 655 Main St.
506/853-3590

Fort Beauséjour
www.pc.gc.ca
 55 B3
✉ Exit 550A of Hwy.
106 in Aulac N.B.
☎ 506/364-5080
🕐 Closed mid-Oct.–May

Acadian Shore
 55 B5

FORT BEAUSÉJOUR

Overlooking the marshlands at the head of the Cumberland Basin is **Fort Beauséjour,** which commands the Chignecto isthmus, the neck of land separating New Brunswick from Nova Scotia. Four years after its completion by the French in 1751, it was attacked by a party of British regulars and Massachusetts volunteers led by Col. Robert Monckton, and fell after a siege of two weeks. The French commandant, De Vergor, who was allowed to march his men out with banners flying and band playing, was fated to meet the British once again, in 1759, on the Plains of Abraham at Québec. As for Monckton, his name, misspelled, was given to the nearby settlement previously known as The Bend; his action, carried out in time of peace, helped precipitate the Seven Years' War.

In 1776, refortified, renamed Fort Cumberland, and commanded by Col. Joseph Goreham of the Royal Fencible Americans, the stronghold successfully beat off an attack by rebel New Englanders. Strengthened again against a possible U.S. attack in the War of 1812, it was finally abandoned in 1835.

The fort's star-shaped hilltop earthworks are still an imposing sight, and cannon and mortar evoke its days of action. The visitor center has excellent displays, not only on military history, but on the deportation of the Acadians and on the surrounding landscape, which still bears the imprint of the Acadians' extensive dike and drainage systems.

THE ACADIAN SHORE

Appreciated for its sandy beaches, warm water, and abundant seafood, the eastern coast of New Brunswick facing the Northumberland Strait and the Gulf of St. Lawrence is the heartland of the Maritimes' Acadian population. The Acadian tricolor flies from many a residence, there are Acadian festivals and blessings of the fishing fleet, and numerous attractions have a distinctive Acadian flavor.

The province makes much of the coast, enjoying some of the warmest saltwater swimming north of Virginia. Because of the shallowness of the sea, water temperatures can indeed reach 70°F or more in summer. From Moncton it is a short drive to the resort of **Shediac** and the fine sand of the extremely popular **Parlee Beach Provincial Park** (Tel 506/533-3363). Farther north is **Kouchibouguac National Park** (Tel 506/876-2443, visitor center closed mid-Oct.–mid-May),

A solitary walker savors the sandy shoreline of Kouchibouguac National Park.

with a landscape of forest, bog, marsh, and meadowland, and a shoreline of sandy beaches and warm water lagoons, protected by barrier islands and sand dunes.

There are plenty of accessible beaches along the shores of the Acadian Peninsula, whose north coast faces the long inlet of the sea named Baie des Chaleurs (Warm Bay) by Jacques Cartier. Lovers of solitary walks by the sea will head for remote Miscou Island at the very tip of the peninsula, accessible by bridge from Petit-Shippagan.

It is easy for visitors to make contact with some aspect of Acadian life, past or present. At **Bouctouche,** the **Musée de Kent** realistically re-creates the regime endured by girls at a 19th-century Roman Catholic boarding school, while the **Pays de la Sagouine** *(Tel 506/743-1400,*

closed Oct.–mid-June) is a theme park devoted to the doings of the colorful characters created by the popular novelist Antonine Maillet. On the Acadian Peninsula, **Caraquet** has a rambunctious Festival Acadien on the Feast of the Assumption (August 15), as well as the fascinating **Acadian Museum** *(15 blvd. Saint-Pierre East, tel 506/726-2682, closed winter)* and the nearby **Village Historique Acadien** *(6 miles W of Caraquet on Rte. 11, tel 506/726-2600, closed mid-Oct.–late May).* This excellent counterpart to Kings Landing Historical Settlement (see p. 64) in the southwest offers an array of traditional buildings from all over New Brunswick, all set in a re-created landscape and "populated" by 19th-century folk who help bring alive the Acadia of yesteryear. ■

The Village Historique Acadien evokes the simple life of Acadian countryfolk.

Musée de Kent
✉ 150 rue du Couvent
☎ 506/743-5005
🕐 Closed Oct.–May

Acadie & after

Acadia (Acadie in French) was the name given to the Atlantic region of New France to distinguish it from Canada, which in those days consisted only of the settled area of the St. Lawrence Valley. At the beginning of the 17th century, Acadia was the site of the first permanent European settlement north of Florida. Although its population was subjected to massive deportation by the British in the mid-18th century, the name and a distinctive francophone culture live on in the Maritime Provinces.

Acadia's origins

The word "Acadia" is derived from Arcadia, the province that the ancient Greeks thought of as an earthly paradise. The term was used in 1524 by Giovanni da Verrazano (1485–1528) to describe the coastline well to the south of present-day Acadia—the "r" in the name was lost by mapmakers long ago. French colonization of the area began in 1604, with the establishment by explorers Sieur des Monts and Samuel de Champlain of the short-lived Habitation on Île Sainte-Croix, followed by

the more permanent fortified settlement at Port Royal the following year. More colonists arrived in the 1630s, mostly from the western regions of France, but disputes between its leaders held back the colony's development. Franco-British rivalry was present from the earliest days; Port Royal was sacked in 1613 by raiders from Virginia, and parts of the colony passed between the French and British several times before the definitive establishment of British rule in 1763.

The Acadians concentrated on making a living by farming the marshlands they expertly reclaimed from the sea around the Bay of Fundy. Trading relations were closer with New England, the home of *nos amis l'ennemi* (our friends the enemy), than with far-off France. The British rulers of Nova Scotia attempted to extract an oath of unconditional loyalty from their Acadians, but they refused, preferring to remain neutral in what to them seemed irrelevant struggles between imperial powers. As tensions rose in the buildup to the Seven Years' War (1756–1763), the British felt unable to tolerate the threat from what they saw as a potentially hostile population. In 1755 the majority of the Acadians were rounded up and deported, some to France, some to Britain, some to the American Colonies. A significant number escaped into the forests or made their way to Québec. Many ended up in Louisiana, where their name metamorphosed into "Cajun." Their homes were destroyed to discourage any thoughts of returning.

Despite the rigors of the *Grand Dérangement* (the Deportation), in which many perished of hunger and disease, the Acadians proved tenacious. Many made the journey back to their lands, only to find them in the hands of New England colonists encouraged to move north by the British. Joined by released prisoners and others emerging from the shelter of the forests, the returnees settled on far less fertile lands and found new livelihoods in fishing and lumbering—important occupations to this day.

For decades, the Acadians accepted their lot as second-class citizens in a conquered land, unable to vote, exploited economically, and

The expulsion depicted at the Museum of the Acadians in Bonaventure, Québec

The Acadian Village at Miscouche on Prince Edward Island is an evocative and informative reminder of the Acadian presence in the Maritimes.

with no institutions of their own other than the Roman Catholic Church, which itself was largely staffed by clergy from Québec.

But revival began in the 19th century. A wider world became aware of Acadian identity through the 1847 sentimental epic *Evangeline* by Henry Wadsworth Longfellow (1807–1882), which dramatized the Deportation. Acadians won the right to vote, and by the end of the century they had adopted a flag (a French tricolor with the Marian star), a national holiday (August 15, the Feast of the Assumption), and a national anthem ("Ave Maria Stella"). As in Québec, population increased rapidly, from about 8,500 at the start of the 19th century to around 300,000 today. During the 20th century, economic underprivilege was reduced by the establishment of cooperatives, political representation improved, and language rights were legislated.

A vigorous middle class came into being as Acadians moved away from farming, fishing, and forestry into administrative and professional work. Their vital folk culture continued to thrive, supplemented by new initiatives in theater, literature, film, radio, and television.

Today's Acadians live all over the Maritime Provinces. The greatest concentration (one-third of the province's total population) is in New Brunswick, particularly in the south around Moncton and along the "Acadian shore" in the northeast. The city of Moncton serves as a focus of francophone culture, with its university and TV and radio stations. Smaller numbers of Acadians also live on the west side of Prince Edward Island and on Cape Breton Island and the "French shore" of Nova Scotia.

To understand the Acadians and their eventful history, it is worth a visit to Grand-Pré National Historic Site (see p. 80). ■

Saint John River Valley drive

Between the headwaters of its several branches in the wooded wildernesses of Maine and Québec and its mouth on the Bay of Fundy, the Saint John River drains a basin of some 25,000 square miles, passing through some of the most attractive and agriculturally rich countryside in New Brunswick. This driving route covers about 175 miles, following Trans-Canada 2 and linking Edmundston, near the Québec border, with Fredericton.

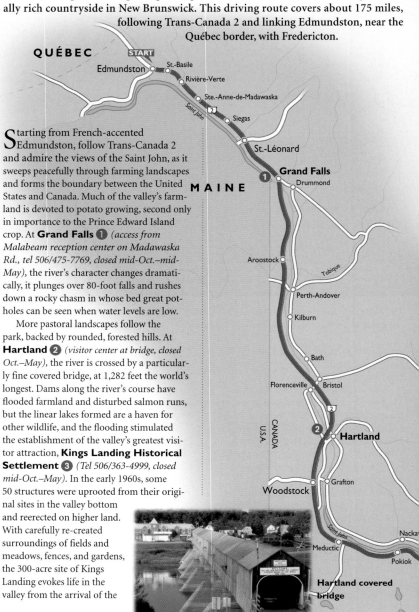

QUÉBEC START
Edmundston   St.-Basile
              Rivière-Verte
                  Ste.-Anne-de-Madawaska
              2   Siegas
                  St.-Léonard
              ❶ **Grand Falls**
MAINE   Drummond

Aroostock
              Tobique
          Perth-Andover
       Kilburn
              Bath
Florenceville Bristol
              2
          ❷ **Hartland**
    CANADA
    U.S.A.
Woodstock   Grafton

              Saint John
                      Nacka
  Meductic
                  Pokiok

Starting from French-accented Edmundston, follow Trans-Canada 2 and admire the views of the Saint John, as it sweeps peacefully through farming landscapes and forms the boundary between the United States and Canada. Much of the valley's farmland is devoted to potato growing, second only in importance to the Prince Edward Island crop. At **Grand Falls** ❶ *(access from Malabeam reception center on Madawaska Rd., tel 506/475-7769, closed mid-Oct.–mid-May)*, the river's character changes dramatically, it plunges over 80-foot falls and rushes down a rocky chasm in whose bed great potholes can be seen when water levels are low.

More pastoral landscapes follow the park, backed by rounded, forested hills. At **Hartland** ❷ *(visitor center at bridge, closed Oct.–May)*, the river is crossed by a particularly fine covered bridge, at 1,282 feet the world's longest. Dams along the river's course have flooded farmland and disturbed salmon runs, but the linear lakes formed are a haven for other wildlife, and the flooding stimulated the establishment of the valley's greatest visitor attraction, **Kings Landing Historical Settlement** ❸ *(Tel 506/363-4999, closed mid-Oct.–May)*. In the early 1960s, some 50 structures were uprooted from their original sites in the valley bottom and reerected on higher land. With carefully re-created surroundings of fields and meadows, fences, and gardens, the 300-acre site of Kings Landing evokes life in the valley from the arrival of the

Hartland covered bridge

Loyalists in 1784 to the end of the 19th century. As well as a variety of houses, there is a sawmill, gristmill, forge, store, church, pub, and theater with live performances. Attention to detail and costumed villagers going about their everyday tasks help make this one of the best re-creations of traditional rural life in North America.

From Kings Landing the highway follows the river northeast until it reaches the genteel capital of New Brunswick. With its population of academics and civil servants, **Fredericton** ❹ *(Visitor Center, 11 Carleton St., tel 506/460-2041)* stands on a bend of the Saint John River close to the river's tidal limit. Well inland, and thus relatively safe from American incursions, it seemed to the Loyalists who established it in 1784 a better choice as provincial capital than coastal Saint John. A grandiose **Provincial Legislative Assembly Building** *(Queen & St. John Sts., tel 506/453-2527)* in Second Empire style, the stately stone-built **Christ Church Cathedral** *(Church & Brunswick Sts., tel 506/450-8500)* with a tall spire, and remnants of the British garrison's presence in the **Historic Garrison District** *(Tel 506/460-2041)* set the tone of the place, as do elm-lined streets and a number of Regency houses. To complete the neocolonial picture there is a ceremonial **Changing of the**

Guard *(twice daily)* in July and August. The British garrison departed following the Confederation in 1867, but Fredericton retained its military importance; Canadian forces trained here in both world wars, and in the 1950s nearby Camp Gagetown became the country's largest army base.

In the **York-Sunbury Historical Society Museum** *(Queen St., tel 506/455-6041, closed Jan.–Mar.)* the town possesses an intriguing local museum, crammed with curiosities. The exhibit everyone comes to see, however, is Fred Coleman's giant frog, fed lovingly until it attained a weight of 44 pounds, then stuffed.

Fredericton's art collection is equally compelling. The city benefited greatly from favors bestowed by politician and newspaper magnate Lord Beaverbrook (1879–1964), a resident of New Brunswick. Along with university buildings and a theater, Beaverbrook gave Fredericton its **Beaverbrook Art Gallery** *(703 Queen St., tel 506/458-8545, closed Mon. Nov.–Mar.).* The gallery has old masters, the country's largest collection of British art, and an array of Canadian pictures. ■

See area map pp. 54–55
► Edmundston
◄► 175 miles
⏱ Allow 2–3 days
► Fredericton

NOT TO BE MISSED
- Grand Falls
- Hartland covered bridge
- Kings Landing Historical Settlement
- Beaverbrook Art Gallery

Fredericton lighthouse

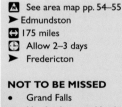

NEW BRUNSWICK

Grand Lake

Fredericton

Saint John

Oromocto

Longs Creek
ngs Landing
st. Settlement

nce
liam

0   30 kilometers
0   20 miles

Prince Edward Island

PHYSICALLY LINKED TO THE REST OF CANADA BY THE Confederation Bridge since 1997, Prince Edward Island strives to maintain the offshore identity of which it is so proud and which kept it aloof from the Confederation until there seemed no alternative to joining. That identity is partly the land, partly human.

P.E.I. has been an island since about 5,000 years ago, when the sea level rose to create the Northumberland Strait. Its glaciated surface is flat or gently rolling. Beneath the distinctive red soil, in which the famous potatoes flourish, are layers of soft red sedimentary rock, exposed in crumbling cliffs at many places along the shore. Though some woodland remains, it is agriculture that has determined the patchwork pattern of fields and farms, so much in contrast to the endless forest blanketing much of the Maritimes.

P.E.I.'s first European settlers came directly from France, brought here in 1720 to secure the island for the mother country after it had lost Acadia and Newfoundland to Britain in 1713. Like the rest of the francophone population of the Maritimes, this community was deported in midcentury as tensions rose between Britain and France. But many later returned, and today some 12 percent of the population is of French or Acadian descent, though only a fraction still have French as their mother tongue. Otherwise it is the British Isles that have supplied the island with its European inhabitants. The English mainly arrived after the Acadian deportation in 1755, when it was decided to replace the French with a more docile population. When Charlottetown was founded as the island's capital in 1768, the English were followed by Scots, the majority of them Gaelic-speaking Highlanders, then later by the Irish,

both Protestant and Catholic. This settlement and the maintenance of cultural tradition has made the island one of the most Anglo-Celtic areas of Canada.

CONFEDERATION BRIDGE

It is still possible to travel to P.E.I. by ferry *(Tel 888/249-7245)* but since 1997 most visitors' introduction to the island has been via the **Confederation Bridge** *(CAN$40.50 toll payable on leaving only; pedestrians and cyclists must take bus),* which leaps 8 miles across the Northumberland Strait between Cape Tourmentine, New Brunswick, and Borden-Carleton, P.E.I. The longest continuous marine span bridge in the world over ice-covered waters, it has a two-lane highway supported on 65 piers and rises to a height of nearly 200 feet to allow shipping to pass below.

One of the terms of entry into the Confederation insisted on in 1873 by the island's leadership was that the federal government should provide "continuous communication" between the island and the mainland. The merits of a "fixed link" were the subject of endless debate, some people favoring a rail tunnel, others a bridge. In the meantime, ferries maintained a link that, given winter ice floes, was far from reliable. Nevertheless, the 1993 decision to build the link in the form of a bridge was not greeted with universal acclaim. There were deep fears about the possible effects of the bridge

⚠ 55 C3–C4

Visitor information for Prince Edward Island & Charlottetown
www.peiplay.com
✉ 178 Water St., Charlottetown
☎ 902/368-4444

Above: Prince Edward Island's coat of arms mixes oak trees and the British lion.

Right: Since the opening of the Confederation Bridge in 1997, ice floes in the Northumberland Strait no longer cut off links with the mainland.

Charlottetown

55 C3

Province House National Historic Site

www.pc.gc.ca

✉ Richmond St.

☎ 902/566-7626

🕐 Closed weekends mid-Oct.–May

Province House is one of Charlottetown's fine public buildings designed by P.E.I.'s leading early 19th-century architect, Isaac Smith.

on the strait's environment, in particular on its potential to prolong the presence of ice in the strait and thus possibly shorten the island's growing season. Its impact on the equally crucial lobster fishery was also a source of worry, while some islanders feared the effect of unrestrained tourism on a relatively protected way of life.

The **Gateway Village Complex** (Tel 902/437-8570) by the Borden-Carleton toll plaza has an exhibition entitled "Our Island Home," whose displays and artworks make an excellent introduction to the island and its links to the mainland.

CHARLOTTETOWN

Prince Edward Island's miniature capital was founded in 1768, the successor to the nearby French settlement of Port La Joye, abandoned at the time of the Acadian deportation. Well sited on the natural harbor formed by the confluence of the Hillsborough River and its north and west tributaries, Charlottetown has preserved its original layout. A typical example of the British colonial gridiron plan, it

has refinements in the shape of a central square for civic edifices and four smaller squares symmetrically placed. From the town's **Victoria Park** (Lower Kent St.) there is a fine view across the water to the site of **Fort Amherst** (off Rte. 19, 25 miles W of Charlottetown, tel 902/566-7626), built by the British over the remains of Port La Joye to guard the approaches to the harbor. Only the earthworks of the fort remain, but there is a panorama of Charlottetown and an interpretive center with displays on the history of the site.

The dignified white neoclassic edifice of **Government House,** one of a number of prestigious buildings in Charlottetown designed by the local architect Isaac Smith (circa 1795–1871), stands among the trees of Victoria Park. Close by is **Beaconsfield** (2 Kent St., tel 902/368-6603), a handsome villa from 1877, now the headquarters of P.E.I.'s Museum Service. There are more well-preserved 19th-century structures around early 20th-century Gothic **St. Dunstan's Basilica** and along Great George Street, the route linking the harbor to the central square. But the building everyone is urged to see in Charlottetown is **Province House National Historic Site,** considered to be one of the most elegant examples of Georgian architecture in the Maritimes. Completed in 1848 by Isaac Smith, it still houses the provincial legislature and was the site in 1864 of the first of the meetings held to discuss the Confederation. The island may have hesitated to join with the other provinces to form a united Canada, but it is proud of its role as the "Cradle of Confederation," and of the hospitality that was offered to the provincial premiers when they met here. On the upper floor

of Province House is the Confederation Chamber, where they held their deliberations, as well as other rooms (Library, Secretariat) with exhibits recalling these stirrings of Canadian unity. Close by is the bunker-like **Confederation Centre of the Arts** (*Richmond St., Tel 902/628-1864*), built in 1964 to commemorate the centenary of the Charlottetown Conference. With its library, theaters, and art gallery arranged around a memorial hall, it is as representative of its time as was Province House. The musical version of *Anne of Green Gables* (*Tel 800/565-0278 for ticket information*) plays every summer to packed audiences in its theater.

ANNE'S ISLAND

Lucy Maud Montgomery (see p. 71) described her beloved Prince Edward Island as an "Emerald, Ruby and Sapphire land," and the island repays the compliment with an array of attractions that should satisfy even the most devoted follower of the cult of *Anne of Green Gables.*

In addition to summer performances of a musical version of Anne's adventures and an annual Lucy Maud Montgomery festival in the Cavendish area, there are several sites with Montgomery and Anne associations. They include: the **Lucy Maud Montgomery Birthplace** (*Jct. of Rtes. 6 & 20, tel 902/886-2099, closed mid-Oct.–early May*) in New London, which houses many of the author's personal effects including her wedding dress; the **Lucy Maud Montgomery Heritage Museum** (*in Park Corner on Rte. 20, tel 902/886-2807*), a farmhouse where she was brought up by her grandparents; and her uncle and aunt's house (also at Park Corner), "the big white beautiful house which was the wonder castle of my childhood," now the **Anne of Green Gables Museum at Silverbush** filled with much memorabilia.

Pilgrims will find their way to these and other sites, while those ignorant of Montgomery and her fictional offspring would do well to visit **Green Gables House** in

Attractive and productive farmland makes up much of the landscape of Prince Edward Island.

Anne of Green Gables Museum at Silverbush

✉ Park Corner (Route 20)

☎ 902/436-7329

🕐 Closed mid-Oct.–mid-May

💲 $

The ocean eats away steadily at the soft sandstone cliffs of P.E.I. National Park.

Cavendish. The centerpiece of the extensive site managed by Parks Canada is the white house (with green gables) once lived in by the cousins with whom Lucy Maud spent many happy times, and that she used as the setting of her novel.

Originally built in 1830, their residence has been restored and refurbished to suggest scenes from the novel. Extensive restoration work has been carried on around the house to complete the picture of an Edwardian childhood, and the imposing farm buildings have been saved from dereliction. The visitor center has displays that give an excellent introduction to the whole Anne phenomenon. Those who wish to immerse themselves further into her world will take a stroll along nearby Lovers' Lane or venture into the Haunted Wood.

PRINCE EDWARD ISLAND NATIONAL PARK

One of the smallest of Canada's National Parks is also one of the most popular, its dunes and beaches drawing thousands of visitors. The park is a long and narrow strip, stretching along the island's northern coast for some 25 miles between Cavendish Beach and Stanhope Beach. The Gulf of St. Lawrence is shallow here, no more than 50 feet deep 12 miles out from the shore, and its waters warm up quickly in summer.

Most of the park's beaches are backed by dunes, which you can reach on boardwalks, but in places there are low cliffs. These make fine viewpoints, but be warned—their red sandstone is being continually undercut by the sea and crumbles easily. The cliffs are liable to sudden collapse, and visitors should keep away from the edge. Behind the cliffs and dunes is a wooded strip of spruce forest, interspersed with meadows, salt marsh, and freshwater ponds, all connected by interpretive trails.

The popularity of this coastline has led to intensive development of its hinterland, in particular along Rte. 6, where multiple attractions compete for the visitor's attention.

ISLAND EXTREMITIES

Both Prince County in the west of the island and Kings County in the east have their share of man-made attractions. Between the Nova

Green Gables House
www.pc.gc.ca
✉ off Rte. 6 just west of Rte. 13
☎ 902/963-7874
🕐 Closed Nov.-Apr.
💲 $

Prince Edward Island National Park
www.pc.gc.ca
🅰 55 C4
✉ 15 miles north of Charlottetown on Rte. 15
☎ 902/672-6350

Scotia ferry terminal at Wood Islands and Charlottetown is **Orwell Corner Historic Village** *(Off Trans-Canada 1, tel 902/651-8510, closed mid Oct.–mid-May)*, once abandoned but now restored, while farther east, beyond the port of Souris, is the **Basin Head Fisheries Museum** *(Off Rte. 16, tel 902/357-7230, closed mid-Oct.–May)*, detailing the life and work of inshore fishermen, and the **Elmira Railway Museum,** in what was P.E.I.'s easternmost station *(Rte. 16A, tel 902/357-7234, closed Oct.–mid-June)*. In the west, as well as **"Canada's only Potato Museum"** *(Heritage Ln in O'Leary, tel 902/859-2039, closed mid-Oct.–mid-May)*, there is the modern **Acadian Museum** at Miscouche *(Rte. 2, W of Summerside, tel 902/432-2880, fee May-Oct.)* telling the story of the P.E.I. Acadians, most of whom live on this part of the island. But the real point in moving on from the more crowded center of the island is to meander along quiet side roads, wiggle your toes in the sand of unpeopled beaches, brace yourself on a cliff top against the sea breeze, and set off for the brightly painted beacon of a lighthouse on a distant headland. ■

Lucy Maud, Anne, & their island

Although the latter part of her life was spent in Ontarian exile, Lucy Maud Montgomery (1874–1942) never forgot the island where she was born, and 19 of her 20 novels were set here, most famously those that record the doings of the mettlesome little lass known as Anne of Green Gables.

Born in P.E.I.'s New London (then called Clifton), the young Montgomery was brought up in Cavendish by her elderly and severe maternal grandparents. She found solace and stimulation in the landscape, and in books and writing. Her emotional life was far from untroubled; she had a history of secret loves and broken engagements, and the clergyman she finally did marry fell prey to religious melancholia. But her books, letters, and journals are full of spirit and sensitivity, as well as humor. A prolific writer, she penned 450 poems, 500 short stories, and 5,000 diary pages as well as her novels. *Anne of Green Gables*, published in 1908, was an instant best-seller, and was

followed by numerous sequels. Described by Mark Twain as "the sweetest creation of child life ever written," the tale of irrepressible orphan Anne has been translated into 20 languages. The little girl herself enjoys cult status, particularly among young Japanese women, who can be seen around P.E.I. wearing her trademark boater and pigtails. ■

An irresistible attraction to all "Anne" fans: the green-gabled farmhouse at Cavendish

Nova Scotia

THE BEST INTRODUCTION TO NOVA SCOTIA—AND IN many ways the ideal way to grasp the significance of the sea to all the Maritime Provinces—is Halifax. Virtually a creation of the sea itself, and with a sometimes explosive history, the provincial capital sets the tone for the rest of this fascinating and attractive province.

HALIFAX

Although possessing many of the attributes of a modern metropolis, Halifax remains deeply marked by its history; after two and a half centuries, warships still shelter in its superb natural harbor, and a grim citadel still commands the city from its hilltop site. Cheek by jowl with glittering downtown office towers are venerable Georgian and Victorian edifices. The waterfront is dominated by the 19th-century warehouses and other immaculately restored buildings known as the Historic Properties. The city's suburban fringe with its malls and freeways may be unremarkable, but just beyond begins the boundless forest that cloaks so much of the Maritimes, and on either side of the city the coastline has a timeless air, with innumerable bays, coves, and fishing villages.

Dominance by the ocean explains Halifax's creation. The city's gaze is still turned resolutely toward the Atlantic, beyond the headlands and islands guarding the deep inlet leading to Bedford Basin. In the mid-18th century, prompted by New Englanders, the British decided to counter continuing French command of the eastern seaboard and move the capital of Nova Scotia from Annapolis Royal. In 1749, H.M.S. *Sphinx* led a convoy of 13 ships into the deep inlet that the native Mi'kmaq had called Chebucto; aboard was a motley crew of would-be settlers, led by a future governor, Col. Edward Cornwallis. They laid out a ten-acre grid of streets on the slopes leading from the waterfront to the hilltop, where they placed a timber stockade, the predecessor of today's much larger citadel.

From its foundation, the city's fortunes fluctuated with the tides of international and national history. Wartime brought prosperity, from the early days when soldiers and sailors sallied forth to besiege Louisbourg (see p. 84) and capture Québec to the world wars of the 20th century, when the convoys that kept Britain alive assembled in Bedford Bay before braving the U-boat wolf-packs of the North Atlantic.

Explorations of this salty city are best begun at the waterfront. Here, the **Historic Properties** *(below Upper Water St., N of Maritime Museum)* comprise an array of

---

The Town Clock has told the time to Haligonians since 1803.

Halifax
🗺 55 C2

Visitor information
www.novascotia.com
www.halifaxinfo.com
✉ 1595 Barrington & Sackville
☎ 902/490-5946

sturdy stone or timber buildings saved from the threat of a waterside freeway in the late 1960s. One, the **Privateer's Warehouse,** was used in Napoleonic times to store the plundered cargoes of enemy ships, often American, during the War of 1812.

Even more intriguing is the waterfront itself. The famous *Bluenose II* (*Tel 866-579-4909*) is moored here when in Halifax; the chubby ferries linking Halifax to Dartmouth (*leave from bottom of George St. every 15 minutes*) bustle to and fro; historic vessels, including the World War II H.M.C.S. *Sackville*, form the outdoor exhibits of the **Maritime Museum of the Atlantic;** and there may even be a visiting warship to be boarded. The rich collections of the museum bring to life much of the eventful story of Halifax's relationship with the sea; as well as any number of superb ship models, actual crafts range from humble vessels like jolly boats, skiffs, and gigs to Queen Victoria's elegant royal barge. Paneling from the *Titanic* is a poignant reminder that the bodies

of many of the great liner's drowned passengers were brought to Halifax for burial in the city's cemeteries. Other displays include shipwrecks and lifesaving, the Age of Steam, the achievements of Halifax-born Samuel Cunard and his shipping line, and Halifax's role as the most important Canadian naval base—its dockyard was founded in 1759 as the home of the Royal Navy's North American Squadron. The Halifax explosion of 1917 (see p. 74) is evoked in a dramatic audiovisual presentation.

Inland from the waterfront, in the 19th-century courthouse building, is the **Art Gallery of Nova Scotia**. It has a good general selection of Canadian art, from the cheery snowbound scenes of Cornelius Krieghoff (1815–1872) to the Ontario-based Group of Seven (see pp. 186–87). There are plenty of local works, including early ones that attempted to fit Halifax and its surroundings into the European picturesque tradition; lively etchings of city life by Donald C. MacKay (1906–1979); and some charming examples of folk and naive art.

Maritime Museum of the Atlantic
www.maritime.museum
.gov.ns.ca
✉ 1675 Lower Water St.
☎ 902/424-7490
🕐 Closed Mon. Nov.-Apr.
💲 $

Art Gallery of Nova Scotia
www.agns.gov.ns.ca
✉ 1723 Hollis St. at Cheapside
☎ 902/424-7542
💲 $

Contemporary high-rises dominate the skyline above Halifax's historic waterfront.

people could see them. The Town Clock has become one of the great emblems of Halifax, even if it has had no noticeable effect on punctuality in this resolutely laid-back city.

The clock stands at the foot of the steep grassy slope below the **Halifax Citadel National Historic Site** *(Tel 902/426-5080)*. This formidable-looking star-shaped stronghold, the fourth to be built on the site, was constructed between 1828 and 1856 to defend both the landward approach to the city and its harbor. One of the most visited of Canada's national historic sites, it is full of the atmosphere of the British presence in North America. There are kilted sentries, a ceremonial firing of the noonday cannon, and a number of fascinating displays and exhibits, including an exciting audiovisual show "The Tides of History." The fort's placement is stunning, and there is an incomparable panorama of Halifax in its magnificent setting from the ramparts.

Province House, on Hollis Street, is the home of the Nova Scotia legislature, an institution that has existed since 1758. Built in 1819, the present sandstone structure was once described as a "gem of Georgian architecture" by British novelist Charles Dickens (1812–1870). ■

Saved from destruction for an expressway, Halifax's Historic Properties are now a magnet for locals and visitors alike.

Province House
www.gov.ns.ca/legislature
✉ 1726 Hollis St.
☎ 902/424-4661
🕐 Closed Sat.–Sun. Sept.–June

THE HISTORIC CENTER
The best way to get the feel of the historic center of Halifax city is to stand by St. Paul's Anglican Church and City Hall on the **Grand Parade.** From here, walk up George Street to the **Town Clock** bequeathed to the city in 1803 by Edward, Duke of Kent. A punctilious disciplinarian, Edward found Haligonians, or natives of Halifax, very casual about time. The faces on the north and east sides are bigger than the other two, because these were the sides that faced the town, and Edward wanted to make sure

The Halifax Explosion

Before Hiroshima, the world's most devastating man-made explosion occurred in Halifax. On the morning of December 6, 1917, the French ship *Mont Blanc,* fully laden with a cargo of mixed explosives, collided with the Norwegian vessel *Imo* at the entrance to the Narrows. Fire broke out aboard the *Mont Blanc,* and 20 minutes later, abandoned by her crew, she blew up, completely destroying 1,630 houses and instantly killing some 1,400 people, with many more dying in the tidal wave. Buildings 60 miles away lost their windows, and the explosion was heard as far away as Prince Edward Island. Relief efforts came from all over the Maritimes and New England; a Nova Scotia Christmas tree stands every year in central Boston, a symbol of Haligonians' gratitude. ■

Atlantic coast drive: Halifax to Barrington

This drive southwest of Halifax takes in some of the finest coastal scenery on Nova Scotia's Atlantic shore and introduces a number of the province's most attractive harbor villages and small towns.

Leave Halifax via Hwy. 3. Join Rte. 333 at the turnoff and head southwest to **Peggys Cove ❶**. Elemental harshness and cozy domesticity exist side by side in this tiny fishing port; battered by the ocean, a treeless landscape of monstrous glacier-scraped boulders is humanized by a scattering of colorful cottages and by fishermen's shacks perched precariously over the waters of the tiny harbor. A red-capped, brilliant white lighthouse crowns a granite outcrop made slippery by sea spray, a trap for the unwary scrambler. Fishing tackle on the dockside and boats in the water are evidence that hard work is still carried on here, but Peggys Cove's main role nowadays is to be admired. The village has long attracted the attention of visitors. By the mid-20th century, writers, artists and photographers had made the place famous, and you are unlikely to be able to enjoy it on your own, except perhaps when a sea mist rolls in (as it frequently does) and your fellow tourists seek refuge in the big café on the headland.

From Peggys Cove rejoin Hwy. 3, and follow this road north and gradually east around the shore of St. Margarets Bay and Mahone Bay. Among the charming villages that line this coast is **Chester ❷** *(Visitor information Old Station, Hwy. 3, tel 902/275-4616, closed mid-Oct.–mid-May)*. Its tree-lined streets and elegant residences have been a favorite summer resort for vacationers from America's East Coast for more than a century and a half. With two harbors, Front and Back, and access to the bay with its 365 islands, handsome Chester is a yachtsman's paradise, at its liveliest during mid-August's Race Week.

About 14 miles along the old coast road is the equally distinguished but much smaller town of **Mahone Bay ❸** itself, once famous for its shipbuilders, who are celebrated in the annual Wooden Boat Festival in July *(Tel 888/624-0348)*. The best view of the town is from the far side of the fine harbor; rising over the well-treed waterfront in friendly proximity are the towers of the town's three churches, a much photographed scene. A few miles to the south along Hwy. 3, the fishing port of **Lunenburg ❹** *(Visitor information Blockhouse Hill Rd., tel 902/634-8100, closed*

Filled with colonial buildings, Lunenburg's grid of streets climbs steeply from the waterfront.

mid-Oct.–mid-May) is the undoubted star of the Atlantic coast, its unique character given international recognition by its designation in 1995 as a UNESCO world heritage site. The area had long been frequented by natives and Acadians, before the town itself was founded in 1753. Most of the settlers who built their timber houses along its grid of streets were Germans, intermixed with people from Switzerland and the Montbéliard district of France, all categorized as "foreign Protestants," whom the British regarded as reliable to populate and control the coast.

The layout of old town Lunenburg, with its rectangular residential plots and space reserved for public buildings, is a classic example of British colonial town planning, perhaps the best preserved of its kind in the whole of North America. The architecture is equally remarkable. The oldest structure, perhaps built as early as the 1770s, is the gambrel roofed **Romkey House,** but most of Lunenburg's houses are late 19th century. Timber-built, painted in cheerful colors, they rise up the slope overlooking the wharves of the Front Harbour. Many have intriguing details borrowed from the shipwright's craft, but the most characteristic feature is the mildly ostentatious "Lunenburg Bump," a dormer window extended out over the front door. **St. John's Church** has been described as "Carpenter-Gothic style at its finest."

Originally farmers, Lunenburg's settlers soon turned to the sea for their living. In the 1850s they sent the first schooner fleet to the Grand Banks; in the 1870s they introduced double-dory trawl fishing, then in the 1920s pioneered fresh-fish processing. The famous racing schooner *Bluenose* was built here in 1921, and Lunenburgers' shipbuilding and repairing skills are still much in demand, not only for routine tasks. The beautiful *Bluenose II* was built here in 1963 *(see p. 79),* as was an equally exact reproduction of H.M.S. *Bounty;* in 1997, the copy of Cabot's *Matthew* called in for repairs.

The **Fisheries Museum of the Atlantic** *(Tel 902/634-4794, closed Sat.–Sun. Nov.-Apr.),* housed in the Salt Hall, Ice House, and other waterfront buildings of the former fish processing plant, is one of the most rewarding museums in the Maritimes. As well as an aquarium, there are fascinating displays on the history of the Grand Banks fishery, rum-running, and the life of the community. The *Bluenose,* the only man-made artifact to be featured on a Canadian coin (the dime), is celebrated in style, and there are real vessels tied up along the dockside.

Leave Lunenburg via Hwy. 3 and follow it west to Bridgewater. Pick up Rte. 331 and enjoy the coastal views. If you're interested in natural attractions, this drive south has splendid sandy beaches. A picture of one of them, **Crescent Beach,** once graced the $50 bill.

After 28 miles turn south on Hwy. 103 toward **Liverpool** ❺ *(Visitor information White Point Rd., tel 800/655-5741).* Located at the mouth of the Mersey, like its English counterpart, this port specialized in that licensed system of piracy known as privateering. One of its vessels, the *Liverpool Packet,* captured no fewer than 100 American ships. Yankee patience ran out, and in 1780 the town had to swallow its own medicine when it was sacked by a fleet of American privateers. These stirring times are evoked in the **Queen's County Museum** *(109 Main St., tel 902/354-4058)* and the adjacent 1766 **Perkins House** *(105 Main St., tel 902/354-4058, closed mid-Oct.–May),* one

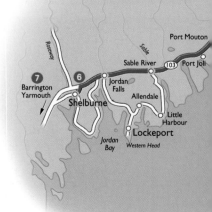

of the finest late 18th-century residences in eastern Canada.

As you depart Liverpool keep following Hwy. 103 west to **Shelburne** ❻ *(Visitor information: north end of Dock St., tel 902/875-4547, closed mid-Oct.–mid-May).* Founded in 1783, this town was built when thousands of New York Loyalists arrived and rapidly assembled a town. For a brief moment, it was the largest in British North America. Like Halifax, Shelburne has a superb natural harbor, but this failed to save it from the decline that perhaps preserved its charm. There are fine houses, and among the attractions is the **Dory Shop** *(Dock St., tel 902/875-3219, closed Oct.–May),* now a museum,

but still producing the sturdy fishing craft that were so vital to the fishery. The drive ends here but you could continue along the coast to Yarmouth, the workaday terminus for the ferries from Maine. It is worth stopping in the tiny town of **Barrington** ❼, with its historic woolen mill, replica lighthouse, and **Old Meeting House** of 1765, the oldest Nonconformist place of worship in Canada. ■

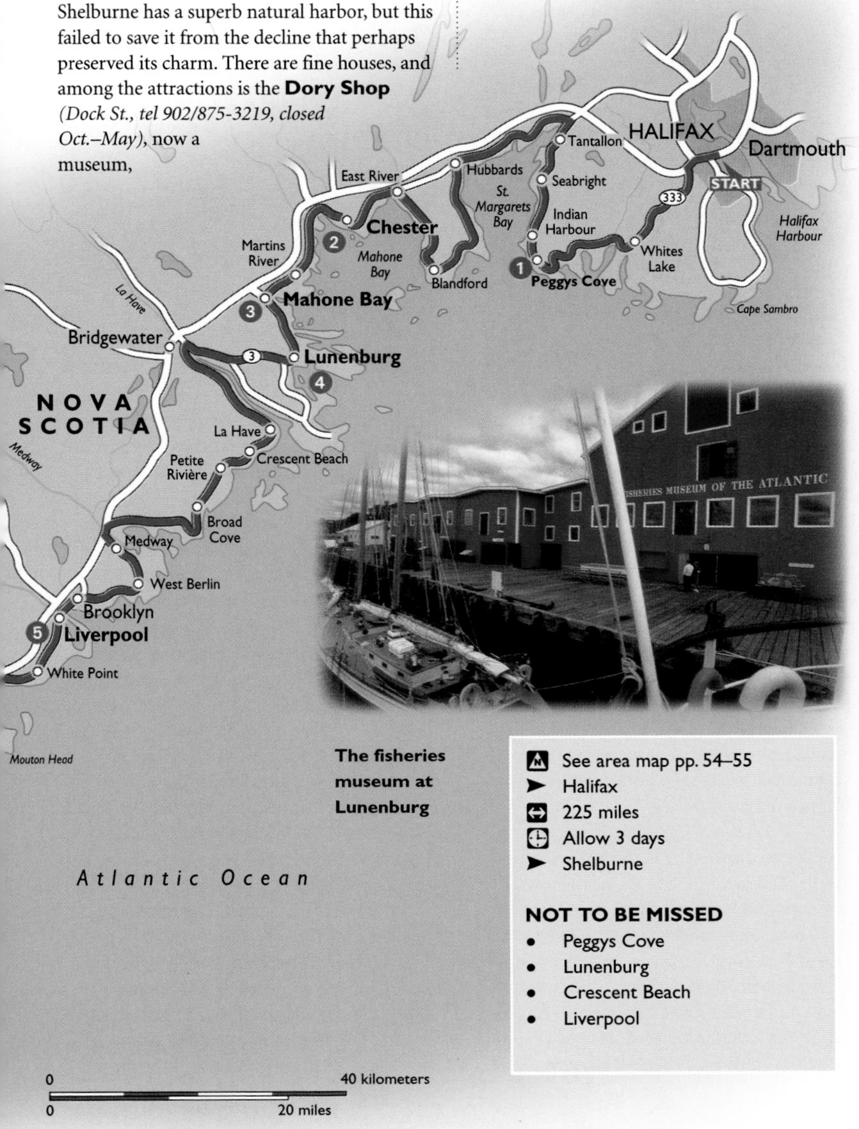

The fisheries museum at Lunenburg

- ▣ See area map pp. 54–55
- ► Halifax
- ↻ 225 miles
- ⊕ Allow 3 days
- ► Shelburne

NOT TO BE MISSED
- Peggys Cove
- Lunenburg
- Crescent Beach
- Liverpool

Maritime heritage

Not without reason are Canada's eastern provinces called the Maritimes. European colonists came here from across the ocean, and for many years remained dependent on the sea routes from France and Britain. Travel by sea and inland waterway was the principal means of communication within the region, and in the 18th century the combined operations of sea and land forces characterized the Franco-British struggle for supremacy. Settlement in this forested, largely infertile area was concentrated along the long and complex coastlines and to a lesser extent along accessible river valleys. Most towns were ports, and many villages lived from fishing.

From the very earliest days, ships were built here. In 1606, a year after Champlain's establishment of his Habitation (see pp. 80–81), two small crafts were launched into the Annapolis Basin at Port Royal. At first, craftsmen replicated European boat plans, but using local designs and timber harvested from the hinterland. By the late 18th century, shipbuilding was well established, local skills supplemented by the migration northward of New England shipwrights and carpenters. The glory days of Maritime shipping came in the 19th century, when some 200 shipyards were operating, turning out a huge tonnage of timber vessels and contributing to Canada's position as the world's fourth largest ship-owning nation.

As well as countless small "home-built" fishing vessels, there were sloops and schooners handling coastal commerce. Larger ships traded wherever a cargo was to be found and carried local fish and timber to Britain, the Mediterranean, the Caribbean, and South America. The 1,625-ton *Marco Polo*, built at Saint John in 1851, was claimed to be the fastest ship in the world, and in 1858, of the vessels over 500 tons on the Liverpool (England) *Register*, more than three-quarters were Canadian built.

But toward the end of the century, ships of iron and steel began to dominate the shipping scene, and this Canadian preeminence disappeared, though maritime yards continued to build timber sailing vessels well into the 20th century. The most famous ship of all, the elegant schooner *Bluenose*, came off the slip at

The sea has shaped the character of the Maritimes and remains their defining feature. Lighthouses, such as this one (opposite left), line the treacherous rocky coast. A Nova Scotian skipper (opposite right), dressed in traditional Sou'wester, gazes seaward. The elegant schooner _Bluenose II_ (above) enters Halifax harbor.

the Smith and Rhuland yard in Lunenburg in 1921. She repeatedly won the annual Fishermen's Trophy against the stiffest competition New England could muster. Despite being wrecked off Haiti in 1944, the _Bluenose_ has joined the immortals, gracing the ten cent coin and reincarnated in _Bluenose II_, an exact replica built at the same yard in 1963, and frequently on show in both Lunenburg and Halifax (see p. 76).

More modest craft command almost as much affection as the thoroughbred _Bluenose_. Archetypal Maritime vessels include the _Cape Islander_ with its high bow and cabin well forward, first developed by Ephraim Atkinson on Cape Sable Island, or the ubiquitous flat-bottomed dory. The skills that built such boats

are still practiced today, in places such as the Dory Shop in Shelburne (see p. 77) or alongside the splendid Fisheries Museum of the Atlantic (see p. 76) in Lunenburg. Both the Fisheries Museum of the Atlantic and the Halifax Maritime Museum of the Atlantic have fine collections of historic ships.

Together with Newfoundland, the Maritimes are the closest lands on the North American continent to Europe, and in two world wars their waters have been the scene of intense naval activity. In both conflicts, U-boats sowed mines and sank both merchant vessels and warships; techniques of anti-submarine warfare and convoy management were developed and applied to protect the endless stream of vessels supplying Britain with essential provisions and war material. The focus of much of this activity was the magnificent natural harbor of Halifax, and these tense times are recalled not only in the Maritime Museum (see p. 73) but also in the Maritime Command Museum _(Admiralty House, 2725 Gottingen St., Halifax, tel 902/427-0550, closed weekends)_, devoted to the city's naval history. ◼

Annapolis Valley & the French shore

55 A2, B2–B3

ITS FLANKS PROTECTED BY THE NORTH AND SOUTH mountain ranges running parallel to the Fundy shore, the Annapolis Valley is the sunniest and most fertile part of Nova Scotia. The valley is famous for its apple orchards, less extensive than they once were, but still a glorious show of blossom in springtime. Many visitors start a tour of the area at Grand-Pré.

Gently rolling hills flank the fertile farmlands of the Annapolis Valley.

Grand-Pré National Historic Site
www.pc.gc.ca
55 B3
2.5 miles east of Wolfville off Hwy. I
902/542-3631
Closed Nov.-Apr.
$

Port Royal National Historic Site
www.pc.gc.ca
55 B2
8 miles west of Annapolis Royal
902/532-2898
Closed mid-Oct.—mid-May
$

GRAND-PRÉ NATIONAL HISTORIC SITE

Once a flourishing Acadian town of 5,000 inhabitants, **Grand-Pré** is now a national historic site, surrounded by the rich agricultural landscape of the Annapolis Valley. It is a tiny yet poignant memorial to one of the most tragic Maritime events, the Deportation of 1755 (see pp. 62–63).

There is not a lot to see here, but you will not forget your visit. Few people leave unmoved. Take a walk to the tiny chapel to see lists of the families deported and maps showing where they went. You can even read a copy of Governor Lawrence's Deportation Order. Take a look at the marvelous life-size sculpture of Evangeline by Louis-Philippe Hébert, the great Montréal sculptor who was himself of Acadian descent.

Close to Grand-Pré is the refined little town of **Wolfville** *(Visitor information, tel 902/542-7000, closed mid-Oct.–mid-May)*, its

elegant streets lined with Victorian villas and shaded by great trees. Home to **Acadia University,** whose origins go back to 1838, Wolfville is also known for the annual Atlantic Theatre Festival.

ANNAPOLIS VALLEY

The many attractive communities that line Highway 1 make a drive to the southwestern end of the valley delightful. The one with the most small town charm is **Bridgetown.** Stop to admire the fine houses built by Loyalists on elm-lined streets.

Farther southwest, where the Annapolis River broadens into a great tidal basin, are two of Nova Scotia's outstanding sights—the superb reconstruction of Port Royal Habitation and the tiny town of Annapolis Royal.

Port Royal Habitation

After passing the disastrous winter of 1604–1605 on Île Sainte-Croix in Passamaquoddy Bay, the party led by Sieur des Monts and Samuel de Champlain crossed the Bay of Fundy and rebuilt their habitation in a more clement location on the bluff looking south over the Annapolis Basin. "Ten fathoms in length and eight in breadth," according to Champlain's account, the Habitation was a survival capsule, containing all that European culture and technology could devise to sustain life in these unexplored surroundings.

While relatively short-lived (des Monts departed in 1607 when his fur-trading license was revoked, and a raiding party from Virginia sacked the place in 1613), the Habitation was the first successful European colony north of St. Augustine, predating the founding of Jamestown, Virginia, by two years.

No trace of the Habitation remained above ground until the meticulous reconstruction of the buildings in 1939. Nowadays at **Port Royal National Historic Site,** visitors can see an almost exact re-creation of the site as it would have looked in the 17th century. Traditional techniques have helped rebuild the central well and courtyard, the palisade guarding the entrance, the accommodation of all ranks and the storehouse and service wing—all of which make this one of the most evocative historical sites in Canada.

Annapolis Royal

On the far side of the Annapolis Basin, just beyond the power station that harnesses the energy of the massive Fundy tides, stands **Annapolis Royal,** the successor to Port Royal, renamed after Britain's Queen Anne when it briefly became the capital of Nova Scotia in 1713. Once a bustling port and garrison town, Annapolis Royal is now a showcase of heritage restoration.

At its heart, commanding the waters of the basin, are the remaining buildings and earthworks of **Fort Anne National Historic Site** *(295 St. George St., tel 902/532-2321, closed mid-Oct.–mid-May),* much fought over by the French and British. Nearby are the extensive **Annapolis Royal Historic Gardens** *(441 St. George St., tel 902/532-7018, closed mid-Oct.–mid-May),* which were established in 1981 to illustrate the development of horticulture.

The French coast

Of all the areas in Nova Scotia resettled by returning Acadians in the 1760s and later, **Clare County,** on the coast between the ports of Digby and Yarmouth, has the most distinctively French character and the greatest concentration of Acadian population. The thin soils along the shoreline of St. Marys Bay forced the resettled Acadians to abandon their farming skills and turn to lumbering and fishing. Their villages along the old Highway 1 run into one another, only grandly scaled churches distinguishing one parish from another. At **Pointe de l'Église** (Church Point) is Sainte-Marie, the largest timber church in North America, its 185-foot spire steadied against the coastal gales by 40 tons of ballast, while St. Bernard can shelter a congregation of 1,000, three times the population of the parish. ■

A European outpost in the Canadian wilderness—Port Royal Habitation

A bust of Longfellow honors the poet of *Evangeline* at Grand-Pré National Historic Site.

Cape Breton Island & the Cabot Trail

Rugged Cape Breton Island is a rocky finger pointing northward across the Cabot Strait, which links the Gulf of St. Lawrence with the Atlantic. The northwest section of Cape Breton Island has a spectacular circular drive known as the Cabot Trail.

In spite of its name, Cape Breton has not been an island since 1955, when a 2-mile causeway, the deepest in the world (217 feet), was constructed across the Strait of Canso. After crossing it, look back at the cliffs which supplied the ten million tons of rock required for its construction. The signs proclaim "Cead Mile Failte" ("a hundred thousand welcomes" in Gaelic). You have entered a fiercely independent part of the province where natives, many of whom are descendants of settlers from the Scottish Highlands, often have little time for their fellow "mainland" Nova Scotians.

This memorable drive passes through Cape Breton Highlands National Park and is undoubtedly one of the most beautiful and dramatic drives of eastern North America. With whales offshore, moose inland, and bald eagles circling above you, the Cabot Trail is a paradise for nature lovers. The wary drive it in a clockwise direction away from the some-times precipitous drops to the sea. But it is even more spectacular if taken counterclock-wise. Be warned that fog can roll in and obscure views, especially on the eastern side.

The starting point of the trail is the resort of **Baddeck ❶** (*Visitor information, Chebucto St., tel 902/295-1911*), charmingly sited on the shore of Cape Breton's inland sea, the Bras d'Or. Much cherished by locals for his appreciation of the attractions of his adopted home ("For simple beauty, Cape Breton Island outrivals them all"), Alexander Graham Bell (1847–1922) first came here in 1885, building his home, Beinn Bhreag ("Beautiful Mountain" in Gaelic), and conceiving and testing some of his myriad inventions here.

The **Alexander Graham Bell National Historic Site** *(Hwy. 205, tel 902/295-2069)* is comprehensive in scope; there are telephones, but much else besides, including a splendid reproduction of the 60-foot-long HD-4.

Driving west on Trans-Canada 105 you join the Cabot Trail. Beyond the Margaree River, with its unrivaled salmon fishing, and the Acadian port of **Chéticamp ❷**, the trail enters **Cape Breton Highlands National Park** *(Tel 902/224-2306).* "Where the moun-tains meet the sea" is the apt description applied to this park, which has hardwood forest, mountain plateau, and a rugged but beautiful coast. The trail winds through the park between Chéticamp and **Pleasant Bay.** Stop at the designated pulloffs to admire the superb views of the dramatic coastline.

A short walk inland takes you to the **Lone Shieling,** an evocative reconstruction of a Highland crofter's cottage. On the inland section between **Cape North** and Neil's Harbour, look out for moose by the road.

From Pleasant Bay the trail heads east and inland, following the park's northern bound-ary until it reaches Neil's Harbour. Here the trail hugs the east coast again. **Black Brook Cove** is splendid, with pink rocks stretching into the sea and views ahead of Ingonish Bay, dominated by the slopes of Cape Smokey.

The resort hotel **Keltic Lodge ❸** *(Visitor information, tel 902/285-2880)* has a spectacular location on **Middle Head,** which cuts Ingonish Bay in two. Park at the lodge and follow the trail to the end of the peninsula for views of Cape Smokey and Tern Rock, a nesting place for common and arctic tern *(path closed in nesting season, mid-May–July),* as well as other seabirds.

In the summer taking part in one of the popular **whale-watching boat tours** can be a highlight of your trip *(Cape Breton Information, tel 800/565-0000).* After

The Cabot Trail and the scenic grandeur of the Cape Breton Highlands National Park

0 20 kilometers
0 10 miles

Cape St. Lawrence
St. Lawrence Bay
Cape North
Capstick
Bay St. Lawrence
Aspy Bay
Cape North
South Harbour
Cape Egmont
Neils Harbour
Black Brook Cove

Nova Scotia's flag

Pleasant Bay
Gulf of St. Lawrence
CABOT TRAIL
Lone Shieling

CAPE BRETON HIGHLANDS NATIONAL PARK
532m

Ingonish
North Bay Ingonish
3 Keltic Lodge

Atlantic Ocean

Not a typical Nova Scotian doorway!

Presqu'ile
Chéticamp Island
Chéticamp
Chéticamp 2

Ingonish Ferry
4 Cape Smokey

N O V A   S C O T I A

Point Cross
Grand Etang
St. Joseph du Moine
19
Margaree Harbour
Belle Côte

495m
CABOT TRAIL
Wreck Cove
French River
Skir Dhu
Breton Cove
North Shore

CAPE BRETON ISLAND

Indian Brook

Indian Brook

Tarbotvale

Northeast Margaree
Margaree Forks
Margaree

North River Bridge
St. Ann's
St. Ann's Bay

Finlayson
CABOT TRAIL

Middle River
105
5
South Gut St. Ann's

St. Andrews Channel

Sydney

Hunters Mountain
1
Alexander Graham Bell Nat. Hist. Site
Baddeck

START

Yachts moored at Baddeck

	See area map pp. 54–55
▶	Baddeck
⬌	186 miles
⏱	Allow 2 days
▶	South Gut St. Anns

NOT TO BE MISSED
- Alexander Graham Bell National Historic Site
- Cape Breton Highlands National Park
- Whale-watching

Ingonish, follow the trail south. Over **Cape Smokey 4** it passes through a series of Gaelic fishing villages and precariously clings to the sides of St. Anns Bay. At **South Gut St. Anns 5** visit the **Gaelic College of Arts and Crafts** *(Tel 902/295-3441).*

Founded in 1938, it has been the driving force behind the Gaelic revival. As well as promoting the Gaelic language, virtually extinct here by the early 20th century, it has courses in traditional Highland activities like bagpiping and tartan-weaving. ■

Louisbourg

Fortress of Louisbourg National Historic Site
www.pc.gc.ca
🅰 55 E3
✉ 22 miles south of Sydney on Rte. 22
☎ 902/733-2280
🕐 Closed Nov.–Apr.
⑤ $$$

Completed in the early 1730s, Louisbourg's Château Saint-Louis was the most imposing building in all of New France.

ONCE A PAWN IN THE DEADLY GAME OF CONTINENTAL domination played by Britain and France, the great coastal fortress of Louisbourg has been rebuilt in one of the most ambitious historical reconstruction projects ever undertaken in North America.

Covering more than 12 acres, with more than 50 restored buildings, and staffed in season with costumed townsfolk and soldiers, **Fortress of Louisbourg National Historic Site** offers visitors a compelling experience of the 18th-century colonial world.

In 1713, driven out of Newfoundland and faced with the loss of peninsular Nova Scotia and its capital, Port Royal, France tried to safeguard its position in North America by establishing a new stronghold on Cape Breton

Island. The site of Louisbourg was selected in 1715. It had a fine harbor and was well located in relation to the Grand Banks fishery and the Cabot Strait, which guarded the sea route to Québec. By the 1730s, the bastion town of Louisbourg had a thriving population of some 4,000 civilians and the same number of military personnel.

A BARGAINING CHIP
The strength of Louisbourg provoked the very reaction it was intended to deter. In 1745, alarmed by its menacing presence, a force of New Englanders, supported by a British naval squadron, attacked the fortress—not from the sea as the French had expected, but from the land. In the first of two successful siege actions, Louisbourg surrendered, but was returned to France in 1749, having served as a useful bargaining chip in one of the perennial redrawings of the European political map. A second siege, in 1758, in which James Wolfe played a key role, led to a more decisive result: After its surrender, its garrison and inhabitants were deported to France, then, in the following year, Louisbourg served as the base for Wolfe's victory on Québec's Plains of Abraham. Having no further need of it (Halifax was now established as Nova Scotia's capital and major port), the British razed the fortifications to the ground.

Allow a whole day to savor fully this remarkable reconstruction, with its dockside, its Citadel, its gateways, walls and bastions, and numerous residences. ■

This great island out in the cold waters of the North Atlantic, part of Canada only since 1949, is utterly distinctive. So, too, are its inhabitants, their warmth and humor contrasting with the harshness of their vast and open land.

Newfoundland & Labrador

Introduction & map **86–87**
St. John's **88–91**
Avalon Peninsula **94–96**
Bonavista Peninsula **97**
Terra Nova National Park
  & the interior **98**
Gros Morne National Park **99**
Norsemen in Newfoundland
  100–101
Labrador **102**
Hotels & restaurants in
  Newfoundland & Labrador
  351–352

Waves crash on Cape Spear's rocky coast.

Newfoundland & Labrador

NO NEWFOUNDLANDER WOULD CLAIM THEIR ISLAND TO BE A PRETTY place. "A monstrous mass of rock and gravel … like a strange thing from the bottom of the great deep" is one telling description. Despite its long history of European settlement, Newfoundland bears fewer traces of human occupation than most of the continent. Much of its sparsely scattered population clings to the coast as it always has done, looking to the sea for sustenance and for connections to the outside world.

The outport is the characteristic Newfoundland settlement, a clutch of raggedy fishermen's houses clinging to the water's edge or strewn over the nearby slopes, inhabited because of the once abundant fishery that brought settlers sailing across the Atlantic hundreds of years ago. The only really substantial city is St. John's, with its wonderful sheltered harbor and long-standing dominance of the island's fishing economy. Inland places are few—Gander, with its strategic airport, and Grand Falls, with its pulp mill processing the interior's main crop, coniferous forest. Away from the often spectacularly rugged 6,000-mile coast, much of the landscape of scrub, rock outcrops, ponds, and bogs seems to have only just emerged from the crushing weight of the Ice Age glaciers. With a climate whose harshness can be felt even in the summer months, Newfoundland is a place for those in search of all kinds of outdoor challenges, whether hunting or fishing, canoeing or hiking into the wilderness. The somber mountains of Gros Morne National Park offer a special kind of wilderness experience, while bird-watching or whale-spotting can be enjoyed by every visitor.

The fish-rich waters of the Grand Banks may have been known to fishermen from the northwest coasts of Europe even before John Cabot made his historic voyage in 1497, but it was in the following centuries that the fishery thrived (see pp. 92–93). Despite the disapproval of the English government, what was supposed to be a strictly seasonal activity soon led to permanent settlement, quite apart from the less successful, officially sponsored colonial developments such as Ferryland on the Avalon Peninsula. Early Newfoundlanders were mostly of English West Country origin, followed by Scots, and, in the early 19th century, a flood of Irish, who soon formed the majority of the population in St. John's and along much of the coast. Many immigrants moved on elsewhere, establishing a tradition that still sends young Newfoundlanders southward to the northeastern states of the U.S. or westward to Ontario and Alberta. In time a characteristically

In spring and summer, the Labrador Current brings icebergs to the Newfoundland coast, such as this one in Trinity Bay, near Old Bonaventure.

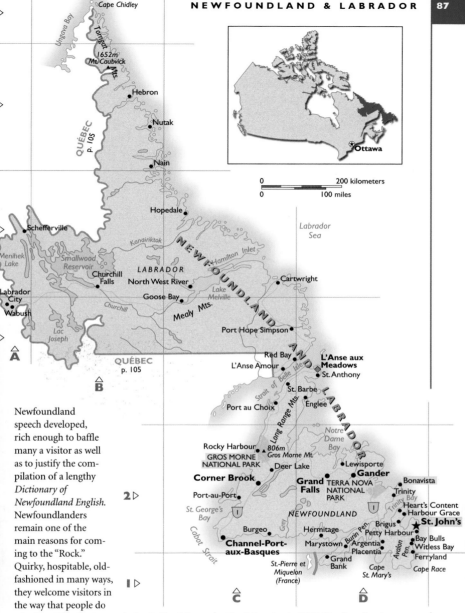

Cape Chidley
Ungava Bay
Torngat Mts.
1652m Mt. Caubvick
Hebron
Nutak
QUÉBEC p. 105
Nain
Hopedale
Labrador Sea
Schefferville
Kanairiktok
Menihek Lake
Smallwood Reservoir
LABRADOR
Hamilton Inlet
Churchill Falls
North West River
Lake Melville
Cartwright
Labrador City
Goose Bay
Churchill
Wabush
Mealy Mts.
Lac Joseph
Port Hope Simpson
NEWFOUNDLAND AND LABRADOR
A
QUÉBEC p. 105
Red Bay
L'Anse aux Meadows
L'Anse Amour
St. Anthony
B
St. Barbe
Strait of Belle Isle
Englee
Port au Choix
Long Range Mts.
Notre Dame Bay
Rocky Harbour
806m Gros Morne Mt.
GROS MORNE NATIONAL PARK
Deer Lake
Lewisporte
Gander
Bonavista
Corner Brook
Grand Falls
TERRA NOVA NATIONAL PARK
Trinity
Trinity Bay
Port-au-Port
St. George's Bay
Grey R.
NEWFOUNDLAND
Heart's Content
Harbour Grace
★ **St. John's**
2
Burgeo
Hermitage
Brigus
Petty Harbour
Bay Bulls
Channel-Port-aux-Basques
Cabot Strait
Marystown
Argentia
Placentia
Burin Pen.
Avalon Pen.
Witless Bay
Ferryland
St.-Pierre et Miquelon (France)
Grand Bank
Cape St. Mary's
Cape Race
C
D

Ottawa

0   200 kilometers
0   100 miles

Newfoundland speech developed, rich enough to baffle many a visitor as well as to justify the compilation of a lengthy *Dictionary of Newfoundland English.* Newfoundlanders remain one of the main reasons for coming to the "Rock." Quirky, hospitable, old-fashioned in many ways, they welcome visitors in the way that people do who live off the beaten track. Annie Proulx's novel The Shipping News provides a droll introduction to their ways.

"Come near at your peril, Canadian wolf" chanted 19th-century Newfoundlanders, and it was only by a narrow margin that this erstwhile British colony decided to join the Confederation in 1949. Newfoundland remains defiantly different from the rest of Canada, determined, with its newfound oil wealth, to make its way in the world.

This province, as its name indicates, includes a vast tract of the Canadian mainland—Labrador, a rugged environment. ■

St. John's

St. John's

⚐ 87 D2

Visitor information

www.stjohns.ca

✉ 348 Water St.

☎ 709/576-8537

🕐 Closed Sat.–Sun.

✉ Destination St.
John's, Murray
Premises,
5 Beck's Cove

☎ 709/739-8899 or
877/739-8899

Whale-watching tours

✉ Adventure Tours on
the Scademia

☎ 709/726-5000

🕐 Closed Nov.–Apr.

💲 $$$$$

WELL-SHELTERED FROM THE ATLANTIC GALES IN ITS fjordlike harbor, Newfoundland's atmospheric capital city boasts a history going back to 1583 when Sir Humphrey Gilbert sailed in and took possession of the island in the name of Queen Elizabeth I. Its harborfront site, like those of most other sizable cities along Canada's Atlantic coast, determined its growth and subsequent history. Today the sea remains as all-pervasive to the residents of St. John's as it does for townsfolk in the most remote coastal Newfoundland settlements.

Fishermen from Normandy, Brittany, and Portugal as well as England had wintered here before Gilbert's arrival, but it was only after Sir Humphrey's visit in 1583 that permanent buildings were erected. A history of attacks by the French, raids by pirate gangs, and a series of devastating fires has left little trace of the early architecture of North America's earliest urban settlement. In any case, much building tended to be of a temporary or makeshift nature, and for centuries Mother England remained hostile to the idea of permanent settlement. Early houses clustered around Fort William, a compact stronghold built in 1689 on the site of the present **Hotel Newfoundland,** while later development took place along **Water Street.** Here rose the warehouses, offices, and commercial premises that controlled the island's fishing economy and ensured the town's prosperity.

As late as the early 19th century there were virtually no structures built of stone, and Water Street, the principal thoroughfare, remained unpaved, unlighted, and in places no more than six feet wide. Even after the great fires that raged on several occasions in the early part of the 19th century, many residents steadfastly refused to rebuild in anything but timber, preparing the way for the greatest conflagration of all, in 1892, which destroyed

two-thirds of the town and left 10,000 homeless.

St. John's may appear a jumble of unregulated building, but its layout is in fact logical. A series of long thoroughfares such as Water Street and **Duckworth Street** run along the contours of the steep slope rising from the waterfront, linked by short cross streets or

flights of steps. With the vast reserves of offshore oil, the city's focus remains the harbor, tidied up, with the old finger jetties replaced by a continuous dockside. There's a variety of craft including coast guard cutters, fishing boats, tankers, and research vessels as well as conventional freighters and ships serving the offshore oil rigs and the occasional warship. Sailboats lie ready to take visitors iceberg-spotting or whale-watching, perhaps combined with a mildly embarrassing "screech-in," involving the consumption of rum and intimate contact with a codfish.

Just behind the dockside stand the venerable **Murray Premises** (*between Water St. & Harbour Dr.*), the last of the city's mid-19th-century waterfront mercantile complexes. Housing a luxury hotel, boutiques, and restaurants, today its solid stone walls and charming cobblestone courtyard make an atmospheric start to an exploration of the city. A block or so inland, beyond **George Street's** pubs and restaurants and next to the brutalist concrete of the modern City Hall, a marker defines Mile 0 of the Trans-Canada Highway, which stretches 4,857 miles west from here to far-off Victoria, B.C. East along Water Street stands the **Courthouse,** a substantial granite structure built in 1901 and once used by the prime minister and cabinet.

The streets climbing the slopes above Duckworth Street are lined with charming clapboard houses, reminiscent of a miniature San

A kaleidoscope of colors, the rowhouses in St. John's terrace up the town's slopes.

Cathedral of St. John the Baptist

✉ Church Hill on Gower Street
☎ 709/726-5677
🕐 By appointment only Sept.–June
💲 Donation

Basilica of St. John the Baptist

✉ Military Road
☎ 709/754-2170
💲 Guided tours $$$, Museum $

The Rooms

www.therooms.ca
✉ 9 Bonaventure Ave.
☎ 709/757-8000
🕐 Closed Mon. mid-Oct.–May
💲 $

At St. John's Signal Hill, a simple memorial commemorates Marconi's historic achievement in receiving a radio signal from across the Atlantic.

Francisco. Substantial churches dot the neighborhood, including the Anglican **Cathedral of St. John the Baptist** and the Roman Catholic **Basilica of St. John the Baptist.** Both churches are dedicated to the saint, from whom the city supposedly takes its name. The cathedral is the successor to earlier timber churches, while its parish, established in 1699, is the oldest Anglican parish in North America. The present imposing building was begun in 1846 by the great British architect of the Gothic Revival, George Gilbert Scott (1811–1878). Subsequent work, including extensive reconstruction following the great fire of 1892, was continued by the Scott family firm, who remained cathedral architects into the 1950s.

An even greater landmark, the basilica, commands a position farther up the slope, where its twin towers have served as beacons to seamen since the building's completion in 1892. Within the ornate interior is a figure of Our Lady of Fatima, a gift from the Portuguese fishermen of the White Fleet that once put in regularly at St. John's.

Since 2005, the vast structure known as **The Rooms** has towered high above the city. It houses the Provincial Museum, Art Gallery, and archives. On a massive scale, it represents the fishing rooms where families got together to process their catch in times past. It is well worth visiting for the view and to see the museum's extensive collection, which gives an excellent overview of Newfoundland's ecology and unique history.

To the north cluster historic structures built to serve official functions. The neoclassic **Colonial Building** of 1850 (Military Rd., tel 709/729-3065, closed weekends) housed Newfoundland's parliament until 1969, when it moved to the modern Confederation Building

on the outskirts of town. Even grander than this is **Government House** (Military Rd., tel 709/729-4494, grounds only). The fine red sandstone edifice was the lieutenant governor's residence until 1949. It was begun in 1827 to plans supplied from England by the prospective governor, Sir Thomas Cochrane. Sir Thomas's willful changes in the design of his future residence were the despair of the engineer in charge of the works, who eventually obtained a transfer elsewhere. It still remains unclear why a building in Newfoundland should be surrounded by a moat (seemingly designed to deter poisonous snakes and other undesirable tropical creatures). Both buildings contain ceiling frescoes painted by Alexander Pindokowski, a convicted forger whose jail sentence was reduced to reward the quality of his work.

Close to the Church of St. Thomas, Newfoundland's oldest surviving church, is another handsome Georgian-style structure, **Commissariat House** (Kings Bridge Rd., tel 709/729-6730, closed mid-Oct.–May). Built in 1820 and used by the British military until their withdrawal from the colony in 1870, it boasts interiors restored to their early 19th-century appearance, a re-created Victorian garden, and a small interpretive center housed in a coach house.

C.A. Pippy Park occupies an elevated position to the north of the center of St. John's. It is the location of the Newfoundland Freshwater Resource Centre, with its main attraction, the **Fluvarium.** This fascinating three-level series of displays provides a detailed introduction to the freshwater ecology of Newfoundland, with informative exhibits on fish, plants, bogs, and streams and even a model iceberg.

Although modern St. John's has acquired extensive suburbs, it is still a small town, at least in capital city terms, and nature is never very far away. Rising some 500 feet over the constricted entrance to the harbor known as the Narrows, windswept **Signal Hill National Historic Site** is a wild landscape on the very edge of town, with the characteristic Newfoundland scrub of partridge-berry and rowan among outcrops of bare rock. The hill is topped by the **Cabot Tower,** erected in 1897 to mark Queen Victoria's Diamond Jubilee as well as the 400th anniversary of Cabot's voyage. From the beginning of the 18th century, lookouts manned the summit, signaling the approach of ships to owners and merchants in the city below. Almost every visitor to St. John's makes it to the hilltop—the more energetic by a spectacular footpath, others by the winding road. Halfway up the road is the modern Parks Canada Visitor Centre, whose well-presented exhibits make it one of the best places to become acquainted not only with Signal Hill but with the history of Newfoundland in general.

But the real attraction of the site is the stunning panorama from the summit: To the west spreads the harbor and the whole of the city, to the east the infinite Atlantic rimmed by rugged cliffs. An occasional ship threads its way through the rocky Narrows far below.

Perhaps the most epoch-making occurrence on the hill took place on December 12, 1901, when Guglielmo Marconi (1874–1937) launched a kite 400 feet into gale-force winds and received the first-ever transatlantic wireless signal in Morse code from England. Just north of Signal Hill is the pleasant fishing village of **Quidi Vidi.** Tidy cottages and fishing shacks nestle beneath dramatic cliffs and a reconstructed 18th-century gun battery (*Tel 709/729-2977*) guards the coast. To the north, beyond Quidi Vidi Lake, lies the suburb of **Pleasantville,** successor to a big U.S. base established in World War II.

Every summer the Signal Hill Tattoo (*July–mid-Aug. Wed., Thurs., Sat. & Sun.*) recalls aspects of the long British military presence in St. John's. ■

Cabot Tower atop Signal Hill recognizes John Cabot's 1497 voyage as well as Marconi's achievements.

Fluvarium
✉ Nagles Pl.
☎ 709/754-3474
$ $

Signal Hill National Historic Site
www.pc.gc.ca
✉ Cabot Tower & Visitor Reception Centre (closed Jan.–Mar.)
☎ 709/772-5367
$ $

Fish & more fish

"The fisheries of Newfoundland are inexhaustible and are of more value to the Empire than all the silver mines of Peru," declared the English essayist Francis Bacon (1561–1626) in the early 17th century. Even today, despite a disastrous decline in stocks and the much-resented 1991 federal moratorium on fishing for cod, Newfoundland manages to export millions of dollars' worth of seafood annually, although much of the catch consists of crab and other shellfish.

Crab was once despised by Newfoundlanders. The only sea creature worth talking about was cod, to the extent that in local parlance the word "fish" became synonymous with cod. It was cod that filled the basket hoisted from the waters off Newfoundland by Cabot's sailors in the course of his 1497 voyage, and it was cod that drew myriad fishing boats from the ports of northwest Europe to the banks. The cod congregated here for the same reason as the fishermen: the presence of abundant food. The shallow waters of the continental shelf known as the Grand Banks are where the warm waters of the Gulf Stream and the chilly Labrador Current meet and mix, stirring up minerals from the ocean floor and providing nutrients for the plankton, which, in turn, feeds the smaller fish preyed on by the cod.

In its beginnings the fishery was a seasonal one. Flotillas of vessels from Portugal, Brittany, the Basque country of Spain, and the West Country of England would set out for the Grand Banks in early spring and remain until September. (A custom was initiated by which the first sea captain to arrive in harbor was made Fishing Admiral, with full authority for the season over his fellow fishermen.) The French first ran a "wet" fishery, cleaning their catch on board and preserving it in salt. The English fishery, by contrast, was "dry." With less salt at their disposal, they landed their catch on the coast, cleaned it there and cured it by laying it out to dry on the timber "flakes" that were a feature of Newfoundland's outports for centuries.

Permanent settlements

Rivalry between English and French characterized the early years of the fishery. As autumn set in and the fleets returned to Europe, the English left behind a small work force to guard and repair installations and tackle. Such supposedly temporary footholds developed over the years into more permanent settlements, consolidating the English presence despite government attempts to maintain the strictly seasonal character of the fishery. A series of treaties throughout the 18th century and into the 19th allowed the French to use parts of the Newfoundland coast for fishing purposes, but not permanent settlement. These rights along the "French shore" lasted until 1904, when they were extinguished by the Anglo-French Convention. (France retains the islands of St. Pierre and Miquelon, see p. 96.)

By the 19th century the fishery, always the basis of the Newfoundland economy, was largely controlled by merchants based in St. John's. They marketed the catch supplied by the fishermen working out of the 600 or so villages, or outports, around the island's long coastline. In return, the merchants provided goods in kind—fishing equipment, clothing, rum, and all the many foodstuffs that could not be grown on the thin soils of outport small holdings. This system guaranteed good profits for the merchants while keeping the outporters in a more or less permanent state

Despite depleted stocks and moratoriums, fishing is still important in Newfoundland.

of debt and dependence. But even in the hardest of times, men could always set out in tiny boats they had built themselves and catch enough fish to feed the family on brewis, the Newfoundland national dish of cod, hardtack, and crisp-fried pork fat.

Cod moratorium

Previously, the hard times came when markets failed. More recently, it is the fish themselves that have failed. Whether this is because of overfishing, particularly by high-tech foreign fleets, or as a result of natural causes, remains a matter of dispute. What is clear is the deep resentment felt by most Newfoundlanders at the fishing moratorium instituted by a federal government that in their view has consistently mismanaged Newfoundland's greatest asset, its immensely productive fishery. However much money Ottawa pumps into the provincial economy in the form of income support or retraining schemes, it cannot compensate for the loss of a livelihood that goes to the very root of a Newfoundlander's identity. ■

While it is a rare sight nowadays, cod laid out to dry on "flakes" (above and below) have been a familiar feature of the Newfoundland fisheries since the 16th century.

Avalon Peninsula

Avalon Wilderness Reserve
🏞 87 D1–D2

Visitor information
www.gov.nf.ca/parks&reserves
✉ Parks Division, Dept. of Tourism, Culture, & Recreation
☎ 800/563-6353

Colony of Avalon Archaeology Site
🏞 87 D2
✉ The Pool, Ferryland
☎ 709/432-3200
🕐 Closed mid-Oct.–mid-May
💲 $$

Puffins, commonly seen along the Avalon coastline

CONNECTED TO THE CENTRAL PART OF THE ISLAND BY A narrow isthmus, the Avalon Peninsula is Newfoundland's most densely settled and history-rich area, while still encompassing wild and spectacular landscapes and lonely places. A number of fascinating excursions revealing the peninsula's essential character can be undertaken from St. John's.

NORTH & SOUTH OF ST. JOHN'S

A 40-plus-mile trip northward along Marine Drive reveals the Atlantic in all its majesty, bounded by high cliffs and wave-battered beaches. However, the most popular nearby destination is southeast at **Cape Spear National Historic Site** *(Tel 709/772-5367, closed mid-Oct.–mid-May)*, the easternmost point in North America. Its lighthouse, built in 1836, has been restored to its original condition, although its warning functions are now undertaken by a modern light station. It is the oldest surviving lighthouse in Newfoundland. The domed light itself is surrounded by the two-story keeper's house, its classical proportions enhanced by false windows.

To the south, Hwys. 11 and 10 reveal more of Newfoundland's coastal scenery. The little outport of **Petty Harbour** with its fish-drying flakes is picturesque enough to have featured in a number of films. The deep harbor of **Bay Bulls** is bigger altogether, proud of having the earliest known English place-name in Newfoundland (the bull bird, or dovekie, was once common here). Together with Witless Bay and Cape Broyle, this is one of the starting points for a boat trip *(O'Briens Whale & Bird Tours, tel 709/753-4850; Gatheralls Puffin & Whale Watch, tel 709/334-2887)* around Great, Green, and Gull Islands, collectively known as the **Witless Bay Ecological**

Reserve *(Tel 709/277-1666).* The islands are home to countless gulls, razorbills, murres, guillemots, kittiwakes, and above all, puffins, one of the emblems of Newfoundland. Whales, too, are much in evidence from around mid-June to the end of July, devouring the capelin that run at this time.

The interior

Hwy. 10 runs away from the coast, with side roads leading down to such melancholy and half-deserted outports as little **Brigus South.** Inland, the desolate 385-square-mile tract of the **Avalon Wilderness Reserve** *(Tel 709/635-4520),* accessible only by permit, offers a haven for wildlife including a large caribou herd. Some 40 miles south of St. John's, an ongoing archaeological dig, **Colony of Avalon Archaeology Site,** continues to reveal fascinating details about the early European colonization of North America. Now the town of **Ferryland,** it was established as the colony of Avalon in 1621 on the orders of Sir George Calvert, later the first Baron Baltimore. A four-acre enclosure, defended by a palisade, contained a mansion house, other dwellings, a forge, saltworks, and a wharf. Other amenities included what was probably North America's first flushing toilet (worked by the action of seawater). Despite his followers' efforts, this environment proved too inhospitable for Calvert's liking.

After the rigorous winter of 1628–29 he took his family to Maryland, whose largest city still bears his name. Some of the more elegant of the half million objects uncovered can be viewed in the attractive visitor center.

WEST OF ST. JOHN'S

Only 10 miles west of St. John's lies the deeply indented far shore of **Conception Bay,** site of some of Newfoundland's earliest and most fascinating settlements. Attractive **Brigus** is associated with the American artist Rockwell Kent (1882–1971), who had a summer studio here, as well as with the indomitable Arctic mariner Captain Bob Bartlett (1875–1946), whose **Hawthorne Cottage National Historic Site** *(South St., tel 709/528-4004, closed mid-Oct.– May)* is open to the public.

Stunning coastal scenery at Bird Rock, Cape St. Mary's Ecological Reserve

Brigus
🗺 87 D2

St.-Pierre and Miquelon

🗺 87 D1

Incipient allies: Roosevelt and Churchill confer aboard the battleship H.M.S. Prince of Wales in Placentia Bay.

The nearby town of **Cupids** was the site of a very early plantation. In 1610 the Bristol merchant venturer John Guy landed here with 39 colonists, founding the first formal English colony in Newfoundland. A year later, the "Pirate Admiral," the renegade Royal Navy man Peter Easton, erected a stronghold at **Harbour Grace** to the north. The scale and success of his subsequent operations allowed him to retire and live in splendor in Europe. The site of his fort is now occupied by the **Conception Bay Museum** (*Water St., tel 709/596-5465, closed Oct.–May*), which among other themes recalls the town's role in transatlantic aviation—many pioneering flights started here, including Amelia Earhart's historic crossing to Ireland in 1932.

A further reminder of Newfoundland's relative closeness to Europe may be found at **Heart's Content,** overlooking Trinity Bay. It was here in 1866, after previous attempts had failed, that the first transatlantic telegraph cable was successfully hauled ashore from the majestic S.S. *Great Eastern*, the largest ship of her day. Only superseded a century later, in 1965, by a modern installation, the **Cable Station** (*Hwy. 80, tel 709/583-2160 June–mid-Oct., and 709/729-0592 off-season*) exhibits equipment and displays on the impact the cable had on North America and Europe.

Also connecting Newfoundland and the world beyond is the ferry service to North Sydney, Nova Scotia. Boats dock at **Argentia** on rocky Placentia Bay. This was the center of Allied anti-U-boat operations during World War II. Earlier, when Placentia was known as Plaisance, it was central to France's attempts to turn Newfoundland into a French colony. To that end, Castle Hill was fortified in 1692, and served as a base for attacks on the English in St. John's. The **Castle Hill National Historic Site** (*Tel 709/227-2401*), which is built bunkerlike into the hillside, tells the poignant story of this part of the French empire in North America. To the south of Placentia, a switchback road gives plunging views of the gloriously rugged coves of **Cape Shore** far below. The tip of the peninsula holds what is probably Newfoundland's most spectacular bird sanctuary, **Cape St. Mary's Ecological Reserve** (*Hwy. 100, tel 709/277-1666, closed Nov.–April*). Its Bird Rock, reached by cliff-top footpath, hosts one of the largest colonies of gannets in North America. (See also Bonaventure Island, p. 154.)

St.-Pierre & Miquelon
After passing from French to British rule and back several times, these islands off Newfoundland's Burin Peninsula have stayed definitively French since 1814, when the Treaty of Paris recognized their pivotal role in the French Atlantic fishery. A political deputy is sent to Paris, the streets of St. Pierre are lined with archetypal French buildings and patrolled by gendarmes, and gourmet meals are served in atmospheric bistros. This tiny remnant of the once extensive French North American empire can be reached by air from St. John's, and by ferry from Fortune (*St. Pierre Tours, tel 800/563-2006*). Bring a passport (or other means of identification if you are a U.S. or Canadian citizen). ∎

Bonavista Peninsula

"O BUONA VISTA!" WAS JOHN CABOT'S HEARTFELT CRY ON reaching this wild and rocky coastline in 1497. At least that is the generally accepted version of where and how the great navigator first came upon the New World. In 1997 the fifth centennial of his arrival was celebrated in style when a reproduction of his ship *Matthew* sailed into Bonavista harbor after repeating his epic voyage.

**Bonavista
Peninsula**
🅰 87 D2

Close to the tip of the peninsula dividing Bonavista Bay from Trinity Bay sprawls the village of **Bonavista,** the peninsula's principal settlement, established in the late 16th century. Its long history can be traced by visiting the group of old buildings known as the **Mockbeggar Property** *(Off Rte. 230, tel 709/468-7300, closed late Oct.–mid-June);* and, most evocatively of all, the restored **Ryan Premises National Historic Site** *(Ryan's Hill & Old Catalina Rd., tel 709/468-1600, closed late Oct.–mid-May),* which includes a shop, fish store, and salt shed.

Battered by wind and spray, the cape to the north of the village is graced by the bold, red-and-white-striped **Cape Bonavista Lighthouse** *(Tel 709/468-7444, closed Nov.–May)* dating from 1843. It has become one of the emblems of Newfoundland.

Many of the little villages clinging to this desolate coastline deserve more than a casual visit, but one particularly attractive to visitors is **Trinity.** Set among coves and inlets and backed by low hills, Trinity once rivaled St. John's in importance. Its name may date to when the Portuguese sailor Gaspar Corte-Real sailed into the bay on Trinity Sunday in 1500. By the end of that century it had been fortified by the English, and in 1615 Newfoundland's first Court of Admiralty was held here

to adjudicate disputes between migratory fishermen and permanent settlers. Trinity's golden age came in the late 18th and early 19th centuries when prosperous merchants made their fortunes here, but subsequent decline has merely added to the township's charm.

Today this backwater of delightful clapboard houses linked by picket fences and winding lanes offers many attractions, including the **Trinity Interpretation Centre** *(West St., closed mid-Oct.–mid-June),* and the **Green Family Forge** *(West St., tel 709/464-3599).* The **Trinity Historical Society Museum and Archives** *(Church Rd., tel 709/464-3599, closed mid-Sept.–mid-June)* is crammed full of memorabilia. The Roman Catholic church is the island's oldest, and the Anglican church is a carpentry tour-de-force. ∎

One of Newfoundland's oldest lighthouses warns ships of the dangers posed by Cape Bonavista's rugged coast.

Bonavista Peninsula visitor information
✉ Trans-Canada 1 near Clarenville
☎ 709/466-3100
🕐 Closed mid-Oct.–May

Trinity
🅰 87 D2

Terra Nova National Park & the interior

**Terra Nova
National Park**
www.pc.gc.ca
87 D2
✉ 25 miles north
of Clarenville on
Trans-Canada 1
☎ 709/533-2801
$ $ mid-May–mid-Oct.

Grand Falls
87 D2

Gander
87 D2

Deer Lake
87 C2

Corner Brook
87 C2

Lewisporte
87 D2

**Terra Nova
National Park
presents an
array of
beautiful and
diverse
landscapes.**

FROM THE BASE OF THE BONAVISTA PENINSULA, TRANS-Canada 1 cuts through the 150-square-mile Terra Nova National Park. With its well-marked trails, campgrounds, and a new visitor center overlooking Newman Sound, the park is one of the best places to explore a variety of Newfoundland landscapes.

The highly indented coastline shelters fjordlike inlets, beaches of sand and pebble, caves, cliffs, and sea stacks, while inland lie the bogs, barrens, and boreal forest, so characteristic of the island's rugged landscape. One of the best places to learn about this environment is the **Marine Interpretation Centre** (Salton's day-use area, off Trans-Canada 1, tel 709/533-2801, closed mid-Oct.–early June), in the heart of the Terra Nova National Park.

Trans-Canada 1 continues to **Gander.** Developed in the 1930s as a relatively fog-free refueling base for transatlantic air traffic, the airport came into its own in wartime, retaining its importance as "Crossroads of the World" until well into the postwar period, when jets developed the range enabling them to fly direct from Europe into the heart of North America. A short distance north off Hwy. 340 is **Lewisporte,** the embarkation point for ferries to the Labrador coast.

Developed in the early 20th century as a company town to supply newsprint to British newspapers, **Grand Falls** (Tel 709/489–6332) is one of the few settlements in Newfoundland built away from the sea. It has a reproduction **Beothuk Village** (St. Catherine St., tel 709/292-4523, closed Oct.–May). The **Mary March Provincial Museum** (16 St. Catherine St., tel 709/292-4523, closed Nov.–April) recalls the sad fate of one of the last of these unfortunate people, along with displays on regional history. **Deer Lake** (Visitor information, off Trans-Canada 1, tel 709/635-2202, closed Nov.–June), with its airport, is gateway to the great northern peninsula and one of Newfoundland's greatest attractions, Gros Morne National Park, reached via Hwy. 430. Trans-Canada 1 continues to busy **Corner Brook** (Visitor information, Confederation Dr., tel 709/639-9792), the island's second largest city (population about 25,000), past the Port au Port Peninsula, where French can still be heard, and on to Channel-Port aux Basques and its ferry service to Nova Scotia's North Sydney (Tel 800/341-7981 for schedules). ∎

Gros Morne National Park

A HIGH POINT OF ANY VISIT TO NEWFOUNDLAND, GROS Morne National Park, on the exposed west coast of the island's great northern peninsula, holds some of eastern Canada's most spectacular scenery as well as an array of unique geological features—all contributing to its designation as a UNESCO world heritage site.

Gros Morne N.P.
www.pc.gc.ca
🄰 87 C2
☎ 709/458-2417
💲 $ mid-May–mid-Oct.

Reached via Hwy. 430 from Deer Lake, this park has a variety of landscapes: a coastline of cliffs, dunes, sea stacks, beaches, and fjords penetrating deep inland. The coast formed part of the French shore, where, in the 19th century, France was granted special fishing rights. Although permanent settlement was forbidden, some of the villages clinging to the shore attest to the defiance of this proscription. Inland, a narrow plain with mixed woodland and bogs blooms with orchids and Newfoundland's provincial flower, the pitcher plant, in season. To the east rise the **Long Range Mountains,** the northernmost extension of the Appalachians; their flat tops form a vast plateau some 2,000 feet above sea level. Southwest spread the desolate **Tablelands,** a high plateau formed from toxic peridotite, a rock normally only present in the earth's mantle but here forced to the surface when the ancient continents of North America and Eurafrica collided.

The best place to start exploring the park is in **Rocky Harbour,** with its excellent visitor center. Nearby is the starting point of the demanding James Callaghan Trail, which brings determined hikers scrambling to the top of Gros Morne Mountain. Its 2,644-foot-high summit, a chaos of frost-shattered rock, offers magnificent views over uplands, coastline, and the pond-filled glacial valleys all around. An equally unforgettable, and less demanding, excursion is to hike the 2-mile trail across the

wetlands to the tip of Western Brook Pond, then board one of the **Western Brook Pond Boat Tours** (*Bontours, Rocky Harbour, tel 709/458-2730*). These explore this superb landlocked fjord.

Beyond Gros Morne, Hwy. 430 continues north, hugging the coast much of the way. Important evidence of the presence here nearly 4,000 years ago of Maritime Archaic people and of the Dorset Eskimo community that followed them is displayed at **Port au Choix National Historic Site** (*Off Hwy. 430, tel 709/861-3522, closed mid-Oct.–mid-June*). Farther north, **St. Barbe** is a departure point for the Labrador ferry (*Tel 709/724-9173 or 866/535-2567, no service Jan.–March*), and beyond the township and port of **St. Anthony** is a site resonant with meaning for all North Americans—the Viking settlement excavated at **L'Anse aux Meadows National Historic Site** (see pp. 100–101). ∎

The sun sets over one of the coast's many lighthouses.

L'Anse aux Meadows National Historic Site
www.pc.gc.ca
🄰 87 D3
✉ Rte. 436, 27 miles from St. Anthony
☎ 709/623-2608
🕐 Closed mid-Oct.–May

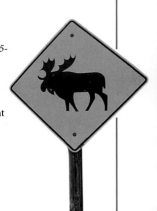

Norsemen in Newfoundland

Near the tip of Newfoundland's great northern peninsula stands a cluster of sod-built structures huddling from the winds blowing off rocky Epaves Bay. L'Anse aux Meadows is one of the most evocative sites in North America, a place touched by the restless questing of European mariners a full 500 years before the voyages of Columbus and Cabot but forgotten for nearly a millennium.

Around A.D. 985–86, the Norsemen who had colonized Iceland ventured even farther from their Scandinavian homeland, founding settlements on the Greenland coast. Blown off course, one of their number, the trader Bjarni Herjolfsson, discovered a well-wooded coastline, almost certainly that of Newfoundland. This, the first recorded sighting by a European of the continent of North America, encouraged a bold spirit by the name of Leif Eriksson to undertake a voyage of southward exploration. Starting out around the turn of the millennium, in the course of his travels he wintered in "Vinland," seemingly a frost-free land of vines, a place evidently far to the south of chilly Newfoundland. Its exact location—not to mention its translation—remains a subject for scholarly dispute to this day.

A year or two later, in 1004, another expedition from Greenland set off southward, evidently with a longer stay in mind, as women and cattle accompanied the warrior-sailors led by Thorfinnr Karlsefni. But the semi-permanent base established at Straumfiord (most likely the Strait of Belle Isle between Newfoundland and Labrador) was abandoned after a few years. Bloody encounters with native groups may have contributed to the decision to discontinue this colonizing endeavor, though it seems certain that Greenlanders continued to make occasional visits to the mainland in the years that followed, using it as a fishing base.

The historical source for all these ventures are the medieval Icelandic sagas, and much skepticism has been expressed about their literal accuracy. Norwegian explorer and writer Helge Ingstad had no such doubts; for years he traveled the coasts of eastern North America looking for evidence of Vinland. Encouraged by an alternative interpretation of "vin" as meaning "meadow" rather than wine, and led to what local people had always thought to be an aboriginal site haunted by ancient ghosts, Ingstad concluded that the humpy grassland overlooking Epaves Bay was, if not Vinland, certainly a Norse site of some kind. The excavations he undertook in the early 1960s with his wife, archaeologist Anne Stine, proved him right; the remains of eight sod-built huts were found, together with artifacts of indisputable Norse origin such as a bronze pin, sewing

Above: At L'Anse aux Meadows, a woven fence defines the enclosure occupied a thousand years ago by the Vikings.
Left: A reproduction Norse boat
Below: Vikings may have sheltered from the storms inside a house like this reconstructed version.

implements, and a soapstone spindle whorl.

This was no temporary camp. Sod walls and sod roofs built over a timber frame indicate buildings substantial enough for permanent occupation. Eight in number, they included three long and narrow dwellings with features similar to those found in Norse buildings in Greenland and Iceland. Other, smaller buildings, used mainly as stores and workshops, include a forge that used iron ore extracted from peat bogs—thrilling evidence of the first iron-working on the North American continent.

Today the site is managed by Parks Canada. Within the enclosure of a woven wood fence, three sod houses have been painstakingly reconstructed using such traditional techniques as wooden "nails" and fastenings made from roots or sealskin. Roofs and walls are of sod, the latter up to 6 feet in thickness. The interiors have been furnished as authentically as possible to convey the living conditions of these pioneers who, a thousand years ago, crossed stormy seas in open boats to seek a foothold in an utterly unknown land. ■

Labrador

Labrador
🗺 87 A3-4, B3-6,
   C3-4, D3-4

A VAST AREA OF SUBARCTIC WILDERNESS, LABRADOR
stretches northward more than 600 miles from the Strait of Belle Isle
to Cape Chidley, overlooking the icy waters of Ungava Bay some 500
miles from Greenland. Only a few permanent residents brave the
fierce climate to live here, most of them dependent on fishing,
forestry, iron-ore extraction, and hydropower generation.

**Scattered
dwellings and
rudimentary port
facilities on Red
Bay typify settle-
ments along the
inhospitable
Labrador coast.**

Much of Labrador is inaccessible
except by air, although Rte. 389
(gravel in part) runs 380 miles from
Baie Comeau on the St. Lawrence
River to Labrador City and
Wabush, townships that owe
their existence to the iron-ore
deposits that have been exploited
commercially since the 1950s.

A gravel road (Rte. 500), the
Trans-Labrador Highway, runs
eastward from **Labrador City**
about 325 miles to **Goose Bay,**
the embarkation point for ships
serving the rugged north coast or
linking with Lewisporte in
Newfoundland.

The leisurely ferry trip northward (*Labrador coast ferries, tel
709/724-9173 or 866/535-2567*) up
the coast to **Nain** stops at tiny set-

tlements, some with roots in the fur
trade, others established by the
Moravian Brethren. The landscape
becomes even more spectacular farther north, where fjords cut deeply
into the rocky terrain. Here are the
highest Canadian peaks east of the
Rockies (Mount Caubvick: 5,420 ft).

Far to the south, and much
more accessible, a string of settlements is linked by a paved highway along the Belle Isle Strait and
reached by ferry from **St. Barbe**
(see p. 99) on the Newfoundland
shore. In the mid-16th century, this
coastline witnessed activity on an
almost industrial scale, conducted
by whalers from the Basque country. The evocative remains of their
main base at Red Bay are part of
**Red Bay National Historic
Site** (*Off Rte. 510, tel 709/920-
2051, closed mid-Oct.–mid-June*).

Of far greater antiquity is the
burial mound at the **Maritime
Archaic Burial Mound
National Historic Site** (*Tel
709/920-2142*) in L'Anse Amour.
The oldest of its kind in North
America, it is a reminder of the presence of the Maritime Archaic people
who established coastal settlements
here some 7,500 years ago.

North of Red Bay at St. Mary's
Harbour, you can take a ferry
(*June–Sept.*) to **Battle Harbour,**
once considered the "capital of
Labrador" because so much cod
was processed here. Now deserted,
some of the former mercantile
premises can be visited and there
are fishery-related displays. ■

Goose Bay
🗺 87 C3
Nain
🗺 87 B5
St. Barbe
🗺 87 C3

Canada's most distinct province is evoked by the words that used to grace its license plates, "*La Belle Province*." The current "*Je me souviens*" (I remember) recalls the history of a land first settled by the French four centuries ago.

Québec

Introduction & map 104–105
Montréal 108–25
A walk in Old Montréal
    110-111
The Laurentians 126–27
Richelieu River Valley 128–29
The Eastern Townships 130–31
Trois-Rivières 132–33
Québec City 134–41
A walk around Old Québec
    138-39
Île d'Orléans & the Beaupré shore
    142–43
Charlevoix 144–45
Saguenay Fjord & the Lac
    Saint-Jean region 146–47
Côte Nord 148–49
Île d'Anticosti 150
Îles de la Madeleine 151
Gaspésie 152–54
Hotels & restaurants in Québec
    353–359

Statue at Notre-Dame-de-Bonsecours, Montréal

Québec

QUÉBEC EXTENDS FROM THE FER-
tile and populous St. Lawrence lowlands
across miles of forest and tundra to the
desolate coastline of the Hudson Strait.
Still part of Canada despite a quarter century of uncertainty, the province has
become more distinctively French in character since the changes began in the period of the 1960s Quiet Revolution.

Language laws ensure the visual dominance of
French in advertising and signs of all kinds,
while the long-lasting domination of business
life by English speakers has been brought to an
end. This doesn't mean you have to speak
French in order to enjoy a stay in Québec.
Virtually everyone an English-speaking visitor
is likely to meet will understand English and
probably speak it as well as you do. And despite
rumors to the contrary, the anglophone population of Montréal has not decamped en masse
to Toronto. The signs may be in French in the
city's downtown, but you're just as likely to
hear English spoken as French. Adding to the
charm and diversity of rural Québec are many
pockets of English-speaking communities
dotted around the countryside, descendants of
Loyalist, Irish, Scottish, or Channel Islands
settlers, and just as proud of their Québec
identity as any Québécois.

The Québec countryside is one thing, the
cities another. Montréal and Québec City
attract international visitors by the million,
and once you've arrived in either of them it
is easy to see why. Montréal is a great metropolis, whose deep-rooted past is reflected in its
claim to the biggest concentration of historic
buildings in North America, but whose future
aspirations are expressed in a skyline of skyscrapers, some of great elegance and beauty.
At its foot swirls a cosmopolitan population,
intent on getting the most out of life, especially where food and drink are concerned; the
city claims the finest array of restaurants outside New York. You can eat well in Québec
City, too, but the great attraction in the continent's only walled city is a sense of history.
Even in Europe there are few places that match
Québec City's marvelous fusion of human

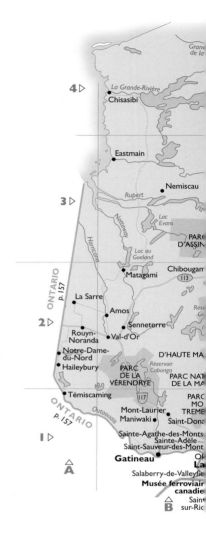

handiwork and nature: A great rock commanding the St. Lawrence, a Lower Town
huddling at its foot, and an Upper Town
crowning the heights with steep roofs,
towers, and a great Citadel.

The Québécois are very attached
to their countryside. Although the province
is highly urbanized, rural roots count for
a lot. City dwellers dream of owning an
old *maison québécoise*, built in fieldstone
under a steep-pitched roof. They flock to
weekend homes and chalets in the delightful rural areas on the fringe of the cities:

Lac Bienville

Schefferville

Réservoir de Caniapiscau

Lac Nichicun

Lac Naococane

NEWFOUNDLAND AND LABRADOR
p. 87

Blanc Sablon

QUÉBEC

Monts Otish

Lac Plétipi

Réservoir Manicouagan

Romaine

Natashquan

Petit Mécatina

PARC DE MISTASSINI

Lac Manouane

Manic-Cinq

Réservoir Pipmuacan

: DE OUGAMAU

ie-du-ste

Hauterive

Lac Saint-Jean

PARC DU SAGUENAY

Chicoutimi

erval

Sainte-Rose-du-Nord

Tadoussa

Port-au-Persil

PARC DES LAURENTIDES

St-Siméon

Sainte-Anne-de-Beaupré

Île d'Orléans

arlesbourg

Montmagny

rois-ières

ôme

orel

Drummondville

NTRÉAL

court

Chambly

rt

nnox

Magog

Knowlton

.A.

RÉS. DE SEPT-ÎLES-PORT-CARTIER

Longue-Pointe

Sept-Îles

Port-Cartier

Baie-Comeau

Havre-Saint-Pierre

Archipel-de-Mingan

Détroit de J.-Cartier

Port-Menier

Île d'Anticosti

Sainte-Anne-des-Monts

Matane

PARC DE LA GASPÉSIE

Gaspé

Cap des Rosiers

PARC NAT. DE FORILLON

Gulf of St. Lawrence

Jardins de Métis

Rimouski

Chandler

Carleton

New Richmond

Percé

I. Bonaventure

Bonaventure

Baie Sainte-Catherine

Rivière-du-Loup

Pointe-à-la-Croix

Miguasha

Baie des Chaleurs

Grosse Île

Îles de la Madeleine

La Malbaie

St-Joseph

Baie-Saint-Paul

Edmundston

NEW BRUNSWICK
p. 54

QUÉBEC

Lévis

U.S.A.

Sherbrooke

Manic-Cinq

Détroit d'Honguedo

0   200 kilometers
0   100 miles

Montréalers to the Laurentian Uplands, Richelieu Valley, and Eastern Townships; Québec City folk to the villages and countryside of Charlevoix. Weekend escapes are fine at any time of year, but perhaps best of all in winter; the many ski resorts may get crowded, but you can always slip away on cross-country skis or snowshoes and find unexplored places and perfect silence.

A second trip to Québec might take you along the north shore of the St. Lawrence, where some villages can still only be reached by boat, or to the islands of the gulf (Îles de la Madeleine and Anticosti). A third trip might lead northward, to the great hydroelectric projects of James Bay, or, properly equipped and advised, farther north still, to the Inuit and Cree villages of one of the last frontiers of travel. ■

Ottawa

The administrative center of New France—Québec City in 1720

New France

Farmhouses strung out along the riverside, their long and narrow lots reaching far inland, gray stone churches with glittering roofs and steeples, fine town houses that would not be out of place in Brittany or Normandy—there is a lot in the landscape of Québec that still breathes the spirit of the French North America of 300 years ago.

New France was intended to dominate the continent. French settlers lived on the Atlantic coast, traders pushed west to the Great Lakes and beyond, Détroit was a French fort, and the Mississippi a potential link to the southern colony of Louisiana. But the French presence was strongest in the lower valley of the St. Lawrence. Here were large towns: the capital, Québec, profiting from its position at the head of navigation for oceangoing ships, and, not far behind it in terms of population, Montréal, founded as the City of Mary (Ville-Marie) by the devout De Maisonneuve as a missionary city in the wilderness, but increasingly the capital of the fur trade, which was the single greatest source of the colony's wealth.

In its early years, the life of the colony was dominated by the fur trade and the companies that ran it (see pp. 220–21), particularly the Compagnie des Cent-Associés. In 1663 their failure to attract settlers—by that time the

population amounted to a mere 3,000—prompted Louis XIV to take control. From then until the British conquest a century later, New France was ruled as a royal province of the mother country. The king's representative was the governor general, supported (and sometimes undermined) by the intendant, in charge of day-to-day administration. Beneath these high officials, an urban aristocracy of mostly military men formed the top layer of society, pushing the frontier of French control farther into the continent and securing the colony against Iroquois and British attack. They shared the towns with a merchant class and with the Church, which sent missionaries to evangelize the natives and dispatched priests to the countryside to remind the rural population of their religious duties, a frequently unrewarding task.

Because the first priority of New France was trade and not settlement, the countryside was slow to develop, but following the term in office of the vigorous Jean Talon, the first royal intendant, immigrants from France arrived in greater numbers, the birth rate rose, the population increased substantially, and pressure for land grew. The way in which farmland was allocated was semifeudal. The land granted to a seigneur (not necessarily an aristocrat) was parceled out in long lots to tenants in return

A romanticized view of French-Canadian life by Cornelius Krieghoff

for annual, usually not very substantial, tithes, and the obligation to use the mill that the seigneur, in turn, was obliged to build.

Farmhouses were built along the river, close, but not too close, to the neighboring family's dwelling. The government would have preferred the rural population to have lived in villages, where they could be supervised more keenly, but the habitants (as they liked to call themselves) preferred to live in this semi-autonomous way, enjoying their freedoms but able to call on neighbors for help when necessary. Many of them had memories of being the outcasts of French society, as orphans, exprisoners, or soldiers, and enjoyed their independence. Urban officialdom worried about habitants having their throats cut by people lurking in the forest, but many Canadians admired those they called *les sauvages* for their pride, bushcraft, and refusal to be bound by routine.

In his homespun coat and moccasins, the typical habitant was quite content if his land yielded sufficient food for his family, and was rarely tempted to try and enrich himself by farming for the market. His sons might well take to the woods, disappearing for a season, or perhaps forever, in search of beaver pelts and other furs. With their adoption of native ways and their willingness to trade with anyone who would pay well (like the otherwise scorned New Englanders), these unlicensed *coureurs de bois* were a constant headache for the authorities, who wished to keep the fur trade under their control.

After the British conquest, the representatives of French authority were shipped back to France. The habitants stayed, adjusting to the new regime, but continuing their settled ways, living in a landscape that they created and whose patterns persist today. ■

Stalwart French habitants adapted perfectly to their harsh environment.

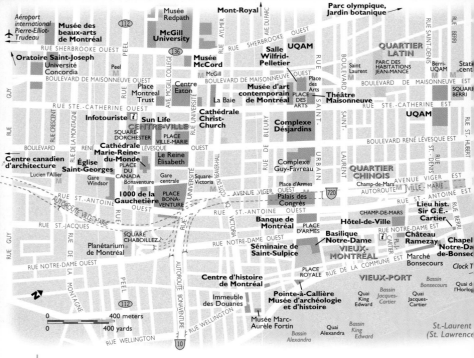

Montréal

Montréal
🅰 105 C1

**Visitor
information**

www.tourism-montreal.org

✉ 1001 Square-
   Dorchester
☎ 514/873-2015
📠 Metro: Peel

**Vieux-Montréal
Visitor
information**

✉ 174 Rue Notre
   Dame Est
☎ 514/873-2015
📠 Metro: Champ-
   de-Mars

TORONTO MAY HAVE SNATCHED THE BATON FROM Montréal as Canada's biggest city, but Montréal remains the country's most diverse and fascinating metropolis, an extraordinary fusion of rich European tradition and North American modernity. Montréal is on an island, the biggest in an archipelago downstream from the confluence of the Ottawa River and the St. Lawrence.

For a seat-of-the-pants understanding of why there is a city here at all (if you don't mind a bit of a soaking), take the powerboat ride from the Old Port to the Lachine Rapids. The foaming water blocked further navigation upstream by oceangoing vessels, making it necessary to reload, store, and supervise goods going to and from the continent's interior. So the mission of Ville-Marie established in 1642 by Paul de Chomedy Maisonneuve (1612–1676) soon developed as the base for explorers and for the *coureurs de bois* and voyageurs who ran the fur trade (see pp. 220–21).

Though Ville-Marie was soon renamed Montréal, the power of the Catholic Church remained strong. Missionaries had their headquarters here, and the Sulpician Order, which had sponsored Maisonneuve, stayed seigneurs of the city for more than 200 years. Their seminary of 1685 still stands next to their glorious basilica of Notre-Dame in the heart of Old Montréal.

TODAY'S MONTRÉAL
Once defended by a double line of stone walls, Vieux-Montréal has the biggest collection of 19th-

century buildings in North America. No longer the powerhouse of the Canadian economy—though its Wall Street, Rue Saint-Jacques, is still dominated by banks—it has been rescued from mid-century decay to become a focal point of the city for locals and visitors alike. The resurrection of the adjacent Vieux-Port (Old Port) as a leisure and recreational area has only added to its attraction.

The 19th-century development of Montréal as the nation's commercial and industrial capital and its greatest port saw the bypassing of the rapids on the St. Lawrence by the Lachine Canal (1825) and the extension of the city's influence by the building of railroads, including the Canadian Pacific, which had its headquarters here. Immigrants arrived from Britain and Ireland and for a few decades the city had an anglophone majority. The balance changed as burgeoning industries sucked in a francophone work force from the countryside. French speakers lived east of St. Lawrence Boulevard, English speakers to the west, where the wealthiest of them built the great mansions of the "Golden Square Mile" at the foot of leafy Mont-Royal, the city's great natural landmark.

In the early 20th century the city's center of gravity shifted to the west, reflecting the realities of anglophone dominance of the economy. But from the late 1950s Montréal was the focus of Québec's Quiet Revolution, which coincided with the physical transformation of the cityscape. The cross-shaped tower of Place Ville-Marie was among the first of a forest of skyscrapers, some of great architectural beauty. Beneath the streets the Underground City (p. 116) began to form, connecting stores, stations, places of entertainment, and the sparkling new Metro. An almost completely self-contained subterranean world, insulated from the rigors of the Montréal winter, came into being. This was the era of Mayor Jean Drapeau, flamboyant ruler of the city for 29 years, who not only gave Montréal the Metro, but also presided over Expo 67 and the summer Olympics of 1976. When, vexed by the promotion of French in public life from the mid-1970s onward, English speakers began to quit the city in large numbers, Drapeau commented "Let Toronto become Milan, Montréal will always be Rome."

Montréal may not have Rome's seven hills, but it is home to some 200,000 Italians, the largest of the migrant communities attracted here since World War II. The ethnic diversity of immigrants, who now make up nearly a fifth of the city's population, has not only diluted the intensity of the French-English polarity, which was once so dominant, but has added immensely to the richness of the city's cultural scene. Montréal is currently only one step behind New York as North America's capital of gastronomy.

Once you've finished eating, it is time to party. This is truly one of those cities that never sleeps, with an almost infinite choice of bars, cafés, cabarets, night spots, and entertainment. And when you've recovered from partying, there is an array of museums awaiting—some, like the Fine Arts Museum or the Museum of Contemporary Art, in world-class new buildings. ■

Street scene in Old Montréal

Nighttime in downtown Montréal from the heights of Mont-Royal

A WALK IN OLD MONTRÉAL

A Walk in Old Montréal

The historic core of Montréal, with its wonderful array of old buildings, is once more a fashionable place to live and work, and is the best place to begin your exploration of this fascinating, many-sided metropolis. The 18th-century stone walls have long since been pulled down, but Old Montréal, on its low ridge overlooking the St. Lawrence, is still well defined and a pure delight to stroll around.

The main east–west streets, Rue Saint-Jacques, Rue Notre-Dame, and Rue Saint-Paul, still follow the alignment traced out in the 1670s. There are boutiques, bars, restaurants, the occasional bed-and-breakfast in an 18th-century house built from Montréal's hard, gray limestone. Running north–south, the cross streets descend to what was once a busy dockside. Commerce has retreated from the Vieux-Port, giving way to riverside parkland and recreational facilities.

Take Montréal's squeaky clean Metro to **Champ-de-Mars ❶** and leave the station by the south exit. Walk diagonally across the Champ-de-Mars, the old parade ground that for many years served as a popular space for gatherings of all kinds.

From here there are views westward of the soaring towers of the downtown area, but below and in front of you are the bases of Montréal's old walls, a double line of defense erected early in the 18th century. Resist the temptation to go down Place Jacques-Cartier and instead walk east along Rue Notre-Dame, past bulky **Hôtel-de-Ville** on the left and modest **Château Ramezay** on the right (see p. 112).

Some of the numerous cafés on Rue Crescent in downtown Montréal

As you turn right on the **Rue Bonsecours,** there is a charming view downhill of the **Chapelle Notre-Dame-de-Bonsecours ❷** (see pp. 112–13) at the foot of the street. Rue Bonsecours has a number of fine old houses, including the 1785 **Maison Papineau** (No. 440) and the **Maison du Calvet** (No. 401) at the corner by the chapel.

Walk west past the 500-foot facade of **Marché Bonsecours,** then turn left and cross the railroad track to get a taste of the **Vieux-Port.** From the upper levels of the **Pavillon Jacques-Cartier** unfolds a panorama of the long, irregular line of mostly 19th-century shipping offices and storehouses that once marked the boundary between city and waterfront.

Recross the railroad tracks and enjoy the lively (summertime) ambience of **Place Jacques-Cartier ❸.** Walk west along narrow Rue Saint-Amable, then down Rue Saint-Vincent and west again on Rue Saint-Paul, perhaps the most picturesque of all the streets in Old Montréal. At Place Royale, turn left to Pointe-à-Callière and the **Musée d'archéologie et d'histoire de Montréal** (see p. 113–14). Go west again on **Place d'Youville ❹,** where, as well as the **Centre d'histoire**

- 🗺 See area map pp. 104–105
- ▶ Champ-de-Mars
- ↔ 1.7 miles
- ⏱ 3 hours
- ▶ Basilique Notre-Dame

NOT TO BE MISSED
- Chapelle Notre-Dame-de-Bonsecours
- Musée d'archéologie et d'histoire de Montréal
- Basilique Notre-Dame

A view from the port illustrates the architectural contrasts of Montréal.

de Montréal (see p. 114), there are splendid old stone buildings that once housed the **Écuries d'Youville** (Nos. 298–300) and the **Grey Nuns' Convent** founded in 1693 (Rue Saint-Pierre).

Go north on Rue Saint-Pierre and turn right onto Rue Saint-Jacques, which, under its English name of St. James' Street, was the Wall Street of Canada until well into the 20th century.

Among the ostentatious bank buildings the Banque de Montréal (No. 119) is outstanding, a Roman temple built to house the financing of Canada's imperial expansion. Its neighbors on **Place d'Armes** include the city's first sky-scraper, the New York Life Insurance Building of 1889, and the art deco Aldred Building. To the south are the twin towers of the **Basilique Notre-Dame 5** (see p. 114). ■

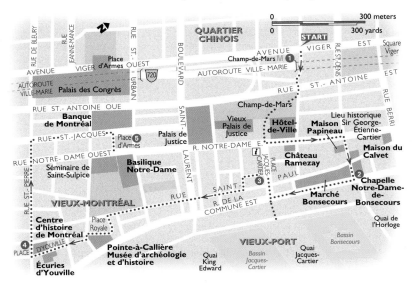

Old Montréal

Château Ramezay

✉ 280 Rue Notre-Dame Est

☎ 514/861-3708

🕐 Closed Mon. Oct.–May

💲 $

🚊 Metro: Champ-de-Mars

Lieu Historique Sir George-Étienne-Cartier

✉ 458 Rue Notre-Dame Est

☎ 514/283-2282

💲 $

🚊 Metro: Champ-de-Mars

Chapelle Notre-Dame-de-Bonsecours

✉ 400 Rue Saint-Paul Est

☎ 514/282-8670

🕐 Closed Mon. & restricted hours in winter

💲 Museum $

🚊 Metro: Champ-de-Mars

THE OBVIOUS FIRST CHOICE FOR MANY PEOPLE FINDING their bearings in Old Montréal is Place Jacques-Cartier *(Metro: Champ-de-Mars).* Named after the great French explorer, the square descends from the Nelson statue at the top of the slope to Rue de la Commune along the line of the old dockside. You are unlikely to be alone here; this is where city visitors hop aboard a horse-drawn carriage, watch the street entertainers from an outdoor café, and admire the offerings of the street artists in narrow Rue Saint-Amable just to the west.

But the square is far from being just a tourist trap. Half the city turns out here on summer days, overflowing across Rue de la Commune to the generous spaces of the the Vieux-Port. Before you join them, make sure you have had a good look at some of the fine old buildings lining the square, like No. 410, the restored **Maison Viger** at the corner of Saint-Amable, or No. 404, the **Maison del Vecchio,** also from the early years of the 19th century.

Nearby is the **Hôtel-de-Ville.** Dating from 1878, this monumental city hall in Second Empire style was rebuilt after burning down in 1922. The focus of Montréal's often convoluted city politics, it enjoyed a moment of international glory in 1967 when visiting President of France Charles de Gaulle cried *"Vive le Québec libre!"* from its balcony to the huge crowd assembled below. Apparently surprised at their ecstatic reaction, De Gaulle turned to his host, Québec premier Daniel Johnson, for an explanation. "You've just repeated the slogan of my opponents at the last election!" was the mortified reply.

Château Ramezay is one of the oldest and most evocative buildings in North America. This long, low, farmhouse-like structure in gray fieldstone has had an illustrious history. Completed in 1705 as the home of Claude de Ramezay, the 11th governor of Montréal, it was successively the headquarters of the Compagnie des Indes, the great fur-trading company, then the residence of the British governor-general. Benjamin Franklin lodged here during the 1775 American occupation of Montréal, but failed in his mission to persuade the citizens to sign up as the 14th state. The château has been a museum for over a century. Among its exhibits on domestic and First Nations themes is superb early 18th-century paneling from France.

A more recent place in Canadian history is preserved at **Lieu Historique Sir George-Étienne-Cartier**. Revered as a Father of Confederation by federalists, denounced as a stooge and collaborator by Québec nationalists, Sir George Étienne-Cartier (1814–1873) attracts controversy long after his death. The point of this charming museum, set out in the adjacent houses where he lived and worked, is not politics so much as the comfortable upper-middle-class life led in Montréal in the mid-19th century, with a wealth of period furniture and other artifacts.

Chapelle Notre-Dame-de-Bonsecours is also known as the Sailors' Church. This delightful 18th-century chapel is topped by a tall copper statue of the Virgin Mary, her arms outstretched to all

those who sail on the St. Lawrence. Grateful seafarers donated the ship models displayed inside. The building is a successor to the wooden chapel built in 1657 on the initiative of Marguerite Bourgeoys. Canonized in 1982, this indomitable lady from Troyes in France made her mark on Ville-Marie in all sorts of ways, not only founding an order of nuns, but establishing schools for both French and local girls and, most famously, shipping in young women *(Les filles du Roy)* as wives for bachelor colonists.

The Old Port

Summer is the time to enjoy the park laid out on the docksides of the **Vieux-Port,** when thousands of city dwellers congregate to stroll, cycle, Roller-blade, lounge around, see and be seen, and enjoy the cooling breezes. The breezes are a bit too cool in the winter, but hardy souls can still be seen skating and sliding. There is open-air entertain-

ment, and an interpretive science center called Centre des sciences de Montréal *(Tel 514/496-4724),* which incorporates an IMAX cinema. Of the various boat trips offered, the most exciting dares passengers to brave a soaking on the famous Lachine Rapids *(Tel 514/284-9607).*

POINTE-À-CALLIÈRE

All levels of Montréal's history come together in the fascinating complex of buildings known collectively as the **Musée d'archéologie et d'histoire de Montréal,** where there is an intriguing underground display of archaeological excavations. The area known as **Pointe-à-Callière** is the very birthplace of the city, the spot at which Champlain landed in 1611 and where Maisonneuve and his party of settlers landed in 1642. This, and much more, is entertainingly brought to life in a witty audiovisual show which painlessly

Montréalers reconstructed their Second Empire-style city hall after a fire in 1922.

Musée d'archéologie et d'histoire de Montréal
www.pacmuseum.qc.ca
✉ 350 Place Royale
☎ 514/872-9150
🕐 Closed Mon. mid-Sept.—late June
💲 $$
🚇 Metro: Place-d'Armes

The sumptuous interior of the Basilique Notre-Dame

combines English and French and in the space of a few minutes tells you most of what you need to know about Montréal's three-and-a-half centuries of existence. From here, you go beneath the surface to an atmospheric crypt, with evocative remains of walls, water conduits, sewers, even a cemetery. Back up on ground level, you find yourself inside the dignified old **Customs House** overlooking Place Royale, site of Maisonneuve's first residence.

To complete the history lesson begun at Pointe-à-Callière, go inside the splendidly ornate old fire station that now houses the **Centre d'histoire de Montréal.** Full of displays on all aspects of Montréal's past, its 11 rooms evoke the texture of urban life as you ride a trolley, climb up one of the city's famous outside staircases, or eavesdrop in a 1940s living room.

The **Basilique Notre-Dame** is one of the outstanding architectural achievements in a city that has more than its share of lovely buildings. In 1824 the Sulpician seigneurs who ruled Montréal ordered the building of a great church that would accommodate all the faithful of the parish (which covered the whole city). Their

chosen architect was an Irish-American Protestant named James O'Donnell, who was so moved by the magnificence of his achievement that he converted to Catholicism and was eventually buried here. For half a century, the twin-towered, Gothic Revival basilica was the biggest church in North America, and it remains a Montréal landmark despite the proliferation of skyscrapers. Its interior is of the utmost sumptuousness, a fusion of richly detailed carving, stained glass, and subtly controlled natural and artificial lighting. The gilt of woodwork and the mystic blue of vaults and altarpiece create an atmosphere of great serenity. The sanctuary is a masterpiece, carved by the sculptor Henri Bouriché. The windows, from Limoges in France, tell the tale of early Montréal.

The basilica is flanked by Montréal's oldest building, the **Vieux Séminaire de Saint-Sulpice,** erected by the Sulpician Order in 1685. The seminary is still in use by the order and is not open to the public. Behind its courtyard wall the symmetrical freestone building breathes the spirit of 17th-century New France. Its elegant clock is reputed to be the oldest of its kind in North America. ■

Centre d'histoire de Montréal

✉ 335 Place d'Youville

☎ 514/872-3207

🕐 Closed Mon. year-round, & Tues. mid-Sept.–April

💲 $

🚇 Metro: Square Victoria

Basilique Notre-Dame

www.basiliquenddm.org

✉ 110 Rue Notre-Dame Ouest

☎ 514/842-2925

💲 $

🚇 Metro: Place d'Armes

Square-Dorchester
& downtown

TOGETHER WITH PLACE DU CANADA ON THE FAR SIDE OF
Boulevard René-Lévesque, leafy Square-Dorchester *(Metro: Peel or
Bonaventure)* is traditionally held to be the heart of Montréal, though
it has to be said that the city's vibrant pulse beats in many places. For
visitors, it is a good place to start exploring the downtown area, not
least because of the presence of the visitor information center (Centre
Infotouriste) in the Dominion Square Building on the north side of
the square.

A glance at the buildings around
the square takes in much of
Montréal's recent history. Starting
with **Place du Canada,** nothing
could be more British than the oldest structure, **St. George's
Church,** a fine example of Gothic
Revival architecture, with a ham-
merbeam roof. Next to the church
is **Windsor Station,** a splendid
Romanesque Revival building of
1889, once the grand terminus of
the Canadian Pacific Railway.

Despite the presence of several
skyscrapers, the most compelling
building is still the **Cathédrale
Marie-Reine-du-Monde,** consecrated in 1894 and dedicated to
Mary, Queen of the World. A
scaled-down copy of St. Peter's in
Rome, it is an emphatic statement
of the power of the Catholic
Church here in the western part
of the city center, once the stronghold of British Protestantism.
Gesticulating from the cornice are
the patron saints of the various city
parishes that helped finance the
construction of the monumental
building, while inside is a magnificent reproduction of the balda-
chino (altar canopy) in St. Peter's.

On the east side of the square, a
whole block is occupied by the pale
granite **Sun Life Building,** begun
in 1914 and progressively added to
until it reached its present huge size.
It is easy to believe the claim (made

for quite a number of buildings in
Canada) that it was once the biggest
building in the British Empire.
Bigger, but slimmer, is Montréal's
tallest (672 feet) structure, **1000 de
la Gauchtière,** with a quietly
sumptuous interior incorporating a
skating rink.

OTHER DOWNTOWN
SIGHTS

Begun in 1958, I.M. Pei's **Place
Ville-Marie** *(On Blvd. René-
Lévesque at Rue Université)* ushered
in the modern transformation of

**St. George's
Church**
- Corner of Peel
  & de la Gauchetière
- 514/866-7113
- Closed Mon.
- Metro: Bonaventure

**Cathédrale Marie-
Reine-du-Monde**
- Boulevard René-
  Lévesque at
  Mansfield
- 514/866-1661
- Metro: Bonaventure

**A monument to
former Prime
Minister Sir
Wilfred Laurier
(1841–1919)
stands in Square-
Dorchester.**

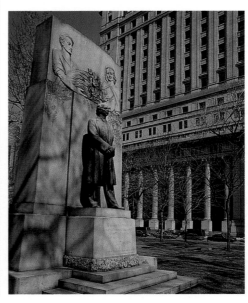

McGill University

✉ 805 Rue Sherbrooke Ouest

☎ 514/398-6555

🚇 Metro: McGill

Musée McCord

www.mccord-museum.qc.ca

✉ 690 Sherbrooke Ouest

☎ 514/398-7100

🕐 Closed Mon.

💲 $$

🚇 Metro: McGill

Christ Church Cathedral

✉ 635 Ste.-Cathérine Ouest

☎ 514/843-6577

🚇 Metro: McGill

In Montréal's vast underground network, interconnected levels house offices, stores, and places to eat.

Montréal's center. Above the esplanade with its fine vista up **Avenue McGill College** rises the 42-story cruciform tower in glass and aluminum topped by a rotating searchlight. Below the esplanade is a covered shopping center. The first of its kind, this now forms the nucleus of the Underground City.

Leading north from Place Ville-Marie is Avenue McGill College, which was widened in 1988 in order to create a visual link between the city center, **McGill University,** and Mont-Royal. The avenue provides a dignified setting for a number of highly individual contemporary buildings. They include **Place Montréal Trust,** with its spectacular five-story atrium, and the crystalline blue glass **BNP/Laurentian Bank Tower,** *(corner of Ave. McGill College & Ave. du Président Kennedy)* with its landmark sculpture, "The Illuminated Crowd" by the British-born sculptor Raymond Mason.

Avenue McGill College ends, not surprisingly, at McGill University. You're free to walk through the campus of this world-famous university, although you may stand out among the throng of students. There are about 30,000 of them, most, but not all, English-speaking. The campus is a wonderful oasis of green space in downtown Montréal, with an amazing variety of buildings that somehow blend effectively together to create an archetypal university atmosphere.

The Underground City

*M*on pays c'est l'hiver (Winter is the name of my country) sang *chansonnier* Gilles Vignault in the 1960s, and Québecers certainly know how to make the best of their fierce climate, what with superlative winter sports and rambunctious carnivals. But you don't want to struggle through snow and slush when you're doing the shopping or going to the theater. Montréalers have solved this problem by going underground. Since the Place Ville-Marie mall was completed in the early 1960s, a 20-mile network of weatherproof passageways has spread all over the city center, linking Metro and train stations, shops and stores (1,700 of them), theaters, hotels, offices, and apartments. In winter it is possible to enjoy city life to the fullest without ever having to venture outside, and the air-conditioned underground is equally welcome during Montréal's humid summer. ∎

The **Arts Building** tops the rise. Although much modified, this is the oldest structure, dating from 1839, not long after the university was founded in 1821 with resources from the estate of prominent Scottish fur-trader James McGill.

Musée McCord is a testament to the inveterate collector David McCord. Despite this museum's modern extension, only a fraction of the tens of thousands of objects assembled by him can be shown at any one time. Their richness and variety enables the museum to stage fascinating exhibitions on all kinds of themes, from ice hockey to satirical cartoons, and you should certainly check on what is currently on display. One of the museum's great strengths is its array of First Nations artifacts, symbolized by the magnificent cedar totem pole from far-off Queen Charlotte Islands. Another is the unique **Notman Photographic Archives,** an astonishingly complete record of Canadian life in the 19th and early 20th centuries.

Christ Church Cathedral (Cathédrale Christ Church), Montréal's splendid Gothic Revival Anglican cathedral, was built in 1859 and has led a rather precarious existence. The stone spire turned out to be too heavy for the foundations to bear, and an aluminum replacement had to be fitted. A solution to the sinking of the foundations was found in the 1980s, when the whole building, all 9,000 tons of it, was jacked up and a new basement was constructed. This underground addition houses **Promenades Cathédrale,** a shopping mall, though no stores were permitted to be built directly below the church.

In the days of Québec's Quiet Revolution, a concerted effort was made to revitalize the eastern, more francophone part of the city center. The **Université du Québec à**

Montréal (UQAM) was established here, as was the **Complexe Desjardins** *(corner of Rue St.-Urbain & Ste.-Cathérine Ouest),* its huge atrium a forum for popular events and entertainment. Arranged around a public square, which is at its liveliest in summer, the **Place des Arts** *(Tel 514/842-2112, Metro: Place des Arts)* comprises several auditoriums and the lavish **Musée d'art contemporain de Montréal.** Opened in 1992, this museum is a spacious home for the province's extensive collection of post-1945 works, mostly but not exclusively by artists from Québec. Visiting exhibitions are a major feature of its program.

The largest of the auditoriums is the **Salle Wilfrid-Pelletier,** where up to 2,892 spectators can watch performances by the resident ensembles, l'Orchestre symphonique de Montréal, l'Opéra de Montréal, and les Grands ballets canadiens.

Christ Church Cathedral is dwarfed by one of Montréal's many contemporary towers.

Musée d'art contemporain de Montréal
www.macm.org
✉ 185 Rue Ste-Cathérine Ouest
☎ 514/847-6226
🕐 Closed Mon.
💲 $$
🚇 Metro: Place des Arts

Musée des beaux-arts de Montréal

www.mmfa.qc.ca

- ✉ 1379–1380 Sherbrooke Ouest
- ☎ 514/285-2000
- 🕐 Closed Mon.
- 💲 $$$ (temporary shows only)
- Ⓜ Metro: Guy-Concordia

Centre canadien d'architecture

www.cca.qc.ca

- ✉ 1920 Rue Baile
- ☎ 514/939-7026
- 🕐 Closed Mon. June–Sept., Mon.–Tues. rest of year
- 💲 $$
- Ⓜ Metro: Georges-Vanier or Guy-Concordia

Oratoire Saint-Joseph

www.saint-joseph.org

- ✉ 3800 Chemin Queen Mary
- ☎ 514/733-8211
- 💲 Museum donation requested
- Ⓜ Metro: Côte-des-Neiges

WEST OF DOWNTOWN

The **Musée des beaux-arts de Montréal** is one of the most distinguished collections in North America, in terms of both the quality of its art and its architectural setting. The pictures, sculptures, drawings, and other art objects are housed in two very different buildings, linked by underground galleries beneath busy Sherbrooke Street. The 1912 North Pavilion is a neoclassic temple to the arts, as grandiose inside as out. Completed in 1991, the striking South Pavilion is the work of Montréal architect Moshe Safdie.

The South Pavilion has space for prestigious temporary exhibitions as well as for its extensive collection of European art, which ranges from superb medieval sculpture to Old Master paintings, including works by Memling, Mantegna, Rembrandt, El Greco, and Gainsborough. In addition there is a fine selection of 19th- and early 20th-century pictures. Contemporary Canadian and international art is represented too. The intimate spaces of the below-ground galleries seem just right for treasures from the ancient world, Asia, and Oceania.

The North Pavilion houses the comprehensive collection of Canadian art, comprising paintings, drawings, sculpture, and furniture. In addition, a wonderful series of decorative arts galleries display masterpieces from medieval times to the present day, notably a fine collection of 20th-century objects donated by Liliane Stewart that once formed part of the now-defunct Decorative Arts Museum.

Concerned at the loss of so much of Montréal's fine architectural heritage, Phyllis Lambert saved the historic **Shaughnessy House** of 1874 from demolition, and incorporated it into the sensitively designed complex known as the **Centre canadien d'architecture.** This fascinating center sees its mission as promoting a humane approach to architecture and its allied disciplines like urban planning and landscape design.

Mont-Royal

Known affectionately as "the mountain" though it only rises 768 feet above sea level, leafy Mont-Royal is a wonderful asset in a city where there is less public open space per head than in any other Canadian metropolis. Responsible for the tree-planting and subtle layout of roads, paths, and viewpoints was North America's greatest landscape architect, Frederick Law Olmsted, designer of New York's Central Park.

From downtown you can climb the mountain via a footpath and steps from the top of Rue Peel, but the easy way up is to take the No. 11 bus (which connects with the Metro at Mont-Royal station), get off at Lac-aux-Castors (Beaver Lake), and walk up the gentle slope to the big, stone-built **Chalet.** The lookout here gives a superb panorama of the city. A further climb brings you to the 120-foot metal cross, a great landmark especially at night, when it is illuminated. It is the 20th-century successor to the cross erected here by Paul de Maisonneuve in 1642 in thanksgiving for Ville-Marie's escaping a Christmas flood.

Popular all year round, the mountain is just as crowded in winter, with skaters on the lake, skiers on the slopes and trails, and visitors in horse-drawn carriages.

Oratoire Saint-Joseph, the massive pilgrimage church on the northwestern ridge of Mont-Royal, grew from the humblest of beginnings. In 1904, Brother André, porter at Notre-Dame College opposite the oratory, built a small shrine to St. Joseph to receive the

growing number of sick people who benefited from his healing powers. As the crowds of pilgrims increased, work was begun in 1924 on a great oratory to accommodate them. Interruptions and difficulties were triumphantly overcome by Dom Paul Bellot (1876–1944), the architect-monk also responsible for the abbey at St.-Benoît-du-Lac.

The interior is sparsely decorated with artwork and stained glass. Brother André's remains are here, and there is a small museum dedicated to him. The original shrine is outside the main building, where there are Stations of the Cross, too. The oratory stands at the top of a flight of 99 steps, which some pilgrims still climb on their knees. There is a view of all of northern Montréal from the terrace; the most prominent feature is the complex of the Université de Montréal, the largest francophone university in the world outside Paris. ■

The massive bulk of Oratoire Saint-Joseph dominates the high ground on the northwest side of Mont-Royal.

Two solitudes

The title of Montréal author Hugh McLennan's 1945 novel has become synonymous with the awkward relationship that has always existed between Canada's two founding nations. Translated into many languages (*Deux Solitudes* in French), the book deals with the identity crisis faced by a young man from the Québec countryside who, despite his bilingualism, is as ill at ease among his own folk as with the Montréal English speakers with whom he associates.

Montréal has long been the place where the two solitudes have confronted or, more often, failed to confront each other. Canada's economic development in the 19th and early 20th century was directed from here by a business class almost entirely of British origin, and for many years it was English-speaking immigrants who provided the necessary working-class manpower. For a while, in the middle of the 19th century, the city had an anglophone majority.

Elsewhere, especially in the countryside, French Canadians seemed trapped in a mid-18th-century time warp. After the British conquest, the community had turned in on

itself, protecting its identity by clinging to traditional ways and looking for leadership to the powerful Roman Catholic Church. The Church promoted a high birthrate, not least in order to ensure the survival of the community among the more numerous English speakers of Canada as a whole. But as Montréal grew in the late 19th century, more and more French-speakers were drawn in from the rural hinterland to man the new industries. Once described as "hewers of wood and drawers of water," they now formed the majority of the working class, toiling in enterprises whose bosses and managers were English Canadians, if not British or American.

Language & prestige

Inevitably, it was the English language that gave status. To get on in the dominant world of business, a French speaker would have to become bilingual, but even then career opportunities were limited. Downtown Montréal wore an almost entirely English face: Signs and advertising were in English, anyone a visitor might encounter would be an English speaker, and altogether there was little that distinguished Montréal from any other large North American city.

French Canadians might be at home in the countryside, but their big city was slipping away from them. Whatever their origin, successive waves of immigrants naturally identified with the dominant culture and sent their children to English schools. Securely on top, comfortable folk living in exclusive suburbs such as Westmount needed to have little more contact with their French-speaking fellow citizens than their anglophone equivalents in Toronto. The preferred picture of a French Canadian was a patronizing one, that of the habitant with his sash and clay pipe, living with his enormous family in picturesque squalor in an overcrowded farmstead. In town, he was an irritant: "Speak white!" was a not infrequent retort to someone who failed to understand English.

Whether or not French speakers understood English, their language was increasingly influenced by it, much to the chagrin of intel-

Unusually united—the federal maple leaf and the Québec fleur-de-lis fly from the same flagpole.

Only signs in French may appear on Montréal streets.

lectuals. The vocabulary of work, technology, and material progress generally was English, and French Canada had no equivalent of the Académie Française to police the entry of undesirable words into general use. A real fear arose that French could be swamped by the more powerful and prestigious language.

French resurgence

But with the coming of the Quiet Revolution in the 1960s, the French-speaking community emerged from its solitude. Even before the election of the Parti Québécois in 1976, the process that has been called "the reconquest of Montréal" had begun. A huge expansion of the public sector gave a growing French-speaking middle class jobs in schools, universities, hospitals, and administration generally. Steps were taken to promote the use of French in business, schools, and in signs and advertising. With the P.Q. in power, these processes intensified, finding their most complete expression in the ominously Orwellian-sounding Bill 101. Much to the dismay of many anglophones, this Charter of the French Language asserted the primacy of French in all spheres of life in Québec. Some found the situation intolerable, and set off down Highway 401 to Toronto or to other places in the rest of Canada where English solitude could still be enjoyed. Other perhaps braver spirits stuck it out, abandoning that solitude to learn French themselves, seeing advantages for their children in becoming bilingual and accepting, with varying degrees of reluctance, their minority status.

With the passing of time, and the increase in both the non-English and the non-French population of Montréal, attitudes have softened. Today, most Montréalers speak two or more languages with pleasure and they revel in their uniquely bilingual community. In the end, they enjoy life too much to let language tensions get out of hand. ∎

Shanghai Dream Lake Garden in the Jardin Botanique de Montréal

More places to visit in Montréal

OLYMPIC STADIUM

One of the world's most spectacular follies, the huge stadium built for the 1976 Olympic Games is dominated by an extraordinary leaning tower from which a fiber-glass roof is suspended by 26 cables. Endless difficulties attended the building of the stadium, designed by an architect hired from France. The tower and roof, made of a woven synthetic material, were only completed in 1987, more than a decade after the Games, and the city was burdened with the billion-dollar bill for the complex until 2006. Postgames, the stadium hosts concerts and gatherings of all kinds, including the Pope's visit in 1984. For those with no fear of heights, a strange self-righting vehicle crawls up the spine of the tower to an observation deck giving an unparalleled view of Montréal's east end and far beyond. www.rio.gouv.qc.ca ✉ 4141 Ave. Pierre-de-Coubertin ☎ 514/252-4737 💲 $$ 🚇 Metro: Pie IX

BIODÔME

The elegant concrete shell of the velodrome built for the 1976 Olympic Games now covers an ambitious and very convincing re-creation of four characteristic ecosystems of the Americas. You can step straight from the rigors of the Montréal winter into the warmth and humidity of a tropical forest inhabited by sloths, monkeys, and some 350 bats, or alternatively escape from the city's scorching July to the shores of the polar world, where a blizzard rages and penguins show their paces. Equally fascinating are the Laurentian forest and the ecosystem of the St. Lawrence. www.biodome.qc.ca ✉ 4777 Ave. Pierre-de-Coubertin ☎ 514/868-3000 💲 $$ 🚇 Metro: Viau

JARDIN BOTANIQUE DE MONTRÉAL

This paradise of plants, one of the world's great botanical gardens, extends over 185 acres to the north of the Olympic complex. Even if you go around on board the little sightseeing train, it is not possible to do justice to the whole of the gardens, so begin your exploration at the Reception Centre, where a giant model will help you decide what to see. The conservatories contain an array of plants from all over the world, while the gardens boast the biggest Chinese garden outside China, an equally fascinating and authentic Japanese garden, a total of 30 thematic gardens, a forest arboretum with more than 10,000 trees, and the fascinating Insectarium. www2.ville.montreal.qc.ca/jardin ✉ 4101 Rue Sherbrooke Est ☎ 514/872-1400 💲 $$ 🚇 Metro: Pie-IX

PARC-JEAN-DRAPEAU

Straddled by the Jacques-Cartier Bridge, Île Sainte-Hélène is a natural island, extended when it was chosen as the site for Expo 67. The hills and trees of Île Sainte-Hélène create an atmosphere far removed from the city's center, visible just across the water. One of the most admired structures at Expo was Buckminster Fuller's great geodesic dome, housing the U.S. pavilion. Now called the **Biosphere** *(160 chemin du Tour-de-l'Île, tel 514/283-5000)*, it contains an elaborate and user-friendly ecowatch facility, devoted to raising the profile of the St. Lawrence ecosystem.

Built on the orders of the Duke of Wellington, a fort houses one of Montréal's most appealing history museums, the intimate

Musée David M. Stewart *(Tel 514/861-6701)*. The museum draws on its extensive collections of maps, weapons, and navigational aids to illustrate aspects of the discovery and exploration of the New World. On the far side of the Pont Jacques-Cartier is the vast amusement park of **La Ronde** *(Tel 514/397-2000)*.

Neighboring **Île Notre-Dame** is entirely artificial. It features a beach, Formula One racing, extensive gardens, and the Montréal Casino *(Tel 514/392-2746)*, housed in the striking building that was the French pavilion in 1967.

☎ 514/872-6120 🚇 Metro: Jean-Drapeau ■

Runners pause for a break outside Montréal's Olympic Stadium.

Terre des hommes—Man & his world

This was the theme of *Expo 67*, the world's fair so triumphantly staged by Canada toward the end of the optimistic 1960s to celebrate the country's hundredth birthday. The construction of Montréal's Metro provided the fill to extend Île Sainte-Hélène and make the completely artificial Île Notre-Dame. The Canadian provinces, private bodies, and dozens of countries sprinkled their often exciting pavilions across the islands, which were lavishly landscaped and linked by futuristic transportation systems. Some 50 million visitors came to the show and apparently enjoyed themselves immensely, spending far more than the fair had cost to put on. But Expo was followed by the October Crisis (see p. 39) and by the gross overspending on the 1976 Olympic Games, for which the city paid for until 2006. ■

Montréal streets & suburbs

**Downtown
Montréal**
🅰 105 C1 & 108

Parc des Rapides
✉ Corner of Boulevard
LaSalle & 6th
Avenue, LaSalle
☎ 514/367-6351
Ⓜ Metro: de l'Église,
then 58 bus west

THE DOWNTOWN STRETCH OF RUE SAINTE-CATHÉRINE
Ouest still attracts the city crowds with its stores and places of entertainment. Celebrated by Québec-Irish singers Kate and Anna
McGarrigle, it is a bit seedy in places and has lost some of its vitality
to indoor malls and the Underground City, but a stroll here is an
essential part of the Montréal experience. Between St. Catherine and
Sherbrooke is Rue Crescent, which has kept most of its late 19th-
century charm. Winter evenings and summer days see it blossom as
a focal point of local social life.

Traditionally the dividing line
between French east Montréal and
the Anglo-dominated west,
Boulevard Saint-Laurent, or the
"Main" as it is known, has been the
conduit along which successive
waves of new Montréalers have
moved inland from the port to
found their new communities. Hop
aboard a No. 55 bus *(Tel 514/288-
6287 for schedule)* near Saint-
Laurent Metro station and travel
north past vendors of smoked meat
and bagels, Greek travel agents,
Portuguese restaurants, a branch of
the Ukrainian National Bank, and a
whole medley of multicultural shop
signs. The **Marché Jean-Talon**
(Tel 514/277-1599) is at the heart of
the Italian quarter.

An island of an independent
municipality in the ocean of
Montréal, **Westmount** took over
the role of the Golden Square Mile

**Diners enjoy the
cafés along Rue
Prince-Arthur.**

as the favored residential area of
English-speaking Montréal and for
many years its name was synonymous with anglophone style and
power. Leafy streets lined with
prosperous-looking villas climb the
western slope of Mont-Royal
toward Oratoire Saint-Joseph. By
contrast, **Westmount Square**
has a metropolitan atmosphere, its
exclusive shops and Metro station
topped by a trio of elegant black
towers by the great modern architect Mies van der Rohe.

Between Sainte-Cathérine and
Duluth, **Rue Saint-Denis** runs
through Montréal's Latin Quarter,
thronged by students from the university (UQAM). There are cafés,
bistros, galleries, bookstores, and
restaurants galore, some occupying
the charming old town houses built
here in the 19th century when this
was the fashionable francophone
suburb.

Carré Saint-Louis is the prettiest square in Montréal, lined with
row houses that somehow combine
extreme picturesqueness with good
manners. Running west from the
square to Boulevard Saint-Laurent,
pedestrian-only **Rue Prince-
Arthur** (Prince Arthur Street)
offers a bewildering choice of places
to eat.

PARC DES RAPIDES
The great rapids in the St.
Lawrence, which prevented the

early explorers and fur traders from continuing upstream, still exist even though damming of the river has reduced their ferocity. The early explorers baptized them "les rapides de Lachine" because they believed that China (La Chine) was just beyond them. Thrilling jet boat rides (see p. 383) are one way to experience the rapids but, for the less adventurous, it is possible to admire them from the shore. This park in the Montréal suburb of LaSalle offers a landscaped lookout, explanatory panels, and the possibility of seeing great blue herons. The largest heron colony in Québec inhabits the islands and rocks of the rapids feeding on the fish.

LACHINE NATIONAL HISTORIC PARK

Built in 1803, the park's centerpiece, a stone fur trade warehouse, was important in fur trade days. Here bales of pelts were stored before being taken into Montréal for transhipment to Europe and trading goods waited their transportation to the interior by canoe. Run by Parks Canada, this colorful era of Canada's history is marvelously brought to life. If possible, view the film on the Voyageurs, the people who transported the furs and trade goods by canoe.

EXPORAIL/MUSÉE FERROVIAIRE CANADIEN

Railroads were vital to growth of Canada. The **Musée ferroviaire canadien** is the country's major railroad museum, with a superb array of locomotives, rolling stock, and all kinds of railroad memorabilia. In addition to the giants of steam that conquered the Rockies, there are engines from abroad, including the British locomotive that once hauled the *Flying Scotsman*. The director's car used by Sir William Van Horne in the building of the Canadian Pacific Railway across the continent is also on show. On weekends there are live steam train and streetcar rides. ∎

Lachine National Historic Park
www.pc.gc.ca
✉ 1255 Boulevard Saint-Joseph, Lachine
☎ 514/637-7433
🕐 Closed Nov.–March & Mon.–Tues. mid-Oct.–Nov.
💲 $

Exporail/Musée ferroviaire canadien
www.exporail.org
✉ 110 Rue Saint-Pierre, Saint-Constant
☎ 450/632-2410
🕐 Closed Nov.–mid-May
💲 $$

The Laurentians (Les Laurentides)

The Laurentians
🅐 104 B1

Saint-Jérome
🅐 105 C1

Visitor Information
www.laurentides.com
✉ Maison de Tourisme des Laurentides, Autoroute 15, exit 15
☎ 450/224-7007 or 800/561-6673

Saint-Sauveur-des-Monts
🅐 104 B1

Sainte-Adèle
🅐 104 B1

Sainte-Agathe-des-Monts
🅐 104 B1

PART OF THE CANADIAN SHIELD, THE LAURENTIAN UPLANDS reach right across Québec from near Ottawa in the west to the Saguenay in the east. But for Montréalers, and for countless winter and summer vacationers from Canada and the United States, the bit of the Laurentians that counts is the hilly country northwest of Montréal, once reached by *l'petit train du Nord* (the little train of the north) and now by Autoroute 15.

The region has been developed with lodges, ski resorts, weekend homes, and recreational facilities of all kinds, including water sports on the rivers and many lakes. An elevation of 3,175 feet makes Mont Tremblant, the highest point in the area, a real mountain, but the rolling, humpbacked uplands, delightful though they are, don't quite have the drama of alpine terrain. Their slopes are fine for skiing, though, and the once continuous forest cover is now patched with stripes where trees have given way to pistes.

Vacationers have been the salvation of the region. In the second half of the 19th century Father Antoine Labelle made heroic attempts to stem the flow of young folk away from Québec to the mills of New England by opening up the area for agriculture. His efforts were largely in vain. Though he brought the railroad here and created many new parishes, the infertile soils resisted cultivation and much cleared land was eventually abandoned. But even in the 1890s, the wealthy had begun to come here for summer vacations. Winter sports developed in the 1920s, and in the 1960s the construction of the Autoroute des Laurentides brought the region within the reach of all.

The substantial town of **Saint-Jérôme,** situated 32 miles from Montréal at the point where the Rivière du Nord leaves the uplands, acts as the gateway to the Laurentians. Father Labelle was its parish priest for many years, and his statue stands in front of the cathedral. The fun really begins at **Saint-Sauveur-des-Monts** *(Visitor information, Parc Filion, tel 450/227-2564)*, the oldest of the Laurentian resorts, the most fashionable, and one of the best equipped both for skiing and après-ski. The imposing timber ski-lodge called **Pavillon Soixante-Dix** is an acclaimed work by the postmodern Montréal architect Peter Rose.

Sainte-Adèle (43 miles from Montréal) is a small and leafy town with a pretty location on its lake. It is famous as the hometown of the writer Claude-Henri Grignon, whose 1933 novel *The Woman and the Miser* inspired both radio and television shows, and added the word to be a *"séraphin"* (miser) to the Québec language.

HEART OF THE LAURENTIANS

One focal point of tourism in the Laurentians is **Sainte-Agathe-des-Monts** *(Visitor information 24 Rue Saint-Paul Est, tel 819/326-0457)*, a bustling little place with a wide range of services and facilities. Its attractive situation on the shores of Lac des Sables has made it a

favored location for prestigious second homes, but there are public beaches, too, and a lakeside drive taking in the lovely views.

Mont Tremblant

After the crossroads town of **Saint-Jovite,** Rte. 327 leads past picturesque Lake Ouimet to the huge **Mont Tremblant Resort** on its long and narrow lake. Mont Tremblant acquired its name—"shaking mountain"—from the natives, who thought that the wickedness of men would cause the mountain to shake in anger. So far Mont Tremblant has tolerated the

thousands of skiers who frequent its dozens of runs, among them one of the longest in Québec. Covering 930 square miles of superb forested upland, and at its most glorious when suffused with autumn color, **Mont Tremblant Provincial Park** *(Tel 819/688-2281, some park roads closed in winter)* was the first of its kind (1894) to be designated by the government of Québec. It is possible to see some of its splendid lakes and waterfalls by car, but for the best of the park and the chance of seeing deer, moose, and bears, take to the trails. ∎

Richelieu River Valley

RUNNING NORTHWARD 80 MILES FROM LAKE CHAMPLAIN and the U.S. border to the St. Lawrence at the town of Sorel, the valley of the Richelieu River has long served as a corridor of movement and as a focal point of national rivalries. Its contemporary role is an entirely peaceful one. The agricultural lands of its lower course are some of the most fertile in Québec, while its waterways and country-side form a popular recreational area for its many visitors.

Blockhaus de Lacolle
- ⚿ 105 Cl
- ✉ 1 Rue Principale
- ☎ 450/246-3227
- ⏱ Closed mid-Oct.–mid-May & weekdays mid-Sept.–mid-Oct.

Fort Lennox National Historic Site
www.pc.gc.ca
- ⚿ 105 Cl
- ✉ Ferry service from village of Saint-Paul-de-l'Île-aux-Noix
- ☎ 450/291-5700
- ⏱ Closed mid-Oct.–mid-May & weekdays mid-Sept.–mid-Oct.
- 💲 $$

One of the attractive features of the Richelieu River is the way in which its course is diversified by numerous islands. The first island downstream from Lake Champlain, **Ash Island,** used to bear the grisly name of Île aux Têtes (Island of the Heads). After a bloody battle between the Algonquin and Iroquois around 1580, the defeated Iroquois had their heads impaled on stakes here. The movement of Europeans into the area brought other rivalries with it, and led to the construction of so many defense works that this southern part of the Richelieu is known as the "valley of forts."

Nearby, close to the confluence of the Richelieu with its tributary the Lacolle, is the timber-built **Blockhaus de Lacolle,** the only one of its kind still standing in Québec. Constructed in 1781, it formed part of the British defense system against American attack and saw action during the War of 1812, as bullet holes in its walls testify.

The French were the first to fortify the Richelieu Valley, one of their strongholds being **Fort Lennox National Historic Site,** built on this 210-acre island. But the imposing buildings and earth-works that can be seen today are the result of the British refortification of the site after the island had been occupied by the Americans in 1775–76. Protected by a typically baroque star-shaped moat and ramparts, a series of military

Quashed rebellion

In 1837 the lower Richelieu Valley was the scene of fighting between French Patriote rebels and British forces. Alarmed by a mass meeting at the village of Saint-Charles at which Patriote leaders pledged to "direct not words, but bullets against our enemies," the British sent out a force from Montréal. Despite their numerical superiority over the Patriotes, who had assem-bled at Saint-Denis, and some of whom were only armed with pitch-forks, the British were forced to retreat. But this was the Patriotes' only victory. Within days they were overwhelmed at Saint-Charles and again in the Deux-Montagnes region, where 70 of them were slaughtered as they tried to escape from the burning parish church at Saint-Eustache. ■

structures in an austere classical style include barracks, officers' quarters, and guardhouse. It is quite a thrill to take the ferry across the Richelieu, cross the moat, enter the fort through its severe stone gateway, and inspect the buildings where the harsh conditions of soldierly life have been convincingly re-created.

Founded by the French in 1666 as a link in their system of defenses against the Iroquois, **Saint-Jean-sur-Richelieu** became an indus-trial town famous for its pottery and ceramics. In 1775 the British garrison of the fort here withstood 45 days of an American siege before surrendering. The history of the region is explained with special emphasis on ceramics at the **Musée du Haut-Richelieu.**

Chambly is only a short drive via Hwy. 10 from the center of Montréal and attractively located at a point where the Richelieu widens out into a broad basin. This historic center is now a popu-lar residential town for city com-muters. It is famous for its fort, first built in 1665, and for the **Chambly Canal,** completed in 1843 to bypass the rapids between here and Saint-Jean, and now restored by Parks Canada. With its nine locks, the canal was an important link on the trade route between Montréal and towns along the Hudson, but nowadays its still substantial traffic consists purely of pleasure craft.

Originally a timber structure, **Fort Chambly National Historic Site** was rebuilt in stone in 1711, and it is to its 18th-century state that the rectangle of walls and corner bastions have been restored.

Mont-Saint-Hilaire imposes a massive presence on the surround-ing plain and on the charming village (St.-Hilaire) at its foot—a favorite haunt of artists. The near-pristine state of the forest led to its being designated Canada's first UNESCO biosphere reserve. Part of it is sealed off for scientific research, but you can wander an extensive trail network, climb to little glacial **Lake Hertel** or to the top of **Pain de Sucre** (Sugarloaf), where there are magnificent views over the plains. ■

Musée du Haut-Richelieu
www.museeduhautrichlieu.com
✉ 182 Jacques Cartier Nord
☎ 450/347-0649
🕐 Closed Mon.
💲 $

Chambly
🅰 105 C1

Fort Chambly National Historic Site
www.pc.gc.ca
✉ 2 Rue de Richelieu
☎ 450/658-1585
🕐 Closed Nov.–March and Mon. & Tues. April–mid-May & Sept.–Oct.
💲 $

Mont-Saint-Hilaire
www.centrenature.qc.ca
✉ 422 Chemin des Moulins
☎ 450/467-1755
💲 $

Long gone cold, a cannonball heater drawn up in the central enclosure of Fort Lennox.

The Eastern Townships (Cantons de l'Est)

Regional visitor information

www.easterntownships.org

✉ 20 Rue Don-Basco Sud, Sherbrooke

☎ 819/820-2020

Musée des beaux-arts de Sherbrooke

🅰 105 C1

✉ 241 Rue Dufferin

☎ 819/821-2115

🕐 Closed a.m. & Mon.

💲 $

SOME OF THE MOST ATTRACTIVE COUNTRYSIDE IN QUÉBEC can be seen among the Eastern Townships, the rolling wooded uplands and lake- and river-filled valleys along the Vermont border. A couple of hours' drive from Montréal, the area is popular with weekenders from the city, as well as with visitors enchanted by the comfortable, well-lived-in landscape with its farmlands, charming villages, clapboard churches, covered bridges, and round barns.

The area owes much of its character to the Loyalists who settled here after the American Revolution. Other Americans, mostly New Englanders, followed in search of cheap land when the British government lifted restrictions after the War of 1812, and well into the 19th century the townships looked south for economic and cultural sustenance rather than to Lower Canada. By the middle of the century, nearly 100,000 English speakers lived here, but they were soon outnumbered by French-Canadian immigrants who came to farm or to work in the many small-scale industries. Today the population of the townships is overwhelmingly French-speaking, but there are many places that will remind New Englanders of home, like the village of **North Hatley** 12 miles south of Sherbrooke.

The region welcomes guests at all times of the year. The fall colors of the forest make a lovely backdrop to the ripening fruit of orchards and vineyards, best seen around little **Dunham,** the very first township to be established in the region. Winter brings both downhill and cross-country skiers; there are popular resorts at **Sutton, Mont Orford** (*Visitor information, off Rte. 141, tel 819/843-9855*), and a number of other small resorts.

Owl's Head Mount rises beyond the Abbaye de St.-Benoît-du-Lac.

Snowmobile center

If you've ever wondered where Skidoos came from, it is here! Bombardier is one of Québec's big industrial names, with headquarters in Montréal and a manufacturing plant in the Townships village of Valcourt, the birthplace of its founder, Joseph-Armand Bombardier. In 1937 the inventive Joseph-Armand put together an all-terrain vehicle using skis and a tracked drive, but it was his world-beating Skidoo of 1959 that caught everyone's imagination, revolutionizing mobility in the winter countryside. Full tribute is paid to the man and his invention in Musée J.-Armand Bombardier. ■

Sold by the thousands, snowmobiles have transformed life in the winter countryside.

Industrial **Sherbrooke,** located at the meeting-point of the Magog and Saint-François Rivers, is the capital of the Eastern Townships. As well as an imposing cathedral, there is the very American-looking **Plymouth Trinity Church,** built in 1848 for a congregation with roots in Massachusetts. Among the attractions of mainly local interest is the **Musée des beaux-arts de Sherbrooke,** which has a fascinating collection of international naive art as well as many fine pictures by Québec artists. In the 19th and early 20th centuries, Sherbrooke's captains of industry built their mansions in a variety of extravagant styles in the **Quartier du Vieux-Nord** (Old North Ward district). The best way to explore this and other historic parts of town is to take an audio tour; inquire at the **Centre d'interpretation de l'histoire de Sherbrooke.**

Lake Memphremagog is the largest lake in the Eastern Townships, extending into the United States to Newport, Vermont. Between the northern end of the

lake and Mont Orford is the resort of **Magog,** the main visitor center in the townships. A 12-mile drive down the west bank of the lake brings you to **Abbaye de Saint-Benoît-du-Lac** *(Tel 819/843-4080).* In an idyllic situation among the woods, the abbey was founded in 1924 and extended in the 1930s by architect-monk Dom Bellot, designer of the dome of Oratoire Saint-Joseph in Montréal. Visitors can attend some services and the abbey shop sells an excellent cheese made by the monks.

One of several little towns around the shores of Lake Brome, **Knowlton** (now officially called Lac-Brome) has kept its strongly Loyalist flavor with a largely anglophone population, fine old 19th-century houses, and a fascinatingly heterogeneous local museum—the **Brome County Historical Museum,** housed in a number of heritage buildings. There is a courthouse, a restocked village store from long ago, and a collection of militaria including a World War I German pursuit plane. ■

Centre d'interpretation de l'histoire de Sherbrooke
- ✉ 275 Rue Dufferin, Sherbrooke
- ☎ 819/821-5406
- 🕐 Closed Mon.
- 💲 $

Brome County Historical Museum
- ✉ 130 Lakeside, Lac-Brome
- ☎ 450/243-6782
- 🕐 Closed mid-Sept.–mid-May
- 💲 $

Musée J.-Armand Bombardier
www.fjab.qc.ca
- ✉ 1001 ave. J.-Armand Bombardier, Valcourt
- ☎ 450/532-5300
- 🕐 Closed Mon. mid-Sept.–May
- 💲 $$

Trois-Rivières

Trois-Rivières

⛰ 105 C1

Visitor information

www.v3r.net

✉ 1457 Rue Notre-Dame

☎ 819/375-1122

🕐 Closed weekends Oct.–May

Centre d'Exposition sur l'Industrie des Pâtes et Papiers

✉ 800 Parc Portuaire

☎ 819/372-4633

🕐 Closed Oct.–mid-May

💲 $

Musée des Ursulines

✉ 734 Rue des Ursulines

☎ 819/375-7922

🕐 Closed Mon. in summer, Mon.–Tues. off-season & Nov.–Feb.

💲 $

Forges-du-Saint-Maurice National Historic Site

www.pc.gc.ca

✉ 10,000 Blvd. des Forges

☎ 809/378-5116

🕐 Closed mid-Oct.–April

💲 $

TROIS-RIVIÈRES OWES ITS NAME AND ITS FORTUNE TO THE Saint-Maurice River. As the Saint-Maurice joins the far larger St. Lawrence, it divides into three branches (*trois rivières*) to flow around a pair of islands, and for many years the town has been the world's foremost producer of newsprint, made from the timber floated down the river from the forests to the north.

The origins of Trois-Rivières go back much further than the timber industry established in the 19th century. It is in fact the second oldest settlement in Québec, founded as a fur-trading post in 1634 only a few years after Québec City. Despite the ravages of a great fire in 1908, there remain enough old buildings in the center to give you a strong sense of the city's long past.

The historic core of Trois-Rivières was built on a terrace high above river level. The site of the original fort overlooking the St. Lawrence is known as **Le Platon** and has a bust of the founder, Nicolas Goupil, Sieur de Laviolette. Also overlooking the river is the elaborate terracing of the **Parc Portuaire** (waterfront park). From here there is access to the **Centre d'Exposition sur l'Industrie des Pâtes et Papiers,** which does a workmanlike job on all aspects of the industry that sustains Trois-Rivières and its region.

One block inland from the waterfront is venerable Rue des Ursulines, which runs parallel to the river. The domed **Monastère des Ursulines,** founded in 1700, dominates the street and the attractive gardens laid out in front of it. Inside, there is an ornate chapel and the **Musée des Ursulines,** a museum with a wonderful assortment of religious objects and furniture from the 17th century forward. Opposite Anglican St. James' Church are particularly fine examples of 18th- and early 19th-century

houses, and to the west is **Manoir de Tonnancour** (*864 Rue des Ursulines, closed Mon.*), a distinguished stone edifice dating from the early 18th century but rebuilt in 1795 after a fire. It now houses an art gallery. There is another superb manor house a little farther inland; follow Rue Bonaventure to the **Manoir Boucher-de-Niverville** (*168 Rue Bonaventure, tel 819/375-9628*), which is now the home of the regional Chamber of Commerce. Built in 1730, it breathes the atmosphere of New France.

On the edge of the old quarter of Trois-Rivières stands the **Musée québécois de culture populaire** (*200 Rue Laviolette, tel 819/372-0406, www.culturepop.qc.ca, closed Mon. mid-Sept.–mid-June, $$*). Devoted to folk culture, it features changing exhibits on day-to-day experiences, concerns and values of Québecers. The old city jail of 1822 is also part of the museum and it offers a visit entitled "Go to Jail" with former inmates.

For nearly a century, the people of New France paid high prices for any objects made of metal, all of which had to be imported from the mother country. At last, in 1734, a Canadian ironworks was established at **Forges-du-Saint-Maurice National Historic Site.** For its raw material it used the bog-iron along the riverbank. For 150 years the works turned out metal objects ranging from ax heads to the engines for the 1809 steamboat *Accommodation*. The *grande maison*

that housed the offices and living quarters still stands, while imaginative symbolic structures evoke the outline of the other buildings of the complex. Excellent interpretive displays help bring to life this pioneering New World industrial site.

The atmosphere of religious devotion once so prevalent in Québec is still very present at **Sanctuaire Notre-Dame du Cap** *(3 miles east of Trois-Rivières, tel 819/374-2441, www.sanctuaire-ndc.ca)*, the third most important place of pilgrimage in the province. A little, early-18th-century church still stands here, but it is the imposing octagonal basilica, completed in 1964 by a student of architect-monk Dom Bellot, that draws the crowds to celebrate the miracles witnessed here in the late 19th century by Father Luc Désilets.

OTHER ATTRACTIONS

The St. Maurice River flows through one of Québec's most industrial regions, with pulp mills, smelters and hydro-electric power stations. This industrial heritage is celebrated at the **Cité de l'énergie** in Shawinigan where you can enjoy video presentations and exhibits. The highlight is the elevator ascent of a massive 377-foot hydro pylon for splendid views of the area.

Just to the north, industry is left far behind in the 210-square-mile **La Mauricie National Park,** which protects a superb tract of the Canadian Shield country of mixed forest and more than 150 lakes. The park is best appreciated from a canoe, but a parkway does connect the entrances at Saint-Jean-des-Piles and Saint-Mathieu. ■

Paddling through La Mauricie National Park

Cité de l'énergie
www.citedelenergie.com
- ✉ 1000 Ave. Melville, Shawinigan
- ☎ 819/536-8516
- 🕐 Closed mid-Oct.– mid-June & Mon. in June, Sept. & Oct
- 💲 $$$

Parc National de la Mauricie
www.pc.gc.ca
- 🅰 105 C1
- ✉ 30 miles N of Trois-Rivières, Hwy. 55 (exit 217 or 226)
- ☎ 819/538-3232
- 💲 $

Québec City

Québec City
105 C1

Visitor information
www.quebecregion.com
12 Rue Sainte-Anne
418/641-6290

835 Ave. Wilfred-Laurier
418/649-2608

Château Frontenac
1 Rue des Carrières
418/692-3861
Guided tours $$$

Basilique de Notre-Dame-de-Québec
www.patrimoine-religieux.com
20 Rue de Buade
418/694-0665. For son-et-lumière shows call 418/694-4000

Séminaire de Québec and Musée de l'Amérique Française
www.mcq.org
2 Côte de la Fabrique
418/692-2843
Museum: closed Mon. late Sept.—early June
$$

QUEBEC'S PROVINCIAL CAPITAL HAS LONG OUTGROWN ITS walls. Residential and commercial areas sprawl over the surrounding countryside. The Assemblée Nationale (Provincial Legislature) dominates the Grande Allée, the hub of the city's life today. Within the walls of the Upper Town, all is enchantment: Old stone houses cozy up to the great religious institutions built from the same gray stone. Above it all rises Château Frontenac, the ultimate in romantic hotel architecture. Below it, down the steps and stairways to the foot of the cliff, are the even more romantic old streets of the Lower Town.

UPPER TOWN (HAUTE-VILLE)

The sloping square of the Place d'Armes is as good a place as any to get your bearings in this city. The dominant structure is the **Château Frontenac.** With its outline of towers, steeply pitched roofs, and dormer windows, it is the archetype of the château-style hotel and an unmistakable symbol of Québec. Built between 1893 and 1924, with a wing added in the 1990s, it is named after Louis de Buade, Comte de Frontenac, a 17th-century governor of New France.

Along the clifftop stretches **Terrasse Dufferin,** a boardwalk leading to the stairways of the Promenade des Gouverneurs, clinging to the cliffs beneath the Citadel (see p. 140). Laid out in its present form in the 1870s, Terrasse Dufferin bears the name of the governor-general of Canada at the time, Lord Dufferin, who worked to preserve the city's historic character. With its little market stands and other urban furniture, it has the character of a resort, and for many years was very fashionable.

After admiring the view down to the Lower Town and across the St. Lawrence to Lévis on the far bank, visit one of several nearby establishments that stand ready to deliver a painless history lesson. There is a wax museum, the **Musée de Cire** (*22 Rue Ste.-Anne, tel 418/692-*

2289) housed in a fine 18th-century dwelling; the **Musée du Fort** features a model of the city in 1750, (*10 Rue Ste.-Anne, tel 418/692-2175*); and **Québec Expérience** (*8 Rue du Trésor, tel 418/694-4000*), the best of them all, which explores the city's history with inventive use of multimedia.

The forerunner of today's cathedral was New France's first parish church, built of stone in 1647, itself a replacement for a timber church erected by the Jesuits in 1633. In 1657 the church became a cathedral. Badly damaged in the course of the British bombardment in 1759, the **Basilique de Notre-Dame-de-Québec** was rebuilt over a period of nearly two centuries by the Baillairgé dynasty of architects. Their work formed the basis of reconstruction after a fire in 1922. The best way to appreciate the interior is to attend one of the daily *son-et-lumière* shows. The cathedral has been the scene of many funeral masses for the great and good of Québec, from Samuel de Champlain to René Lévesque.

The austere stone walls of the **Séminaire de Québec** and **Musée de l'Amérique française** sheltered the first educational institution in New France, a training school for priests. Founded in 1663 by Monsignor de Laval (who became New France's first bishop), it is now the home of

Laval University's school of architecture. Look for the sundial on the wall of the late 17th-century Procure Wing; its inscription means "Our days pass like a shadow." The museum deals in a lively way both with its own history and with the stirring tale of the settlement and culture of New France.

Begun in 1800, **Holy Trinity Anglican Cathedral** (Cathédrale épiscopale de la Sainte-Trinité) was modeled on London's famous Church of St. Martin-in-the-Fields, and was the first Anglican cathedral to be built outside the British Isles. Its simplified classical architecture served as a model for many more churches across Canada. Hardly altered in 200 years, the interior features furniture, including a royal pew made from English oak.

Still caring for today's patients, the **Hôtel-Dieu Hospital** (*Rue Charlevoix, closed to public*) was founded by Augustinian nuns around 1640. Its church, begun in 1800, has a splendid interior with carvings by Thomas Baillairgé. A number of religious paintings confiscated by anticlerical zealots during the French Revolution eventually found a home here. There are more paintings, in this case from the early days of New France, in the **Musée des Augustines de l'Hôtel-Dieu de Québec,** which is devoted to the life of the nuns who founded this hospital in 1639, one of the first in North America. An array of early medical instruments are among the museum's varied collections.

While the Augustinians cared for the sick, the Ursulines, who also landed in the new colony in 1639, concerned themselves with the education of girls, both French and native. The oldest institution of its kind in North America, the **Couvent des Ursulines** (*Rue Donnaconna*) is housed in buildings erected at various times during the monastery's three and a half centuries of existence. The **Chapelle des Ursulines**

Holy Trinity Anglican Cathedral
www.ogs.net/cathedral
✉ 31 Rue des Jardins
☎ 418/692-2193

Musée des Augustines de l'Hôtel-Dieu de Québec
✉ 32 Rue Charlevoix
☎ 418/692-2492
🕐 Closed Mon.

Street life on Rue Petit Champlain

Musée des Ursulines de Québec
✉ 12 Rue Donnaconna
☎ 418/694-0694
🕐 Closed Mon. & Dec.–Jan.
💲 $

Place-Royale Information Centre
www.mcq.org
✉ 27 Rue Notre-Dame
☎ 418/646-3167
🕐 Closed Mon., mid-Sept.–mid-June

Église Notre-Dame-des-Victoires
✉ Place Royale
☎ 418/692-1650

(Tel 418/694-0413, closed Mon. & Nov.–April) dates from the beginning of the 20th century and incorporates the decorated interior of the 18th-century chapel it replaced. Much of the carving is the work of Québec's master-sculptor Pierre-Noël Levasseur. The **Musée des Ursulines de Québec** contains many items evocative of early days in New France, including exquisite embroidery worked by the nuns.

LOWER TOWN (BASSE-VILLE)

Reached from the Upper Town via the steep and winding street called Côte de la Montagne and Escalier Casse-Cou (Breakneck Stairs), or by funicular from Terrasse Dufferin *(Tel 418/692-1132),* the Lower Town is the nucleus from which Québec grew. Here you will have a thrilling sense of New France's earliest days. The focal point is Place Royale, but be sure to stroll streets such as Rue du Petit-Champlain, Rue Saint-Pierre, and Rue Saint-Paul, get a whiff of the sea from the boardwalks of the Old Port, and visit the Musée de la Civilisation.

Place Royale is lined with fine stone houses and dominated by the church of Notre-Dame-des-Victoires. It was laid out in 1688 on the site of the garden of Champlain's Habitation of 1608, and, as market square and public forum, was the epicenter of life in Québec for many years. A reconstruction from the late 1960s forward has returned it to the appearance it had at the time of the conquest. As well as being the starting point for guided walks, the **Place-Royale Information Centre** gives a full account of the Lower Town's history.

Originally dedicated to the infant Jesus, Bishop Laval's chapel was rededicated in 1690 as **Église Notre-Dame-des-Victoires** when 34 British ships withdrew after a five-day siege of the city. "Victory" singular became "victories" plural in 1711 after a British naval attack was disrupted by a violent storm. When the British came a third time, in 1759, they stayed, and the church was almost completely destroyed by their bombardment. Rebuilt more than once since, it presents a steep gable to the square, topped by a spire. Inside, a large model ship is suspended in the nave, while the altarpiece symbolizes the fortified city of Québec.

Housed in a superb modern building, the **Musée de la Civilisation** offers up to 12 exhibits at any one time. Wonderfully integrated into the urban fabric of the Lower Town, the museum incorporates the 18th-century **Maison Estèbe.** In the spacious lobby, a striking, concrete sculpture evokes the springtime breakup of the ice on the St. Lawrence. The permanent exhibits will intrigue anyone interested in what it is that makes up the identity of Québec. They trace the history of

New France to the present day and explore the lifestyle of the First Nations peoples of the province. Among the vast array of objects, one outstanding exhibit is *La Barque*, a boat that was discovered on the actual site of the museum during construction. The numerous temporary exhibits feature elements of civilizations of all ages and parts of the world.

Québec boomed as a port city in the early 19th century, when raftsmen steered their long timber bundles down the St. Lawrence and St. Charles Rivers to be loaded aboard ships bound for Britain. In the other direction came immi-

grants looking for a new life. Activity fell off toward the end of the century, but you can still see freighters from the observation deck of the **Old Port of Québec Interpretation Centre.** Housed on the dockside of the Bassin Louise in what used to be a cement plant, the center brings to life the glory days of the port and the work of loggers, raftsmen, and shipbuilders. To the east of the lock connecting the Bassin Louise to the St. Lawrence, broad boardwalks give access to the riverside, whose performance area, Agora du Vieux Port, is popular in summer. ∎

Musée de la Civilisation

www.mcq.org

☒ 85 Rue Dalhousie

☏ 418/643-2158

🕐 Closed Mon. late Sept.–early June

💲 $$

Old Port of Québec Interpretation Centre

www.pc.gc.ca

☒ 100 Quai St.-André

☏ 418/648-3300

🕐 Closed late Oct.–mid-May except by appt.

💲 $

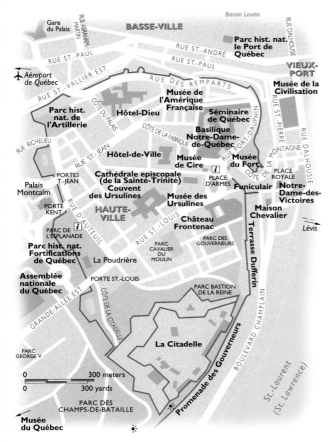

A walk around Old Québec

This walk explores both the Upper and Lower Towns, but leaves you with plenty more to discover. After a brief circuit of the Upper Town, capitalizing on its marvelous views over the great river, the walk goes downhill to meander through the streets and squares of the Lower Town.

Begin the walk in the **Place d'Armes** ❶ by the Champlain memorial and the monument commemorating Québec's UNESCO designation as a world heritage site. After admiring the view of the Lower Town and the St. Lawrence, go along the righthand side of the square and turn right down narrow Rue du Trésor and left along the flank of the **Notre-Dame basilique** (see p. 134).

Go down Rue Sainte-Famille past the high walls of the Seminary, turn left along Rue Couillard, then right down Rue Saint-Flavien to the **ramparts** ❷ and their view of the port. Rue Hamel and Rue Charlevoix lead to the **Musée des Augustines.** Come back uphill via Côte de la Fabrique and follow Rue des Jardins to the **Place de l'Hôtel de Ville,** dominated by the grandiose late 19th-century **Hôtel de Ville,** or City Hall. In its basement, the **Urban Life Interpretation Centre** (43 Côte de la Fabrique, tel 418/641-6172) has displays on the development, past and present, of this uniquely fascinating city. To the left of City Hall is the Price Building, an art deco skyscraper that fits into the urban scene remarkably well. Nearby is the monument to Cardinal Taschereau, the first Canadian cardinal.

Follow Rue Donnaconna to the Ursuline Monastery, and from there, walk back to your

Street cafés abound in Old Québec.

starting point, passing what may well be the city's oldest house, the **Maison Jacquet** ❸ (34 Rue Saint-Louis), now a classy restaurant.

Descend the cliff separating the Upper and Lower Towns by flights of steps down Côte de la Montagne. At the foot of the precipitous second flight of steps (Casse-Cou or "Breakneck") is the charming **Rue du Petit-Champlain** ❹, lined with craft shops and cafés. At the end of Petit-Champlain, make a 180-degree turn and follow Boulevard Champlain, turning left past the imposing **Maison Chevalier** and its exhibits from the **Musée de la Civilisation** (see pp. 136–37). To the right, Rue Sous-le-Fort leads to the Batterie Royale, with its cannon trained on former foes approaching from the river. Walk along Rue Saint-Pierre, turn left, and end the walk in **Place Royale** ❺. ■

- ▲ See area map p. 137
- ► Place d'Armes
- ↔ 3 miles
- ⏱ 2 hours
- ► Place Royale

NOT TO BE MISSED
- Basilique de Notre-Dame
- Urban Life Centre
- Maison Chevalier

The recognizable Château Frontenac rises above the rooftops of Old Québec.

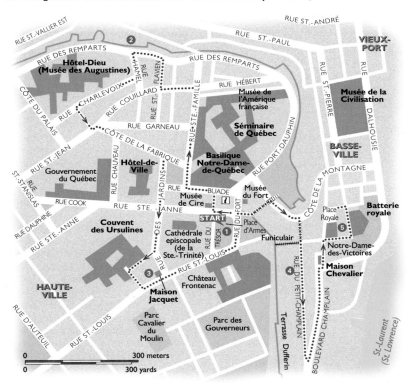

RUE ST.-ANDRÉ

RUE ST.-VALLIER EST

RUE ST.-PAUL

VIEUX-PORT

RUE DES REMPARTS

Hôtel-Dieu
(Musée des Augustines)

RUE DES REMPARTS

RUE HÉBERT

Musée de la
Civilisation

RUE FLAVIEN

RUE HAMEL

RUE CHARLEVOIX

RUE COUILLARD

RUE ST.-FLAVIEN

RUE ST.-PIERRE

RUE DALHOUSIE

CÔTE DU PALAIS

RUE

Musée de
l'Amérique
française

RUE GARNEAU

RUE STE.-FAMILLE

Séminaire
de Québec

CÔTE DE LA FABRIQUE

BASSE-
VILLE

CÔTE DE LA MONTAGNE

RUE PORT-DAUPHIN

RUE ST.-JEAN

RUE CHAUVEAU

Hôtel-de-
Ville

Basilique
Notre-Dame-
de-Québec

Gouvernement
du Québec

RUE ST.-STANISLAS

RUE COOK

RUE

BUADE

Musée
de Cire

ℹ

Musée
du Fort

RUE STE.-ANNE

RUE DES JARDINS

RUE

Place
d'Armes

Place
Royale

Batterie
royale

RUE DAUPHINE

RUE STE.-ANNE

START

RUE DU FORT

⑤

RUE DU TRÉSOR

Couvent
des Ursulines

Cathédrale
episcopale
(de la
Ste.-Trinité)

Funiculair

Notre-Dame-
des-Victoires

③

RUE ST.-LOUIS

Maison
Chevalier

HAUTE-
VILLE

Maison
Jacquet

Château
Frontenac

④

RUE DU PETIT-CHAMPLAIN

RUE D'AUTEUIL

RUE ST.-LOUIS

Parc
Cavalier
du
Moulin

Parc des
Gouverneurs

Terrasse Dufferin

BOULEVARD CHAMPLAIN

St.-Laurent
(St. Lawrence)

0   300 meters
0   300 yards

Québec's fortified defenses

Artillery Park
www.pc.gc.ca
✉ 2 Rue d'Auteuil
☎ 418/648-4205
🕐 Closed Nov.—April
💲 $

Fortifications Interpretation Centre
www.pc.gc.ca
✉ 100 Rue St.-Louis
☎ 418/648-7016
🕐 Closed Nov.—March
💲 $

Citadel
www.lacitadelle.qc.ca
✉ Access from Rue St.-Louis via Côte de la Citadelle
☎ 418/694-2815
🕐 Closed Nov.—April except by appt.
💲 $$

National Battle-fields Park Inter-pretation Centre
www.ccbn-nbc.gc.ca
✉ Musée du Québec (see p. 141)
☎ 418/648-5641
🕐 Closed Mon., late Sept.—mid-May
💲 $

Military pride on display at Québec's Citadel

NEVER REALLY FREE FROM THE THREAT OF ATTACK BY THE Iroquois or the British, the capital of New France was constantly improving and adding to its defenses. Walls were built and strengthened, but the plan to construct a great citadel on the highest point of Cap Diamant failed to attract funds from a parsimonious Paris, and it was left to the British to build the great star-shaped stronghold that overlooks both the city and the St. Lawrence today.

It is a real thrill to walk around the fortifications of what is the only walled city in North America, one of the chief reasons for its designation by UNESCO as a world heritage site. There are interpretive panels along the nearly 3-mile circuit, while guided walking tours set off from the **Frontenac kiosk** *(Tel 418/648-7016)* on Dufferin Terrace. Each stretch of the circuit has its own interest, but be sure not to miss the giddy boardwalk called **Promenade des Gouverneurs** suspended from the cliff face below the Citadel.

Fascinating stops en route include **Artillery Park,** a complex of military installations that evolved over three centuries and is now a national historic site. There is a 500-foot-long, 18th-century barracks, a massive redoubt of the same period, and an old foundry housing a magnificent model of the city as it appeared at the beginning of the 19th century. Between here and the Citadel, the formidable walls are pierced by a number of gateways. Close to the St. Louis Gate, the **Fortifications Interpretation Centre** has displays on the development of the city's defenses.

THE CITADEL

After the conquest, the British inherited the much battered French defenses but only began work on a temporary stronghold following the American attack in 1775–76. The present 40-acre **Citadel** was only completed in 1831. Its design follows the classical star-shape baroque pattern perfected in Europe, with projecting bastions commanding a field of fire over walls, ditches, and the exposed earthworks beyond.

The Citadel is the home of the Van Doos *(Vingt-deux),* the Royal 22nd Regiment, the prestigious French-speaking regiment of Canadian Forces. In summer, the Changing of the Guard *(June–Aug. 10 a.m.)* and the Beating of the Retreat *(Fri.–Sun. July–Aug. 7 p.m.)* draw crowds.

The 250 acres of rolling parkland on the Plains of Abraham have been preserved as the **Parc des Champs-de-Bataille**—the site of the 15-minute battle that led to the end of the French regime in North America. It was here, in the early morning drizzle of September 13, 1759, that British General Wolfe's troops stood in line ready to resist the defending French under General Montcalm. Wolfe's men had made their way up from the St. Lawrence with great stealth, easily overcoming the sleeping Canadiens supposed to be on guard at the top of the cliff. Taken by surprise, Montcalm's mixed force of regulars and militiamen advanced in disorder and were cut to pieces by the redcoats' sustained fire. Wolfe perished on the field of battle; Montcalm died from his wounds the following day. The

events of this most decisive day in Canadian history are recounted in the **National Battlefields Park Interpretation Centre,** housed in the **Musée du Québec** on the town edge of the park.

The comprehensive collections of Québec art in the Musée du Québec were revitalized in 1991 when its original neoclassic building was dramatically linked to the former prison by a new Great Hall, a crystalline structure that allows the landscape of the battlefields park to flow over and around it.

The expanded museum now displays many more of its 22,000 works than before. There are sculptures, drawings, prints, photographs, and many items of decorative art, but it is the splendid painting collection that most captures the attention. It is a lesson in how artists have seen the Québec landscape (look specially for pictures by Arthur Lismer and Clarence Gagnon) and the province's past (king-size history pictures by Henri Beau and Marc-Aurèle Suzor-Côté). ■

The ramparts of Québec's Citadel still loom over the city and the Plains of Abraham (top of picture).

Musée du Québec
www.mnba.qc.ca
✉ Battlefields Park
☎ 418/643-2150
🕐 Closed Mon.
   late Sept.–May
💲 $$

Île d'Orléans & the Beaupré shore

This day drive takes you downstream from Québec City to the tranquil Île d'Orléans (Orleans Island) and then along the Beaupré shore to one of North America's great centers of pilgrimage, the shrine of Sainte-Anne.

Jacques Cartier is supposed to have cried *"Quel beau pré!"* (What lovely meadows!) on sighting the lush grasslands along the shore of the St. Lawrence, downstream from where Québec stands today.

Leave Québec City heading north via Hwy. 440 and, after about 6 miles, cross the bridge over the northern arm of the St. Lawrence. At the junction, turn right toward **Sainte-Pétronille ❶**. It was here that farmers laid out the island's first settlement, and it was here that General Wolfe pondered his assault on the city which so splendidly fills the view upstream.

Continue your tour around the island in a counterclockwise direction. In the 19th century, **Saint-Laurent ❷** was a famous boatbuilding center, with 20 yards turning out *chaloupes* (longboats) in great numbers. The yard once known as the Chalouperie Godbout is now a museum, the **Parc Maritime de Saint-Laurent** *(Tel 418/828-9672)*. The next parish, Saint-Jean, has one of the finest examples of an

early manor house, the imposing **Manoir Mauvide-Genest** *(Tel 418/829-2630),* now an interesting museum. Climb up the viewing tower in the parish of **Saint-François ❸** at the downstream tip of the island and savor the superb views in all directions.

Sainte-Famille ❹ boasts the largest collection of French regime buildings, including the **Maison Drouin**, and, above all, the twin-towered **Sainte-Famille** parish church, consecrated in 1749. The north side of the island gives splendid views of the Beaupré shore. Just before the bridge, Saint-Pierre boasts the island's oldest church (St.-Pierre church), now a museum *(Tel 418/828-9824)*.

Cross the bridge back to the mainland, and turn right along Hwy. 138. After about 18 miles turn into the parking lot for the great pilgrimage church of **Basilique Sainte-Anne-de-Beaupré ❺** *(Ave. Royale, tel 418/827-3781)*. This great basilica is dedicated to the patron saint of Québec and attracts pilgrims from all over North America. Its

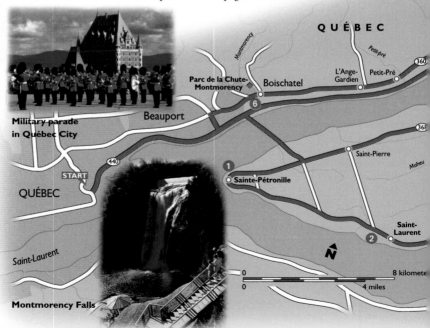

Military parade in Québec City

Montmorency Falls

QUÉBEC

Parc de la Chute-Montmorency

Boischatel

L'Ange-Gardien   Petit-Pré   360

Beauport   ❻

368

Saint-Pierre   Maheu

START   440

QUÉBEC

❶

Sainte-Pétronille

Saint-Laurent   ❷

Saint-Laurent

N

0   8 kilometers
0   4 miles

legendary origins go back to the mid-17th century, when storm-tossed sailors were delivered from disaster by praying to Saint Anne, mother of the Virgin Mary. Other miracles and healings followed, and successively greater shrines were built on the site. The present, magnificent building was completed in 1934 and rivals the great cathedrals of Europe in splendid proportions and opulent decor.

Unless you are in a hurry, go back in the direction of Québec City along Rte. 360, the **Avenue Royale**, laid out in the late 17th century by Bishop Laval as one of the first roads in Québec and originally known as le Chemin du Roy (the King's Road). Close to the bridge to the Île d'Orléans lies the parking area for **Parc de la Chute-Montmorency** ⑥ *(Tel 418/663-3330)*—where you will find one of the area's great natural attractions, the **Montmorency Falls.** These spectacular 272-foot waterfalls have long been a popular tourist site and have featured in many a painting. At the top of the falls, the elegant **Manoir Montmorency** *(Tel 418/663-3330)* houses a visitor center with displays on the falls and their history. ■

🅼 See area map pp. 104–105
▶ Québec City
↔ 75 miles
🕐 Allow 1 day
▶ Québec City

NOT TO BE MISSED
- Parc Maritime de Saint-Laurent
- Basilique Sainte-Anne-de-Beaupré
- Montmorency Falls

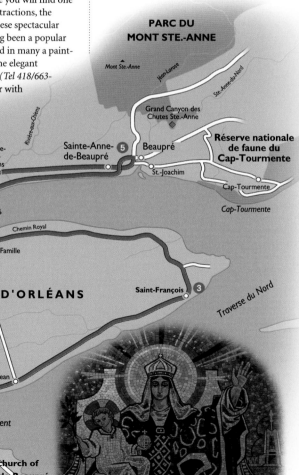

PARC DU MONT STE.-ANNE

Mont Ste.-Anne

Jean-Larose

Ste.-Anne-du-Nord

Grand Canyon des Chutes Ste.-Anne

Rivière-aux-Chiens

Rivière-aux-Chiens

Sainte-Anne-de-Beaupré ⑤   Beaupré

Réserve nationale de faune du Cap-Tourmente

Sault-à-la-puce

Sault-à-la-Puce   AVENUE ROYAL

St.-Joachim

Cap-Tourmente

Château-richer   138

Cap-Tourmente

Chenal de l'Île d'Orléans

Chemin Royal

Saint-Famille

④

ÎLE   D'ORLÉANS

Saint-François   ③

Traverse du Nord

Rivière-Lafleur   Saint-Jean   368

Saint-Laurent

Art in the church of Ste.-Anne-de-Beaupré.

Charlevoix

A harmonious landscape of forests, farms, and country cottages at Saint-Siméon, near the northern end of the Charlevoix Coast

Baie-Saint-Paul
🅰 105 C2

Visitor information
www.tourisme-charlevoix
.com
✉ 444 Blvd. Mgr.-de-Laval (Hwy. 138), Baie-St-Paul
☎ 418/435-4160

THE EVER BROADENING SWEEP OF THE ST. LAWRENCE bordered by the plunging slopes of the Canadian Shield, deep forests, old villages set in farmland—all this has given the Charlevoix coastline an irresistible appeal. Such landscapes, combined with a timeless way of life, inspired artists like Clarence Gagnon a century ago. The region continues to work its charm, not only on artists but on vacationers, who have been coming here even longer in search of fresh air, abundant game, pristine scenery, and a warm welcome.

Part of the seemingly unchanging charm of Charlevoix can be traced to an event that occurred around 350 million years ago. Traveling at a speed of 6 miles a second, a meteorite some 7,000 feet across hit the Earth with unimaginable force. In less than a minute, its 3-mile-deep crater was formed, creating the land forms that exist to this day. The **Charlevoix crater** is one of the biggest in the world; some 35 miles in diameter, it consists of a central upland surrounded by a deep trench and an outer escarpment. Half of this formation has disappeared into the St. Lawrence; the rest forms an exceptionally varied habitat in which all the ecosystems of Québec are present, from maple forest to tundra. This great diversity in a relatively small space led in 1988 to the designation of the Charlevoix area as a UNESCO world biosphere reserve.

BAIE-SAINT-PAUL

Before descending the steep hill into this artists' village, pause at the **Centre d'histoire naturelle de Charlevoix** *(444 Blvd. Mgr.-de-Laval, tel 418/435-6275)*. From the balcony there is a fine view of coast and uplands. Inside, displays recount the unique geology and natural history of the area, including the dramatic impact of the meteorite and its consequences.

Take time to stroll the streets of Baie-Saint-Paul. Plenty of delightful dwellings date from the 19th century, and it is easy to appreciate the appeal the village has always exercised on artists. A modern note is struck by the award-winning **Centre d'Exposition de Baie-Saint-Paul** *(23 Rue Ambroise-Fafard, tel 418/435-3681, closed Mon., $)*, opened in 1992 as a setting for changing art shows. A number of other establishments draw on Baie-Saint-Paul's artistic heritage.

Traditional ways of life lasted longer on seven-mile-long **Île-aux-Coudres** (Hazel Island) than on the Baie-Saint-Paul mainland, and were memorably filmed by documentarians in the 1960s. The island was famous for building the schooners that, for many settlements along the St. Lawrence, were the only means of communication with the outside world. Clamber aboard a *voiture d'eau* (water-wagon) at the museum devoted to these everyday runabouts, the **Musée les Voitures d'Eau.** Otherwise people come here for peace and quiet. To best savor the island, pedal slowly around it by bike.

Between Baie-Saint-Paul and the resort of **La Malbaie-Pointe-au-Pic,** the scenic Rte. 362 follows a switchback course along the spectacular coastline, passing through delightful villages such as **Les Éboulements** and **Saint-Irénée. Saint-Joseph,** where the ferry leaves for the Île-aux-Coudres, once earned its living from boatbuilding, and you can see abandoned schooners lying around. This resort's glory days came in the early 20th century, when wealthy vacationers arrived by elegant steamship and either stayed in the château-style grand hotel called the **Manoir Richelieu** or, like U.S. President William Howard Taft, in the fine vacation homes they built themselves on the upper slopes. The little **Musée de Charlevoix,** set in a striking modern building, puts on temporary exhibitions.

One of the most spectacular sights in eastern Canada is the gorge of the Malbaie River. Now forming Québec's most extensive regional park, the **Parc régional des Hautes-Gorges-de-la-Rivière-Malbaie,** and reached by a 20-mile unpaved road, the gorge is an ideal place to appreciate the variety of vegetation in the Charlevoix area. Great elms grow in the sheltered valley, while above the 2,000-plus-foot sides of the gorge are plants of the arctic-alpine zone. ∎

Musée les Voitures d'Eau

- ✉ 1922 Chemin des Coudriers
- ☎ 418/438-2208
- ⏱ Closed mid-Oct.—mid-May
- 💲 $

Musée de Charlevoix

- ✉ 10 Chemin du Havre, La Malbaie
- ☎ 418/665-4411
- ⏱ Closed Mon. Sept.—June
- 💲 $

Parc régional des Hautes-Gorges-de-la-Rivière-Malbaie

- ✉ Via Rte. 138 & Sainte-Aimée-des-Lacs on unpaved roads
- ☎ 418/439-1730
- ⏱ Closed mid-Oct.—mid-May
- 💲 $

The grand château-style Manoir Richelieu now houses a casino.

Saguenay Fjord & the Lac Saint-Jean region

Saguenay Fjord
📷 105 C2

Baie-Sainte-Catherine
📷 105 C2

Tadoussac
📷 105 C2

Centre d'interprétation des mammifères marins
✉ 108 Rue de la Cale-Sèche, Tadoussac
☎ 418/235-4657
🕐 Closed mid-Oct.–mid-May
💲 $$

Sainte-Rose-du-Nord
📷 105 C2

Chicoutimi
📷 105 C2

THE SAGUENAY RIVER FINDS ITS WAY INTO THE ST. Lawrence along a great crack in the Canadian Shield, a fault whose waters fill to a depth of 800 feet. Almost a mile wide in places, this 60-mile stretch of the river is bordered by superb forested cliffs rising to a height of 1,500 feet. The area around Lac Saint-Jean provides an altogether different experience—a restful oasis of fertile soil in the unforgiving Canadian Shield.

SAGUENAY FJORD

The occasional villages huddled in coves along the Saguenay Fjord can be reached by road, but the best way to experience this majestic waterway is to take one of the many boat cruises offered. A mini-cruise, a mere eight minutes long and costing nothing, crosses the mouth of the Saguenay 24 hours a day. It links the villages of **Baie-Sainte-Catherine** and **Tadoussac** and keeps traffic moving along Hwy. 138, the shoreline road.

This meeting point of two great rivers is one of the most popular whale-watching spots in all of Canada. Five species of whale—fin, minke, beluga, humpback, and blue—frequent the area, drawn by the rich crop of krill and caplin that develops as a result of the mixing of icy cold salt water from the St. Lawrence with the fresh water of the Saguenay (see p. 147).

If you can't take one of the highly recommended whale-watching trips *(details available from Maison du Tourisme, Tadoussac, tel 418/235-4744),* you may well see some of these wonderful mammals from a number of lookouts; try the **Pointe-Noire Interpretation and Observation Centre** *(Tel 418/237-4383, closed winter months)* on its cliff-top site close to the southern terminal of the free ferry. The attractive little resort of Tadoussac has the excellent **Centre**

d'interprétation des mammifères marins, with displays explaining why the Saguenay-St. Lawrence has been established as a marine park. Its strategic position made Tadoussac a focal point of trade among natives, leading Pierre Chauvin to establish Canada's very first fur-trading post here in 1600. Reconstructed, the steep-roofed timber building houses a little museum on these earliest days of native/European contact.

THE UPPER REACHES OF SAGUENAY FJORD

Rte. 172 from Tadoussac runs mostly out of sight of the river, so make sure you turn down the side road to the village of **Sainte-Rose-du-Nord** *(53 miles W of Tadoussac).*

Rte. 170 leaves the coastal highway at Saint-Siméon *(25 miles S of the mouth of the Saguenay)* and parallels the southern bank. For some of the finest views of the fjord, go down side roads, first to the tiny settlement of **L'Anse-Saint-Jean,** then, at Rivière-Éternité, to **Cap Trinité,** where a 26-foot-tall statue of the Virgin Mary graces a ledge in the 1,700-foot-high headland.

CHICOUTIMI

Capital of the Saguenay/Lake Saint-Jean region, Chicoutimi makes its living from industry, and it is industry, in the form of the fine

old granite buildings of a former **pulp mill,** that makes up the city's main visitor attraction. As well as housing displays of local interest and all kinds of cultural events, the mill tells the story of its past as the very first industrial enterprise founded by French-Canadians. Also here is the Arthur Villeneuve House, gloriously decorated with the naive murals of this barber-turned-painter.

LAC SAINT-JEAN

An isolated pocket of reasonably fertile clay soil in the Canadian Shield, the shore of this 520-square-mile lake was settled from the mid-19th century by French-Canadian farmers unable to find land in the overcrowded valley of the St. Lawrence. It is a popular summer vacation spot for visitors from the rest of Québec, with attractions that include the **Zoo sauvage de Saint-Félicien,** where native Canadian animals such as bears, wolves, and moose range freely while visitors admire them from a sort of mobile cage. This is particularly impressive in the winter months. ∎

Saguenay Fjord can best be seen from the deck of a cruise boat.

Chicoutimi Pulp Mill (La Pulperie)
www.pulperie.com
✉ 300 Rue Dubuc
☎ 418/698-3100
⊕ Open year-round, but no activities Nov.–March
$ $

Maison Arthur Villeneuve
✉ Part of La Pulperie
☎ 418/698-3100

Zoo sauvage de Saint-Félicien
www.borealie.org
✉ 2230 Blvd. du Jardin, Saint-Félicien
☎ 418/679-0543
⊕ Reduced schedule Oct.–May
$ $$$

Whales of the St. Lawrence

More than 30 species of whale live in or migrate through Canadian waters. Whale-watching, or whale-contact, has become popular ever since the 1972 moratorium on hunting. The little beluga or white whale (up to 16 feet long) has become one of the most cherished inhabitants of the St. Lawrence, though its numbers are down to about 500, from a former high of several thousand.

Other species encountered in the river include the minke whale (up to 35 feet long), the humpback (up to 50 feet), the fin whale (up to 65 feet), and occasionally the blue whale, the largest creature in the world, which can reach a length of 100 feet and weigh up to 150 tons. ∎

Côte Nord

Côte Nord

105 D2, D3, E3

Manic 2 & 5

Inquiries to Hydro-
Québec, Rte. 389,
Baie-Comeau

866/526-2642

UNTIL A 400-MILE HIGHWAY WAS BUILT AS FAR AS Havre-Saint-Pierre in the 1960s, any trip along the Côte Nord (North Shore) of the St. Lawrence beyond Tadoussac had to be undertaken by boat. The road now stretches to Natashquan, but if you wish to venture farther along the wild shoreline, you will have to board the weekly boat that takes two days to reach Blanc Sablon on the border with Labrador. Here, a stretch of highway crosses the border, giving access to some of the remarkable sights along the Labrador coast. There is also a ferry connection with St. Barbe in Newfoundland.

The strange shapes of the Mingan Archipelago monoliths result from the weathering of limestone formed 500 million years ago.

FIRST SETTLERS

Now settled in a series of reserves scattered along the coast, the Montagnais have lived along the North Shore for more than 8,000 years and were among the first natives to have contact with Europeans. The Basque fishermen who set up their processing plants on the Labrador coast in the 1400s were active along this shore as well.

They were followed by a handful of French and English fishermen and traders, but it was only in the 20th century that large-scale developments took place, based first on pulp mills, then on the discovery of iron-ore inland and the harnessing of water resources for hydroelectric power.

The town of **Baie-Comeau** *(125 miles east of Tadoussac via Rte. 138)* was largely the creation of Colonel Robert McCormick, publisher of the *Chicago Tribune*, and the place is still dominated by a huge pulp mill.

On an even greater scale are the hydroelectric installations inland from the town, reached by virtually the only road to penetrate the wilderness that stretches out endlessly to the north of the St. Lawrence. Known collectively as the **Manic-Outardes Complex,** they consist of several dams and power stations along the Manicouagan and Outardes Rivers. **Manic 2,** 14 miles north of Baie-Comeau, can be visited. But the most spectacular feature of this gigantic undertaking is **Daniel Johnson Dam** of the Manic 5 generating complex, which is well worth the trip up the long and winding road. With a height of 702 feet and a length of 4,307 feet, the largest of its kind in the world, it bears the name of the prime minister of Québec who unfortunately died here on the day it was to open in 1968. A breezy walk along the top of this titanic construction reveals something of the 770-square-mile reservoir, which, far upstream, has created a ring of water 40 miles across, outlining what is probably a gigantic meteorite crater.

The town of **Sept-Îles** *(142 miles east of Baie-Comeau)* has a fine deepwater port sheltered by the seven islands that give it its name. The railhead for the iron-ore line that reaches far inland to Shefferville and Labrador City, Sept-Îles has a couple of museums that between them show how a seemingly inhospitable land has been lived in, first by the native Montagnais **(Vieux-Poste),** then by Europeans **(Musée régional de la Côte-Nord).**

Havre-Saint-Pierre *(132 miles east of Sept-Îles via Rte. 138)* is not only the port for the weekly ferry service to Blanc Sablon *(mid-April–mid-Jan.),* but also the point of departure for trips to the fascinating Mingan Archipelago and Anticosti Island (see p. 150). The highway continues another 100 miles to Natashquan.

MINGAN ARCHIPELAGO

Strung out along the Côte-Nord between Longue-Pointe and Baie-Johan-Beetz, these 40 islands have formed a national park reserve since 1984. Their ecology is unique: The combination of the cold waters of the Labrador Current, harsh winters, and limestone soil means that an arctic-alpine flora flourishes here well to the south of its normal boundary. Some species, such as the Mingan thistle, are very rare, if not unique. Seabirds abound, notably the Atlantic puffin, and seals can be seen. But the most extraordinary natural features are the monoliths that have been weirdly sculpted in the limestone. Given fanciful names by local people, their fascinating shapes have been formed over millennia by the abrasive forces of wind and water. The Mingan Archipelago can be reached by boat from Longue-Pointe and Havre-Saint-Pierre, where Parks Canada operates two visitor centers. ■

The Canadian Shield has huge potential for hydropower.

Daniel Johnson Dam
- ✉ 133 miles N of Baie-Comeau via Rte. 389
- ☎ 866/526-2642

Vieux-Poste
- ✉ Blvd. des Montagnais
- ☎ 418/968-2070
- 🕐 Closed off-season
- 💲 $

Musée Régional de la Côte-Nord
- ✉ 500 Blvd. Laure
- ☎ 418/968-2070
- 🕐 Closed Mon. Sept.–June
- 💲 $

Mingan Archipelago NP
www.pc.gc.ca
Longue-Pointe
- ✉ 625 Rue du Centre
- ☎ 418/949-2126

Havre-Saint-Pierre
- ✉ 975 Rue de l'Escale
- ☎ 418/538-3285 or 800/463-6769

Île d'Anticosti

Île d'Anticosti

🗺 105 E2

Port-Menier

🗺 105 E2

Visitor information

✉ Île d'Anticosti Tourist Office, 36 Chemin des Forestiers, Port-Menier

☎ 418/535-0250

🕐 Closed winter months

The lighthouse at Cap-du-Rabast is one of many erected in response to Anticosti Island's reputation as the Graveyard of the Gulf.

LARGER THAN PRINCE EDWARD ISLAND, THE ISLAND OF Anticosti has a population of only a few hundred people. Extending for nearly 140 miles between the Straits of Jacques-Cartier and Honguedo in the Gulf of St. Lawrence, it has been known as the Graveyard of the Gulf because of the hundreds of vessels wrecked on its reefs. The fossil-rich limestone foundation of the island has been shaped into cliffs, canyons, and caverns. Coniferous forest covers much of the surface, while the eastern part of the island is marshy.

After many changes of ownership (for a while it was part of Newfoundland) and mostly fruitless efforts to develop Anticosti's economy, the island now belongs to the province of Québec. The proprietor who had the most dramatic impact was the French chocolate tycoon, Henri Menier, who acquired it in 1895 and set about converting it into an immense private game park. The 220 white-tailed deer he introduced have multiplied to a herd of more than 100,000 animals, but Menier's fabulous hunting lodge at

Port-Menier, the island's only village, was burned down in 1953. The foundations are a poignant reminder of his grandiose ambitions to make Anticosti a kind of feudal domain. Menier first rebuilt the village at Baie-Sainte-Claire (originally English Bay, but renamed in honor of his mother) close to the western tip of the island, but then moved to Port-Menier. Baie-Sainte-Claire now lies in ruins, but the **Pointe de l'Ouest lighthouse** is still here, as well as a cemetery.

In the graveyard of the ocean, the remains of the *Calou,* wrecked in 1982, are visible. With its deep-water harbor and shopping and other facilities, Port-Menier is the only settlement on the island, with a ferry link *(Tel 418/723-8787)* to Havre-Saint-Pierre, Sept-Îles, and Rimouski.

People come here mainly to hunt the deer and fish in the island's many rivers, but if you're looking for a unique experience, and are well equipped, rent a four-wheel-drive and head off down the only road leading east from Port-Menier. As well as lonely beaches, dramatic cliffs, and the occasional shipwreck, you will find the phenomena characteristic of limestone country, including the **La Patate** cave system, only discovered in 1981, and the **Vauréal Canyon,** with its sheer limestone walls and 230-foot falls. ∎

Îles de la Madeleine

IN THE MIDDLE OF THE GULF OF ST. LAWRENCE, CLOSER TO
Prince Edward Island than to any part of Québec, this intriguing
archipelago consists of a crescent of islands, some linked by
immensely long sandbars enclosing lagoons.

Everything contrives to make this a special place: Trees cut by the wind into contorted shapes; red sandstone cliffs carved into arches, caves, and columns; emerald green grass contrasting with a brilliant blue sea and with the bright paintwork of the fishermen's houses.

Although some of the islands' population are English speakers, most are descendants of the Acadians who fled here from Nova Scotia or Saint-Pierre and Miquelon, preferring to live under the British Crown than submit to the rule of republican France.

Each of the islands has its own delights. **Cap-aux-Meules** *(Visitor information, tel 418/986-2245)* is the most populated island. As well as having a fascinating fishing port, it is the terminal for the ferry *(Tel 888/986-3278)* from Souris on Prince Edward Island and the weekly freighter *(Tel 888/986-3278)* from Montréal. The best all-round view in the islands is from the summit of nearby **Butte-de-Vent** hill, and some of the most spectacular cliff formations are at **Cap au Trou** and **L'Étang-du-Nord** on the west coast. **Notre-Dame-du-Rosaire,** the church at the settlement of Fatima, is one of the most extraordinary modern buildings in Québec. Every feature, from its shell-like outline to its interior decoration, speaks of the islanders' relationship with the sea. **Havre-Aubert** island, to the south, has gentler scenery, an aquarium, a maritime museum, and **La Grave,** a medley of old fishing installations. **Île d'Entrée** (Entry Island) has grassy hills culminating in **Big Hill** (571 feet), with splendid views of the archipelago. The island has an Anglican church serving its 200 or so inhabitants, most of whom are descended from Scottish settlers.

To the north, **Havre-aux-Maisons** island has perhaps the most harmonious landscapes of the archipelago, with old farm structures and characteristic houses as well as rugged rock formations. Reached via the long and narrow Dune du Nord, the **eastern islands** have sand dunes, superb beaches, and some of the best walking trails. The vast sandy beach of **Grande Échouerie** is the finest on the islands. ∎

Îles de la Madeleine

🅜 105 E2, 55 D4–5

Visitor information
www.tourismeilesdela
madeleine.com

✉ Tourist Office, 128 Chemin Principal, Cap-aux-Meules

☎ 418/986-2245 or 877/624-4437

Above: White-tailed deer on Anticosti Island

Gaspésie

Gaspésie

△ 105 D2, E2

**Grosse-Île
& the Irish
Memorial National
Historic Site**

✉ 3 Rue de Buade,
Québec

☎ 418/248-8888 or
800/463-6769

🕐 Closed mid-
Oct.–mid-May

💲 $$$

Musée de la Mer

✉ 1034 Rue du Phare,
6 miles E of
Rimouski

☎ 418/724-6214

🕐 Closed mid-
Oct.–May

GASPÉSIE (THE GASPÉ PENINSULA) CONSISTS OF A forested mountain backbone sweeping down to a rugged, sparsely inhabited coastline of cliffs and coves and the occasional fishing village. Its remoteness, natural grandeur, and the traditional ways of its inhabitants have long attracted visitors. Built in the 1920s, in a vain attempt to bring settlers to the area, the contour-hugging road along the north shore is one of the most splendidly scenic routes in Canada, especially as it nears the tip of the peninsula.

Gaspésie is approached from Québec City by Hwy. 20 to just beyond the town of Rivière-du-Loup, and then by Hwy. 132 along the shore. At **Berthier-sur-Mer,** about 30 miles from Québec, boats take visitors to the old immigrant quarantine station on **Grosse-Île,** Canada's equivalent of Ellis Island, preserved as the **Grosse-Île and the Irish Memorial National**

Historic Site. It is a poignant spot, evoking the hopes and tribulations of more than four million immigrants, many of them Irish. **Rivière-du-Loup** and **Trois-Pistoles,** 30 miles farther on, both have ferry services to the north shore of the St. Lawrence. Just beyond the industrial town of Rimouski, in the village of Pointe-au-Père, the **Musée de la Mer**

commemorates the 1914 sinking of the *Empress of Ireland*. When the fog-bound liner was rammed by a freighter in the St. Lawrence, 1,014 lives were lost. The disaster was comparable to that of the loss of the *Titanic* only two years earlier.

Six miles east of the resort of Sainte-Flavie on Rte. 132 are the **Jardins de Métis** *(Tel 418/775-2222, closed Nov.–May)*. The variety and luxuriance of these superb gardens owe much to the humid microclimate of the site at the mouth of the Métis River, but much more to the enthusiasm and horticultural genius of Elsie Reford. Already well into middle age, she inherited what had been a fishing lodge from her uncle, George Stephen, the first president of the Canadian Pacific Railway. From 1929 to 1954 she transformed it

into the gardeners' paradise that welcomes visitors today.

For a chance to see something of the bleak interior of the Gaspé Peninsula, make the short detour into the provincial park known as the **Parc de la Gaspésie.** This is the dramatic border where forest gives way to tundra on one of the highest points in eastern Canada, Mont Jacques-Cartier (4,159 feet). Uniquely, deer, moose, and caribou flourish here in close proximity.

THE OUTER PENINSULA

Designated a national park in 1970, the 93-square-mile **Parc National de Forillon** *(Tel 418/368-5505)* protects the rocky peninsula where the mountainous spine of the Gaspé finally meets the Gulf of St. Lawrence in sheer limestone cliffs. Seabirds are abundant, and a variety of land animals, including lynx and black bear, inhabit the densely forested interior of the park. The interpretation center near **Cap-des-Rosiers** has displays on the ecology and human history of the area.

To experience something of the traditional life of the area, try to stop by the old fishing community of **Grande-Grave National Historic Site,** founded by immigrants from the Channel Islands and now restored by Parks Canada. Reached by a spectacular footpath, one of Canada's tallest lighthouses perches on the clifftop at the very tip of the peninsula.

The deepwater port of **Gaspé** is worth a stop for its strikingly modern **Cathedral of Christ the King**, its excellent local museum, and for its historical associations, since it was here that Jacques Cartier landed in 1534 to claim the land for France by erecting a huge wooden cross in the name of his king, François I. An

Parc de la Gaspésie
www.sepaq.com
⊠ Visitor center 24 miles south of Sainte-Anne-des-Monts on Rte. 299
🕐 Park open daily, visitor center closed mid-Oct.–May
☎ 418/763-3181

Parc National de Forillon
www.pc.gc.ca
🅰 105 E2
⊠ Visitor center, 122 Blvd. de Gaspé
☎ 418/368-5505

Cap-des-Rosiers
🅰 105 E2

Gaspé
🅰 105 E2

Percé Rock was given its name in 1607 by Samuel de Champlain because of its pierced (*percé*) profile, though one of its original arches has since collapsed. The stack at the seaward end of the great rock is called the Obelisk.

Centre de l'Heritage Britannique de la Gaspésie

Musée de la Gaspésie

- ✉ 80 Blvd. Gaspé
- ☎ 418/368-1534
- 🕐 Closed Mon. mid-Oct.–late June
- 💲 $

Percé

- 🗺 105 E2

Musée acadien du Québec

- ✉ 95 Ave. Port-Royal, Bonaventure
- ☎ 418/534-4000
- 🕐 Ltd. hours in winter
- 💲 $

Centre de l'Héritage Britannique de la Gaspésie

- 🗺 105 D2
- ✉ 351 Blvd. Perron Ouest, New Richmond
- ☎ 418/392-4487
- 🕐 Closed late Sept.–mid-June
- 💲 $$

equally massive cross, this time in granite, was installed near the cathedral 400 years later. A contemporary monument stands outside the **Musée de la Gaspésie.** The museum displays explain all about Jacques Cartier and his voyages.

Percé

The long haul up the coast road is a reasonable price to pay for a sight of the great **Percé Rock** stretching its 1,500-foot-length just offshore. A compelling presence, altering its appearance as the light changes, the rock exercises a potent fascination on all who see it. It can be reached on foot at low tide, perhaps the best way to appreciate the grandeur of its cliffs, nearly 300 feet high in places. For a broader perspective of this geomorphological marvel, climb to the top of **Mont-Sainte-Anne,** the 1,050-foot mountain that rises behind the town. Another way to experience the rock is from a boat (*Details from the Percé Tourist Office, tel 418/782-5448*) that takes visitors around **Bonaventure Island** and its colony of tens of thousands of gannets, the largest in America.

Baie des Chaleurs

With a less severe climate and gentler landforms than the north shore of the peninsula, Baie des Chaleurs faces the coast of New Brunswick. It was named by Jacques Cartier for its (relatively) warm waters. While the population of the north shore is now almost entirely French-speaking, this coastline has many traces of its settlement by Scots, Irish, Channel Islanders, and Loyalists, as well as Acadians. Visit the **Musée acadien du Québec** and the **Centre de l'Héritage Britannique de la Gaspésie,** with its restored traditional buildings.

Attractively located at the foot of the coastal hills is the resort of **Carleton,** which enjoys both Acadian and Loyalist heritage. Rising 1,830 feet above the town, **Mont-Saint-Joseph** can be reached by road or on foot and has the best all-around view of the bay. The little **Miguasha Peninsula** is internationally famous for its fossils from the Upper Devonian period some 370 million years ago, many of which were removed by collectors before the area was protected as the provincial park, **Parc de Miguasha** (*15 miles W of Carleton, tel 418/794-2475, closed mid-Oct.–May*). Spectacular fossil examples are displayed in a visitor center, and there are supervised tours of the site. At **Pointe-à-la-Croix** (*Rte. 132, tel 418/788-5676*) a strikingly modern building overlooks the mouth of the Restigouche River. Here in 1760, one year after the Battle of the Plains of Abraham, the French fleet sent belatedly to the succor of Québec was overcome by ships of the Royal Navy. Thus died the last hope of recovering New France from the British. Among the fascinating displays are recovered sections of the French vessel *Le Machault.* ■

Ontario took its name from the Iroquois word meaning "shining waters," and here you can enjoy the grandeur of lake and forest, as well as Canada's greatest metropolis and a crown of smaller cities and towns.

Ontario

Introduction & map 156–57
Upper Canada 158–59
Ottawa 160–67
Kingston & the St. Lawrence 168–69
Toronto 170–83
Toronto walk: Union Station to City Hall 176–77
The Great Lakes 178–79
Outer Toronto excursions 184–85
Niagara Falls 188–93
Huron-Erie Peninsula 196–99
Southern Ontario's weekend paradise 200–203
North by Northwest in Ontario 206–210
Hotels & restaurants in Ontario 358–64

The Skylon Tower near Niagara Falls

Ontario

ONTARIO COVERS AN AREA BIGGER THAN FRANCE and Spain combined. It stretches 1,000 miles from the barren coast of Hudson Bay in the north to the crowded cities of the south. Most of this vast province is part of the Canadian Shield, where two-billion-year-old rocks underlie a landscape of forest, muskeg, and countless lakes. Few people live here, although the rocks yield some of the most abundant mineral wealth on earth. The shield extends almost to the gates of Ottawa, once a rowdy logging town, now a true capital city with museums and other attractions to match.

To the south, a 500-mile strip of fertile land forms a peninsula bounded by three of the Great Lakes: Huron, Erie, and Lake Ontario itself. Clearance of the peninsula's dense forest and its conversion into farmland began only at the end of the 18th century, when Loyalists fled north from the newly formed United States. Known as Upper Canada until the mid-19th century, southern Ontario rapidly filled up with immigrants, mostly from the British Isles. Railroad and canal construction laid the foundation for the modern commerce and industry that has since made Ontario the powerhouse of the Canadian economy, producing more goods than the other provinces and territories combined.

With more than 12 million inhabitants, Ontario is the most populous of Canada's provinces. More than 80 percent of Ontarians are town dwellers, nearly four million of them living in Toronto alone. Until quite recently, most were of British stock, ties to the old country were assiduously cultivated, and Ontarian life had a decidedly British "tone," though the Germanic character of the Kitchener area was reflected in its original name of Berlin. The province has a substantial minority of French speakers. Some descended from farmers who settled in the Windsor area long before British rule; others moved up the Ottawa River in search of farmland; others still helped provide the labor force for such mining towns as Sudbury. A late 20th-century wave of multi-ethnic immigration has transformed the character of many Ontarian cities, especially Toronto, which has become one of the most multiethnic cities on the continent. With the decline of anglophone Montréal, Toronto has also become the focal point of English-speaking Canada, the capital of press and electronic media, with office towers housing national and international headquarters. By contrast, time seems to have stood still in some of the province's smaller places, notably Niagara-on-the-Lake, apparently untouched since its rebuilding early in the 19th century.

There's a certain intimacy with the United States at Niagara Falls, where little Goat Island separates the Horseshoe Falls in Canada from the American Falls. The falls are a spectacular attraction, but if your stay in Ontario is limited to a day trip here from Toronto, you will miss out

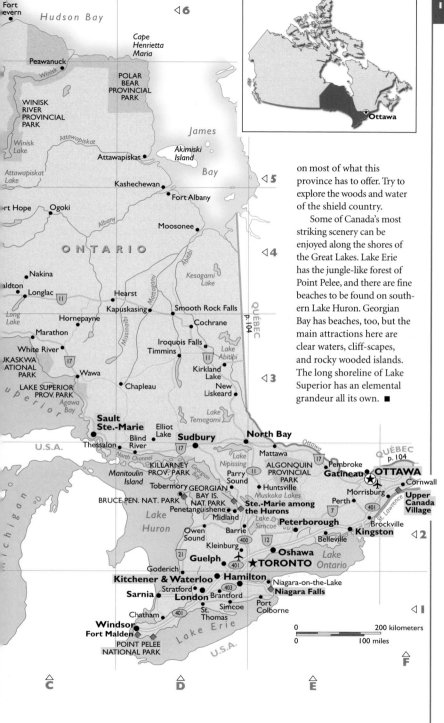

on most of what this province has to offer. Try to explore the woods and water of the shield country.

Some of Canada's most striking scenery can be enjoyed along the shores of the Great Lakes. Lake Erie has the jungle-like forest of Point Pelee, and there are fine beaches to be found on southern Lake Huron. Georgian Bay has beaches, too, but the main attractions here are clear waters, cliff-scapes, and rocky wooded islands. The long shoreline of Lake Superior has an elemental grandeur all its own. ∎

Hudson Bay

Fort Severn

Cape Henrietta Maria

Peawanuck

Winisk

POLAR BEAR PROVINCIAL PARK

WINISK RIVER PROVINCIAL PARK

Winisk Lake

Attawapiskat

Akimiski Island

James

Bay

Attawapiskat Lake

Attawapiskat

Kashechewan

Fort Albany

rt Hope

Ogoki

Albany

Moosonee

Nakina

Kesagami Lake

aldton

Longlac

11

Hearst

ONTARIO

Mattagami

Abitibi

Smooth Rock Falls

Kapuskasing

Long Lake

Hornepayne

Cochrane

Marathon

Missinaibi

Iroquois Falls

Timmins

Lake Abitibi

White River

Kirkland Lake

11

JKASKWA ATIONAL PARK

17

Wawa

Chapleau

New Liskeard

LAKE SUPERIOR PROV. PARK

Agawa Bay

Lake Temagami

uperior

Sault Ste.-Marie

Elliot Lake

U.S.A.

Thessalon

Blind River

Sudbury

North Bay

Ottawa

North Channel

17

Mattawa

17

QUÉBEC p. 104

Lake Nipissing

KILLARNEY PROV. PARK

Pembroke

Manitoulin Island

Parry Sound

11

ALGONQUIN PROVINCIAL PARK

Gatineau

OTTAWA

Cornwall

Tobermory

GEORGIAN BAY IS. NAT. PARK

Huntsville

Morrisburg

Upper Canada Village

BRUCE PEN. NAT. PARK

Penetanguishene

Muskoka Lakes

Perth

7

Midland

Ste.-Marie among the Hurons

Lake Huron

Owen Sound

Lake Simcoe

Peterborough

Brockville

Kingston

Barrie

400

12

Belleville

Kleinburg

Oshawa

Lake Ontario

Guelph

21

TORONTO

401

Goderich

Kitchener & Waterloo

Hamilton

Stratford

403

Niagara-on-the-Lake

Sarnia

London

Brantford

Niagara Falls

Chatham

401

St. Thomas

Simcoe

Port Colborne

Windsor

Lake Erie

Fort Malden

POINT PELEE NATIONAL PARK

U.S.A.

QUÉBEC p. 104

Michigan

0   200 kilometers
0   100 miles

6 ◁
5 ◁
4 ◁
QUÉBEC p. 104
3 ◁
2 ◁
1 ◁

C   D   E   F

Ottawa

Upper Canada

By the middle of the 19th century, a million and a half people lived in the land bounded by Lakes Huron, Erie, and Ontario. Farms and towns had replaced the forest that once covered the landscape. They were linked by roads that included what was reputedly the longest street in the world, Yonge Street, running between Toronto and Lake Simcoe.

A century earlier, southern Ontario had been almost devoid of human habitation. Once numbering perhaps 25,000, the Huron had disappeared in the middle of the 17th century, massacred or absorbed by the Iroquois League, who themselves then left the area. The Iroquois forced the retreat of the Jesuits from the mission now known as Sainte-Marie among the Hurons, established early in 1639 on the shores of Georgian Bay. Fur traders crisscrossed the area, but the only permanent population consisted of a few hundred French settlers, whose farmsteads were laid out along the Detroit River.

The transformation of an empty land began with the arrival of some 10,000 Loyalists fleeing the American Revolution and its aftermath. Among them were Iroquois, who had fought with the British under the leadership of the war-chief Joseph Brant. Many others of American origin came for the cheap land. By the time war broke out in 1812, the area had a population of some 80,000 people, more than three-quarters of them of American origin.

On his arrival in 1792, the first lieutenant governor, John Graves Simcoe (1752–1806) thought of establishing the capital of the newly created colony of Upper Canada at the appropriately named city of London. However, this was not to be. Upper Canada's first capital was Newark (Niagara-on-the-Lake), which turned out to be much too close to the United States for comfort, and the honor was given to York (Toronto).

During the War of 1812 between Great Britain and the United States, a majority of the new settlers remained loyal to the crown, and the warriors of Shawnee chief Tecumseh, whom the Americans had crushed at Tippecanoe a year earlier, rallied to the British cause. Upper Canada saw most of the fighting. Armies marched across the Niagara peninsula, and Canadian heroes were created, like Laura Secord, who warned of an impending American attack (see p. 192). The British were driven out of York, and the town partly burned down. Newark suffered even more complete destruc-

The Battle of the Thames River, 1813, where the British ally Tecumseh (top left) was killed.

The Ontario wilderness witnessed many of the key moments in the War of 1812.

tion when the occupying force withdrew.

The defeat of the Royal Navy at the Battle of Lake Erie in 1813 gave the Americans naval control of the lake. Determined to maintain their hold on Lake Ontario, the British feverishly built ships at their naval yard at Kingston, but the war was over before the massive 112-gun man-of-war *St. Lawrence* could see action.

After the war, the British restricted immigration from the south, encouraging new immigrants from the United Kingdom, and to a lesser extent from Germany. The policy was a success; in the 1840s up to 100,000 people a year crossed the Atlantic to Canada and while some moved on to the United States, many stayed. Only about a fifth were English. Most came from the western fringes of the British Isles—Highland and Lowland Scots as well as Catholic and Protestant Irish. The last were

particularly numerous and dominant in areas such as the Ottawa valley and western Ontario.

The British had been anxious to ensure that the developing colony did not fall prey to the democratic tendencies that had subverted their rule in the 13 Colonies. They attempted to create a social hierarchy whose status and privileges would encourage imperial loyalty. The layout of townships included blocks of land reserved for substantial landowners and the clergy. Town meetings were not permitted, and every effort was made, in the words of the first lieutenant governor, "to inculcate British Customs, Manners & Principles in the most trivial, as well as serious matters." The result was that for most of its existence, Upper Canada was a Tory society, ruled by a small group of interconnected families who came to be known as the Family Compact. ∎

Ottawa

"WESTMINSTER IN THE WILDERNESS" OR "WASHINGTON OF the North." Both epithets have been applied to Canada's capital city; the former is an accurate enough description of Ottawa's origins, while the latter is more of a goal to which it has aspired, often with impressive results. In the century and a half since it was declared capital of newly united Canada, Ottawa has changed from a brawling lumber town to a city of some refinement, with a full array of national institutions that include not just the famous buildings on Parliament Hill but a number of excellent museums.

Ottawa

▲ 157 E2

Capital Infocentre
www.canadascapital.ca

✉ 90 Wellington St.

☎ 613/239-5000 or
800/465-1867

It was not Ottawa but Hull (now called Gatineau), on the Québec bank of the Ottawa River, that saw the beginnings of urban settlement in the area at the very start of the 19th century. Then, the first rafts of lumber were floated downstream and the important Ottawa Valley lumber industry got under way. Not long after, the War of 1812 made Britain nervous about the proximity of the strategic route along the St. Lawrence to the U.S. border. The need for a more secure link between Upper and Lower Canada led to the construction between 1826 and 1832 of the Rideau Canal. The waterway used existing rivers as well as new construction between the Royal Navy's Lake

Ontario base at Kingston and the head of navigation near Hull. In charge of this engineering wonder was a Colonel By, whose splendid run of locks connecting the canal to the river were in effect Ottawa's foundation stone. On either side of the canal, the colonel laid out a township. Named Bytown, the new settlement soon overtook Hull in size, though with a population of laborers, lumbermen, and river rats, its character remained resolutely rough. When the time came for a capital of the new United Province of Canada to be chosen, both Toronto and Québec City were disgusted with Queen Victoria's seemingly willful choice of Ottawa. In retrospect, however, the

Like the federal flag, Ontario's coat of arms includes the maple leaf.

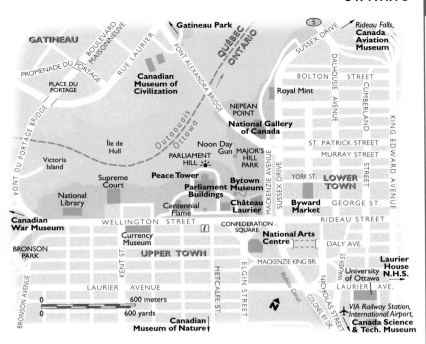

Empress's hatpin could be said to have landed in the right place, safe both from American incursions and, on the border between Ontario and Québec, safe from excessive Anglo-French rivalry.

The wilderness can still be sensed, not least in the broad waters of the Ottawa River flowing down from the Canadian Shield. The forest seems to close in from all around. A longstanding National Capital Commission has protected Ottawa with a green belt, torn up the railroad tracks, and laid out parks and parkways along waterways. The magnificent location of the parliament buildings overlooking the river is hardly matched anywhere else in the world. A splendid cliff-top route *(Rte. 17)* winds along the river to the east, past the famous Rideau Falls and the prime minister's residence to Rockcliffe Park. In winter, civil servants skate to work along the frozen canal through the heart of the city.

For many years Ottawa had the reputation of being a dull, provincial town. The place closed down early in the evening, and night owls would take flight across the river to Hull (Gatineau), where Québec laws allowed bars and nightspots to stay open an hour or two longer. As the city has grown, a certain liveliness has crept in. There's lots of entertainment, interesting shops, and plenty of eating places, especially around the city's colorful Byward Market. Today Ottawa and Gatineau have taken on something of each other's coloring; government buildings have partly replaced the lumber yards and mills that dominated Gatineau's townscape, and Ottawa is a place where bilingualism seems to thrive. In the old days, visitors came here mainly to see red-coated guardsmen and Mounties in front of the Houses of Parliament. This is still a great attraction, but Ottawa has become a city to be savored in its own right. ■

Parliament Hill

Parliament Hill visitor information

www.parl.gc.ca

✉ Info-Tent between West and Centre Blocks on Parliament Hill.

☎ 613/992-4793

🕑 Closed Mid-May–mid-Sept. (go directly to Centre Block)

THE LIMESTONE BLUFF OVERLOOKING THE BROAD REACHES of the Ottawa River is crowned by an extraordinary group of neo-Gothic buildings, an expression in stone of Canada's aspirations to nationhood. Almost every visitor to the country's capital climbs the gentle slope up to "The Hill," which offers not only the richly decorated interior of the Houses of Parliament but also an array of statuary and, in summer, a colorful display of pageantry with watchful Mounties and a ceremonial Changing of the Guard.

Parliament Hill rises gently from Confederation Square, the centerpiece of which is the **National War Memorial,** a 70-foot granite arch topped by bronze figures of Peace and Freedom and with sculpted figures of World War I combatants and auxiliaries. The memorial was dedicated by King George VI just before the outbreak of World War II; it is the focus of Remembrance Day observations every November 11. Around the square are a number of buildings with some national significance. The most remarkable of them is an institution in its own right: The **Château Laurier Hotel** (*1 Rideau St., tel 613/241-1414*) was built by the Grand Trunk Railway in 1912 and, with its towers, turrets, steep pitched roofs, and dormer windows, is a fine example of the Canadian château style. The first person to sign the guest register was the hotel's namesake, Prime

Minister Sir Wilfred Laurier, and the interior of the great building is said to have seen as much politicking as parliament itself, probably because many politicians lived here. The Grand Trunk complemented its castle hotel with a palatial railroad terminus, but Ottawa's trains have been banished to the distant suburbs, and the neo-classic Union Station is now the **Government Conference Centre** (*2 Rideau St.*). Next to it is the **National Arts Centre** (*53 Elgin St., tel 613/947-7000*), which dates from 1967.

The parliamentary buildings form three sides of a great open forecourt some 650 feet square. The dominant feature is the slim **Peace Tower,** 300 feet high, offering an unrivaled view of Ottawa from its viewing gallery. The tower rises from the **Centre Block,** rebuilt in the 1920s after a disastrous fire had destroyed the original 1866 building. Housing both the Commons and Senate, the Centre Block is flanked by the East and West Blocks, once capable of accommodating the whole apparatus of government and civil service, but today providing office space for members of parliament and senators, committee rooms, and the like. A number of rooms in the East Block have been restored to their 19th-century appearance. Linked to the far side of the Centre Block is the great **Library,** which, with its flying but-

Red carpets, murals, and a gilded ceiling make a dignified setting for the deliberations of the nation's Senate.

tresses and conical cap, is perhaps the most extraordinary of all these great Gothic Revival structures.

Choice of the Gothic style seems to have been influenced by two great building complexes nearing completion at the time—Britain's Houses of Parliament and Washington's neoclassic Capitol. Given that Canada's parliamentary structures were to be closely modeled on those of the mother country and that the new Palace of Westminster was the supreme example of Gothic Revival, there could have been little doubt about the outcome of the architectural competition, though the designs submitted included styles ranging from Norman to Venetian. The buildings are as rich in intriguing detail as they are in grandiose spaces for the rituals of rule. Carvings include humorously grotesque gargoyles and other figures, while interior decorations endeavor to express the character and history of the nation. Thus stained-glass windows in the House of Commons display the floral emblems of the country's provinces and territories, while the Senate has a frieze carved with Canadian plants and animals, as well as large-scale murals with scenes from World War I. The white-pine paneling of the library matches the magnificence of its exterior; a pale statue of Queen Victoria seems to admonish readers to silence.

Victoria appears again outside, her statue gracing the grounds to the left of the Centre Building, while her great-great-granddaughter, Elizabeth II, can be seen astride her mount, Centennial, in a similar location to the right. There's equal symmetry in the statues of two of the Fathers of Confederation, Sir John A. Macdonald (to the right) and Sir George-Étienne Cartier (to the left). Many other statues on the grounds commemorate Canada's leading figures. ■

The Centre Block of Ottawa's neo-Gothic parliamentary buildings house the Senate and the Commons.

Museums of the capital

AS BEFITS A CAPITAL CITY, THE OTTAWA AREA HAS MORE museum space per capita than any other Canadian city. Superbly housed in impressive modern buildings, the Canadian Museum of Civilization and the National Gallery of Canada attract visitors from all over the world, but there are many other collections of interest too.

NATIONAL GALLERY OF CANADA

Since 1988 the country's national art collections have been magnificently housed in this monumental modern building of granite, glass, and concrete, a masterpiece by Israel-born Moshe Safdie, the architect who first strode onto the Canadian scene with Expo 67's Habitat. Looking across an inlet of the river toward Parliament Hill, the gallery stands on what is probably the capital's second most prominent site. The glittering prisms of Safdie's Great Hall pay homage to the forms of the parliamentary library opposite, while the immensely long, sloping corridor leading to it was inspired by the Scala Regia in the Vatican.

The gallery has fine collections of paintings, sculpture, prints, drawings, and Inuit art. It mounts an ambitious program of temporary exhibits. There is an Asian Gallery with mostly Indian artworks spanning the period from the third century A.D. to modern times, while the extensive contemporary art collection focuses on American as well as Canadian art of the last few decades. The European and American Galleries house a fine collection representing many aspects of the evolution of Western art from medieval times to the present. There are paintings by Simone Martini, Hans Memling, Cranach, Rembrandt, and El Greco, and a superb bust by Bernini. The original of one the most famous Canadian history pictures is here,

"The Death of General Wolfe," painted by American artist Benjamin West in 1770. Constable and Turner are represented, as are many 19th-century French painters, among them Corot, Cezanne, Monet, Pissarro, and Dégas, as well as Van Gogh ("Iris"). The 20th-century art extends from a decorative Klimt ("Hope I") to a dynamic Jackson Pollock ("No. 29").

Inevitably and rightly, the heart of the gallery is its vast and comprehensive Canadian collections. The paintings and other works benefit enormously from the sophistication of the surroundings in which they are displayed. Highlights from early days include a sumptuous mid-18th-century tabernacle from Québec, charming portraits by William Bercy (1744–1813) and Antoine Plamondon (1804–1895), and immensely appealing naive wall paintings, which once decorated the living room of a Nova Scotia shipowner. Perhaps the most extraordinary single exhibit in the whole gallery is the **Rideau Street Convent Chapel** of 1888, a glorious neo-Gothic fantasy of slim columns and fan vaults saved from demolition and reerected here.

Plenty of space is given to innovative artists like Montréal's Paul-Emile Borduas (1905–1960), pioneer of Automatisme, but many visitors will be drawn again and again to the rooms containing works by those most Canadian of all painters, the Group of Seven and their associates (see pp. 186–87).

National Gallery of Canada
www.national.gallery.ca
✉ 380 Sussex Drive
☎ 613/990-1985
🕐 Closed Mon.–Tues. Oct.–April
💲 $ (temporary exhibits $$)

Right: Artist Paul Kane (1810–1871) made many trips across a Canada still largely unknown, recording people and landscapes. His majestic portrayal of Blackfoot Chief Big Snake was painted in 1856.

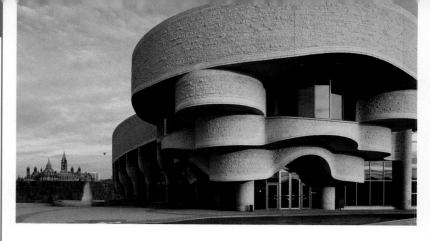

The superb Canadian Museum of Civilization is separated from Parliament Hill (visible in the background) by the Ottawa River.

They are all here, represented by some of their finest and most famous works ("The Jack Pine" by Tom Thomson, "Red Maple" by A.Y. Jackson, "North Shore, Lake Superior" by Lawren S. Harris, "Tangled Garden" by J.E.H. MacDonald). Sketches painted on wood shingles are a special treat, as are the panels painted to decorate the summer cottage of the group's patron, Dr. James MacCullum.

CANADIAN MUSEUM OF CIVILIZATION

In contrast to the rational, crystalline character of the National Gallery of Art, this distinctive building complex takes its inspiration from flowing sculptural forms that resemble rock outcrops molded by the action of wind, rain, and ice. Designed by the Blackfoot architect Douglas Cardinal, it was inaugurated in 1989 to house almost four million pieces explaining Canadian history and, to a lesser extent, world history and ethnology.

Framing a classic view of the parliament buildings atop the bluff on the far bank of the Ottawa River, the museum consists of two main parts linked by a basement: To the north, the serpentine terraces of the six-story Canadian Shield Wing housing administration, conservation, and storage functions, and to

the south the columns, high glazed walls, sinuous roofline, and copper domes of the Glacier Wing: This makes a dramatic setting for the museum's extensive displays, as well as housing a conventional auditorium, an IMAX theater, the **Canadian Postal Museum,** and the always lively **Children's Museum.**

The foyer, entered at street level, commands a view down into the curvilinear Grand Hall, its tall columns matched by a splendid line of totem poles. The hall is devoted to the art and culture of the native peoples of British Columbia's northwest coast, and also features copies of several chieftains' houses. While other galleries have both temporary and permanent exhibitions, the museum's other main display space is the third-floor Canada Hall, which takes visitors on a highly enjoyable trip through a thousand years of the country's history. The elaborately staged scenes feature both reconstructed buildings and a host of authentic artifacts. They include a Viking encampment, a Basque whaling station, a town square in New France, a voyageurs' camp, British officers' quarters, an early Ontario street, and a prairie settlement with railroad station, Ukrainian church, and grain elevators. ■

Canadian Museum of Civilization

www.civilization.ca

✉ 100 Rue Laurier, Gatineau

☎ 819/776-7000

🕐 Closed Mon. Oct.–April

💲 $$

More places to visit around Ottawa

BYTOWN MUSEUM

Colonel By's canal descends to the level of the Ottawa River down a stately flight of eight locks, massively built out of limestone hewed from the adjacent bluff. The three-story stone structure that served as his commissariat is now the Bytown Museum, the oldest remaining building in the capital, with displays on the canal and those who constructed it.
☎ 613/234-4570 🕐 Closed Dec.–March & weekends April–mid-May, mid-Oct.–Nov.
💲 $

CANADIAN WAR MUSEUM

Housed in a spectacular building designed by Raymond Moriyama beside the Ottawa River, the museum's state-of-the-art dioramas and displays bring to life Canada's military history from the early days of New France through both World Wars to present-day peace-keeping duties for the U.N. Highlights include a re-enactment of the 1759 Battle of the Plains of Abraham, the 1917 Battle of Vimy Ridge, the 1944 D-Day landings, and tributes to Canadian soldiers killed in Afghanistan in 2003. There is also a huge collection of military vehicles.
www.warmuseum.ca ✉ 1 Vimy Place.
☎ 819/776-8600 or 800/555-5621 🕐 Closed Mon. mid-Oct.–April 💲 $$$

CANADIAN MUSEUM OF NATURE

The displays of the Museum of Nature occupy a splendid early 20th-century building. The exhibits tell the story of the earth and its creatures in an often fascinating way. The dinosaur gallery is outstanding, and there is a very full account of Canada's wonderfully varied wildlife. One gallery takes visitors into the frozen, but far from lifeless, northland.
✉ 240 McLeod St. at Metcalfe. ☎ 613/566-4700 🕐 Closed Mon. Oct.–April 💲 $

GATINEAU PARK

One of the great attractions of life in the Ottawa area is this splendid 135-square-mile forest park on the Québec side of the Ottawa River. Prime Minister Mackenzie King was largely responsible for its preservation, and his estate at Moorside *(Tel 819/827-2020, closed mid-Oct.–mid-May)* has an odd collection of ruins on the grounds. The name of the government retreat at Meech Lake entered the language after the accord reached here in 1979 failed to solve the country's perennial constitutional crisis regarding Québec.

LAURIER HOUSE NATIONAL HISTORIC SITE

This villa of 1878, with its charming verandas, became the home of Prime Minister Sir Wilfred Laurier in 1897 and passed to his successor William Mackenzie King in 1921. Now a national historic site, it contains many mementos of these two great prime ministers, among them the famous crystal ball used by Mackenzie King, a noted spiritualist.
✉ 335 Laurier Ave. East ☎ 613/992-8142 🕐 Closed mid-Oct.–March & weekends April–May. 💲 $

CANADA AVIATION MUSEUM

Beneath the roof of this huge, triangular hangar is a superb array of aircraft that gives a very complete picture of how aviation has evolved in the 20th century. A copy of the *Silver Dart* that flew over Nova Scotia's Baddeck Bay in 1909 evokes the early days of heavier-than-air flight in Canada. There are aircraft from both world wars, as well as the commercial planes that opened up the north. The greatest bush plane of them all, the De Havilland Beaver, has a prominent place. By contrast, there are only fragments of the Avro Arrow, the supersonic interceptor whose cancellation on Black Friday (February 20, 1959) ended Canada's aspirations as an air superpower.
✉ Rockcliffe Airport, 3 miles NE of downtown off Rockcliffe Pkwy. ☎ 613/993-2010 🕐 Closed Mon., & Tues. Sept.–April 💲 $

CANADA SCIENCE & TECHNOLOGY MUSEUM

A lighthouse moved from Nova Scotia signals the site of this museum, whose exhibits include many hands-on attractions as well as vintage vehicles, magnificent steam locomotives, shipping exhibits, and much more.
✉ 1867 St. Laurent Blvd., 3 miles east from downtown ☎ 613/991-3044 🕐 Closed Mon. Sept.–April 💲 $$ ∎

Kingston & the St. Lawrence

Kingston
   157 E2

**Visitor
information**
www.kingstoncanada.com

✉   209 Ontario St.

☎   613/548-4415 or
888/855-4555

🕐   Closed Sat.–Sun. in
winter months

SITED AT THE POINT WHERE THE ST. LAWRENCE FLOWS
out of Lake Ontario and at the terminus of the Rideau Canal, this
old harbor town enjoyed a brief moment of glory between 1841 and
1843, when it served as the capital of the Province of Canada.

KINGSTON

The Loyalist settlement founded as
"King's Town" in 1784 had been
preceded by a French fur-trading
post established in 1673, which, as
Fort Frontenac, fell to the British in
1758. During the War of 1812,
Kingston became an important
military and naval base. The Royal
Navy sailed away in 1852, but there
is still a strong military presence in
the shape of the Royal Military
College and a nearby Canadian
Forces base.

Early Kingston was built of
timber, but by the 19th century
masons were fashioning the local
blue-gray limestone into fine houses
and public buildings. Enough
remain today to justify the town's
appellation as the "Limestone City."
Dominating the waterfront parkland, the massive neoclassic **City
Hall** (216 Ontario St.) begun in
1842 embodies Kingston's aspirations as a capital city. Built later in
the century and almost matching
City Hall in grandeur is nearby

St. George's Cathedral, while
the earlier **Court House** of
1826 is a model of Georgian
restraint. Architectural restraint
had flown out of the window by
the time **Bellevue House** (35
Centre St., tel 613/545-8666) was
built for a wealthy local grocer in
1841. In 1848–49 this extravagantly
picturesque Italianate residence
was let to future Prime Minister
John A. Macdonald, who called it
his "Eyetalian Willa." The house
has been refurbished in the style
of his time there.

A stroll along Kingston's waterfront is full of interest. There is a
busy marina, the ferry terminal to
Wolfe Island, and a clutch of
museums. The **Marine Museum
of the Great Lakes** (55 Ontario
St., tel 613/542-2261, closed weekends Nov.–April) tells the fascinating story of hundreds of years of
navigation on the lakes, and close
by is the **Pump House Steam
Museum** (23 Ontario St., tel
613/542-2261, closed Oct.–mid-
May), where pride of place
is occupied by massive stationary
steam engines. The museum in the
Murney Tower (Tel 613/544-
9925, closed mid-Sept.–mid-May)
explains the military significance of
this martello tower, one of several
built in 1846–48 at a time of border
tensions with the United States.

But Kingston's most imposing
stronghold is on the far side of the
harbor, beyond the Royal Military
College on the promontory. Formidable **Fort Henry** (Tel 613/542-
7388, closed mid-Sept.– mid-May)
was built overlooking Navy Bay in

**The sharp
marching
precision of the
military parades
at Fort Henry
keeps the province
in step with its
past.**

1832–36 to protect the naval ship-yard there. No shot was ever fired in anger at Fort Henry, but you would-n't know that to judge from the gunfire accompanying the summer-time military parades and maneu-vers staged here, much to the delight of younger tourists.

THE THOUSAND ISLANDS

The first 35 miles of the St. Lawrence downstream from Kingston was known to the French as *le lac des mille îles*, the Lake of the Thousand Islands, and most visitors agree that a four-figure total can be justified. American raiders lurking among the islands harassed British convoys as they made their way up and down the St. Lawrence during the War of 1812. After the war the frontier was settled in an amicable way; the boundary line follows the main channel, and no island is divided between the two countries.

The prettily wooded islands have been a playground for a century and a half. The wealthy got here first, staying in luxury hotels or building extravagant residences, of which none was more extrava-gant than **Boldt Castle,** built by the Austrian owner of New York's Waldorf-Astoria, whose chef, it is

said, was inspired by sojourns here to invent Thousand Island salad dressing. Nowadays it's mostly weekenders who throng the islands, arriving here by cruiser or canoe. Other visitors wanting to get onto the water can take a boat cruise from Kingston *(Tel 613/549-5544)* or Gananoque *(Tel 613/382-2146)*. Landlubbers can enjoy this wonderful watery landscape from the **Thousand Islands Parkway** and from the viewing tower *(Closed Nov.–mid-April)* close to the Thousand Islands International Bridge connecting Ontario and New York State.

UPPER CANADA VILLAGE

The area along today's Thousand Islands Parkway was settled by Loyalists in the late 18th century. Upper Canada Village is one of the most entertaining restorations of its kind in Canada. Consisting of some three dozen buildings rescued from flooding by the St. Lawrence Seaway project, as well as dwellings ranging from the primitive structures of early days to fine houses in brick and stone, it has mills, schools, stores, churches, and a forge, print-ing press, and tavern, all staffed by convincingly clad 19th-century folk engaged in appropriate activities. ■

One of the St. Lawrence River's Thousand Islands

Upper Canada Village
🅰 157 F2
www.uppercanadavillage .com
✉ 7 miles E of Morrisburg on Hwy. 2
☎ 613/543-4328 or 800/437-2233
🕐 Closed mid-Oct.–mid-May
💲 $$$

Toronto

Toronto
157 E2

Visitor information
www.torontotourism.com
✉ 207 Queens Quay West, Ste. 590
☎ 416/203-2600 or 800/363-1990

OTTAWA MAY BE THE NATION'S CAPITAL, BUT TORONTO IS the epicenter of Canada's financial and commercial life, and, as far as Anglo-Canada is concerned, its cultural life, too. Following its latest (1997) amalgamation with outlying municipalities, Toronto has become North America's fourth largest city, its dynamism proclaimed by its splendid cluster of downtown skyscrapers, its aspirations indicated by the immensely tall CN tower. Despite its great size, it's a livable city, with clean and relatively safe public spaces, cohesive neighborhoods, every imaginable kind of shopping and entertainment opportunity, lakeside amenities, and other green spaces. Some of the country's finest museums and galleries are here, too, most notably the Art Gallery of Ontario and the magnificent Royal Ontario Museum.

Apart from the lakeside, there seem to be few natural features to compete with the dominance of man-made structures: To the north of downtown, the ancient shoreline of the prehistoric ancestor of Lake Ontario is marked by a ridge that makes a site for prestige houses, but otherwise Toronto is flat. However, threading through the built-up area is a network of wooded ravines carved out by streams, such as the Don, that flow south into the lake, an asset described as equivalent to Venice's canals and San Francisco's hills.

The first European to visit the site of present-day Toronto seems to have been the Frenchman Étienne Brulé, who came here in 1615 along an old native trail from Lake Huron, later used by English and Dutch fur traders from New York. In the early 18th century, the French built a fort to interfere with this trade, but it was abandoned in 1759. In the late 18th century, British interest in the area was boosted by the arrival of Loyalists who settled along the shore of Lake Ontario; in 1794 the choice of a capital of newly created Upper Canada finally fell on Toronto, renamed York in honor of George

Toronto's contemporary skyline, seen from the islands sheltering the harbor

Toronto's downtown towers now completely hide the once dominant bulk of the Royal York Hotel (1929).

Lester B. Pearson International Airport

0   600 meters
0   600 yards

Summerville

Casa Loma   Steps   Spadina House
Corso Italia

VERMONT SQUARE

Dupont
RAMSDEN PARK
Rosedale

SIBELIUS SQUARE
Spadina

KETCHUM PARK

Metro Toronto Library
Ontario Science Centre

Spadina
Bathurst   St. George   Bay   Bloor Yonge

YORKVILLE

BLOOR STREET WEST

Bata Shoe Museum   Royal Ontario Museum   Gardiner Museum of Ceramic Art   St. Paul's Church

BLOOR STREET EAST

Museum
QUEEN'S PARK

University of Toronto

Ontario Legislative Building
Wellesley

Ontario Hydro

Queen's Park

Maple Leaf Gardens

COLLEGE STREET   COLLEGE STREET
College
CARLTON STREET

ALLAN GARDENS

Kensington Market

CHINATOWN

DUNDAS STREET

ALEXANDRA PARK
Art Gallery of Ontario
The Grange
GRANGE PARK
Toronto City Hall
Campbell House

St. Patrick   Eaton Centre
Textile Museum of Canada   Dundas   DUNDAS ST. E.
Mackenzie House
NATHAN PHILLIPS SQUARE
Queen

QUEEN   STREET   WEST   Osgoode

Old City Hall

QUEEN ST. EAST

Royal Alexandra Theatre
St. Andrew

ST. JAMES PARK

KING   STREET   WEST
VICTORIA MEMORIAL SQUARE
CLARENCE SQUARE
Roy Thomson Hall
Royal Bank Plaza
T.D. Centre   KING ST. EAST
King
BCE Place   FRONT ST. EAST

FRONT   STREET   WEST
Union
St. Lawrence Market

Fort York

CN Tower
Union Station
GARDINER EXPRESSWAY

Rogers Centre
GARDINER EXPRESSWAY
QUEENS QUAY E.

Ontario Place
QUEENS QUAY W
HARBOURFRONT
York Quay Centre
Queen's Quay Terminal
Island Ferry Docks

Toronto Harbour

Toronto Islands

N

III's second son (the native name Toronto was reinstated in 1834, when it was incorporated as a city).

Well into the 19th century, growth was slow, and the little frontier settlement seems to have deserved the derisive epithet of "Muddy York." But it was as if the inhabitants were aware of the place's destiny; the sacking of the town by the Americans during the War of 1812 was soon made good, and the attempt by Kingston to usurp York's capital city status was beaten off. For many years, a tightly knit group of mostly British merchants (collectively known as the Family Compact) dominated government and social life as well as commerce, and made quite sure that the bulk of Upper Canada's trade passed through their hands.

When the Erie Canal was completed in 1825, Toronto no longer had to rely on Montréal as a port of entry but could use New York, the beginnings of an American tie which has remained important ever since. As Ontario developed throughout the 19th century, Toronto became the natural focus for its agricultural products, its industry, and its commerce. The violence and disorder of the Mackenzie Rebellion of 1837 (see p. 36) was seen as a disgraceful interruption of the city's stately progress, based on virtue as much as effort. Muddy York metamorphosed into "Toronto the Good," a sternly Protestant town of moral rectitude and the strictest Sunday observance.

Only in the mid-20th century was its utterly Anglo-Saxon ethos diluted, as immigrants arrived, first from northern, then from southern Europe, then from all around the world. Today's Toronto has a population of striking diversity, visible over the city as a whole, and not just in the lively neighborhoods with their distinctive Greek, Italian, Portuguese, Indian, and Chinese communities.

No visit to Toronto is complete if just the center and the lakefront are explored. Among the inner suburbs, choose from **Yorkville** (once hippy, now just hip), **Corso Italia** on St. Clair Street, **Chinatown** between the University of Toronto and Spadina Avenue, or **Kensington Market,** the arrival point for many of the successive waves of immigrants, once Jewish, then Portuguese, now predominantly Caribbean. The inner city is served by excellent public transportation *(Visitor information, tel 416/393-4636, www.toronto.ca/ttc),* but to reach some of the many attractions in the outer suburbs or beyond, it may pay to rent a car. ■

One of the many vessels that dock at Toronto's Queen's Quay Wharf

Toronto's lakefront & islands

OVER THE YEARS TORONTO HAS STEADILY EXTENDED itself southward into the lake, leaving Front Street (once lapped by water) high and dry and creating a long sliver of man-made land up to 1,800 feet across. Mainly a working area, with docks, commercial buildings, and railroad tracks, it was also the embarkation point for the pleasure steamers that used to ply the lake. As the St. Lawrence Seaway neared completion in 1959, plans were made to extend docking facilities, but the expected boom in harbor traffic never came. From the 1970s on, the waterfront has been colonized by hotels, offices, apartments, and a mixture of marinas, cafés, restaurants, shops, and places of entertainment. New paving, landscaping, and placing of public sculpture has added to the area's attractiveness, and what is now called the Harbourfront Centre is an essential part of any tour of Toronto. As well as a stroll along the waterfront, there are two other unmissable experiences: a dizzy trip up the CN Tower for a vertiginous view of the city, and a ride on one of the ferries to the miniature Toronto Islands archipelago, with the shining towers of the downtown as a magnificent backdrop.

CN Tower
www.cntower.ca
- 301 Front St. W.
- 416/868-6937
- Subway: Union, then CN Skywalk
- $$$

Rogers Centre
www.rogerscentre.com
- 1 Blue Jays Way
- 416/341-3663
- Subway: Union, then CN Skywalk
- $$$

Toronto Islands
www.toronto.ca/parks
- Ferry: 416/392-8193
- Island Ferry Docks, Queens Quay at Yonge
- $

CN TOWER
Toronto's unmistakable urban icon shoots an extraordinary 1,815 feet into the air, a fluted concrete column contrasting with the bulbous Rogers Centre crouching nearby. As of press time, it is still the tallest freestanding structure in the world, high enough for the Skypod and its minaretlike spike to pierce low cloud cover, or for visitors to look down on aircraft heading for the city's international airport. The tower was built in 1976, not only as a telecommunications facility but as the centerpiece for a vast urban redevelopment project. In any event, it has more than earned its keep as a visitor attraction.

The view is the thing, of course, both from the observation decks of the Lookout (1,136 feet up) or the even higher Skypod (1,465 feet). For those unscathed by vertigo on the ride up on the outside elevator, there is the additional challenge of the glass floor, with only space between your feet and the Rogers

Left: The sleek steel-and-glass towers of Toronto's financial district frame a view of the CN Tower.

Centre's infield far below. There's a revolving restaurant, and, at the base of the tower, more thrills such as laser games.

ROGERS CENTRE

The former SkyDome bills itself as the World's Greatest Entertainment Centre, but everyone knows it as the shrine where up to 53,000 of the faithful can express their devotion to the Blue Jays, World Series champions in 1992 and 1993. The Toronto Argonauts (Canadian football) also play here; other entertainment ranges from circuses to pop concerts and ice shows. The Rogers Centre is an attraction in itself, with guided tours taking in a video show and explanations of how the world's largest retractable roof is made to open and close.

The roof of the Rogers Centre weighs 12,100 tons and rises to a height of 300 feet.

TORONTO ISLANDS

The 18 verdant islands sheltering the broad waters of Toronto's fine natural harbor have long been a valuable refuge from the pressures of city life. The ramshackle but charming residences on **Ward's Island** and **Algonquin Island** at the eastern extremity of the archipelago are the remains of a more extensive settled area that the Parks Department is converting to public open space over a period of years. The ferries terminate at Ward's Island, at Hanlan's Point near the busy Island Airport, and at the Centre Island Dock, close to the popular amusement park. With no competition from cars, the best way of exploring the nearly 4-mile-long crescent of islands is by renting a bicycle. ■

Toronto walk: Union Station to City Hall

The streets in Toronto's heart are lined with buildings that provide ample evidence of Canada's architectural heritage. Between Union Station and the Eaton Centre are treasured landmarks, innovative skyscrapers, and fine examples of modern architecture.

Linked by underground passageway, both the **Royal York Hotel** and **Union Station** ❶ recall the great days of train travel and tourism. The station—the third Union Station to stand on this site—was begun in 1913 and took 17 years to complete. Behind its long facade with its central colonnade is an imposing ticket hall 88 feet high and lit from each end by tall arched windows.

Built in 1929, the dignified art deco giant of a hotel makes a fine partner for the station, and is one of several buildings in Canada that for a while could boast of being the largest in the British Empire. The Canadian Pacific later added the steep roof to harmonize with its other château-style hotels. From the level beneath the hotel's sumptuous lobby, the city's downtown walkway (called PATH) leads through the Royal Bank Plaza, then, on the far side of Bay Street, up into **BCE Place.** This

development of 1993 with its stunningly elegant galleria incorporates one of the oldest surviving stone buildings in Toronto, the Commercial Bank of the Midland District, which had to be dismantled and moved south 20 yards to fit into the new scheme.

At the corner of Front and Yonge Streets, another old bank building, the ornate Bank of Montréal, houses the **Hockey Hall of Fame.** Walk east along Front Street past the **St. Lawrence Centre for the Arts.** The south side of the street has a number of 19th-century warehouses and former chandlers' stores, reminders of the one-time proximity of the lakeside. There's now an intriguing mix of shops and cafés. The rear of the 1892 Flatiron or **Gooderham Building** has a wonderful mural, with its turret making an appealing composition when seen against the background of the office towers to the west.

Old City Hall, one of the landmark structures of late 19th-century Toronto

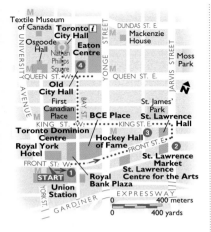

See city map p. 172

► Union Station (Subway: Union)

↔ 1.8 miles

⏱ Allow 1 day

► Nathan Phillips Square
  (Subway: Dundas or Queen)

NOT TO BE MISSED

- BCE Place
- St. Lawrence Market
- Eaton Centre

Follow Front Street East for another 400 yards to the corner of Jarvis Street and find **St. Lawrence Market ❷** *(92 Front St. E., tel 416/392-7219, closed Sun.)*. This cornucopia of tempting comestibles is at its liveliest on Saturdays, when people come from all over town to pick and choose from the marvelous fresh produce in the North Building's farmers market. The South Building incorporates parts of the 1845 City Hall, and the old council chamber is now the **Market Gallery** with exhibits on historical themes.

Just a few paces north of the St. Lawrence Market is the corner of Jarvis Street and King Street East, featuring the richly decorated **St. Lawrence Hall ❸**. Splendidly restored for the 1967 Centennial, the hall was the city's mid-19th century social and cultural center. The little oasis of **St. James' Park**, behind it, is an excellent place to pause and take stock. To the west, the spire of **St. James'**

Cathedral *(65 Church St., tel 416/364-7865)* rises more than 300 feet and for many years was Toronto's principal landmark.

Continue west along King Street West, where the early evolution of the skyscraper can be traced. The 15-story **Canadian Pacific Building,** 400 yards along at the corner of Yonge Street, was one of the tallest buildings outside New York when completed in 1911. It was outdone in 1931 by the **Bank of Commerce** at No. 25 King Street West, a stylish tiered tower of 34 stories with a wealth of Canadian symbolism in its fascinating decoration. This really was the tallest building in the British Empire, not only at the time of its completion but for 35 years thereafter. Continue along King Street West for another hundred yards; on the south side, beyond the intersection with Bay Street, is the group of classic modernist towers in black metal and bronze glass that make up the **Toronto Dominion Centre.** The first two towers to be built, between 1963 and 1969, were the work of Mies van der Rohe, famous for his minimalist approach to architecture. The shopping concourse beneath the plaza is part of the PATH system.

Continue a half mile north along Bay Street to **Old City Hall ❹**. With its beckoning tower, this center of municipal government was ceremonially opened in 1899, after taking ten years to build and going more than ten times over the original budget. It's a splendid example of the late 19th-century Richardson Romanesque style, built in textured two-toned sandstone. The extravagantly ornate interior now serves as law courts.

Public protests saved Old City Hall from demolition as part of the site clearance for the construction of the Eaton Centre, its immediate neighbor to the east. The multilevel **Eaton Centre** *(Yonge St., tel 416/598-8700)* itself, spreading 900 feet along Yonge Street, is worth more than a casual glance. Beneath its glazed roof is one of the finest—and most popular—shopping centers in Canada, with more than 300 stores as well as a famous flight of sculpted Canada geese.

At the Eaton Centre follow Queen Street West 200 yards west to **Nathan Phillips Square,** the plaza fronting **City Hall,** to end the walk (see p. 182). ∎

The Great Lakes

The massed towers of Toronto's downtown look southward over oceanlike Lake Ontario toward the shore of New York State, 35 miles away. Vast though the lake is, it is the second smallest in area of the five Great Lakes, which collectively make up the largest body of freshwater in the world. Connected by waterways and discharging into the mighty St. Lawrence River, the lakes formed a natural route, tempting European explorers into the heart of the continent. Today, the basin in which they lie is the home of no less than half of the population of Canada and one-fifth of that of the United States, a focus of commerce, industry, communications, tourism, and of cross-border cooperation.

The shape of the lakes reflects the underlying geological structure. While Lakes Huron and Michigan arc around the Michigan basin, Erie and Ontario share the southwest–northeast axis of the Appalachian Mountains. The outline of austere Lake Superior is influenced by the structure of the ancient Precambrian rock of the Canadian Shield (see p. 20). The largest (31,700 square miles) and deepest (average 483 feet) of the lakes, Superior is also the most elemental, a true inland sea where waves can reach 50 feet in height, and whose chill waters are reputed never to give up the bodies of the drowned. Michigan (22,300 square miles) is the only lake with no Canadian shore. The main body of Lake Huron (23,000 square

miles) is almost separated from the North Channel and Georgian Bay by the line of the Niagara Escarpment that forms the Bruce Peninsula and Manitoulin Island. Bigger than Lake Ontario in area, Erie is shallow (average depth 62 feet), and contains by far the smallest quantity of water of all the lakes (116 cubic miles compared with Superior's 2,900 cubic miles). So it regularly freezes over in winter.

The change in level from Lake Superior (about 600 feet above sea level) to Lake Ontario (about 243 feet above sea level) is taken up by rapids at Sault Ste. Marie between Lakes Superior and Huron, and along the Niagara River between Lakes Erie and Ontario. But the most dramatic change of level is the 160-foot drop of the world-famous Niagara Falls. Natives and early explorers overcame these obstacles to navigation by

laborious portages. Canals were built at an early stage—1798 at Sault Ste. Marie, the first Welland Canal (see p. 192) bypassing Niagara in 1829. They steadily improved, enabling increasingly larger ships to travel not only from lake to lake, but, via the St. Lawrence River, to and from the Atlantic. The final, triumphant stage in improvement of the waterway was the completion of the St. Lawrence Seaway in 1959. This monumental joint Canada-U.S. venture involving the construction of new canals, locks, and channels between Montréal and Lake Ontario allowed oceangoing vessels ("salties") to make the 2,355-mile journey inland from Anticosti at the river's mouth to Duluth, Minnesota, at the far western end of Lake Superior. It was hailed at the time, not only as a stupendous engineering achievement but also as a symbol of goodwill and cooperation; both Queen Elizabeth II and President Dwight D. Eisenhower attended the opening ceremony, on June 26, 1959. Much was made of the effective addition of 8,300 miles of coastline to the two countries and of the galvanizing effect the seaway would have on their economies. But time has shown that the seaway has its limits. Ice impedes navigation for part of the year, and salties are limited to about 30,000 tons, thus excluding the largest ocean vessels.

The seaway was a symbol of 1950s and 1960s optimism about economic growth. In the 1970s, 1980s, and 1990s, the Great Lakes were seen more as an object lesson in the dire environmental effects of that growth. Eutrophication, the reduction in fish numbers, and the identification of more than 300 potentially harmful chemical compounds and of 42 "hot spots" of concentrated pollution all contributed to public concern. The Great Lakes Water Quality Agreement, signed by Canada and the United States in 1972, has led to the expenditure of billions of dollars to improve water quality, with sometimes dramatic results. But there is still a long way to go before the lakes are once more the "sweetwater seas," about which French Jesuit missionaries rhapsodized. ■

**A rocky view of Ontario's inland sea—
Lake Superior**

Royal Ontario Museum

Royal Ontario Museum

www.rom.on.ca

✉ 100 Queen's Park, but in 2007 the entrance will be on Bloor St.

☎ 416/586-8000

🚇 Subway: Museum

💲 $$$

SIX MILLION OBJECTS AND MORE THAN 40 GALLERIES make the largest museum in Canada a place for repeat visits. The ROM is presently undertaking a major expansion. When complete in 2007, the ROM will boast more than 300,000 square feet of gallery space and a host of new or refurbished galleries. The spectacular Michael Lee-Chin Crystal, five unique crystalline forms designed by Daniel Libeskind that rise to a height of 117 feet, will take center stage, covering the new main entrance on Bloor Street.

Originally part of the University of Toronto, the ROM remains an important research organization with an encyclopedic collection. Its world-famous Chinese collection can be viewed in the Galleries of World Culture. It features a spectacular Ming Tomb, the only complete example in the Western world; an ornate reconstruction of a 17th-century Imperial palace from Beijing's Forbidden City; and the awe-inspiring Bishop White gallery, with temple wall paintings from the Yuan dynasty (A.D. 271–1386) and large wooden sculptures representing bodhisattvas. Japanese ceramics and Buddhist art from Korea occupy adjoining galleries.

As well as being a popular visitor attraction, the ROM is an important research center.

Among the natural history displays, the perennially popular dinosaurs draw crowds of all ages. A dozen-plus skeletons are artfully posed in settings resembling the Jurassic and Cretaceous landscapes in which these doomed giants roamed. The Bat Cave treats you to an unnervingly realistic encounter with thousands of bats and other denizens, while stuffed Canadian birds and an elaborate diorama show the life of Ontario wetlands.

The ancient world of the Mediterranean can be thoroughly explored thanks to the museum's exceptionally wide-ranging collection of Egyptian antiquities and Greek and Roman artifacts. There are masks and mummies of outstanding quality, as well as casts of wall reliefs from the famous temple of Queen Hatshepsut. Greek sculptures are arranged to superb effect in a court. In the Gallery of Islam, visitors weave their way through a bazaar and a mosque with illuminated Qur'ans and glassware on display. The evolution of European decorative arts from the Middle Ages onward is traced in the Samuel European Galleries, where exhibits include arms and armor, selections from Canada's largest costume collection, and a series of elaborately re-created period rooms.

Last but not least, the ROM's Canadian galleries house decorative arts of both French and English Canada from the 17th to the 19th centuries, as well as a splendid First Nations collection of both traditional and contemporary art. ∎

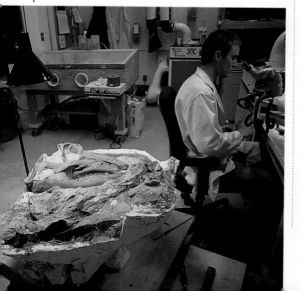

Art Gallery of Ontario

Art Gallery of Ontario

www.ago.net

✉ 317 Dundas St. W
(temp. entrance on
McCaul St.)

☎ 416/979-6648

🚇 Subway: St. Patrick

💲 $$

TORONTO'S GREAT GALLERY OF ART, STRONG IN EUROPEAN and Canadian art, has been enriched and extended many times since the early 20th century, when it inherited the splendid Georgian mansion, The Grange. It is at present undergoing a major expansion to house the Thomson Collection of about 2,000 works given to the gallery by Canadian millionaire and art collector, Kenneth Thomson.

Note: Until the new Frank Gehry designed wings are complete in 2008, only part of the permanent collection will be displayed. Reduced admission fees and hours will apply.

The gallery's collection of Henry Moore's works contains several "Reclining Figures," one of the sculptor's favorite themes.

The European collections include many old masters, among them Brueghel the Younger, Tintoretto, Rembrandt, Frans Hals, de la Tour, and Poussin. Most of the late 19th- and early 20th-century movements in painting are represented; among the pictures by the French Impressionists are canvases by Monet, Gauguin, Dégas, and Renoir, and there are works by Chagall, Picasso, Dufy, and Modigliani. This collection will be enhanced by the addition of such works as the "Massacre of the Innocents" by Peter Paul Rubens, part of the Thomson Collection. The evolution of Canadian art can be followed, both in Québec, with fine pictures by artists such as Joseph Legaré and James Morrice, and most comprehensively of all, in English Canada, where there is a splendid selection of works by the Group of Seven (see pp. 186–87) and their associates. A real attraction is an innovative installation where you are taken through an intimate encounter with one of Canada's modern masterpieces.

The setting for the magnificent and unrivaled collection of Henry Moore sculptures dates from 1974 and was designed by the artist himself. Bronzes, plasters, and plaster maquettes are displayed in a large space with natural light entering from the ceiling. ∎

More places to visit in Toronto

BATA SHOE MUSEUM

From modest beginnings in what is now the Czech Republic, the Bata firm became the world's largest shoe manufacturer. With more than 10,000 items in the witty shoebox building designed by Raymond Moriyama, the museum tells an informative and highly entertaining story of footwear. Popular displays include the footwear of Pablo Picasso, Mikhail Barishnikov, Elizabeth Taylor, Indira Gandhi, Winston Churchill, Pierre Trudeau, and Elton John.
www.batashoemuseum.ca ✉ 327 Bloor St. W. ☎ 416/979-7799 🕐 Closed Mon. Sept.–May 🚇 Subway: St. George 💲 $$

CASA LOMA

Casa Loma, the "house on the ridge," was built in 1914 to satisfy the architectural fantasies of Sir Henry Pellatt and show off the vast fortune he accumulated in developing hydroelectricity in Ontario. The mammoth edifice is a sort of souvenir of Sir Henry's trips around the monuments of Europe. It was designed by E.J. Lennox, previously employed by Pellatt to build the even more monumental hydropower station at Niagara Falls. There are 98 lavishly furnished rooms, a 70-foot-high ceiling in the Great Hall, and all the latest conveniences. Poor Sir Henry came to grief in the early 1920s when the province took public ownership of the power supply, and Casa Loma was repossessed for unpaid debts.
www.casaloma.org ✉ 1 Austin Terrace ☎ 416/923-1171 🚇 Subway: Dupont 💲 $$$

CITY HALL

In 1957 the architectural competition for a new headquarters for city government attracted an astonishing 510 entries from all around the world. The winner was a Finn, Viljo Revell; his astonishingly original design has long been accepted as one of the city's great civic symbols. It's an exercise in sculptural concrete, with a saucer-shaped Council Chamber embraced by two curving towers of unequal height. It's worth going inside, perhaps taking the elevator to the amphitheater-like Council Chamber, or just admiring the great mushroom-shaped column that supports it. In front is **Nathan Phillips Square,** named for the mayor who insisted the city have a building worthy of a modern metropolis. In winter, it becomes a skating rink. The sculpture that adorns the square, the bronze "Archer" by Henry Moore, stirred up as much controversy as the building itself.
✉ 100 Queen St. W. ☎ 416/338-0338 🚇 Subway: Osgoode or Queen

FORT YORK

Squashed between railroad tracks and dominated by the multilane Gardiner Expressway, Fort York appears even less menacing today than it did to the well-armed American troops who stormed ashore in the early morning of April 27, 1813, easily overcoming its feeble defenses and putting the raggle-taggle Canadian force of regulars, militiamen, and natives to flight. Before retreating across the Don River and abandoning the town to its fate, the American-born commander of the Canadian troops ordered the fort's 500 gunpowder barrels to be blown up.

The fort was subsequently rebuilt and improved. There are ramparts, blockhouses, and magazines, and the officers' barracks have been refurbished in the style of the period. The Blue Barracks contain exhibits on early days in Toronto and on military history. In summer there are soldierly drills and displays.
www.toronto.ca/culture ✉ 100 Garrison Rd. at Fleet St. ☎ 416/ 392-6907 💲 $$

GARDINER MUSEUM OF CERAMIC ART

When it reopens in late 2006 (or early 2007), this gem of a museum will have doubled in size, allowing it to display more of its stunning collection, which ranges from pre-Columbian pottery through Italian Renaissance majolica and delftware to the classic porcelain of Meissen, Sèvres, Chelsea, and Bow. Highlights include a display of exquisite scent bottles made in different parts of Europe, with elaborate rococo models from England and delightful Commedia Dell'Arte figurines made by Johann Joachim Kändler. There are also a few examples of contemporary ceramic ware.
www.gardinermuseum.on.ca ✉ 111 Queen's Park ☎ 416/586-8080 🚇 Subway: Museum 💲 $$

Military history is brought to life in Fort York by its authentically costumed militia.

THE GRANGE

Revealed in all its pedimented Georgian splendor from the fragment of its once extensive grounds, the Grange was built in 1818 by D'Arcy Boulton, a member of what a political rival described as "one of the most unprincipled families of the Tory compact." One of the oldest and finest of the city's historic buildings, it has been furnished in the style of the 1840s, when the power and prestige of the Family Compact was at its zenith and much of what happened in Toronto was decided in its elegant rooms.

✉ 317 Dundas St. W., entry via Art Gallery of Ontario (AGO) ☎ 416/979-6648 ⊕ Closed until 2008 during renovation of AGO 🚇 Subway: St. Patrick 💲 $

ONTARIO LEGISLATURE

This massive sandstone structure dominating Queen's Park and the University quarter to the west is the seat of a legislature that governs a province of some 12 million inhabitants, more than the population of many European countries. Originally Ontario was to be ruled from a Gothic edifice modeled on the British Houses of Parliament, but the U.S.-based architect Richard Waite succeeded in pushing through his more up-to-date Romanesque Revival design of 1893, overcoming the united opposi-

tion of the province's architects. The somber exterior belies the opulence of the interior with its rich and, in places, playful decoration.
www.ontla.on.ca ✉ Queen's Park
☎ 416/325-7500 ⊕ Closed weekends in winter 🚇 Subway: Queen's Park

ONTARIO PLACE

Toronto's riposte to Montréal's 1967 Expo, this amusement park is laid out on a series of islands offshore from the somewhat rundown Canadian National Exhibition Centre. With its array of structures in steel and glass, Ontario Place was truly innovative when built in the early 1970s by Eberhard Zeidler, architect of the Eaton Centre. Since then it has strived to keep abreast of the trends. There are restaurants, a large amphitheater for outdoor performances, and a six-story-high IMAX cinema.
✉ 955 Lake Shore Blvd. W. ☎ 416/314-9900
⊕ Closed Sept.–mid-May

SPADINA HOUSE

A grocer-turned-banker, James Austin acquired the Spadina estate in 1866 on the ridge overlooking the city. Extended by his heirs, the original house is opulent enough, but contrasts with nearby Casa Loma in the refinement of its decorative objects, furnishings, and architecture.
www.toronto.ca/culture ✉ 285 Spadina Rd.
☎ 416/392-6910 ⊕ Closed Mon., & weekdays Jan.–March 🚇 Subway: Dupont 💲 $$

HOCKEY HALL OF FAME

The ultimate tribute to the popular Canadian sport, this is the most comprehensive collection of hockey artifacts and memorabilia in existence. Learn all about stars such as Maurice "The Rocket" Richard, Bobby Orr and Wayne Gretzky. Then visit the former locker room of the fabled Montréal Canadiens from the old Montréal Forum, or try your hand at interactive displays and games. Major National Hockey League (NHL) trophies are on display in the Great Hall. The highlight is the original Stanley Cup, North America's oldest sports trophy. It was donated to the sport by Governor General, Lord Stanley, in 1893.
www.hhof.com ✉ 30 Yonge St. (in BCE Place) ☎ 416/360-7765 🚇 Subway: Union
💲 $$ ■

Outer Toronto excursions

The Dominion Carriage Works is one of a number of industrial and commercial buildings rebuilt at Black Creek Pioneer Village.

BLACK CREEK PIONEER VILLAGE

This open-air museum of Ontarian rural life centers around the original farmstead of a Pennsylvania Dutch family that erected a log house here in 1816. In addition to their second house, smokehouse, and barn, another 30 or so mid-19th-century buildings—including a substantial mill building, a printshop, and the Half Way House, a tavern which once stood midway between York and Scarborough—have been brought here from other sites. Gardens, fences, and boardwalks complete the rustic scene, and the village is given added authenticity by the presence of old breeds of farm animals.

www.blackcreek.ca ✉ 1000 Murray Ross Pkwy., Downsview, 18 miles NW of downtown ☎ 416/736-1733 🕐 Closed Jan.–April 💲 $$

McMICHAEL CANADIAN ART COLLECTION

In 1954 Bob and Signe McMichael bought their first painting—"Montréal River" by Lawren Harris. The $250 it cost them was paid off on the installment plan. Over the years, they collected further works by the Canadian artists known as the Group of Seven (see pp. 186–87) and in 1965 donated this unique collection to the province of Ontario. What eventually became the country's largest collection of paintings by this renowned group is housed in several timber and fieldstone structures clustered around the McMichael's original 1951 cabin. Plenty of windows look out over the densely wooded Humber Valley, a landscape quite similar to the wilderness that inspired the artists. Now in provincial care, the collection consists of nearly 6,000 works, most of them donated by private collectors.

In addition to the paintings by the Group of Seven, there is an extensive collection of works by First Nations and Inuit artists and exhibitions of works by modern and living Canadian artists. But it is the evocations of the Canadian landscape by group members Lawren Harris, A.Y. Jackson, J.E.H. MacDonald, Franklin Carmichael, Arthur Lismer, Frederick Varley, and Frank Johnston that compel the greatest attention, together with work by their precursor, Tom Thomson, and those they influenced, like Emily Carr.

www.mcmichael.com ✉ 10365 Islington Ave., Kleinburg, 25 miles NW ☎ 905/893-1121 🚇 Subway: Yorkdale and long bus ride 💲 $$

METRO TORONTO ZOO

This magnificent zoo occupies over a square mile of parkland, within which superbly designed pavilions and external spaces house more than 4,000 animals in natural habitats. Thus the luxuriant vegetation of the Africa pavilion provides a home to monkeys, gorillas, pygmy hippos, and pythons, while outside roam zebras, lions, cheetahs, and elephants. Other pavilions are devoted to the wildlife of Eurasia, the Americas, the Indo-Malayan Peninsula, and Australia. www.torontozoo.com ✉ 361A Old Finch Ave., Meadowvale Road, Scarborough, about 24 miles NE of downtown ☎ 416/392-5900 💲 $$$

ONTARIO SCIENCE CENTRE

One of the first of its kind, the lavishly equipped Ontario Science Centre makes science and technology not just fascinating, but fun. Opened in 1969, it is housed in an early masterpiece by architect Raymond Moriyama, a series of glass-walled pavilions that respects the natural forms and vegetation of the ravine in which it is set. Inside are more than 800 interactive exhibits, embracing every aspect of the human relationship with the physical world. You can land on the moon, keep a hot-air balloon in flight, instigate an earthquake, and enjoy a hair-raising electrical charge. There is also an OMNIMAX theater. www.ontariosciencecentre.ca ✉ 770 Don Mills Rd., Don Mills, 7 miles NE of downtown via Don Valley Pkwy. ☎ 416/696-1000 💲 $$$

OSHAWA

Oshawa *(www.oshawa.com)* began as a port, but owes its fortune to the automobile works created by Robert S. McLaughlin (1871–1972). Responsible for shifting the emphasis of the family firm from carriages to cars, McLaughlin sold the business to General Motors in 1918, becoming G.M.'s vice president. His opulent estate and luxurious gardens at **Parkwood** *(270 Simcoe St. North, tel 905/433-4311)* attest to his wealth and fine taste. The products that he helped to found are on display at the **Canadian Automotive Museum** *(99 Simcoe St. South, tel 905/576-1222),* which traces the evolution of the car in Canada. ■

Sure to shock—the Van de Graaff Generator at the Ontario Science Centre

Canadian painting & the Group of Seven

Until the early 20th century, Canadian art was strongly tied to European models. Canadian artists were trained in the traditions and techniques of the Old Masters and of contemporary art movements on the far side of the Atlantic. This did not, however, inhibit an open-hearted response to the special character of the Canadian landscape or its inhabitants. Between them the country's major art galleries give a comprehensive and fascinating account of the changing ways in which artists have seen this vast country.

Of German ancestry, the highly accomplished Cornelius Krieghoff (1815–1872) painted countless picturesque scenes—especially snowscapes—of life in Québec, in a style owing much to Dutch genre paintings. Krieghoff's contemporary Paul Kane, who was born in Ireland in 1810, accompanied fur traders across the prairies and over the Rockies to the Pacific coast, sketching all he saw en route (including the last great bison hunt). Still in the genre mode, his works

constitute a wonderful record of the West as it stood on the brink of change. At the end of the 19th century, painters from Québec were strongly influenced by the French Impressionists, whose techniques they applied to the landscapes and cityscapes of eastern Canada. The way Montréalers look at their winter city will probably always be influenced by the urban snowscapes of Maurice Cullen (1866–1934), while Québec City and its surroundings received a similar treatment from James Wilson Morrice (1865–1924).

A later generation of artists, based in Toronto, deliberately set out to create a school of painting that would not only record the Canadian scene, but would reinforce a distinctive Canadian identity. Calling themselves the Group of Seven, they proclaimed in their exhibition catalog of 1920 that they were "imbued with the idea that an Art must grow and flower in the land before the country will be a real home for its people."

The group's origins date back to the 1911 showing in Toronto of "At the Edge of the

Maple Wood" by the Montréal painter A.Y. Jackson. Its vibrant color and texture made a deep impression on local artists, who persuaded Jackson to come to Toronto. Here he shared studio space with his admirers, and began to accompany the self-taught Tom Thomson on sketching trips to Algonquin Park to the north of the city. Thomson was a countryman, an expert with rod, gun, and canoe paddle; his crude style was refined thanks to the influence of Jackson and the other painters, who in turn were inspired by Thomson's understanding of land and landscape and by his bold technique.

A prosperous patron, Dr. James MacCallum, lent the group his summer residence on Georgian Bay. Together with the wealthy artist Lawren Harris (1885–1970), who was connected with the agricultural machinery firm of Massey-Harris, MacCallum provided the painters with the famous Studio Building overlooking Toronto's Rosedale Ravine. Holed up in a shack on the studio's grounds, Thomson worked up some of his finest paintings from oil sketches made in the wild; among them were some of the nation's most loved pictures, including "The West Wind" and "The Jack Pine." Thomson's death by drowning in 1917 was a terrible shock to his friends, who nevertheless came together in 1920 to formally found the Group of Seven. In addition to Jackson and Harris, they included Frederick Varley, Frank Johnston, Arthur Lismer, Franklin Carmichael, and J.E.H. MacDonald. They devoted themselves to the wild Canadian Shield, often depicting it in a way that owed much to Thomson's vigorous handling of color and texture. But each member of the group had his own distinctive vision and his own technique. Macdonald's painting was perhaps the closest to Thomson's, while Lismer's depictions of the "Canadian Jungle" have an intensity all their own. Varley excelled at portraiture, while Carmichael was as much at home among farmsteads and mining towns as in nature. Harris developed even more elemental landscapes of the far north before turning to complete abstraction. ■

Left: The Group of Seven at Toronto's Arts and Letters Club (ca 1920)
Below: "In Algonquin Park" (ca 1914, oil on canvas) by Tom Thomson, precursor of the Group

Niagara Falls

🄰 157 E1

Niagara Falls Visitor & Convention Bureau
www.niagarafallstourism.com

✉ 5515 Stanley Ave.
☎ 905/356-6061 or 800/563-2557

Maid of the Mist
www.maidofthemist.com

✉ Access by elevator from 5920 River Rd.
☎ 905/358-5781
🕐 Operates daily late April–late Oct., weather permitting
💲 $$$

American Falls illuminated

"TO SAY ANYTHING ABOUT THIS WONDROUS PLACE would be sheer nonsense," exclaimed Charles Dickens upon visiting Niagara Falls in 1842. In fact, the great Victorian wordsmith did go on to remark that "it would be harder for a man to stand nearer to God than he does here." Few people fail to be deeply stirred by this awesome manifestation of elemental forces, though they might share Dickens' modesty in putting it into adequate words.

Although the days of tightrope-walking and barrel-riding are long since past, the falls can be experienced in a number of ways. Since 1876 the sturdy little *Maid of the Mist* boats have nudged their way through the spray, past the **American Falls** to the very foot of the **Horseshoe Falls.** An elevator decants its passengers onto an outdoor observation platform or into tunnels that lead to miraculous views from behind the Horseshoe Falls. Rising from the top of the steep slope marking the edge of the town of Niagara Falls are observation towers that give spectacular panoramas of the falls. Finally, a promenade and parkway accompany the Niagara River as it accelerates toward the falls, crashes into the depths, then reconstitutes itself as a river and foams down the gorge toward its outlet into Lake Ontario. The most crowded spot is **Table Rock,** where the promenade directly overlooks the very lip of the cataract.

Niagara Falls are the result of dynamic geological processes that continue to this day. As the glaciers retreated at the end of the last ice age, about 12,000 years ago, the waters of Lake Erie, which had previously drained southward, found an outlet over the Niagara Escarpment into Lake Ontario. Since then the softer underlying shales and sandstones of the escarpment have been continuously eroded by the action of falling water, causing the harder upper layer of limestone to collapse. The vertical face of the falls is maintained, but the falls themselves slowly move back upstream, leaving

behind a steadily lengthening gorge, now some 7 miles from **Queenston,** the original point of entry to the then much higher Lake Ontario.

The abstraction of water to generate hydroelectricity has slowed the rate of erosion, originally about 3 feet a year, to about one foot every ten years. Nevertheless, the southward retreat of the falls is destined to continue. At some point in the distant future, **Goat Island,** which at present separates the American Falls (1,000 feet long) from the Horseshoe Falls (2,600 feet long) will disappear, and

the falls will eventually meet Lake Erie and probably become a series of rapids.

Originally the home of the Neutral Indians, who were largely wiped out by the Iroquois, the Niagara area had a mild climate, fertile soils, and a strategic location between two of the Great Lakes. Early explorers had been intrigued by local tales of a great cataract somewhere in the heart of the continent. Récollet Father Louis Hennepin wrote in 1678 about "Waters which fall from a horrible Precipice … making an outrageous Noise, more terrible than that of

Canadians take pride in noting that "their" falls are more dramatic than those on the U.S. side.

Thunder." Hennepin's fellow Frenchmen founded a trading post at Lewiston in 1721, then built Fort Niagara (now on the U.S. side) to guard the river's outlet into Lake Ontario. In 1759 the British took control of the Niagara area from the French; during the Revolutionary War and later, during the War of 1812, the area was the scene of much conflict between the combatants. The peace established in 1814 allowed both Canadians and Americans to concentrate on the problems and opportunities presented by the falls. The barrier they presented to navigation was overcome, first by the construction of the Erie Canal in 1825 (see p. 192), which linked the upper Niagara River to the Hudson, then by the Welland Canal (1829), which connected Lakes Erie and Ontario across the Niagara Peninsula.

Sightseers have visited the falls ever since they were first discovered. A crude inn was built at Table Rock at the end of the 18th century, but the real commercialization began in the early 19th century.

By the 1870s, squalid shacks and tawdry booths aimed at exploiting visitors had reached such proportions that a commission (predecessor of today's Niagara Parks Commission) was founded to regulate the needs of ever increasing numbers of visitors (currently more than 14 million a year).

The viewing areas and manicured **Niagara Parkway** showcases the commission's efforts; meanwhile, the showmen and hucksters have retreated to the city of Niagara Falls, where the attractions range from honeymoon hotels to Dracula's Castle and the Believe It Or Not Museum.

The doughty *Maid of the Mist* is an enduring symbol of Niagara Falls.

WELLAND CANAL

Completed in 1932, the present canal, the fourth to link Lakes Erie and Ontario, runs 28 miles from Port Colbourne, Ontario, to Port Weller, Ontario. Part of the St. Lawrence Seaway, its eight locks overcome a height difference between the two lakes of 326 feet and accept "salties" (oceangoing ships) and "lakers" weighing 30,000 tons or more and as long as two football fields. View some of the passing vessels from the visitor center at Lock No. 3, near the city of St. Catharines. ∎

Maj. Gen. Sir Isaac Brock, the fearless British commander who fell at the Battle of Queenston Heights

ALONG THE NIAGARA PARKWAY

The 35-mile parkway along the Niagara River between Lakes Erie and Ontario completed in 1923 was enjoyed by Winston Churchill, who described it as "the prettiest Sunday afternoon drive in the world."

Restored **Fort Erie** *(Tel 905/871-0540)* marks the southern limit of the drive, 20 miles south of the falls. First built by the British in 1764, the fort was twice destroyed by masses of ice driven ashore from the lake. U.S. forces captured the third fort in 1814, and demolished it before their withdrawal.

Just upstream from the falls stands the enormous neoclassic **Toronto Power Generating Station,** completed in 1913. Its generators shut down in 1974, but it remains an imposing relic of the numerous schemes on both sides of the border to harness the power of the falls to generate electricity. In order to maintain the flow of water over the falls and give visitors the spectacle they have come here for, the amount of water diverted is strictly regulated by international treaty, with greater quantities drawn off at night and outside the main visitor season. Downstream from the falls, the river narrows and foams over rapids. The elevator of the **White Water Walk** *(Tel 905/374-1221)* descends to a boardwalk with a close-up view of the angry-looking waters. At a bend a half mile farther north, cables slung across the gorge carry the charming old **Whirlpool Aero Car** *(Tel 905/354-8983)* high above the Whirlpool Rapids, where the agitated river swirls in a spiral before resuming its course downstream.

At the **Niagara Glen Nature Reserve,** it is possible to escape the crowds by hiking into the gorge and wandering through a landscape of fallen boulders and luxuriant deciduous forest. More trees, as well as immaculately maintained flowers and shrubs, are on show at the delightful botanical gardens of the **Niagara Parks Commission's School of Horticulture** *(Tel 905/371-0254).*

The original location of the falls was at **Queenston Heights** on the Niagara Escarpment, now an attractive and popular park *(8 miles N of the falls, tel 877/642-7275)*. The heights were fiercely contested in the War of 1812, and it was here that Maj. Gen. Sir Isaac Brock fell while leading a Canadian counterattack against the Americans. Narrow stairs lead to Brock's statue atop the 184-foot column commemorating him. Another heroic figure is remembered by a memorial on the heights, as well as at the **Laura Secord Homestead** *(29 Queenston St., tel 905/262-4851)* in the pretty village of Queenston itself. In 1813, having overheard American officers discussing their plans, Laura Secord rushed 20 miles through difficult terrain to warn the British of the impending attack, enabling them to ambush and defeat their opponents at the Battle of Beaver Dams.

NIAGARA-ON-THE-LAKE

Elegant, early 19th-century brick and clapboard houses line tree-shaded streets, making this little town at the outlet of the Niagara River into Lake Ontario one of the most charming in Canada. Originally called Newark, it was the first capital of Upper Canada in 1792, but within two years fears about its proximity to the American frontier had ceded that role to York (later renamed Toronto). The fears were very well grounded; in 1813

the Americans burned the town to the ground and consequently destroyed some of the finest Georgian mansions in Canada. Rebuilding took place almost immediately, in the best possible taste, and the look of the town has hardly changed since. This is partly thanks to the fact that, from the late 1820s on, commerce no longer flowed this way, but along the new Welland Canal. Among the refined shops on broad Queen Street—with its central clock tower—is the delightful **Apothecary**, dating

from 1866 *(Tel 905/468-3845, closed mid-Sept.–mid-May)*. **St. Andrew's Church** is a particularly impressive example of a Georgian church building.

Just outside the town is **Fort George National Historic Site** *(Queens Parade, tel 905/468-4257, closed Nov.–March)*. Burned during the War of 1812, its earthworks survived and in the 1930s its palisade and most of the structures within it, including barracks, artificer's shop, and powder magazine, were rebuilt. ∎

Early 19th-century elegance at Niagara-on-the-Lake

Niagara-on-the-Lake
🅰 157 E1
Visitor information
www.niagaraonthelake.com
✉ 26 Queen St.
☎ 905/468-1950

Canadian wines

To the surprise of many visitors, this northern land not only produces wine of fine quality (and in some quantity, too), but also has vineyards and wineries that are attractive places to visit. Vineyard tours and tastings enhance a stay in the two main production areas, southern Ontario and southern British Columbia.

With vineyards covering about 18,000 acres, southern Ontario is the heartland of Canadian wine. Most of the vines are concentrated on the Niagara Peninsula, but there are also vineyards on the north shore of Lake Erie near Windsor and on Pelee Island. The success of viticulture in the area is not surprising, given its location at the same latitude as Spain's Rioja, France's Languedoc-Roussillon, and northern California. The difference, of course, is the climate. But the harsh Canadian winter is tempered by the presence of Lakes Erie and Ontario, which absorb heat in the summer and slowly release it as the land cools down in winter. The lakes also produce refreshing breezes to mitigate the effects of the fierce summer sun.

The first vines were planted in the area more than 150 years ago. But for a long time Canadians' favorite tipples were beer and whiskey; wine was only drunk in tiny quantities, and Canadian grapes were mostly turned into fortified sherry- or port-type beverages that wine connoisseurs would hardly recognize. All this has changed in recent decades; palates have become more sophisticated and local growers, stimulated by the increased import of American wine thanks to the Canada-U.S. Free Trade Agreement, have looked for ways to satisfy them.

Some wineries got clever, abandoning the reliable but boring labrusca grape for hybrid or European grape varieties adapted to the particular soil and microclimatic conditions of individual vineyards. The results were dramatic. Since the early 1990s, Ontario wines have been winning prizes at international events and have been gaining the approval of seasoned wine drinkers. The cellars of the prestigious Royal York Hotel in

Connoisseurs can be surprised by the fine wines of these seemingly northern latitudes.

Toronto may still be full of fine Burgundy and Bordeaux, but the establishment is also proud to offer the wines of the Niagara peninsula.

The well-marked **Wine Route** (For information contact Niagara-on-the-Lake visitor center. See p. 193) around the Niagara peninsula is an excellent way of getting to know this fascinating area, with its rich mixture of vineyards and wineries, orchards, natural attractions, historic places, and numerous festivals. The wineries are open to the public, offering tastings and vineyard tours, as well as bistros, restaurants, events and entertainment, and even bed-and-breakfasts.

Most Niagara wines are whites, Chardonnays, Pinot Blancs, Rieslings, and Vidals, but there are fine reds, too: Cabernets, Gamay Noirs, and Merlots. Ice wine has become a specialty. In Germany, its country of origin, Eiswein can only be made when winter sets in early. As a result, it is incredibly expensive. Canadian ice wine is more affordable, thanks to the reliable frostiness of the Canadian winter. The grapes are left on the vine until December or even January, picked (by freezing hands!) and pressed while still frozen. With most of the water in the grape

Predictable summer sun and an abundance of moisture help mature the grapes in the vineyards of southern Ontario.

locked up in crystals, the resulting syrupy liquid is rich and luscious. But there's not much of it, and the delicious wine (usually presented in 375 ml half-bottles) is best reserved for an extra special occasion.

Far to the west of Ontario, British Columbia's vineyards are concentrated in the Okanagan area, close to the U.S. border, though vines also grow in the lower Fraser Valley and on Vancouver Island. If southern Ontario corresponds with Bordeaux, the more northerly Okanagan is close to the latitude of France's Champagne and the Rhine Valley in Germany. As in Ontario, a great lake tempers winter cold, while irrigation helps to overcome the dearth of rain, which in the south sometimes amounts to only six inches a year. Most of the province's wines are whites, but there is an increasing number of rather light but sophisticated reds. ■

Huron-Erie Peninsula

Kitchener & Waterloo

 157 D1

Visitor information

www.kw-visitor.on.ca

✉ 191 King St..

☎ 519/745-3536 or 800/265-6959

🕐 Closed weekends Sept.—June

A place for quiet contemplation as well as serious horticultural study and research— Hamilton's immaculate Royal Botanical Gardens

JUTTING SOUTHWEST FROM METROPOLITAN TORONTO toward the U.S. border with Michigan, the Huron-Erie Peninsula divides two Great Lakes and ends in the southernmost point on Canada's mainland. The character of the peninsula changes along the way, beginning with the commercial centers of Kitchener, Waterloo, and Hamilton, and becoming increasingly more rural.

KITCHENER & WATERLOO

Until the outbreak of World War I, when the city patriotically adopted the name of a British field marshal, Kitchener was known as Berlin, a reflection of its predominantly German character. The first German speakers, Mennonites from Pennsylvania, came to this area in 1805, their pacifism having made them unwelcome in the United States. They were joined by German immigrants who farmed or, as skilled workers and entrepreneurs, built the city's commercial and industrial reputation. Today, people of German descent make up roughly half of the population of Kitchener and its twin, Waterloo. The dark-clad and plain-living Mennonites have mostly retreated to the countryside; their little black, horse-drawn buggies can sometimes be seen on back roads, perhaps heading to the market town of **St. Jacobs,** where many of their crafts are displayed for sale.

Kitchener is at its most Germanic on Saturdays (and Wednesdays in summer months), when the sausage stalls of the **Farmers' Market** *(Market Sq., 300 King St. E.)* present a tempting array of wurst. Every fall, wurst is consumed in quantity with

the limitless flow of beer at the Oktoberfest, second only to Munich's famous festival for general enjoyment and *Gemütlichkeit* (amiability).

The oldest building in town was the home of the first sausage king, Joseph Schneider. His attractive frame farmhouse, built around 1816, is now a museum with German-Canadian memorabilia *(Joseph Schneider Haus, 466 Queen St. S., tel 519/742-7752)*. Another residence open to the public is **Woodside National Historic Site** *(528 Wellington St. N., tel 519/571-5684)*, the completely rebuilt boyhood home of long-serving Prime Minister William Lyon Mackenzie King. In old age, King was consulted about the restoration and furnishing of the brick-built house, which among other items includes some belongings of his equally eminent grandfather, William Lyon Mackenzie, leader of the ill-fated Rebellion of 1837 (see p. 36).

HAMILTON

At the western end of Lake Ontario, the steel town of Hamilton claims two outstanding attractions in addition to the **Art Gallery of Hamilton** *(123 King St. West, tel 905/527-6610, closed Mon.)*, which showcases a fine collection of Canadian and international art.

The splendid porticoed neo-classic villa known as **Dundurn Castle** *(610 York Blvd., tel 905/546-2872, closed Mon. Sept.–May)* was built in 1835 for Sir Allen Napier MacNab, one of the most powerful members of Upper Canada's oligarchy, the Family Compact. MacNab rose from humble beginnings to great wealth, to a knighthood conferred for his part in crushing the Mackenzie Rebellion, and finally to high office as prime minister of what by then had become the province of Canada.

The park around his castle provides fine views over Hamilton Harbour and the city where he made his fortune in land dealings.

On the far side of the isthmus linking Hamilton with Burlington are the **Royal Botanical Gardens** *(680 Plains Rd. W., tel 905/527-1158)*. Extending along the shoreline of the harbor and covering a total area of 2,700 acres, this is a vast and exceptionally fine collection of trees, shrubs, and flowers, impossible to take in on a single visit. Features of special interest include a lilac garden with more than 800 varieties, a lavish rock garden in a former quarry, a two-acre rose garden, and a terraced Mediterranean garden that enjoys southern Ontario's Mediterranean light but is protected from its winter by a great conservatory.

STRATFORD

A former railroad town, Stratford has acquired an international reputation for its annual **Shakespeare Festival** *(Tel 800/587-1600, www.stratford-festival.on.ca)*. The festival was first staged in 1953, when Sir (then Mr.) Alec Guinness

The great blue heron thrives in the wetlands of southern Ontario.

Hamilton
🅼 157 D1
Visitor information
www.hamiltonundiscovered.com
✉ 34 James St. S.
☎ 905/546-2666

Stratford
🅼 157 D1
Visitor information
www.city.stratford.on.ca
✉ York St.
☎ 519/273-3352

✉ 47 Downie St.
☎ 519/271-5140
🕐 Closed weekends

starred in *Richard III*, beneath a huge tent. In 1957 a permanent building was completed, inspired by the layout of the Elizabethan theater, with the audience sitting around three sides of the stage.

The festival has gone from strength to strength, and can claim to be one of the foremost classical theater festivals in North America, with an annual attendance of more than 600,000 people.

Mohawk chief Joseph Brant, Brantford

Brantford
🅰 157 D1
Visitor information
www.visitbrantford.ca
☎ 519/751-9900

Point Pelee NP
🅰 157 D1
Visitor information
www.pc.gc.ca
☎ 519/322-2365
💲 $

Point Pelee National Park

BRANTFORD

This country town owes its name to Mohawk war chief Joseph Brant, who fought on the British side in the American Revolution. Forced to leave the United States after the war, he and his followers resettled here on land granted by the British government. King George III paid for **Her Majesty's Chapel of the Mohawks** (*355 Mohawk St., tel 519/756-0240*), a modest clapboard structure built in 1785 and the oldest place of worship in Ontario.

Brantford was also the home of the inventor of the telephone, Alexander Graham Bell (1847–1922), who moved here from Scotland in 1870. The **Bell**

Homestead (*94 Tutela Heights Rd., tel 519/756-6220, closed Mon.*) chronicles the inventiveness of this extraordinary man, as well as showcasing his family's comfortable lifestyle. The world's first long-distance telephone call was made from here to Paris, Ontario, 7 miles away, in 1876.

POINT PELEE NATIONAL PARK

Point Pelee, the southernmost point in mainland Canada, is a sand spit extending 10 miles into Lake Erie. Designated a national park in 1918, the southern part of the peninsula claims a greater variety of flora and fauna than anywhere else in Canada. In some places, luxuriant near-jungle growth tangled with vine-draped trees resemble the southern United States more than Canada. Even more compelling is its overlapping position on the Mississippi and Atlantic flyways, making it a stopover for vast numbers of migrating birds in spring and fall. Bird-watchers from all over North America and from as far away as Europe crowd the park to observe at least some of the 350 species that have been recorded here. The spring migration, in May, is the more colorful, with the birds decked out in their mating plumage; the fall scene is equally impressive and lasts longer, usually through September and October. Another fall migrant, the monarch butterfly, congregates on the hackberries near the tip of the peninsula before setting off on the long flight to Mexico's Sierra Madre.

Stopping points along the road fringing the western shore of the peninsula give access to trails into the different habitats, which include shifting shorelines and extensive wetlands. From the visitor center, a shuttle takes visitors to the tip of Point Pelee. ∎

More places to visit on the Huron-Erie Peninsula

FORT MALDEN

Forced by Jay's Treaty of 1794 to abandon their Detroit base, the British withdrew to this splendid site overlooking the Detroit River as it flows into Lake Erie. In addition to the fort, they established a naval dockyard that turned out vessels of up to 400 tons to secure British interests on the Great Lakes. The fort saw action in the War of 1812, when it was occupied by U.S. forces, and during the Mackenzie Rebellion of 1837 (see pp. 36 & 173). Barracks as well as substantial earthworks are on view.
157 D1 www.pc.gc.ca ⊠ 100 Laird Ave., Amherstburg ☎ 519/736-5416 $ $

GODERICH

This port and resort town on the shore of Lake Huron was the terminus of the famous Huron Road, cut through the primeval forest of western Ontario in the 1820s to encourage pioneer settlement. The town has kept its planned layout, with leafy streets radiating from a central octagonal square. The splendid stone-built 1842 **Huron Historic Gaol** *(181 Victoria St. North, tel 519/524-6971, closed Nov.–May)* combined cells and courtroom. The country's last public hanging took place here in 1865. The displays in the local **Huron County Museum** *(110 North St., tel 519/524-2686, closed Sun. Dec.–March)* bring home the immense effort that went into the conversion of the forest into today's neat pattern of fields and farmsteads.
157 D1 **Visitor information** www.town.goderich.on.ca ⊠ 91 Hamilton St. ☎ 519/524-6600

WINDSOR

Looking north across the Detroit River to its far larger neighbor on the American shore, Windsor is Canada's southernmost city. The town's origins go back to the early 18th century, when French settlers established themselves on the southern bank of the river.

Vehicle manufacture began in Windsor in 1904, when the Ford Motor Company of Canada joined the town's previous largest employer, the distillery, which now houses the **Windsor Community Museum** *(254 Pitt St. W., tel 519/253-1812, closed Mon., & Sun. Oct.–April)*. By the 1920s, Windsor liked to call itself the Auto Capital of the British Empire, and had dozens of car plants and component producers.

The town is connected to Detroit by rail, by the Ambassador road bridge, and by the world's first (1926) international road tunnel.
157 D1 **Visitor information** www.visitwindsor.com ⊠ 333 Riverside Dr. W. ☎ 519/255-6530 🕐 Closed weekends ∎

The Windsor Community Museum is housed in this attractive early 19th-century brick house built by François Baby.

Southern Ontario's weekend paradise

Peterborough

🅰 157 E2

Visitor information

www.thekawarthas.net

✉ 175 George St. N.

☎ 705/742-2201

🕐 Closed Sun.

Petroglyphs Provincial Park

✉ 34 miles NE of Peterborough via Hwy. 28

☎ 705/722-8061

🕐 Closed mid-Oct.–mid-May

💲 $$

Peterborough Lift Lock Visitor Centre

www.pc.gc.ca

✉ Hunter St. E., Peterborough

☎ 705/750-4950

🕐 Closed mid-Oct.–March

💲 $$

VISITORS MAY MAKE THE LAKESHORE DRIVE TO NIAGARA a priority, but come the weekend, the inhabitants of urban Ontario head north to the fringe of the Canadian Shield, where cottage country gives way to real wilderness only two to three hours' drive from the metropolis.

PETERBOROUGH

Growing up as a logging center, Peterborough became the largest town along the 240-mile **Trent-Severn Canal,** which linked Trenton on Lake Ontario to the eastern shore of Georgian Bay. The Peterborough canoe, a particularly efficient example of that archetypal Canadian craft, was developed here. The town is now best known as the urban center for the **Kawartha Lakes,** the popular recreation and weekend cottage region that stretches westward to **Lake Simcoe.**

The freight once carried on the canal has long since transferred to road and rail, and the waterway is now used instead by leisure craft making the week-long trip between Lakes Ontario and Huron. The most impressive structure in Peterborough is the canal's **Lift Lock No. 21,** at 65 feet the highest hydraulic elevator in the world at the time of its construction in 1904 and the first of its kind in North America. Boats are raised and lowered simultaneously in twin chambers, each of which holds 1,700 tons of water. A modern visitor center has displays on this century-old engineering marvel.

In the forest close to **Stony Lake,** 34 miles northeast of Peterborough, is Canada's biggest concentration of native stone carvings. Now protected in **Petroglyphs Provincial Park,** more than 800 petroglyphs were carved in the bedrock of this southernmost extension of the Canadian Shield up to one thousand years ago, probably by Algonkian-speaking people. For the contemporary Ojibwa people, this is a sacred place, its symbolic shapes and figures full of significance.

Muskoka Lakes is cottage country par excellence, a gorgeous chunk of Canadian Shield whose

lakes and forests are a mere two-hour drive north of Toronto.

The area's rise to recreational paradise began in the late 19th century, when luxury hotels attracted wealthy guests in search of wilderness plus comfort from as far afield as Europe. Changing lifestyles, combined with the destruction by fire of many of the original hotels, has altered the character of the area; some 20,000 weekend and vacation houses now occupy the wooded shorelines of Lakes Joseph, Rosseau, and Muskoka. The towns of **Bracebridge, Gravenhurst,** and **Huntsville** help cater to the needs of up to a million and a half visitors a year. In summer, it is still possible to board the pleasure steamer **Segwun** *(Tel 705/687-6667)* built in 1887 for an old-fashioned trundle among the myriad wooded islands.

GEORGIAN BAY

Virtually separated from Lake Huron by the Bruce Peninsula and Manitoulin Island, this vast stretch of water is sometimes referred to as the sixth Great Lake. Its rugged eastern shore and myriad islands are extremely popular with vacationers; their landscape of shining water, bare rock, and wind-blasted pines were favorite subjects of the Group of Seven painters.

Midland

A popular launch for boat trips around the Georgian Bay islands, this port and manufacturing town makes the most of its location in former Huronia, where the Huron,

Georgian Bay
⚐ 157 D2

You can easily find solitude in the woods and waterways of southern Ontario.

Midland
📍 157 D2
Visitor information
www.town.midland.on.ca
✉ 208 King St.
☎ 705/526-7884
🕐 Closed weekends Oct.—May

Sainte-Marie among the Hurons
📍 157 D2
www.saintemarieamongthe hurons.on.ca
✉ 3 miles E of Midland on Hwy. 12
☎ 705/526-7838
🕐 Closed Nov.—April
💲 $$

Penetanguishene
📍 157 D2

Georgian Bay Islands National Park
📍 157 D2
Visitor information
www.pc.gc.ca
✉ P.O. Box 9, Midland
☎ 705/526-9804

or Wendat, people lived during the period of French contact. There is a **Huronia Museum** and a reconstructed **Huron Indian Village** (both in Little Lake Park), but the best place to become acquainted with the area's troubled past is the reconstructed Jesuit mission known as Sainte-Marie among the Hurons.

Sainte-Marie among the Hurons

In the early 17th century, the Huron people of the Huron-Erie Peninsula led a settled life, practicing agriculture around their palisaded villages and acting as middlemen in the European fur trade (see pp. 220–21). Their social cohesion was undermined by the French missionaries' attack on ancestral beliefs as well as by a panoply of European diseases. These factors made them easy prey for the invading Iroquois from the south, who either killed them or absorbed them into their own society. By the 18th century, the area was almost completely depopulated.

These events and the context in which they took place are brilliantly evoked at Sainte-Marie among the Hurons, a reconstruction of the mission established in 1639 by Jesuits on the banks of the Wye River near present-day Midland. An enthralling audiovisual presentation precedes a visit to the settlement, which has some 20 rebuilt structures within its timber palisade. There were separate quarters for missionaries and their helpers and for the natives, who lived in tepees and longhouses that some Jesuits only entered with reluctance.

Increasingly harassed by the Iroquois, the Jesuits and many of their Huron protégés abandoned the mission in 1649, first setting it on fire. The failure of the mission

and the savagery of the Iroquois attack made a lasting impression on the European mind. The torturing to death of several of the Jesuit missionaries was depicted by Goya, and in 1930 several of them were canonized by Pope Pius XI. They are also commemorated at the nearby **Martyrs' Shrine,** a twin-towered church erected in 1926.

Penetanguishene

This bilingual little town on an inlet of Georgian Bay began as a community of French fur traders and voyageurs. In 1817 they were joined by the soldiers and sailors of the Royal Navy base established to keep a watchful eye on American activities on the Upper Lakes at **Discovery Harbour** (93 Jury Dr., tel 705/549-8064). More than a dozen buildings at the base have been rebuilt, and a number of vessels are moored at the dock. Among them are authentically rigged reproductions of the supply schooners that once sailed the lake. Today, the schooners are available for pleasure tours conducted by equally authentic-looking jolly Jack Tars.

GEORGIAN BAY ISLANDS NATIONAL PARK

The starting point for a boat ride to this string of some 60 islands along the east coast of Georgian Bay is little Honey Harbour, at the end of Rte. 3 off Hwy. 69. The biggest island is **Beausoleil,** where walking trails lead through two distinct landscapes. To the south, a mixed forest of conifer and hardwood grows on deep soil deposited by retreating glaciers, while to the north the same glaciers scoured the granite, gneiss, and quartz bedrock, creating the elemental shield landscape that the Group of Seven painters (see pp. 186–87) found so inspiring.

BRUCE PENINSULA

Partly separating Georgian Bay from the main body of Lake Huron, the tip of the 50-mile-long Bruce Peninsula holds two of Ontario's most fascinating national parks. The main feature of "The Bruce" is the Niagara Escarpment, which here forms 200-foot cliffs along the eastern shore of the peninsula, their bleached limestone contrasting with the intense blues of the clear water and with the dark greens of the trees. Along the escarpment runs Canada's first long-distance hiking path, the **Bruce Trail**. Beginning at Queenstown more than 400 miles away, the trail reaches a scenic climax here before terminating at **Tobermory,** the ferry port for the crossing to Manitoulin Island *(Tel 519/376-6601)*. The final, spectacular section of the trail can be reached from **Cyprus Lake** in **Bruce Peninsula National Park** *(P.O. Box 189, Tobermory, tel 519/596-2233)*, 55 square miles of forest and wetland, where more than 40 species of orchid flourish.

The peninsula's other protected area, **Fathom Five National Marine Park** *(Tel 519/596-2233)*, is Canada's first park of its kind, set up in 1987 to preserve the pristine lake environment. In addition to underwater caves and other submerged features of the Niagara Escarpment, there are dramatically sculpted freestanding limestone columns known as "flowerpots" because of their topping of scraggy tree growth. Scuba divers come here to enjoy the exceptionally clear water and to admire the many shipwrecks, some of which can also be seen from glass-bottomed boats.

ALGONQUIN PROVINCIAL PARK

Covering an area greater than Prince Edward Island, this 2,934-square-mile park on the edge of the Canadian Shield marks the transition between northern coniferous forest and the southern forest of maple, beech, and birch. Its wildlife is accordingly rich and varied, with some 250 species of birds as well as moose, deer, beavers, bears, and wolves. More than 2,500 lakes stud its surface, many linked along 1,000 miles of canoe trails.

Its designation in 1893 was intended not just to conserve nature, but also to satisfy timber interests; logging continues today, though careful management ensures minimal impact on the most visited places.

Algonquin celebrated the 100th anniversary of its designation with the opening of a lavish **visitor center.** It is located on the Parkway Corridor, the sliver of land along Hwy. 60 in the southwestern corner of the park where most facilities are concentrated. ∎

Camping by the Barron River in Algonquin Provincial Park

Bruce Peninsula
🅰 157 D2

Algonquin Provincial Park
🅰 157 E2
Algonquin visitor center
www.algonquinpark.on.ca
✉ 30 miles from West Gate (Hwy. 60)
☎ 705/633-5572
🕐 Closed weekdays Nov.–April

Minerals & mining towns

When incredibly hot magma flows welled up from the earth's interior and forced apart the hard and ancient rocks of the Canadian Shield, they created ideal conditions for the formation of mineral veins. Indeed, in the 19th and 20th centuries, rich veins of gold and silver, nickel, cobalt, zinc, copper, and iron lured prospectors to northern Ontario's shield country, an otherwise inhospitable region. Many mines have long since been worked out and abandoned; some have disappeared, reclaimed by the ubiquitous forest, others have been turned into visitor attractions. Elsewhere, the shield continues to give up its riches, in places such as Sudbury (see p. 206), with its billion-dollar nickel production, transforming the landscape on a truly gigantic scale.

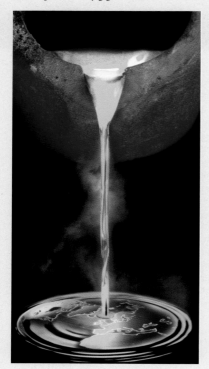

Molten gold, glowing symbol of Canada's mineral wealth

Measuring 35 miles long and 16 miles across, the Sudbury Basin may have been created by volcanic processes or by the devastating impact millions of years ago of a meteorite. Interestingly, it was here that NASA astronauts Neil Armstrong and Buzz Aldrin familiarized themselves with North America's closest approximation to a lunar environment before their epoch-making trip to the moon in 1969. Sudbury has made amends for a century of reckless mineral exploitation, and much of the scraped and polluted surface of the surrounding country is green once more. The city also brings five billion years of the region's geological history alive with Science North's 3-D film and laser show (see p. 208).

Gold & silver

Next to nickel in terms of production, and far ahead in glamour, is Ontario's gold, the search for which led to the establishment of mining camps across the whole of northern Canada from the Québec border to Manitoba.

Nowadays you are unlikely to meet more than a handful of other vehicles on the road running north from Ignace (150 miles north of Thunder Bay) to Pickle Lake, but in the early 1900s it was packed with people heading to Ontario's Gold Belt, whose mines produced more of the precious metal than all the other mines in the province combined. The largest camps sprang into existence when the South Porcupine strike of 1909 unearthed an exceptionally rich deposit, and mines were sunk to a depth of 5,000 feet. The scattered mining settlements in the area were amalgamated in 1971 to form Timmins, which, covering 1,240 square miles, is the second largest city in North America, though its population amounts to fewer than 50,000 people.

Timmins is named for one Noah Timmins, who settled there after making his fortune in the Cobalt silver rush a few years earlier. The silver had been discovered in 1903 by workmen building the Ontario Northland Railway close to the Québec border. Within months dozens of shafts had been sunk, and by 1910 Cobalt was one of the largest silver producers in the world. The price paid was a ruined

Entering the tunnel of an Ontario gold mine

landscape stripped of trees, covered in slag, and undermined by abandoned pits and shafts. Those who could kept their distance from the workings, preferring to live in Haileybury and New Liskeard on the nearby shore of Lake Temiskaming.

Cobalt's fortunes swung with the changing value of silver on the world market; it once supported a population of 7,000, but today only a thousand or so live here, despite a recent upturn that permitted a limited reopening of the works. Visitors can tour the Heritage Silver Trail, a 4-mile drive around abandoned headframes and mine shafts. In Timmins, you can don miner's overalls, boots, lamp and helmet, and go down into the old Hollinger Gold Mine *(220 Algonquin Blvd. E., tel 705/360-8500, www.timminsgoldminetour .com).* After a walk through low-ceilinged tunnels, you can watch machinery at work, brace yourself for underground explosions, and even perhaps take some gold away as a souvenir. ■

North by Northwest in Ontario

WHILE MUCH OF NORTHERN ONTARIO IS INACCESSIBLE TO visitors, transcontinental roads and railroads access a scattering of towns of distinct character, national and provincial parks, and other areas where the magnificent Canadian Shield country can be easily enjoyed. Motorists heading westward can make for North Bay or Sudbury, or alternatively take the ferry from Tobermory on the Bruce Peninsula to 100-mile-long Manitoulin Island, which the Ojibwa called Island of the Great Spirit.

On the mainland, facing the north shore of Georgian Bay and reached from Sudbury, sprawls **Killarney Provincial Park** (*Tel 705/287-2900*). Promoted as the crown jewel of Ontario's parks, its delights—including the many lakes and spectacular quartzite ridges—are really accessible only on foot or by canoe.

The 350-mile stretch of Lake Superior shorelines between Sault Ste. Marie and Thunder Bay is one of the most spectacular in Canada. The lake, however, is not a hospitable environment. Blowing winds can be fierce—whipping waves up to 50 feet in height. Some of the finest stretches of shore are protected in **Lake Superior Provincial Park** (*Tel 705/856-2284*), which lies about 70 miles northwest of Sault Ste. Marie and is crossed by Trans-Canada 17. Here is Agawa Rock, a fearsome cliff rising 100 feet from the water, and painted with pictographs, one of which represents Mishipizjhiw, the "god of troubled waters." At **Pukaskwa National Park** (*P.O. Box 212, Heron Bay, tel 807/229-0801*), the granite of the shield meets the lake in massive headlands and boulder beaches, while **Sleeping Giant Provincial Park** (*Tel 807/977-2526*) consists of a tableland jutting 25 miles into the lake and shielding Thunder Bay from some of its storms.

NORTH BAY

Located on Lake Nipissing, North Bay's road and rail links underpin its claim to being the gateway to Ontario's "Near North." Vacationers enjoy the lake and the rivers that flow from it, once used by the traders who came this way on the fur route between the Ottawa River and Georgian Bay. The town is famous as the birthplace of the Dionne quintuplets (see p. 209), born here on May 28, 1934. Their birthplace is now the **Dionne Quints Museum** (*1375 Seymour St., tel 705/472-8480, closed mid-Oct.–mid-May*).

SUDBURY

Built on the ruthless exploitation of mineral resources (see p. 204) and the relentless destruction of the environment, Sudbury has metamorphosed into a regional capital with a wide range of amenities.

The Sudbury Basin's mineral wealth was discovered during the construction of the Canadian Pacific Railway, and has since been worked for its nickel, cobalt, gold, lead, platinum, selenium, silver, tellurium, and zinc. By the early 20th century, Sudbury was producing more than three-quarters of the world's nickel, while the impact of huge open-cast mines—severe air pollution from the ore roasting processes, and unchecked urban

North Bay
157 D3
Visitor information
www.city.north-bay.on.ca
City Hall, McIntyre St. E.
705/474-0400

Sudbury
157 D2
Visitor information
www.sudburytourism.ca
Welcome Centre, S of Sudbury on Hwy. 69
705/523-5587 or 877/304-8222

Right: The loneliness of a long-distance driver...the Trans-Canada Highway threads its way through northern Ontario.

center, you can descend to the bottom of a rock chasm where a multimedia presentation on mining is projected on the rock face, and former miners recount tales from Sudbury's mining history.

This mine visit is organized by Sudbury's justly famous **Science North** *(Ramsey Lake Rd., tel 705/523-4629).* On the shore of Lake Ramsey, this ambitious science center is housed in two structures: an extraordinary snowflake-shaped structure designed by Toronto architect Raymond Moriyama and in a chamber hewn into the lakeside rock outcrop. Inside, all kinds of "-ologies" are brought to life by means of vivid hands-on displays. A fascinating 3-D show takes you back through billions of years of geological time to the formation of Sudbury's mineral resources.

SAULT STE. MARIE

Known affectionately as The Soo, Sault Ste. Marie stands on the north bank of the St. Mary's River, which flows from Lake Superior into Lake Huron and forms the boundary with Michigan. The river's rapids had long attracted native fishermen before French explorers came here and called the place Sault ("falls" in French). To make navigation easier, the first lock was constructed by the North West Company in 1798. It was destroyed by U.S. forces during the War of 1812. It became clear a new Canadian lock was needed when, in 1870, Canadian troops on their way west to crush the Red River Rebellion (see p. 228–29) were refused passage through the lock in U.S. territory. Construction began in 1887. With a mile-long channel cut through solid rock, the largest lock chamber in the world, and machinery operated by electricity, the lock was an engineering won-

The striking building of Science North and its array of attractions has put workaday Sudbury firmly on the tourist map.

Sault Ste. Marie
157 C3
Visitor information
www.sault-canada.com
261 Queen St. W.
705/945-6941 or 800/461-6020

sprawl—devastated the surrounding land forms, lakes, and vegetation. Beginning in the 1970s, the city began to clean itself up, restoring thousands of acres of degraded land and, in the process, gaining an international reputation for the environmental technology involved. Even many lakes within the city limits have lost much of their acidity, thanks in part to the construction of the city's most prominent landmark, the world's tallest smokestack, which rises to an astonishing 1,250 feet above International Nickel's huge plant.

Sudbury's other nickel landmark, also a giant of its kind, is the 30-foot-high five-cent coin overlooking the Trans-Canada 17 beside **Dynamic North** *(122 Big Nickel Rd., tel 705/523-4629, closed Nov.–March).* From this exhibition der that functioned for nearly a century before a structural fault closed it down. It is now the **Sault Canal National Historic Site** *(1 Canal Dr., tel 705/941-6262),*with original buildings constructed from the red sandstone excavated from the channel.

The Soo is far from being a backwater. More ships pass through the four American locks than through the Suez or Panama Canal, and upstream there is a huge steel-works, now employee owned. Overlooking the river, the stately, five-bay **Ermatinger House** was built in 1814 by a Swiss director of the North West Company and his Ojibwa wife, Charlotte. It is the old-est stone house in Canada west of Toronto and has been restored to its original appearance.

Sault Ste. Marie is the starting point for a rail tour that repeats trips taken by the Group of Seven painters. Between 1918 and 1923 Lawren Harris, A.Y. Jackson, Frank Johnston, J.E.H. MacDonald, and

Arthur Lismer hired a boxcar that they used as a mobile studio on sketching expeditions to the Algoma wilderness, to the north.

The **Algoma Central Railway** still exists, and, although no boxcars are rented, passenger excursions head out on day trips to explore the rocks, ravines, and primeval forests of this pristine part of Ontario.

THUNDER BAY

Poised at the geographical center of Canada, and at the Canadian head of navigation on Lake Superior, Thunder Bay could hardly avoid becoming a transshipment center between the eastern and western halves of the country.

During the first decades of the 19th century, the North West Company post built here, known as Fort William, was the summer rendezvous point between voyageurs bringing up supplies from Montréal and traders return-ing from the wilderness with their

Ermatinger House
✉ 831 Queen St. E.
☎ 705/759-5443
🕐 Closed Dec.—mid-April
💲 $

Algoma Central Railway
www.agawacanyontourtrain.com
✉ 129 Bay St.
☎ 705/946-7300 or 800/242-9287
🕐 Closed mid-Oct.—mid-June
💲 $$$

Thunder Bay
🅰 156 B3
Visitor information
www.thunderbay.ca
✉ Terry Fox Centre, E of town on Hwy. 11
☎ 807/983-2041 or 800/667-8386

Canada's Quints

Annette, Émilie, Yvonne, Cécile, and Marie were five little rays of sunshine in Depression-era Canada when they were born on May 28, 1934, to Ontario franco-phones Elzire and Oliva Dionne. Not only Canadians but many people around the world were fas-cinated by the quintuplets, a rare phenomenon at the time. Fearful of commercial exploitation, the Ontario government moved the lit-tle girls to a specially built hospital, where hundreds of thousands of people could view them. All seemed for the best, or so it was thought. Accusations of childhood abuse have since been made, and funds set aside for the girls' welfare were woefully mismanaged. Émilie

died in 1954, Marie in 1970. After an attempt at reparation was bungled, Ontario Premier Mike Harris traveled to Montréal in 1998 to make a public apology to the three remaining sisters for the government's part in blighting lives that had started so brightly. ∎

No hint here of the less than happy fate that awaited the Dionne quints

Outside Old Fort William, where every July the rambunctious rendezvous of fur traders and voyageurs is enthusiastically reenacted

Fort William Historical Park

www.fwhp.ca

✉ 10 miles SW of Thunder Bay on Hwy. 61

☎ 807/473-2344

🕐 Closed mid-Oct.–mid-May

💲 $$$

year's supply of furs (see pp. 220–21). In 1870 the force heading west to counter the Red River Rebellion (see pp. 228–29) disembarked 4 miles north, at a place subsequently named Port Arthur. Fierce competition broke out between fort and port, which intensified when the former was chosen as the starting point for the construction of the Canadian Pacific Railway to the west. The railroad brought grain from the prairies to Thunder Bay's developing harbor facilities, which by the early 20th century included the massive grain elevators that still dominate the townscape. Their contents are discharged into ships that then head down the seaway to Great Lakes harbors and the ocean beyond.

Forced into union under the name of Thunder Bay by an insistent provincial government, Fort William and Port Arthur have given up their old rivalry, together offering visitors a number of attractions. Thunder Bay promotes itself as the Sports Capital of Canada, with an impressive array of sports facilities. There is also a fine new auditorium where the city's symphony orchestra performs, and a public gallery devoted to First Nations art. But the great attraction is **Fort William.** Within its palisade, this lavish reconstruction of the North West Company's trading post has more than 40 structures, seemingly staffed by the traders of old, their servants, and native helpers (who are actually convincingly clad actors and students). ■

Its endless grasslands replaced a century ago by wheat fields and cattle ranches, the stretch of country between the Canadian Shield and the Rockies forms Canada's heartland, prefiguring in its ethnic variety the multicultural nation of today.

The Prairies

Introduction & map **212–13**
Manitoba 216–23
Winnipeg **216–18**
Churchill **219**
Lower Fort Garry NHS
    & Mennonite Heritage
    Village **222**
Riding Mountain National
    Park **223**
Saskatchewan 224–30
Regina **224–25**
Saskatoon **226–27**
Saskatchewan parks **230**
Alberta 231–40
Edmonton **231–32**
Alberta badlands **233–34**
Calgary **235–40**
Hotels & restaurants
    in the Prairies **365–67**

Prairie agriculture in Saskatchewan

The Prairies

SOMETIMES PASSED OVER BY VISITORS CAPTIVATED BY THE OBVIOUS charms of the Rocky Mountains or eastern cities, Canada's Prairie Provinces—Manitoba, Saskatchewan, and eastern Alberta—offer landscapes far more varied than commonly supposed, as well as a human heritage of exceptional interest.

Flatness, the overwhelming characteristic of the prairie landscape, presents a world in which any vertical element takes on a special significance—be it a grain elevator, an onion-domed church, or the surprise of a city skyline seen from far away. Skies are magnificent, with what writer Wallace Stegner called "whole navies of clouds" moving across them.

But flatness is not the whole story, nor is prairie the only landscape of this part of Canada. From sea level on Hudson Bay, the terrain rises in a succession of steps, first to the Manitoba Escarpment, then to the Missouri Coteau, and finally to the Rockies' foothills.

Along the way rivers have carved deep valleys, and isolated upland blocks, such as the Cypress Hills, are shared between Saskatchewan and Alberta. A mantle of boreal forest covers the greater part of the surface of the three provinces, stretching southward from a thin strip of tundra vegetation along the shore of Hudson Bay. This largely uninhabited land of rivers, countless lakes, rock outcrops, and muskeg is crossed in Manitoba by a solitary railroad line to the Hudson Bay port of Churchill, famous for its polar bears (see p. 219).

To the southwest the spruce, pine, and tamarack of the boreal forest give way to a crescent-shaped zone of aspen parkland roughly 100 miles across, most of which is now given over to farming or urban development. The true prairie lies southwest, or rather, what is left of it, since virtually the whole of what was once a sea of grass and wildflowers extending from Manitoba to the Rockies has been turned over to cultivation. A few fragments of native grassland remain, in Grasslands National Park in southwestern Saskatchewan, for example. But the development of hardy varieties of grain and the irrigation of the drier areas has made cereal farming here some of the most profitable in the world, while other areas, notably around the Cypress Hills, provide extensive grounds for cattle.

Grain and cattle have taken the place of the bison that once roamed the prairies by the millions. The bison formed an invaluable resource for the nomadic tribespeople, providing food, clothing, and the material for cladding tepees. Techniques of hunting included the use of jumps, cliffs over which the herds were driven to their death as at the famous Head-Smashed-In Jump in southwestern Alberta. In Mesozoic times, between 225

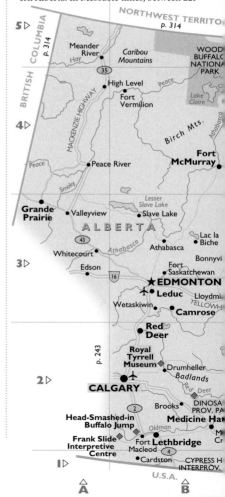

and 63 million years ago, Alberta was a landscape of warm seas and swamps, the home of many different species of dinosaur. Today the terrain of the Alberta badlands has some of the richest fossil beds in the world. Current excavations can be seen at Dinosaur Provincial Park, while the spectacular displays of the Royal Tyrell museum at Drumheller bring to life not only the world of the dinosaurs but the whole story of the evolution of life on Earth.

The prairies were the fulcrum of the modern Canadian nation and their history is fascinating. The North West Mounted Police (see p. 225) were established to control this vast territory; many of their forts can still be seen, either in their original isolation or re-created in the cities where they were the nucleus. The Métis' resistance to settlement can be traced at Batoche, site of the battle that ended their 1885 rebellion. Also evocative is the annual reenactment of Louis Riel's trial in Regina.

Today most people travel across the prairies by airplane or highway. Linking Winnipeg and Calgary, the Trans-Canada 1 follows a southerly alignment, while farther north the Yellowhead Highway passes through Saskatoon and gives access to two outstanding national parks, Riding Mountain in Manitoba and Prince Albert in Saskatchewan. ∎

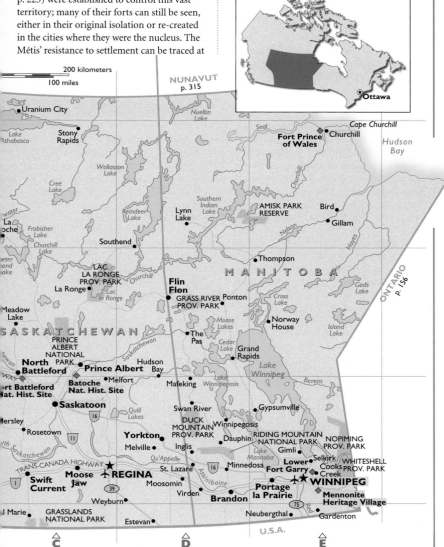

Populating the Prairies: Métis to the Human Mosaic

Conventional maps of the southern Prairie provinces are painted with a broad brush, showing great swaths of grassland and parkland stretching for hundreds of miles. The ethnic map, by contrast, is a kaleidoscope of colors, the outcome of Canada's call to land-hungry farmers from Europe to colonize the sparsely populated land.

The Métis, the offspring of European fur traders and native women, had long developed their unique way of life, and a small number of settlers had established themselves in the Red River Colony. But when seen from Ottawa in the 1870s, the prairies remained an "Empty Quarter." Strenuous efforts were made to encourage settlers: A land survey divided the terrain along the American checkerboard model, and potential farmers were offered 160 acres of land—provided they brought it into cultivation within a specified period and built a dwelling. A trickle of anglophone immigrants moved into Manitoba from Ontario, Britain, and the United States, joined by French speakers, Mennonites from Russia, Scandinavians, Belgians, Germans, and even Icelanders, who established the Republic of New Iceland at Gimli on the shore of Lake Winnipeg.

In the last years of the 19th century, an economic upturn combined with the work of Clifford Sifton, the energetic minister of the interior, to boost immigration. Though preferring settlers of Canadian or American stock, Sifton encouraged immigrants from the Slav lands of east-central Europe: "A stalwart peasant in a sheepskin's coat, born on the soil, whose forefathers have been farmers for ten generations, with a stout wife and half a dozen children, is good quality."

Most settlers had to build a farm out of whatever materials came to hand: timber in the wooded areas; sod, mud, and thatch in the grasslands. Later, more permanent structures drew on vernacular building traditions in the immigrant's country of origin until the availability of standardized materials and even complete prefabricated buildings encouraged, in the words of writer Harold Kalman, the "Bodnarchuks, Tatasoffs, and Silbersteins...to keep up with the Joneses." A few examples can be seen outside museum villages.

In the 1870s the first non-French or non-English people to arrive were the Mennonites, members of a German-speaking cultural-religious group from Russia and central Europe. Their settlements in the East and West Reserves south of Winnipeg are street villages, with farmsteads in sociable proximity, rather than scattered over the landscape. A characteristic example with typical Mennonite house barns has been preserved at Neubergthal, Manitoba. Toward the end of the century, the Doukhobors, an egalitarian and pacifist sect from southern Russia, were also allowed to establish communal settlements; in early photographs, their village at Khristianovka in Saskatchewan looks as if it belongs on the shores of the Black Sea, with more than 40

Cathedrals of the Prairies

Impacting the landscape on an even greater scale than that of the Ukrainian churches was a very different building type, the grain elevator. These superb timber structures, nicknamed the "Cathedrals of the Prairies," were built at intervals along the railroad tracks, usually within horse-drawn carting distance of local farms. They were brightly painted, and carried company names and sometimes the name of the railroad station. Some rose to a height of 100 feet, although 65 feet was more typical. Their simple, unmistakable outline concealed quite elaborate machinery to weigh, hoist, store, and discharge the grain. There were some 6,000 by the 1930s; they have since decreased to about 1,500, many made obsolete by motor transportation, closure of branch lines, and advances in agriculture. To prevent this symbol of the Canadian prairies from disappearing altogether, a row of five of them in Manitoba has been designated the Inglis Elevators National Historic Site *(Tel 204/564-2243).* ∎

thatched-roof houses and newly planted trees lining a tidy main street. Together with other immigrants, the Doukhobors arrived in such numbers that in the 20 years between the completion of the main railroad network and the outbreak of war in 1914, the population of the prairies had increased almost five-fold, from about 150,000 to 1.5 million.

Equally exotic, and now an integral part of the prairie image, are the Ukrainian churches that raise their onion domes toward the huge vault of the prairie sky. Built from the earliest days of the massive Ukrainian influx that began toward the end of the 19th century, they house congregations of both the Roman Catholic and Russian Orthodox faiths. A well-conserved early example with a richly decorated interior is St. Michael's at Gardenton, Manitoba, completed in 1899. Many Ukrainian churches are the work of one man, the extraordinary Father Ruh. This self-taught architect and tireless laborer built places of worship all across the Prairie provinces during his 50-year ministry. ∎

Winnipeg
🅰 213 E2

Tourism Winnipeg
www.destinationwinnipeg.ca
✉ 259 Portage Ave.
☎ 204/943-1970 or
800/665-0204

Winnipeg

STILL THE "GATEWAY TO THE PRAIRIES" DESPITE THE growth of great cities farther west, Winnipeg, Manitoba, is strategically located at the crucial point where the Canadian Shield meets the Canadian frontier. This is also the junction of some of North America's coldest winds, and the city has come up with an imaginative way of sheltering itself—by moving much of its business underground.

Each of the Prairie Provinces boasts a splendid neoclassic edifice built to house its parliament. Completed in 1920, Manitoba's Legislative Building was the last to be finished.

The confluence of the Assiniboine and Red Rivers had long served as a meeting place for aboriginal people. Later it was the site of forts built by both the Hudson's Bay Company and the North West Company. Today this historic core is known as **The Forks,** a cheerful gathering ground for townsfolk and visitors, with a covered market, boutiques, restaurants, and cafés, as well as riverside open spaces that include a national historic site and a pedestrian bridge to St. Boniface.

To the west, off Broadway, only a 19th-century gateway remains from the Hudson's Bay Company's Upper Fort Garry, but the real nucleus of the modern metropolis is about a mile to the north; here, at the crossroads of Portage Avenue and Main Street, is Henry McKenney's Royal Hotel, built in 1862 when the Red River Colony was evolving from an isolated frontier settlement into a modern commercial city.

Winnipeggers take a perverse pride in the fact that the **Portage and Main** intersection is reputed to be the windiest corner in North America. Pedestrians can now escape into the city's extensive underground walkway system.

In addition to modern office towers, Winnipeg holds a fascinating array of older buildings, many from the late 19th- and early 20th-century boomtown days, when settlement of the prairies led to an insatiable demand for goods and services of all types. Grand banks and ornate warehouses reflect the dynamism of these pioneering times, particularly in the **Exchange District** area just north of Portage and Main. Beyond downtown lie several distinctive neighborhoods: Only incorporated into Winnipeg since 1971, French-speaking **St. Boniface** on the east side of the Red River traces its heritage from the mission founded in 1818. In contrast, the **North End** received its decisive imprint from the stream of Scandinavian and Slavic immigrants in the early 20th century.

Winnipeg's cultural dynamism is reflected in its **Folklorama festival** every August, and in its array of institutions—theater, opera, symphony, and above all, the Royal Winnipeg Ballet *(Tel 204/956-0183).*∎

Manitoba Museum

THIS MODERN MUSEUM, OPENED TO COMMEMORATE Winnipeg's 1974 centennial, succeeds magnificently in its aim of interpreting the complex relationship between humankind and the natural environment of this part of Canada.

Vivid dioramas enliven many of the museum's galleries, though few surpass the impact of the Red River Buffalo Hunt, with a Métis horseman closing in on his charging prey. Others depict an ice cave in the Arctic with a polar bear settling down to a meal of ringed seal, or caribou migrating through the subarctic landscape of the Wolverine River, among other scenes. Visitors walk past a waterfall in the boreal forest and enter a scene populated by moose and by a Cree band, some of whom are engaged in pictograph painting.

But even more striking than these dioramas is the extraordinary full-size reproduction of the Nonsuch. Built in Devon, England, to mark the 300th anniversary of the voyage that opened up Hudson Bay and its vast hinterland to the fur trade, the 50-foot ketch sailed the English Channel in the summer of 1969, was shipped across the Atlantic, and came to rest here, deep in the interior of the continent, on the artificial mud of a meticulously re-created English harbor complete with dockside Boar's Head tavern. The efforts paid off and the vessel seems quite at home.

These are the highlights, but the museum holds much more. A strangely man-shaped inukshuk, an Inuit marker built of stone, guards the entrance to the Arctic/Sub-Arctic Gallery. The haunting cry of the loon evokes the loneliness of the northern wilderness, while other displays bring home the

nature as well as the nastiness of the biting flies that infest it—punkies, gnats, sandflies and no-see-ums, in addition to mosquitoes, blackflies, and horseflies. A section on the winter landscape shows how snow and frozen soil shelter an amazing variety of life, while other exhibits demonstrate the extraordinary root depth of prairie grasses. There's an example of the famous Red River cart, the region's primary mode of transportation before the coming of the railroad. Poignant pamphlets proclaiming "Canada, Deine Neue Heimat" or "Canada, your new homeland" recall the Europe-wide appeal for hardy settlers to populate and cultivate the hitherto untouched Prairie provinces. ∎

Manitoba Museum
www.manitobamuseum.ca
✉ 190 Rupert Ave.
☎ 204/956-2830
  or 204/943-3139
🕐 Closed Mon. mid-
  Sept.–mid-May
💲 $$

Visitors to the Manitoba Museum are greeted by its dramatic diorama of stampeding bison.

More places to visit around Winnipeg

THE FORKS
NATIONAL HISTORIC SITE

Winnipeg's **Union Station** is one of the grandest in Canada, built in beaux arts style in 1911 by architects also involved in the design of New York's Grand Central. Once occupied by countless boxcars and grain wagons, the vast tract of land between the station and the Red and Assiniboine Rivers has been renamed The Forks and reclaimed for public use. Archaeologically the richest part of the riverside is the Forks National Historic Site, complete with an amphitheater, a striking "Path of Time" sculpture, and landing stages for river trips. Old railroad storage buildings now house a market, specialty shops, and cafés, as well as the elaborate displays of the Manitoba Travel Ideas Centre, a children's museum, and a pedestrian bridge to St. Boniface. The Forks are frequented all year, but are at their best during the many events that take place in summer.

www.pc.gc.ca ✉ Off Main St. at Water Ave. ☎ 204/983-6757

MANITOBA
LEGISLATIVE BUILDING

Rising over a 30-acre parkland that extends to the banks of the Assiniboine, the home to Manitoba's parliament is built on a truly imperial scale. It was completed in 1920, and is one of a number of beaux arts structures intended to express civic pride and consolidate urban civilization in the prairies. Richly decorated with allegorical sculpture, it has a tall dome capped by the famous "Golden Boy," a spirited, gilded youth bearing a torch (representing economic progress) and a wheat sheaf (agriculture). Beyond the classical portico is a triumphal stairway guarded by a brace of bronze bison cast in New York.

✉ 450 Broadway Ave. ☎ 204/945-5813

RIEL HOUSE
NATIONAL HISTORIC SITE

The modest home of the Riel family (see pp. 228–29) has been restored and refurbished to its original appearance. Built in 1881, mostly of timber from the family's previous dwelling, the house was never actually lived in by Louis Riel, though he came here briefly in the summer of 1883, and it was here that he lay in state after his execution in 1885.

www.pg.gc.ca ✉ 330 River Rd., St. Vital ☎ 204/257-1783 🕐 Closed Sept.–mid-May 💲 $

ST. BONIFACE MUSEUM

The former Convent of the Gray Nuns was completed in 1851. Winnipeg's oldest building, and a fine example of Red River frame construction, it now houses a museum that tells the story of the frontier past of Western Canada through the eyes of the Métis and of Manitoba's francophone community. They now form some ten percent of the province's population, mostly resident in St. Boniface and other districts of Winnipeg. Close by looms the modern St. Boniface Cathedral, the sixth place of worship to stand on this site. Built in 1972, it incorporates the imposing twin-towered facade in pale stone of the old cathedral, gutted by fire in 1969.

✉ 494 Ave. Taché, St. Boniface ☎ 204/237-4500 🕐 Closed Sat. in winter months 💲 $

WINNIPEG ART GALLERY

This major gallery is as notable for its architecture as for its excellent specialist art collections. An assertive triangular structure terminating in a knife-edge, its design was hailed at the time of its implementation in 1971 as a "brilliant symbolization of contemporary Winnipeg." Thanks to the enthusiasm of its Viennese curator in the early 1950s, the gallery has an unequaled collection of Inuit art, some 10,000 sculptures, prints, drawings, textiles, and paintings. Selections from this treasure store are exhibited in rotation. There's also a fine collection of other Canadian paintings, but the gallery's second great strength, hardly paralleled in Canada, is the Gort Collection of Gothic and Renaissance paintings. Still glowing with vitality, these mostly German and Flemish masterworks include paintings by Cranach and an outstanding "Adoration of the Magi" by the group of artists called the Master of the Heilige Sippe.

www.wag.mb.ca ✉ 300 Memorial Blvd. ☎ 204/786-6641 💲 $ ∎

Churchill

THIS URBAN OUTPOST, CLINGING TO THE BLEAK southwestern shore of Hudson Bay, has a long history as a trading post, fort, and harbor and, more recently, as a major vacation center. Links by rail and air make its extraordinary arctic and subarctic wildlife and landscape accessible to a growing number of visitors eager to see the "Polar Bear Capital of the World."

Churchill
🗺 213 E4

Visitor information
www.townofchurchill.ca
✉ Town Centre
Complex
☎ 204/675-8871
🕐 Closed Sat.–Sun.

The Danish explorer Jens Munck first visited the site at the mouth of the Churchill River in 1619, but no permanent European settlement was established until the Hudson's Bay Company built a post here in 1717. Anglo-French competition for control of the bay led to construction of the huge star-shaped Prince of Wales Fort—a task which took more than 40 years. It still broods over the tundra and the entrance to the harbor. Despite the fort's 40-foot thick walls, it meekly surrendered to the French on the only occasion it was ever attacked, in 1782.

In the late 19th century, the prairies buzzed with talk of a rail and harbor link to free them from control by eastern Canadian interests and give them an outlet to the sea and to Europe. After several false starts, resources were found and the problem of laying track on permafrost overcome. The Hudson's Bay Railroad opened to Churchill in 1929; the first cargo of prairie wheat reached England two years later.

The port has never enjoyed the expected success, not least because it is icebound for eight months of the year. But the trains making the journey from Winnipeg (*VIA Rail, tel 888/842-7245*) bring visitors eager to see the abundant bird life (more than 200 species), the seals, the beluga whales, which play in the (relatively) warm water of the estuary in the summer, and above all, the polar bears. A short boat trip across the river mouth gives access to the **Prince of Wales Fort National Park** (*Tel 204/675-8863*). The riches of the **Eskimo Museum** (*242 La Vérendrye Ave., tel 204/675-2030, closed Sun.*) can be enjoyed in town and at the **Parks Canada Visitor Reception Centre** (*Tel 204/675-8863*), which is the best place to begin a visit to what is, for most people, an unfamiliar environment. ■

Above: Winter displays of aurora borealis are a highlight of Churchill.

Below: Polar bear

Churchill's bears

Polar bears are big as well as beautiful. A female weighs an average of 660 pounds, a male more than 1,300 pounds. From September to early November, bears returning from their summer ranges to the south of Churchill congregate along the shore of the bay, waiting for the water to freeze and give them access to their favorite food, the seal.

Contemporary environmental impact studies would probably have ruled out Churchill as a suitable site for a town, as it lies directly on the bears' route to the shore. Locals are wary of these large and fearless carnivores, and visitors need to heed advice before attempting to get close to them. The tundra buggy tours (*Tel 204/949-2050 or 800/663-9832*) are the best way to enjoy a unique experience of bear contact. ■

The Hudson's Bay Company & the fur trade

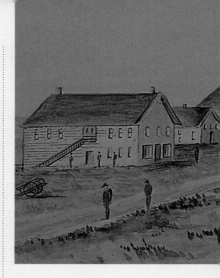

Fish brought Europeans to the coasts of Canada, fur to the interior. Far from empty, the vast land proved to be teeming with animals whose pelts commanded high prices in Europe, where the most desirable of all furbearing animals, the beaver, was on the point of extinction. Beaver pelts were particularly valuable because, once subjected to expert processing by natives, they could be made into a durable, malleable felt—the ideal material for the styles of hats worn by European gentlemen throughout the 18th and 19th centuries.

The French dominated the fur trade at first, establishing good relations with the natives, whose expertise in hunting, trapping, and processing was an absolute prerequisite for success. Trade routes led west far into the interior from just above the famous rapids at Lachine near Montréal. The trade reached Lakes Michigan and Superior, and, in the middle of the 18th century, even farther, across the prairies and into the far northwest. Here waited a formidable adversary—the Hudson's Bay Company (HBC).

The English quest for the elusive Northwest Passage leading from the Atlantic to the Pacific Ocean brought their sailors through the long strait and into the great bay named for Henry Hudson, who explored its shores in 1610. But it was left to a pair of Frenchmen to point out the bay's significance as a doorway to the riches of the fur trade. Médart Chouart, sieur des Groseilliers, and Pierre Esprit Radisson had learned of the existence of the bay from the Cree, but could not obtain backing for its exploration from the French authorities. A more enthusiastic reception awaited them at the English court, and, backed by a consortium of businessmen and nobles, the pair set off from London in 1668 aboard the *Nonsuch* and the *Eaglet*. Only the *Nonsuch* made it to

Hudson Bay; it returned laden with furs of such quality and in such quantity as to delight the backers. Formed in 1670, the Hudson's Bay Company was granted far-reaching powers and a trading monopoly over the whole of the drainage basin of the bay, a vast area now given the name of Rupert's Land.

A style of trading developed, quite distinct from that of the questing, adventurous French, with their intimate contact with natives and willingness to learn their ways. The Hudson's Bay officials tended to remain in the forts built at the mouths of the rivers running into the bay, content to await the arrival of the natives with their annual consignment of furs. Transactions were often carried out through a hatch in the wall of the fort, rather than with the elaborate ceremony preferred by the natives and enthusiastically taken up by the French. Company employees were forbidden to cohabit with native women.

This ponderous approach proved inadequate as the French extended their sphere of operations into the northwest, and the company began to move out from its bayside bases to establish trading posts far inland. Rivalry failed to diminish when Québec fell to the British; the Montréal base of the trade might now be dominated by Scottish fur barons, but business was business, and conflict continued—the HBC on one side and the newly formed North West Company on the other.

The half century after the conquest by the British marked the final, glorious years of the

Above: Fort Garry in the 19th century
Right: Fur trappers had a solitary existence in the 18th and 19th centuries.

Montréal-based fur trade. French voyageurs with their unparalleled skills still formed the elite of the traders. Great prestige attached to those who had wintered at least once in the far northwest, the *pays d'en haut*, while a lower status was enjoyed by the *mangeurs de lard* (pork-eaters) who returned in the fall to the comforts of civilization. The Beaver Club was founded in Montréal, with membership limited to those who had experienced the hardships of the northwest. The arduous route between Montréal and Fort William on Lake Superior was improved with roads around portages and with locks at Sault Ste.-Marie. By the first decade of the 19th century, North West Company men had traced routes through the mountains to the Pacific, 3,000 miles from Montréal, opening up the last untapped reserves of furbearing animals to the trade.

Company rivalries came to an end in 1821, when the Hudson's Bay Company absorbed the Nor' Westers. For a while the HBC continued to exercise its near-dictatorial powers over its huge domain. By mid-century, however, as it became ever more clear that the future of the prairies belonged to the farmer rather than the bison hunter or fur trader, this role had become an anachronism. In 1870 the HBC sold Rupert's Land to the Canadian government.

Thanks largely to the prime lands it was allowed to retain, the company remained prosperous. Shortened to The Bay (or *La Baie*), its name still dominates many a shopping district, although its sale to American interests in 2006 makes its future uncertain. The records kept by its army of administrators and employees form a huge archive, perhaps the most important single source for Canadian history. And in the Manitoba Museum in Winnipeg (see p. 217), a full-size copy of the 50-foot ketch that began it all, the *Nonsuch*, sails on forever. ■

Lower Fort Garry National Historic Site

Lower Fort Garry National Historic Site

🅰 213 E2

www.pc.gc.ca

✉ 20 miles N of Winnipeg on Hwy. 9

☎ 888/773-8888

🕐 Closed early Sept.–mid-May

💲 $$

Mennonite Heritage Village

🅰 213 E2

www.mennoniteheritage village.com

✉ Just N of Steinbach on Hwy. 12

☎ 204/326-9661

🕐 Buildings closed Oct.–April

💲 $$

Traditional farm buildings rebuilt at the Mennonite Heritage Village

In 1826 one of the Red River's periodic floods caused severe damage to Fort Garry at the confluence of the Red and the Assiniboine Rivers. Already concerned at the effect raw frontier society was having on his young wife, Governor George Simpson decided to move his headquarters downstream to a less vulnerable site, one that could be developed not just as a fort and trading post, but also as the center of a refined country estate.

Construction began on what came to be called Lower Fort Garry in 1831; restored by Parks Canada, the complex of buildings is today inhabited by 19th-century folk who role-play and help interpret life as lived here before railroads and steamships displaced the Red River cart and York boat.

The heart of the complex is the Big House, a substantial one-and-a-half story stone structure with high roof and veranda. Elegantly furnished, it nevertheless failed to become the sophisticated social center Simpson planned, and, disappointed with his endeavors, he sailed home to England in 1833. Around it stand the more workaday buildings in which the functions of the trading post were carried out: warehouses, a granary, and a well-stocked fur loft. ∎

Mennonite Heritage Village

Beyond the modern visitor center that tells the often troubled story of the Mennonites from 1500 onward sprawls a 40-acre site. Here one of their prairie villages has been reconstructed in its original form, using reproductions as well as buildings saved from other sites. There are opportunities to sample typical Mennonite fare, hear the German Mennonite dialect spoken, and enjoy a range of special events.

Houses, churches, schools, shops, workshops, and farm buildings are primarily arranged in typical fashion along a street, very different from the isolated farmsteads dictated by the surveyors' plans in most parts of the prairies. The first building encountered is a copy of a semlin, one of the sod houses hastily built as temporary shelters when the pioneers first arrived in their new environment. These were quickly replaced by more permanent structures such as the substantial combination house and barn known as the Hochfeld House, with its characteristic central brick heater system. This type of building can be traced back to medieval Frisia on the North Sea coast. Dominating the village is an exact reconstruction of the Steinbach windmill, the only one of its kind in Canada. ∎

Riding Mountain National Park

THIS NATIONAL PARK WEST OF LAKE MANITOBA INCLUDES some of the highest land in the province—part of the upland known as the Manitoba Escarpment, which runs 1,000 miles from North Dakota to Saskatchewan. Here the escarpment rises 1,500 feet above the flat farmland of the adjoining prairie, forming a dramatic contrast to the tamed landscape.

Riding Mountain National Park
🗺 213 D2
www.pc.gc.ca
✉ Wasagaming
☎ 204/848-7275
$ $$

The park's 1,150 square miles have been protected since 1906, when it was designated as a forest reserve. National park status followed in 1930, when the Wasagaming town site was laid out and a number of buildings, including the Interpretive Centre, were designed in a distinctively Canadian rustic style. The park, long a favorite recreation and vacation area locally, has made the town at its entrance a busy summer resort, with sunbathers and swimmers crowding the beach at **Clear Lake.** In winter, **Agassiz Ski Hill** offers downhill skiing with a modest 500-foot vertical drop.

But Riding Mountain's real fascination lies in its juxtaposition of three very different ecosystems. On its eastern edge, at the foot of the escarpment, a tract of deciduous woodland thrives far to the west of its normal occurrence. Elm, oak, and maple shelter a rich lower level of vines, shrubs, and ferns—a habitat that has virtually disappeared from the prairie. West of the escarpment the plateau has been scraped by glaciers, leaving rock outcrops, countless prairie potholes, and a mantle of boreal forest. Farther west still are stands of aspen intermixed with grassland.

Riding Mountain has partly recovered from the trapping that threatened to eliminate much of its wildlife in the 19th century. There are bears, moose, elk, lynx,

beaver, and wolves, as well as a bison herd in a large enclosure at **Lake Audy.** Some 250 miles of trails offer hiking in summer, and some are groomed in winter for cross-country skiing or snowshoeing. The pathways enable visitors to explore the park and even visit the cabin at **Beaver Lodge Lake** built by the early conservationist Grey Owl (1888–1938) during his brief stay as park warden. ■

Largest of the bodies of water in Riding Mountain National Park, Clear Lake is fringed with glorious conifer forest.

Regina

Regina
🅰 213 C2
Visitor information
www.tourismregina.com
✉ E of town
on Hwy. 1
☎ 306/789-5099 or
800/661-5099

Saskatchewan Legislative Building
✉ Wascana Centre
☎ 306/787-5358

Royal Saskatchewan Museum
www.royalsaskmuseum.ca
✉ Wascana Centre,
College Ave.
& Albert St.
☎ 306/787-2815
💲 Donation

R.C.M.P. Training Academy
✉ Dewdney Ave. W.
☎ 306/780-5838

Wheat sheaves grace Saskatchewan's coat of arms.

"THE CITY THAT DID THE MOST WITH THE LEAST" WAS Pierre Berton's tribute to the capital of Saskatchewan, a city founded in the middle of a treeless plain, virtually without water, on soil that turned to mud after rain and to dust when the sun shone. Just over a century after the Canadian Pacific Railway arrived in this desolate spot, Regina prides itself on fine civic buildings and facilities, nearly as much parkland as Ottawa, and an urban forest of 350,000 trees. The regional center for the wheat producers of southern Saskatchewan, Regina is the home of many government institutions.

The town began life in 1883 as the capital of the Northwest Territories, on a spot by the Wascana Creek named Pile O'Bones for the bison remains left by Cree hunters. At first growth was as sluggish as the muddy waters of the creek, but Regina boomed at the turn of the century as settlers flooded to the plains. In 1905 it became capital of the new province of Saskatchewan.

Regina's distinctiveness lies less in the grid of streets that make up its commercial core than in the 2,300-acre park known as the **Wascana Centre.** Partly in order to solve the problem of water supply, the creek was dammed to form a large serpentine lake. The surrounding parkland was the subject of a typically ambitious beaux arts landscaping scheme by Thomas Mawson in the course of his trans-Canada journey, of which the much admired formal gardens around the legislative building survive. The park provides a green setting for many of the city's foremost attractions.

LEGISLATIVE BUILDING

Completed in 1912, the home of the Saskatchewan legislature is a splendidly self-confident structure in classical style, its long wings firmly anchored by a great portico and high dome. In addition to visiting the Legislative Chamber, the guided tour reveals some of the building's rich collection of artwork.

ROYAL SASKATCHEWAN MUSEUM

Excellent displays in the museum's Earth Sciences Gallery reveal the region's extraordinary geological past, with particular attention paid to Saskatchewan's unusually rich fossil deposits. Visitors can even design their own dinosaur. Nearby, the acclaimed First Nations Gallery tells the story of the province's aboriginal heritage in a comprehensive and accessible way, with lifelike dioramas and an array of other exhibits. The Life Sciences Gallery is also outstanding.

ROYAL CANADIAN MOUNTED POLICE TRAINING ACADEMY

An inspection of the place where future Mounties get their training has to be a highlight of any stay in Regina. There's a Sergeant Major's Drill at 12:45 *(weekdays)* on the Parade Ground and on Tuesdays in July and August the splendid spectacle of the Sunset Retreat as the flag is lowered. The **R.C.M.P. Centennial Museum** gives a thorough account of the force's history, with emphasis on such episodes as the 1885 Riel Rebellion and the Klondike Gold Rush. A new RCMP center will open in 2007. ∎

Horses and riders perform at a Mounted Police show.

The Mounties

Few figures symbolize a country so effectively as the Mountie in his (or her) red tunic and stiff-brimmed Stetson hat. Originally called the North West Mounted Police, the force was hurriedly organized to deal with the aftermath of the Cypress Hills Massacre in the 1870s and to bring law and order to the west generally. The color of the uniform was calculated to carry with it a potent whiff of British imperial authority. The Mounties' network of forts brought a skeletal settlement pattern to the west (Fort Edmonton, Fort Calgary, Fort Macleod), while the men themselves acquired a reputation for fearlessness and evenhanded meting out of justice.

A Blackfoot chieftain declared: "The police have protected us as the feathers of a bird protect it from the frosts of winter" and the fact that the settlement of the west proceeded so peacefully has been attributed to the respect all parties felt for these near-legendary figures. Surprisingly, the NWMP was almost disbanded on more than one occasion, but survived to acquire its "Royal" title in 1920 and play the role of a federal force. It has survived being mythologized (by comic books, novels, films, and even TV sitcoms) and in the 1980s spying and phone-tapping scandals to retain a place in most Canadian hearts. ■

Reconstruction of an NWMP office at Fort Calgary

Saskatoon

Saskatoon
⚊ 213 C2

Tourism Saskatoon
www.tourismsaskatoon.com
✉ 6–305 Idylwyld Dr. N.
☎ 306/242-1206 or 800/567-2444

STILL SMARTING SOMEWHAT AT REGINA'S CAPITAL CITY status, and larger than its southern Saskatchewan competitor, Saskatoon nevertheless prides itself on its fine setting on both banks of the South Saskatchewan River, on its elegant university campus, and on a longstanding tradition of civic improvement and urban landscaping. The city was founded in 1882 by sober-minded Ontarians as the center of a temperance colony. Growth was slow; by the turn of the 20th century there were only 100 or so inhabitants. But boom time came suddenly; lines of two Canadian railroad companies met here and settlers flocked in to farm the surrounding prairie. By the outbreak of World War I, the population numbered nearly 20,000. Recently, the city has taken on a vital role in the development of the province's potash reserves and uranium deposits.

The winding South Saskatchewan River, crossed by seven bridges, is accompanied by the **Meewasin Trail,** a 33-mile hiking and biking route that links many of the city's attractions. The **Meewasin Valley Centre** (3rd Ave. S., tel 306/665-6888) on the west bank introduces visitors to the city and its surroundings. On the same side of the river is one of Saskatoon's Ukrainian museums, the **Ukrainian Museum of Canada** (910 Spadina Cres. E., tel 306/244-3800), with traditional artifacts and displays on the evolution of the sizable Canadian-Ukrainian community and its culture. Farther north the **Mendel Art Gallery** (950 Spadina Cres. E., tel 306/975-7610) offers a luxuriantly planted conservatory as well as the exceptionally rich collection of Canadian art assembled by Fred Mendel, a public-spirited local millionaire. On the grounds of the University of Saskatchewan on the far bank of the river, the **Diefenbaker Canada Centre** (101 Diefenbaker Pl., tel 306/966-8384) commemorates "The Chief," politician John

Saskatoon's popular Farmers' Market

The modern
facade and
gardens of
City Hall

Diefenbaker from the prairies, who was Canada's prime minister between 1957 and 1963.

Away from the river, Saskatoon's other sights include the **Western Development Museum** *(2610 Lorne Ave. S., tel 306/931-1910)* and **Wanuskewin Heritage Park** *(3 miles north by Wanuskewin Road and Hwy. 11, tel 306/931-6767)*. The former celebrates the European settlement of the prairies through its collections of agricultural equipment and its Boomtown, a copy of an early 20th-century street. The latter explores the far older heritage of the Plains Indians.

BATOCHE NATIONAL HISTORIC SITE

Overlooking the South Saskatchewan River, the village of Batoche was a center of Métis settlement and the short-lived capital of Louis Riel's "provisional government of the Saskatchewan." It was here in 1885 that his followers made their last stand under the command of the skilled guerrilla leader Gabriel Dumont against the force led by Maj. Gen. Frederick Middleton. The outnumbered Métis held up Middleton's advance on Batoche, but after four days inferior

weaponry and lack of ammunition made their defeat inevitable (see pp. 228–29).

Visitor center displays and audiovisual presentations provide an excellent introduction to this evocative national historic park. Although most of the village of Batoche has disappeared, the church and rectory that served as Riel's headquarters are intact, along with traces of the defenders' rifle pits and a poignant cemetery.

FORT BATTLEFORD NATIONAL HISTORIC SITE

For a brief period following the construction of the North West Mounted Police post at this site on the North Saskatchewan River in 1876, Battleford became the capital of the Northwest Territories; an honor it lost to Regina when the Canadian Pacific Railway decided to build its line far to the south. During the Northwest Rebellion of 1885, the Cree sacked the town while its inhabitants huddled in the shelter of the fort. Within the reconstructed stockade several of the fort's original structures have been refurbished, and the barrack building outside the perimeter houses a visitor center. ■

Batoche National Historic Site
- 213 C2–3
- www.pc.gc.ca
- 55 miles NE of Saskatoon on east bank of South Saskatchewan River
- 306/423-6227
- Closed Oct.– mid-May
- $$

Fort Battleford National Historic Site
- 213 C2
- www.pc.gc.ca
- Off Yellowhead Hwy. 16, 85 miles NW of Saskatoon
- 306/937-2621
- Closed Oct.– mid-May.
- $$

Louis Riel & rebellion

A controversial figure well over a century after his death, Louis Riel (1844–1885) led not one but two rebellions against the Canadian advance into the prairies. A sorry sequence of misunderstanding and poor communications, combined with Riel's own erratic behavior, led to his tragic trial and execution.

Seven-eighths French and one-eighth Indian, Riel trained in Montréal for the Catholic priesthood, but found his vocation in politics when called upon in 1869 by Métis anxious about the activities of Canadian surveyors on their traditional lands. Though there was no intention on the part of Ottawa to dispossess the Métis, fears had been fanned—Riel's National Committee prevented the lieutenant governor of Rupert's Land from entering the territory, then seized Fort Garry at the confluence of the Red and Assiniboine Rivers. While Riel issued proclamations and Ottawa made soothing statements, a number of free-booting Ontarians made what seemed to be threatening noises from nearby Portage La Prairie. Captured by Métis, they were imprisoned in Fort Garry and one, a troublesome Orangeman named Scott, was executed. This was Riel's undoing in the eyes of Anglo-Canada, and he was never forgiven. Although the Manitoba that came into existence in 1870 may have owed much to his successful negotiations with the Canadian government, unrelenting Ontarian animosity left him unable to take the seat he had won in Parliament, and he was forced into American exile.

By the mid-1880s, history was about to repeat itself. Many Métis had moved northward from the Red River area, where they had been cheated by speculators out of the lands granted them by the government, to the banks of the South Saskatchewan River, where they hoped to continue living their traditional way of life undisturbed by the western march of progress. The hope was a vain one. Once more, survey parties invaded the area, the advance guard of land speculators and settlers. Riel, by now a U.S. citizen and long since amnestied for his part in the Red River

Above: Louis Riel, who was executed after leading not one, but two, rebellions against insensitive central authority
Top right: Native Canadian and Métis rebels were forced to yield to the overwhelming force of the 3,000 troops sent from Ontario.
Bottom right: Louis Riel was laid to rest outside St. Boniface Basilica, Winnipeg.

Rebellion, was called from his Montana exile to help in the defense of land rights. In 1884 he arrived in Batoche on the South Saskatchewan River, investigated the situation, and sent a petition to Ottawa.

Irritated by apparent government inaction, and taunted by some of his followers for his seeming ineffectiveness, Riel appeared to lose the balance he had recovered following a nervous breakdown ten years earlier. Declaring himself the "Prophet of the New World," he set up a military headquarters at the parish church of Batoche and ordered the North West Mounted Police to leave the area or face extermination. Ottawa, not inclined to leave this threat unanswered, now had the means of rapid reinforcement, since the rails

of the Canadian Pacific were being swiftly laid across shield and prairies. A force of 3,000 men rushed from Ontario and despite a skilled, guerrilla-type defense conducted by Riel's military commander, Gabriel Dumont, the rebellion was doomed.

As the four-day battle ended, Dumont fled to the United States and Riel, who had encouraged his followers with cries of "Fire in the name of the Father! Fire in the name of the Son! Fire in the name of the Holy Ghost!," was captured and brought to trial in Regina.

Inevitably, the charge against him was that of treason. Though he had never fired a shot himself, he had raised a rebellion, in the course of which perhaps a hundred people had lost their lives. Sympathy for his cause, particularly in Québec, contrasted with Ontario's implacable hostility. Riel's lawyers pleaded insanity, but the defendant himself spoke so eloquently that the plea failed. Despite the jury's recommendation of mercy, Riel was hanged on November 16, 1885. ■

A lone bison roams the empty acres of Saskatchewan's Grasslands National Park.

Saskatchewan parks

PRINCE ALBERT NATIONAL PARK

The particular fascination of this 1,500-square-mile national park, established in the very heart of Saskatchewan in 1927, lies in its embrace of two of Canada's major ecosystems.

In the south, aspen parkland intermixes with swaths of prairie grasslands, habitat of creatures from ground squirrels to an introduced herd of plains bison. (The wood bison is more at home in this habitat.) To the north, parkland gives way to a boreal forest of spruce, tamarack, and jack pine—the domain of mink, otters, foxes, black bears, and wolves. The once rare beaver is common again, not least thanks to the pioneering conservation work of Grey Owl, whose cabin stands at the end of one of the park's many trails. Myriad lakes, rivers, and other bodies of water attract numerous vacationers and pleasure-seekers, particularly around the **Waskesiu Lake** town site. **Lavallée Lake,** however, is out of bounds, since it is the home of a flock of white pelicans.

🏕 213 C3 www.pc.gc.ca ✉ 56 miles N of Prince Albert via Hwy. 2 ☎ 306/633-4522 💲 $$

GRASSLANDS NATIONAL PARK

This national park's mandate is to conserve significant remnants of the once extensive mixed-grass prairie. A visitor center in **Val Marie** *(closed Sat.–Sun. in winter months)* provides insight into this quintessential prairie landscape, with its wildflowers and 40-plus species of grasses forming the tough cover known as "prairie wool." Fauna includes gophers, pronghorn, mule deer, and Canada's only colony of black-tailed prairie dogs.

🏕 213 C1 www.pc.gc.ca ✉ Between Val Marie & Kildeer S of Hwy. 18 ☎ 306/298-2257

CYPRESS HILLS INTERPROVINCIAL PARK

Shared by Saskatchewan and Alberta, these hills are the highest land between Labrador and the Rockies, rising to more than 4,800 feet. With a moister climate, richer vegetation, and a delightfully varied relief, they seemed "a perfect oasis in the desert" to the surveyor John Palliser in 1859.

🏕 212 B1 www.cypresshills.com ✉ 17 miles S of Maple Creek via Hwy. 21 & 271 ☎ 306/662-5411 ∎

Edmonton

"A CITY YOU COME FROM, NOT A PLACE TO VISIT," WAS Montréaler Mordecai Richler's grumpy dismissal of the capital of Alberta, one of the northernmost big cities in the world, with a ferocious winter climate to match. Yet Edmonton has much going for it: The checklist of the usual metropolitan amenities is full enough, with museums, a symphony orchestra, a year-long round of festivals, and a wonderful network of green spaces based on the valley of the North Saskatchewan River that bisects the built-up area. In addition to a light rail rapid transit line, one of the first of its kind in North America, a citywide system of "ped-ways" offers refuge from the rigors of winter.

Edmonton
🅐 212 B3
Visitor information
www.edmonton.com
www.infoedmonton.com
✉ 9990 Jasper Ave. N.W.
☎ 780/496-8400 or 800/463-4667
🕐 Closed Sat.–Sun.

Gateway Park
✉ 2404 Gateway Blvd. S.W.
☎ 780/496-8400

The valley of the North Saskatchewan attracted early human occupation for thousands of years, with its relatively abundant resources of water, wood, and wildlife. Trading posts arrived late in the 18th century, and were rebuilt several times before Fort Edmonton was consolidated on the site now occupied by the provincial legislative building *(97th Ave. & 107th St.)*. Always the Gateway to the North, Edmonton lost out when the Canadian Pacific routed its tracks on the southern alignment through Calgary in 1883. The arrival of the other transcontinental railroads in the early 20th century was some compensation, as was the city's selection as provincial capital (1905) and site of the University of Alberta. During World War II Edmonton was the operations base for the construction of the Alaska Highway and the Canol oil pipeline. In 1947 the first of several oil fields was discovered—dictating the city's fortunes ever since.

The core of the city is formed by **Churchill Square,** dominated by modern structures including the acclaimed City Hall (1993), the five-auditorium **Citadel Theatre** *(9828–101 A Ave., tel 780/425-1820),* the Court House, and the **Art Gallery** *(2 Churchill Sq., tel 780/422-6223),* with its changing exhibits of mainly Canadian art. Stepping down the 200-foot-deep valley of the North Saskatchewan River is the unusual Convention Centre, greeted from the far bank by the equally striking glass pyramids of the **Muttart Conservatory** *(9626–96 A St., tel 780/496-8787),* which contain the exotic plant communities of arid, temperate, and tropical climates. From here there is a striking panorama of the bulky building blocks of the city center. Upstream, around the bend in the river, stands the massive beaux arts **Alberta Legislative Building.** Completed in 1913, its grandiose portico and dome made it perhaps the most imposing of all the prairie parliaments—a far cry from the crude fort that once occupied the site. ∎

Referred to by some as "Giza on the Saskatchewan," the glass pyramids of Muttart Conservatory (1977) make a dramatic addition to the Edmonton townscape.

More places to visit around Edmonton

FORT EDMONTON PARK

What is claimed to be Canada's largest living history park is a thorough attempt to re-create Edmonton's past by means of authentic-looking reproductions of buildings and authentically costumed and scripted townsfolk. The trip in time is based on four periods: the 1846 fur-trading post of Fort Edmonton with the Big House of the chief factor; Jasper Avenue of 1885 with its stores and NWMP post; a 1905 Street with its tramway; and 1920 Street. www.edmonton.ca/fort ✉ Off Whitemud Dr., 5 miles SW of downtown ☎ 780/496-8787 🕐 Closed Oct.–April 💲 $$$

ROYAL ALBERTA MUSEUM

This museum offers a fine introduction to the human and natural history of the province. A highlight is the Syncrude Gallery of Aboriginal Culture and Wild Alberta, which features all aspects of the lives of the original inhabitants of the western plains. Other galleries explain the major ecosystems of the province, its exceptional wealth of natural resources, its prehistory, and the story of European settlement. www.royalalbertamuseum.ca ✉ 12845 102nd Ave. ☎ 780/453-9100 💲 $$

WEST EDMONTON MALL

More than 800 stores, 100 or more eating places, late night spots, a huge covered amusement park and indoor water park , an NHL-size skating rink, and an indoor lake complete with submarines (more, some would jest, than the Canadian Navy owns) … the list of superlatives goes on. The 5.2 million-square-foot mall may be architecturally undistinguished, but its sheer size and popularity (more than six million visitors a year) make a visit almost an obligation. www.westedmontonmall.com ✉ 170th St. & 87th Ave., 5 miles W of downtown ☎ 780/444-5300 or 800/661-8890 ■

Thriving West Edmonton Mall has defied critics who said that the sparsely populated provinces would never support such a massive commercial venture.

Alberta badlands

FOR MANY MILES ALONG THE VALLEY CARVED BY THE RED Deer River, gullies, buttes, flat-topped mesas, and the mushroom-shaped pinnacles known as hoodoos form a weird moonscape known as the Alberta badlands. One of the world's richest sources of dinosaur remains, the area includes the world heritage site of Dinosaur Provincial Park as well as the Royal Tyrrell Museum of Palaeontology, one of the finest of its kind.

Alberta badlands
🅰 212 B2

In complete contrast to the feature-less prairie all around, the deep channel carved by the glacial ancestor of today's Red Deer River is full of strange, even uncanny, forms, made all the more stark in appearance by the lack of vegeta-tion and the somber coloring of the exposed rocks. The hoodoos are the most spectacular, their caps of resistant red ironstone protecting softer layers of sandstone or silt-stone beneath—at least temporari-ly, since this whole landscape is in a constant state of transformation.

The rate of erosion here is rapid, up to one-fifth of an inch a year, 2,000 times more than the far harder rocks of the mountains to the west. There is also human interference in the form of trampling and tamper-ing, and visitors are asked to respect these strange and beautiful—but ultimately, delicate—features.

The badlands extend along creeks and gullies some distance from the main valley. An impressive introduction to the area can be seen on the approach from Calgary, at the lookout giving a panoramic view over **Horseshoe Canyon** (Hwy. 9). Northwest of where the old mining town of **Drumheller** spreads out along the valley floor is the **Dinosaur Trail**, a 32-mile circular driving route offering an overview of the changing land-scapes of the valley and a ferry ride across the river. The best hoodoos are 10 miles southeast of Drumheller, just off Hwy. 10. And an essential stop along the Dinosaur Trail is the magnificent Royal Tyrrell museum.

Formed from sediments deposited in an ancient inland sea, Alberta's badlands have been eroded into their present strange forms by the action of water and weather.

Most terrible of all the dinosaurs, *Tyrannosaurus rex* evokes awe even as a skeleton.

ROYAL TYRRELL MUSEUM OF PALAEONTOLOGY

Guarded by sprinting sculptures of dinosaurs, this long and low museum building echoes the shapes and colors of its setting.

Visitors can admire the colorful denizens of a Devonian reef, wander among the primeval plants of the Paleo-conservatory, plunge their hands deep into a pile of simulated *Triceratops* dung to identify its diet, enjoy audiovisual shows, work at computer stations, and even watch laboratory experts preparing fossils for preservation. But the heart of the museum is the superb array of skeletons in the Dinosaur Hall. Thirty-five in all, they constitute the largest display of its kind in the world. Here is *Albertosaurus* with its daggerlike fangs and clawed hind feet, and the weak-toothed but well-armored *Edmontia*, as well as *Quetzacoatlus*, the largest flying creature ever, and, of course, *Tyrannosaurus rex.*

Another exhibit devoted to the Burgess Shale (see p. 265) provides a 3-D look at the unusual creatures which swam in prehistoric waters. In addition to the museum, the Royal Tyrrell runs a field station in Dinosaur Provincial Park (see below) where most of its 150,000-item fossil collection comes from.

DINOSAUR PROVINCIAL PARK

Established in 1955, the 18,000-acre park was given world heritage status in 1979 in recognition of its extraordinary wealth of dinosaur remains, unequaled except in the Nemegt Valley of Mongolia. The park's badland scenery includes stately stands of plains cottonwoods, a valuable habitat for the area's rich bird life.

There are campsites and other services, but the focal point of the park is the **Field Station** of the Royal Tyrrell museum. A base for continuing scientific work, it also displays skeletons and other material in an exhibit building. There are self-guided trails, conducted hikes, and, most interesting of all, bus tours to areas under excavation not otherwise accessible to the public *(reservations needed).* ■

Royal Tyrrell Museum of Palaeontology

🗺 212 B2

www.tyrrellmuseum.com

✉ 4 miles NW of Drumheller in Midland Provincial Park

☎ 403/823-7707 or 888/440-4240

🕐 Closed Mon. mid-Oct.–mid-May

💲 $$

Dinosaur Provincial Park

🗺 212 B2

www.cd.gov.ab.ca/parks /dinosaur

✉ 30 miles NE of Trans-Canada 1 from Brooks

☎ 403/378-4342

🕐 Park open year-round; visitor center closed Oct.–May

💲 $$

Calgary

CALGARY IS SET 3,000 FEET UP AMID THE COWBOY country of the Alberta ranch lands, with the eastern range of the Rockies as an incomparable backdrop. Its strong identity has in recent years been enhanced by a cluster of handsome office towers. Despite the city's historic reliance on vulnerable, resource-based industries—first agriculture, then oil—it survived sometimes violent fluctuations in prosperity to maintain its cheerful, very Western spirit, best experienced during its world-famous Calgary Stampede. Even the climate is friendly: The sun shines here more than in the rest of Canada, and the winter cold is often relieved by the warm wind from the west known as the Chinook.

Calgary

🗺 212 B2

Visitor information

www.tourismcalgary.com

✉ Calgary Tower Centre, 101 9th Ave. S.W.

☎ 403/263-8510 or 800/661-1678

The city's beginnings go back to 1875 and the construction of the North West Mounted Police fort at the confluence of the Bow and Elbow Rivers. When the tracks of the Canadian Pacific reached Fort Calgary in 1883 the railroad craftily built its station on its own land, across the Elbow and opposite the settlement that had grown up around the fort. Residents soon migrated to what was obviously going to be a boomtown, roping up their dwellings and dragging them across the frozen river.

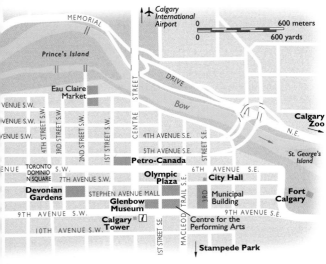

Spectators at the Calgary Stampede, with the aptly named Saddledome Stadium in the background

Calgary's distinctive skyline rises above a dual-tram and pedestrian bridge.

Calgary prospered because of its strategic position on the transcontinental railroad and, as the western prairies filled up with ranchers and other settlers, became a great agricultural center. Oil, the region's other major source of wealth, was tapped in the Turner Valley southwest of the city as early as 1914. But the real oil boom came after World War II, boosting population growth and fueling construction of glamorous corporate buildings as well as urban expressways and an efficient public transportation system based on light rail rapid transit.

DOWNTOWN

The city's closely spaced high-rise buildings give it an instantly recognizable profile, whether seen from far across the prairie or close up, from the high rim of the valley carved by the Bow River. A number of older structures remain from the late 19th century, many built from excellent local sandstone. Several stand along **Stephen Avenue Mall,** one of the main east–west streets, now open only to pedestrians. East beyond **Olympic Plaza,** built for the ceremonies of the Winter Games hosted here in 1988, the rugged sandstone of the old **City Hall** makes a fascinating contrast with the sleek blue glass of its new annex. To the west, the most distinguished of the towers gracing the townscape are probably those of the chisel-topped **Petro-Canada complex,** completed in 1984.

As in several other Canadian cities, Calgary has a weather-proof circulation system for pedestrians, known here as Plus-15, since its 40 or so bridges and 7 miles of walkways are built 15 feet above street level. Offering access to most shops and offices is **Devonian Gardens,** a 2.5-acre paradise of water features and luxuriant plant growth above the streets. ■

More places to visit in Calgary

CALGARY TOWER

Its impact somewhat diminished by the office towers, the Calgary Tower nevertheless offers the best all-around view of the city and its setting. Completed in 1968, its 626 feet are topped by a revolving restaurant.
www.calgarytower.com ✉ 9th Ave. & Centre St. S. ☎ 403/266-7171 $ $$$

CALGARY ZOO, BOTANICAL GARDEN, & PREHISTORIC PARK

Well located on an island in the Bow River, Calgary's zoo hosts animals from all over the world. But its originality lies in a bold re-creation of characteristic habitats, featuring not just the animals but the landscapes in which they live. You can visit Eurasia, Australia, and Africa, as well as the Canadian wilds complete with grizzly bears. Also popular is Prehistoric Park, although the artificial dinosaurs seem incongruous in an institution otherwise populated by live animals.
www.calgaryzoo.org ✉ 1300 Zoo Rd. N.E., Whitehorn C-Train to Zoo Station ☎ 403/232-9300 $ $$$

FORT CALGARY

The stockade surrounding the NWMP fort was torn down as early as 1882 and the fort itself rebuilt after destruction by fire in 1887. It finally disappeared under the installations of the Grand Trunk Railroad in 1914. This historic site, the nucleus of today's city, was turned into parkland as part of Calgary's centennial celebrations in 1975. This reconstruction of the 1875 fort is complemented by an interpretive center that gives a good account of the city's evolution from simple stockade to metropolis.
www.fortcalgary.com ✉ 750 9th Ave. S.E. ☎ 403/290-1875 $ $$

GLENBOW MUSEUM

A giant, icicle-like sculpture representing the aurora borealis rises up through all floors of this modern building named for the ranch of the oil tycoon who assembled many of the varied collections of this fine museum.

A wonderful array of artifacts illustrates

Calgary Zoo specializes in re-creating convincing western habitats.

the lives of the varied human groups that have made an impact on the Canadian West. The First Nations Gallery features objects of rare beauty and interest such as a superb Stony Indian headdress of 96 eagle feathers, and a big tepee, its flaps east-facing to welcome the sun and the Creator. The ethnic and cultural diversity of European settlers is effectively communicated in the domestic objects piled high in "Homage to the Homeland," while the golden age of ranching in the 1880s is evoked, as are the sodbusters, homesteaders who followed the cattlemen and plowed up the prairie after fencing it off with barbed wire.

Among other interestingly arranged and interpreted displays is a celebration of West African cultural achievements, and "Warriors," a fascinating cross-cultural account of combat.
www.glenbow.org ✉ 130 9th Ave. S.E. ☎ 403/268-4100 $ $$

HERITAGE PARK HISTORICAL VILLAGE

Among the largest of its kind in Canada, this site is a thorough attempt to re-create the atmosphere of the pre-1914 Canadian West—more than 150 buildings and exhibits, plus stagecoaches, trams, a steam train, and an antique fairground, attended by people in period garb.
www.heritagepark.ca ✉ 1900 Heritage Dr. S.W. ☎ 403/268-8500 🕑 Closed Nov.–April & Mon.–Fri. Sept.–Oct. $ $$ ■

Calgary Stampede

Every July the sleek skyscrapers of Calgary look down on a colorfully chaotic scene as business suits give way to western outfits—Stetsons, blue jeans, bolo ties, and hand-heeled boots—and citizens join genuine cowboys in a ten-day celebration of the city's cowtown heritage. Billed as the greatest out-door show on earth, the Calgary Stampede offers thrills galore: bronco busting, bull riding, steer wrestling, calf roping, and, most heart-stopping of all, chuck-wagon racing.

Organized by American rodeo cowboy Guy Weadick, the very first stampede opened on September 2, 1912, with a spectacular parade of 1,000 cowboys and 3,000 Indians in full ceremonial dress, as well as veterans of the early days of the North West Mounted Police and even survivors of the Riel Rebellion. Rodeo stars flocked in from all over Canada and the United States. Skeptics had prophesied a flop, saying that the great days of ranching and cowboys were over, and that the future belonged to the sodbusters and their wheat crop. "All the more reason to stage a show," was Weadick's retort. In fact, ranching survived while many homesteaders failed in the dry years of the Dirty Thirties. This first stampede was a great success, with an estimated 40,000 spectators at a time when Calgary counted only 60,000 inhabitants. A special thrill was the subjugation of the legendary black bronco Cyclone by the little-known rodeo rider Tom Three Persons, who outperformed established stars to win a purse of one thousand dollars.

World War I stopped the shows, but the stampede was revived and, in 1923, linked with the big annual agricultural fair to become the Calgary Exhibition and Stampede. Today prize money amounts to some $600,000, and visitor numbers reach the million mark. They fill Stampede Park just south of downtown not just for the thrills and spills of the rodeo and chuck-wagon races, but also to enjoy the livestock shows, the amusement park, and a myriad of other attractions. In the evening the Stampede Grandstand features precision kicking dancers and other spectacular entertainment. Downtown streets come alive with revelers and country music as bars, restaurants, and night spots do a roaring trade. Strict vegetarians wrestle with their principles at the sight of beef-dominated menus.

Wild and chaotic chuck-wagon racing can be a dusty affair. The wagon's original role was to carry food and other supplies to the men on the range.

By morning it's time to begin all over again, fortified with a free breakfast of pancakes and coffee.

First featured in the 1923 stampede, chuck-wagon races evolved from what was originally a stagecoach race. Each team consists of a driver, four horses, and four outriders. Before setting off, the wagon is loaded with tent poles and a stove, all of which must remain well stowed during the contest. The wagon is then steered around a figure-eight course marked by barrels before tearing around the half-mile-long main track. Casualties among riders and horses are not uncommon, despite a tightening-up of rules. Animal-rights activists have intervened on behalf of the horses, but the human participants pursue the race with a passion that defies the risk of broken bones.

Ranching legacy

Beef came in quantity to the Calgary area in the 1880s, when cattle were driven up from Montana to satisfy the healthy appetites of the

Staying on a bronco for eight seconds or more is achievement enough for even an ambitious rider.

newly arrived Mounties and provide an alternative source of protein to the once-plentiful bison. Great ranches were established, many by wealthy landowners from Britain as well as eastern Canada. Early difficulties and the arrival of homesteaders intent on crop farming seemed to spell ranching's demise. But it survived to play an important role in the economic life of the province, and an even more pervasive cultural role, as any visitor to the stampede will realize.

Several of the most famous ranches are open to the public. For example, the 100,000-acre **Cochrane Ranch** *(Tel 403/932-2902)* on the Bow River just to the west of Calgary has lavish displays on the history of the rodeo and livestock farming, while the equally prestigious **Bar U Ranch** *(Tel 403/395-2212 or 800/568-4996)* is now run by Parks Canada as a national historic site . ■

Calgary excursions

Head-Smashed-In Buffalo Jump was exploited masterfully by early hunters.

HEAD-SMASHED-IN BUFFALO JUMP

The bison jump in the Porcupine Hills of southwestern Alberta is one of the most evocative Plains Indian sites in Canada, its importance recognized in the granting of UNESCO world heritage status in 1981. An interpretive center, inserted into the escarpment with consummate skill, tells the story of the site's use as a bison-killing ground for several millennia.

The long period of use beginning some 5,700 years ago left 35-foot-thick bone beds at the base of the cliffs over which the bison were driven. This invaluable resource for archaeological investigation is especially intriguing for the light shed on the evolution of tool making and use. Inside the center's seven-tiered building superb displays give a comprehensive account of the techniques of the jump and of its material and spiritual significance. A path leads from the building's uppermost terrace along the top of the cliff, offering wonderful views of the prairies to the east and, to the west, of the terrain so expertly used to drive the bison herds to their doom.

🅰 212 B2 www.head-smashed-in.com ✉ 11 miles NW of Fort Macleod via Rte. 785 ☎ 403/553-2731 💲 $$

FORT MACLEOD

The kernel of the Canadian presence in the West, the fort was named in honor of NWMP Assistant Commissioner Macleod, who helped lead the epic expedition of 1874 when the Police made their way to the West. Its timber stockade, together with a number of buildings, have been reconstructed to make a setting for musical rides 1876-style *(July–Aug.)* and other events.

🅰 212 B2 www.nwmpmuseum.com ✉ Fort Macleod ☎ 403/553-4703 🕐 Closed Jan.–Feb.

FRANK SLIDE INTERPRETIVE CENTRE

The road to the **Crowsnest Pass,** part of the southernmost route through the Canadian Rockies, links a number of poignant reminders of the coal industry that briefly thrived here in the early years of the 20th century.

As you approach the fine old powerhouse building of the **Leitch Collieries,** a great mass of rock appears to block the way ahead. This is the Frank Slide, more than a billion cubic feet of limestone that in April 1903 detached itself from Turtle Mountain and crashed into the valley, instantly burying 70 people in their homes.

The story of this horrific event, together with other aspects of the area's history, is told in the modern interpretive center built high on a bluff overlooking the valley.

🅰 212 B2 www.frankslide.com ✉ Crowsnest Pass on Hwy. 3 ☎ 403/562-7388 💲 $

REMINGTON-ALBERTA CARRIAGE CENTRE

Founded in 1887 by Mormons who arrived in one of the very last covered wagon treks, the little town of **Cardston** is an appropriate home for this magnificent array of horse-drawn vehicles, the largest in North America. Displayed in a modern building with state-of-the-art techniques, the collection ranges from crude carts to elaborate vehicles such as park drags and sumptuous hearses, many shown in carefully re-created settings.

www.remingtoncarriagemuseum.com ✉ 623 Main St., Cardston ☎ 403/653-5139 💲 $$ ∎

The gleam of snowcapped peaks and the glitter of ice fields is reflected in the aboriginal name for the Canadian Rockies, the "Shining Mountains." Today, these same glories attract thousands of visitors from all over the world.

The Rockies

Introduction & map **242–43**
Alberta 244–61
Banff National Park **244–49**
Lake Louise **250–51**
Icefields Parkway drive **252–55**
Jasper National Park **258–61**
British Columbia 264–69
Yoho National Park **264–65**
Kootenay National Park **266–67**
Glacier & Mount Revelstoke
    National Parks **268–69**
Waterton Lakes National Park
    270
Hotels & restaurants
    in the Rockies **367-69**

**Maligne Lake,
Jasper National Park**

The Rockies

IT IS NOT HARD TO SEE WHY THE CANADIAN ROCKY MOUNTAINS have become one of the country's most mesmerizing attractions, even drawing visitors from other mountainous countries to marvel at their untamed splendor. Most come to the mountain core formed by the national parks of Banff, Jasper, Yoho, and Kootenay, whose global significance (together with the provincial parks of Mounts Robson and Assiniboine) was designated in 1985 as a world heritage area. Rising from the rolling prairies in the east, the Rockies are bounded to the west by the great rift valley known as the Rocky Mountain Trench. Beyond are the Columbia Mountains, embracing Glacier and Revelstoke National Parks, which, together with Alberta's Waterton Lakes National Park, are described here because of their strong links with the Rocky Mountains.

The natural wonders of the Rockies combine to form a pristine landscape that was the birthplace in Canada of what elsewhere seem incompatible twins, tourism and conservation. In the late 19th century and early 20th century, as the railroads approached the Rockies from the east, government and business capital joined forces both to attract visitors and to protect the environment. Clever publicity encouraged the leisured classes of Europe and North America to visit what was billed as a mountain wilderness while staying in the luxury of château-style hotels. At the same time, reserves were established that were later expanded to become forest parks, then national parks; Banff was among the very first of the world's great landscapes to be so protected.

A century of conservation means that today's visitors can come into easy contact with superlative scenery still in its near-natural state. A network of roads such as the Icefields Parkway not only leads along the river valleys but crosses high passes and even gives access to the awesome Athabasca Glacier. The Canadian Pacific still threads its way through some of the harshest terrain ever penetrated by a railroad, though the only passenger trains to use its track these days are visitor specials. Few experiences could be more sublime than watching the peaks roll past from the comfort of the panorama car attached to such a train, though a leisurely drive along the incomparable Icefields Parkway comes close.

Road and rail are not the only ways to see the Rockies; at Banff and Jasper gondolas float above it, while the Snocoaches at the Columbia Icefield grind over it. But in order to be really "in" the landscape, there is no alternative to

The sublime beauty of Lake Louise in Banff National Park

walking. This does not necessarily mean hiking into the backcountry with a tent and several days' supply of food, though some of the finest wilderness trails in North America can be explored here, and for even more adventurous spirits there are both summer and winter mountaineering. The majority of visitors are more than satisfied with the superb network of footpaths, which range from lakeside strolls with full wheelchair access to half- and whole-day hikes. Bicycling is becoming an increasingly popular way of getting around—the Icefields Parkway is recognized as one of the best routes in the world. For those attracted to water, there is everything from paddling a canoe on a tranquil lake to braving the fiercest white water.

Banff's Sunshine Village downhill ski area has the second longest season of anywhere in Canada. As well as many cross-country ski trails, there are three other downhill areas within the national parks, and another one in

P. 314

Chetwynd

Fort McLeod

Tumbler
Ridge

ARP LAKE
OV. PARK

Murray

Parsnip

R
O
C
K
Y

97

MONKMAN
PROV. PARK

Wabiti

Ottawa

McGregor

YELLOWHEAD HIGHWAY

Kakwa

Smoky

P. 212

P. 273

Fraser

Cariboo

Bowron

Grande Cache

16

WILLMORE
WILDERNESS
PROVINCIAL PARK

Athabasca

BOWRON
LAKE
PROV. PARK

JASPER
NATIONAL
PARK

16

Hinton

Edson

3954m
Tête Jaune Cache • Mt. Robson

BRITISH

Quesnel Lake

Mts.

Valemount

Yellowhead
Pass

Miette Hot Springs

Cadomin

Maligne Canyon

Medicine Lake

Jasper

MT. ROBSON
PROV. PARK

2495m

Azure Mt.

WELLS GRAY
PROV. PARK

Clearwater

Blue River

Mica
Dam

Mica Creek

3363m ▲
Mt. Edith Cavell

HAMBER
PROV. PARK

North Thompson

Kinbasket
Lake

Adams

M
o
u
n
t
a
i
n

Athabasca
Falls

Maligne Lake

3470m
Mt. Brazeau

Sunwapta Falls

Columbia
Icefield

3747m

Mt. Columbia

93

ALBERTA

North Saskatchewan

Saskatchewan
River Crossing

Rocky
Mountain
House

COLUMBIA

Monashee Mts.

Lake
Revelstoke

5

Shuswap
Lake

Rogers Pass

Columbia

ICEFIELD PKWY

Kicking
Horse Pass

BANFF
NATIONAL
PARK

5

MT. REVELSTOKE
NAT. PARK

Selkirk

GLACIER
NATIONAL
PARK

Field

YOHO
NAT. PARK

Lake Louise

Moraine Lake

Castle Junction

Vermilion Pass

Minnewanka

Sicamous

1

Revelstoke

Upper
Arrow
Lake

Shelter Bay

Galena Bay

Purcell Mts.

Duncan

Marble Canyon
& Paint Pots

MT. ASSINIBOINE
PROV. PARK

Bow

Banff

Cochrane

Canmore

1

P. 273

KOOTENAY
NAT. PARK

PETER
LOUGHEED
PROV. PARK

Radium
Hot Springs

Invermere

Kootenay

ELK LAKES
PROV. PARK

P. 212

95

TOP OF THE
WORLD
PROV. PARK

Elkford

Sparwood

Crowsnest
Pass

3

Fernie

WATERTON LAKES
NAT. PARK

U.S.A

0 ——— 100 kilometers
0 ——— 50 miles

P. 273

Kananaskis Country. This is the name of the
1,550-square-mile area of provincial parkland
southeast of Banff. It has the same superlative
landscape as the national parks, but encour-
ages controlled development of recreational
facilities, thereby relieving more vulnerable
areas. Look here for accommodations, especially in Canmore (www.canmorealberta.com),
when Banff and Jasper are booked solid, as
they often are in summer. ■

A   B

C

2 ▷

I ▷

A   B   C   D   E

Banff National Park

Banff NP
▲ 243 D3
**Park
information**
www.pc.gc.ca
✉ 224 Banff Ave.
☎ 403/762-1550
⑤ $$

**Town
information**
www.visitors-info.com
✉ 224 Banff Ave.
☎ 403/762-8421

CANADA'S FIRST AND MOST FAMOUS NATIONAL PARK combines some of the most spectacular scenery in the Rockies with ease of access and a long tradition of catering to visitors.

The park's origins go back to 1883. Construction of the Canadian Pacific Railway up the valley of the Bow River had stopped for the winter, and a pair of workers occupied themselves with prospecting for minerals around the recently completed Siding No. 29. Instead of precious metals, they came upon an equally valuable resource, the hot sulfurous springs noted by an earlier explorer. The men's attempt to stake a claim came to nothing: Within two years the area around

OUTDOOR ACTIVITIES

For those looking for a break from the pampered luxury of the Banff Springs Hotel—or who simply want to make the most of the magnificent surroundings—Banff offers a wide choice of exhilarating pastimes. The Banff Visitor Centre (see above) provides information on these activities, with whitewater rafting and helihiking topping the list for many thrill-seekers. There are also a number of recommended climbs and hikes in the surrounding mountains. Horseback riding and mountain biking are also popular around Banff. Less strenuous, but no less enjoyable, are glacier ice-field tours aboard Snocoaches and boat trips on Lake Minnewanka. ■

the springs was designated as the Banff Hot Springs Reserve, and then, in 1887, renamed the Rocky Mountains Park. After Yellowstone and Australia's Royal, it was only the third area in the world to be protected as a national park. It was extended to its present size, 2,563 square miles, in 1902.

By 1887, the Canadian Pacific's energetic general manager, Van Horne, had already commissioned his architect to design a 250-bed spa hotel, part of his plan to lure the rich and famous to the "Mountain Playground of the World," by CPR train, of course. The trek from Siding No. 29 up to the **Banff Springs Hotel** proved inconvenient and the station was soon moved to its present location, though it no longer has regular passenger train service. The hotel, by contrast, has gone from strength to strength; successive extensions have made it a supreme example of what has been termed the Canadian château style, and it is as dominant

Banff Springs Hotel

www.fairmont.com

✉ Spray Ave.

☎ 403/762-2211

💲 $$ (tours of the complex)

A solitary hiker admires Banff National Park's incredible panoramas.

Banff townsite

243 D2

Archetypal château-style architecture—the Banff Springs Hotel

a feature in the landscape of Banff township as the surrounding mountains.

BANFF TOWNSITE
The vast majority of visitors arrive in the resort of Banff by road, most of them along Trans-Canada 1, as it climbs away from the prairie up the valley of the Bow River. The town's permanent population of about 5,000 swells to more than 30,000 in summer. Most of the national park's nearly four million annual visitors spend at least some time here.

The town has a fair number of man-made attractions, and it is perfectly possible to spend a stay here strolling the streets, shopping, seeing and being seen, all against the backdrop of fabulous mountain scenery. But Banff's main role is as a starting point for the excellent drives and trails that bring visitors into immediate contact with the mountains. Not surprisingly, Parks Canada runs a very full interpretive program, and a visit to the Banff Visitor Centre makes a worthwhile start to any stay in the national park. ■

Around Banff townsite

BANFF PARK MUSEUM
NATIONAL HISTORIC SITE

This is western Canada's oldest natural history museum, founded in 1903. The array of stuffed native animals is evidence of a now-outdated approach to wildlife interpretation, but the museum has lots of character.
✉ 91 Banff Ave. ☎ 403/762-1558 🕒 Closed Nov.–April 💲 $

BOW FALLS

Just before it joins the Spray River at the foot of the Banff Springs Hotel, the Bow River has cut these falls into an outcrop of Sulphur

Mountain siltstone. Trails along both sides of the Bow River allow access to overlooks and superb views of the Banff Springs Hotel.

CAVE AND BASIN
NATIONAL HISTORIC SITE

The first facilities to take advantage of Banff's hot springs were bath houses built in 1887. These were replaced in 1914 by a more elaborate structure and swimming pool, which eventually became unsafe due to the weakness of the tufa deposits on which it was built. A rebuilding project has restored the site to its glamorous 1914 appearance—although you may not swim. Displays tell the story of the site, the starting point of Banff and the whole Canadian parks movement.
www.pc.gc.ca ✉ End of Cave Ave.
☎ 403/762-1566 💲 $

BUFFALO NATIONS MUSEUM

Norman Luxton settled here in 1901 and devoted most of his life to promoting Banff as a resort. On good terms with the First Nations people of the area, he organized the town's Indian Days and dedicated a museum to their heritage. After his death, Luxton's collections were managed by Calgary's Glenbow Museum, but they are now cared for by local First Nations people.
✉ 1 Birch Ave. ☎ 403/762-2388 🕒 Closed mid-Oct.–mid-May 💲 $$

WHYTE MUSEUM
OF THE CANADIAN ROCKIES

Born in Banff, Peter Whyte and his American wife, Catherine, both of them artists, devoted their lives to portraying local people and land-scape and collecting documents and artifacts relating to the region. Their collection forms the basis of the Archives of the Canadian Rockies, an important research resource. Displays give an overview of how the Rockies were conquered and how Banff developed as a resort. Together with the library of the Alpine Club of Canada and galleries for temporary exhibitions on local themes, the archives are housed in a fine modern building.
www.whyte.org ✉ 111 Bear St. ☎ 403/762-2291 💲 $ ■

Short excursions from Banff townsite

BOW VALLEY PARKWAY

The original road built in 1920 to link Banff and Lake Louise, 30 miles away, has become a relaxed alternative to the more recent Trans-Canada 1, a busy road used by heavy trucks. Numerous turnoffs offer views of the valley and its dramatic mountain backdrop, and there is a chance of encountering wildlife such as caribou, deer, or moose.

At **Johnston Canyon,** 16 miles from Banff, Johnston Creek has eroded a deep cleft in the limestone, which is made accessible by a carefully constructed catwalk. Waterfalls occur where the flow of water encounters layers of harder dolomite, as at the 50-foot high **Lower Falls** (just over 0.5 mile from the parking lot) and at the 100-foot **Upper Falls** (just over 1 mile). Farther still (3.5 miles from the parking lot) are the **Ink Pots,** a series of cold-water springs, normally clear blue in color, but sometimes changing to an inky black.

Continuing along the parkway as far as **Castle Junction,** the serrated mountains to the northeast belong to the distinctive Sawback Range, which make up part of the front ranges of the Rocky Mountains. At Castle Junction, the fault line is crossed, separating the front ranges from the eastern main ranges to the west. Part of the eastern main range, the great landmark of Castle Mountain (9,075 feet), 21 miles northwest of Banff, is a supreme example of a castellated mountain, with its typical layer cake appearance produced by a series of cliffs and ledges.

THE HOODOOS

A short interpretive trail along the Bow River leads to a viewpoint overlooking these strange columns, a geological freak sculpted in debris-flow deposits.

✉ 2.5 miles from Banff townsite on Tunnel Mountain Drive

LAKE MINNEWANKA LOOP DRIVE

The largest water body in the national park is a reservoir, used to generate hydroelectric power and a popular venue for boating and fishing.

🗺 243 D3 ✉ 12-mile round-trip from Banff townsite

MOUNT NORQUAY

A well-engineered road with a series of hair-pin bends climbs steeply up the northern flank of the Bow Valley to give ever wider views of the mountain landscape. The Mount Norquay Ski Area saw the beginnings of the sport here in the early 20th century. A network of trails leads into the mountains from the parking lot.

🗺 243 D2 ✉ 5 miles from Banff townsite on Norquay Rd.

SULPHUR MOUNTAIN

The 7,497-foot-high crest of Sulphur Mountain, reached by an eight-minute gondola ride, offers those who are not up to a challenging walk a superb high-level panorama of Banff townsite in its mountain setting. There is a restaurant, the highest in Canada, and the mountaintop is a favorite spot for bighorn sheep to hang around and look for a handout. A 0.6-mile trail leads to the restored weather station of 1903.

www.banffgondola.com ✉ 3 miles from Banff townsite on Mountain Ave. ☎ 403/762-2523 💲 Gondola: $$$

UPPER HOT SPRINGS

The Upper Hot Springs have been exploited as a visitor attraction since the start of the 20th century. The water in this large outdoor pool, which was built when the springs were redeveloped in the 1930s, stays at an average temperature of 38°C. A steamroom, massage, and plunge pool complement your swim. There is also a poolside restaurant.

✉ 3 miles from Banff townsite on Mountain Ave. ☎ 403/762-1515 💲 $$

VERMILION LAKES DRIVE

This 2.5-mile drive leads past a series of shallow lakes in the broad floodplain of the Bow River and gives fine views toward Mount Rundle. The lakes are frequented by beavers (responsible for damming two of them), moose, deer, bighorn sheep, and wolves, and they are an excellent spot for bird-watching, particularly in the early morning or at dusk.

🗺 243 D2 ✉ 2 miles west of Banff townsite off Norquay Rd. ∎

The unmistakable peak of Mount Assiniboine stands well clear of its neighbors.

Mount Assiniboine

Part of the world heritage area and a paradise of glacial lakes and alpine meadows, Mount Assiniboine Provincial Park in British Columbia guards its secrets from all but those prepared to backpack. No roads lead to the park, which is named for the Assiniboine, members of the Sioux Confederation. The park has a score of peaks exceeding 8,000 feet. The mightiest of them all is Mount Assiniboine itself (11,870 feet), whose distinctive horn profile recalls that of Switzerland's famous Matterhorn. *(Visitor information, BC Parks, www.env.gov.bc.ca/bcparks)* ■

Lake Louise

243 D3

**Parks Canada
visitor center**
www.pc.gc.ca
Next to
Samson Mall
403/522-3833

**Château
Lake Louise**
www.fairmont.com
Lake Louise Dr.
403/522-3511

FEW SCENES CAN BE MORE PHOTOGENIC THAN THE ONE revealed from the lawns in front of Château Lake Louise. In their frame of dark green forest, the emerald lake and its backdrop of white-capped mountains combine to make an irresistible composition for the cameras of the million or so visitors who come here every year.

The lake, which owes its summer color to the rock flour suspended in its waters, was first seen by a European in 1882, when Tom Wilson, a packhorse owner working for the Canadian Pacific, was brought here by his Stoney guide, Edwin Hunter. The Stoney called it the Lake of Little Fishes, but Wilson could find no better name for it than Emerald Lake. Two years later, the lake was officially renamed after Princess Louise Caroline Alberta, one of Queen Victoria's daughters and the wife of the then Canadian governor-general.

The CPR was quick to see the potential of what Wilson had called "a matchless scene;" its first accommodations were built in the form of a log cabin in 1890. This was succeeded by the **Château Lake Louise,** which, like its counterpart at Banff Springs, was progressively

**A juvenile
black bear**

extended, housing 200 guests by 1900, 400 by 1913, and 1,100 by the 1990s.

The château-style hotel stands in splendid isolation on the moraine at the eastern end of the lake. The township of Lake Louise, with its motels and other facilities, is 2.5 miles away. In the town there is an excellent **Parks Canada visitor center** with displays and an audiovisual show on the natural and human history of the area. The tramline that operated between 1912 and 1930, linking the townsite to the lake, is now an attractive bicycle and walking trail. On the east side of Trans-Canada 1 is the **Lake Louise Ski Area** *(Skiing Lake Louise, tel 403/522-3555, www.skilouise.com).* The **Mount Whitehorn gondola** *(Tel 403/522-3555)* operates in summer, taking visitors to a

Bear safety

Black bears are still quite common in most of Canada's national parks, whereas grizzlies now only live in western and northern mountain parks. Both species are attracted to the aromatic refuse strewn around by careless campers. When camping, keep everything in secure containers or hoist it out of reach, and eat all you cook. Avoid pitching your tent on a trail and do your hiking in groups to announce your presence.

If you do come face to face

with a bear, stop walking and stay calm; sudden movements or noises may provoke an attack. Then move quietly and slowly away, avoiding all eye contact. Make absolutely certain that you don't come between a mother and her cubs. Leaving your pack on the ground could distract the bear. If worst comes to worst, and it is a black bear that's approaching, fight back! You've nothing to lose! If it is a grizzly, play dead; your adversary may accept your submission and leave you alone. ∎

Vast though it is, the Château Lake Louise hotel is dwarfed by its surroundings.

fine viewpoint above Lake Louise.

It is tempting to try to walk around Lake Louise, but there is no recognized path on the south shore. The following day walks are within the capacity of most visitors.

PLAIN OF SIX GLACIERS

The trail along the north shore of Lake Louise flanks 300-foot cliffs near the far end of the lake, then climbs through forest and across avalanche slopes to moraines, from which there are views of six glaciers. The prominent **Victoria Glacier,** which once stretched to the lip of the lake, has receded about half a mile in the last 150 years. The path continues to climb, eventually reaching a teahouse built in 1924.

7 miles round-trip; 1,200-foot ascent

LAKE AGNES

The most popular summer walk in the Rockies leads up through the forest. The trail gives ever more spectacular views, passing little **Mirror Lake** and the **Bridal Falls** before reaching Lake Agnes in its lovely mountain setting. Here, too, is a teahouse, successor to the CPR chalet built in 1901. From here it is possible to take short strolls to the distinctive features known as the **Big** and **Little Beehives,** or a more ardu-

ous walk to link up with the Plain of Six Glaciers teahouse.

4 miles round-trip; 1,300-foot ascent

MORAINE LAKE

Half the size of Lake Louise, Moraine Lake has water of an even more intense blue-green hue. Its setting is equally splendid, if not more so, with great fans of scree at the foot of the 3,000-foot walls of the Wenkchemna Peaks. "No scene has given me an equal impression of inspiring solitude and rugged grandeur," commented explorer Walter Wilcox in 1899. It was he who gave the lake its misleading name: Its waters are held back, not by a moraine, but by a rock slide. The view from the top of the slide was once featured on the back of Canada's $20 bill. A lodge and chalets designed by the Vancouver architect Arthur Erickson blend with the surroundings.

Moraine Lake is the starting point for a number of trails. You can take a short stroll along the western shore of the lake, or a 2-mile walk that leads along **Consolation Valley,** past the pinnacle called the **Tower of Babel** to the little Consolation Lakes. A more demanding but popular excursion is the climb through **Larch Valley** and **Sentinel Pass,** 2,362 feet above the surface of the lake. ■

ICEFIELDS PARKWAY DRIVE

Icefields Parkway drive

To travel this 143-mile route between Lake Louise and Jasper is to experience one of the world's great scenic highways. The careful engineering of the road, and the generous provision of stopping places, viewpoints, and interpretive information allow the sublime scale and wonderful variety of mountain scenery to be fully appreciated.

Linking the valleys of the Bow, Mistaya, North Saskatchewan, Sunwapta, and Athabasca Rivers, the road introduces visitors to the highest mountains in the Canadian Rockies, to glaciers and ice fields, to pristine forests, lakes, waterfalls, and wild rivers.

Begun in the early 1930s as an unemployment relief scheme, the road was opened in 1940 and improved in the 1960s. It is a generously dimensioned two-lane highway with relatively easy grades and paved shoulders, popular with bicycle riders as well as with motorists, a million of whom travel it every year. There is no special advantage in driving from southeast to northwest or vice versa, although if you are bicycling, you may benefit from tailwinds by starting out from Jasper. The description below starts from Lake Louise, and the mileages given are from there. Stopping places are well marked.

Note that between Lake Louise and Jasper the only services are at Saskatchewan Crossing and the Columbia Icefield.

Ten miles along the Icefields Parkway from Lake Louise is **Hector Lake** ❶. Set at the foot of the Waputik Range and ice field, the lake is the second largest in Banff National

Lakes and glaciers appear around the curves of the parkway.

Park. Some 10 miles farther, the parkway rounds the isolated mountain of Bow Peak to reach a viewpoint from which **Crowfoot Glacier,** the first of a series of superb glaciers, can be seen. It originally had three lobes that made it resemble a crow's foot, but the glacier has retreated and no longer resembles its name.

Continue for another 3 miles to reach beautiful **Bow Lake,** which is fed by water from the Bow Glacier, one of the eight glaciers descending from the **Waputik Icefield.** The red roof of the little Num-ti-jah Lodge contrasts strikingly with the blue of the lake, the green of the forest, and the minerals in the rocks. The building is the successor to a cabin built in the early 1920s by a famous trapper and guide, Jimmy Simpson. **Bow Summit,** at 6,850 feet, is the highest point along the route, as well as the watershed between the Bow and Mistaya Rivers. A short trail leads to a viewpoint overlooking **Peyto Lake** with its startlingly blue-green glacier-fed waters.

The road now starts to drop down a long incline into the **Mistaya Valley,** passing a series of lakes for 12 miles before reaching **Upper Waterfowl Lake** ❷. Take

Yellowhead Pass

CONTINENTAL DIVIDE

advantage of the lakeside viewpoint to marvel at the awe-inspiring mountains of the Continental Divide, including a 6-mile ridge—whose highest points are the majestic **Howse Peak** (10,794 feet) and the splendid pyramid-like peak of **Mount Chephren** (10,850 feet).

As it drops from its hanging valley into the basin of the North Saskatchewan River, the Mistaya is hard at work, and 10 miles along it carves itself back into the limestone as the **Mistaya Canyon ❸**. A short footpath leads into the cleft with its vertical walls, potholes and a natural bridge. **Saskatchewan River Crossing** is 3 miles ahead. Some 2,000 feet below Bow Summit, the valley of the North Saskatchewan River belongs to the montane zone of the Rockies, with a mixed forest cover and a less severe climate.

Designated a Canadian heritage river in 1989, the North Saskatchewan runs 760 miles from its source toward Lake Winnipeg and Hudson Bay. Early travelers experienced great difficulty in crossing

the braided stream, especially when it was flooding, and even in the 1930s, highway engineers had trouble finding a suitable spot to construct a bridge. Gas, food, and lodging are available here. Just before the crossing is the junction with Hwy. 11, the David Thompson Highway, named for the great explorer and mapmaker and connecting with the town of **Red Deer,** 159 miles to the east. To the north of the crossing you can see massive **Mount Wilson** (11,880 feet), with its cliffs of yellowish quartzite.

▲ See area map p. 243
► Lake Louise
⟷ 143 miles
⊕ Allow 1–2 days
► Jasper

NOT TO BE MISSED
- Hector Lake
- Peyto Lake
- Columbia Icefield
- Sunwapta Falls
- Athabasca Falls

Hector Lake

(map labels)

JASPER
NATIONAL PARK
Jasper
Medicine Lake
Athabasca Falls
Cavell
Maligne Lake
❼
❻ 3470m
Sunwapta Falls
Sunwapta
ICEFIELDS PARKWAY
Athabasca
C A N A D I A N
❺ Sunwapta Pass
Athabasca Glacier
Columbia Icefield
❹ Weeping Wall
93 Saskatchewan River Crossing
N. Saskatchewan
❸ Mistaya Canyon
Mistaya
R O C K I E S
Upper Waterfowl Lake ❷
Peyto Lake
BRITISH COLUMBIA
Bow Lake
Hector Lake ❶
YOHO NATIONAL PARK
Kicking Horse Pass
START
CONTINENTAL DIVIDE
vapta Falls

3373m
BANFF
Clearwater
Bow Pass
NATIONAL
2669m
Mt. Whitehorn 3315m
Lake Louise
PARK
The Bow River

ALBERTA

0 ——— 50 kilometers
0 ——— 25 miles

By the time it reaches **Weeping Wall** **4**, 17 miles ahead, the valley is much narrower, defined on its eastern flank by 2,000-foot cliffs streaked with waterfalls fed by melting snow high up on Cirrus Mountain. The road climbs the hairpin known as the **Big Bend** to two further viewpoints. The first, the **Cirrus Mountain viewpoint,** commands a splendid panorama of the North Saskatchewan Valley, while the second overlooks **Bridal Veil Falls** and gives access to **Panther Falls** down a roughly constructed path.

Parker Ridge is another 8 miles along. A steep but very rewarding trail (1.5-mile round trip) rises about 900 feet through subalpine forest and tundra to an unforgettable view of the Saskatchewan Glacier, at 6 miles the longest of the glaciers descending from the Columbia Icefield.

At 6,637 feet, **Sunwapta Pass** marks the boundary between Banff and Jasper National Parks and the divide between the North Saskatchewan River and the Sunwapta ("turbulent one"), which drains to the Arctic.

Early travelers found the Sunwapta Valley blocked by the Athabasca Glacier and had to

Ice Explorers offer an easy means of viewing the wonders of the Columbia Icefield's Athabasca Glacier.

climb up and around it. By the time the parkway was built, the glacier had receded, and a detour was no longer necessary.

A 6-mile drive past Parker Ridge leads to the **Columbia Icefield** and **Athabasca Glacier** **5**. Covering an area of about 125 square miles with an estimated maximum depth of more than 1,000 feet, the Columbia Icefield is the most extensive of its kind in the Rockies. Take time to appreciate this awe-inspiring relic of the Ice Age. The ice field gives rise to a whole series of glaciers, some of them unnamed. Visible from the parkway are the Athabasca, **Dome, Kitchener,** and **Stutfield,** while the longest, the **Saskatchewan,** can be viewed from Parker Ridge. Meltwater from the glaciers eventually arrives in three oceans, the Arctic via the Athabasca and Mackenzie Rivers, the Atlantic via the North Saskatchewan, and the Pacific via the Columbia.

Stop at the **Icefields Centre** (*Closed mid-Oct.–April, tel 780/852-6177*) opposite the Athabasca Glacier: It has a full range of interpretive displays. Think about taking a ride in one of the chunky 56-passenger Ice Explorers (*Closed mid-Oct.–mid-April, tel 877-423-7433, www.brewster.ca*) to experience the glacier; the vehicle makes a thrillingly steep descent from the lateral moraine to travel some distance

along the surface of the glacier, allowing passengers a brief walk on the ice before returning. For a more intimate look you can take a three-hour conducted walk; it is also quite possible to make your own way to the toe of the glacier from the parking lot at the glacial tarn known as **Sunwapta Lake.** A series of marker posts shows the extent to which the ice has retreated in recent years.

Superbly engineered, the Icefields Parkway ranks among the world's finest scenic highways.

Continue along the parkway for 30 miles to **Sunwapta Falls** ❻. Here the waters of the Sunwapta River crash into a limestone gorge threaded by a trail, which leads to a series of smaller falls and rapids.

To the north of the falls, the parkway enters the superb **Athabasca Valley,** the longest and widest in the Rockies. Some 764 miles long (its national park section is designated a heritage river), the Athabasca River discharges into **Lake Athabasca** in northwestern Alberta through a delta that gives it its Cree name—"place of reeds."

The **Goats and Glaciers Viewpoint,** 11 miles beyond Sunwapta Falls, provides a magnificent panorama over the valley, its floor covered in a superb forest of lodgepole pine.

A left turn along the Athabasca Parkway, 3 miles beyond Goats and Glaciers Viewpoint, leads a few hundred yards to the parking lot for **Athabasca Falls** ❼. The Athabasca carries the most water of any Rocky Mountain river, and the 70-foot falls present a spectacle of roaring water, spray, and mist.

As you approach Jasper townsite, the dominant feature you see to the north is the mighty outline of Pyramid Mountain. ∎

Rock, ice, & water

The building blocks of the Canadian Rockies are the sediments deposited on the bed of ancient seas by rivers that scoured the surface of the precursor of the Canadian Shield. For about a billion years sands, silts, clays, and lime muds accumulated on the ocean floor, in places reaching a thickness of 12 miles and eventually hardening into sandstones, siltstones, shales, and limestones.

Moraine Lake is a superb example of a glacier-fed body of water.

Around 175 million years ago, the continental plate beneath North America came into collision with offshore land masses, setting in motion a series of moving shocks that buckled the sedimentary layers, uplifting them to form first the Columbia Mountains, then the main ranges of the Rockies. A further collision around 120 million years ago led to more crumpling and folding; the main ranges were uplifted further and the Front Range and foothills created. In places, the force behind these processes was so great that huge sheets of rock were forced over the top of much younger strata. Such overthrusts, like the Lewis Overthrust in Waterton Lakes National Park (see p. 270), moved eastward as much as 60 miles.

Once built, the mountains began to be worn down by the processes of erosion that continue today. Their present outline is the result of the sculpturing that took place during a succession of ice ages that began about a quarter of a million years ago. The final shaping was carried out during the most recent ice age, which ended some 11,000 years ago. The remorseless grinding action of great glaciers widened valleys like that of the Bow, Athabasca, and Kicking

Horse to their characteristic U-shape. Higher up, smaller glaciers worked on tributary valleys left above the main valley; today, streams and rivers escape many of these hanging valleys in spectacular waterfalls like Takakkaw Falls in Yoho National Park (see p. 265). Alternatively, when softer rocks were present, the rivers cut gorges like Maligne Canyon.

Niche glaciers scooped out the sides of mountains, forming the natural amphitheaters called cirques. Some mountains were attacked in this way on several sides, giving them a distinctive pinnacle shape. Known as horn mountains, these great landmarks include Mount Chephren and Mount Assiniboine (see p. 249).

Other characteristic mountain types

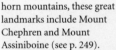

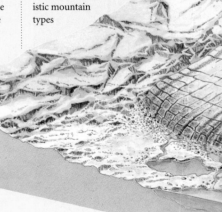

While the glaciers we see in the Rockies today are undoubtedly impressive, they are only the remnants of the vast sheets of ice that sculptured the range millions of years ago.

include the "writing desk" shapes formed by overthrusts, where a southwest-facing slope contrasts with a near-vertical wall facing north-east; a well-known example is Mount Rundle above Banff. Where the once horizontal layers of rock were tilted into a vertical position, the erosion of weaker strata has left more resistant rocks in the shape of pinnacles and spires. Mount Edith Cavell in Jasper National Park is a fine example of such a "dogtooth" mountain. But of all the mountain types that occur in the Canadian Rockies the "castellated" is the most renowned. These natural fortresses are made up of layers of soft shales alternating with harder bands of limestone, dolomite, and quartzite. The shales erode rapidly to form ledges, while the more resistant rocks remain as cliffs, giving a typical "layer-cake" appearance. Few travelers fail to marvel at aptly named

Castle Mountain standing guard over Bow Valley north of Banff.

The severe climate, with its high rain and snowfall, continues the work of erosion. But the Rockies are not ripe for leveling; it is estimated that the mountains are being reduced in height by an average of three feet every 17,000 years. What becomes of the peaks can be seen along rivers like the Sunwapta and Athabasca. These typical glacier-fed watercourses carry mountain debris that fills the valley floor and diverts the river into multiple channels. Water color in the upper reaches of these rivers is gray. But the smallest particles, known as rock flour, metamorphose in the lakes, absorbing all colors in the spectrum except the blue-green that in summer gives them their enchanting emerald sheen. ■

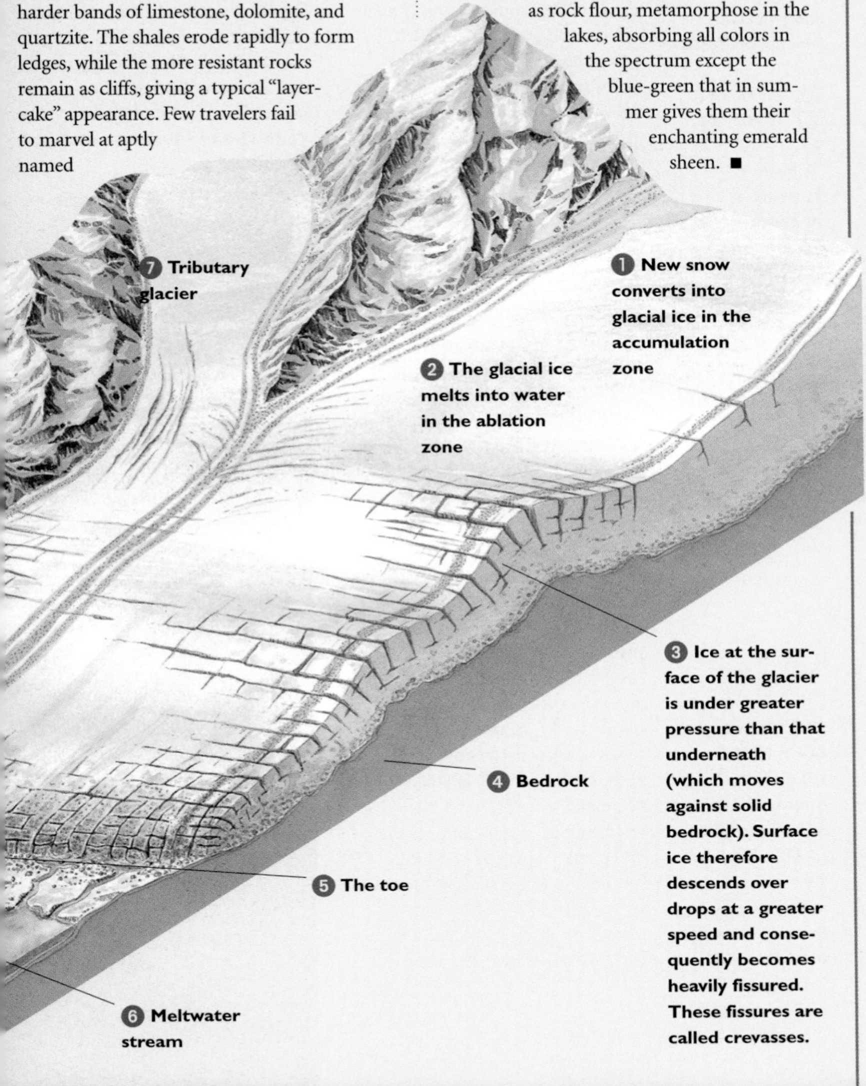

7 Tributary glacier

1 New snow converts into glacial ice in the accumulation zone

2 The glacial ice melts into water in the ablation zone

3 Ice at the surface of the glacier is under greater pressure than that underneath (which moves against solid bedrock). Surface ice therefore descends over drops at a greater speed and consequently becomes heavily fissured. These fissures are called crevasses.

4 Bedrock

5 The toe

6 Meltwater stream

Jasper National Park

Jasper NP
243 C4

Parks Canada Information Centre
www.pc.gc.ca
✉ 500 Connaught Dr.
☎ 780/852-6176
$ Park permits: $$

Townsite visitor information
www.jaspercanadianrockies.com
✉ 409 Patricia St.
☎ 780/852-3858

Yellowhead Museum & Archives
✉ 400 Pyramid Lake Rd.
☎ 780/852-3013
$ $

WITH SOME OF THE FINEST AND WILDEST SCENERY IN THE Rockies, Jasper is the largest (4,199 square miles) of the Rocky Mountain national parks, less frequented by visitors than Banff, but with equally spectacular displays of mountain, lakes, and forest.

Jasper National Park was founded (originally as a forest park) in 1907. The successful establishment of Banff National Park several years earlier had demonstrated the winning combination of railroad construction, tourism, and conservation, and served as a model when the Grand Trunk Pacific Railway began to lay the tracks of a second transcontinental line through the mountains. The railroad's alignment, previously surveyed, then rejected by the CPR, followed the old route used by fur traders and gold seekers along the Athabasca River and its tributary, the Miette. The route crossed the Continental Divide at the lowest pass along its entire length, the Yellowhead Pass.

Both the national park and the townsite, the only settlement within its boundary, were named for Jasper House, a North West Company depot on Brulé Lake.

JASPER TOWNSITE
Jasper townsite is the focal point. It was founded as a railroad town, and its station is still a stopping place for scheduled services linking eastern Canada with Vancouver and Prince Rupert. The equivalent of the Banff Springs Hotel, the famous Jasper Park Lodge hotel, built in 1922 by the Canadian National Railway just outside town, expresses something of the difference in spirit between the two places: While Banff Springs is an assertive citadel of luxury rearing up above the town, Jasper Park Lodge lies low, spreading its

timber structures with great subtlety around Lake Beauvert.

Another building that fits in well with its mountain setting is the **Parks Canada Information Centre,** built in stone and timber in 1914 and now a national historic site in its own right. An excellent source of all kinds of local information, it is complemented for historical background by the **Yellowhead Museum and Archives.** ■

Tiny Spirit Island sits in Maligne Lake, which measures 14 miles long and up to 315 feet deep. The lake is fed by meltwater from the glaciers at its southern end.

Excursions around Jasper

The valley of the Athabasca around Jasper townsite is much broader than that of the Bow around Banff, so the mountains form a relatively distant backdrop. The best excursions require a vehicle, though some of the lakes studding the valley floor are within easy reach of the townsite and have trails along their shores. Among the most popular are **Patricia** and **Pyramid Lakes** (about 3 miles northwest) and **Lakes Edith** and **Annette** (about 4 miles northeast).

JASPER TRAMWAY

Canada's longest cable car ride lifts passengers 3,074 feet in seven minutes to a ridgetop chalet beneath the summit of **Whistler Mountain** (named for the warning call of the local marmots). You can enjoy the all-around view of Jasper in its superb setting, or if you are feeling energetic—and have good hiking shoes—you can make the 600-foot climb up a rocky pathway to the top of the mountain (1.5 hours round-trip—8,084 feet). www.jaspertramway.com ✉ 4.5 miles S on Whistler Mountain Rd. ☎ 780/852-3093 ⏰ Closed mid-Oct.–mid-April 💲 $$$

MOUNT EDITH CAVELL

This drive brings visitors into close contact with the austere north face of this mountain, named for a British nurse executed by the Germans as a spy during World War I and at 11,047 feet the highest near Jasper. The route takes in part of the old alignment of the Icefields Parkway, renamed the Athabasca Parkway, then climbs up a narrow twisting road, not suitable for RVs, above the course of the Astoria River. You can get a fine view of the

mountain from a point close to the **Tonquin Valley** trailhead, with **Cavell Lake** in the foreground. From the end of the road there is a magnificent close-up view of the mountain, its cliffs a challenge even for experienced mountaineers. The Mount Edith Cavell trail, which follows the former course of the Angel Glacier, is an object lesson in the effects of ice retreat. 🏔 243 C4 ✉ 18 miles south off Hwy. 93A 🕐 Closed in winter

MALIGNE VALLEY

One of the most popular excursions in the Rockies, Maligne Valley belies the name (meaning "nasty") given to it by a French missionary, who got into difficulties crossing the river at its confluence with the Athabasca.

Maligne Canyon is up to 180 feet deep, the most spectacular of the accessible canyons in the Rockies, carved into the Palliser limestone by the Maligne River as it drops from its hanging valley to join the Athabasca. Shaded by lush, damp forest, the canyon is so narrow in places that squirrels jump across. If you are hiking, you should not follow their example but keep to the bridges on the 2-mile interpretive trail.

The rocky bed of the Maligne River winds its way through Maligne Canyon in Jasper National Park.

Lovely **Medicine Lake** is remarkable for the fluctuations in its water level. The lake is drained by a series of holes in its bed, a not uncommon feature in limestone country. In periods of high runoff, the capacity of the sinkholes is exceeded and the level rises, sometimes spilling over the lakeside; when there is little flow, the lake almost empties. The sinkholes feed an underground river system, which has so far defeated all attempts to explore it and may well be one of the most extensive in the world.

Nestled in a ring of snowcapped mountains, **Maligne Lake** is impossibly beautiful. It measures 14 miles from end to end—the longest natural lake in the Rockies. Its waters, which originate from the Brazeau Icefield, are held back by a massive landslide. Their color changes southward from green to turquoise as the amount of suspended rock flour increases. Carefully protected from unsuitable development, the lake can only be fully explored on foot or by boat. Beyond **Samson Narrows,** where the lake is constricted by an alluvial fan, lies dreamlike **Spirit Island,** its grassy surface a level platform for a clump of skyward-straining conifers (see photo p. 258).

For many daring visitors to Jasper National Park, white-water rafting on the Maligne River is a must.

📍 243 C4 www.malignelake.com ✉ 55 miles round-trip from Jasper ☎ Maligne Tours 780/852-3370, for boat tours and equipment rental *(closed mid-Oct.–mid-May)*

MIETTE HOT SPRINGS

Tucked away in a gorge running east from the Athabasca Valley, these are the hottest springs in the Canadian Rockies; waters emerge averaging 129°F. The springs had long been known to locals, and in 1910 miners from the Pocahontas Coal Mine built a track to reach them. A projected luxury resort came to nothing when the president of the Grand Trunk Railway perished aboard the *Titanic,* taking the plans with him. Today the springs feed a hot pool kept at 104°F as well as a pool kept at a cool temperature in which you can swim.

The route to the springs takes the Yellowhead Highway eastward along the braided course of the Athabasca in its superb mountain setting, past **Jasper Lake** and a cairn commemorating the old trading post of Jasper House on the far bank of the river. By **Disaster Point** you can see mineral licks frequented by bighorn sheep. The isolated limestone peak of **Roche Miette** (7,599 feet) is a prominent landmark. The winding 11-mile side road to the hot springs leaves the Yellowhead Highway close to the old Pocahontas mine, closed in 1921.

📍 243 C4 ✉ 38 miles E of Jasper via Yellowhead Hwy. ☎ 780/866-3939 🕐 Closed mid-Oct.–April 💲 $ ∎

Mount Robson Provincial Park

At 12,972 feet, Mount Robson is the highest peak in the Canadian Rockies, and was first climbed only in 1913. It is a formidable presence, dominating the British Columbia provincial park that bears its name. The summit is often obscured by clouds, and its ascent is still considered exceptionally difficult. The visual impact of this magnificent mountain is all the more impressive since, for a considerable time, it is hidden from view on the approach from the east.

The Yellowhead Highway follows the valley of the Miette River and the Canadian National railroad to **Yellowhead Pass,** the lowest on the Continental Divide and the border between Alberta and British Columbia. To the west of the pass, the road crosses the **Fraser River** just beyond **Yellowhead Lake,** then reaches 8-mile-long **Moose Lake.** A trail (half-hour round-trip) leads to **Overlander Falls,** where the Fraser River plunges into a deep canyon. From the park visitor center, a short distance along the highway, there is a fine view of Mount Robson, though more intimate contact with the great peak is reserved for serious backpackers. The **Berg Lake Trail** is 14 miles long and climbs 2,600 feet. Your reward is an unforgettable prospect of the mountain's great ramparts, rising a full 8,000 feet from the lake. Two glaciers descend the mountain's flanks, one of them feeding the lake with icebergs.

📍 243 C4 www.env.gov.bc.ca/bcparks ✉ 55 miles W of Jasper via Yellowhead Hwy. ∎

Routes through the Rockies

"All I can say is that the work has been well done in every way" were the sober words with which General Manager William Cornelius Van Horne concluded the simple ceremony on November 7, 1885, that marked the completion of the Canadian Pacific Railway. The president of the CPR, Donald Smith, had just succeeded in his second attempt at securing the last spike (of iron, not gold) on the Eagle Pass in British Columbia. This significant occasion was marked with all due solemnity by Smith and a number of other eminent men, who were surrounded by a small crowd of railroad workers, one of whom had suddenly cried "All aboard for the Pacific!"

Perhaps even the normally exuberant Van Horne was overawed by his achievement—a 3,000-mile railroad built across the continent in far less than the allotted time.

Van Horne was famous for his "can-do" qualities when hired by the CPR in 1882 to complete the transcontinental railroad linking the Atlantic to the Pacific. Drawing on experience gained in the American Civil War, he organized construction along military lines, with impressive results: The iron road advanced across the prairies at rates some-times exceeding 6 miles a day. But the prairies were easy terrain compared to the mighty mountain barrier to the west, much of which remained unknown. In 1872, surveyor Sandford Fleming had recommended a westward rail route to run from Edmonton over the relatively low Yellowhead Pass. Fearful of possible U.S. encroachment on the Northwest, the Canadian government ordered the railroad to be aligned much farther south, regardless of the engineering difficulties.

By 1883 rails were reaching up the Bow Valley toward Kicking Horse Pass. The next year saw the conquest of the pass and the building of the line down the canyon of the Kicking Horse River. Common caution, to say nothing of the railroad rule book, dictated the construction of tunnels on the descent toward the town of Field in order to reduce the steep grade. Van Horne would have none of it; the CPR needed to earn revenue as soon as possible, and building tunnels would delay the opening of the line by at least a year.

The tracks were run directly down to Field at the

One of the most famous photographs in Canadian history shows CPR President Donald Smith hammering home the last spike at Craigellachie, high up on the Eagle Pass, in 1885.

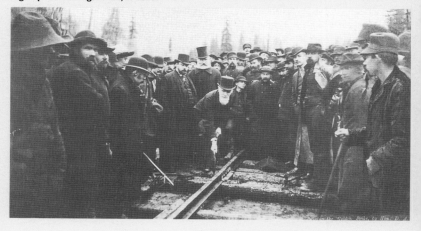

Locomotives winding through the Rockies have been a common sight since the 1880s.

horrendous grade of 4.5 percent. The 4-mile long "Big Hill," as it came to be known, was a nightmare; the first construction train to venture onto it plunged into the canyon, killing three workmen. Trains using the completed line had to be limited in weight and length. Eastbound trains required several locomotives to shove them uphill, while westbound trains were restricted to not much more than a walking pace.

By the early 20th century, the CPR could afford to bypass the Big Hill by building one of the railroad wonders of the world: The famous Spiral Tunnels were completed in 1909, a great figure eight of track built into the flanks of Mount Ogden and Cathedral Mountain. They reduced the grade to a manageable 2.2 percent and offered the spectacle of a freight train locomotive leaving a tunnel while the last car has still to enter.

Farther west, in 1881, surveyor Albert B. Rogers had found a way through a seemingly impenetrable mountain fastness of ice, snow, and avalanche, now known as Glacier

National Park. For 35 years the railroad followed the pass named after him, shielding itself from the elements with a series of tunnels and snowsheds. This old route is now a visitor attraction, accessible from Trans-Canada 1. Now safe from avalanches, the railroad has buried itself deep underground in the 5-mile-long Connaught Tunnel, completed in 1916.

Though it was the railroad that opened up the Rocky Mountains, alternatives had previously been discussed, including a colonization roadway for wagon traffic and even a "perpetual sleigh road," which would whisk passengers along at speeds of up to 100 mph. The first automobile arrived in Banff along the railroad track, provoking a ban on motor traffic that was only lifted in 1915. The forerunner of the Trans-Canada Highway reached Lake Louise in 1921 and crossed the Continental Divide to Field in 1926. The modern Trans-Canada was built in the 1950s and early 1960s, paralleling the route, as well as the achievement, of the CPR. ■

Yoho National Park

Yoho NP
🏔 243 D3

Visitor information
www.pc.gc.ca
✉ 1 mile east of Field
☎ 250/343-6100
💲 Park permit $

BRITISH COLUMBIA'S YOHO NATIONAL PARK LIES AT EITHER side of the valley of the Kicking Horse River, a major route for both road—Trans-Canada 1—and rail—the main line of the CPR. With some of the most spectacular lakes, waterfalls, and mountain scenery, the park more than deserves its name, derived from a Cree word meaning "awe." Road, rail, and a well-developed network of hiking trails give easy access to some of the park's finest features.

As with Banff, the designation of Yoho as a protected landscape was closely linked to the activities of the Canadian Pacific Railway. The railroad's conquest of the Continental Divide was the most heroic episode in its construction, and even today its route over **Kicking Horse Pass** is an object of wonder and admiration. As elsewhere in the mountains, the CPR immediately saw the potential for attracting visitors along its tracks. Stunningly located at the foot of magnificent **Mount Stephen,** the depot town of **Field** (*Visitor information, tel 250/343-6783*) was given a dining room that turned into a hotel. Named Mount Stephen House, this very first of the CPR's Rocky

Mountain hotels soon became a venue for alpinists, artists, and wealthy visitors. Around it, the original 6-square-mile preservation area was extended in 1911 to become the country's second national park.

Trans-Canada 1 climbs parallel to the railroad from Alberta to the B.C. boundary at Kicking Horse Pass, 5,330 feet above sea level and the highest point along its route. The pass and the valley to the west both owe their name to the blow administered to Scotsman James Hector by a horse's hoof, as he and his party explored the area in 1858.

The first of several side valleys leading off the highway from the east is that of the **Cataract**

Yoho National Park has more than 30 "three thousanders"—peaks of more than 9,800 feet (3,000 m).

Brook, which descends from **Lake O'Hara.** The lake is cradled in an incomparable setting, which includes the mountains of the Continental Divide to the north. In contrast to bustling Lake Louise, on the far side of the ridge, Lake O'Hara is secluded. The fragility of the alpine ecosystem has led to restriction of access; cars (and even bicycles) are banned, and the chalet hotel and campsite can only be reached on foot or by a bus service up the 8-mile road *(Reserve in advance: tel 250/343-6433).* A network of trails enables walkers to enjoy the small lakes and flower-rich alpine meadows.

Crowds gather at the **Spiral Tunnel viewpoint** *(6 miles from eastern entrance),* the most popular in any Canadian national park, for the spectacle of immensely long freight trains snaking through the Canadian Pacific's spiral tunnels (see pp. 262–63).

A narrow, winding 8-mile road with hairpin bends runs up **Yoho Valley** *(7 miles from eastern entrance)* to the **Takakkaw Falls.** Fed by meltwaters from the Waputik Icefield, the falls are among the highest in North America, dropping a spectacular 1,247 feet in a series of magnificent cascades.

Dating from the Middle Precambrian period, more than 500 million years ago, the extraordinarily rich fossil beds on **Mount Burgess** above Field have yielded—and are still yielding—important evidence about life on earth. Their palaeontological significance led to the Burgess Shale being designated a UNESCO World Heritage site in 1981. Specimens are on display at the visitor center in Field and also in the Royal Tyrrell Museum (see p. 234). There are guided hikes to the fossil beds *(Tel 800/343-3006).*

Yoho's Emerald Lake

The 5-mile road to **Emerald Lake** *(2 miles W of Field)* leads past a stopping place with a view of a natural bridge, where the Kicking Horse River has cut away soft deposits of shale, leaving an arch of harder limestone. Of stunning beauty, its blue-green waters set among high mountains and surrounded by lush forest, Emerald Lake is the biggest of Yoho's water bodies and is a popular destination.

At the western entrance to the park, look for the trail head to **Wapta Falls** *(3 miles round-trip).* Most of the precipitation falling on Yoho National Park eventually passes over these falls. Though not especially high (100 feet), the sheer volume of the falls is stunning. ■

Kootenay National Park

Kootenay NP
🅰 243 D2

**West Gate
Information
Centre**
www.pc.gc.ca
✉ Off Hwy. 93
☎ 250/347-9615
💲 $$

TO THE WEST OF THE CONTINENTAL DIVIDE OFF Hwy. 93, the 543-square-mile Kootenay National Park links the high mountains to the milder environment of the Rocky Mountain Trench.

Whereas railroads were the reason for the designation of Banff, Jasper, and Yoho National Parks, Kootenay owes its existence to a road. The Kootenay Parkway was originally conceived before World War I as a route for orchard produce from the Columbia Valley to be trucked northeastward. When private promoters and the B.C. provincial government ran out of money, the federal government completed the road, on condition that a strip of land 5 miles wide on either side become a national park. Kootenay National Park was designated in 1920, and the 58-mile parkway opened in 1923.

The road rises out of the Bow Valley from **Castle Junction,** giving fine views back to Castle Mountain. Five miles from Castle Junction, Vermilion Pass (5,412 feet) marks the B.C./Alberta boundary and the border between Banff and Kootenay National Parks. The short **Fireweed Trail,** through an area devastated by a forest fire in 1968, demonstrates how a burn can enhance wildlife diversity and how controlled burns are essential to the mountain environment.

Rushing down from its hanging valley, the **Tokkum Creek** has eroded the 2,000-foot-long **Marble Canyon** (*11 miles from Castle Junction*) in the dolomite and Cathedral limestone, which has been so polished by the silt-rich stream as to resemble marble. The short interpretive trail crisscrosses the canyon and passes a natural bridge.

Twelve miles west of Castle Junction off Hwy. 93 a half-mile

trail crosses a suspension bridge over the **Vermilion River** to a mysterious place, where mineral-rich springs seeping upward have created the **Ochre Beds,** colorful deposits of clay. Nearby, the **Paint Pots** are a series of pools formed by the accumulation of minerals around their rim. An active trade was developed by the Kutenai Indians (after whom the park is named), who processed what they called the "red earth" of this sacred place into pigments for rock-, body-, or tepee-painting. In the early 20th century a short-lived effort was made to mine the deposits on an industrial basis.

After the Paint Pots, Hwy. 93 runs southeast down the valley of

The range of habitats in Kootenay National Park is astonishing. Upland meadows and moist coniferous forest in the valleys contrast with cactus and prickly pear in the warm environment of the Rocky Mountain Trench.

the Vermilion River. To the west, one of the most popular backpacking routes in the Rockies follows the foot of the **Rockwall,** a spectacular 3,000-foot cliff of Ottertail limestone.

Vermilion Crossing has services and a **visitor center** *(just inside entrance, closed winter months),* and offers fine views of one of the park's most spectacular peaks, Mount Verendrye (10,125 feet). At the foot of **Mount Wardle** it is sometimes possible to see moose, deer, or mountain goats—the symbol of the park— taking advantage of the roadside mineral licks. **Kootenay Crossing** marks the start of a run along the **Kootenay Valley,** in the course of which the damp subalpine forest gives way to the drier, more fragmented woodland of the B.C. interior, characterized by Douglas-fir. As the road leaves the river and climbs southwestward, there is a fine panorama.

Sinclair Pass and **Sinclair Valley** are named after the leader of a group of settlers sent this way by the Hudson's Bay Company, in an (unsuccessful) attempt to forestall the colonization of Oregon by the United States.

RADIUM HOT SPRINGS

Emerging via a fault in the earth's crust at a temperature of 104°F, these hot springs were known to local residents, who regarded their outlet as a sacred place. Mineral content is minimal, and consequently the waters are virtually odorless. They are, however, mildly radioactive, a property once considered highly beneficial.

Around the turn of the century, the springs were developed by private interests in a rather fitful way until the government took them over in 1922 as part of the national park. Today there are two popular open-air pools, one hot, one cool. ■

Radium Hot Springs

🄰 243 D2
www.hotsprings.ca
✉ 2 miles east of the town of Radium, off Kootenay Parkway
☎ 250/347-9485
💲 $$

Glacier & Mount
Revelstoke
National Parks
🅰 243 C3
www.pc.gc.ca

Glacier NP
✉ Rogers Pass Visitor
Centre, 0.75 mile W
of Rogers Pass
☎ 250/837-7500
🕐 Visitor center closed
Nov.
💲 $

**Mount Revelstoke
NP**
✉ Park admin. office,
Revelstoke
☎ 250/837-7500
💲 $

A plaque
commemorates
engineer Walter
Moberly's feat
in forging a route
through the
seemingly
impenetrable
Monashee Range.

Glacier & Mount Revelstoke National Parks

CANADA'S ADJOINING NATIONAL PARKS WERE DESIGNATED to conserve the jagged Selkirk Mountains, part of the Columbia range just to the west of the Rocky Mountain Trench. The peaks are at least as formidable as those to the east; the highest point, Mount Dawson, reaches 11,122 feet. The climate here is exceptionally harsh—Glacier's 400-plus glaciers are fed by a snowfall averaging 370 inches a year. The steep valleys are regularly swept by avalanches capable of burying the Trans-Canada Highway under 30 feet of snow.

GLACIER

Glacier National Park shares railroad origins with Yoho and Banff. Its designation as a park in 1886 coincided with the opening of CPR's line through the pass heroically discovered by surveyor Albert Rogers a few years earlier. A visitor boom developed, based on the long-since demolished Glacier House hotel, conceived as a railroad restaurant to save locomotives the burden of pulling dining cars up the severe grades. Climbers flocked here from Europe, and today alpinists consider Glacier to be the birthplace of mountaineering in North America. The area's heyday came to an end in 1916 when the CPR, tired of the wear and tear on its rolling stock and the cost of constantly repairing avalanche damage, abandoned Rogers Pass in favor of a 5-mile tunnel through Mount Macdonald.

After decades of isolation, the construction of the Trans-Canada Highway across the pass in 1962 once more brought visitors into the area. The avalanche problem is kept within bounds by the presence of snowsheds along the road and by the use of artillery; the buildup of snow formations is carefully monitored, and army howitzers are fired to dislodge them in a controlled way.

Much of Glacier is inaccessible except to climbers and serious walkers, but a road or rail journey through the park affords a memorable experience. A number of short trails starting at or near the highway introduce the park's landscapes and history. Among them, the **Abandoned Rails Trail** (0.75 mile one way) follows the old route of the CPR through Rogers Pass. The pass itself is a national historic site, with displays in the visitor center. The **Illecillewaet campground** (*2.5 miles west of visitor center*) is the starting point for trails of varying length, while **Bear Falls Trail** and the **Hemlock Grove Trail** lead through surprisingly lush forest produced by the abundant precipitation.

MOUNT REVELSTOKE

Mount Revelstoke National Park also offers the experience of luxuriant woodland. Not far from the eastern entrance to the park on Trans-Canada 1, the boardwalk of the **Giant Cedars Trail** leads through a majestic stand of 600-year old western red cedar and hemlock, a fine example of British Columbia's interior rain forest. But the main attraction of this tiny national park (100 square miles) is the ease with which visitors can enjoy the floral wealth of its alpine meadows, the chief reason for the

park's creation in 1914.

The 16-mile **Meadows in the Sky Parkway** *(closed winter months)* climbs from the park's western entrance toward the 6,358 feet summit of Mount Revelstoke. The zigzag route offers magnificent views of the great sweep of the **Columbia River Valley** and the **Monashee Mountains** to the west, but the real treat comes at the summit, where the 0.75-mile **Meadows in the Sky Trail** leads through a glorious display of mountain flowers, at their showiest in high summer. Other, longer, trails give access to a number of delightful alpine lakes.

Revelstoke townsite stands where the Illecillewaet River flowing westward from Glacier National Park discharges into the Columbia River. A service center for travelers, the town is named for the man who in the 1880s financed the Canadian Pacific Railway in its most difficult hour, Lord Revelstoke. Eighty-seven miles north of town, the waters of the Columbia are held back by the huge 574-foot **Mica Dam.** A visitor center *(Just N of Revelstoke, tel 250/814-6697, closed mid-Oct.–mid-April)* has displays on the construction of this feat of engineering and on the management of the Columbia River system. ∎

One of Mount Revelstoke's many alpine meadows

Waterton Lakes National Park

Waterton Lakes National Park

243 D1

Visitor information

www.pc.gc.ca

✉ In Waterton

☎ 403/859-2224

🕐 Visitor information closed mid-Oct.– mid-May

Park Admin. Office

✉ 215 Mount View Rd.

☎ 403/859-2224

Waterton Lakes National Park juxtaposes alpine landscapes with the aspen groves and the architecture of the Prince of Wales Hotel.

RISING WITH DRAMATIC SUDDENNESS DIRECTLY OUT OF the prairies of southwestern Alberta, the mountains of Waterton Lakes National Park are unique among the Rocky Mountain parks and are a world heritage area in their own right. Between 175 million and 125 million years ago, a 100-mile-long by 4-mile-thick slab of ancient rock was violently uplifted and pushed 60 miles northeastward atop the much younger rocks of the prairies. Known as the Lewis Thrust, this extraordinary event reversed the usual geologic sequence—young rocks overlying older rocks—and explains the surprising lack of transition between prairie and mountain; in places the elevation changes 4,000 feet only a half mile from the prairie floor.

The park is small (202 square miles) and, unlike the other parks, has no through roads. Visitors relax on the shores of **Lower, Middle,** and **Upper Waterton Lakes** and **Maskinonge Lake** and, above all, make use of the superb 150-mile trail network. The park came into being in 1895 (to preserve it from encroaching settlement); in 1932 it was linked with Montana's **Glacier National Park** to be-come the world's first International Peace Park.

The most prominent man-made feature in the park is the splendid timber structure of the **Prince of Wales Hotel** (*Waterton Lake, tel 403/236-3400*), built by the U.S. Great Northern Railway in 1926 as a base for Rocky Mountain

bus tours. The hotel overlooks Upper Waterton Lake and **Waterton townsite,** the focal point of the park. This is the starting point for a number of trails and for boat trips (*Tel 403/859-2362, closed mid-Oct.–mid-June, $$$*) on the Upper Lake. The boats cross the international border and give access to the spectacular trail leading via a tunnel to **Crypt Lake,** high up in a superb glacial amphitheater (*11-mile round-trip, 2,100-foot ascent*). This is an excursion for determined hikers, but there are plenty of easy walks in the park, including the **Red Rock Canyon trail,** which leads through a 65-foot-deep cleft with rocks of purple, green, yellow, and red. ■

L ying beyond the barrier of the Rocky Mountains, British Columbia, Canada's westernmost and third largest province, is almost a separate country, proud of its 5,000 miles of magnificent coastline.

West Coast

Introduction & map 272–73
Vancouver 276–87
Vancouver Island & Victoria 288–98
A walk around Victoria 292–93
The Inside Passage 299–301
Prince Rupert, Skeena Valley, & Queen Charlotte Islands 302–303
The Cariboo 306–307
Hope to Kamloops drive 308–309
The Kootenays 310–11
Okanagan Valley 312
Hotels & restaurants of the West Coast 369–74

Fall in British Columbia

West Coast

BRITISH COLUMBIA (B.C.) OFFERS A BEWILDERING VARIETY OF CLIMATES
and landscapes. Eternal snows cloak the peaks of the ranges that parallel the Rocky
Mountains, while along the U.S. border scarce water makes irrigation necessary in the
orchards and vineyards. Primeval rain forest spreads inland from the fjord-cut littoral,
while in the interior, deprived of the rain that falls on the Coast Mountains, patches
of near-desert coexist with fine ranch lands. The bleak northern half of the province is
hardly inhabited: More than half the population is crowded into the Lower Fraser
Valley around Vancouver, with another half million in Victoria and the southeastern tip
of Vancouver Island.

It is to this metropolitan region based on the
balmy shores of the Strait of Georgia that
most of the province's visitors come. Many
arrive from the nearby states of the Pacific
Northwest, others from the far side of the
ocean, others still by the east-west road and
rail routes through the mountains that have
become classic journeys in their own right.

With all the allure of a great and growing
city, vibrant Vancouver also enjoys an
unrivaled setting of water and mountains.
On the opposite shore of the strait, and
much smaller, is Victoria—hardly less
enticing, pleased to be the provincial capital,
and coyly playing on its British heritage.
Both cities have outstanding museums:
In Vancouver, the University of British
Columbia Museum of Anthropology houses
an unrivaled collection of Northwestern
native art and artifacts; in Victoria, the lavish
displays of the Royal British Columbia
Museum deal with the same themes, as well
as introducing the province's history and its
richly diverse landscapes.

Neither city is far from wilderness. Most of
the population of Vancouver Island clings to
the east-facing shore of the strait, sheltered by
the island's mountain spine from the rain and
storms of its western coast. Here, Pacific Rim
National Park Reserve protects a savage, surf-
battered shore and its rain forest-clad heights.
Vancouver's urban sprawl threatens the productive farmlands won with much effort from
the swampy levels of the Lower Fraser Valley,
but immediately to the north a whole series of
parks, among them Garibaldi Provincial
Park, enables hikers to escape into the forests
and alpine meadows of the Coast Mountains.

Well-trod visitor routes lead away from the

province's urban heartland. Vancouver
Island's principal highway terminates at Port
Hardy, terminus for the spectacular ferry trip
through the Inside Passage, the easiest way for
visitors to experience something of the
magnificence of the islands and inlets of the

0   200 kilometers

0   100 miles

lonely northwestern coast. To the east of Vancouver, two railroads as well as the Trans-Canada Highway follow the Fraser River upstream, leaving the lush pastures of the lower valley to make their way through the canyons that early explorers and prospectors found so formidable. At Kamloops, the Canadian National turns north to break through the barrier of the Rockies at Yellowhead Pass, while the Canadian Pacific, accompanied by the Trans-Canada, penetrates increasingly dramatic mountain country on its way to Kicking Horse Pass. Originally a fur-trading post, Kamloops thrived as a supply center for the gold rushes that opened up the interior of the province in the mid-to-late 19th century. Most prospectors followed the famous Cariboo Road, striking north from the Fraser's tributary, the Thompson River.

An alternative route into the Cariboo country follows the magnificent ocean inlet of Howe Sound inland, passing the world-famous ski resort of Whistler, and continues on to terminate at the province's largest inland city, Prince George. From here, rail and road accompany each other on the long journey westward to Prince Rupert. The final stretch along the Skeena River passes villages where a revival of Gitksan culture has added new totems to those already there. The Port Hardy ferry docks at Prince Rupert, as does the boat to and from the far-off Queen Charlotte Islands, or Haida Gwaii, stronghold of the once fierce Haida people, whose deserted coastal villages are among the country's most evocative sites.

Along the U.S. frontier in the far south of the province, the north-south river valleys, with their chains of beautiful lakes, made natural routes for the first white settlers. Laid out against the grain of the country, the modern Crowsnest Highway, successor to the Dewdney Trail of the 1860s, is a fascinating alternative to the Trans-Canada between Pacific coast and prairie interior. Overcoming a series of high passes, it gives access to the orchard-patterned lowlands of the Okanagan, with its lakeside resorts, or to fascinating heritage towns such as Nelson, on Kootenay River. ■

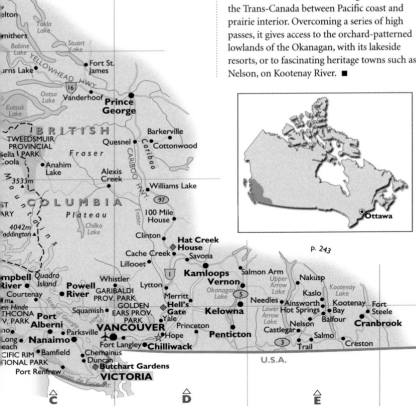

p. 314

p. 243

Super-natural British Columbia

Superabundant natural resources in ocean, rivers, and forests helped Northwestern natives achieve an unusually high standard of material culture long before the arrival of Europeans, drawn here by this same natural bounty. The fur traders were the first to come, followed by mineral prospectors, fishermen, ranchers, and lumbermen. Today's provincial economy still depends largely on the exploitation of what were once seen as almost limitless resources.

Organized mostly in huge conglomerates, forestry still occupies first place among the province's resource-based industries. At the same time, the highly mineralized rocks of the province are mined according to the fluctuating demands of the world market for an A to Z of metals—from antimony to zinc. The rain from Pacific clouds on uplands and mountains feeds lakes and rivers, many of which have been tapped for hydropower, in sufficient quantity for export to the United States.

The stars of the province's fishery are its five species of salmon, once so abundant that at places such as Salmon Arm they were hauled from the water in armfuls and spread on the land as fertilizer. The damming of rivers for hydroelectricity and the consequent barring of the salmons' way upstream to their spawning grounds is one of many factors contributing to a dismaying decrease in their number. Drastic restrictions have been placed on the catch and disputes between U.S. and Canadian fishermen over who is entitled to fish have led to many unpleasant incidents such as the blockade of an Alaska ferry by B.C. fishing boats.

Forestry resources

But it is B.C.'s forestry industry that was the focus of most controversy in the 1980s and '90s. Almost 60 percent of the province is mantled in trees, but the temperate rain forest of the coast, with its red cedar, western hemlock, Douglas-fir, and Sitka spruce, attracts most attention. Here, where the soggy conditions inhibit fires, trees grow to immense size, sometimes reaching a height of 300 feet. Luxuriant undergrowth and the presence of slowly decaying fallen trees act as a filter, ensuring the purity of the runoff feeding streams and lakes. The cedar's aromatic and lightweight wood was a staple of Northwestern First Nations culture—its trunk used for canoes and totem poles; its timber split into planks for house construction, carved into masks, or steam-bent into storage boxes. But lumbermen have found a use for most trees: The straight trunk of the Douglas-fir has always made it ideal for construction, while even the once-despised soft wood of the hemlock can be converted into excellent pulp for paper and synthetics. The attack on the forest began in early colonial days on the coast or along rivers, where trees were easily accessible, and the felled timber could be transported by water. Railroads extended the scope of operation immensely, and nowadays roads and modern machinery mean that virtually no forest is inaccessible, and areas once thought to be remote can be easily reached and exploited.

The environmental effects of logging can be devastating. The removal of tree cover through clear-cutting leads to soil erosion and landslides (often long after the clearing has taken place), the silting of streams, and their destruction as salmon spawning grounds. The loss of wildlife habitat can be particularly serious in the case of large mammals such as grizzlies or mountain lions, which require extensive ranges. The efforts of timber companies to replant require many years, and in any case it is impossible to replicate the ecological or aesthetic value of old-growth forest.

Great Bear Rainforest Park

In 1993, resistance to the destruction of this great natural resource led to Canada's biggest civil disobedience campaign between loggers and environmentalists at Clayoquot Sound on Vancouver Island. Subsequently, protracted

Logging (above) remains a staple of the British Columbian (and Canadian) economy, though it no longer requires the dash and daring of "white-water men" (left) to break up log jams.

negotiations between the government which owns the land, the native peoples who claim the land, and the major forestry companies who log the land (and thereby provide jobs for people in communities where there is often little alternative employment) led to the creation in 2006 of an enormous new park. Great Bear Rainforest covers 8 million acres of coast land and islands stretching north from Vancouver Island for more than 250 miles to the Alaskan border. Logging will not be banned but it will occur only where the forest is sustainable. There will be no more clear-cutting; instead resources will be invested to develop ecotourism. This unique agreement between industry, government, conservationists and local population is considered a model for the 21st century. ■

Vancouver

Vancouver

🅰 273 C1–D1

**Visitor
information**

www.tourismvancouver.com

✉ 200 Burrard St.

☎ 604/683-2000

www.hellobc.com

☎ 800/435-5622
(Tourism B.C.)

CANADA'S WESTERNMOST GREAT CITY REVELS IN ITS glorious setting of sea and mountains, offering its inhabitants a tempting lifestyle in which leisure and pleasure are underpinned by the prosperity engendered by Vancouver's position on the Pacific Rim. The reason for the city's existence, the splendid deepwater harbor formed by fjordlike Burrard Inlet, is backed by the often snowcapped Coast Mountains. To the west, the peaks of Vancouver Island rise over the waters of the Strait of Georgia, while to the south Mount Baker, the giant of the U.S. Cascade Range, can often be seen.

Residents never tire of telling of the wonders of swimming, sailing, or skiing at whim, or of being able to disappear into the wilderness just a few minutes' drive from a city with all the cultural delights of a multi-cultural metropolis. Despite the frequent sight of snow on the mountaintops, Vancouver enjoys a mild climate, though mist is common and rainfall heavy (about 60 inches annually).

The city is built on a peninsula defined by the **Burrard Inlet** on the north and the delta of the **Fraser River** to the south. From the compact downtown core, less than a mile square, the densely built-up and now fashionable West End soon gives way westward to one of the world's great urban green spaces, Stanley Park, the forested tract occupying the tip of the peninsula. To the east is attrac-tively renovated Gastown, where Vancouver began; in 1867 garrulous John Deighton opened the doors of his saloon to workmen from the recently established sawmills near-by. His nickname, "Gassy Jack," is supposed to have influenced the present-day name of the settlement that grew up around his bar. Otherwise the slowly growing town was called Granville, a name discarded in favor of Vancouver on the initiative of William Van Horne, general manager of the Canadian Pacific Railway in the 19th century.

The CPR arrived here in 1886 (see pp. 262–63), much to the cha-grin of the speculators who had bought up land around the original terminus at Port Moody a few miles upstream. Van Horne's choice of name stuck, despite resentful rumblings from Vancouver Island on the far shore of the strait. Though its timber buildings were devastated in a great fire in 1886, Vancouver flourished, rebuilding in stone and brick and soon surpassing Victoria in size and importance.

By the 1920s it had become

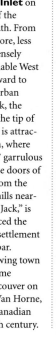

**Downtown
Vancouver,
as seen from
its marina**

Canada's third largest city. Very British at first, Vancouver has inevitably attracted immigrants not only from Europe but from the far shores of the ocean on which it is set; its longstanding Chinese community is now one of the largest in North America. Today, with a metropolitan population approaching two million, it has become an excellent location for many kinds of economic activity, including corporate headquarters. You can see evidence of this in the high-rise structures that dominate the downtown skyline. Some of these, like the chisel-capped Cathedral Place, are fine examples of postmodern elegance, worthy successors to the extravagantly ornamented art deco **Marine Building** of 1930. Another architecturally interesting building is the Public Library; designed by Moshe Safdie in 1995, it resembles the Roman Coliseum.

Vancouver is a pleasure to explore. Downtown is compact, easy to get around on foot, and the shore of Burrard Inlet is becoming increasingly accessible as the redevelopment of old port installations proceeds. Protruding into the waters of the harbor, Canada Place, with its superb views of the city's setting, is one of a number of assets added for Expo '86. No visit is complete without some sort of trip on the water, perhaps an inexpensive ferry ride across to North Vancouver aboard the Seabus, part of a developed public transportation system *(B.C. Transit, tel 604/953-3333, www.translink.bc.ca)* that includes Skytrain, a futuristic driverless train linking downtown with some suburbs.

Beyond the center, some attractions such as the thriving market quarter of Granville Island and the museums in Vanier Park can be reached by bus, but it is far more fun to take the little ferries that ply the waters of False Creek. Farther afield still, but not to be missed for its marvelous collection of

Northwest First Nations artifacts, is the campus of the University of British Columbia and its superb Museum of Anthropology.

Anchored to the shore by a luxury hotel, **Canada Place** resembles a great sailing vessel about to cast off from the dockside. With superlative views of the harbor from its boardwalks, it is perhaps the best place to begin an exploration of the city center, whose clustered towers rise just inland. Designed by Eberhard Zeidler, architect of Toronto's Eaton Centre, as the Canadian pavilion for Expo '86, it now houses a trade and convention center and an IMAX cinema beneath its five great sails of fiberglass fabric. True to the past—it is built on the site of Harbour Pier B-C, where the famous ships of the White Empress Line once docked—Canada Place welcomes cruise liners as well as the occasional naval vessel.

Granville Square, which is graced with an enigmatic modern sculpture, overlooks the embarkation point for the Seabus linking downtown to North Vancouver. Though no longer the terminus for transcontinental trains, the grandiose Canadian Pacific Railroad station of 1914 is still a transport hub, serving not only Seabus but also Skytrain and the regional West Coast Express. Its great halls are decorated with Canadian travel scenes and have earned it a well-merited heritage award.

No city worth its salt lacks a revolving restaurant and observation deck, and here it is called the Vancouver Lookout, an awesome 548 feet above the street via a vertiginous outside elevator. It is the crowning glory of the **Harbour Centre.**

Today's British Columbians are increasingly aware of the First Nations heritage of the West Coast. These totems stand in Vancouver's Stanley Park.

Gastown

Threatened by total redevelopment in the early 1960s, Vancouver's late 19th-century urban nucleus was saved by the efforts of local people and developers, who restored and refurbished old buildings and ensured that most new structures fitted in with the established townscape. Today, Gastown is a

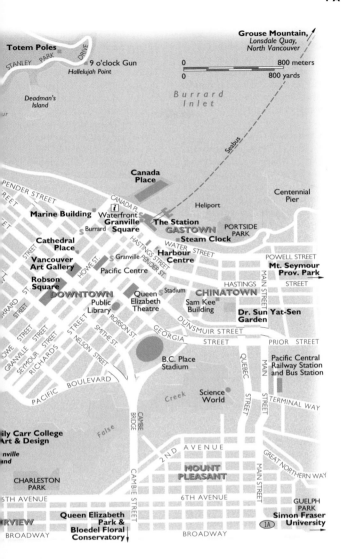

Totem Poles

STANLEY PARK DRIVE

9 o'clock Gun
Hallelujah Point

Deadman's
Island

Grouse Mountain,
Lonsdale Quay,
North Vancouver

0 _____ 800 meters
0 _____ 800 yards

Burrard
Inlet

Canada
Place

Heliport

Centennial
Pier

PENDER STREET

CANADA PL.

Marine Building   Waterfront
                  Granville
Burrard Square

The Station
GASTOWN   PORTSIDE
Steam Clock PARK

Cathedral
Place

HASTINGS STREET

WATER STREET

Vancouver
Art Gallery

Granville PENDER ST.

Harbour
Centre

POWELL STREET

Mt. Seymour
Prov. Park

Robson
Square

Pacific Centre

HOWE ST.

HASTINGS   STREET

MAIN STREET

DOWNTOWN   Public
           Library

Stadium

Queen
Elizabeth
Theatre

CHINATOWN

Sam Kee
Building

Dr. Sun Yat-Sen
Garden

BURRARD STREET

STREET

ROBSON ST.

SMITHE ST.

NELSON STREET

GEORGIA

DUNSMUIR STREET

STREET

PRIOR STREET

GRANVILLE STREET

SEYMOUR STREET

RICHARDS

PACIFIC BOULEVARD

B.C. Place
Stadium

Creek

Science
World

QUEBEC STREET

MAIN STREET

Pacific Central
Railway Station
and Bus Station

TERMINAL WAY

CAMBIE BRIDGE

False

ily Carr College
Art & Design

nville
nd

2ND   AVENUE

MOUNT
PLEASANT

GREAT NORTHERN WAY

MAIN STREET

CHARLESTON
PARK

CAMBIE STREET

5TH AVENUE

6TH AVENUE

GUELPH
PARK

IRVIEW

BROADWAY

Queen Elizabeth
Park &
Bloedel Floral
Conservatory

BROADWAY

Simon Fraser
University

1A

busy and rather self-conscious heritage area with trendy boutiques, souvenir shops, bars, and restaurants, saved from smugness by its proximity to the city's east end and its numerous skid row residents.

The basic grid of Gastown's streets is angled to accommodate the outline of the waterfront, and the odd angles of some of the junctions are occupied by flatiron buildings like the **Europe Hotel.** Tidewater once lapped the very edge of **Water Street,** now the main thoroughfare. At the corner with Cambie Street stands the **Steam Clock,** a favorite spot for photographs. Inaugurated in 1977, the clock powers its old paddle-

**Harbour Centre–
Vancouver Lookout**
www.vancouverlookout.com
✉ 555 W. Hastings St.
☎ 604/689-0421
💲 $$

Dr. Sun Yat-Sen Garden
www.vancouverchinese garden.com
✉ 578 Carrall St.
☎ 604/662-3207
🕐 Closed Mon. in winter
💲 $$

Art Gallery
www.vanartgallery.bc.ca
✉ 750 Hornby St.
☎ 604/662-4719
💲 $$$

steamer whistle with steam from the district heating system. The improbable founder of the area, loquacious saloon owner "Gassy Jack," is commemorated in **Maple Tree Square** by a statue atop a whiskey barrel.

Chinatown

Just east of Gastown is Canada's largest Chinatown, the focal point of a 250,000-plus community whose origins go back to the gold rush and the construction of the CPR. Behind high white walls is the **Dr. Sun Yat-Sen Garden,** an exquisite reproduction of a Ming Dynasty landscape, constructed for the Expo '86 by an expert team of horticulturalists from the People's Republic of China.

Cathedral Place

Completed in 1991, this elegant office tower with its chiseled copper cap has become a city landmark. It exemplifies postmodernist concern for context by incorporating details from the much-loved art deco structure it replaced and with its sensitivity to its long-established neighbors, **Christ Church Cathedral** and the **Hotel Vancouver.**

Vancouver's public art collection, known simply as the **Art Gallery,** is housed in the former city courthouse, a neoclassic structure designed by Francis Rattenbury and carefully converted into an elegant setting for art by local architect Arthur Erickson. Most of the usual Canadian figures are represented, as are a number of European and American artists, but the greatest attraction for visitors is the extensive collection of the works of Emily Carr (see below).

A tour-de-force of progressive architect and landscape designer Arthur Erickson, **Robson Square** comprises a 7-story law court building and extensive and attractive outdoor spaces on several levels. With its lush planting and extensive use of water, the complex occupies two whole city blocks and leads under Robson Street via a skating rink and convention center to the Art Gallery, making a fascinating sequence of urban spaces.

Stanley Park

The 1,000-acre Stanley Park, which covers an area as large as Vancouver's downtown, is a wonderful asset for a city already bountifully blessed with natural

Emily Carr

Born of English parents in Victoria, Emily Carr (1871–1945) was one of the most fascinating figures in Canadian art. It was only in middle life that her utterly original talent was recognized. Up to then, she had followed a lonely path, recording the villages and the art of the First Nations of the Northwest and supporting herself by running a lodging house. On meeting members of the Group of Seven (see pp. 186–87) in 1927 and seeing their work she exclaimed,

"Oh, God, what have I seen? Where have I been?" Encouraged by Lawren Harris, a member of the group, she returned to her earlier themes, painting monumental pictures of the totems that are her best known works and that "throb and sway with the vital energy of conviction." Her later works apply the same intensity to the depiction of the deep forests of British Columbia and capture the transcendental qualities of the open sky. ■

landscape. Mostly forested, the park extends to the very tip of the peninsula at the **Narrows,** the entrance to Burrard Inlet. The peninsula was a military zone that would have no doubt been clear-cut, but it was saved by the foresight of the city fathers, who petitioned to preserve it within a month of Vancouver's founding in 1886. Facilities and attractions abound, but the main function of Stanley Park is as a vast open space, directly accessible from the city, in which people can do as they want—jog, walk, Rollerblade, cycle, swim, or just laze. You can take the 6-mile Stanley Park Drive, or follow the Seawall Promenade around the perimeter of the park. This essential experience for all visitors is best undertaken by rented bicycle (the bike path is one way, running counter-clockwise) with frequent stops to savor the ever changing views of city, sea, and mountain.

As Stanley Park Drive curves around **Coal Harbour** with its Royal Yacht Club and Rowing Club, bird-rich **Lost Lagoon** is to the left, a former inlet that almost dries up at low tide. Among the trees just short of **Hallelujah Point** is a brightly painted group of totem poles. Near **Prospect Point,** the road crosses over the approach to the 5,000-foot-long **Lions Gate Bridge** over First Narrows, built in 1938 to link the city with the exclusive residential area of West Vancouver. There is a fine view of ships passing in and out of Burrard Inlet from Prospect Point. Between here and west-facing Ferguson Point, the forest of cedar, hemlock, and Douglas-fir gives a good idea of what the site of Vancouver must have looked like before clearance began in the 1880s.

Within Stanley Park is one of Vancouver's most popular attractions, the internationally renowned **Vancouver Aquarium Marine Science Centre**. Emphasis is on the marine life of the Northwest and Arctic, with sea otter, octopus, and beluga whale, but this magnificent institution has much else besides, including a convincingly steamy re-creation of the Amazon rain forest with its abundant bird, fish, and reptilian life, as well as a reproduction of an Indonesian coral reef. ∎

The balcony of Canada Place affords dramatic sunset views over Vancouver's waterfront.

Vancouver Aquarium Marine Science Centre
www.vanaqua.org
☎ 604/659-3474
🕐 Closed Mon. mid-Sept.–mid-June
💲 $$$

More places to visit in Vancouver

GRANVILLE ISLAND

Granville Island, a 20-acre landfill site in **False Creek** created in 1915 for industrial purposes, is now a vibrant meeting place, which has admirably fulfilled the Granville Island Trust's aim of making it a place of "randomness, curiosity, delight and surprise." The remains of industry coexist happily with a whole array of other activities, including shops, studios, restaurants, galleries, theaters, a marina, brewery, and large indoor **Public Market.** On fine weekends, everyone who's not on the beach seems to head here, and the island becomes almost impossibly crowded, but no one complains. Hardly heritage material, the old industrial buildings have been brightly reclad and repainted to house their new uses; the market, with its array of tempting comestibles and other articles, still has pulleys and derricks hanging from the ceiling. There are no sidewalks, but people and cars mingle in friendly proximity in the spaces between the buildings, where railroad tracks still run. In the middle of it all and setting the tone is the **Emily Carr College of Art and Design.**

VANCOUVER MUSEUM

Fronted by a glittering giant sculpture of the crab that, in First Nations legend, is the guardian of the harbor, the museum presents a dutiful account of the history of Vancouver from the earliest European incursions onward, as well as rotating displays from its splendid collection of First Nations art and artifacts. There are reconstructions of a fur-trading post, the steerage quarters in an immigrant ship, the interior of a railroad

Outdoor performers make the most of a sunny day to entertain the weekend crowd on Granville Island.

sensational delights as a virtual voyage to Mars. On it they brave a close shave with the sun and a brush with a meteor shower to bring relief to the inhabitants of a late 21st-century colony on the surface of the red planet.
www.vanmuseum.bc.ca; www.spacecentre.ca ✉ 1100 Chestnut St., Vanier Park ☎ 604/736-4431 (museum), 604/738-7827 (space center) 🕐 Closed Mon. Sept.–June 💲 $$

MARITIME MUSEUM

This relatively small museum in a striking A-frame building has as its superb centerpiece the RCMP vessel *St. Roch*. In 1940, concerned enough to emphasize its presence in the far north, Canada dispatched this large supply and patrol boat from Vancouver on the first west–east voyage through the Northwest Passage. The epic trip took 27 months to reach Halifax, but, undaunted, the *St. Roch* returned to Vancouver, the first vessel ever to sail the passage in both directions. The return journey lasted a mere 86 days. The *St. Roch* has been fully restored to its appearance in 1944, down to a team of huskies on deck.

The museum's other exhibits are minor compared with the *St. Roch*, but there is plenty of maritime memorabilia (including items from Canada's worst shipping disaster, the sinking of the *Empress of Ireland* in the St. Lawrence in 1914), lots of fascinating ship models (and a glimpse into the modelmakers'

"colonist car," all in great contrast to opulent urban interiors from the early 20th century. A thought-provoking model of the site of Vancouver shows what is now a great metropolis when it was nothing more than a thickly forested peninsula with a solitary trail leading to a tiny harbor.

Attached to the museum is the lavishly equipped **H.R. MacMillan Space Centre,** which incorporates a planetarium. Visitors are invited to "boldly go" and enjoy such

Bill Reid's "Bear" at the U.B.C. Museum of Anthropology. The sculptor, of Haida descent, devoted his working life to reviving and reinterpreting the First Nations' artistic tradition.

workshop), and a chance to skipper a tugboat as it noses out of False Creek.

A dock on English Bay has a number of small vessels, most of them in working order. www.vancouvermaritimemuseum.com ✉ 1905 Ogden Ave., Vanier Park ☎ 604/257-8300 🕐 Closed Mon., early Sept.–mid-May 💲 $$

UNIVERSITY OF BRITISH COLUMBIA

Almost a city in its own right, the vast campus of the University of British Columbia, with nearly 500 buildings, is located on Point Grey overlooking the Georgia Strait and the mountains of Vancouver Island. From early days, agriculture and forestry played an important role in the life of the university, and 70 acres of the campus are given over to the marvelous trees and shrubs of the **University of British Columbia Botanical Garden** (Tel 604/822-3928). In addition, there is the exquisite **Nitobe Japanese garden** (Tel 604/822-9666), but most visitors come to the campus for the unrivaled collections of First Nations art in the **Museum of Anthropology** (6393 Northwest Marine Dr., tel 604/822-5087, www.moa.ubc.ca, closed Mon. mid-Sept.– mid-May).

Embedded in woodland with a prospect of sea and mountains, the museum building is a superb showcase for a fascinating array of sculptures, carvings, totem poles, and other art and craft objects. The building was designed by Arthur Erickson and completed in 1976. Its inspiration was the traditional post-and-beam structures of the Kwakwaka'wakw people; the concrete posts of the glass-walled and top-lit Great Hall are up to 50 feet high, matching in scale the imposing totems assembled within and allowing their full grandeur to be appreciated. The totems are complemented by other large carvings, but there are objects of all sizes, some, in precious metals, argillite, or bone, of great intricacy and delicacy. Although the emphasis is on peoples of the Northwest, the collections include items from the Arctic and from all around the world. In addition, the magnificent European ceramics of the Koerner Collection, their centerpiece a huge and elaborate 16th-century Central European tiled stove, are housed in a side gallery. The

Visible Storage Galleries allow visitors access to more than 15,000 objects that might otherwise be hidden.

At the very heart of the building, in a rotunda lit dramatically from above, is the powerful presence of Bill Reid's "Raven and the First Men." Sculpted in cedar and weighing 4.5 tons, the piece is dominated by the massive figure of Raven atop a clam shell from which human figures struggle to emerge, an allegory of creation by this world-famous artist who died in 1998, many of whose other works are on display.

Outside the Great Hall, on top of the low cliffs dropping to the water, are more totems as well as two Haida houses.

QUEEN ELIZABETH PARK

Running south from the Vancouver city center, the otherwise ruler-straight Cambie Street curves round in obeisance to this superb hilltop park. Competing for attention are the magnificent views of the city, the richly planted sunken gardens, and the geodesic dome of the **Bloedel Floral Conservatory** (West 33rd Ave. & Cambie St., tel 604/257-8584) with its luxuriant vegetation.

SIMON FRASER UNIVERSITY

Few contrasts could be greater than between the campuses of the University of British Columbia and Simon Fraser, Vancouver's "other" university. Begun in 1914, the former is laid out along beaux arts lines, with long vistas and sweeping avenues. The latter, a product of the 1960s, based on a concrete spine of interconnected structures crowning the ridge of Burnaby Mountain. An "Acropolis for our time," Simon Fraser pioneered not just architectural but also academic structures and has a reputation as a progressive institution. ☎ 604/291-3210

THE NORTH SHORE

The mountains of the North Shore are not simply there to be looked at, but can be easily explored due to their proximity to the city and accessibility by road. The excursion to the top

Right: A short ferry and bus ride from downtown, Grouse Mountain can be climbed via this high-capacity cable car.

of **Grouse Mountain** *(8 miles from Lions Gate Bridge, tel 604/980-9311, www.grouse mountain.com)* is popular in both summer and winter thanks to the aerial tram that whisks passengers up to the summit station (3,700 feet). At the top, visitors can enjoy wining and dining, "Theatre in the Sky," helicopter tours, logging shows, and floodlit skiing, but the view's the thing, a wonderful panorama extending on clear days as far as Vancouver Island. A network of walking trails leads into the mountains.

With fine stands of fir and cedar, **Capilano Canyon** *(6 miles from Lions Gate Bridge on Capilano Rd., tel 604/985-7474)* is also accessible on foot from Grouse Mountain, and has a number of fascinating features including a salmon hatchery. But the feature that attracts most visitors is the spectacular suspension footbridge, at 450 feet the longest of its kind in the world. An almost constant stream of daring individuals pays a not inconsiderable sum to defy vertigo and walk across the bridge as it sways 250 feet above the floor of the canyon. Lookouts along the winding Mount Seymour Parkway in **Mount Seymour Provincial Park** *(10 miles via Second Narrows Bridge off Mount Seymour Parkway, tel 604/986-2261)* give splendid views of the city and Indian Arm, the prolongation of Burrard Inlet. The parkway climbs to a height of more than 3,300 feet before terminating at the base of a chairlift, much used by skiers in season. There is an excellent choice of day and half-day hikes, including one to the summit of Mount Seymour (4,767 feet). ■

Excursions from Vancouver

Vancouver is also a good base for a number of longer excursions. Some merit an overnight stop, although most can be treated as day trips, or possibly combined as a tour.

HOWE SOUND & THE SEA TO SKY HIGHWAY

An excursion up the fjordlike Howe Sound to the logging town of Squamish and the internationally renowned ski resort of Whistler encompasses many of the attractions that make West Coast life so enjoyable.

Grandly named the Sea to Sky Highway, Hwy. 99 is not the only way to make this trip. The Whistler Mountaineer is a 3-hour train excursion between Vancouver and Whistler run by the Rocky Mountaineer Company (see p. 387).

North of Horseshoe Bay, a ferry port for boats to Vancouver Island, road and rail squeeze together between cliff and shoreline with spectacular views of Howe Sound in its mountain setting.

BRITANNIA BEACH

In its heyday in the 1920s and '30s, the Britannia Copper Mine was the most productive in the British Empire. Altogether some 56 million tons of copper were extracted before prices fell and the ore dwindled. Closed in 1974, it is now the **British Columbia Museum of Mining** (*Britannia Beach, tel 604/896-2233, closed Sat.–Sun. Nov.–April),* a national historic site offering a fascinating account of its often troubled history (accidents, rock slides, fire and floods) as well as underground tours.

SQUAMISH

In a splendid setting beneath snow-tipped Mount Garibaldi (8,786 feet), Squamish has a developing railroad museum at the **West Coast Railway Heritage Park** *(39645 Government Rd., tel 604/898-9336).* Squamish means "Mother of the Wind" in Coast Salish, and windsurfers make use of the stiff breezes of the sound to achieve speeds of nearly 40 mph.
🏔 273 C1 ✉ Visitor Information, Cleveland Ave. ☎ 604/892-9244

GARIBALDI PROVINCIAL PARK

This park encompasses 750 square miles of mountain wilderness in the heart of the Coast Mountains just north of Vancouver. Snow-capped mountains, glaciers, lakes, alpine meadows full of flowers and wildlife make it not only immensely beautiful but extremely popular. Dominated by Mount Garibaldi (8,786 feet), named for the 19th century Italian patriot, and Wedge Mountain (9,485 feet), the park is also known for geological features such as Black Tusk and the Barrier created by volcanic action. There are many miles of hiking trails of varying length and difficulty.
🏔 273 D2 www.bcparks.ca ✉ 44 miles N of Vancouver via Hwy. 99 ☎ 604/898-3678

WHISTLER

This world-famous ski resort promotes itself with an array of well-founded superlatives reflected in its consistently high ranking in international skiing surveys. Forgetting jet lag, people fly here from Europe as well as from all over North America to enjoy the superb

Unbeatable snow cover and superlative scenery draw many to Whistler Mountain. Opposite: The *Queen of Surrey* ferries passengers to and from Vancouver Island.

quality of the skiing. Overlooked by the two great peaks of **Whistler Mountain** (7,160 feet) and **Blackcomb Mountain** (7,494 feet), the resort boasts the largest ski area on the North American continent, a long season, an astounding 30-foot snowfall, high speed lifts, and amazing downhill runs (Mount Blackcomb is 5,280 feet—nearly a vertical mile). There is skiing in summer, too. It is the only place in North America offering the chance to ski or snowboard on a glacier. It will host the winter Olympic Games in 2010

🅰 273 D2   www.tourismwhistler.com
☎ 800/WHISTLER

FORT LANGLEY NATIONAL HISTORIC SITE

In 1858 this Hudson's Bay Company fort on the Fraser River only just failed to become the capital of newly created British Columbia. This focal point of the HBC's supply operations for the whole of the Columbia District was originally built in 1827, 2.5 miles down-stream from its present location. As the fur trade flagged, the importance of the fort's farm and its salmon-packing business grew; provisions from here were exported to Hawaii and Australia as well as to San Francisco and the Russian outposts in North America.

Within the stockade, now a national historic site, the only original building is the storehouse dating from 1840. It has the distinction of being the oldest nonnative structure in British Columbia, and served for a while as a cooperage, barrel production being crucial for the successful export of fish. The other buildings, including the factor's Big House, have been carefully rebuilt, and are peopled by a variety of costumed characters who give a lively impression of the life that went on in the mid-19th century in this mainland nucleus of Canada's western-most province.

🅰 273 D1   www.pc.gc.ca   ✉ 23433 Mavis St.
☎ 604/513-4777   🕐 Closed Mon. Nov.–mid-March ■

Vancouver Island & Victoria

SOME 300 MILES IN LENGTH AND WITH A TOTAL AREA OF about 12,000 square miles, Vancouver Island is the largest of the islands off the western coast of North America. Mountains of volcanic origin form the island's spine, part of a mostly submerged formation that includes the Queen Charlotte Islands and the Wrangell Mountains of Alaska. Luxuriant rain forest thrives in the generally damp and mild climate, and though much of it has been logged, fine stands of fir, cedar, and hemlock still thrive.

The population is overwhelmingly concentrated in Victoria and in the lowlands along the Strait of Georgia. Few people live very far from the highway linking Victoria at the southern tip of the island to Port Hardy in the north, embarkation point for the Inside Passage ferry.

Virtually every visitor to Vancouver Island is drawn to Victoria, which assiduously cultivates the Britishness of its heritage. Others head for the breakers and beaches of the spectacular coastline of Pacific Rim National Park or the wilderness of Strathcona Provincial Park, which has the island's highest peak, Golden Hinde (7,218 feet).

Abundant marine and forest resources helped the First Nations people here reach a high level of cultural and economic development and there are a number of places on the island where their heritage is readily accessible.

VICTORIA

Long since left behind in metropolitan ambition by Vancouver, sedate Victoria remains the capital of British Columbia, quite content to polish its image as a welcoming haven for the retired and its many visitors from all over the world. The image is based on realities: A wonderful site on a splendid natural harbor, a climate classed as Mediterranean, a gentlemanly pace of life, and a carefully tended downtown where high-rises are few

Vancouver Island

272–273 C1–C2, B2

Visitor information
www.tourismvictoria.com

Victoria Infocentre, 812 Wharf St.

☎ 250/953-2033

Victoria's Parliament building overlooks the city's inner harbor.

and flowers many. An array of other attractions includes the Royal British Columbia Museum, held by many to be the country's finest institution of its kind.

Victoria's much vaunted Britishness has some foundation in fact as well as in double-decker buses and afternoon tea and crumpets at the Empress Hotel. "Cheltenham with sea air" was one American's epithet, and Victoria's clement weather is not unlike (though definitely superior to) that of the famous English spa town and retirement spot and is equally kind to old bones. After working lives spent battling the rigors of other Canadian climates, many Anglo-Canadians were more than happy to settle here and spend their declining years in a neo-Tudor mansion or reproduction Cotswold villa, perhaps cultivating one of the English-style gardens for which this southeastern part of Vancouver Island is famous. The tone of the place had been set at the beginning in the mid-1800s: Charged with producing as much food as possible from the company's farms, Hudson's Bay Company chief bailiff Kenneth McKenzie found that his colleagues were more inclined to

Forests, mountains, and coastlines similar to Half Moon Bay in Pacific Rim National Park Reserve characterize Vancouver Island.

Fort Rodd Hill National Historic Site

www.pc.gc.ca

✉ 603 Fort Rodd Hill Rd.

☎ 250/478-5849

$ $

"introduce the outlook, the pleasures, and the customs of the English gentry, and with complete indifference to profit-making, live a life of comparative ease."

Bastion Square and Fort Street recall Victoria's origin as a fortified post of the Hudson's Bay Company (see pp. 220–21), moved here in 1843 from Fort Vancouver in what is now Washington State as the company's Pacific coast base. Long since demolished, the fort was the nucleus from which the town developed from the early 1850s on; **Government Street,** laid out in 1851, was the very first street in British North America west of the Rockies. The 1858 Gold Rush, with the sudden arrival of between 20,000 and 30,000 feverish prospectors on their way to the Fraser River, gave the town's development a kick start, and also led to the establishment of Victoria's substantial Chinatown. The insubstantial one- and two-story buildings of

this era with their flat-topped boomtown fronts rising over the raised boardwalks gave the town a very un-British look.

The rambunctious behavior of the mostly American prospectors was considered by the authorities to be very un-British, too; it was primarily to maintain law and order that the government took over control of Vancouver Island from the Hudson's Bay Company and created the new colony of British Columbia. Victoria's vocation was henceforth that of a government town; a first set of colonial administration buildings was replaced in 1897 by the enormously imposing Parliament Building that still dominates the harbor today. **Fort Rodd Hill,** now a national historic site and still a magnificent vantage point, was developed as a part of a system of defenses, and the Royal Navy made its Pacific base on the southwestern corner of the harbor at Esquimault.

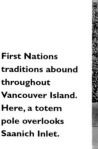

First Nations traditions abound throughout Vancouver Island. Here, a totem pole overlooks Saanich Inlet.

ROYAL BRITISH COLUMBIA MUSEUM

Built on a grand scale in the late 1960s, the museum hosts temporary exhibitions of international importance as well as a permanent collection. The permanent displays include the superb natural history dioramas and models, as well as galleries covering the modern history of the province and, above all, the First Peoples Gallery, a comprehensive and thrilling account of early Pacific coast life and heritage. The light and airy entrance hall of the museum has space enough for tall, 19th-century totems, whose fascinating detail can be examined close-up from the upper floor.

With its huge tusks pointing ominously at the visitor, a woolly mammoth makes an impressive guardian to the **Living Land, Living Sea Gallery.** This exhibition explores the forces that have shaped the land that is British Columbia for 90 million years, and which continue to do so.

The **Natural History Gallery** has great dioramas, with impeccable attention to detail, sound effects, and lighting. They make a marvelous introduction to the extraordinary array of natural environments in this huge province, which boasts Canada's wettest mountains, driest valleys, deepest snows, and warmest coast. The dominant features of the dioramas are the great trees of the various types of forest—coastal, Columbia, subalpine, boreal— which cloak much of the province, making it all the more thrilling to emerge on the simulated shore of Vancouver Island, with its guano-streaked headland, playful seals, and triumphant bull sea lion atop his rock.

The exhibits in the **Modern History Gallery** deal with the province's relatively short but colorful history in reverse, from modern times backward. The most striking exhibit is perhaps the reconstruction of an early 20th-century street, with shops, offices, dimly lit Chinatown, and plush interior of the Grand Hotel. The telegraph taps away in the railroad station until drowned out by the noisy arrival and departure of a train.

Other displays convincingly re-create the ambience of the Tremblay Farmstead in the Peace River District, the inhospitable landscape of the Stikine Country that was the scene of Anglo–Russian rivalry, and a fish-canning plant complete with seagull scavengers and slimy fish-gutting bench. The gallery ends at the beginning of B.C.'s European history, aboard the three-master sloop *Discovery*, in which Captain Vancouver's quarters served as charthouse and botanical laboratory as well as cabin.

The dimly lit spaces of the **First Peoples Gallery** heighten the impact of the superbly presented exhibits. Divided into two main sections, the gallery shows the art and culture of the nations of the Northwest before and after the arrival of the Europeans, their technology, and their diseases. It is the best possible introduction to the subject, with an array of objects that demonstrates the richness and diversity of the material culture of the different groupings and gives some insight into magic, ritual, and the spiritual life. The centerpiece is the reconstructed full-size plankhouse of Chief Kwakwabalasami with its glowing fire. Don't miss the audiovisual presentation on cosmology, myth, and image, where the supernatural is evoked by song, dance, costume, and eerily illuminated masks. ∎

Royal British Columbia Museum
www.royalbcmuseum.bc.ca
✉ 675 Belleville St.
☎ 250/356-7226 or 888/447-7977
💲 $$

A walk around Victoria

This short walk introduces the staid downtown of this miniature provincial capital, its fascinating harbor, and the clutch of grandiose buildings dominating the waterfront. With comfortable walking shoes you should have no trouble completing this tour in just over an hour, having worked up enough appetite for afternoon tea at the Empress Hotel, one of this pleasant city's defining experiences.

⊞ See area map pp. 272–73
► Parliament Buildings
⟷ 1.5 miles
⊕ Allow 1 hour
► Empress Hotel

NOT TO BE MISSED
- Parliament Buildings
- Thunderbird Park
- Crystal Garden
- Empress Hotel
- Maritime Museum

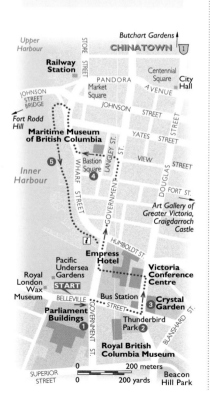

Begin at the **Parliament Buildings ❶** *(South side of James Bay, tel 250/387-3046),* completed in 1898 by a young English architect, Francis Mawson Rattenbury, who used local granite, slate, and andesite for his ambitious scheme—three wings beneath a central dome topped by a gilded statue of Captain Vancouver. The building launched Rattenbury's career as Victoria's civic architect.

To the east, along Belleville Street and beyond the archives building with its belfry is **Thunderbird Park ❷** *(In front of Royal British Columbia Museum).* Around the reproduction Bighouse is a fine collection of totems, some of them superb copies from the hand of Kwakwaka'wakw master carver Mungo Martin. Close by are Victoria's two oldest buildings, the cabinlike **St. Anne's Schoolhouse** and a modest dwelling built by pioneer doctor John Sebastian Helmcken in 1852.

Walk north on Douglas Street. The great days of the **Crystal Garden ❸** *(317 Douglas St., tel 250/360-2055)* on the right were between the wars, when it was enlivened with tea dances and swimmers frolicking in the country's biggest indoor pool. Now renovated, it houses the BC Experience, a discovery center, and a teahouse. Go up the steps into the 1989 **Victoria Conference Center,** which has been sensitively integrated into the venerable **Empress Hotel** *(721 Government St., tel 250/384-8111),* and walk through the palatial ground floor spaces of this great Edwardian institution. Leave by the front doors and head up **Government Street,** with its clipped and disciplined trees and harmonious heritage buildings. There's even a shopping mall discreetly hidden behind the original 19th-century facades. Turn left into **Bastion Square ❹,** named for the Hudson's Bay Company's fort, whose northeast bastion was sited where the square meets

Adding to Victoria's atmosphere of Britishness, double-decker buses await sightseers outside the stately Empress Hotel.

Empress of Victoria

Architect Francis Rattenbury followed the completion of Victoria's legislative buildings with a monumental château-style design for the Canadian Pacific Railway's Empress Hotel. Begun in 1904, the hotel was seen as a "fitting companion to the historic pile on the heights of Québec," that is, Château Frontenac, completed a decade earlier. It was built on piles sunk 125 feet into what was then a tidal swamp, and has always been as much a civic institution as a hotel. No visit to Victoria is complete without a stroll through its halls and lobbies, or, better still, a drink in the Bengal Lounge with its memories of an empire whose way of life lingered longer here than almost anywhere else. ∎

Government Street. The square has a number of attractive old edifices, including the former courthouse, now the home of the **Maritime Museum** *(Tel 250/385-4222)*.

Walk along Wharf Street with its renovated warehouses. To the east, both Yates and Johnson Streets have fine examples of late 19th-century commercial buildings. Cross Wharf Street and descend past rock outcrops to the **waterfront boardwalk.** The **Johnson Street Bridge** carries the single track of Vancouver Island's only railroad. Walk south along the waterfront and enjoy the varied activity of the **harbor** ⑤—training sloops, the Seattle catamaran, and floatplanes taking off and landing. Climb the steps by the art deco tower of the **Tourist Information Centre** *(Tel 250/478-5849)* and finish the walk by the statue of Captain Cook opposite the Empress Hotel. If your timing is right, this could be the moment to indulge in afternoon tea in the hotel's sumptuous surroundings. ∎

Excursions from Victoria

CRAIGDARROCH CASTLE

Scottish-born Robert Dunsmuir commissioned this hilltop castle in 1887, but died before it was completed in 1890. Dunsmuir's story seems to encapsulate much of B.C.'s early social history. A penniless arrival in the province was soon overcome when he made a fortune from Nanaimo coal. He and his son James built the Nanaimo and Esquimault Railway to export the coal, receiving a huge land grant amounting to about a quarter of the area of Victoria. Ownership of an iron foundry, a fleet of ships, and a newspaper followed, as did James's appointment as provincial lieutenant governor. The house has been described as Richardsonian Romanesque, but its exaggerated proportions speak more of arriviste pretensions than architectural taste.
www.thecastle.ca ✉ 1050 Joan Crescent
☎ 250/592-5323 💲 $$

ART GALLERY OF GREATER VICTORIA

This substantial clapboard house of about 1890 was built by a banker and served for a few years as Government House. In 1958 it was extended to house the city's art gallery, which has a small collection of European art as well has two great strengths: A fine collection of Asian art and works by Emily Carr, born in Victoria in 1871 (see p. 280). The paintings, sketches, and other memorabilia here remind visitors of her passion for the Northwest and its First Nations heritage and of how she "clung to earth and her dear shapes."
www.aggv.bc.ca ✉ 1040 Moss St.
☎ 250/384-4101 💲 $$

BUTCHART GARDENS

The mild, damp climate of southeastern Vancouver Island is particularly favorable to plant growth, and English-style gardening began as soon as the first settlers had established themselves.

Government House in Victoria marries a degree of formality with informal use of native plants, while the city's **Beacon Hill Park** has showpiece gardens as well as wildflower meadows. The **University of Victoria** boasts a superb rhododendron

Butchart Garden's ever popular centerpiece—the Sunken Garden

Early locomotive's run through Duncan's Forest Museum Park

collection, and the Royal British Columbia Museum has an array of native plants.

The greatest of all island gardens is a private venture: Butchart Gardens on the Saanich Peninsula to the north of Victoria. The gardens had a utilitarian origin in the quarry of Robert Pim Butchart, who had established a Portland cement plant at Tod Inlet. In 1904 the worked-out quarry, a ready-made sheltered habitat for a variety of plants, inspired his wife, Jenny Butchart, to start creating the gardens that have become one of western Canada's foremost visitor attractions.

The gardens' centerpiece is the splendid **Sunken Garden** laid out on the floor and sides of the original quarry. Sumptuous floral displays are set off by immaculate lawns and tree growth. An imposing rock garden recalls the site's industrial beginnings. But the 50-acre grounds include much more, from the aromatic rose garden where the perfume of the blooms assails the senses, to exquisitely planned Japanese and Italian gardens.

The huge popularity of the gardens makes savoring them in solitary peace unlikely. In summer, a late afternoon visit is advised.

🅼 273 C1 www.butchartgardens.com
✉ 13 miles N of Victoria off Hwy. 17A
☎ 250/652-5256 💲 $$$

DUNCAN
The town of Duncan pays tribute to the Cowichan on whose land it stands by calling itself "the town of totems" and by displaying an array of poles, many of them along the Trans-Canada 1. The **Qmw'utsun' Cultural Centre** (*200 Cowichan Way, tel 250/746-8119*) is one of the best places to get the flavor of First Nations life today, watch totem carving and other crafts being practiced, take part in events, or visit Vancouver Island's largest native arts and crafts shops.

Also close to the town, the **British Columbia Forest Discovery Centre** (*1 mile N of Duncan on Trans-Canada 1, tel 250/715-1113, closed mid-Oct.–mid-April*) tells visitors everything they are ever likely to want to know about forestry. A narrow-gauge railroad runs around the 100-acre site, past the working sawmill and a host of other logging installations and demonstrations.

🅼 273 C1 ✉ Visitor information, 381 Trans-Canada Hwy. ☎ 250/746-4636

CHEMAINUS
Claiming to be the oldest deepwater port in British Columbia, this small town came to depend on its huge sawmill, and faced disaster when it closed in 1983. A concerted campaign to put the place back on the map involved covering as much wallspace as possible with murals. The results are impressive, as well as entertaining, and have helped bring some new life to the town.

🅼 273 C1 ✉ Visitor information, 9796 Willow St. ☎ 250/246-3944 ■

Western & Northern Vancouver Island

PACIFIC RIM NATIONAL PARK RESERVE

Some of the finest stretches of Vancouver Island's wild western coast are protected by this reserve, which consists of three distinct units. In the north, great waves beat on the sands and rocky headlands of **Long Beach;** to the south an archipelago, the **Broken Group Islands,** adorns the waters of **Barkley Sound;** farther south still, the **West Coast Trail** created for shipwrecked sailors threads its way through the wilderness. The narrow coastal strip has cliffs, caves, rain forest, and waterfalls, while inland rise snow-covered mountaintops. The park is reached via Hwy. 4 from **Parksville** on the east coast. The route cuts across the grain of Vancouver Island and introduces some of its most characteristic landscapes.

273 C1 www.pc.gc.ca Park headquarters at Ucluelet; Visitor center at Wickaninnish off Hwy. 4 250/726-7721 Visitor center closed mid-Oct.–mid-March $

ENGLISHMAN RIVER & FALLS PROVINCIAL PARK

The name of the river recalls the anonymous Englishman who perished in its waters, which tumble over the upper and lower falls set among the luxuriant trees, shrubs, and ferns of the rain forest of this park.

5 miles along side road 2.5 miles W of Parksville

LITTLE QUALICUM FALLS PROVINCIAL PARK

Between its upper and lower falls, the Little Qualicum River foams through a canyon,

visible from a trail though the forest. The falls themselves add a note of noisy grandeur within this primeval setting.

✉ 16 miles W of Parksville via Hwy. 4

CATHEDRAL GROVE

Just beyond the western end of Cameron Lake, a short trail gives access to this famous stand of Douglas-fir. Perhaps as much as a thousand years old, these forest giants induce in most visitors the reverence that is suggested by the grove's name.

✉ 22 miles W of Parksville via Hwy. 4

PORT ALBERNI

On a long inlet connecting it to Barkley Sound stands workaday Port Alberni. It is famous for its salmon fishing, but its role as a logging center is equally important. One of the easiest ways of seeing something of the sound and its scattering of islands is to travel

Stretching along the western coast of Vancouver Island, Pacific Rim National Park receives a rainfall averaging 120 inches a year, which nourishes a dense temperate rain forest comprising western redcedar, western hemlock, and more.

aboard M.V. *Mary Rose (Tel 250/723-8313),* which makes a daily trip from Port Alberini to **Bamfield** or **Ucluelet** and back. Local lumber mills offer tours and a former logging locomotive, the 1929 Baldwin, offers rides through the town from the 1912 rail station to the **McLean Mill** *(5 miles N via Beaver Creek Rd. & Smith Rd., tel 250/723-1376, www.alberniheritage.com).* This operation is Canada's last operating steam-powered sawmill, which cuts wood for demonstration and sale.

🏕 273 C1 ✉ Visitor information, 2533 Redford St. ☎ 250/724-6535

LONG BEACH

On its way to Tofino, the fishing village just beyond the northern boundary of the national park reserve, the highway passes a number of short trails leading to the pristine shore of Long Beach, stretching some 10 miles northward, from Ucluelet. One of the best overall views of coast and mountain is from the World War II military site at **Radar Hill.** Excellent displays at the **Wickanninish Interpretive Centre** (see p. 296) explain the complex and fascinating ecology of the area; from it, a trail leads to a superb pebble beach among rocky bluffs, where the waves surge in through a natural arch. En route is **Lismer Beach,** named for painter and Group of Seven member Arthur Lismer, who came here often. Up to 20,000 gray whales swim past between February and May in the course of their annual migration from Baja California to Alaska. Other whales can be seen, too, including killer whales, or orcas, in pursuit of the sea lions, whose favorite spot is **Sea Lion Rocks.**

Tofino (*Visitor information, 1426 Pacific Rim Hwy., tel 250/725-3414*) itself stands on a narrow neck of land at the end of Hwy. 4, looking out over **Clayoquot Sound.** Crowded in summer, the village is the point of departure for explorations, not only of the national park reserve's shoreline, but also of the superb and still intact rain forest of Clayoquot Sound, once a subject of controversy over the conflicting claims of loggers and conservationists. Some of the finest old-growth forest can be seen on **Meares Island,** just offshore from Tofino.

🅰 273 C1

BROKEN GROUP ISLANDS

The Broken Group Islands are most easily visited in the course of a day trip aboard the M.V. *Mary Rose* (see p. 297), though their special delights are reserved for kayakers and scuba divers. With many wrecks to be explored, the name Graveyard of the Pacific is well deserved.

WEST COAST TRAIL

After the *Valencia* disaster of 1906 when all hands perished, the predecessor of today's 45-mile **West Coast Trail** between **Bamfield** and **Port Renfrew** was equipped with cabins with emergency supplies for shipwrecked survivors and with telephones for them to contact the outside world. As rescue services improved, the trail fell out of use. Restored today, it tempts hikers prepared to rough it.

🅰 273 C1

CAMPBELL RIVER

The southern Kwakwaka'wakw people had fished for salmon here for many years before the first white visitor landed a 66 pounder in 1891. A ferry service links the town with **Quadra Island,** a First Nations village site for more than 2,000 years; the seashell-shaped **Kwagiulth Museum** (*Cape Mudge Village, tel 250/285-3733, call for hours in winter*) has potlach regalia (see pp. 304–305) and other fascinating objects confiscated by the government in 1922 but subsequently returned.

🅰 273 C2

STRATHCONA PROVINCIAL PARK

Designated in 1911, British Columbia's oldest provincial park protects some of Vancouver Island's grandest scenery. Many peaks rise from the forest and alpine meadows, among them the island's summit, Golden Hinde (7,216 feet). Wildlife includes deer, elk, wolf, and even the elusive mountain lion. Many trails are for experienced backpackers only, but short walks are found around popular **Buttle Lake.**

🅰 273 C1 www.env.gov.bc.ca/parks
✉ Visitor information, jct. of Hwy. 28 & Buttle Lake Rd.

PORT MCNEILL

A modern logging town, Port McNeill has a ferry to the fishing village of **Alert Bay** on Cormorant Island. The **U'Mista Cultural Centre** (*Front St., tel 250/974-5403, closed weekends off-season*) derives its name from a native word meaning "those returned from slavery." Local people were at the center of the events that resulted in the Kwakwaka'wakw being deprived of their potlatch artifacts in 1922; the returned objects are displayed in the center, which also hosts events and courses.

Also near Port McNeill is the delightful village of **Telegraph Cove,** dating from the early years of the 20th century and which still has its boardwalk and many of its stilt buildings intact.

🅰 272 B2 ✉ 112 miles N of Campbell River ∎

The Inside Passage

Although discovering the Northwest Passage proved an unattainable goal for European explorers in North America, finding the Inside Passage along Canada's Pacific coast proved to be an achievable—and scenic—aim. Today it is one of the most dramatic voyages in the world, tracing a route north from the tip of Vancouver Island to Canada's border with Alaska.

The waters of Hecate Strait, which separates the Queen Charlotte Islands from the host of small islands that line Canada's Pacific shore, and of Queen Charlotte Strait, which separates Vancouver Island from the same small islands, are treacherous. Despite the fact that the Haida (closely related to the Tlingit), who settled the Queen Charlotte Islands, are known to have traveled these waters, and later explorers such as the Russians and Captain Cook also sailed them, a calmer, less dangerous route along the Pacific coast was needed. The Haida had, in fact, established it before Europeans settled the area, showing those early settlers the Route of the Haidas, as it was known for many years. The Inside Passage is a less romantic but more descriptive name for a sea route that threads a way between the islands and mainland of Canada's Pacific coast.

NORTH TO ALASKA

The Inside Passage can be followed from Vancouver all the way to the Lynn Canal in Alaska, the canal being a dead-end fjord that ends at Skagway. For many travelers, the Canadian passage starts with a boarding of the ferry that travels the route from **Port Hardy** ❶ on Vancouver Island's northern coast, to Prince Rupert at the mouth of the Skeena River. The 15-hour trip—all of it in daylight during the summer months—takes in beautiful scenery rich in both human and natural history.

Port Hardy was named for Thomas Masterman Hardy, the captain of H.M.S. *Victory* at the Battle of Trafalgar in 1805. Today the town is a center for mining, logging, and fishing. From the port the ship crosses **Queen Charlotte Strait,** an exposed piece of water that occasionally tests the sea legs of travelers.

Green Island Lightstation in Chatham Sound is one of several lighthouses along British Columbia's west coast that provide navigational aid to boats plying the Inside Passage.

Chatham Sound

Prince Rupert

16

Skeena River

BRITISH
COLUMBIA

PORCHER
ISLAND

Kitimat

QUEEN
CHARLOTTE
ISLANDS

Hecate Strait

Grenville Channel

HAWKESBURY
ISLAND

BANKS
ISLAND

PITT
ISLAND

4

GRIBBELL
ISLAND

GILL
ISLAND

PRINCESS
ROYAL
ISLAND

Fraser Channel

C
O
A
S
T

M
O
U
N
T
A
I
N
S

SARAH
ISLAND

ARISTAZABEL
ISLAND

SWINDLE
ISLAND

PRICE
ISLAND

3

Milbanke
Sound

Dean Channel

CAMPBELL
ISLAND

Bella Bella

KING ISLAND

Burke Channel

Fishing vessel at Prince Rupert.

HUNTER
ISLAND

Fitzhugh Sound

Namu

2

Queen Charlotte Sound

CALVERT
ISLAND

Cape Scott

Pacific Ocean

Queen Charlotte Strait

Port Hardy

1

START

19

N

0   80 kilometers
0   40 miles

VANCOUVER
ISLAND

See area map pp. 272–73
► Port Hardy
⟷ 310 miles
🕐 Allow 15 hours
► Prince Rupert

INFORMATION
Information on all British Columbia
Ferries is available from:
www.bcferries.com
✉ B.C. Ferries, 1112 Fort St.,
   Victoria, B.C.
☎ 250/386-3431 or 888/223-3779
   (toll free in B.C.)

Here the ship is plying the Pacific Ocean: To
the west, there is only water until the eastern
coast of Russia is reached. At the far side of the
sound is the highly exposed lighthouse on **Egg
Island.** In 1948 a storm blew the lighthouse
away, fortunately just after it had been abandoned by the keeper and his wife.

The lighthouse marks the approach to
Fitzhugh Sound ❷ and the true entrance
to the Inside Passage. Toward the northern
end of Fitzhugh, to the right, is **Namu.** The
First Nations' name of the town, meaning
"whirlwind," reflects the sound's famous
winds. The locals refer to them as *williwaws.*
The ship now rounds the northern end of
Hunter Island: Ahead here, the waterway
leads to the **Dean Channel** where,
Alexander Mackenzie reached the Pacific at
the end of the first land crossing of the North
American continent on July 22, 1793.

You now turn north, passing **Bella Bella**
village, then rounding **Campbell Island** to
reach **Milbanke Sound** ❸. Here, again, the
ship is exposed to the Pacific, another trial in
poor weather. But on a good day, the sound is a
wonderful place. When Pacific salmon—the
chinook, sockeye, pink, coho, and chum—are
making their spawning run, fishing boats compete for the fish with nature's predators. If you
are lucky, you will see orca (the correct name
for the usually, and inappropriately, named
killer whale), Steller sea lion, and northern fur
seal. The orca, in particular, is a magnificent
sight—25 feet long and patterned in black and
white, its high dorsal fin scything the sea. You
may also see bald eagles fishing. The sound's

famous herring shoals attract humpback
whales that can often be seen breaching—hurl-
ing themselves out of the water. The energy
required to lift a 50-foot, 40-ton whale out of
the water is colossal, and no one knows exactly
why they do it. All these animals can be seen at
various points along the passage—the hump-
backs infrequently in the narrower channels.

Northward, you follow the Finlayson
Channel to reach the **Boat Bluff lighthouse** on the southern tip of Sarah Islands.
Boat Bluff is the most picturesque of all the
passage's lighthouses. To the left, **Princess
Royal Island** is the home of white black
bears and black gray wolves. Beyond the
island, the ship crosses the **Whale Channel**
to reach the **Grenville Channel** ❹, named
by Capt. George Vancouver for William
Grenville (1759–1834), briefly a British prime
minister. Grenville Channel is 11 hours' sailing
from Port Hardy and just a couple of hours
from Prince Rupert, but travelers are well
rewarded for the wait. The channel has the
most spectacular scenery on the entire passage, with mountains up to around 3,500 feet
high on each side, their flanks covered in pine
and cedar forests. The channel is remarkably
deep (about 1,600 feet) and sharp-sided, so
the ship can travel extremely close to the
shore. At the narrowest point, the channel is
only 600 yards wide. Beyond the Grenville
Channel, the scenery is no less breathtaking,
but set farther back: It is just a few minutes
now to the terminus at **Prince Rupert.**

Prince Rupert is the end of the true Inside
Passage, but it is possible to continue on the
Alaska Marine Highway *(Tel 800/642-0066,
www.ferryalaska.com)* along an inner channel,
crossing Chatham Sound to reach the Canada-
U.S. border and continuing to **Ketchikan,** the
first town in Alaska. Northward, the Clarence
Strait is followed to Wrangell, from where
island-hopping reaches **Petersburg.** The
Alaskan passage now splits into two, an outer
route visiting **Baranof Island** before reaching the **Lynn Canal,** an inner route reaching
Juneau, Alaska's capital. The Lynn Canal to
Skagway is the last stretch of the inner
passage, but as a fine alternative many will
want to take in the spectacular sights in the
magnificent **Glacier Bay National Park**
(Tel 907/697-2230, www.nps.gov/glba). ∎

Prince Rupert, Skeena Valley, & Queen Charlotte Islands

Prince Rupert
🅰 272 B3
Visitor information
www.tourismprincerupert.com
✉ 215 Cow Bay Rd.
☎ 250/624-5637

Museum of Northern British Columbia
www.museumofnorthernbc.com
✉ 100 1st Avenue W.
☎ 250/624-3207
🕐 Closed Sun. in winter
💲 $$

North Pacific Historic Fishing Village
✉ 1889 Skeena Dr., Port Edward
☎ 250/628-3538
💲 $$
🕐 Closed mid-Oct.–mid-May

'Ksan Historical Village Museum
www.ksan.org
✉ Northwest of New Hazleton
☎ 250/842-5544
💲 $$

PRINCE RUPERT IS A PORT THAT MISSED ITS APPOINTMENT with destiny when it lost out to Vancouver as the Pacific end of the transcontinental rail line. However, it remains a vital link to the less explored extremities of British Columbia. The valley of the mighty Skeena River has been a corridor for trade for many centuries, with a long history of skillful native transportation along its rushing waters. Offshore lie the rain-soaked and geologically fascinating Queen Charlotte Islands, where traces of the original temperate rain forest are still host to a number of species that are extinct elsewhere.

PRINCE RUPERT

Superbly located among mountains on an island at the mouth of the Skeena River, Prince Rupert owes its existence to the Grand Trunk Railway's hope that the western terminus of its transcontinental line would rival Vancouver's port and metropolis and have the advantage of being 500 miles nearer Japan. But in 1912 the railroad's president, Charles M. Hays, went down with the *Titanic*. The town's layout followed his commissioned plan, but the port has yet to achieve the potential he envisaged. Today, its population is barely a hundredth of that of Vancouver. Nevertheless, Prince Rupert is a significant communications hub; the Yellowhead Highway terminates here, as does VIA Rail's remaining transcontinental service, exchanging passengers with the ferries to and from Vancouver Island, Alaska, and the Queen Charlotte Islands. Prince Rupert is also front and center in the **Great Bear Rainforest Park** (see pp. 274–275), which was created in 2006 to protect British Columbia's coast and islands.

For centuries before the arrival of Europeans, the site of the town had been a meeting place for the Tsimshian and Haida peoples. The **Museum of Northern British Columbia** has excellent First Nations collections that bring alive 10,000 years of settlement history along this northwestern coast. Craftspeople can be seen at work, and the museum also runs tours to some of the many archaeological sites in the area.

Fish-canning was one of British Columbia's staple industries, and in its late 19th-century heyday, more than 200 canneries operated along the coast. Near **Port Edward,** 13 miles southeast of Prince Rupert, one of the last canneries is now a national historic site known as the **North Pacific Historic Fishing Village.**

SKEENA VALLEY

The second longest river (after the Fraser) to run entirely within British Columbia, the turbulent and beautiful **Skeena River** has long been a corridor for trade and travel. The often mist-shrouded stream was named "water of the clouds" by the Tsimshian. It was navigated by 60-foot-long native canoes long before the 1870s, when sternwheelers brought prospectors upstream en route to the goldfields of the Omineca region inland. Today it is followed through the 6,000-foot **Coast Mountains** by the Yellowhead Highway.

The valley has a strong First Nations presence. The national historic site at **Fort Kitwanga** *(Tel 250/559-8818)* was a stronghold built atop a glacial mound by the Gitwangak people, who devised ingenious ways of crushing any attackers by releasing stacked-up logs onto them. But the real draw of the Skeena lies in its concentration of totem poles, some modern, some dating back to the mid-19th century. There are poles at Kitwanga itself, and at Kitwancool, Kispiox, and Kitseguecla. The reconstructed traditional village of **'Ksan** lies at the confluence of the Skeena and Bulkley Rivers. It has poles and a series of stately longhouses sheltering a carving school, as well as an extensive collection of artifacts.

QUEEN CHARLOTTE ISLANDS

Separated from the mainland by the broad waters (up to 80 miles across) of Hecate Strait, this remote and rain-soaked archipelago of some 150 islands remained largely untouched by glaciers, leaving it with an exceptionally rich ecology with many relict species such as deer mouse, Lairly woodpecker, and black bear. Homeland of the ethnically distinct Haida people, who call it Haida Gwaii ("islands of the people"), the islands bear witness to their past and present creativity. Logging has diminished some of the glory of the islands' rain forest, but much remains, particularly in the **Gwaii Haanas National Park Reserve** *(Tel 250/559-8818)*, which covers a large part of **Moresby Island.**

The ferry *(B.C. Ferries, tel 250/386-3431)* from Prince Rupert to **Graham Island,** the largest and most populous in the archipelago, terminates at Skidegate landing. To the west, **Queen Charlotte City,** a community of a thousand or so inhabitants, serves as the non-First Nations administrative center of the islands. At Skidegate itself, the **Haida Gwaii Museum** *(Tel 250/559-4643)* offers a fine introduction to Haida culture. ∎

Devastated by disease, many Haida abandoned their coastal villages at the end of the 19th century, leaving remains such as this mortuary pole on the fringe of the encroaching forest.

Queen Charlotte Islands
▲ 272 A3
Visitor information
✉ Infocentre, 3220 Wharf St., Queen Charlotte City
☎ 250/559-8316

First Nations peoples of western British Columbia

The First Nations residents of western British Columbia are geographically and culturally unique. The province's collection of First Nations historical sites makes it ideal for the visitor interested in this aspect of Canadian history.

In the northern interior were the Athapaskan, who occupied a vast area of forest and plains. The Athapaskan were a seminomadic people who are usually credited with having introduced the potlatch—a ritual ceremony involving feasting and dancing. The European settlers, fearing the potential for inciting rebellion, banned the potlatch between the 1880s and the 1950s. Recently, many of the ceremonial objects for the potlatch, confiscated and placed in museums, have been returned. One collection can still be seen in the Kwagiulth Museum on Quadra Island (see p. 298) at the north end of the strait of Georgia, between Vancouver Island and the mainland.

Another famous coastal First Nations people are the Tlingit, who inhabited the area north of (and including) the Queen Charlotte Islands. Though the coast was a rugged one, and a harsh place in winter, it was also an area well stocked with food. Of the shoreline it was said that "when the tide goes out, the table is set," so abundant were the shellfish. These Tlingit are famous for weaving Chilkat blankets from the wool of the mountain goat (three goats for one blanket). The blankets are still produced in the traditional way: Panels are woven on a primitive loom and then stitched together.

Even more famous are the Tlingit's totem poles. There are several misconceptions about totem poles, many claiming that all First Nations peoples carved them, and that they were a religious object. In fact, totem-carving was almost exclusively a North American west

Left: Historic Edward S. Curtis photo of a Kwakiuti bridal group. The bride is pictured between two dancers, hired especially for the celebration.
Right: A typical west coast totem

coast tradition. Totems represented a family's pride in its ancestry, rather than performing ritual or religious functions. The various carvings on an individual pole represented supernatural creatures (humans and animals), and the form was specific to a family and group. Totem pole carving, like potlatch, was banned for many years, and as a result few older poles exist. One place where they can be seen in this original setting is in Hazleton near the 'Ksan Historical Village Museum (see p. 303), close to New Hazleton in the Skeena River Valley. The site also has traditional Tlingit longhouses. Totems can also bee seen at the Quw'utsun' Cultural Centre (see p. 295) near Duncan on Vancouver Island.

At both 'Ksan and Duncan you'll also find examples of the beautiful wood carvings of the coastal peoples. Also notable are those at the Kwagiulth Museum. Many of these are of monsters and supernatural creatures, the most famous being the Thunderbird, the lord of the sky, the most powerful spirit of the spirit world. Though the Thunderbird is the most famous of the carvings, the most exotic is the raven of the Kwakwaka'wakw peoples who inhabited the coast to the south of the Tlingit (to whom they were related). The raven mask is a five-foot-long head and beak in black, red, and white, with "feathers" of shredded cedar bark that fell to the shoulders of the dancer who wore it. During the dance, the wearer would "clack" the hinged beak.

But to feel more of the spirit of Haida Gwaii, it is necessary to venture farther afield. Close to the town of Masset, at the north end of Graham Island, is the largest Haida community in the Queen Charlottes. Once known as Old Masset, it is now usually called Haida. Its people not only produce souvenirs for visitors, but have added an array of fine new totems. To the south, Moresby Island in the Queen Charlotte Islands has poignant testimony to the high level of development reached by the Haida in the late 19th century, before death and disease forced them from

their villages. With their ruined houses and well-weathered totem poles, these villages are extraordinarily evocative sites. Some, guarded by the Haida Gwaii Watchmen, are accessible by sea and air to visitors, but in restricted numbers only. Skedans is one such village, while another, Ninstints, is protected as a world heritage site. ■

Historic photo of performers re-creating the legend of the mythological birds Kotsuis and Hohhuq, by Edward S. Curtis

The Cariboo

The Cariboo
273 D2–D3

THE CARIBOO IS THE NAME GIVEN TO THE ROLLING uplands of the interior plateau, bounded on the west by the Coast Mountains and on the east by the Cariboo range. Threaded by the Fraser River, this is gold rush, forestry, and ranching country, with many traces still of the days when prospectors flocked northward by the tens of thousands in search of fortune.

The key to the area was the **Cariboo Road,** surveyed and built in part by the Royal Engineers. By 1863 it extended from Yale as far as **Soda Creek,** where passengers boarded the steamship for Quesnel in the heart of the goldfields. Roadhouses were built at more or less regular intervals to serve as rough hotels and livery stables. The pioneers had to make their own way to the area. The first gold strike was in 1860, but the biggest find of all came two years later, when Billy Barker, a Cornishman after whom the archetypal gold rush town of Barkerville was named, struck a rich deposit at a depth of more than 50 feet. As gold rush settlements sprang up, cattle ranchers moved north to supply the prospectors

Barkerville's gold deposits provided 19th-century prospectors with a good living for only ten years, but the town still stands, an intriguing relic of B.C.'s gold rush days.

with beef, the origin of the area's still flourishing ranching activity.

The original single-story cabin known as **Hat Creek Ranch** *(7 miles N of Cache Creek at junction of Hwys. 97 & 99, tel 800/782-0922)* was built as a rough-hewn roadhouse by Donald McLean, but is now embedded in an elegant two-story building with a double veranda. It has been restored, and with its outbuildings now forms a visitor ranch run by the B.C. Heritage Trust. Marking the beginning of the real Cariboo, the little town of **Clinton** began life as the 47 Mile House, and acquired the name of a British duke as it grew.

The Cariboo Road bypassed the site of the workaday town of **Williams Lake,** serving a wide ranching and lumbering area; Williams Lake only developed once the Pacific Great Eastern Railway arrived in 1920. The town is the starting point for the 285-mile, partly paved road that crosses the plateau and the Coast Mountains to the remote fishing village of **Bella Coola,** on the north arm of Burke Channel on the Pacific shore.

Prospectors disembarked in **Quesnel** (*Visitor information, 703 Carson Ave., tel 250/992-8716*) from the stern-wheelers that had brought them up the Fraser River. Quesnel still has its 1867 Hudson's Bay Company depot, but is otherwise dominated by the logging industry, whose activities can be watched from an observation tower 2 miles north of the town.

On its way from Quesnel to Barkerville, Rte. 26 passes relics of gold-mining activity, as well as the restored **Cottonwood House** (*Tel 250/992-2071, closed Sept.–April*). Built in 1864, Cottonwood

House began as a roadhouse and served many purposes before being restored as a provincial historic site.

Barkerville (*Visitor information, Pooley St., tel 250/994-3332, www.barkerville.ca, buildings closed Oct.–mid-May*) is now British Columbia's finest example of a town of its time. Not long after Billy Barker's gold find, the town had more than 10,000 inhabitants and trumpeted itself as the biggest city west of Chicago and north of San Francisco. Nevertheless, it was a makeshift place, with irregular boardwalks high above a narrow street barely wide enough for two carts to pass. In 1868 it burned down, but was substantially rebuilt. By the 1930s, it had almost faded away, but ongoing restoration since the 1950s has added many reconstructed buildings to these surviving originals. Visitors can attend school, go to the theater, ride a stagecoach, or watch mining demonstrations. ■

The simply furnished interior of one of Barkerville's many preserved buildings evokes the town's glory days of the 1860s and '70s.

Hope to Kamloops drive

On its way from Vancouver into the dry interior of British Columbia, the Trans-Canada Highway follows the route taken by 19th-century travelers, who used every conceivable means of transportation to overcome the formidable obstacle of these river canyons. This tour, which calls for none of that 19th-century endurance, follows Fraser and Thompson Canyons.

Today's smooth, four-lane highway belies the difficulties faced by these pioneers. "We had to pass where no human being should venture" was Simon Fraser's comment after completing his epic journey down the river to which he gave his name. His party only descended the Fraser River Canyon with the help of native guides, who made their way along the seemingly impassable cliffs on fragile structures of poles and twigs far above the deadly foaming waters. Below Yale, the Fraser was navigable, and in the 1858 Gold Rush prospectors could get this far by steamboat. From here, a rough mule track northward was constructed by the miners themselves. This precarious trail was replaced, from 1863 onward, by the famous Cariboo Road (see p. 306). Traces of this narrow and vertiginous road can still be seen today.

Construction of the CPR through the canyons posed massive problems. The difficulties were confronted head-on by the contractor, New Yorker Andrew Onderdonk, helped by an army of Canadian, Chinese, local, and Norwegian laborers, who dangled from ropes to blast out tunnels and the narrow ledge on which the railroad runs. Onderdonk completed his epic of construction in 1885. In 1914 the line through the Fraser Canyon was joined by the Great Northern Railway, predecessor of the CNR, and today the two lines, together with the Trans-Canada Highway, make light of this once daunting obstacle.

The drive begins at **Hope ❶,** 93 miles east of Vancouver. Founded as a Hudson's Bay Company post in 1848, this small town is located among mountains at the point where the valley of the Fraser River narrows and turns northward.

From Hope follow Trans-Canada 1 north along the Fraser River for 13 miles until you reach **Yale ❷**. Minuscule today, the town swarmed with "gamblers, ruffians, drinkers,

turncoats, highwaymen, thieves, murderers, and painted women" at the height of the 1858 Gold Rush. Mementoes of gold rush and railroad building days include the **Historic Yale Museum** (Douglas St., tel 604/863-2324).

Leave Yale and keep north, crossing the river on the bridge at Spuzzum. Follow the Fraser Canyon Highway, along the wooded east bank of the river. Here you will find the most spectacular section of the Fraser. The 600-foot-deep chasm of **Hells Gate ❸** forces the river into what seems an impossibly narrow channel, through which it seethes at great speed. It is worthwhile descending by **Airtram** (Tel 604/867-9777, closed mid-Oct.–mid-April) into the gorge, where there is a suspension footbridge.

Then continue north, passing into the dry interior. After about 30 miles, sited at the confluence of the skyblue Thompson River and the muddy waters of the Fraser is **Lytton ❹**—on record as the hottest place in Canada. Dozens of rapids make it the proclaimed "white-water rafting capital of Canada."

Follow the highway northeast from Lytton, through the often barren landscape along the Thompson River. Cross to the west bank at Spences Bridge and continue through the countryside around **Cache Creek**—often referred to as the Arizona of Canada because of its desertlike ecology, with sagebrush,

---

See area map pp. 272–73
Hope
200 miles
Allow 2 days
Kamloops

NOT TO BE MISSED
- Hells Gate
- Rapids at Lytton
- Cache Creek

prickly pear, and even rattlesnakes.

Stay on Rte. 1, which is joined by Rte. 97 at Cache Creek, and follow it east to busy **Kamloops** ⑤. Its name derived from the Shuswap word Cumloops, meaning the "meeting of the waters," it stands at the confluence of the North and South Thompson Rivers, which flow into the 25-mile-long **Kamloops Lake.** From there the Canadian National Railway heads north to Jasper and Edmonton, and the Canadian Pacific goes east to Revelstoke, Banff, and Calgary. ■

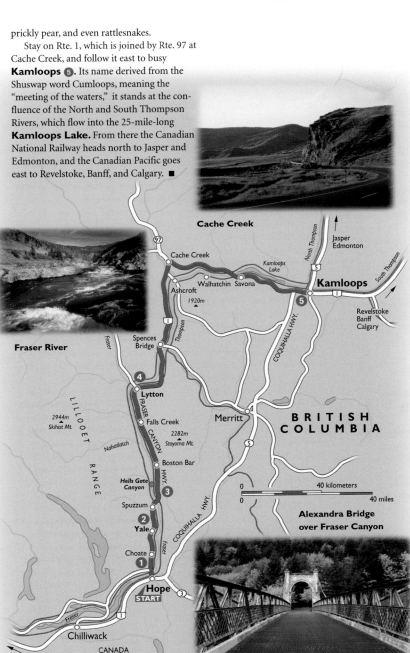

Cache Creek

Fraser River

97
Cache Creek
Ashcroft
1920m

Walhatchin   Savona
Kamloops Lake
North Thompson
Jasper Edmonton
5
Kamloops
⑤
South Thompson
Revelstoke Banff Calgary

Thompson
Fraser
Spences Bridge

④
Lytton
FRASER CANYON HWY.
Falls Creek
2282m
Stoyoma Mt.
Merritt
④
COQUIHALLA HWY.
5

2944m
Skihist Mt.
LILLOOET RANGE
Nahatlatch

Boston Bar
Hells Gate Canyon
③

**B R I T I S H
C O L U M B I A**

Spuzzum
②
Yale
COQUIHALLA HWY.
Fraser

0   40 kilometers
0   40 miles

Choate
①

**Alexandra Bridge
over Fraser Canyon**

Hope
START
3

Fraser
Chilliwack
Vancouver
CANADA
U.S.A.

W A S H I N G T O N

The Kootenays

The Kootenays
🅼 273 E1–E2

Castlegar visitor information
🅼 273E1
www.castlegar.com
✉ 1995 6th Ave.
☎ 250/365-6313

Doukhobor Heritage Museum
✉ 112 Heritage Way, off Hwy. 3 near Castlegar Airport
☎ 250/365-6622
🕐 Closed Oct.–April
💲 $$

Nelson visitor information
🅼 273 E1
www.discovernelson.com
✉ 225 Hall St.
☎ 250/352-3433

Balfour
🅼 273 E1

Ainsworth Hot Springs
🅼 273 E2

Kaslo
🅼 273 E2

IN THE FAR SOUTHEASTERN CORNER OF BRITISH COLUMBIA, the Kootenay River almost joins the Columbia River at Canal Flats before flowing south in a great bend that takes in part of the United States, finally making its junction at Castlegar. In most of what is loosely called Kootenay Country, the roughly north-south valleys are defined by mountains and receive heavy rain and snow, while to the south, a strip of land along the U.S. border enjoys a mild and sunny climate like that of the neighboring Okanagan Valley (see p. 312).

After David Thompson had mapped the region in 1808, it was ignored by Europeans until the mid-1860s, when the Dewdney Trail was built from Hope to the Rockies. Then, in the 1880s, a series of mineral finds began: Many of the towns that sprang up as a result of this boom have disappeared; others, like pretty little Nelson, have survived, though logging and tourism have replaced mining almost everywhere.

On its plateau at the confluence of the Columbia and Kootenay Rivers, the site of **Castlegar** lay at the division between Interior Salish and Kutenai territory, and both groups came here to fish for the rivers' abundant salmon. The modern settlement grew up as a communications center, when stern-wheelers ferried passengers up the Columbia and Arrow Lakes (now dammed) to Revelstoke. Many Doukhobors settled in the area, and the **Doukhobor Heritage Museum** introduces visitors to the sect's spartan way of life. Reached by a little suspension bridge, wooded **Zuckerberg Island** still has the delightful church built by a Russian mystic who came here in the 1930s to teach Doukhobor children.

Attractively located at the point where the Kootenay River flows out of the western arm of Kootenay Lake, **Nelson** sprang up when a silver deposit was discovered on nearby **Toad Mountain** in 1886. The town flourished as a service center for this and other mineral workings and hence survived their demise. Today it is justifiably proud of the sustained restoration program that has given new life to its late 19th-century townscape, comprising no fewer than 350 heritage buildings. Among them, a sign of early 20th century civic pride, is the **Courthouse,** the work of British Columbia's premier architect, Francis Rattenbury, designer of the province's Parliament Buildings in Victoria.

Rte. 3A running north from Nelson along the lakeshore passes **Balfour,** the terminus for the free ferry across Kootenay Lake. This is part of an optional east-west route to Hwy. 3 over the Kootenay Pass, which, at 5,820 feet, is Canada's highest paved roadway and is subject to frequent closures. Nine miles beyond Balfour is **Ainsworth Hot Springs,** a little settlement that began as a mining town and continued as a spa (*Ainsworth Hot Springs Resort, tel 250/229-4212*). The waters have a higher mineral content than any other hot springs in Canada. Farther north is **Kaslo** (*Visitor information, 324 Front St., tel 250/353-2525*), a miniature version of Nelson with a similar charm, despite having only a tenth of the population of its heyday as a center for the silver mines to the west. A

reminder of the glory days floats on the lake: The S.S. *Moyie (Visitor information, Kaslo visitor center, closed mid-Oct.–mid-May)* is a fine example of the stern-wheelers that once plied the lake. Launched in 1898, it is the oldest surviving craft of its kind in Canada.

In a superb setting at the foot of the Rockies, **Fort Steele Heritage Town** originated as a ferry crossing over the Kootenay River and gained its name when famous Superintendent Sam Steele came this way in 1887 to settle a dispute between settlers and Kutenai people. In 1898 the Canadian Pacific Railway's decision to bypass the town in favor of running its line through nearby Cranbrook sounded Fort Steele's death knell. Today its collection of early buildings is in the care of the province, which has supplemented them with other structures to make the splendid provincial heritage park, with costumed inhabitants, stagecoach rides, and a steam train. There are other trains in **Cranbrook,** where the **Canadian Museum of Rail Travel** features a tour through a complete set of luxury passenger coaches of the early 1900s. ∎

Some B.C. landscapes are best experienced on horseback. Riders from the Top of the World Ranch near Fort Steele pause in awe at the snow-capped Rockies.

Cranbrook & Fort Steele
🅰 273 E1

Fort Steele Heritage Town
www.fortsteele.bc.ca
✉ 10 miles NE of Cranbrook via Hwy. 95
☎ 250/426-7352
💲 $$ (May–mid-Oct.)

Canadian Museum of Rail Travel
www.trainsdeluxe.com
✉ Hwy. 3/95 in Cranbrook
☎ 250/489-3918
💲 $$

The Doukhobors

Some 7,500 members of this pacifist sect, dissenters from the Russian Orthodox Church, were helped by Russian author Leo Tolstoy and American and British Quakers to resettle in Saskatchewan at the end of the 19th century. When their exemption from the oath of allegiance was revoked, many moved to southern British Columbia under the leadership of Peter Vasilevitch Verigin, who established an initially successful self-contained community of some 6,000 people. But when Verigin was killed in a train explosion, the community was split by internal rifts that included protests by naked members of a fanatical subsect. In 1939 the Doukhobors' land was confiscated by the provincial government. ∎

Okanagan Valley

Okanagan Valley
 273 D1/D2

Penticton
273 D1

Kelowna
273 D2

Vernon
273 D2

Historic O'Keefe Ranch
www.okeeferanch.bc.ca
✉ 7 miles N of Vernon off Hwy. 97
☎ 250/542-7868
🕐 Closed mid-Oct.–April
💲 $$

Wines from the vineyards of Okanagan Valley are popular in Vancouver restaurants.

THE SUNNY CORRIDOR OF THE OKANAGAN VALLEY, WITH its river and chain of lakes, leads northward from the U.S. border through a smiling countryside of irrigated orchards and vineyards. The mild climate, delightful landscape, and easy access from north and south draw vacationers as well as retired people. There are attractions and recreational activities aplenty, from water sports to zoo parks. One of the best ways to explore the Okanagan is to follow the signed Okanagan Wine Route, which takes in 25 of the region's wineries, now enjoying a renaissance after the introduction of new vines and advanced winemaking techniques.

Known to the Salish as Pen-Tak-Ton, meaning a "place to live in forever" (because its favorable climate was conducive to year-round living), **Penticton** is built between two lakes, **Skaha Lake** and the much larger **Okanagan Lake.** Originally a center for the surrounding ranching and orchard country, it has developed rapidly as a summer resort, with marinas and miles of sandy beaches. The visitor center shares a stylish modern building with the **British Columbia Wine Centre** (Tel 250/490-2006), offering a full range of information on wineries, wine

tours, and events. At one end of the poplar-lined lakefront is the beached 500-passenger stern-wheeler S.S. *Sicamous* (Tel 250/492-0403). Dating from 1914, the vessel can be boarded and toured.

Rapidly expanding **Kelowna,** approached from the west bank of Lake Okanagan by an unusual floating bridge, was where the valley's modern history began. In 1859 a mission founded near here by members of the Oblate Order was the first European settlement established in British Columbia independently of the Hudson's Bay Company. Oblate Father Charles Pandosy is credited with planting the first vines and fruit trees. Then in the 1890s, Canada's governor general, Lord Aberdeenr, together with his energetic wife, Isabel, bought a ranch here and promoted orchards on a large scale.

The resort town of **Vernon** (Visitor information, 701 Hwy. 97 S., tel 250/542-1415), north of Kelowna, was founded in the 1860s by the Vernon brothers, miners-turned-ranchers. The O'Keefe Ranch also goes back to the 1860s and remained family owned for 100 years. It is now open to the public as the **Historic O'Keefe Ranch,** and is a great place to enjoy the atmosphere of early ranching days. A dozen original buildings include the family mansion, a forge, general store, and St. Anne's Church. ■

The northern territories are a complete contrast to the south's orderly cities and the fertile plains that separate them, but their harsh beauty makes them equally alluring. Adventurous visitors will be well rewarded.

The North

Introduction & map 314–17
The Alaska Highway 320–22
Yukon 323–328
Whitehorse 323
The Klondike Highway 324–25
Dawson 328
Northwest Territories 329–338
Inuvik 329
Mackenzie River 332
Nahanni National Park 333
Yellowknife 336
Baffin Island 337–38
Hotels & restaurants in the North 374

Stone *inukshuk*, Northwest Territories

The North

THE NORTHERN TERRITORIES OF YUKON, THE NORTHWEST
Territories (N.W.T.), and Nunavut make up around 40 percent of
Canada's land area. Yet apart from a few cities, the subarctic region is
an empty land, where miles of unspoiled landscape separate small
communities still imbued with the pioneering spirit. North of
the Arctic Circle there are even fewer settlements, mostly
belonging to the Inuit. Canada's Arctic islands are largely
uninhabited, a wilderness where animals have had
to battle and evolve to survive the savage
environment.

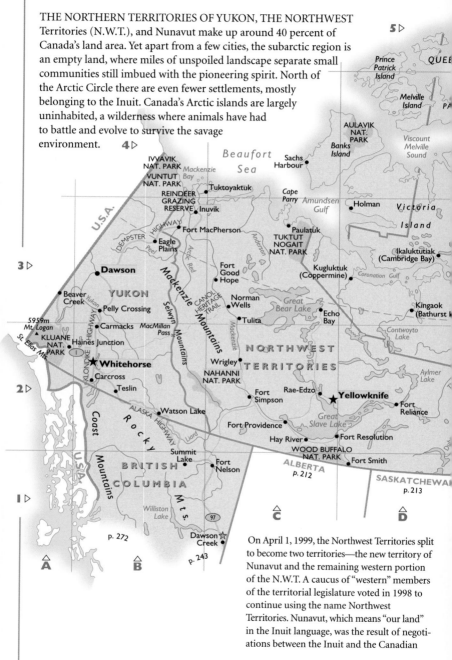

On April 1, 1999, the Northwest Territories split
to become two territories—the new territory of
Nunavut and the remaining western portion
of the N.W.T. A caucus of "western" members
of the territorial legislature voted in 1998 to
continue using the name Northwest
Territories. Nunavut, which means "our land"
in the Inuit language, was the result of negotiations between the Inuit and the Canadian

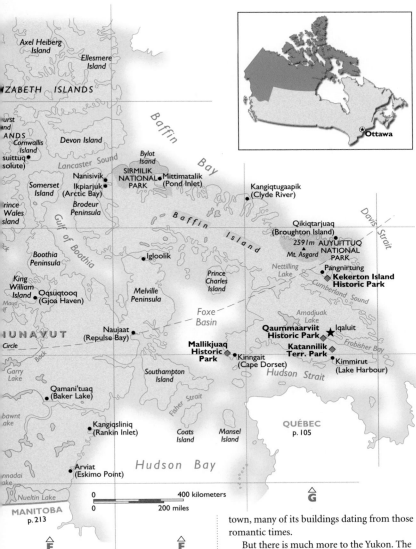

Axel Heiberg
Island

Ellesmere
Island

ZABETH ISLANDS

urst
and
ANDS
Cornwallis
suittuq Island
solute)

Devon Island

Lancaster Sound

Baffin Bay

Nanisivik

Somerset
Island

Ikpiarjúk
(Arctic Bay)

Brodeur
Peninsula

Bylot
Isand

SIRMILIK
NATIONAL Mittimatalik
PARK (Pond Inlet)

Kangiqtugaapik
(Clyde River)

rince
Wales
sland

Gulf of Boothia

Baffin Island

Davis Strait

Qikiqtarjuaq
(Broughton Island)

2591m AUYUITTUQ
▲ NATIONAL
Mt. Asgard PARK

Boothia
Peninsula

Igloolik

Prince
Charles
Island

Nettilling
Lake

Pangnirtung

Kekerton Island
Historic Park

King
William
Island
Maud
f

Oqsuqtooq
(Gjoa Haven)

Melville
Peninsula

Cumberland Sound

IUNAVUT

Circle

Naujaat
(Repulse Bay)

Foxe
Basin

Amadjuak
Lake

Qaummaarviit
Historic Park

Iqaluit

Bock

Mallikjuaq
Historic
Park

Kinngait
(Cape Dorset)

Katannilik
Terr. Park

Frobisher Bay

Kimmirut
(Lake Harbour)

Garry
Lake

Southampton
Island

Hudson Strait

bawnt
ake

Qamani'tuaq
(Baker Lake)

Fisher Strait

QUÉBEC
p. 105

Kangiqsliniq
(Rankin Inlet)

Coats
Island

Mansel
Island

nnadai
ake

Arviat
(Eskimo Point)

Hudson Bay

Nueltin Lake

0   400 kilometers
0   200 miles

△
G

MANITOBA
p. 213

△
E

△
F

government to return to Inuit control a land
first peopled by them thousands of years ago.

YUKON

When people think of the Yukon, its association with the Klondike Gold Rush springs to
mind. It is true that the gold rush built some
of the territory's roads and it is likewise true
that Dawson still has the feel of a gold rush

town, many of its buildings dating from those
romantic times.

But there is much more to the Yukon. The
highways that traverse it allow visitors to
explore its subarctic wilderness more easily
than any other part of the Canadian north.
Travelers can go from the Kluane National
Park, where wild sheep roam a land close to
Canada's highest mountains, to the Arctic
Circle. This is a harsh land, home to the
migrating herds of barren-ground caribou,
whose territory stretches all the way to the
shores of the Arctic Ocean. The Dempster

Highway traverses this land to reach Inuvik, N.W.T., a town on the Mackenzie Delta.

NORTHWEST TERRITORIES

The N.W.T. is crossed by the Mackenzie River system which, at 2,600 miles, is longer than either the Mississippi or Missouri Rivers. At the headwaters of the Mackenzie, on the Great Slave Lake, lies Yellowknife, the territorial capital. Viewed from the lake shore Yellowknife's log cabins and skyscrapers characterize the N.W.T.— a mix of the pioneering spirit of the region's early settlers, and the modern world of Canadian commerce. The N.W.T. is less accessible to the visitor than its Yukon neighbor: Fewer roads mean that the traveler has to be more adventurous in exploring. The Mackenzie River can be followed in the comfort of modern transportation—a wonderful journey—but to enjoy the awesome beauty of the Nahanni National Park you must simply use a canoe or walk.

During the summer caribou migrate en masse over the Arctic tundra.

NUNAVUT

Although the Inuit settled the shoreline of the Arctic Ocean several thousand years ago, the present inhabitants are descended from Thule peoples who crossed the Bering Strait about 4,500 years ago. These people were given the name Eskimo by Cree Indians, a name meaning "those who eat their meat raw." The Cree used it to express their distaste and over the years it became a term of abuse. As such its use is rightly decried today, and it has been replaced by "Inuit," which means "the people" in their Inuktitut language. The creation of Nunavut was a landmark for the Inuit: At last they control the evolution of the land their ancestors settled so long ago. And a magnificent land it is, a rugged wilderness of incomparable beauty studded with settlements in which Inuit arts and crafts flourish. ■

Arctic animals

Of the more than 4,000 species of animal that exist on the earth, fewer than 50 live all or part of their lives in the Arctic. Of these, 31 inhabit the Canadian Arctic. This small fraction indicates how harsh the Arctic environment is—plant-eating animals have to exist on a few scattered plants, while the carnivores find little to prey on. The animals have adapted remarkably to the environment.

Most of Canada's Arctic animals are rodents that are found close to tree line or in the tundra. But for most people, it is the big animals of the high Arctic that define the region.

Polar bears

The polar bear evolved from the same ancestor as the brown bear but is now quite distinct from its land-based cousin. To survive the Arctic cold, the bear has a layer of blubber below its skin and a thick coat of hair which covers its entire body apart from the nose and pads of the feet. The bear's skin is black, a good color for absorbing heat from the sun, and the coat has some hollow hairs that

Adult male polar bears engage in a bit of recreational wrestling.

transport sunlight to the skin. The coat is white—though it can appear cream or even pale yellow as the light changes—an adaptation for camouflage on the Arctic ice rather than insulation. As with all Arctic animals, evolution has reduced the size of the bears' extremities—small ears and short tails help to reduce heat loss. An exception to this rule are the bears' enormous feet, which spread their considerable weight on thin ice and also act as paddles when the bears are swimming. The polar bear is so much at home in water that some naturalists classify it as a sea mammal. The polar bears' diet has also been subject to adaptation—it is the world's only wholly carnivorous bear, consuming the seals that it hunts on the sea ice.

On land, polar bears are often followed by arctic foxes, who scavenge on the bears' leftover kills. While bears spend almost their entire lives on the ice, the fox is a land mammal. Consequently its coat changes color season by season, dark in summer for camouflage against the earth, changing to a denser (and much warmer) white coat when the winter snows fall.

The ragged coats of musk-oxen may look scruffy, but they are vital to the creatures' survival in the harsh climate.

Musk-oxen

Another typically Arctic animal is the musk-ox. Musk-oxen have a permanently dark brown coat. This coat is made up of an inner layer of fine hair protected by long, silky "guard" hairs. The outer coat extends almost to the ground, giving the animal an almost comical appearance. The undercoat molts annually; the hair falls away in huge tufts, leaving the animal looking decidedly unkempt.

Musk-oxen have huge horns whose weight is concentrated across the forehead. The males use these during the rut, when two animals crash against each other in a fierce and noisy trial of strength. The females use theirs to protect the young. To combat the threat occasionally offered by wolves, adult musk-oxen form circles facing outward with their young safe in the center—the attackers are confronted by a barrier of heavy, pointed horns. Only if the wolves can spook the musk-oxen into fleeing will they be able to grab a sick or young animal. This circle formation is very effective against wolves, but useless against a man armed with a rifle. Consequently, musk-oxen were exterminated in much of their former range. Today, with active protection, numbers are on the increase.

Arctic birds

Birds differ greatly from land-based mammals in their ability to migrate easily from the Arctic at the onset of winter—a strategy adapted by all but a very few species. Of the resident species, both the rock and willow ptarmigan turn white in winter; they also increase their feather volume and lower their metabolic rate. The snowy owl is white at all times: Its feathers have the highest insulation quality of any bird species' plumage. The owl's feathers extend right down the bird's legs to the claws. The bill is also very short and almost hidden by the dense plumage covering the face. Despite these adaptations to the Arctic cold, snowy owls head south in winter, where they are sure to find enough lemmings, their major prey, to sustain them through the Arctic night. ■

The Alaska Highway

After the heady days of the gold rush, mining and the Yukon declined. For 40 years the area was left alone. Then, in the wake of the attack on Pearl Harbor, the fear that the Japanese might invade the continent via Alaska prompted President Franklin D. Roosevelt to order the construction of a highway linking Dawson Creek, British Columbia (which was already linked by road and railroad to Washington state), to Fairbanks, Alaska.

The highway was a massive project, involving the building of more than 100 bridges and the creation of more than 1,500 miles of road. Astonishingly, in only eight months the road was fit for military traffic, and it was officially opened in November 1942 at a ceremony on **Soldiers' Summit** *(Mile 1061)* above Kluane Lake; it was another year before the road was

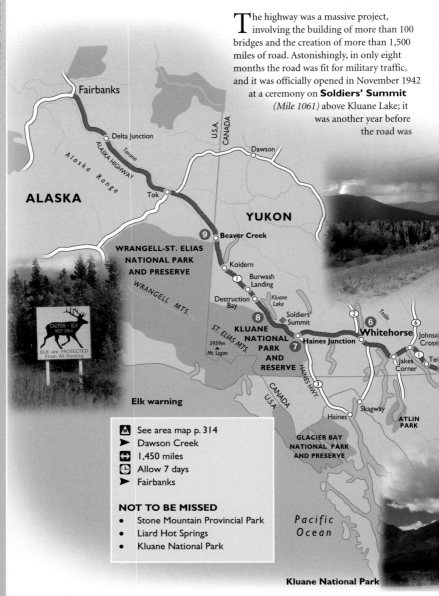

Elk warning

Kluane National Park

- See area map p. 314
- ➤ Dawson Creek
- ↔ 1,450 miles
- ⏱ Allow 7 days
- ➤ Fairbanks

NOT TO BE MISSED
- Stone Mountain Provincial Park
- Liard Hot Springs
- Kluane National Park

finally completed. The road opened the Yukon, although not until the 1970s was it fully paved. Then in 1996, the highway was granted the status of International Historic Civil Engineering Landmark, one of only 16 projects to be so recognized to date.

The highway is marked with historical mileposts (distances in Canada are given in kilometers) that, while they allow travelers to locate historic sites and provide information, do not accurately reflect current distances.

The logical place to begin an exploration of the highway is Mile 0, located on Tenth Street in the the heart of **Dawson Creek** ➊ *(Visitor information, tel 250/782-9595)* in British Columbia. Follow the road northwest from the town. At Mile 21 stop and admire the elegantly carved **Kiskatinaw Bridge**—the only surviving original bridge. A few miles further north at Mile 35 cross the **Peace River Bridge.**

The First Nations named the Peace River for a treaty that identified the wide river as a frontier between two tribes. The stretch

Crowds gather for the Yukon's Sourdough Rendezvous.

of road halfway between Dawson Creek and Suicide Hill is marked by reminders of the road's military importance. The **Beatton River airstrips** ➋ *(Mile 73)* were for emergency use by the U.S. military and **Blueberry Control Station** *(Mile 101)* was a manned checkpoint maintained 24 hours a day throughout World War II.

Continue northwest, through Wonowon toward Suicide Hill. From here follow the long mountainous section of the highway: A major rerouting in 1992 eliminated many of the curves, but did not spoil the views, which are superb all the way to **Fort Nelson** ➌ *(Visitor information, tel 250/774-6400)* at Mile 300. Follow the highway west of the town—where you find that the vistas before were just a prelude. The scenery improves even more on the approach to **Stone Mountain**

NORTHWEST TERRITORIES

The Alaska Highway

Black

Watson Lake ➎

ALASKA HWY.

Liard Hot Springs ➍

Coal River

Liard River

Liard

Muncho Lake Provincial Park

Muncho Lake

2972m   **Stone Mt. Provincial Park**

BRITISH COLUMBIA

Summit Lake

77

Fort Nelson ➌

ROCKY MOUNTAINS

Prophet

ALASKA HWY.

Sikanni Chief

Pink Mountain

Wonowon

Suicide Hill

Beatton River ➋

97

ALBERTA

Peace

Fort St. John ➊   **Kiskatinaw Bridge**

Dawson Creek

START   2

97

0   150 kilometers

0   150 miles

Beautiful panoramas are commonplace in Kluane National Park.
Right: Whitehorse's famous Anglican log cathedral

Provincial Park (*Mile 392*), which represents the high point of the road, at 4,250 feet. The views on this section of the highway are among the most magnificent along its length. Keep west as the road threads through **Muncho Lake Provincial Park,** cross the Liard River and you will reach **Liard Hot Springs** 4 at Mile 496. During the highway's construction the soldiers used these springs as a natural bath on six days of the week, the seventh day being reserved for female staff.

From Liard Hot Springs, remain on the highway as it follows the north bank of the Liard River. Though the highway crosses the British Columbia-Yukon border seven times between Miles 588 and 627, 627 represents the official crossing. From here it is only a short drive to **Watson Lake** 5 (*Mile 635*), the Yukon's first town. Leaving westward you will find that the highway actually dips back into British Columbia again before reaching **Teslin** (*Mile 804*), a lake taking its name from the First Nations' description—"long, narrow lake." After rounding the lake, the highway heads west to **Whitehorse** 6 at Mile 918 (see p. 323).

From Whitehorse, some travelers switch to the Klondike Highway, a more romantic road (see pp. 324–25). But, if you remain on the Alaska Highway, you will also be rewarded as it enters one of its most majestic sections.

At **Haines Junction** 7 (*Mile 1016*), the highway meets the Haines Highway (from the south and the Lynn Canal) and turns north along the border of **Kluane National Park** 8 (*Visitor information, tel 867/634-7207*). Together with Wrangell-St. Elias National Park, just across the border in Alaska, this breathtaking park preserves one of the world's most pristine wilderness areas.

Follow the highway along the park's edge to Kluane Lake. **Destruction Bay** (*Mile 1083*), by the lake, is so named because a winter storm all but destroyed the camp and machinery of the highway's builders.

Farther on, at **Beaver Creek** 9 (*Mile 1202*), the construction crews pushing the road northward met those working their way south from Fairbanks. The Alaskan border is just a short distance away now (*Mile 1221*), but the highway continues for another 220 miles or so to Fairbanks. ■

Whitehorse

THE FORTUNE-SEEKING HORDES WHO BRAVED THE Chilkoot Trail on their way to Dawson spent the early spring camped by Lake Bennett, waiting for the Yukon River to thaw and for rafts to be built to run it. The river journey was fraught with danger, one of the biggest hazards being Miles Canyon near the lake. The canyon held the Yukon's roughest waters and was christened White Horse Rapids because rafters likened them to the white manes of horses.

The rapids ended many expeditions, some of them tragically. The Mounties tried to control rafters, discouraging the foolhardy and encouraging experienced boatmen: Jack London is said to have earned $3,000 as a boatman in 1898. Then an enterprising group laid a 5-mile tramway around the canyon, reaching the river again at a site where a town rapidly grew up. The town's founders called it Whitehorse as a reminder of the rapids.

While the best place to begin a visit to Whitehorse is at the **Tourist Information Centre,** many visitors go straight to the **S.S. Klondike** (*Waterfront, tel 800/661-0486, closed mid-Sept.–mid-May*), a stern-wheeler built in 1937 to travel between Whitehorse and Dawson. The downriver trip took one and a half days and burned 40 cords of wood; the upriver return took three times longer and required 120 cords. Visitors can join a tour around the boat.

Back toward the center of town and close to the river, the **MacBride Museum** (*1st Ave., tel 867/667-2709, closed Sun.–Mon. Oct.–mid-May*) has a wonderful collection of gold rush photographs and some remarkable items—Sam McGee's cabin, an engine from the White Pass & Yukon Railroad, and a fine (mounted) collection of Yukon wildlife. Whitehorse's **log "skyscraper"** stands on the corner of Lambert and Second. Just before the skyscraper, a right turn on Elliott reaches the town's **Log Church** (*3rd Ave., tel 867/668-2555, closed mid-Sept.–mid-May*). Built in 1900, this beautiful church is now a religious museum. ■

Whitehorse
🗺 314 B2

Visitor information
www.visitwhitehorse.com
www.touryukon.com
✉ Second Ave., Whitehorse
☎ 867/668-8687 or 867/667-3084 (govt. of Yukon)

Above: Once a main supply ship for Dawson, the S.S. Klondike is now a dockside museum to the old days.

The Klondike Highway

**For information
on the road:**
☎ 800/661-0494

TECHNICALLY, THE KLONDIKE HIGHWAY STARTS AT Skagway, Alaska. But for most people the real Klondike Highway is the road between Whitehorse and Dawson, a route that closely follows the trail of the gold rush hopefuls of the late 1890s.

The Klondike Highway branches off the Alaska Highway a little north of Whitehorse, soon reaching the shore of lovely **Lake Laberge;** in gold rush times the lake's trout were transported to Dawson in bargeloads. Laberge is also famous as the actual scene of the cremation of Sam McGee, the event immortalized in Robert Service's famous poem. Beyond the lake, a side road at the Fox Lane campground leads up to picturesque **Little Fox Lake.**

The highway now follows the Nordenski River, which flows into the Yukon at **Carmacks,** 118 miles

from Whitehorse. **Five Fingers Rapids,** 16 miles farther north, is the halfway point between Whitehorse and Dawson, and a section of the Yukon feared by rafters. Here the river forms five parallel channels of dangerous rapids.

The highway now follows the majestic river through unspoiled country, passing **Minto** and **Pelly Crossing,** each little more than a provision stop, before reaching **Stewart Crossing.** Adventuring American author Jack London's only Yukon winter was spent in Stewart Crossing; his cabin has since been

This mountain goat appears to be blissfully unaware of the disruption it is causing.

Above: Dall's sheep are found in abundance throughout the Yukon.

Left: In Dawson, the cabin of Robert Service, poet, adventurer, and author of "The Cremation of Sam McGee," remains exactly as he left it.

dismantled and reassembled in **Dawson** (see p 328). Stewart is named for the discoverer of the Stewart River. The next town, **McQuesten,** also remembers a Yukon pioneer, Leroy (Jack) McQuesten, who discovered gold in the Stewart River. Beyond McQuesten the highway reaches the Klondike River. The river's name derives from a mispronunciation of its native name, thron diuck—hammer water—so called because the First Nations hammered stakes into its waters to catch salmon. The same people also named the Yukon: To them it was yuckoo—clear water. In just a few miles now, the hammer water will reach the clear water at Dawson. ■

The Gold Rush

Many legends surround the discovery of gold in the Canadian north, so many that the whole truth concerning this fascinating moment in the region's history will never be revealed. A likely story began in 1895 when Robert Henderson, a Nova Scotia-born prospector, arrived near what is now Dawson and began to pan the local creeks for gold. He had little success in his first summer, but the following spring he climbed King Solomon Dome, a 4,048-foot peak to the east of the junction of the Klondike and Yukon Rivers. From the peak a series of creeks ran off in all directions. Henderson chose one and began to pan. In his first wash he found more gold than he had ever seen before in a single pan.

In those early days, with few prospectors in the area, it was an unwritten rule among pioneers that such news was shared. Henderson immediately told his fellow prospectors, and they worked the creek until the next August. Henderson then journeyed south to pick up fresh supplies. While returning to his creek, he met George Washington Carmack, who was traveling with his Athapaskan wife and two of her native relatives, Tagish Charlie and Skookum Jim. Henderson told them about the new find and returned to his creek.

Carmack and his companions headed for the peak, but instead of following Henderson they chose a creek on the west side of the mountain—soon known as Bonanza Creek, for the three men's first pan revealed more gold than even Henderson had found. This find consequently helped spark the Klondike Gold Rush. Ironically, the only person who did not benefit from the new find was Henderson. Carmack and his partners staked three claims and headed south to file them. They revealed all to those in the supply villages—who promptly deserted their houses and shops and headed north—but they neglected to cross King Solomon Dome to tell Henderson.

The outside world did not know about the find until the summer of 1897, when the first prospectors, carrying vast quantities of gold, arrived by steamer in Seattle and other ports along the U.S. West Coast. Within days those hopeful of getting rich quickly had set off northward. It is estimated that at least 100,000 people began the trek to Dawson. So many of them moved so fast that they resembled a cattle stampede, earning the nickname Klondike Stampeders. Some went via Edmonton, others via Anchorage, but those anxious to be first to arrive went by ship to Skagway and then walked over the Chilkoot or White Pass to reach Lake Bennett and the Yukon River.

Many arrived in late summer and reached the passes in early winter. With little sustenance available near the Klondike River, they carried huge quantities of supplies. Many were unprepared for the snow and bitter cold of winter. On the passes and the frozen shores of Lake Bennett and the Yukon River, many froze to death, died of disease, or committed suicide to escape the appalling conditions. Others simply turned back. And even those who survived until the ice on the Yukon thawed were not saved. Having built rafts, they ran the river to Dawson, but most had no idea of raft design and even less about navigating a river. The White Horse Rapids of Miles Canyon and the Five Fingers Rapids farther north smashed boats and drowned men. Not until the Mounties arrived to regulate the Stampeders, turning back those with inadequate clothing and supplies and setting up a team of qualified boatmen, did the death toll fall.

Many found their fortune in gold. In 1896 some 14,000 ounces were extracted from the streams and frozen ground around Dawson. By 1897 this rose to more than 120,000 ounces; by 1900 it was more than a million ounces. In Dawson the gambling halls and good-time girls did their best to relieve the wealthy of their gold, often successfully. Fortunes were sometimes made on the turn of a card—but just as often lost.

By 1901 the amount of gold extracted from the Klondike decreased, and three years later all the Stampeders had gone as large companies with steam-powered dredging machines took over. The Klondike Gold Rush was short lived, but it remains one of the most colorful episodes in North American history. ∎

WILL'S CIGARETTES.

PANNING AT KLONDYKE.

The early gold-seekers panned the streams, but the search soon became more intensive, with huge spoil heaps created by digging machines.

GOLD DUST BOUGHT AND SOLD

Dawson

Dawson
314 B3

**Visitor
information**
www.dawsoncity.ca
Front St.
867/993-5575
Closed mid-
Sept.–mid-May

DAWSON'S GOLD BOOM LASTED JUST A COUPLE OF YEARS, during which time the town was built and burned three times. After the third fire there were barely enough people left to do the rebuilding: News of a gold strike at Nome, Alaska, had taken them all west. Dawson's population fell to a few hundred. Today, some 1,800 people call Dawson home.

Set where the Klondike River joins the Yukon River, Dawson is built on permafrost. From October to April or May temperatures in the town are below freezing, while in summer temperatures rise to 60°F, making the ground boggy. Dawson's roads are unpaved, and its houses rest on wooden pads, to prevent sinking and to block heat from the houses thawing the ground surface more than once.

The town is laid out on a grid between the two rivers. The ferry crossing the Yukon to reach the Top of the World Highway leaves from Front Street, where the Tourist Information Office stands near the **Dänoja Zho Cultural Centre** (*Tel 867/993-6708, closed late Sept.–late May*), where the history of the area's first inhabitants is explored. On King Street is an exact replica of the **Palace Grand Theatre** built

in 1899 by Arizona Charlie Meadows, Dawson's most famous bartender (and gunfighter); the original was demolished in 1959. Ahead is **Diamond Tooth Gerties** (*Corner of 4th & Queen Sts., tel 867/993-5575*), Canada's first casino. It was named for Gertie Lovejoy, who had a diamond wedged between her front teeth. Closer to the Klondike River is the **Dawson City Museum** (*Tel 867/993-5291, closed mid-Sept.–mid-May*) by **Minto Park,** on the other side of which is **Robert Service's Cabin** (*8th Ave.*), looking just as the famous poet/adventurer (author of "The Cremation of Sam McGee") left it. Close by is **Jack London's Cabin** (*8th Ave., tel 867/993-5575, closed mid-Sept.–mid-May*), brought from Stewart Crossing; daily readings are given here from works of the Yukon's most famous writer. ■

The Midnight Dome above Dawson City offers a magnificent view of the town sitting at the confluence of the Klondike and Yukon Rivers.

Inuvik

FOR 700 YEARS, THE GWICH'IN DENE INUIT, COASTAL AND tundra hunting people, left their settlements on the Peel River and the delta of the Mackenzie River (a river the Inuit called Deh Cho) and drove their dogsleds to the Yukon River to trade furs. One of their principal settlements, now Inuvik in the Northwest Territories, has enjoyed a resurgence as a base for exploring the vast Arctic region with its delicate ecosystems.

Some years ago Inuvik was a rather disappointing place, the Inuit occupying poor housing with inadequate facilities at one end of town, and the more prosperous white population residing in better places at the other end. Recent and progressive changes of policy and attitude have ended this anomaly: Today Inuvik is a much more lively town, its buildings a cheerful splash of color in the barren wilderness. Look on Mackenzie Road for the circular **Our Lady of Victory** "igloo" church, with its roof of domes and cupolas, just as innovative a design as can be found anywhere below the Arctic circle. Its Stations of the Cross, by local Inuit artist Mona Thresher, are masterpieces.

ARCTIC BASE

As the visitor center for the western Arctic, Inuvik has excellent accommodations and offers many opportunities for day or longer trips to the several surrounding national parks that have been set up to preserve the region's fragile Arctic ecosystem. **Aulavik National Park** *(Tel 867/690-3904)*, with its brief growing season, supports grasses, sedges, heathers, and the dwarf willows that become food for the population of several thousand musk-oxen. Located on the Bank's Island across the Amundsen Gulf, the park is the breeding ground for numerous arctic birds. There is also an excellent bird reserve at **Cape Parry,** east of Inuvik, close to the **Tuktut Nogait**

National Park *(Tel 867/580-3233)*, the newest of the Arctic reserves. In the park's southern region, between the Peel and Arctic Red Rivers, roam Dall's sheep, caribou, grizzly bears, and the elusive gyrfalcon. On the Beaufort coast, close to the Inuit settlement of **Tuktoyaktuk** *(www.tuk.ca),* is a famous collection of pingos—cones of gravel or soil forced up by the pressure of underlying ice. The pingos of the Mackenzie Delta, some of which reach 130 feet in height and measure almost 1,000 feet across the base, are among the most impressive in the whole Arctic. ■

Inuvik

⚠ 314 B3

Visitor information

www.inuvik.ca

✉ Inuvik Visitor Centre, Mackenzie Rd.

☎ 867/777-4727 or 867/777-7237 (off-season)

🕐 Closed Oct.–May

www.pc.gc.ca

✉ Parks Canada Infocentre, Mackenzie Rd. (above post office)

☎ 867/777-8800

Inuit art evocatively integrates myth and reality, sometimes merging prey animals with imagined events.

The Inuit people

The Arctic's unforgiving environment ensured that northern Canada was one of the last places on earth in which humans settled permanently. It also meant that those who settled did so in very small numbers in comparison to the vastness of the land. Other continents' populations expanded as they filled the landscape, but in the Arctic the population never rose beyond the scattered handful of settlements and nomadic groups who first occupied the area.

As the ice sheets of the last ice age retreated small groups of Paleo-eskimo peoples arrived in Arctic Canada. The settlers had come from Alaska, having earlier crossed the Bering Sea from Siberia.

The earliest inhabitants probably lived in tents year-round, using animal skins stretched over a framework of lashed-together bones. In winter they would have used double skins with an insulating layer of heather or other vegetation between them. These people crafted tools from ivory, bone, antler, and stones; they hunted land and sea mammals and took freshwater fish as they migrated up or down rivers. They were a nomadic people, traveling mostly on foot, although they did use a one-person boat called a qajaq (kayak) for fishing. Then, about 2,800 years ago, a people now known as "Dorset" (named after Cape Dorset on Baffin Island) gradually emerged, probably as a result of a cooling in the local climate that induced a change in lifestyle. People of the Dorset constructed the first igloos, the most well-known feature of the Inuit to outsiders, using them as winter quarters. They did not use the bow and arrow, perhaps because the change in climate meant there were fewer land animals to hunt. Instead they harpooned sea mammals from ice floe edges or at breathing holes. The Dorset people also produced exquisite ritualistic art work—carving bone, ivory, and antler.

The Dorset culture existed for about 2,000 years. Then, with the warming climatic trend, Neo-eskimo peoples migrated from the west bringing larger boats (called *umiat*—skin-covered vessels capable of ferrying an entire family) and sleds pulled by dogs. Excavations at Thule on Greenland's west coast led to this people being named the Thule. Like people of the Dorset culture, the Thule also hunted sea mammals, but instead of limiting their catch to walrus, seal, beluga, and narwhal they were technologically advanced enough to hunt the huge bowhead whale. The Thule people were also nomadic, dwelling in stone or sod dwellings and igloos (in winter) and skin tents (in summer). Their campsites have been excavated in a number of locations like Ellesmere Island—the untouched stone circles used to anchor the bottom of the skins can still be seen, together with the weathered bones of slaughtered whales. A surprising aspect of Thule culture is how little artwork they created; however, they were capable of producing marvelous carvings in bone, ivory, and wood. This aspect of Thule culture is still apparent in the Inuit population today, who produce wonderful works of art in ivory, soapstone, and serpentine. Many of the works illustrate aspects of the rich Inuit culture, featuring men or women in ritual dances or dressed in ritual masks. They also portray the Inuit myths about the creation of the arctic animals, or of the spirits of those animals.

The Thule Inuit settled in Arctic Canada about 1,000 years ago but within 600 years their way of life received a shock from which it could never recover—the first meeting with Europeans. In seeking a passage between the Atlantic and the Pacific explorers like Martin Frobisher inevitably encountered the Inuit, although these early Europeans had little effect on Inuit life and culture. The pace of change was accelerated in the early 19th century when British whalers began exploiting the west coast of Baffin Island. While Europeans brought improved weapons for hunting, they also brought new diseases that the Inuit were unable to tolerate.

In the 20th century the changes were almost overwhelming, as the Inuit way of life was increasingly threatened by industrial mineral extraction and, more importantly, continued whaling—the wholesale slaughter of these creatures by Europeans brought them to the

An important lesson Inuit children must learn is how to recognize the safe forms of sea ice.

brink of extinction. For the Inuit, whose reliance on hunting whales was incalculable, the effects were devastating. Communities were uprooted, moved, and resettled. Employment within the mining industry forced young men into the new economy and consequently many traditions were lost. More recently, conservationists have threatened the hunting and trapping lifestyle.

The creation of Nunavut, the Canadian territory that came into existence on April 1, 1999, returned much of the Arctic lands to their Inuit owners. It is hoped that Nunavut will provide a more positive future for the Inuit peoples, one in which they will be able to control their own destiny. ■

Mackenzie River

Mackenzie River

🅰 314 B3, C2–C3

Visitor information

www.explorenwt.com

✉ N.W.T. Tourism, P.O. Box 610, Yellowknife

☎ 867/873-7200 or 800/661-0788

M.S. Norweta

www.norweta.com

✉ 8 Riverview Circle, Cochrane, Alberta

☎ 403/932-7590 or 866/667-9382

On its way to Inuvik, the Dempster highway crosses the Mackenzie River at the tiny village of Tsiigehtchic (formerly Arctic Red River).

ONE OF NORTH AMERICA'S GREAT RIVERS, THE MACKENZIE traces its way from Great Slave Lake northwestward for 1,068 miles before emptying into the Beaufort Sea. It takes its name from the Scottish-born explorer Alexander Mackenzie whose 18th-century voyage along the river rivaled Meriwether Lewis and William Clark's 1804–1806 exploration of the Pacific Northwest for scientific inquiry. The Mackenzie remains an untamed feature of Canada's north.

As a young employee of a fur-trading company, Mackenzie led an expedition from **Lake Athabasca** (on the Alberta-Saskatchewan border) to continue the exploration of the Canadian north. Between June 3 and September 12, 1783, the expedition traveled the length of the river, following it for over 1,000 miles all the way to the Arctic Ocean. Mackenzie's diary details the birds and fish caught for food each day, as well as the weather.

The Mackenzie has been canoed many times since, but an easier way to enjoy this massive river system is aboard the 20-passenger **M.S. Norweta,** which makes round-trips each summer between **Hay River** on Great Slave Lake and **Inuvik.** The downriver journey takes 10 days, the upriver 12.

From the town of **Norman Wells,** real adventurers can tackle the **Canol Heritage Trail** (*"A Hikers Guide" available from Govt. of N.W.T., P.O. Box 130, Norman Wells, tel 867/587-3500*), which follows a roadbed built during World War II and abandoned in 1945. The trail heads southwest to the **MacMillan Pass** (the border with the Yukon). Few will have the time or energy to walk its entire 230-mile length, but airstrips allow sections to be walked; the lucky walker sees moose, wolf, black bear, woodland caribou, and perhaps even a grizzly. ■

Nahanni National Park

**Nahanni
National Park**

🏕 314 B2, C2

www.pc.gc.ca

✉ Box 348,
Fort Simpson

☎ 867/695-3151

💲 $$$

NORTHERN CANADA IS A LAND OF SUPERLATIVES: IT IS EASY to think that the panorama you are currently viewing is the finest in the country, only to discover another, better, farther along. While many of the landscapes are breathtaking, the South Nahanni River, much of which is protected by the Nahanni National Park, capitalizes on the repeated discovery of magnificent scenery.

The park is best viewed from the river, and there are many opportunities for canoe trips lasting from a single day to several weeks.
Virginia Falls is the park's most famous attraction. Here the river drops in two mighty falls, the upper one 295 feet high, the lower 171 feet, the two separated by a vast pillar of rock known (locally) as Mason Rock. The total height of the falls is twice that of Niagara. Upriver are the **Rabbitkettle Hotsprings,** volcanic springs that gush water at a temperature of 70˚F. In winter Virginia Falls freezes almost solid—a wonderful sight—while the hot springs continue non-stop. The hot water deposits calcium carbonate around the vents, creating tufa in weird shapes.

The park also has an area of karst landforms: As water dissolves the limestone, it produces vast canyons and gorges with steep cliffs; sinkholes into which rivers disappear and where they then carve huge caves; and unusual rock formations such as the double arch near Raven Lake.

As a complete contrast, just outside the national park stands one of the world's most impressive series of rock walls, the hard granite cliffs of the **Cirque of the Unclimbables.** These vast walls, many hundreds of feet high, were so intimidating to those who first saw them that they assumed no one would be skilled (or mad) enough to climb them. History has proved them wrong. Add the beautiful

canyons through which the Nahanni River flows and the glaciers from the high peaks at the river's head, and the landscape is seen to be one of the most comprehensive in the world, and was designated a World Heritage site in 1978. ■

The sheer power of Virginia Falls has carved a narrow canyon (Fourth Canyon) for the Nahanni River.

The Northwest Passage

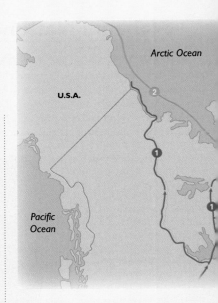

Arctic Ocean

U.S.A.

Pacific Ocean

In the 15th century, faced with hostile kingdoms to the east, the countries of western Europe sought an alternative route to the fabulous wealth of China and Japan. Spurred by this, rather than by the idea of a New World, Christopher Columbus set out on the journey that ended on the northern shore of Cuba. Many other Europeans followed Columbus in the search for the western route to the east, but it soon became clear that America was a solid barrier to progress westward, and the search began for a way around the continent. The route around the Cape of Good Hope was long, that around Cape Horn dangerous. Was there a route linking the Atlantic to the Pacific around the northern edge of Canada? The search for the Northwest Passage had begun.

Throughout the 16th century the Spanish, French, and Portuguese all sent expeditions to explore the northern Atlantic shores of what is now Canada. These were all driven back by the ice, as were those of the English, whose first attempts to reach China involved exploring the northern coast of Norway and Russia in the hope of finding a northeast passage.

Spanish successes in Latin America ensured that if England was to retain its position as an important European (and therefore world) power, it had to control trade routes to the East. So by the late 16th century they, too, were seeking the Northwest Passage. The early English explorers gave their names to the places they discovered—Frobisher (Bay), Davis (Strait), Baffin (Island) and, most famous of all, Hudson (Bay).

In 1607 Henry Hudson began his exploration of the Canadian Arctic, returning again in 1609 and 1610. On the final voyage he discovered the bay to become known as Hudson Bay, but it ended in tragedy when his crew mutinied. Hudson's ship was inadequately stocked with food and his men were poorly clothed. When, after a winter locked in ice, his ship was freed, Hudson declared his intention of continuing the search for the passage rather than returning home. Appalled by this prospect, the crew put him, his 14-year-old son, and seven other men into an open boat and set them adrift on the bay with just one musket and a kettle. They were never seen again.

In 1631, with Charles I's backing, the rival ports of London and Bristol sent ships (Luke Fox in the *Charles* and Thomas James in the *Henrietta Marie*, named for Charles's Queen) on a race for the passage. Each captain carried a letter of greeting to the Japanese Emperor, signed by the king. The letters were in English, since it was assumed that the Emperor, being a noble, cultured man, would speak the language. Captain James also has the dubious distinction of almost roasting his men to death (on an island in what is now James Bay). When they were half frozen in the grip of an Arctic winter, James started a fire that went out of control, burning down the island's forest and forcing the men to flee the flames.

Just when the English realized that even if there was a passage it would not be a practical trade route is not clear. The problem was, and is, that the line of the passage is dictated by the ice. This may force ships to travel one side of an island one year, but on the other side the

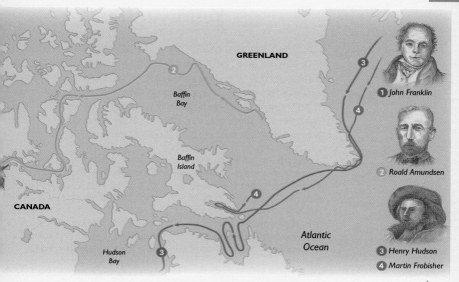

GREENLAND

Baffin
Bay

Baffin
Island

CANADA

Hudson
Bay

Atlantic
Ocean

1 John Franklin

2 Roald Amundsen

3 Henry Hudson

4 Martin Frobisher

Left: Over
the course of
several voyages
in the 1850s,
Francis Leopold
McClintock
(1819–1907)
investigated the
fate of Sir John
Franklin's
expedition. The
tragic story
unfolded through
conversations
with the region's
Inuit population.

next. In the following year it may stop them altogether. The passage is also tortuous, weaving a route through the maze of islands that lie off Canada's northern coast.

By the time of Sir John Franklin's famous 1845 expedition, the purpose was scientific research and national prestige. Unfortunately, Franklin, his ships *Erebus* and *Terror*, and all his men disappeared, leading to a search for survivors that included such experiments as the sending of dozens of messages to the expedition in small balloons. The truth emerged— that the expedition succumbed to the Arctic winter and scurvy, and, in a desperate overland trek, had been forced into cannibalism.

But the search for Franklin had one significant outcome. By approaching the northern waters from the Pacific end, the Bering Strait, Robert McClure discovered the final leg of the passage, although it was not until 1903-06 that Roald Amundsen, the Norwegian who was the first to the South Pole, completed the journey. Today, icebreakers can follow the passage with ease, but to try it without such modern devices still requires great courage and endurance. ∎

Yellowknife

City of Yellowknife

🗺 314 C2

Visitor information

www.northernfrontier.com

✉ Northern Frontier Visitors' Association 4-4807 49th Street, Yellowknife

☎ 867/873-4262 or 877/881-4262

Regional visitor information

www.explorenwt.com

✉ N.W.T. Tourism, P.O. Box 610, Yellowknife

☎ 867/873-7200 or 800/661-0788

To explore the area around Yellowknife, visitors might use floatplanes and canoes.

VISITORS TO YELLOWKNIFE ARE GREETED BY A LARGE *inukshuk*—a "man" built of stone blocks. Such statues are ancient markers erected to guide travelers across a landscape devoid of distinguishing features. Founded on gold mining, the capital of the N.W.T. jumped to prominence in the 1990s when diamonds where discovered to the northeast. The first mine opened in 1998; the N.W.T. is now the third greatest diamond producer in the world.

Yellowknife is a hub for exploring the north; the excellent **Prince of Wales Northern Heritage Centre** (*Off Ingraham Trail, tel 867/873-7551*) is a good place to start. More than that, though, it is a lively place, especially during one of its numerous festivals. In March, a three-day, 150-mile dogsled race, offering the largest purse in Canada, begins and ends here. At the same time, the **Caribou Carnival** enlivens the city with ice sculpting, dancing and feasting, and much more. In July, the **Festival of the Midnight Sun** is a weeklong festival that celebrates the culture of the north.

From Yellowknife, scheduled flights allow visitors to reach places that are as different from each other as is imaginable. A short flight south reaches **Fort Smith,** where

visitors can drive through subarctic **Wood Buffalo National Park** (*Fort Smith, tel 867/872-7960*). Here Canada's largest herd of bison roams—and is hunted by wolves. A flight north, via Cambridge Bay to **Resolute,** brings you to the real Arctic. Situated on **Cornwallis Island,** less than 200 miles from the North Magnetic Pole, Resolute is an Inuit settlement where residents follow the old ways, hunting and trapping on the tundra and sea ice. There are comfortable accommodations at Resolute for those wanting to use it as a center for trips of a lifetime—to see belugas and polar bears on the north coast of **Somerset Island,** narwhals near **Devon Island,** or the graves of members of Franklin's ill-fated expedition (see pp. 334–35) on nearby **Beechey Island.** ∎

Baffin Island

BAFFIN IS THE LARGEST ISLAND OF THE CANADIAN ARCTIC. Indeed, at over 190,000 square miles, it is the fifth largest on earth. Yet for all its vast size, it has only a scattering of settlements, some on the north coast, twice as many on the south, and only one main settlement in its center. That central region settlement is also coastal: A place of majestic beauty, with a wild, rugged terrain, inland Baffin supports little life, offering few hopes for the hunter or trapper.

In northern Baffin, **Sirmilik National Park** *(Tel 867/899-8092)* protects the rugged cliffs of Bylot Island where 300,000 thick-billed murres and 80,000 black-legged kittiwakes nest. In the waters of **Pond Inlet,** between Bylot Island and the mainland, and in **Lancaster Sound,** to the north of Bylot, there are walruses, beluga and bowhead whales, narwhals and orcas, and several species of seals, on which polar bears prey. Trips to Bylot to see the birds and to watch whales can be organized in the village of

Mittimatalik *(Visitors center, tel 867/899-8225)*. The village has several hotels and regular flights from Iqaluit in southern Baffin and from Resolute, N.W.T. The other two settlements in the north may also be reached by regular flights. Each year **Nanisivik** hosts the world's most northerly marathon.

Central Baffin is a remote, isolated wilderness, although the area to the north of **Cumberland Sound** is becoming increasingly popular, with hikers and climbers visiting the **Auyuittuq National Park.** Auyuittuq means "the land

Baffin Island

315 F3–F4, G3

Visitor information

www.nunavuttourism.com

Nunavut Tourism, P.O. Box 1450, Iqaluit

867/979-6551 or 866/686-2888

Visitor Centre, Iqaluit

876/979-4636

Native Inuit seal hunting on Baffin Island

Auyuittuq National Park

www.pc.gc.ca

✉ P.O. Box 353, Pangnirtung

☎ 867/473-2500

that never melts" and it was the first Arctic national park in Canada, set up in 1972. The most popular hiking trail traverses the park from **Broughton Island** to **Pangnirtung,** but many walkers prefer to follow a shorter route, heading north from

Babysitting on Baffin Island

Pangnirtung to **Summit Lake,** where the huge, vertical walls of Mount Asgard can be seen. **Mount Thor** has the highest uninterrupted rock face in the world.

Pangnirtung, a small village reached by regular flights from Iqaluit, is the starting point for visiting **Kekerton Island Historic Park** (*Angmarlik Interpretive Centre, Pangnirtung, tel 867/473-8737*). Here the ruins of a whaling station can still be seen. Between the late 1850s and early 1860s, whalers virtually exterminated the bowhead whale from habitats such as the one on Kekerton.

Lying at the head of Frobisher Bay, **Iqaluit,** the main settlement on Baffin, is the capital of Nunavut. It is a lovely place with a population of more than 4,400, more than 60 percent of them Inuit. It has a range of good hotels and restaurants, and the **Nunatta Sunakkutaangit Museum** (*Tel*

867/979-5537), housed in an old Hudson's Bay Company trading post, is worth a visit for its collection on the history of southern Baffin. In addition to Pangnirtung and Auyuittuq, Iqaluit is also the starting point for trips to several other parks. At **Qammaarviit Historic Park** (*Unikkaarvik Visitor Centre, Iqaluit, tel 867/979-4636*)—about 7 miles by boat from the town— are the remains of Inuit turf houses dating from the Thule period, perhaps 1,000 years ago. About a half-hour's walk north from Iqaluit leads to the **Sylvia Grinnell Territorial Park** (*Unikkaarvik Visitor Centre, Iqaluit, tel 867/979-4636*), a quiet spot renowned for its fishing and populations of caribou and arctic fox.

To the south of Iqaluit is **Kimmirut** (formerly Lake Harbour), a beautiful village at the edge of the **Katannilik Territorial Park** (*Park Interpretive Centre, Kimmirut, tel 867/939-2416*). The name means "place of waterfalls," and the falls add to the beauty of a surprisingly fertile area. Arctic fox and hare, caribou, peregrine and gyrfalcons, and rough-legged hawk can all be seen here.

Finally, to the west of Iqaluit is **Kinngait** (formerly known as Cape Dorset), the famous center for Inuit artists. Museums throughout Canada display the works of these artists, who work in antler, bone, ivory, and stone. The artists' studios can (and should) be visited. To the north-west of the village—about 45 min-utes on foot—is **Mallikjuaq Historic Park** (*Mallikjuaq Visitors Centre, Kinngait, tel 867/897-8996*), where the 1,000-year-old remains of a Thule settle-ment have been preserved. ∎

Travelwise

Travelwise information 340–47
Planning your trip **340**
How to get to Canada **341–42**
Practical advice **342–46**
Emergencies **346–47**
Hotels & restaurants 348–74
Shopping in Canada 375–79
**Entertainment & activities
    380–89**

**Floatplane on the Thelon
River**

TRAVELWISE INFORMATION

PLANNING YOUR TRIP

WHEN TO GO

Any time is a good time to visit Canada, depending on your interests. Cold winter weather produces some spectacular skiing, and the warmth of summer gives rise to a myriad of outdoor festivals and activities.

As a general rule, the climate is mildest on the country's coasts, especially on Vancouver Island. However, what the East and West Coasts don't get in snow is made up for in rain and fog. The landlocked prairies have bitterly cold and drawn-out winters but beautiful warm summers. Ontario and Québec can be a little humid in mid-summer and their winters are cold, but these are punctuated by short crisp springs and brilliant mild falls with stupendous colors. In the north of the country, summers are short and warm with 24 hours of daylight, winters are long and Siberianlike.

With the huge size of some provinces and territories, there is considerable variation within their borders. Québec, for example, stretches from the temperate south to the Arctic, and the weather varies accordingly.

The vast majority of tourists visit Canada between mid-May and mid-October. Outside these months, facilities might be reduced, unless you are going to a ski area or major city. Thus, it is advisable to check in advance that hotels and sights are open during the off-peak season.

WHAT TO TAKE

Most of southern Canada has a climate similar to the northern U.S., so you should dress accordingly. Expect hot summer days with cooler evenings. If you are staying in the Rockies or beside a lake or the ocean, evenings tend to be cool even in mid-summer. A sweater or light jacket is recommended.

On the coasts, rain is frequent and a raincoat is essential, plus an umbrella if you are in a city. In Vancouver natives never seem to use umbrellas. So be forewarned that if you buy an umbrella there, it is likely to say "visitor to Vancouver" inside.

In May or June in the north, or in lake country, you will need insect repellent, especially if you are camping or planning a wilderness excursion. Sometimes, depending on the rainfall, biting insects can be so ferocious near lakes or streams that a hat with mosquito netting attached is a good idea.

Sunglasses are important, not only in the south as you would expect, but the light of the north is surprisingly bright, and it lasts for 24 hours a day in summer. Sunscreen is also a good idea if you are going to spend lengthy periods outside.

For winter visits, your car should be winterized. Snow tires are essential except in the major cities. You should have warm mittens, a hat, a scarf, a warm coat, boots, and long johns, to save your legs from freezing.

BEFORE YOU GO

PASSPORTS

U.S. citizens do not need a passport or a visa to visit Canada. However, proof of citizenship and photo identification are essential. Identifying papers such as a passport or birth, baptismal, or voter's certificate should be carried. U.S. residents who are not U.S. citizens should carry their Alien Registration cards.

Any person under 19 traveling alone or in a group requires a letter from a parent or guardian giving permission to visit Canada, in addition to proof of identity. Such a letter should state the traveler's name and the duration of the trip. Canadian officials are very cautious when it comes to children traveling across the border.

CUSTOMS

Certain restrictions apply to goods that you bring into Canada. Smokers can bring in a maximum of 200 cigarettes, 50 cigars, or 400 grams of tobacco. The limit on alcoholic beverages and wine is a one-liter bottle; for beer it is 24 regular-size cans or bottles.

There are very strict regulations concerning the importation of plants, flowers, and other vegetation. It is not advisable to bring anything of this sort into Canada. Likewise check with customs before bringing firearms into Canada.

Obtain details concerning restrictions or regulations from the Canadian Border Services Agency: Tel 800/461-9999 or 204/983-3500 (within Canada); 506/636-5064 (outside Canada); or www.cbsa-asfc.gc.ca/travel/visitors-e.html.

VACCINATIONS

No vaccinations are required before entering Canada from the United States.

PETS

Americans may bring their dogs and cats with them on a visit to Canada as long as they have a health certificate (issued by a veterinarian) and a valid vaccination certificate against rabies. Such a vaccination has to have been administered at least 30 days before departure and should not be more than a year old.

Restrictions on animals vary from province to province. In Québec, for example, dogs are not allowed in national or provincial parks at all, even on leashes. However, they are allowed in parks on leashes in Ontario. Pets are not allowed in restaurants with the exception of guide dogs. Some hotel chains permit pets—often for an extra charge. It is advisable to check when making your reservation.

HOW TO GET TO CANADA

AIR

Since Canada is such a huge country (the second largest in the world), air travel is generally the fastest and most practical means of transportation. For some northern communities, it is the only means of visiting.

The major international airports in Canada are:
Pierre Elliott Trudeau International Airport,
  tel 514/394-7377
  Montréal, Que.
Lester B. Pearson International Airport, tel 416/247-7678 (Terminal 1 & 2) or 416/776-5100 (Terminal 3), Toronto, Ont.
Vancouver International Airport, tel 604/207-7077
  Vancouver, B.C.

In addition, major cities like Halifax, N.S., Edmonton, Alta., Calgary, Alta., and Winnipeg, Man. have important airports, which are connected to each other and to neighboring U.S. cities.

There is only one major carrier in Canada: Air Canada (Tel 888/247-2262 or www.aircanada.ca). With headquarters in Montréal, Air Canada has a vast network of routes serving more than 120 destinations across Canada and around the world. Air Canada also offers low-fare alternatives through its subsidiaries: Air Canada Jazz (Tel 888/247-2262, www.flyjazz.ca) and Air Canada Tango (Tel 800/315-1390, www.flytango.com).

Regional carriers in Canada include WestJet with headquarters in Calgary (Tel 403/250-5839 and 888/937-8538, www.westjet.com); CanJet with headquarters in Nova Scotia (Tel 902/873-7800 or 800/809-7777, www.canjet.com); and Air Transat with headquarters in Montréal (Tel 514/636-3631 or 877-872-6728, www.airtransat.com).

In northern Canada—the Yukon, Northwest Territories, and Nunavut—the major carriers are Canadian North (Tel 867/669-4000) and First Air (Tel 867/669-6600). In addition, many charter companies provide air service to remote areas; the provincial tourist offices are the best places to obtain further information about these.

In addition, many U.S. airlines offer regular flights between the United States and Canada. American Airlines, Continental Airlines, Delta Air Lines, Northwest Airlines, United Airlines, and US Airways all serve Canada's major airports. Connecting flights within Canada serve some 75 additional places.

It is worthwhile shopping around to get the best price for international connections on the busy U.S. to Canada routes; there are many special offers that require you to fly at certain times or on particular dates. In addition, domestic flights within Canada generally cost less than flying from U.S. cities. Thus, in certain cases, you may find it cheaper to drive across the border and then pick up a flight.

DRIVING YOUR OWN CAR

Driving across the border into Canada from the United States is no problem. There are more than a dozen major entry points, and numerous others are open limited hours.

Driving in Canada is always done on the right with passing on the left. Speed limits are posted in kilometers (see conversion chart p. 343).

Speed limits vary slightly between provinces, but the uniform top speed on expressways is 100 kph (about 60 mph); 90 kph (55 mph) on the Trans-Canada and Yellowhead highways; 80 kph (50 mph) on most rural roads; and between 40 and 60 kph (25 to 35 mph) in urban areas. Speed limits are rigidly enforced.

Fuel or gas is sold by the liter in three grades of octane levels, as well as in diesel.

Drivers and passengers are required by law to wear seat belts in every province. Drivers must also carry proper vehicle registration and proof of insurance. Right-hand turns are allowed on red lights, except in Montréal.

RENTING A CAR

Renting a car in Canada can be quick and easy. You must be over 21 years of age and produce identification and a valid driver's license (a U.S. license is acceptable), which has been held for at least one year.

Car rental companies will expect you to have a credit card; if you don't have one, you may have to leave a hefty deposit. Look out for additional charges, notably GST, provincial taxes, and "drop-off" charges, often equivalent to a week's rental, when you rent the car in one town and leave it in another.

For an additional charge, collision or "Loss Damage Waiver," an insurance against accident or damage, is worth considering. Check with your credit card company or insurance agent about automatic coverage. Also check to see whether the rental includes unlimited mileage, or whether you incur an additional charge after reaching a set mileage.

Car rental rates vary widely across the country, ranging from a starting rate of about $30/day in the large cities to $40/day in more remote areas.

All the major car rental companies are represented in Canada. They can be reached at the following numbers:
National: Tel 800/361-5334 (Canada)
Dollar: Tel 800/800-4000

Hertz: Tel 800/263-0600
(worldwide)
Budget: Tel 800/268-8900
(Canada), 800/527-0700
(U.S.A.)
Thrifty: Tel 800/367-2277
Avis: Tel 800/879-2847
(worldwide)
In case of a car breakdown,
contact the Canadian Automobile Association (Tel 800/268-
3750) or its local affiliate. AAA
members are entitled to full
service with the CAA.

RAIL

Train travel is a pleasant
alternative to driving and is
usually cheaper than flying. It is
often slower and more
expensive than the equivalent
journey by bus, but it can be a
pleasant and scenic way to view
the country, especially when
using the "Silver and Blue" first-
class service on trans-Canada
trains, which offers exclusive use
of the famous domed cars that
allow an uninterrupted rooftop
view of the countryside.

AMTRAK
From the U.S., Amtrak (Tel 800/
872-7245 or www.amtrak.com)
has regular train service to both
Montréal and Toronto from
New York, also to Toronto from
Chicago and to Vancouver from
Seattle.

VIA RAIL
Once in Canada, most passenger
services are operated by VIA
Rail Canada (Tel 888-VIA-RAIL,
in Canada). (In the U.S. contact
Amtrak or www.viarail.ca.) It
offers a good standard of
comfort and service. Reserve
seats whenever possible,
certainly for the trans-Canada
service (Toronto–Vancouver).
Via Rail services more than
400 communities in every
province except Newfoundland
and Labrador and Prince Edward
Island. The most popular route is
The Canadian (Montréal to
Vancouver) but there are many
other scenic routes such as The
Ocean (Montréal to Halifax) and

The Skeena (Jasper to Prince
Rupert).

FERRIES

Ferries form part of the highway
system in much of Canada,
providing vital links in the
country's road network. They also
offer connections to islands off
both the East and West Coasts.

WEST COAST
Several ferry companies operate
between Washington State and
Victoria, the capital of British
Columbia: Black Ball Transport
(Tel 250/386-2202) runs
between Port Angeles, Wash.
and Victoria; Washington State
Ferries (Tel 888/808-7977)
between Anacortes, Wash. and
Victoria; and Victoria Clipper
between Seattle, Wash. and
Victoria (Tel 250/382-8100).
Once in Canada, the main
West Coast company, with some
42 ports of call, is the British
Columbia Ferry Corporation
(1112 Fort Street, Victoria, BC
V8V 4V2, tel 888-BCFERRY [in
B.C.] or 250/386-3431 [else-
where], www.bcferries.com). Its
key services operate between
the British Columbia mainland
and Vancouver Island (Horse-
shoe Bay, North Vancouver, to
Nanaimo and Tsawwassen to
Swartz Bay); between Vancouver
Island and Prince Rupert (the
Inside Passage); and between
Prince Rupert and the Queen
Charlotte Islands.

EAST COAST
Two services link Nova Scotia
and the state of Maine:

Scotia Prince Cruises (P.O. Box
609, Yarmouth, NS, B5A 4B6 or
P.O. Box 4216, Station A,
Portland, ME, 04101, tel 866/412-
5270, www.scotiaprince.com)
operates between Portland,
Maine. and Yarmouth, N.S.

Bay Ferries (94 Water St., P.O.
Box 634, Charlottetown, PE,
C1A 7L3, tel 888-249-7245 or
902/566-3838) operates
between Bar Harbor, Maine, and

Yarmouth, N.S., and between
Digby, N.S., and Saint John, N.B.

Once in Canada, there are
ferries to the province of
Newfoundland from Nova Scotia
operated by Marine Atlantic
(355 Purves St., North Sydney,
NS B2A 3V2, tel 800/341-7981,
www.marine-atlantic.ca). These
ferries run between North
Sydney, N.S., and either Port-
aux-Basques or Argentia, Nfld.
Despite the construction of
the Confederation Bridge, the
province of Prince Edward Island
is still accessible by ferry.
Northumberland Ferries (94
Water St., P.O. Box 634,
Charlottetown, PE C1A 7L3, tel
902/566-3838) operates the only
remaining ferry service between
Caribou, N.S., and Wood Islands,
P.E.I.

BUSES

Travel by long-distance bus is
relatively cheap and provides
access to most of Canada. There
is no national transportation
company. Greyhound Canada
(Tel 800/661-8747, www.grey
hound.ca) provides service in
Western Canada, Yukon, and
most of Ontario (in alliance with
Voyageur). In Western Canada,
Brewster Transportation (Tel
877/791-5500, www.brewster.ca)
is a major player; whereas Coach
Canada (Tel 800/461-7661,
www.coachcanada.com) is an
alternative in Ontario. In
Québec, Orléans Express (Tel
888/999-3977, www.orleans
express.com) is the major
carrier; and in Atlantic Canada,
service is offered by Acadian
Lines (Tel 800/567-5151,
www.smtbus.com).
If you plan to cover a lot of
ground, consider purchasing a
long-distance bus pass.
Greyhound has several different
plans. Certain restrictions apply
so it is best to contact them
before doing detailed planning
for a trip. There can also be
considerable savings if tickets are
purchased in advance.

PRACTICAL ADVICE

BEER, WINE, & ALCOHOL

Across Canada, provincial governments are responsible for regulating alcohol. It is sold in special liquor stores across the country. Beer and wine can be purchased in grocery stores in Québec and in special government beer and wine stores in other provinces.

The legal drinking age in Canada is 19, except in Québec where it is 18. Certain northern communities are "dry" towns, where the sale or consumption of alcohol is strictly forbidden.

COMMUNICATIONS

POST OFFICES

It costs a minimum of 51 cents to mail a regular letter within the country, about 89 cents to send it across the border to the U.S., and $1.49 to send it abroad. Priority Post is a fast and rather expensive service which promises "next day delivery" within Canada. It is available 24 hours a day, seven days a week. Otherwise, there is one mail delivery per day, Monday through Friday.

Post offices are generally open Monday to Friday 8:30 a.m. to 5:30 p.m. Some larger branches in the major cities are open Saturday, Sunday, and holidays. Stamps can also be purchased at designated retailers often found in hotel lobbies, airports, and news stands. Certain small stores are licensed to sell stamps, and post offices are often found inside larger stores and railway stations, so be on the lookout for the Canada Post sign.

TELEPHONES

Public phones work the same as they do in the U.S. and are widely available and relatively cheap. Pay phones accept American coins and U.S. telephone credit cards. There

are no problems dialing direct to the United States. If you have any problems placing an international call (outside Canada and the U.S.), dial "0" and ask for the international operator.

For directory assistance, dial 1, the area code, and 555-1212. Provincial telephone area codes:
Alberta—Calgary and Southern Alberta 403; Edmonton and northern Alberta 780
British Columbia—Vancouver 604; rest of BC 250
Manitoba 204
New Brunswick 506
Newfoundland and Labrador 709
Northwest Territories 867
Nova Scotia 902
Nunavut 867
Ontario—Toronto 416 and 647; Central and North 705; SW peninsula 519; Ottawa region 613; South 905 and 289; northwest Ont. 807
Prince Edward Island 902
Québec—Montréal 514; metro region 450, Central and North 819; East 418
Saskatchewan 306
Yukon 867

CONVERSIONS

All across Canada today, the metric system is in use.

On the roads, speed limits are given in kilometers per hour; gasoline is sold in liters; and things are weighed in kilograms.
1 kilometer = 0.62 miles
100 kilometers = a little more than 60 miles
1 meter = 3.28 feet or 39.37 inches
1000 meters = a little more than 3000 feet
1 liter = 0.264 U.S. gallons
10 liters = a little more than 2.5 gallons
1 kilogram = 2.20 pounds
2 kilograms = nearly 4.5 pounds

Weather forecasts and reports in Canada are given in Celsius. The freezing point is 0° Celsius so for an approximate conversion from Fahrenheit to Celsius, subtract 30 and divide by 2. To

convert Celsius to Fahrenheit multiply by 2 and add 30.

0°C = 32°F; 100°C = 212°F
10°C = 50°F
20°C = 68°F
30°C = 86°F

ETIQUETTE & CUSTOMS

Canadian culture and manners are similar in many ways to those of Americans and British, but you should be sensitive to the more traditional ways of life encountered in many rural areas. It is also important to respect the customs of the First Nations and Inuit—native Canadians— who are increasingly asserting their rights and distinct cultural identities. It is an insult, for example, to address an Inuit as an Eskimo, or First Nations as Indians.

In the French-speaking parts of Canada, notably Québec, you should be prepared to acknowledge French as the first, and sometimes only, language. French is the official language of the province, and all road signs and other indications are given in this language. Outside the main tourist areas (Montréal, Québec City) and major resort hotels, you may have difficulty being understood in English. Visitors are advised to learn a few phrases to help them in these situations. Most restaurants, certainly in the tourist areas, will have English versions of the menus, but you may have to ask for them.

FESTIVALS

A list of the major festivals in each region is included in the Entertainments section (see pp. 380-89).

HUNTING & FISHING

Hunting is regulated by federal, provincial, and territorial laws. You must obtain a permit from the province or territory in which you plan to hunt. Hunting of certain species is severely restricted, and, in some cases, only a few permits are given every year. For information about this, contact the appropriate provincial or territorial tourist office, which can tell you how to obtain your permit.

Fishing is regulated by law, and again you must obtain a non-resident permit for the province or territory in which you want to fish. In most cases, permits are on sale at sports stores and local outfitters. The tourist office can help you choose the most convenient place to obtain your permit.

MEDIA

NEWSPAPERS

Canada has two national newspapers, *The Globe & Mail* and *The National Post*. They are both on sale at newsstands and newspaper and magazine stores across the country.

All large cities boast their own newspapers, often with a circulation as large as that of the nationals. Examples include the *Toronto Star*, the *Calgary Herald*, the *Edmonton Journal*, the *Winnipeg Free Press*, the *Ottawa Citizen*, the *Vancouver Sun*, *The Gazette* in Montréal, and the *Chronicle Record* in Halifax. In Montréal, the major French newspapers are *Le Devoir*, *Le Journal de Montréal*, and *La Presse*.

Again in the major cities, English and French-language newspapers are often supplemented by a wide variety of ethnic publications.

The major U.S. newspapers (*New York Times*, *Wall Street Journal*, etc.) are available in the large cities as well as the publications of neighboring cities (*Detroit Free Press–Detroit News* in Windsor, etc.).

TELEVISION & RADIO

Today, television reaches everyone in Canada even in the extreme north where service is assured by satellite, which offers a wide range of channels.

The Canadian Broadcasting Corporation (CBC), a publicly funded television and radio network, has channels throughout the country broadcasting in both English and French. Their radio stations broadcast hourly news updates, general information programs, and commercial-free music. The CBC also has a 24-hour news channel on the cable network which broadcasts in both English and French.

Other major Canadian television channels include the CTV and Global. Among cable stations, the most popular are: the Weather Network; Bravo (an arts channel); TSN (sports); MuchMusic (rock music); Discovery Channel (Canadian science); the Canadian History Channel; and Life Network (Canadian lifestyles channel).

In addition, the four major U.S. television networks are widely available throughout Canada, supplemented by local American stations broadcasting near the border.

MONEY MATTERS

U.S. currency is widely accepted in Canada. At the present time (2006) the Canadian dollar is worth about $0.86 U.S. Exchange rates are notoriously variable, so it is wise to check the current rate just before leaving on a trip. Check the Bank of Canada website (www.bank-banque-canada.ca/en/exchform.htm) for the current exchange rate.

Canadian currency has almost the same denominations as American money, with the exception of the paper $1 and $2 notes, which no longer exist in Canada. Single Canadian dollars come in the form of a gold-colored coin bearing a picture of a loon (thus their nickname "loonie"), two-dollar coins have gold centers and silver rims.

Outside the major cities and resort areas, there are relatively few places devoted just to currency exchange in Canada. Exchange facilities can usually be found in large hotels, airports, and railway stations, but rates are often poor and commission fees high. In addition, most banks offer exchange facilities, and many charge a fee.

A good way to carry money is in the form of travelers' checks, which, if made out in Canadian dollars, can be used as cash in most shops, restaurants, and service stations across the country (change is given in cash). American Express and Visa checks are the most common. There is no limit to the amount of Canadian or foreign currency that can be exchanged or brought into or taken out of the country.

Automated Teller Machines
The simplest method of obtaining money is by using an automated banking machine. This avoids hassles with curren-cy exchange rates and service charges, since your own bank does the exchange. Nonetheless, there is usually a charge for their use.

To use your bank or credit card at an ATM in Canada, it needs to have been programmed with a personal identification number, or PIN. This enables you to withdraw money directly from your account or get cash advances on a credit-card account. Before leaving home, it is wise to check for restrictions such as how much money you can withdraw at any one time or on any one day.

NATIONAL HOLIDAYS

There are seven national holidays celebrated in every province and territory of Canada:

New Year's Day (January 1)
Good Friday
Victoria Day (Third Monday in May)
Canada Day (July 1)
Labour Day (First Monday in September)
Thanksgiving Day (Second Monday in October) Please note this is not at the same

as American Thanksgiving.
Christmas Day (December 25)

Some provinces also celebrate
the following days as holidays:
Easter Monday
Remembrance Day (November
11)
Boxing Day (December 26)
January 2

In addition, there are also
holidays specific to certain
provinces:
John the Baptist Day (June 24):
    Québec
Civic Holiday (First Monday in
    August): Alberta, British
    Columbia, Manitoba,
    Northwest Territories,
    Nunavut, New Brunswick,
    Nova Scotia, Ontario, and
    Saskatchewan

On these holidays, you are likely
to find banks and government
offices closed, but increasingly
stores, tourist sights, and other
services are staying open.

OPENING TIMES

In general, stores are open
9 a.m.–6 p.m. Mon.–Sat., with
later evening hours Thurs.–Fri. If
open on Sunday, store hours are
usually noon–5 p.m.

Shopping malls tend to have
longer hours than downtown
shops, and often close between
7:30 and 9 p.m. In some suburban areas of big cities, super-
markets stay open until 10 or 11
p.m. nightly. In addition, most
towns have all-night pharmacies
and stores.

Bank hours are generally
10 a.m.–3 p.m. Mon.–Fri.,
although this can vary by branch
(some open 9 a.m.–4 p.m.). There
are often extended hours (10
a.m.–5 or 6 p.m.) on certain days,
usually Thursday or Friday.

PLACES OF WORSHIP

Major hotels in all Canadian
cities list the places of worship
close to them. If this is not the
case, the local Tourist Office can

always supply a list. There will
normally be a Roman Catholic
Church, an Episcopal Church
(Anglican), a United Church
(Methodists and Presbyterians),
and sometimes a Baptist Church.
In addition, the major cities have
synagogues and most of them
mosques, and Buddhist and Hindi
temples, too.

SMOKING

Many Canadians still smoke, but
smoking in public places is
increasingly forbidden. It is
prohibited in most shopping
centers, in government offices,
banks, and hospitals, and on
buses and subway systems.

Several provinces (notably
British Columbia, Ontario, and
Québec) have implemented a
no-smoking policy for all
restaurants and bars. Elsewhere,
it is the law that public places
(including restaurants, bars, and
cafés) have both smoking and
non-smoking sections.

Cigarettes are for sale in
grocery stores, bars, newspaper
and magazine stores, and most
corner stores.

TAXES

A 7 percent Goods and Services
Tax (GST) is added to everything
you buy in Canada except food
from the grocery store. (It is
applicable on all hotel and
restaurant bills, all transportation
tickets, and on admissions to
tourist sights. In addition, most
provinces add their own sales
tax. So you may find yourself
paying a surcharge of anything
between 7 percent (GST) in
Alberta, where there is no sales
tax, to 19 percent in Newfoundland where the sales tax is 12
percent plus 7 percent GST.

These are not hidden taxes.
They are added to the bill and
explained as such on the sales
slip. In some cases, the GST is
refundable to visitors taking
goods out of the country.
Certain conditions apply (type of
product, minimum purchase,
etc.) so it is best to obtain the

sales slip at the time of making a
purchase. All major hotels and
tourist offices have a supply of
refund forms. The provincial
sales tax (PST) is also refundable
in Québec and Manitoba.

For more information on
refunds, contact Revenue
Canada, Visitor Rebate Program,
Summerside Tax Centre, 275
Pope Road, suite 104
Summerside, P.E.I. CIN 6C6, tel
800/668-4748 (Canada) or
902/432-5608 (elsewhere),
www.cra-arc.gc.ca.

TIME ZONES

Canada is divided into six time
zones. The list below shows each
zone with its time relationship
to Eastern Standard Time (EST).

Atlantic Standard Time:
The Maritime Provinces,
Labrador, and the most easterly
part of Québec (EST +1 hour)
**Newfoundland Standard
Time:** The Island of Newfound-
land has its own time zone half
an hour ahead of the Maritimes.
(EST +1.5 hours)
Eastern Standard Time:
Most of Québec and Ontario
east of Thunder Bay (EST)
Central Standard Time:
The extreme northwest of
Ontario, Manitoba and Nunavut
(EST –1 hour)
Mountain Standard Time:
Saskatchewan, Alberta, the
southeast corner of British
Columbia and the Northwest
Territories (EST –2 hours)
Pacific Standard Time:
The rest of British Columbia and
the Yukon (EST –3 hours)

Daylight Saving Time: Similar
to U.S., all provinces except
Saskatchewan put clocks
forward at some point
March/April to some point
October/November.

TIPPING

As in the rest of North America,
tipping is a fact of life in Canada,
and many people in service jobs
depend on it to make ends

meet. That being said, tipping is an acknowledgment of good service. If the service is not satisfactory, don't tip.

Service charges are not automatically added to restaurant bills except in a few rare cases. It is customary to leave a tip of about 15 percent (of the bill before taxes) for waiters and waitresses.

As a general rule, hotel porters should be given about $1 a bag, room service staff 10 percent of the bill before taxes, and cab drivers 15 percent of the total. Tour guides should be given a little something also; in general, if you are satisfied with the service, $1 per person is adequate.

TRAVELERS WITH DISABILITIES

Canada has become increasingly sensitive to the needs of visitors with disabilities. Today, all public buildings must have wheelchair accessibility and provide special toilets. Curbs in most cities and large towns are dropped at corners to meet the needs of wheelchair users. Difficulties may still be encountered on public transportation, although buses are increasingly being adapted to accommodate wheelchairs. VIA Rail trains can accommodate wheelchairs up to 250 pounds in weight, and measuring no more than 2.6 feet by 6 feet. However, 48 hours notice is required on all routes.

Visitors may find barriers in older accommodations and restaurants, but for new properties, there are now strict compliance codes in effect, and some hotels even provide special suites for guests with disabilities. Details of suitable hotels can usually be obtained from Provincial tourist offices.

The following agencies in Canada and the U.S. provide information on tour operators, special guides, and other aspects of traveling abroad for visitors with disabilities:
Canadian Paraplegic Association,

230-1101 Prince of Wales Dr., Ottawa, ON K2C 3W7, tel 613/723-1033, www.canparaplegic.org

Council of Canadians with Disabilities, 926-294 Portage Ave., Winnipeg, MB R3C 0B9, tel 204/947-0303, www.ccdonline.ca

SATH (Society for Accessible Travel & Hospitality), 347 Fifth Ave, Suite 610, New York, NY 10016, tel 212/447-7284, www.sath.org

VISITOR INFORMATION

All the Canadian provinces and territories have government operated tourism bureaus, which welcome American calls. They also all have internet web sites. However, the amount of information on the latter varies tremendously across the country. Some provinces have full lists of accommodations and sights and are user-friendly; others are more complicated and less helpful.

Alberta: Travel Alberta, P.O. Box 2500, Edmonton, AB T5J 2Z4, tel 800/252-3782, www.travelalberta.com

British Columbia: Tourism British Columbia, Box 9830, 1803 Douglas St., Ste. 300, Victoria, BC V8W 9W5, tel 800/435-5622 or 604-435-5622, www.helloBC.com

Manitoba: Travel Manitoba, 7th Fl., 155 Carlton St., Winnipeg, MN R3C 3H8, tel 800/665-0040, www.travelmanitoba.com

New Brunswick: Tourism and Parks, Centennial Bldg., P.O. Box 6000, Fredericton, NB E3B 5H1, tel 800/561-0123, www.tourismnbcanada.com

Newfoundland: Newfoundland and Labrador, Dept. of Tourism, Recreation and Culture, P.O. Box 8700, St. John's, NF A1B 4J6, tel 800/563-6353, www.gov.nf.ca/tourism

Northwest Territories: Northwest Territories Tourism, P.O. Box 610, Yellowknife, NWT X1A 2N5, tel:800/661-0788, www.explorenwt.com

Nova Scotia: Nova Scotia Tourism, P.O. Box 456, Halifax, NS B3J 2R5, tel 800/565-0000, www.novascotia.com

Nunavut: Nunavut Tourism, P.O. Box 1450, Iqaluit, NU X0A 0H0, tel 867-979-6551 or 866/686-2888, www.nunavuttourism.com

Ontario: Ontario Tourism 10th Fl., Hearst Block, 900 Bay St., Toronto, ON M7A 2E1, tel 800/668-2746, www.ontariotravel.net

Prince Edward Island: Department of Tourism, P.O. Box 2000, Charlottetown, PEI C1A 7N8, tel 888/PEI-PLAY (734-7529), www.peiplay.com

Québec: Tourisme Québec P.O. Box 979, Montréal, QC H3C 2W3, tel 877/266-5687 or 514/873-2015, www.bonjourquebec.com

Saskatchewan: Tourism Saskatchewan, 1922 Park St., Regina, SK S4N 7M4, tel 877/237-2273, www.sasktourism.com

Yukon: Department of Tourism and Culture, P.O. Box 2703, Whitehorse, YK Y1A 2C6, tel 800/661-0494, www.touryukon.com

EMERGENCIES

CONSULATES

U.S. Embassy Ottawa 490 Sussex Dr., Ottawa, ON, tel 613/238-5335, www.usembassycanada.gov

In addition to its embassy in Ottawa, the United States maintains consulates in the following cities:

Calgary, 615 MacLeod Trail SE, tel 403/266-8962

Halifax, 1969 Upper Water St., Ste. 904, tel 902/429-2485

Montréal, 1155 rue St. Alexandre, tel 514/398-9695

Québec City, 2 Pl. Terrasse Dufferin, tel 418/692-2095

Toronto, 360 University Ave., tel 416/595-1700

Vancouver, 1095 W. Pender St., tel 604/685-4311

Winnipeg, 860-201 Portage Ave., tel 204/940-1800

CRIME & P.O.LICE

For the most part, Canada is a remarkably crime-free country. The streets of the larger cities are considerably safer than those of most American cities. However, reasonable caution should be exercised. It is wise to avoid parks, back streets, and unlit areas after dark. In all large cities, where there is always a danger of pickpockets, visitors need to be aware in crowded areas and on the subway. Avoid leaving luggage or valuables in cars, do not carry large quantities of cash or wear expensive-looking jewelry, and keep passports and credit cards out of sight. If you do have anything stolen, report it immediately to the police and/or your hotel.

For fast access to police, fire department, and ambulance services, call 911. Except in the Northwest Territories, Nunavut, and Yukon (outside Whitehorse), where you should dial 0 for the operator, this is the best way to report an emergency situation and saves you hunting for a police station or hospital.

The Royal Canadian Mounted Police are Canada's federal police force. The "Mounties" also act as the regular police in all provinces except Ontario and Québec, which have their own provincial forces. On duty, RCMP officers look just like any other police officers and drive cars. The red jackets, Stetsons, and horses are only used on ceremonial occasions.

HEALTH & HEALTH INSURANCE

The health service in Canada is government-supported and free for Canadian citizens. It is generally of a very high standard, but foreigners requiring treatment on vacation will not get it for free, so it is advisable to take out full travel insurance before a visit. If you become ill on vacation and are hospitalized, you will be treated and charged later; in some provinces, there is a surcharge of as much as 30 percent for the treatment of non-residents.

Traveler health insurance should be as complete as possible. Make sure it covers all types of medical costs—hospitalization, nursing services, doctors' fees, etc. A medical transportation clause is also important in case sufficient care is not available on site and you need to return home.

If you require medical help in Canada, the best thing to do is to consult your hotel. Most hotels keep a list of doctors and medical centers, which can save considerable time. Otherwise, consult the Yellow Pages of the telephone book. You should also keep any receipts or paperwork for future insurance claims.

Another wise precaution to take in case of emergency is to make a note of the generic name of any prescription medications you take before you leave home. They may be sold by a different trade name in Canada.

Canada's main health hazards are associated with the outdoors. *Giardi lamblia* (beaver fever) is a parasite that thrives in warm water so any small stream or shallow lake can be a breeding ground in summer. Check tap water at campsites and boil water when camping in the backcountry to guard against it. Medical help should be sought if the fever persists.

Lyme disease is also increasingly common in the woods of the south. It is caused by bites from woodland ticks. Signs of infection include a rash and flu-like symptoms. Tick repellents are available, and you can reduce the risk of bites by wearing thick socks, long pants, and long-sleeved shirts. Again, medical help should be sought if the fever persists.

In the wooded areas of southern Ontario and Québec, clumps of poison ivy can cause rashes, blisters, and sores. Creams and ointments are widely available to help ease discomfort. Rashes will clear up after about 10 days, so it is not essential to seek medical attention unless the irritation persists.

Less unpleasant, but equally irritating, are the hordes of blackflies and mosquitoes that are common in the north any time after April, but especially in May and June. All kinds of insect repellents are available for purchase.

HOTELS & RESTAURANTS

Accommodations in Canada are varied, reasonably priced, and normally of a high standard. But there are differences between the types of facilities available, and it will help you to understand these differences when deciding where to stay. Remember that large areas of the country are remote, so the available accommodations may fill quickly during the busy summer months. Therefore it is always best to check the availability of rooms before setting off.

Eating out can be a great pleasure, with most major cities offering a wide variety and range of eating possibilities. Menu prices are usually reasonable, and there are often appetizing regional specialties available.

Accommodations

There are three general types of accommodations: 1) low cost, basic rooms usually found in less desirable locations, frequently sought by students; 2) mid-range hotels and motels that are widely available, easy to find and to contact, and of consistent format and quality; and 3) large, top-of-the-range city and resort hotels that offer high international standards of quality and service. Listed below are some of the up-market and reliable mid-priced hotel chains with toll-free telephone numbers:

Best Western International, tel 800/358-7234; www.bestwestern.com

Choice Hotels International, tel 800/4CHOICE; www.choicehotels.ca

Days Inn, tel 800/329-7466; www.daysinn.com

Delta Hotels, tel 877/814-7706 (cities) or 888/778-5050; www.deltahotels.com

Fairmont, tel 800/441-1414; www.fairmont.com

Four Seasons Hotels, tel 800/819-5058; www.fourseasons.com

Hilton Hotels, tel 888/HILTONS; www.hilton.com

Holiday Inns, tel 800/HOLIDAY; www.ichotelsgroup.com

Hyatt Hotels, tel 800/223-1234; www.hyatt.com

Marriott Hotels, tel 888/236-2427; www.marriott.com

Novotel Hotels, tel 800/668-6835; www.novotel.com

Radisson Hotels, tel 800/333-3333; www.radisson.com

Ramada Hotels, tel 800/272-6232; www.ramada.com

Renaissance Hotels, tel 800/HOTELS1; www.marriott.com/renaissancehotels

Sheraton Hotels, tel 800/598-1753; www.starwoodhotels.com/sheraton

Travelodge, tel 800/578-7878; www.travelodge.com

Westin Hotels, tel 800/228-3000; www.starwoodhotels.com/westin

Bed-and-breakfast lodgings are numerous and available in most Canadian towns, cities, and rural backwaters. When reserving, remember to inquire about details that will affect your stay, such as whether smoking is permitted, whether credit cards are accepted, and the rates. For help in booking these, you can contact the relevant tourist board, which may be able to provide you with a listing of B&Bs or refer you elsewhere for information on availability and reservations. Also, there are associations you can contact directly; the telephone numbers for these associations are listed under the regional headings. Please note that **unless otherwise stated:**

1. All hotel rooms have dining rooms and private bathrooms.
2. Hotels are open year-round.

Restaurants

Except for fast-food establishments, reservations are recommended for lunch during the week and for dinner on Friday and Saturday evenings. Most restaurants open from noon–10 p.m., longer on weekends;

dinner-type establishments in small towns and villages may close earlier (8–9:30 p.m.). The following listings contain a selection of good quality restaurants throughout the country. Wherever possible we have chosen establishments that are both individual and typical, perhaps with notable local associations.

Tipping

Tipping is widely prevalent in Canada. Service charges are rarely added to the check, and even in the most humble diners and restaurants—where waitresses rely heavily on tips—it is usual to leave around 15 percent of the total bill. The tip should reflect the standard of service, so there is no need to tip at all if the service is substandard. In bars drinks are often brought to the table and here, as well, bar staff should always be tipped.

Credit cards

It is virtually essential to have at least one credit card when traveling in Canada. Giving a card number is usually the only way to reserve hotels rooms. The most commonly accepted cards are Visa, Mastercard, Diners Club, and American Express.

PRICES

HOTELS
An indication of the cost of a double room without breakfast is given by $ signs.

$$$$$	Over $280
$$$$	$200–$280
$$$	$120–$200
$$	$80–$120
$	Under $80

RESTAURANTS
An indication of the cost of a three-course dinner without drinks is given by $ signs.

$$$$$	Over $80
$$$$	$50–$80
$$$	$35–$50
$$	$20–$35
$	Under $20

MARITIMES

Maritime hospitality eschews formality in favor of a warm and friendly atmosphere. The local shellfish and fish—lobster, mussels, salmon, scallops, oysters—are outstanding. Be careful not to mistake St. John's, Nfld. for Saint John, N.B.

B&B and Country Inns Association of P.E.I., www.bandbpei.com

FREDERICTON, N.B.

🏨 DELTA FREDERICTON
$$$
225 WOODSTOCK RD.
TEL 506/457-7000 or
888/462-8800
www.deltafredericton.com
Award-winning property bordering the majestic Saint John River and featuring elegant French country decor, situated just five minutes from the city core.
🛏 223 🅿 🔁 🖥 🏊 🏋
🚫 All major cards

🏨 CARRIAGE HOUSE INN
$$
230 UNIVERSITY AVE.
TEL 506/452-9924
www.carriagehouse-inn.net
A Victorian mansion refitted in 1987 and furnished with antiques. Delicious made-from-scratch breakfasts are served in the glassed-in solarium.
🛏 10 🅿 🖥 🚫 All major cards

🍴 LUNA PIZZA
$
168 DUNDONALD ST.
TEL 506/455-4020
Enjoy the enormous portions of Caesar salad, pizza, pasta, steak, and seafood. In fine weather you can dine on the outdoor terrace.
🍽 110 🅿 🖥 🚫 All major cards

MONCTON, N.B.

🏨 RAMADA PLAZA CRYSTAL PALACE
$$
499 PAUL ST., DIEPPE
TEL 506/858-8584
www.crystalpalacehotel.com
This property in suburban Dieppe has a dozen elaborate theme rooms, of which the "Victorian fantasy" is by far the most popular. There are also plenty of regular guest rooms.
🛏 115 🅿 🔁 🖥 🏊
🚫 AE, MC, V

🏨 HOTEL DELTA BEAUSÉJOUR
$$
750 MAIN ST.
TEL 506/854-4344 or
888/351-7666
www.deltabeausejour.ca
Downtown, contemporary property with country touches and views of the river. The elegant Windjammer Restaurant serves contemporary cuisine.
🛏 310 🅿 🔁 🖥 🏊 🏋
🚫 All major cards

🍴 FISHERMAN'S PARADISE
$$
330 DIEPPE BLVD., DIEPPE, MONCTON
TEL 506/859-4388
This is a popular restaurant specializing in local dishes, including a selection of fish and shellfish.
🍽 350 🚫 All major cards.

🍴 PASTALLI PASTA HOUSE
$$
611 MAIN ST.
TEL 506/383-1050
An inexpensive Italian restaurant that serves a wide variety of pizzas and pastas.
🍽 54 🚫 All major cards

ST. ANDREWS, N.B.

🏨 THE FAIRMONT ALGONQUIN
$$$$
184 ADOLPHUS ST.
TEL 506/529-8823 or
800/441-1414
www.fairmont.com
A stately "castle-by-the-sea," this famous hotel in neo-Tudor style was built in 1889 and rebuilt after a fire in 1914. Fully renovated with a modern wing, it dominates this charming and tranquil New Brunswick community. Golf course, tennis courts, and whale watching. Full restaurant facilities.
🛏 234 rooms and suites 🅿
🔁 🏊 🚫 All major cards

🏨 SEASIDE BEACH RESORT
$$
339 WATER ST.
TEL 506/529-3846 or
800/506-8677
www.seaside.nb.ca
Charming rustic housekeeping chalets beside Passama-quoddy Bay with waterfront boardwalk and barbecue pits. Magnificent views and sunsets. Freshly caught fish for sale nearby. Note—no swimming.
🛏 24 🅿 🕐 Some chalets closed Jan.–March 🚫 MC, V

SAINT JOHN, N.B.

🏨 SAINT JOHN HILTON
$$$
1 MARKET SQ.
TEL 506/693-8484 or
800/561-8282
www.hilton.com
With the majority of rooms overlooking the harbor, this waterfront hotel is connected to shopping via the inside walkway network. The Turn of the Tide restaurant specializes in Bay of Fundy lobster and salmon.
🛏 197 🅿 🔁 🖥 🏊 🏋
🚫 All major cards

🏨 SHADOW LAWN COUNTRY INN
$$
3180 ROTHESAY RD.
TEL 506/847-7539 or
800/561-4166
www.selectinns.ca

HOTELS & RESTAURANTS

Old Victorian home located in a genteel suburb 15 minutes from downtown. Elegant dining room specializes in seafood dishes such as salmon en croûte.

🛈 10 🅿 🚻 🅰 All major cards

🍴 D'AMICO
$$
33 CANTERBURY ST.
TEL 506/648-2377
This downtown restaurant offers authentic Italian cuisine. The pizzas from the wood-burning oven are excellent.

🍽 100 🅰 All major cards

🍴 MEXICALI ROSA'S
$
88 PRINCE WILLIAM ST.
TEL 506/652-5252
California-Mexican dishes such as chimichangas are served up with flair in an adobe room that looks and feels as if it is straight out of New Mexico. Fixed-price menu.

🍽 92 🅿 🅰 All major cards

BAY FORTUNE P.E.I.

🏨 INN AT BAY FORTUNE
$$$
RTE. 310
TEL 902/687-3745 or
860/563-6090 (OFF SEASON)
www.innatbayfortune.com
This inn with stunning views of Fortune Harbor and the Northumberland Strait was once home to Broadway playwright Elmer Harris and later to Canadian actress Colleen Dewhurst. Superb restaurant (dinner only; fixed-price menu available),

🛈 18 🕓 Closed mid-Oct.–late May 🅰 MC, V

BRACKLEY BEACH, P.E.I.

🍴 DUNES CAFE
$$
RTE. 15
TEL 902/672-1883 (IN SEASON ONLY)
Dine on local produce, seafood, and great desserts

while overlooking the dunes of Covehead Bay outside Prince Edward Island National Park.

🍽 53 to 75 🅿 🕓 Closed Oct.–May 🅰 AE, MC, V

CHARLOTTETOWN, P.E.I.

🏨 RODD CHARLOTTETOWN
$$$$
75 KENT ST.
TEL 902/894-7371 or
800/565-7633
www.roddhotelsandresorts.com
Centrally located and oozing old-fashioned charm. The Victorian furnishings include crystal chandeliers and plenty of wood.

🛈 115 🅿 🛗 🚻 🏊 📺 🅰 All major cards

🏨 DUNDEE ARMS
$$
200 POWNAL ST.
TEL 902/892-2496
www.dundeearms.com
Two contrasting styles of accommodation available under one management; choose from a cozy Victorian inn or a 1956 drive-up motel.

🛈 22 🅿 🚻 🅰 AE, MC, V

🏨 PRINCE EDWARD DELTA HOTEL
$$$
18 QUEEN ST.
TEL 902/566-2222 or
866/894-1203
www.deltaprinceedward.com
A modern property situated right on the waterfront, with a spectacular lobby complete with a towering waterfall. The majority of rooms have harbor views.

🛈 211 🅿 🛗 🚻 🏊 📺 🅰 All major cards

🍴 OFF BROADWAY
$$
125 SYDNEY ST.
TEL 902/566-4620
Fine dining in Olde Charlottetown. Private booths and well-priced continental cooking featuring steak,

seafood, crêpes, and excellent homemade desserts.

🍽 50 🅿 🚻 🅰 All major cards

🍴 THE SELKIRK
$$
PRINCE EDWARD HOTEL
18 QUEEN ST.
TEL 902/894-1208
Sophisticated menu highlights regional produce and seafood. Live piano music and comfortable wing chairs.

🍽 126 🅿 🚻 🅰 All major cards

TYNE VALLEY, P.E.I.

🍴 THE LANDING
$$
RTE. 167
TEL 902/831-3138
This popular oyster house and pub offers a diverse menu with fresh seafood such as Malpeque oysters, lobster, mussels, and quahogs predominating. They also serve Island draft beer.

🕓 Closed mid-Oct.–mid-May 🅰 All major cards

CHESTER, N.S.

🍴 THE GALLEY
$
130 MARINA RD.
TEL 902/275-4700
Fresh fish from local waters and seafood chowder are menu highlights at this nautical-themed eatery on Mahone Bay popular with sailors and yachters. Reservations strongly recommended.

🍽 100 🅿 🕓 Closed Nov.–March. 🚻 🅰 All major cards

DIGBY, N.S.

🏨 PINES RESORT HOTEL
$$$$
SHORE RD.
TEL 902/245-2511 or
800/667-4637
www.signatureresorts.com
Elegant hotel and attractive cottages on wooded site

overlooking Digby Gut. Walking trails, golf, and tennis courts. Close to ferry to Saint John, N.B. For Annapolis Dining Room see below.

🛈 83 (lodge), 30 cottages (61 rooms) 🅿 🕭 Closed mid-Oct.–mid-May 🅰 All major cards

🍽 ANNAPOLIS ROOM
$$$$
PINES RESORT HOTEL
TEL 902/245-2511 or
800/667-4637
The main dining room at the Pines Resort overlooks the Annapolis Basin. It features local seafood, notably the prized Digby scallop caught just offshore and served in a number of innovative ways. Reservations suggested for dinner and Sunday brunch.

🍴 180 🅿 🕭 Closed mid-Oct.–mid-May 🅰 All major cards

HALIFAX, N.S.

🏨 DELTA HALIFAX
$$$
1990 BARRINGTON ST.
TEL 902/425-6700 or
800/268-1133
www.deltahalifax.com
Large rooms with stunning harbor views distinguish this well-located property.

🛈 299 🅿 🖨 🅰 🌊 🛐 🅰 All major cards

🏨 CASINO NOVA SCOTIA HOTEL
$$$–$$$$$
1919 UPPER WATER ST.
TEL 902/421-1700 or
888/782-9439
www.casinonovascotiahotel.com
This waterfront hotel is linked to the casino. Historic location, modern amenities.

🛈 325 🅿 🖨 🅰 🌊 🛐 🅰 All major cards

🏨 THE HALLIBURTON
$$$
5184 MORRIS ST.
TEL 902/420-0658
www.thehalliburton.com
Three 19th-century town-

houses seamlessly renovated. Two blocks from the water.

🛈 29 🅿 🅰 🅰 All major cards

🍽 GEORGIO'S RESTAURANT
$$
PRINCE GEORGE HOTEL
1725 MARKET ST.
TEL 902/425-1986
A fusion of different cuisines is offered in this restaurant in the Prince George Hotel, but Asian predominates. Try the Thai scallops, rack of lamb, or pork tenderloin and finish your meal with one of the fabulous desserts.

🍴 78 🅿 🅰 🅰 All major cards

🍽 MACASKILL'S RESTAURANT
$$
88 ALDERNEY DR.
DARTMOUTH FERRY TERMINAL BUILDING
TEL 902/466-3100
Romantic dining room overlooking Halifax Harbor. Local ingredients are used to create a selection of seafood, chicken, beef, and pasta dishes.

🍴 150 🅿 🕭 Closed L Sat.–Sun. 🅰 🅰 All major cards

🍽 SALTY'S ON THE WATERFRONT
$$
1869 UPPER WATER ST.
TEL 902/423-6818
The views from floor-to-ceiling windows overlooking Privateer's Wharf compete for attention with the skillfully prepared fish, pasta, and steak dishes. The premier dessert—a Belgian chocolate mousse served over a white chocolate praline crust—is justifiably famous.

🍴 120 🅿 🅰 🅰 All major cards

INGONISH, N.S.

🏨 KELTIC LODGE
$$$$
MIDDLE HEAD PENINSULA,
INGONISH BEACH

TEL 902/285-2880 or
800/565-0444
www.signatureresorts.com
Spectacular location on a peninsula commanding views of mountains and sea in all directions. Situated on the scenic Cabot Trail in part of Cape Breton Highlands National Park. Close to hiking trails good for viewing sea birds, famous golf course, whale watching, and ski center in winter.

🛈 32 (lodge), 10 cottages (30 rooms) 🅿 🕭 Closed late Oct.–mid-May 🅰 🌊 🅰 All major cards

🍽 PURPLE THISTLE ROOM
$$$
KELTIC LODGE
INGONISH BEACH
TEL 902/285-2880 or
800/565-0444
Seafood stars on the menu of this eatery perched on the cliffs in the middle of the Cabot Trail in Cape Breton Highlands National Park.

🍴 160 🅿 🕭 Closed late Oct.–mid-May 🅰 🅰 AE, D, DC

LISCOMB MILLS, N.S.

🏨 LISCOMBE LODGE
$$$$
LISCOMB MILLS,
GUYSBOROUGH COUNTY
TEL 902/779-2307 or
800/665-6343
www.signatureresorts.com
On the Liscomb River near Chedabucto Bay, this modern lodge is a perfect retreat for nature lovers. Facilities include a marina, canoe and bicycle rentals, and tennis.

🛈 68 units (lodge and cottages) 🅿 🕭 Closed mid-Oct.–mid-May 🌊 🅰 All major cards

NEWFOUNDLAND

Fellow Canadians like to tease Newfoundlanders about eating cod's tongues and seal flipper pie, but the

---

commitment to fresh seasonal food is no laughing matter. Sadly, cod is no longer widely available.

CAPE ONION

🏨 TICKLE INN
$
R.R. I
TEL 709/452-4321 (JUNE–SEPT.)
or 709/739-5503
www.tickleinn.net
Inexpensive dishes are served in the dining room of this renovated fisherman's house, just a 25-minute drive from the L'Anse aux Meadows National Historic Site.
🛏 4 🅿️ 🕐 Closed Oct.–May 🍴 MC, V

CORNER BROOK

🍴 THE CARRIAGE HOUSE & THE WINE CELLAR
$$
GLYNMILL INN, RTE. I
TEL 709/634-5181 or
800/563-4400
The Tudor-style Glynmill Inn offers a choice of restaurants. The family-oriented Carriage House features Newfoundland specialties such as fish cakes, cod tongues, and desserts made with local partridge-berries and baked apples. Tucked away in the basement, the Wine Cellar serves char-grilled steaks and seafood—reservations recommended.
🍴 80 🅿️ 🕐 Wine Cellar closed Sun. 🍴 AE, MC, V

GROS MORNE NATIONAL PARK

🏨 SUGAR HILL INN
$$$
115–129 SEXTON RD.
NORRIS POINT
TEL 709/458-2147
www.sugarhillinn.nf.ca
An enchanting inn with cathedral ceilings and modern conveniences; the dining room, for guests only, specializes in health-conscious gourmet meals. Sea kayaking and guided wilderness hikes available.

🛏 7 🅿️ 🕐 Closed
Nov.–Feb. 🍴 AE, MC, V

ST. JOHN'S

🏨 DELTA ST. JOHN'S
$$$$
120 NEW GOWER ST.
TEL 709/739-6404 or
800/263-1133
www.deltahotels.com
Close to the business and entertainment districts, this convention hotel has special amenities in its guest rooms.
🛏 403 🅿️ 🍽 🍴 🚇 🛗
🍴 All major cards

🏨 FAIRMONT NEWFOUNDLAND
$$$$
CAVENDISH SQ.
TEL 709/726-4980 or
800/441-1414
www.fairmont.com/newfoundland
Comfortable, modern rooms overlooking the harbor. Fine dining in the award-winning Cabot Club; Sunday brunch at the Bona Vista Restaurant is a local tradition.
🛏 301 🅿️ 🍽 🍴 🚇 🛗
🍴 All major cards

🏨 COMPTON HOUSE BED & BREAKFAST
$$
26 WATERFORD BRIDGE RD.
TEL 709/739-5789
Charming property within walking distance of down-town; rooms are uniquely furnished and can include whirlpool, fireplace, kitchen facilities, or sunroom.
🛏 11 🅿️ 🍴 All major cards

🍴 THE CELLAR RESTAURANT
$$
152 WATER ST.
TEL 709/579-8900
Continental fine dining with local influences. Excellent wine list with 250 labels. Despite its name, it's on the fourth floor. Reservations essential.
🍴 100 🅿️ 🕐 Closed L Sat. & Sun. 🍴 All major cards

🍴 THE HUNGRY FISHERMAN
$$
MURRAY PREMISES,
5 BECK'S COVE
TEL 709/726-5791
Delights of the deep as well as lamb, chicken, veal, and steak. Seafood pot in tomato sauce with filo pastry is a best-seller, as is the chocolate-rum "screech" pie.
🍴 75 🅿️ 🍴 🍴 All major cards

🍴 BLUE ON WATER RESTAURANT
$$$
319 WATER ST.
TEL 709/754-2583
Located in the hotel of the same name, this popular restaurant serves the freshest local and imported seafood in the city. The presentations are original and distinctly gourmet. Reservations suggested.
🍴 34 🍴 All major cards

QUÉBEC

Gracious, European-style hospitality abounds in La Belle Province. English is widely spoken in Montréal and Québec; you may have to brush up on your high school French to help smooth things over outside the major cities. But what could be more *charmant* than ordering a *tartine de jambon,* even if it is simply a ham sandwich?

AYER'S CLIFF

🏨 RIPPLECOVE INN
$$$$
700 RIPPLECOVE RD.
TEL 819/838-4296 or
800/668-4296
www.ripplecove.com
Attractive inn at south end of Lake Massawippi set in lovely gardens. Finely furnished interior, dining room, summer terrace.
🛈 35 🅿 📶 🏊 🅰 AE, MC, V

BAIE-ST.-PAUL

🏨 AUBERGE LA MAISON OTIS
$$$
23 RUE ST.-JEAN-BAPTISTE
TEL 418/435-2255 or
800/267-2254
www.maisonotis.com
Quiet, romantic hostelry offering rooms with verandas and/or fireplaces. Dining room serves traditional French fare with local touches.
🛈 30 🅿 📶 🏊 🅰 MC, V

KNOWLTON

🏨 AUBERGE LAKEVIEW INN
$$$
50 RUE VICTORIA
TEL 450/243-6183 or
800/661-6183
www.aubergelakeviewinn.com
Splendid example of Victorian architecture built in 1874, with attractively renovated rooms within walking distance of the boutiques and antique stores. Dining room, pub, garden terrace in summer. Trees block the view of the lake.
🛈 28 🅿 📶 🏊 🅰 All major cards

LAURENTIANS

🏨 CHÂTEAU MONT-TREMBLANT
$$$$$
3045 CHEMIN DE LA CHAPELLE, MONT TREMBLANT
TEL 819/681-7000 or
800/441-1414
www.fairmont.com
Modern hotel decorated with old-fashioned wood paneling and stained glass. Resort activities available year round. Heated whirlpools.
🛈 316 🅿 📶 🏊 🅰 📶 All major cards

🏨 LE CHANTECLER
$$$$
1474 CHEMIN CHANTECLER, STE.-ADÈLE
TEL 450/229-3555 or
888/916-1616
www.lechantecler.com
Twenty-two downhill-ski runs begin right at the door of this comfortable hotel. In summer there is golf, tennis, a beach and boating on Lac Rond.
🛈 216 🅿 📶 🏊 🛈 167 rooms 🏊 📶

🏨 AUBERGE DU COQ DE MONTAGNE
$$
2151 CHEMIN DU VILLAGE, MONT TREMBLANT
TEL 819/425-3380 or
800/895-3380
www.recreation-tremblant.com
Cozy inn on Lac Moore with modern amenities and year-round activities; Nino & Kay's Restaurant offers five-course Italian feasts for under $30 per person.
🛈 16 🅿 🕐 Restaurant closed mid-Oct.–mid-Nov. 📶 🅰 All major cards

🍴 BISTRO À CHAMPLAIN
$$$$
75 CHEMIN MASSON, STE-MARGUERITE-DU-LAC-MASSON
TEL 450/228-4988
French restaurant famous for the wines available by the glass and artwork by Jean-Paul Riopelle. Wine cellar tours are

offered, and reservations are recommended.
🍽 150 🅿 🕐 Closed Mon.–Wed. in winter 📶 🅰 All major cards

🍴 L'EAU À LA BOUCHE
$$$
3003 BLVD. STE.-ADÈLE, STE.-ADÈLE
TEL 450/229-2991
Top-rated dining room show-cases innovative seasonal cuisine and updated traditional Québec dishes; 25 guest rooms available. Reservations recommended.
🍽 75 🅿 🕐 Closed L 📶 🅰 All major cards

🍴 LA CLEF DES CHAMPS
$$
875 CHEMIN PIERRE-PÉLADEAU, STE.-ADÈLE
TEL 450/229-2857
Romantic countryside eatery offering elegant French cuisine. Focus on wild game and locally produced foie gras. Reservations essential.
🍽 50 🅿 🕐 Closed L Mon. 📶 🅰 All major cards

MONTEBELLO

🏨 CHÂTEAU MONTEBELLO
$$$$
392 NOTRE-DAME ST.
TEL 819/423-6341 or
800/441-1414
www.fairmont.com
This extraordinary star-shape wooden structure was built in the 1930s from 10,000 red cedar logs, as a private club. Today a Fairmont resort, it stands on secluded grounds beside the Ottawa River. Golf course, tennis courts, walking trails, and cross-country ski trails. Renowned cuisine.
🛈 214 🅿 📶 🏊 🅰 📶 All major cards

MONTRÉAL

🏨 BONAVENTURE HILTON
$$$$
900 DE LA GAUCHETIÈRE

OUEST
TEL 514/878-2332 or
800/445-8667
www.hiltonmontreal.com
Built on the upper floors of
the huge Place Bonaventure
retail and wholesale center,
this downtown hotel has
extensive roof gardens, an
exterior heated pool used
even in midwinter, and views
of the surrounding city.
ⓘ 395 🅿 🚇 Place
Bonaventure 🛗 🚭 🚶
🃏 All major cards

🏨 LE CENTRE SHERATON
$$$$
1201 BLVD. RENÉ-LÉVESQUE
OUEST
TEL 514/878-2000 or
800/325-3535
www.sheraton.com
Business types and tourists
alike appreciate the downtown location and little extras
provided by this chain
property, such as coffee-
makers in the rooms.
ⓘ 825 🅿 🚇 Peel 🛗 🚭
🚶 🃏 All major cards

🏨 DELTA MONTRÉAL
$$$$
475 AVE. DU PRÉSIDENT-
KENNEDY
TEL 514/286-1986 or
877/286-1986
www.deltamontreal.com
Centrally located modern
hotel with spacious rooms,
most with balconies. Children's creativity and activity
center.
ⓘ 453 + 6 suites 🅿
🚇 Place des Arts 🛗 🚭
🚶 🚴 🃏 All major
cards

🏨 INTER-CONTINENTAL
MONTRÉAL
$$$$
360 RUE ST.-ANTOINE OUEST
TEL 514/987-9900 or
800/361-3600
www.montreal.intercontinental
.com
A luxury property close to
Old Montréal offering
spacious guest rooms overlooking either the downtown

or the waterfront.
ⓘ 357 🅿 🚇 Square
Victoria 🛗 🚭 🚴 🚶
🃏 All major cards

🏨 LOEWS HÔTEL VOGUE
$$$$
1425 RUE DE LA MONTAGNE
TEL 514/285-5555 or
800/465-6654
www.loewshotels.com
Chic and central, this hostelry
features pristine duvets in the
guest rooms and decadently
furnished bathrooms.
ⓘ 142 🅿 🚇 Guy 🛗 🚭
🚶 🃏 All major cards

🏨 MAISON PIERRE DU
CALVET
$$$$
405 RUE BONSECOURS
TEL 514/282-1725 or
866/544-1725
www.pierreducalvet.ca
Romantic European-style
auberge in the heart of Old
Montréal, partially located in a
French-regime house built in
1725. Rooms are furnished
with antiques and heirlooms.
Breakfast is served in the
Victorian conservatory.
Cossetted comfort. For the
Pierre du Calvet Restaurant
see p. 356.
ⓘ 10 🅿 🚇 Champ de
Mars 🚭 🃏 All major cards

🏨 OMNI MONT-ROYAL
$$$$
1050 RUE SHERBROOKE OUEST
TEL 514/284-1110 or
800/843-6664
www.omnihotels.com
English furniture and chintz
mark the guest rooms of this
property, favored by
corporate types during the
week. The downstairs Zen
restaurant serves excellent
Chinese cooking.
ⓘ 300 🅿 🚇 Peel 🛗 🚭
🚴 🚶 🃏 All major cards

🏨 RITZ-CARLTON
$$$$
1228 RUE SHERBROOKE OUEST
TEL 514/842-4212 or
800/363-0366
www.ritzcarlton.com

Personal attention is the
hallmark of this European-style
hostelry. Rooms mix old-world
style with modern touches.
ⓘ 229 🅿 🚇 Peel 🛗 🚭
🚶 🃏 All major cards

🏨 CHÂTEAU VERSAILLES
$$$
1659 RUE SHERBROOKE OUEST
TEL 514/933-3611 or
888/933-8111
www.versailleshotels.com
Choose between rooms in a
modern tower or in an
Edwardian townhouse; either
way, the service is impeccable.
Limited access for disabled.
ⓘ 177 🅿 🚇 Guy-
Concordia 🛗 🚭 🚶 🃏 All
major cards

🏨 FAIRMONT QUEEN
ELIZABETH
$$$
900 BLVD. RENÉ-LÉVESQUE
OUEST
TEL 514/861-3511 or
800/441-1414
www.fairmont.com
Archetypal downtown railway
hotel built over the Central
Station and connected into
the maze of Montréal's
underground city. Although
some rooms have been
renovated, facilities in others
are rather tight. The hotel is
excellently located for
shopping and restaurants.
ⓘ 963 + 57 suites 🅿
🚇 Place Bonaventure 🛗
🚭 🚴 🚶 🃏 All major
cards

🏨 HÔTEL DE LA
MONTAGNE
$$$
1430 RUE DE LA MONTAGNE
TEL 514/288-5656 or
800/361-6262
www.hoteldelamontagne.com
Rococo meets art nouveau in
this quirky hostelry. Rooms
are large and comfortable,
their decor much tamer than
that of the flamboyant lobby.
ⓘ 134 🅿 🚇 Peel 🛗 🚭
🚴 🃏 All major cards

HOTELS & RESTAURANTS

HOTEL NELLIGAN
$$$
106 SAINT-PAUL OUEST
TEL 514/788-2040 or
877/788-2040
www.hotelnelligan.com
A delightful boutique hotel in a renovated 19th-century building in Old Montréal. It features stone and brick walls, an interior atrium with fountain and bar, and the elegant restaurant Verses. Its name refers to Québec poet Emile Nelligan, whose verses are transcribed on the walls.
🛏 64 🅿 🚇 Place d'Armes 🚇
🆎 All major cards

HYATT REGENCY
$$$
4 COMPLEXE DESJARDINS &
1255 JEANNE-MANCE ST.
TEL 514/982-1234 or
800/361-8234
www.montrealregency.hyatt.com
Built atop the Complexe Desjardins, this ultramodern property boasts smart guest rooms with designer furniture.
🛏 600 🅿 🚇 Place des Arts 🚇 🆎 🏊 🆎 All major cards

L'APPARTEMENT-IN-MONTRÉAL
$$
455 RUE SHERBROOKE OUEST
TEL 514/284-3634 or
800/363-3010
www.appartementhotel.com
Well-priced studios with kitchenette, television, and telephone. Maid service available and 24-hour staff.
🛏 126 🅿 🚇 Place des Arts or McGill 🚇 🆎 🏊 🆎 All major cards

AUBERGE DE LA FONTAINE
$$
1301 RUE RACHEL EST
TEL 514/597-0166 or
800/597-0597
www.aubergedelafontaine.com
Charming small hotel in a renovated Victorian house beside La Fontaine Park in the city's east end. Tranquil yet close to vibrant rue Saint-Denis. Breakfast, no restaurant, kitchen for snacks.
🛏 21 🅿 🚇 Mont-Royal 🚇 🆎 All major cards

AUBERGE DU VIEUX-PORT
$$
97 RUE DE LA COMMUNE EST
TEL 514/876-0081 or
888/660-7678
www.aubergeduvieuxport.com
Beautifully renovated warehouse in Old Montréal offers interesting rooms with stone and brick walls and massive wooden beams. Fine dining at Les Remparts Restaurant.
🛏 38 🚇 Place d'Armes 🚇 🆎 All major cards

HÔTEL LE SAINT-ANDRÉ
$$
1285 RUE ST.-ANDRÉ
TEL 514/849-7070 or
800/265-7071
www.hotelsaintandre.ca
Award-winning hotel located close to historic Old Montréal and the Latin Quarter.
🛏 61 🅿 🚇 Berri-UQAM 🚇 🆎 All major cards

LE JARDIN DU RITZ
$$$$$
1228 RUE SHERBROOKE OUEST
IN RITZ-CARLTON HOTEL
TEL 514/842-4212
Exquisite setting, excellent food, impeccable service, high prices. An added attraction is the cute ducklings on the pond in the center of the garden. Reservations essential. Also open for breakfast.
🍴 125 🕐 Closed Oct.–mid-May 🚇 Peel 🆎 All major cards

BEAVER CLUB
$$$$$
HÔTEL REINE ELIZABETH, 900 BLVD. RENÉ LÉVESQUE OUEST
TEL 514/861-3511
Classic dishes such as roast beef *au jus* and duck *à l'orange* are served in this former fur traders' club; the old boys' ambience lives on with the jacket and tie recommendation for men.
🍴 200 🅿 🕐 Closed Sun. & L Sat. 🚇 Bonaventure 🚇 🆎 All major cards

TOQUÉ
Consistently rated as the city's top restaurant, Toqué! (the name means "completely nuts" as well as referring to the hat chefs wear) never ceases to amaze and delight with its original dishes and presentations. Specializing in market cuisine, the menu changes every day but the famous duck foie gras is often featured as well as superlative desserts. To fully appreciate the cuisine, try the chef's sampler menu of seven different courses. Reservations recommended.
$$$$
900 PLACE JEAN-PAUL-RIOPELLE
TEL 514/499-2084
www.restaurant-toque.com
🍴 95 🚇 Place Victoria 🕐 Closed Sun.–Mon. 🆎 All major cards

AUBERGE SAINT-GABRIEL
$$$
426 SAINT-GABRIEL, MONTRÉAL
TEL 514/878-3561
Located in a set of stone buildings, some dating back to the 18th century, the Auberge Saint-Gabriel claims to be the oldest inn in North America. It is certainly charming with its open fireplaces in winter and outdoor terrace in summer. The food tends to be French with a few local Québécois dishes.
🍴 450 🚇 Place d'Armes 🆎 All major cards

BONAPARTE
$$$
443 RUE ST.-FRANÇOIS-XAVIER
TEL 514/844-4368
Exposed brick walls create a warm atmosphere for enjoy-

ing contemporary French cuisine in the heart of Old Montréal. Try the escargots, lobster, or scallops.

⊞ 120 🅿 🚇 Place d'Armes 🛗 🚫 All major cards

🍴 GIBBYS
$$$
298 PLACE D'YOUVILLE
TEL 514/282-1837
Occupying part of the historic d'Youville Stables built in 1800, the restaurant features stone walls in dining rooms on several levels. Famous as a steak house, Gibbys also serves seafood and home-made desserts. Outdoor bar in summer. Reservations recommended.

⊞ 450 🅿 🕐 Closed L 🚇 Place Victoria 🛗 🚫 All major cards

🍴 LA MARÉE
$$$
404 PLACE JACQUES CARTIER
TEL 514/861-9794
In the heart of Old Montréal on busy Place Jacques Cartier, this well-known establishment offers a touch of class in an otherwise touristy area. Formal service in Louis XIII-style dining room, and attractive terrace in summer months. Wonderful seafood. Reservations recommended.

⊞ 90 🅿 🕐 Closed L Sat.–Sun. in winter 🚇 Champ de Mars 🛗 🚫 All major cards

🍴 MILOS
$$$
5357 AVE. DE PARC
TEL 514/272-3522
High-end Greek cooking featuring fresh fish and seafood modestly seasoned and grilled to perfection. Meat-eaters are also well treated in the relaxed setting.

⊞ 180 🅿 🕐 Closed L Sat.–Sun. 🚇 Laurier 🛗 🚫 AE, MC, V

🍴 PIERRE DU CALVET
$$$
405 RUE BONSECOURS

TEL 514/282-1725
Good French food with elegant Victorian decor and huge fireplace (winter) in Old Montréal. Reservations recommended.

ⓘ 100 🅿 🚇 Champ de Mars 🕐 Closed L 🛗 🚫 All major cards

🍴 LES CAPRICES DE NICHOLAS
$$$
2072 RUE DRUMMOND
TEL 514/282-9790
Romantic interior garden and an extensive wine list enhance such dishes as fresh foie gras and wonderful cheeses.

⊞ 65 🅿 🕐 Closed L 🚇 Peel 🛗 🚫 All major cards

🍴 BORIS BISTRO
$$
465 RUE MCGILL
TEL 514/848-9575
At the western end of Old Montréal, this fashionable bistro with its delightful summer terrace features items such as smoked fish, salmon tartare, grilled trout, duck salad, and local sausages. Try the passion mousse for dessert. Be prepared to wait for a lunchtime seat during summer.

⊞ 100 🚇 Place Victoria 🚫 All major cards

🍴 LE BOURLINGUEUR
$$
363 SAINT-FRANÇOIS-XAVIER AT SAINT-PAUL OUEST
TEL 514/845-3646
Simple, almost plain, this charming Old Montréal eatery regularly turns out good food (especially fish dishes) at reasonable prices. Poached salmon is a specialty. Busy at lunchtime.

⊞ 100 🚇 Place Victoria or Place d'Armes 🚫 MC, V

🍴 CHEZ LA MÈRE MICHEL
$$
1209 RUE GUY
TEL 514/934-0473

Excellent French cooking in a converted mansion; enclosed garden with spectacular art nouveau tiled walls. Specialties include coq au vin and buffalo tournedos. Try the remarkable Grand Marnier soufflé.

⊞ 90 🅿 🕐 Closed L Sat. & Sun.–Mon. 🚇 Guy 🛗 🚫 All major cards

🍴 L'EXPRESS
$$
3927 RUE ST.-DENIS
TEL 514/845-5333
Good, simple food arrives quickly in this Parisian-style bistro, complete with tiled floors, mirrored walls, and stamped tin ceiling. Beware, there is no sign out front.

⊞ 85 🅿 🚇 Sherbrooke 🛗 🚫 All major cards

🍴 FOURQUET FOURCHETTE
$$
265 SAINT-ANTOINE OUEST, IN THE PALAIS DES CONGRÈS
TEL 514/789-6370
Run by a small micro-brewery, this restaurant features local cuisine, both traditional and Amerindian, all washed down with their specialty beers. Reservations recommended at lunchtime, especially if

there's a big convention in town.

⊞ 250 🅿 Place d'Armes
🚫 All major cards

🍽 MEDITERRANEO GRILL & WINE BAR

$$

3500 BLVD. ST.-LAURENT
TEL 514/844-0027

Note the absence of traditional pasta dishes at this nouvelle Mediterranean boîte. Partake instead of grilled tuna, *magret de canard,* and rack of lamb. Reservations essential.

⊞ 150 🅿 🕒 Closed L
🚭 St.-Laurent 🚫 AE, MC, V

🍽 MOISHE'S STEAKHOUSE

$$

3961 BLVD. ST.-LAURENT
TEL 514/845-3509

Aged, marbled hunks of beef, complimentary pickles and coleslaw in this family steakhouse with enormous portions. Extensive wine list.

⊞ 200 🅿 🚭 St.-Laurent
🕒 Closed L Sat.–Sun. 🚫
🚫 All major cards

🍽 RESTAURANT LE CAVEAU

$$

2063 RUE VICTORIA
TEL 514/844-1624

Hidden away in the heart of downtown, this charming former town house offers French atmosphere and cuisine at reasonable prices.

⊞ 250 🅿 🚭 McGill 🚫 All major cards

🍽 BENS

$

990 BLVD. DE MAISONNEUVE OUEST
TEL 514/844-1000

Hand-cut smoked meat sandwiches, crunchy potato pancakes, and tangy coleslaw dished out in fifties-style cafeteria; check out those who've come before you on the wall-of-fame photo gallery.

⊞ 211 🚭 Peel 🚫 🚫 MC, V

🍽 SCHWARTZ'S DELICATESSEN

$

3895 BLVD. ST.-LAURENT
TEL 514/842-4813

Officially, this venerable eatery is named Montréal Hebrew Delicatessen, but everybody calls it Schwartz's. Brusque waiters and long lines do little to diminish the pleasures of smoked meat sandwiches, grilled rib-eye steaks, and velvety chicken livers.

⊞ 68 🅿 🚭 St.-Laurent 🚫
🚫 Cash only

NORTH HATLEY

🏨 MANOIR HOVEY

$$$$

575 CHEMIN HOVEY
TEL 819/842-2421 or
800/661-2421
www.manoirhovey.com

Antique-and-lace furnished rooms, some with fireplaces, overlooking Lac Massawippi. Restaurant, open to all, serves excellent French cuisine.

ⓘ 40 🅿 🏊 🏋 🚫 All major cards

QUÉBEC CITY

🏨 CHÂTEAU FRONTENAC

$$$$$

1 RUE DES CARRIÈRES
TEL 418/692-3861 or
800/441-1414
www.fairmont.com

This landmark hotel offers extensive amenities and excellent views. Sunday brunches are famous, and the fine dining room, Le Champlain, serves classic French cuisine.

ⓘ 618 🅿 🚮 🚫 🏊 🏋
🚫 All major cards

🏨 AUBERGE SAINT-ANTOINE

$$$$

8 RUE ST.-ANTOINE
TEL 418/692-2211 or
888/692-2211
www.saint-antoine.com

Charming inn located in an ancient shipping warehouse; modern furnishings mix with

antiques in rooms that offer river views or terraces.

ⓘ 95 🅿 🚮 🚫 🚫 All major cards

🏨 HÔTEL LOEWS LE CONCORDE

$$$

1225 COURS DU GÉNÉRAL MONTCALM
TEL 418/647-2222 or
800/463-5256 (CANADA) or
800/23LOEWS (U.S.)
www.loewshotels.com

Contemporary decor and a great location near the lively Grande Allée make this hotel popular among tourists and business types alike.

ⓘ 409 🅿 🚮 🚫 🏊 🏋
🚫 All major cards

🏨 QUÉBEC HILTON

$$$

1100 BLVD. RENÉ LÉVESQUE EST
TEL 418/647-2411 or
800/HILTONS (U.S.) or
800/447-2411 (CANADA)
www.hiltonquebec.com

Located just outside of the walled city, this property has ultramodern rooms with standard furnishings.

ⓘ 571 🅿 🚮 🚫 🏊 🏋
🚫 All major cards

🏨 HOTEL CLARENDON

$$$

57 RUE STE.-ANNE
TEL 418/692-2480 or
888/554-6001
www.hotelclarendon.com

Centrally located hotel with beautifully renovated rooms and a fine-dining restaurant, Le Charles Baillairgé (see below).

ⓘ 143 🅿 🚮 🚫
🚫 All major cards

🏨 L'HÔTEL DU CAPITOLE

$$$

972 RUE ST.-JEAN
TEL 418/694-4040 or
800/363-4040
www.lecapitole.com

Stars—the decorative kind—abound at this choice hostelry, built within the shell of an abandoned theater.

ⓘ 40 🅿 🚮 🚫 🚫 All major cards

🏨 L'AUBERGE DU QUARTIER
$$
170 GRANDE ALLÉE OUEST
TEL 418/525-9726
www.aubergeduquartier.com
Housed in an 1852 building outside the city walls, this inn offers cheerful rooms.
🛏 15 🅿 🛗 1 room 💳 All major cards

🏨 L'AUBERGE ST-LOUIS
$$
48 RUE ST-LOUIS
TEL 418/692-2424 or 888/692-4105
A central location with small guest rooms, minimalist furniture, and friendly service.
🛏 27, 14 with bath 🅿 💳 MC, V

🏨 LE CHÂTEAU DE PIERRE
$$
17 AVE. STE.-GENEVIÈVE
TEL 418-694-0429 or 888/694-0429
A renovated 1853 manor with ornate chandeliers and Victorian rooms, some of which have a balcony, fireplace, or vanity room. Rooms at the front overlook Governors' Park.
🛏 20 🅿 🛗 3 rooms 💳 AE, MC, V

🏨 HÔTEL CHÂTEAU BELLEVUE
$$
16 RUE DE LA PORTE
TEL 418/692-2573 or 800/463-2617
www.vieux-quebec.com
Comfortable accommodations in an excellent location just behind the Château Frontenac. Modern rooms vary considerably in size.
🛏 57 🅿 🔁 🛗 💳 All major cards

🏨 MANOIR D'AUTEUIL
$$
49 RUE D'AUTEUIL
TEL 418/694-1173
www.manoirdauteuil.com
Stunning art deco and art nouveau details make this

newly restored inn one of the most lavish in town.
🛏 16 🅿 🛗 9 rooms 💳 All major cards

🏨 MANOIR STE-GENEVIÈVE
$$
13 AVE. STE.-GENEVIÈVE
TEL 418/694-1666
Elaborate Victorian furnishings and genteel service create a country inn atmosphere in this 1880 building.
🛏 9 🅿 🛗 8 rooms 💳 All major cards

🍴 LE SAINT-AMOUR
$$$$
48 RUE STE.-URSULE
TEL 418/694-0667
Haute cuisine in a welcoming atmosphere. Specialties include seafood, fish, game, and luscious chocolate desserts. Interior garden, fine wine cellar.
🍽 150 🅿 🕐 Closed L Sat.–Sun. 💳 All major cards

🍴 AUX ANCIENS CANADIENS
$$$
34 RUE ST-LOUIS
TEL 418/692-1627
Traditional French-Canadian favorites such as *tourtière* and *fèves au lard* are showcased in an ancient stone house in the Upper Town.
🍽 115 🛗 💳 All major cards

🍴 LE CHARLES BAILLAIRGÉ
$$$
57 RUE STE.-ANNE
TEL 418/692-2480
Located in the Hotel Clarendon, this restaurant serves refined cuisine in a rich wood-paneled decor, accompanied by piano and chamber music.
🍽 125 🛗 💳 All major cards

🍴 LAURIE RAPHAËL
$$$
117 RUE DALHOUSIE
TEL 418/692-4555

Classical haute cuisine tweaked with international flavors. A toned-down room sets off such dishes as smoked sturgeon, freshwater crayfish, Atlantic salmon, quail, veal sweetbreads, and Alberta beef. Reservations essential.
🍽 90 🅿 🕐 Closed Sun.–Mon. 🛗 💳 All major cards

🍴 LE MARIE CLARISSE
$$$
12 RUE DU PETIT-CHAMPLAIN
TEL 418/692-0857
Singular seafood dishes, such as halibut with nuts and honey, star in this cozy restaurant located in an ancient building in the Lower Town; both lunch and dinner fixed-price menus are real bargains. Summer terrace.
🍽 48 🕐 Closed L Sat. & Sun. in winter 🛗 💳 All major cards

🍴 LE PARIS BREST
$$$
590 GRANDE-ALLÉE
TEL 418/529-2243
Well-executed French dishes with Californian touches served to a lively crowd seated in contemporary decor.
🍽 130 🅿 🕐 Closed L Sat. & Sun. 🛗 💳 All major cards

🍴 RESTAURANT LOUIS HÉBERT
$$$
668 GRANDE-ALLÉE
TEL 418/525-7812
Located in the middle of Québec's famous restaurant strip, this institution stands head and shoulders above its neighbors. The cuisine is basically French, the service is courteous and the decor is charming. Summer terrace.
🍽 100 🛗 💳 All major cards

🍴 L'ECHAUDÉ
$$
73 SAULT-AU-MATELOT
TEL 418/692-1299
A chic Lower Town bistro that

draws both locals and tourists with its dishes of game and fish. Summer terrace.
🍴 70 🕐 Closed L Sat. 🅢 All major cards

QUÉBEC CITY REGION

🍴 AUBERGE BAKER
$$$
8790 AVE. ROYALE, CHÂTEAU-RICHER
TEL 418/824-4478
Occupying a lovely old Québec house, this restaurant offers traditional Québec cuisine as well as some contemporary dishes. Summer terrace.
🍴 100 P 🕐 Closed L in winter 🅢 All major cards

🍴 MANOIR MONTMORENCY
$$
2490 AVE. ROYALE, BEAUPORT
TEL 418/663-3330
Although it is only open for Sunday brunch and service on the terrace in summer, this manoir has a spectacular site overlooking Montmorency Falls. Québec cuisine and produce are emphasized.
🍴 130 P 🕐 Sun. L only; closed Mon.-Sat. Oct.–May 🅢 🅢 All major cards

SAINT-GEORGES-DE-MALBAIE (GASPÉSIE)

🏨 FORT PRÉVEL
$$
2053 BLVD. DOUGLAS, PRÉVEL
TEL 418/368-2281 or 888/377-3835
www.sepaq.com
This resort motel at the tip of the Gaspé Peninsula occupies a former World War II military installation where heavy artillery faced the Atlantic to guard against German attack. Golf course, fine dining.
ℹ️ 58 P 🕐 Closed mid-Sept.–mid-June 🅢 🅢 All major cards

ST.-MARC SUR RICHELIEU

🍴 LES TROIS TILLEULS
$$$
290 RUE RICHELIEU
TEL 514/856-7787 or 800/263-2230
Traditional French preparations served at a 40-room inn overlooking the Richelieu River, about an hour from Montréal. Regional gourmet cuisine, including foie gras, duck, lamb, deer, and guinea fowl. Reservations essential for dinner. Limited access.
🍴 120 P 🅢 🅢 All major cards

ONTARIO

Ontario is one of the country's two wine regions (British Columbia is the other). The vineyards in the province's Niagara peninsula consistently produce excellent wines, some of which have won medals in world competition.

Federation of Ontario Bed and Breakfast Accommodations, 95 King St. W., Gananoque, ON K7G 2G2; www.fobba.com

Ontario Farm and Country Vacations Assoc., 8724 Wellington Rd. 18, R.R. 5, Belwood, ON N0B IJO; www.countryhosts.com

ALLISTON

🏨 NOTTAWASAGA INN
$$$$
6015 HWY. 89
TEL 705/435-5501 or 800/669-5501
www.nottawasagaresort.com
Large resort hotel on 475 acres. Golf course, cross-country skiing, and sports. Facilities for children and activiities.
ℹ️ 269 P 🅢 🅢 🅢 🅢 All major cards

ALTON

🏨 MILLCROFT INN
$$$
55 JOHN ST.
TEL 519/941-8111 or 800/383-3976
www.millcroft.com
Fine hostel made up in part of a converted knitting mill; the Mennonite villages of St. Jacobs and Elmira are 30 minutes away.
ℹ️ 50 P 🅢 🅢 🅢 🅢 All major cards

CAMBRIDGE

🏨 LANGDON HALL COUNTRY HOUSE
$$$–$$$$
I LANGDON DR.
TEL 519/740-2100 or 800/268-1898
www.langdonhall.ca
Magnificent Federal Revival mansion with top-notch amenities, close to Kitchener, Waterloo, and Stratford. The award-winning restaurant uses produce right from the kitchen garden.
ℹ️ 53 P 🕐 Closed 1st week Jan. 🅢 🅢 🅢 🅢 All major cards

COLLINGWOOD

🏨 BLUE MOUNTAIN INN
$$
R.R. 3
TEL 705/445-0231 or 877/445-0231
www.bluemountain.ca/lodging
The largest ski resort in Ontario offers outstanding golf in the summer. Chalets and condos also available.
ℹ️ 93 P 🅢 🅢 🅢 🅢 🅢 All major cards

ELORA

🏨 ELORA MILL
$$
77 MILL ST
TEL 519/846-9118 or 866/713-5672
www.eloramill.com
Converted mill with luxury rooms and superb dining.

Restaurant specialties include lamb, trout, apples, cheese, and maple syrup.

ⓘ 32 🅿 ⬌ Main building 🔲 🗝All major cards

HUNTSVILLE

🏨 DEERHURST RESORT
$$$
1235 DEERHURST DR.
TEL 705/789-6411 or 800/461-4393
www.deerhurstresort.com
Ultra-deluxe resort on 800 acres offering a selection of modern accommodations and year-round activities.

ⓘ 410 🅿 ⬌ 🔲 ⛵ 🗝
🗝All major cards

INGERSOLL

🏨 ELM HURST INN
$$$
415 HARRIS ST.
TEL 519/485-5321 or 800/561-5321
www.elmhurstinn.com
A short drive south of Stratford is this Victorian country inn with charming rooms, and access to a golf course and walking trails.

ⓘ 49 🅿 ⬌ 🔲 📺 🗝All major cards

MCKELLAR

SOMETHING SPECIAL

🏨 THE INN AT MANITOU
Luxurious shoreline resort on Lake Manitouwabing offering gourmet dining, top-notch tennis instruction, spa services, and summer music concerts. Meals included.

$$$$
CENTRE RD.
TEL 705/389-2171 (MAY–OCT.) or 800/571-8818
www.manitou-online.com

ⓘ 33 🅿 🕐Closed mid-Oct.–early May 🔲 ⛵ 📺
🗝All major cards

KINGSTON

🏨 HOLIDAY INN KINGSTON WATERFRONT
$$$
2 PRINCESS ST.
TEL 613/549-8400 or 800/465-4329
www.holiday-inn.com
Great location right on the waterfront with views of Lake Ontario activities.

ⓘ 195 🅿 ⬌ 🔲 ⛵
🗝All major cards

NIAGARA FALLS

🏨 VARIOUS HOTELS
$$$$$
In recent years, a number of the major hotel chains have constructed great tower blocks with rooms offering spectacular views of Niagara Falls. These rooms are extremely expensive. For details, contact Best Western, Hilton, Marriott, Renaissance, and Sheraton (see p. 348). Alternatively, contact Niagara Falls Tourism (Tel 906/356-6061 or 800/563-2557, www.discoverniagara.com).

🍴 TERROIR LA CACHETTE
$$$
1389 LAKESHORE ROAD
TEL 905/468-1222
www.lacachette.com
This restaurant at the Strewn Winery offers local Niagara produce prepared with a Provençale accent. All wines are from the Niagara peninsula. Summer terrace.

🍽 80 🗝All major cards

🍴 HILLEBRAND WINERY RESTAURANT
$$$$
1249 NIAGARA STONE ROAD
TEL 905/468-7123 or 800/582-8412
www.hillebrand.com
Highly rated cuisine is matched with the top wines of the region.

🍽 140 🗝All major cards

PRICES

HOTELS
An indication of the cost of a double room without breakfast is given by $ signs.

$$$$$	Over $280
$$$$	$200–$280
$$$	$120–$200
$$	$80–$120
$	Under $80

RESTAURANTS
An indication of the cost of a three-course dinner without drinks is given by $ signs.

$$$$$	Over $80
$$$$	$50–$80
$$$	$35–$50
$$	$20–$35
$	Under $20

NIAGARA-ON-THE-LAKE

🏨 OBAN INN
$$$
160 FRONT ST.
TEL 905/468-2165 or 866/359-6226
www.obaninn.ca
Broad verandas and mani-cured gardens surround this historic country inn, with lake views and antique-filled rooms. The restaurant serves contemporary and traditional cuisine prepared with local produce.

ⓘ 26 🅿 ⬌ 🔲 🗝All major cards

🏨 THE PRINCE OF WALES
$$$
6 PICTON ST.
TEL 905/468-3246 or 888/669-5566
www.vintageinns.com
Modern annex has less charm than the original 1864 building, but the bright rooms and excellent downtown location can't be beat.

ⓘ 114 🅿 ⬌ 🔲 ⛵ 📺
🗝All major cards

🏨 QUEEN'S LANDING
$$$
155 BYRON ST.

TEL 905/468-2195 or
888/669-5566
www.vintageinns.com
Excellent location and antique
canopy beds. Innovative
cuisine and wines shine in the
award-winning dining room.
[i] 142 P ⬓ ⬓ ⬓ ⬓
⬓ All major cards

OTTAWA

🏨 CHÂTEAU LAURIER
$$$$
1 RIDEAU ST.
TEL 613/241-1414 or
800/441-1414
www.fairmont.com
One of the country's great
railroad hotels, this venerable
property offers great service
and comfortable rooms at the
foot of Parliament Hill. Sunday
brunch at Wilfrid's and afternoon tea at Zoe's are truly
sumptuous.
[i] 428 P ⬓ ⬓ ⬓ ⬓
⬓ All major cards

🏨 WESTIN HOTEL
$$$
11 COLONEL BY DR.
TEL 613/560-7000 or
800/937-8461
www.westin.com
High-rise hotel attached to
the Rideau Centre. Modern
rooms, done up in pastels,
have floor-to-ceiling windows.
[i] 484 P ⬓ ⬓ ⬓ ⬓
⬓ All major cards

🏨 LORD ELGIN HOTEL
$$
100 ELGIN ST.
TEL 613/235-3333 or
800/267-4298
www.lordelginhotel.ca
Good value for its central
location within walking
distance of major sights.
Dining room.
[i] 355 P ⬓ ⬓ ⬓ All
major cards

🍴 LE CAFÉ
$$$
53 ELGIN ST. (IN THE
NATIONAL ARTS CENTRE)
TEL 613/594-5127
Overlooking the Rideau Canal

with an attractive outdoor
terrace in summer, Le Café
specializes in gourmet
Canadian cuisine.
⬓ 160 ⬓ Closed Sun. ⬓ All
major cards

🍴 FISH MARKET
RESTAURANT
$$
54 YORK ST.
TEL 613/241-3474
This popular restaurant in a
former hotel building in
Byward Market offers a wide
variety of fish and seafood,
which it imports from all over
the world. Good wine list too.
⬓ 140 ⬓ All major cards

🍴 COURTYARD
RESTAURANT
$$-$$$
21 GEORGE ST.
TEL 613/241-1516
Located in a 1827 stone
building, the Courtyard serves
international cuisine with a
contemporary flair. Specials
include shrimp and scallops
with a sun-dried tomato
pesto cream sauce, rack of
lamb, and filet of beef with
sesame ginger sauce. Summer
courtyard patio. Live classical
music at Sunday brunch.
⬓ 150 P ⬓ ⬓ All major
cards

🍴 FRESCO CIELLO
$$
354 ELGIN ST.
TEL 613/235-7541
This unpretentious trattoria
serves up Mediterranean
cuisine, notably veal, seafood,
and pasta with different sauces.
⬓ 60 ⬓ ⬓ Closed L
Mon.–Wed. & Sat. ⬓ All
major cards

PICTON

🏨 ISAIAH TUBBS RESORT
$$$
WEST LAKE RD.
TEL 613/393-2090 or
800/724-2393
www.isaiahtubbs.com
Picton on Quinte's Isle was
founded by Loyalists in 1786.

Set among the pine trees
beside West Lake, this resort
occupies an 18th-century inn
and contemporary house-
keeping cottages. Tennis and
cross-country skiing.
[i] 65, 14 cottages P ⬓
⬓ ⬓ ⬓ All major cards

PORT CARLING

🏨 SHERWOOD INN
$$$
1090 SHERWOOD RD.
TEL 705/765-3131 or
800/461-4233
www.deltahotels.com
Beside Lake Joseph in the
Muskoka Lakes region of
Ontario, this is a lovely and
very private resort hotel with
lakeside cottages. Country-
house cuisine and fine wines
complete the experience.
[i] 49 P ⬓ ⬓ All major
cards

ST. JACOBS

🏨 JAKOBSTETTEL
GUEST HOUSE
$$$
16 ISABELA AVE.
TEL 519/664-2208 or
800/431-3035
www.jakobstettel.com
Located on 5 acres of pleasant grounds, this Victorian
guest house is really a large
bed and breakfast with
charming rooms, all with their
own bath.
[i] 10 P ⬓ ⬓ ⬓ AE,
MC, V

ST. MARYS

🏨 WESTOVER INN
$$$
300 THOMAS ST.
TEL 519/284-2977 or
800/268-8243
www.westoverinn.com
Built in Confederation year
1867, this limestone mansion
has wonderful carved
gingerbread decoration
outside, attractive guest
rooms, and two dining rooms.
[i] 22 P ⬓ ⬓ ⬓ All
major cards

STRATFORD

🏨 QUEEN'S INN AT STRATFORD
$$
161 ONTARIO ST.
TEL 519/271-1400 or
800/461-6450
www.queensinnstratford.ca
Country inn in downtown
Stratford offering good value
and easy access to the world-
renowned Stratford Festival.
🛏32 P 🛗 🌊 📺 🚇 All
major cards

TORONTO

SOMETHING
SPECIAL

🏨 FOUR SEASONS TORONTO

This downtown property sets
new standards of luxury and
service, with beautifully
appointed rooms and staff
happy to fulfill any request. See
Truffles restaurant p. 363.
$$$$
21 AVENUE RD.
TEL 416/964-0411 or
800/332-3442
www.fourseasons.com
🛏380 P 🚇 Museum,
Bay 🛗 🌊 🚇 📺 🚇
🌊 All major cards

🏨 INTER-CONTINENTAL
$$$$
220 BLOOR ST. W.
TEL 416/960-5200 or
800/267-0010
www.ichotelsgroup.com
Just one block from the Royal
Ontario Museum and world
class shopping. Inside: well-
furnished guest rooms with
pampered service.
🛏209 P 🚇 St. George
🛗 🌊 🚇 📺 🌊 All major
cards

🏨 WESTIN HARBOUR CASTLE
$$$$
1 HARBOUR SQ.
TEL 416/869-1600 or
800/228-3000
www.starwoodhotels.com/westin

Superb lakefront location and
facilities. Rooms have views of
the lake. Several restaurants,
including the revolving Toula
on the top floor.
🛏977 P 🚇 Union 🛗 🌊
🌊 All major cards

🏨 DELTA CHELSEA
$$$
33 GERRARD ST. W.
TEL 416/595-1975 or
800/243-5732
www.deltahotels.com
A large, efficiently run hotel.
Excellent facilities for children
include a supervised creative
center for 3- to 8-year-olds.
🛏1,590 P 🚇 College 🛗
🌊 🌊2 🌊 All major cards

🏨 LE ROYAL MERIDIEN KING EDWARD
$$$
37 KING ST. E.
TEL 416/863-3131 or
800/543-4300
www.toronto.lemeridien.com
Understated elegance defines
this distinguished hotel, built in
1903. Take tea in the palm-
dotted lobby, or dine on
continental dishes at Chiaro's.
🛏261 P 🚇 King 🛗 🌊
📺 🌊 All major cards

🏨 METROPOLITAN
$$$
108 CHESTNUT ST.
TEL 416/977-5000 or
800/668-6600
www.metropolitan.com
A reasonably-priced hotel
challenging the Four Seasons
in the luxury market.
🛏355 P 🚇 St. Patrick 🛗
🌊 🌊 All major cards

🏨 SUTTON PLACE HOTEL
$$$
955 BAY ST.
TEL 416/924-9221 or
866/378-8866
www.suttonplace.com
Modern high-rise with
antiques-filled guest rooms
close to Queen's Park, the
University of Toronto, and
upscale shops.
🛏230 P 🚇 Wellesley 🛗
🌊 🚇 📺 🌊 All major cards

🏨 PARK HYATT TORONTO
$$$
4 AVENUE RD.
TEL 416/925-1234 or
800/233-1234
www.parktoronto.hyatt.com
This luxury hotel at the
corner of Avenue Road and
Bloor Street sits in the heart
of Toronto's most expensive
shopping area. The guest
rooms are especially large and
each have a self-contained
sitting area.
🛏348 P 🚇 Museum 🛗
🌊 🌊 📺 🌊 All major cards

🏨 HOLIDAY INN ON KING
$$
370 KING ST. W.
TEL 416/599-4000 or
800/268-6364
www.hiok.com
Good value, located near
famous attractions such as the
Rogers Centre, CN Tower,
and the entertainment district.
🛏425 P 🚇 St. Andrew
🛗 🌊 🌊 📺 🌊 All major
cards

🏨 RADISSON PLAZA HOTEL ADMIRAL
$$
249 QUEENS QUAY W.
TEL 416/203-3333 or
800/333-3333
www.radisson.com/torontoca
/admiral
Harborfront hotel with
rooftop pool, bar, and terrace.
Rooms are well furnished and
equipped. Health club, two
restaurants, and bar.
🛏157 P 🚇 Union 🛗 🌊
🌊 🌊 All major cards

🏨 FAIRMONT ROYAL YORK HOTEL
$$
100 FRONT ST. W.
TEL 416/368-2511 or
800/257-7544
www.fairmont.com
Beautifully refurbished to its
original 1929 decor, direct
access to the shops and
businesses of the under-
ground PATH walkway.
🛏1,365 P 🚇 Union 🛗
🌊 🌊 📺 🌊 All major cards

SHERATON
$$
123 QUEEN ST. W.
TEL 416/361-1000 or
800/325-3535
www.starwoodhotels.com
/sheraton
Although a large hotel, the
service is efficient. Three
restaurants on the premises,
plus connections to the
underground PATH network.
[1] 1,377 [P] Osgoode
All major cards

WESTIN PRINCE
$$
900 YORK MILLS RD.,
DON MILLS
TEL 416/444-2511 or
800/437-8461
www.starwoodhotels.com/westin
This Japanese-owned hotel set
on 15 acres in the Don Valley is
a 20-minute drive from downtown Toronto. The Katsura
restaurant offers sushi and
robata bars, a tempura counter,
and teppanyaki-style cuisine.
Tennis courts; putting green.
[1] 384 [P] Slam away!
All major cards

CLARION HOTEL &
SELBY SUITES
$
592 SHERBOURNE
TEL 416/921-3142 or
800/387-4788
www.hotelselby.com
Located in a handsome
heritage Victorian building, this
midtown hotel is one of the
city's best bargains. High-
ceilinged rooms are
individually decorated and
furnished.
[1] 82 [P] Sherbourne
All major cards

HOTEL VICTORIA
$
56 YONGE ST.
TEL 416/363-1666 or
800/363-8228
www.hotelvictoria.sites.toronto
.com
Steps away from the heart of
the financial district, this
intimate hostelry offers clean
rooms at affordable prices.

[1] 56 King All
major cards

TRUFFLES
$$$$$
21 AVENUE RD. (IN FOUR
SEASONS HOTEL)
TEL 416/928-7331
A temple of gastronomy with
flawless service. Couples sit
side-by-side in the sedate and
luxurious dining room,
sampling the masterful,
beautifully presented dishes
from the Provence-inspired
menu. Try their trademark
spaghettini with truffles.
Reservations essential.
80 [P] Closed L & all
Sun. Bay All major
cards

360 REVOLVING
RESTAURANT
$$$$
CN TOWER, 301 FRONT ST. W.
TEL 416/362-5411
Food is expensive but tasty,
the view is simply stunning at
lunch and even better at
night, and well worth the
price. Reservations essential.
400 [P] Closed L
winter months Union
All major cards

AUBERGE DU
POMMIER
$$$$
4150 YONGE ST.
TEL 416/222-2220
Modern French dining in a
romantic cottage in the city's
northern end. Menu changes
regularly; the chef's tasting
menu is popular. Lovely
summer terrace.
160 [P] Closed L Sat.
& all Sun. York Mills
All major cards

AVALON
$$$
270 ADELAIDE ST. W.
TEL 416/979-9918
Top-notch ingredients
prepared with French
techniques and breathtaking
creativity. The serene location
is around the corner from the
Rogers Centre and theater

district.
65 [P] Closed L
(except Thurs.) & Sun. St.
Andrew All major
cards

CENTRO GRILL AND
WINE BAR
$$$
2472 YONGE ST.
TEL 416/483-2211
This is a bustling and popular
place that highlights northern
Italian cuisine with Canadian
elements. The wine bar
downstairs features R&B
music in the late evening.
220 [P] Closed L &
Sun. Eglinton All
major cards

COURTYARD CAFÉ
$$$
18 ST. THOMAS ST.
TEL 416/971-9666
This chic restaurant in the
Windsor Arms Hotel offers
afternoon high tea for tired
shoppers as well as elegant
lunches and dinners.
250 Bay All major
cards

NORTH 44°
$$$
2537 YONGE ST.
TEL 416/487-4897
Creative continental cuisine in
a sophisticated setting. Try the
seared tuna or roasted
Atlantic salmon with miso
glaze. Extensive wine list.
202 [P] Closed L &
Sun. Eglinton All
major cards

OPUS RESTAURANT
$$$
37 PRINCE ARTHUR AVE.
TEL 416/921-3105
Converted brownstone
around the corner from
Yorkville serving Continental
cuisine. Wine connoisseurs
appreciate the thoroughness
of the high-quality cellar.
60 [P] Closed L St.
George All major cards

HOTELS & RESTAURANTS

SCARAMOUCHE RESTAURANT
$$$
1 BENVENUTO PL.
TEL 416/961-8011
Sparkling cuisine, an out-standing view, and candlelit luxury are featured in what some consider Toronto's best restaurant. A pasta bar downstairs serves lighter meals in a more casual setting.
100 P Closed L & Sun. All major cards

SPLENDIDO BAR & GRILL
$$$
88 HARBORD ST.
TEL 416/929-7788
Mediterranean cooking in a sleek contemporary room around the corner from the University of Toronto. Try the chef's daily specials or his tasting menu.
100 P Closed L & Sun. Spadina All major cards

ALICE FAZOOLI'S
$$
294 ADELAIDE ST. W.
TEL 416/979-1910
This restaurant in a converted warehouse features contemporary Italian cuisine with a US Gulf Coast flavor, especially in its fresh fish, seafood, and splendid pasta dishes. Lovely patio in summer.
400 St. Andrew All major cards

ARLEQUIN
$$
134 AVENUE RD.
TEL 416/964-8686
Situated on the edge of Yorkville, this café serves great light lunches and more elegant dinners on weekends. They also have a splendid gourmet take-out service.
46 Closed Mon., L Tues–Thurs., & D Fri.–Sun. Museum All major cards

CAFÉ AGO
$$
ART GALLERY OF ONTARIO
317 DUNDAS ST. W.
TEL 416/979-6648
Popular lunchtime haunt of well-heeled Torontonians, the AGO's restaurant offers inventive cuisine. Note: hours, size, and location will change as the AGO's renovations continue (see p. 181).
70 Closed D & Mon.–Tues. St. Patrick All major cards

CAFÉ BRUSSEL
$$
124 DANFORTH AVE.
TEL 416/465-7363
This stylish Belgian brasserie has a wide variety of mussel-based dishes, which arrive with accompanying *frites*. Wide selection of beers too.
30 Closed D Sun.–Mon. & L Broadview AE, MC, V

FIRE AND ICE
$$
25 COCHRANE DR.
TEL 905/947-1900
This restaurant in suburban Markham specializes in new Asian cuisine. They have no less than 28 stir fries to choose from along with a large selection of seasonal vegetables. Summer patio.
150 All major cards

LA MAQUETTE
$$
111 KING ST. E.
TEL 416/366-8191
Pasta and risotto are offered here, in addition to more classic dishes such as grilled salmon and New York sirloin. The elegant room overlooks a small sculpture garden, and is close to theaters. Fixed-price dinners are available.
200 P Closed Sun. King All major cards

ORO
$$
45 ELM ST.

PRICES

HOTELS
An indication of the cost of a double room without breakfast is given by $ signs.
$$$$$ Over $280
$$$$ $200–$280
$$$ $120–$200
$$ $80–$120
$ Under $80

RESTAURANTS
An indication of the cost of a three-course dinner without drinks is given by $ signs.
$$$$$ Over $80
$$$$ $50–$80
$$$ $35–$50
$$ $20–$35
$ Under $20

TEL 416/597-0155
La nuova cucina Italiana in a sophisticated setting just steps from the Eaton Centre. House specialties include shrimp and lemon balm ravioli and basil and mint-crusted rack of lamb.
120 P Closed L Sat. & all day Sun. Dundas All major cards

PANGAEA
$$
1221 BAY ST.
TEL 416/920-2323
High ceilings and mission-style furniture form the backdrop for well-executed fresh market cuisine from all over the world. Try the muscovy duck or caribou served with truffled whipped potatoes.
160 Closed Sun. Bay All major cards

PAN RESTAURANT
$$
516 DANFORTH AVE.
TEL 416/466-8158
Nouveau Greek cooking served in a funky nightclub that has little in common with its souvlaki house neighbors. Specialties include char-grilled loin of lamb and double

smoked pork chop.

🔟 72 P 🚇 Pape, Chester
🚭 All major cards

🍴 LE TROU NORMAND
$$
90 YORKVILLE AVE.
TEL 416/967-5956
Longtime favorite in the heart of Yorkville, Le Trou consistently serves up the best of the cuisine of Normandy complete with the glass of calvados between courses—familiarly known as the *trou normand* (Normandy hole).
🔟 75 🚭 All major cards

🍴 BLOOR STREET DINER
$
55 BLOOR ST (IN MANULIFE CENTRE)
TEL 416/928-3105
Provençale fare is featured at this popular diner. Try the grilled salmon with pink grapefruit vinaigrette or chicken with sun-dried tomato aïoli. There's a glass indoor patio and a brunch buffet on Sundays.
🔟 100 (50 on patio) P
🚇 Bay or Bloor-Yonge 🚭
🚭 All major cards

🍴 THE ELEPHANT AND CASTLE
$
212 KING ST. W.
TEL 416/598-4455
British pub with traditional restaurant fare (shepherd's pie, bangers and mash, fish and chips) located opposite Roy Thomson Hall, which makes it handy before or after a concert.
🔟 390 P 🚭 All major cards

🍴 THE HOST
$
14 PRINCE ARTHUR AVE.
TEL 416/962-4678
Fine northern Indian cuisine in a rococo setting. Whole barbecued fish, tandoori butter chicken and succulent pakoras. Fixed-price lunch available.
🔟 250 P 🕐 Closed L Mon.
🚇 Bay 🚭 🚭 All major cards

🍴 LEE GARDEN RESTAURANT
$
331 SPADINA AVE.
TEL 416/593-9524
Reservations are not normally accepted at this popular Cantonese restaurant in the heart of Chinatown, which means there is often a wait outside. There's an extensive menu but highlights include clams in a black bean sauce, stir-fried chicken with snow peas, and very ungreasy deep fried shrimp.
🔟 90 P 🚇 St. Patrick 🚭
🚭 AE, MC, V

PRAIRIES

Waves of settlers have left their culinary mark on the Prairie provinces. Ukrainian pierogi, Mennonite preserves, and Chinese fried rice are prevalent, as is locally raised beef. Hotels maintain the standards of their big city counterparts.

For details of bed-and-breakfast associations, contact the tourist offices (addresses p. 346).

Manitoba Country Vacations, tel 204/848-2265, www.countryvacations.mb.ca

Saskatchewan Country Vacations, tel 306/731-2646, www.scva.ca

For ranch and farm vacations in Alberta, contact the tourist office (p. 346)

CHURCHILL, MAN.

🏨 AURORA INN
$$
P.O. BOX 1030
TEL 204/675-2071 or
888/840-1344
www.aurora-inn.mb.ca
Dedicated to hospitality, provides opportunity to experience aurora borealis, whales, polar bears, and caribou in season.
🔟 22 🚭 MC, V

WINNIPEG, MAN.

🏨 HOTEL FORT GARRY
$$$
222 BROADWAY
TEL 204/942-8251 or
800/665-8088
www.fortgarryhotel.com
Historic railroad hotel with large guest rooms decorated in dark wood and florals. The downtown location makes it a popular gathering place.
🛈 243 P 🚭 🚭 🚭 🚭
🚭 All major cards

🏨 FAIRMONT WINNIPEG
$$$
2 LOMBARD PL.
TEL 204/957-1350 or
800/441-1414
www.fairmont.com
Skywalk access to office buildings and retail shops is the payoff for staying at this Fairmont luxury hotel in the city's core.
🛈 340 P 🚭 🚭 🚭 🚭
🚭 All major cards

🏨 SHERATON WINNIPEG
$$
161 DONALD ST.
TEL 204/942-5300 or
800/463-6400
www.starwoodhotels.com/sheraton
Inexpensive option right in the heart of the city within walking distance of major attractions. Restaurant.
🛈 271 P 🚭 🚭 🚭 All major cards

🍴 PROVENCE BISTRO AT NIAKWA
$$$
620 NIAKWA RD. (IN THE NIAKWA COUNTRY CLUB)
TEL 204/254-3500
This country club restaurant prepares and serves with great care and attention to detail Mediterranean specialties such as seafood risotto, mussels, prawns and a splendid bouillabaisse as well as excellent rack of lamb, duck confit and *escargots en croûte*.
🔟 90 🕐 Closed L & Sun.
🚭 🚭 All major cards

🍴 AMICI
$$
326 BROADWAY
TEL 204/943-4997
Sophisticated spot serving northern Italian nouvelle cuisine. The Bombolini Wine Bar downstairs serves simpler dishes at lower prices.
🍽 86 🅿 🕐 Closed L Sat. & all day Sun. 🔗 🆎 All major cards

🍴 MUDDY WATERS SMOKEHOUSE
$$
FORKS PAVILION, THE FORKS
TEL 204/947-6653
A popular place in the summer months with outdoor patios overlooking the marina. House specialty is barbecued ribs from the smoker.
🍽 100 🅿 🆎 All major cards

REGINA, SASK.

🏨 DELTA REGINA
$$$
1919 SASKATCHEWAN DR.
TEL 306/525-5255 or 800/209-3555
www.deltahotels.com
Convenient downtown location near Saskatchewan Trade and Convention Centre and the Cornwall Centre Shopping Mall.
🛏 274 🅿 🔗 🆎 All major cards

🏨 RAMADA HOTEL
$$
1818 VICTORIA AVE.
TEL 306/569-1666 or 800/667-6500
www.theramada.ca
Modern downtown property with airy guest rooms and a dramatic lobby.
🛏 232 🅿 🔗 🆎 🚇 📺 🆎 All major cards

🍴 THE DIPLOMAT
$$
2032 BROAD ST.
TEL 306/359-3366
Upscale setting for an extensive selection of steaks, seafood, chicken, and wild game. Extensive wine list.
🍽 120 🅿 🕐 Closed L Sat.–Sun. 🔗 🆎 All major cards

SASKATOON, SASK.

🏨 DELTA BESSBOROUGH
$$$
601 SPADINA CRES. E.
TEL 306/244-5521 or 800/268-1133
www.deltahotels.com
Castle-like, landmark hotel on the South Saskatchewan River with traditionally-furnished guest rooms and modern amenities.
🛏 225 🅿 🔗 🚇 📺 🆎 All major cards

🏨 RADISSON HOTEL SASKATOON
$$
405 20TH ST. E.
TEL 306/665-3322 or 800/333-3333
www.radisson.com/saskatoonca
Eighteen-story tower in downtown core on the banks of the South Saskatchewan River. Recreational complex.
🛏 291 luxury suites 🅿 🔗 🚇 🆎 All major cards

🍴 ST. TROPEZ BISTRO
$
238 2ND AVE. S.
TEL 306/652-1250
This little downtown restaurant is popular for its reasonably priced pastas, stir-fries, seafood, and French dishes such as peppercorn filet mignon and blackened chicken. The triple-chocolate mousse pie is a great dessert.
🍽 100 🅿 🕐 Closed L 🔗 🆎 AE, MC, V

CALGARY, ALTA.

🏨 FAIRMONT THE PALLISER
$$$$
133 9TH AVE S.W.
TEL 403/262-1234 or 800/441-1414
www.fairmont.com
Grand, historic railroad hotel offering guest rooms with traditional furniture, high ceilings, and ornate moldings.
🛏 405 🅿 🔗 🚇 🆎 📺 🆎 All major cards

🏨 WESTIN HOTEL
$$$
320 4TH AVE. S.W.
TEL 403/266-1611 or 800/WESTIN-1
www.starwoodhotels.com/westin
Luxury downtown high-rise offering large rooms with contemporary decor.
🛏 525 🅿 🔗 🚇 🆎 📺 🆎 All major cards

🏨 5 CALGARY DOWNTOWN SUITES
$$
618 5TH AVE. S.W.
TEL 403/451-5551 or 877/451-5551
www.5calgary.com
Rooms here come with fully equipped kitchens.
🛏 301 🅿 🔗 📺 🆎 All major cards

🏨 HOLIDAY INN AIRPORT
$$
1250 MCKINNON DR. N.E.
TEL 403-230-1999 or 800-465-4329
www.holiday-inn.com
Convenient and comfortable airport location with bright rooms tastefully decorated.
🛏 170 🅿 🔗 🆎 📺 🆎 All major cards

🍴 HY'S STEAK HOUSE
$$$
316 4TH AVE. S.W.
TEL 403/263-2222
Charcoal-broiled steak is king at Calgary's most popular chop house, a franchise eatery done up in dark velvet fabrics and Victorian wood paneling.
🍽 185 🅿 🕐 Closed L Sat.–Sun. 🔗 🆎 All major cards

🍴 O.N. BAR AND GRILL
$$$
WESTIN HOTEL
320 4TH AVE. S.W.
TEL 403/266-1611
Quality continental dining

enhanced by a sweeping wine list and top-notch service. Specialties include Alberta beef, British Columbia salmon, and East coast lobster.
🍴 175 P 🕐 Closed L Sat. & all Sun. 🔵 🔵 All major cards

DRUMHELLER, ALTA.

🏨 DRUMHELLER INN
$$
100 S. RAILWAY AVE.
TEL 403/823-8400
www.reveal.ca/drumhellerinn
The Alberta Badlands are not blessed with great hotels, but this is very satisfactory, with a view overlooking the town and its spectacular natural setting. Restaurant.
🛏 100 P 🔵 🔵 🔵 All major cards

EDMONTON, ALTA.

🏨 FANTASYLAND HOTEL
$$$
17700 87TH AVE.
TEL 780/444-3000 or 800/737-3783
www.fantasylandhotel.com
Part of the West Edmonton Mall. Theme rooms cater to Roman, Victorian, Polynesian, or automotive fantasies.
🛏 354 P 🔵 🔵 🔵 🔵
🔵 All major cards

🏨 FAIRMONT HOTEL MACDONALD
$$$
10065 100TH ST.
TEL 780/424-5181 or 800/441-1414
www.fairmont.com
Landmark hotel with traditionally furnished guest rooms and stunning views of the Saskatchewan River.
🛏 198 P 🔵 🔵 🔵 🔵
🔵 All major cards

🏨 WEST HARVEST INN
$$
17803 STONY PLAIN RD.
TEL 780/484-8000 or 800/661-6993
www.westharvest.com
Modern accommodations, five

minutes from the West Edmonton Mall. Rooms in the new wing are slightly larger and more expensive.
🛏 161 P 🔵 🔵 All major cards

🍴 THE CRÊPERIE
$$
10220,103 ST.
TEL 780/420-6656
This popular French restaurant situated right downtown offers over 20 different dinner and dessert crêpes.
🍴 160 🕐 Closed L Sat. & all Sun. 🔵 All major cards

🍴 UNHEARD OF DINING LOUNGE
$$
9602 82ND AVE.
TEL 780/432-0480
Imaginative cooking in an antique-filled setting. The menu changes with the seasons, but saffron-seasoned Atlantic salmon and herbed seafood crêpes remain perennial favorites. Reservations essential.
🍴 118 P 🕐 Closed L & Mon. 🔵 🔵 All major cards

🍴 BISTRO PRAHA
$
10168 100 A ST.
TEL 780/424-4218
Trendy café serving such Central European favorites as wiener schnitzel, goulash, filet mignon, and roast goose. Pastries are perfect for ending the meal or as a snack with coffee.
🍴 82 P 🕐 Closed L Sun. 🔵 🔵 All major cards

THE ROCKIES

Boasting spectacular skiing and dramatic golf courses, the Rockies attract visitors year round. Casual dining is the rule, and hotel rooms are generally booked well in advance for the summer.

BANFF TOWNSITE, ALTA.

Rooms are scarce in the summer in Banff and Lake Louise. For assistance in locating a room contact:
Banff-Lake Louise Central Reservations, tel 800/661-1676 ext. 2.

🏨 RIMROCK RESORT HOTEL
$$$$$
MOUNTAIN AVE.
TEL 403/762-3356 or 800/661-1587
www.rimrockresort.com
Modern property on Sulphur Mountain offering Bow Valley views and leather and velvet furnishings in guest rooms.
🛏 345 P 🔵 🔵 🔵 🔵
🔵 All major cards

🏨 TUNNEL MOUNTAIN CHALETS
$$$$
TUNNEL MOUNTAIN RD.
TEL 403/762-4515 or 800/661-1859
www.tunnelmountain.com
Attractive wooden chalets, featuring kitchenettes and fireplaces, among the trees.
🛏 95 P 🔵 🔵 All major cards

🏨 FAIRMONT BANFF SPRINGS HOTEL
$$$$$
SPRAY AVE.
TEL 403/762-2211 or 800/441-1414
www.fairmont.com
Majestic building offering more than 80 styles of guest rooms, all with high ceilings and antique furniture.
🛏 770 P 🔵 🔵 🔵 🔵
🔵 All major cards

🏨 RED CARPET INN
$$
425 BANFF AVE.
TEL 403/762-4184 or 800/563-4609
www.banffredcarpet.com
These no-frills motel rooms are a rare lodging bargain in downtown Banff. Rooms on

HOTELS & RESTAURANTS

Banff Avenue can be noisy.
🛈 52 🅿 🔁 🖾 AE, MC, V

BOW VALLEY PARKWAY, ALTA.

🏨 CASTLE MOUNTAIN CHALETS
$$$
BOW VALLEY PKWY. (HWY. IA)
TEL 403/762-3868
www.decorehotels.com
Several types of attractive log cabins with views of Castle Mountain east of Kootenay National Park. All have kitchenettes and fireplaces.
🛈 22 Cabins 🖾 MC, V

🍴 LE BEAUJOLAIS
$$$
212 BUFFALO ST.
TEL 403/762-2712
Neoclassic setting for rich French cooking. Seafood, Alberta beef, veal, and rack of lamb are favorite dishes.
🍽 80 🅿 🕐 Closed L & Sun.–Mon. in winter months
🖾 MC, V

🍴 EDEN RESTAURANT
$$$
RIMROCK RESORT HOTEL
MOUNTAIN AVE.
TEL 403/762-1840
Located high on Sulphur Mountain in the Rimrock Resort Hotel, this restaurant offers magnificent views of the Bow Valley. Its cuisine is French-influenced. There's a chef's tasting menu and an extensive wine list. Reservations recommended.
🍽 64 🅿 🕐 Closed L 🕐
🖾 All major cards

🍴 EARLS
$–$$
229 BANFF AVE.
TEL 403/762-4414
Earls, the popular West Coast chain, offers a casual and more moderately priced dining experience. There's Alberta beef and fresh British Columbia salmon on the menu along with good salads, excellent pizza, and great desserts.
🍽 150 🖾 All major cards

ICEFIELDS PARKWAY, ALTA.

🏨 COLUMBIA ICEFIELD CHALET
$$$
ICEFIELDS PARKWAY, BORDER BANFF/JASPER NATIONAL PARKS
TEL 780/852-6550 or
877/423-7433
www.brewster.ca/columbia_icefield/icefield.asp
This is a spectacular location, overlooking the Athabaska Glacier as it plunges down the valley from the Columbia Icefields.
🛈 32 (17 with glacier view)
🅿 🕐 Closed mid-Oct.–mid-May 🖾 MC, V

🏨 NUM-TI-JAH LODGE
$$–$$$
ICEFIELDS PARKWAY, BANFF NATIONAL PARK
TEL 403/522-2167
www.num-ti-jah.com
Simple rustic accommodation beside beautiful Bow Lake (25 miles N of Lake Louise) overlooking glaciers and peaks. The name refers to the marten, a fast-moving animal. It was the nickname of outfitter Jimmy Simpson, who founded the lodge. Good location for hiking neighboring terrain.
🛈 25 🅿 🕐 Closed Nov.
🖾 MC, V

JASPER, ALTA.

🏨 FAIRMONT JASPER PARK LODGE
$$$$
OLD LODGE RD.
TEL 780/852-3301 or
800/441-1414
www.fairmont.com
A village unto itself. Rooms are modern or rustic in style. Summer activities include golf, horseback riding, and boating on Lac Beauvert.
🛈 451 🅿 🔁 🕐 🔄 🔲
🖾 All major cards

🍴 SORRENTINO'S
$$$
CHÂTEAU JASPER, 96 GIEKIE ST.

TEL 780/852-5644
Located in the Chateau Jasper Hotel, this congenial restaurant offers a wide choice of Italian fare with local specialties such as caribou *escalope* and West Coast salmon *cordon bleu*. The desserts are excellent too.
🍽 120 🅿 🕐 🖾 All major cards

KANANASKIS, ALTA.

🏨 BREWSTER'S KANANASKIS GUEST RANCH
$$$
P.O. BOX 964
TEL 403/673-3737 or
800/691-5085
www.kananaskisguestranch.com
This ranch resort 30 minutes east of Banff offers cabins and chalets, antique furniture, and horseback riding. Some guest rooms with whirlpool. Dining room. Golf course.
🛈 33 🅿 🕐 Closed Oct.–May 🔁 🖾 MC, V

LAKE LOUISE, ALTA.

🏨 POST HOTEL
$$$$$
200 PIPESTONE RD.
TEL 403/522-3989 or

800/661-1586
www.posthotel.com
Choose from 16 types of rooms at this elegant property. All rooms have wood and leather furniture, and decadent bathrooms attached.
[i] 99 [P] [clock] Closed Nov.
[x] [pool] [cards] AE, MC, V

SOMETHING SPECIAL

[building] FAIRMONT CHÂTEAU LAKE LOUISE

World-famous hotel with dramatic location facing the Victoria Glacier and the lake. Guest rooms, some with terraces, have reproduction antique furniture. The dining is excellent and the hotel offers myriad activities including hiking trails to hidden tea houses.
$$$$$
LAKE LOUISE DR.
TEL 403/522-3511 or
800/441-1414
www.fairmont.com
[i] 550 [P] [x] [pool] [health]
[cards] All major cards

[fork] THE STATION
$$
200 SENTINEL RD.
TEL 403/522-2600
Local beef and lamb anchor the expertly prepared menu. Casual dining in the restored log railway station; formal atmosphere in the two heritage dining cars.
[seats] 166 [P] [cards] MC, V

LAKE LOUISE AREA, ALTA.

[building] MORAINE LAKE LODGE
$$$$$
8 MILES FROM LAKE LOUISE ON MORAINE LAKE
TEL 403/522-3733
www.morainelake.com
Spectacular site beside a dramatic lake in the valley of the Ten Peaks. Casually elegant cabins with fireplaces; outstanding food. Naturalists lead

hikes and make evening presentations. Canoes available.
[i] 18 cabins, 6 other units, 8 rooms in lodge, & 1 suite [P]
[clock] Closed Oct.–May [cards] All major cards

YOHO NATIONAL PARK, B.C.

[building] CATHEDRAL MOUNTAIN LODGE AND CHALETS
$$$$
YOHO VALLEY RD.,
2 MILES E OF FIELD
TEL 250/343-6442
www.cathedralmountain.com
On wooded site beside Kicking Horse River with magnificent views of Cathedral Mountain, this lodge has luxury log cabins with fireplaces and cooking facilities. Restaurant. No pets.
[i] 29 [clock] Closed Oct.–mid-May [cards] All major cards

[building] EMERALD LAKE LODGE
$$$$
EMERALD LAKE RD.
TEL 250/343-6321 or
800/663-6336
www.crmr.com
No cars allowed on the grounds of this enchanting resort 20 minutes from Lake Louise. Cabins have fireplaces and balconies. Excellent cuisine in dining room.
[i] 85 [P] [health] [cards] All major cards

[building] LAKE O'HARA LODGE
$$$
7 MILES S OF TRANS-CANADA HWY., E OF FIELD
TEL 250/343-6418
(OFF-SEASON 403/678-4110)
Only accessible by foot, on skis, or by daily reserved bus in summer, this is a real mountain hideaway beside lovely Lake O'Hara. The lakefront cottages and lodge units are perfect base for hiking, climbing or back country skiing. Meals included. No pets permitted. Reservations

essential well in advance.
[i] 23 [clock] Closed mid-Oct.–early Feb. & early April–mid-June [x] [cards] All major cards

THE WEST

Cosmopolitan restaurants and intimate lodgings abound along Canada's West Coast. Vancouver boasts world-class dining in addition to vibrant ethnic eateries. The region's wines are featured on many menus, along with local seafood and game.

Western Canada Bed & Breakfast Innkeepers Association,
tel 604/255-9199;
www.webbia.com

KELOWNA

[building] LAKE OKANAGAN RESORT
$$$
2751 WESTSIDE RD.
TEL 250/769-3511 or
800/663-3273
www.lakeokanagan.com
Located on 300 acres of waterfront with lodging choices from one- to three-bedroom chalets.
[i] 135 [P] [cards] All major cards

NANAIMO

[building] BEST WESTERN DORCHESTER HOTEL
$$
70 CHURCH ST.
TEL 250/754-6835, 800/528-1234, or 800/661-2449
www.dorchesternanaimo.com
Converted opera house in the city center with harbor views. Elegant decor and comfortable guest rooms.
[i] 65 [P] [x] [ac] [health] [cards] All major cards

[fork] MAHLE HOUSE
$$
CEDAR AND HEEMER RDS.
TEL 250/722-3621
Innovative Northwest coast

cuisine served in an intimate, country-style setting.
🍴 65 🕐 Closed L & Mon.– Tues. 🛗 🃏 All major cards

PRINCE RUPERT

🏨 EAGLE BLUFF BED & BREAKFAST
$-$$
201 COW BAY RD.
TEL 250/627-4955 or 800/833-1550
www.citytel.net/eaglebluff
Next to Cow Bay, rooms look out on the yachts only a hundred feet away.
🛏 7 🃏 MC, V

🏨 THE INN ON THE HARBOUR
$-$$
720 IST ST.
TEL 250/624-9107 or 800/663-8155
www.innontheharbour.com
Terrific views of the harbor make this a good base for train and ferry travelers.
🛏 50 P 🛗 🃏 MC, V

SOOKE

🍴 SOOKE HARBOUR HOUSE
$$$
1528 WHIFFEN SPIT RD.
TEL 250/642-3421 or 800/889-9688
www.sookeharbourhouse.com
One of British Columbia's finest restaurants, featuring fresh-caught fish and herbs and vegetables from the kitchen garden.
🍴 75 P 🛗 🃏 All major cards

TOFINO

🏨 THE WICKANINNISH INN
$$$$
OSPREY LANE
CHESTERMAN BEACH
TEL 250/725-3100 or 800/333-4604
www.wickin.com Country inn surrounded by ocean and trees. Spacious rooms have balconies and fireplaces.

Excellent dining room serves West Coast wines exclusively.
ⓘ 75 P 🛗 🃏 All major cards

VANCOUVER

🏨 FAIRMONT WATERFRONT
Elegant, dramatic glass tower with calming views of Burrard Inlet from most guest rooms. Contemporary art in every room.
$$$$$
900 CANADA PLACE WAY
TEL 604/691-1991 or 800/441-1414
www.fairmont.com
ⓘ 489 P 🛗 🛗 🖥 📺
🃏 All major cards

🏨 FOUR SEASONS
$$$$$
791 W. GEORGIA ST.
TEL 604/689-9333 or 800/268-6282
www.fourseasons.com
Central location on top of the Pacific Centre and close to all downtown attractions. Luxurious service.
ⓘ 376 P 🛗 🛗 🖥 🖥 📺 🃏 All major cards

🏨 PAN PACIFIC HOTEL
$$$$$
300-999 CANADA PL.
TEL 604/662-8111, 800/663-1515 (CANADA), or 800/937-1515 (U.S.)
www.vancouver.panpacific.com
Relative quiet in this busy convention area. Elegantly understated rooms.
ⓘ 506 P 🛗 🛗 🖥 📺
🃏 All major cards

🏨 WEDGEWOOD HOTEL
$$$$$
845 HORNBY ST.
TEL 604/689-7777 or 800/663-0666
www.wedgewoodhotel.com
Small, exquisite property run by devoted staff. Extra touches, such as turndown service and morning news-

paper, make it popular.
ⓘ 83 P 🛗 🛗 📺 🖥 🃏 All major cards

🏨 METROPOLITAN HOTEL
$$$$
645 HOWE ST.
TEL 604/687-1122 or 800/667-2300
www.metropolitan.com
Intimate luxury hotel in the heart of downtown Vancouver. Spacious guest rooms with mahogany furnishings.
ⓘ 197 P 🛗 🛗 🖥 📺
🃏 All major cards

🏨 RENAISSANCE VANCOUVER
$$$$
1133 WEST HASTINGS ST.
TEL 604/689-9211 or 800/905-8582
www.renaissancevancouver.com
Overlooking the North Shore Mountains and the busy harbor, this hotel is on the waterfront near the cruise ship terminal. Revolving restaurant.
ⓘ 438 P 🛗 📺 🖥 2
🃏 All major cards

🏨 SUTTON PLACE
$$$$
845 BURRARD ST.
TEL 604/682-5511 or 800/961-7555
www.suttonplace.com
Intimate and aristocratic despite its large size. Rooms are richly decorated with dark woods. Apartment suites available for extended stays.
ⓘ 397 P 🛗 🛗 🖥 📺
🃏 All major cards

🏨 WESTIN BAYSHORE
$$$$
1601 BAYSHORE DR.
TEL 604/682-3377 or 800/228-3000
www.westinbayshore.com
Good location right on the water overlooking North Shore Mountains and downtown skyline, near Stanley Park. Marina, fishing and cruising charters. Restaurant facilities.

ⓘ 510 🅿 🏊 🔲 🔲 All
major cards

🏨 **FAIRMONT HOTEL VANCOUVER**
$$$
900 W. GEORGIA ST.
TEL 604/684-3131 or
800/441-1414
www.fairmont.com
Regal property with
mahogany furniture and deep
bathtubs in guest rooms.
Lobby lounge offers after-
noon tea daily, followed by live
music throughout the evening.
ⓘ 555 🅿 🔲 🔲 🏊 🔲
🔲 All major cards

🏨 **SANDMAN HOTEL**
$$$
180 W. GEORGIA ST.
TEL 604/681-2211 or
800/726-3626
www.sandmanhotels.com
A good mid-price hotel within
walking distance of downtown
attractions.
ⓘ 302 🏊 🔲 🔲 All
major cards

🏨 **SYLVIA HOTEL**
$$
1154 GILFORD ST.
TEL 604/681-9321
www.sylviahotel.com
Very popular hotel over-
looking English Bay near
Stanley Park. Housekeeping
suites; restaurant.
ⓘ 118 🅿 🔲 🔲 All major
cards

🍴 **DIVA AT THE MET**
$$$$
METROPOLITAN HOTEL
645 HOWE ST.
TEL 604/602-7788
Dazzling presentation matches
knockout room. Contempor-
ary international cuisine pro-
duced in an open center-stage
kitchen. Lengthy wine list and
renowned chef's tasting menu.
🍴 108 🅿 🔲 🔲 All major
cards

🍴 **FIVE SAILS**
$$$$
PAN PACIFIC HOTEL,
999 CANADA PL.

TEL 604/891-2892
Pacific Rim cooking with a
panoramic view of Lions Gate
Bridge and the North Shore.
Favorites include balik-smoked
British Columbia salmon blini
with creamed goat cheese.
🍴 120 🅿 🔲 Closed L 🔲
🔲 All major cards

🍴 **LE GAVROCHE**
$$$$
1616 ALBERNI ST.
TEL 604/685-3924
This elegant and longtime
popular restaurant in a
heritage property features
organic contemporary
cuisine—free range beef,
sustainable seafood, organic
vegetables, etc. Reservations
recommended.
🔲 Closed L Sat.–Sun. 🔲 All
major cards

🍴 **LUMIÈRE**
$$$$
2551 W. BROADWAY
TEL 604/739-8185
Considered by some to be
Vancouver's top restaurant,
the elegant Lumière serves
modern French cuisine with
lots of flair. Try the chef's
tasting menu, which can be 8
or 12 courses.
🍴 45 🅿 🔲 Closed L &
Mon. 🔲 AE, MC, V

🍴 **BACCHUS**
$$$
845 HORNBY ST.
TEL 604/608-5319
This European-style restaurant
located in the Wedgewood
Hotel features mainly local
products such as British
Columbia salmon, Pacific
halibut, and Alberta beef and
lamb.
🍴 100 🔲 All major cards

🍴 **BISHOP'S**
$$$
2183 W. 4TH AVE.
TEL 604/738-2025
Pioneering restaurant serving
cutting-edge West Coast
dishes featuring local
ingredients. The menu
changes weekly but Fraser

Valley lamb, Cowichan Bay
duck, and local seafood make
regular appearances.
🍴 48 🔲 Closed L 🔲 🔲 All
major cards

🍴 **LE CROCODILE**
$$$
909 BURRARD ST. (ENTRANCE
ON SMYTHE ST.)
TEL 604/669-4298
Excellent French cuisine.
Alsatian specialties such as
onion tart and smoked goose
breast are often featured.
🍴 85 🅿 🔲 Closed L Sat. &
all Sun. 🔲 🔲 All major cards

🍴 **IL GIARDINO DI UMBERTO**
$$$
1382 HORNBY ST.
TEL 604/669-2422
Contemporary and classic
northern Italian cooking in a
country villa with garden.
Outstanding wine list
🍴 250 🅿 🔲 Closed L Sat.
& all Sun. 🔲 All major cards

🍴 **JOE FORTES**
$$$
777 THURLOW ST
604/669-1940
A popular oyster bar that also
offers a variety of fish and
seafood dishes. Roof garden.
Reservations recommended.
Open for brunch on
weekends.
🍴 365 🔲 Closed L Mon.–
Fri. 🔲 All major cards

🍴 **TOJO'S**
$$$
777 W. BROADWAY
TEL 604/872-8050
This legendary sushi
restaurant also serves many
cooked dishes. The runaway
favorite is the *omakase*
(meaning "you're in chef's
hands"), which features many
original offerings not normally
on the menu.
🍴 95 🅿 🔲 Closed L and
Sun. 🔲 🔲 All major cards

🍴 VILLA DEL LUPO
$$$
869 HAMILTON ST.
TEL 604/688-7436
Romantic setting for top-notch Italian dishes, such as their signature lamb shank *osso bucco* or one of their great pastas.
🍽 77 🕐 Closed L 🅿 ♿
♦ All major cards

🍴 FISH HOUSE IN STANLEY PARK
$$-$$$
8901 STANLEY PARK DR.
TEL 604/681-7275
Overlooking English Bay, this restaurant features fish and seafood from all over the world. The tiger prawns are huge and oysters are shucked to order. Also offers afternoon tea and Sunday brunch.
🍽 150 ♦ All major cards

🍴 A TASTE OF INDIA
$$
1282 ROBSON ST.
TEL 604/682-3894
This Indian restaurant on the trendy part of Robson Street features tandoori, seafood, and vegetarian specialties. Take out also available.
🍽 70 ♦ All major cards

🍴 CARDERO'S
$$
1583 COAL HARBOUR
TEL 604/669-7666
With a superb site on the waterfront facing the North Shore mountains, this restaurant is famous for its salmon baked on a cedar plank in a wood burning oven.
🍽 160 ♦ All major cards

🍴 IMPERIAL CHINESE SEAFOOD
$$
355 BURRARD ST.
TEL 604/688-8191
Tanks of live seafood and fish guarantee fresh-tasting dishes at this Cantonese restaurant with stunning views across Coal Harbour.
🍽 280 🅿 ♿ ♦ All major cards

🍴 LILIGET FEAST HOUSE
$$
1724 DAVIE ST.
TEL 604/681-7044
The only authentic First Nations restaurant in Vancouver and a great dining experience. Feast on their signature dish served on a large wooden platter: alder-grilled salmon, mussels, venison and buffalo strips, duck breast, rice, and vegetables.
🍽 50 🅿 🕐 Closed L & Mon.–Tues. ♦ AE, MC, V

🍴 STAR ANISE
$$
1485 W. 12TH AVE.
TEL 604/737-1485
Contemporary West coast cuisine based on French principles with influences from India and Sri Lanka. Try the star anise and almond-crusted roast duck breast or marinated baked *basa* with wild rice.
🍽 50 🅿 ♿ ♦ All major cards

🍴 ZEFFERELLI'S SPAGHETTI HOUSE
$$
1136 ROBSON ST.
TEL 604/687-0655
Spaghetti, yes, of course, but also other innovative pasta dishes as well as veal scallopine and chicken and lamb plates.
🍽 75 🕐 Closed L Sat.–Sun. ♿ ♦ All major cards

🍴 A KETTLE OF FISH
$-$$
900 PACIFIC ST.
TEL 604/682-6661
Fresh West Coast and international seafood served with house chutneys and salsa. Reservations essential.
🍽 240 🕐 Closed L ♿ ♦ All major cards

🍴 EARLS ON TOP
$-$$
1185 ROBSON ST. (SECOND FLOOR)
TEL 604/669-0020

The Vancouver branch of this popular Western chain is located on Robson Street in the heart of the Downtown restaurant district. It offers fresh ingredients, good value, and quality service.
🍽 250 ♦ All major cards

VICTORIA

🏨 ABIGAIL'S HOTEL
$$$$
906 MCCLURE ST.
TEL 250/388-5363 or 800/561-6565
www.abigailshotel.com
Charming Tudor-style inn close to downtown. Guest rooms feature down comforters; some rooms have spa tubs and fireplaces.
🛏 23 🅿 ♿ ♦ AE, MC, V

🏨 FAIRMONT EMPRESS HOTEL
$$$$
721 GOVERNMENT ST.
TEL 250/384-8111 or 800/441-1414
www.fairmont.com
This grand old Canadian Pacific hotel overlooks the inner harbor. Designed by Francis Rattenbury and built in 1905, the turreted ivy-covered structure typifies

---

Victoria for many people. Afternoon tea at the Empress is a fine tradition and so popular in mid-summer that you must reserve. Dinner in the Empress Room is also a treat (see below).
[i] 477 [P] [=] [♥] [≈] All major cards

HOTEL GRAND PACIFIC
$$$$
463 BELLEVILLE ST.
TEL 250/386-0450 or
800-663-7550
www.hotelgrandpacific.com
Comfort, convenience, close to Parliament Buildings and the harbour, views of the Olympic Mountains mark this elegant property.
[i] 304 [P] [=] [≈] [≈] [♥] [≈] All major cards

OCEAN POINTE RESORT (DELTA)
$$$$
45 SONGHEES RD.
TEL 250/360-2999 or
800/667-4677
www.deltahotels.com
Modern hotel with spectacular views of the Parliament buildings from spacious guest rooms. European spa on site.
[i] 239 [P] [=] [≈] [≈] [♥] [≈] All major cards

COAST VICTORIA HARBOURSIDE
$$$
146 KINGSTON ST.
TEL 250/360-1211 or
800/663-1144
www.coasthotels.com
Serene relaxation and modern comfort next to Fisherman's Wharf.
[i] 132 [P] [=] [≈] [≈] [♥] [≈] All major cards

JAMES BAY INN
$$-$$$
270 GOVERNMENT ST
TEL 250/384-7151 or
800/836-2649
www.jamesbayinn.com
This historic hotel dating from 1911 overlooks Beacon Hill Park and is within walking

distance of downtown attractions.
[i] 45 [≈] All major cards

THE EMPRESS ROOM
$$$$
EMPRESS HOTEL
721 GOVERNMENT ST.
TEL 250/389-2727
Every meal is a special occasion in this sophisticated room serving innovative Pacific Northwest cooking. Fresh local salmon, char, and venison are featured. Reserva-tions essential.
[≈] 125 [P] [⊘] Closed L [≈] [≈] All major cards

CAFÉ MEXICO
$$
1425 STORE ST.
TEL 250/386-1425
Mexican classics such as grilled chipotle chicken served in hearty portions in renovated eatery just off the waterfront in Market Square.
[≈] 100 [P] [≈] [≈] All major cards

IL TERRAZZO
$$
555 JOHNSON ST.
TEL 250/361-0028
This romantic outdoor eatery is tucked off an alley. Modern northern Italian dishes include such specialties as wood-fired pizzas, salmon, and rack of lamb.
[≈] 90–150 (with patio) [⊘] Closed L Sun. [≈] [≈] All major cards

MARINA RESTAURANT
$$
1327 BEACH DR.
TEL 250/598-8555
Extremely popular spot serving Italian cuisine and seafood specialties; there's also a sushi bar.
[≈] 130 [P] [≈] [≈] All major cards

PAGLIACCI'S
$$
1011 BROAD ST.
TEL 250/386-1662
Very lively Italian bistro serving dozens of homemade

pasta dishes, chicken, and veal in a room lined with photos of Hollywood movie stars. Reservations not accepted for groups of less than six people.
[≈] 65 [≈] AE, MC, V

PESCATORE'S SEAFOOD FISH HOUSE AND GRILL
$$
614 HUMBOLDT ST.
TEL 250/385-4512
On the inner harbor, this popular restaurant is noted for its excellent fresh seafood.
[≈] 115 [≈] [≈] All major cards

THE SNUG
$
1175 BEACH DR., IN THE OAK BAY BEACH HOTEL
TEL 250/598-4556
This is Victoria's original English-style pub, complete with Old World ambiance, good pub fare, and local ales. Stunningly located with views across the Haro Strait of northern Washington State's Cascade Mountains, including Mount Baker.
[≈] 75 [≈] All major cards

WHISTLER

FAIRMONT CHÂTEAU WHISTLER
$$$$
4599 CHÂTEAU BLVD.
TEL 604/938-8000 or
800/441-1414
www.fairmont.com
Imposing-looking fortress at the foot of Blackcomb Mountain with year-round outdoor activities.
[i] 550 [P] [=] [≈] [≈] [≈] [♥] [≈] All major cards

LE GROS
$$$
1200 ALTA LAKE RD.
TEL 604/932-4611
A small gem of a restaurant. Splendid portions of French cuisine as only the French can prepare it.
[≈] 100 [P] [⊘] Closed L & all Mon. [≈] All major cards

HOTELS & RESTAURANTS

🍴 TRATTORIA DI UMBERTO
$$$
MOUNTAINSIDE LODGE
4417 SUNDIAL PL.
TEL 604/932-5858
Traditional Italian cooking. Tuscan grilled meats and fish compliment the pasta dishes. Casual, relaxed atmosphere. Reservations essential.
🛏 130 🅿 🐾 🚫 All major cards

THE NORTH

In the far north, the sparsity of the population is echoed in the number of dining and lodging choices. Hotels are generally comfortable, though with fewer amenities than those in the south. Restaurants are casual, with well-prepared, traditional items occasionally enlivened by ethnic influences.

DAWSON, YUKON

🏨 DOWNTOWN HOTEL
$$
2ND AVE. & QUEEN ST.
TEL 867/993-5346 or
800/661-0514
www.downtown.ca
This hotel still retains its gold rush era look, but it has been refurbished since 1898. It stands out among the colorful seasonal places to stay in this community, affected every year by permafrost.
🛏 60 🅿 🔁 🚫 All major cards

🍴 JACK LONDON DINING ROOM
$$
2ND AVE. & QUEEN ST.
TEL 867/993-5346
This restaurant in the Downtown Hotel features fresh Yukon salmon. In summer, barbecue is served on the patio.
🍴 72 🅿 🚫 All major cards

🍴 KLONDIKE KATE'S
$
3RD AVE. AND KING ST.
TEL 867/993-6527
Extremely good, ethnic-influenced dishes served in an friendly, casual atmosphere. Large summertime patio and vegetarian selections are added draws.
🍴 100 🅿 🕐 Closed Dec.–Mar. 🚫 MC, V

WHITEHORSE, YUKON

🏨 EDGEWATER HOTEL
$$
101 MAIN ST.
TEL 867/667-2572 or
877/484-3334
www.edgewaterhotelwhitehorse.com
Large rooms with modern furnishings in a quiet setting.
🛏 30 🅿 🐾 🚫 All major cards

🏨 WESTMARK WHITEHORSE HOTEL
$$
201 WOOD ST.
TEL 867/393-9700 or
800/544-0970
www.westmarkhotels.com
Attractive rooms with wood furniture and coffeemakers. Frequent tour groups sometimes make for crowded hallways.
🛏 181 🅿 🚫 All major cards

🍴 CELLAR DINING ROOM
$$$
101 MAIN ST. (IN THE EDGEWATER HOTEL)
867/667-2572
Popular restaurant serving very good prime rib as well as the Alaska King Crab and sockeye salmon.
🍴 100 🚫 All major cards

INUVIK, N.W.T.

🏨 THE MACKENZIE HOTEL
$$$
P.O. BOX 2303, INUVIK
TEL 867/777-2861
www.inuvikhotels.com
There is really little to choose between this place and the Eskimo Inn, but the Mackenzie wins by a hair because the eating facilities are better.
🛏 33 🅿 🚫 All major cards

YELLOWKNIFE, N.W.T.

🏨 DISCOVERY INN
$$$
4701 FRANKLIN AVE.
TEL 867/873-4151 or
866/873-4151
www.discoveryinn.ca
Newly renovated rooms with kitchenettes right in downtown Yellowknife. Popular for long-term stays.
🛏 41 🅿 🐾 🚫 All major cards

🏨 EXPLORER HOTEL
$$$
4825 49TH AVE.
TEL 867/873-3531 or 800/661-0892
www.explorerhotel.ca
Modern 8-story block in downtown Yellowknife, with all "southern" conveniences and diamond mine executives thrown in for good measure. Full restaurant facilities.
🛏 128 🅿 🔁 🐾 🚫 All major cards

IQALUIT, NUNAVUT

🏨 FROBISHER INN
$$$$
P.O. BOX 4209, IQALUIT
TEL 867/979-2222 or
877/422-9422
www.frobisherinn.com
This centrally-located hotel is connected to government offices and stores. Unparalleled views of Frobisher Bay. Restaurant.
🛏 95 🚫 All major cards

SHOPPING IN CANADA

Browsing in shops and malls has become an acceptable pastime for both Canadian residents and visitors to the country. Sales are advertised in nearly every shop window; closing sales, year-end sales, back-to-school sales, you name it and someone has thought of it. Apart from the shopping malls there are also plenty of smaller specialized shops. In the Prairie Provinces and the North you will find Inuit and First Nations crafts that are always a good souvenir idea.

SALES TAX

Canada is riddled with federal and provincial taxes on goods and services. A general sales tax (GST) of 7 percent is levied on most transactions. Visitors are eligible for a GST rebate on most goods taken out of Canada within 60 days. Claim forms are available at airports, shops, and hotels, and from any Canadian embassy. All receipts must be enclosed with the forms, which should be returned within 60 days of leaving Canada.

In addition to GST a 5–12 percent tax is levied on goods bought in many provinces.

OPENING HOURS

Stores are generally open Monday through Saturday, 10 a.m. to 6 p.m., unless otherwise noted. Many retail stores stay open late on Thursday and Friday evenings. Shopping malls have longer hours than most stores, usually about 7:30–9 p.m., and most towns have 24-hour pharmacies and stores, e.g., Mac's or 7-Eleven. The so-called "blue laws" for shops regarding Sunday opening are no longer in application since they were overthrown by the Supreme Court. In much of Canada, stores are open between 12–5 p.m. on Sundays.

MARITIMES

AREAS TO SHOP
Market Square
Saint John, N.B.
Tel 506/658-3600
Some fascinating small boutiques are housed in the warehouses surrounding the Market Slip in Old Saint John.

St. Andrews, N.B.

This gracious community on the Fundy shore of New Brunswick has an interesting collection of boutiques along Water Street.
Historic Properties
1869 Upper Water St., Halifax, N.S.
This collection of waterfront warehouses is home to a wide selection of interesting shops, cafés, and pubs.
Spring Garden Road
Halifax, N.S.
A fascinating street for wandering and browsing in boutiques and art galleries.

ARTS & ANTIQUES
AGNS Gallery Shop
1723 Hollis St.
Tel 902/424-3003
This art gallery shop features jewelry, sculpture, pottery, textiles, woodwork, folk art, Mi'Kmaq handcrafts, and original prints from Nova Scotia.
Gallery 78
796 Queen St., Fredericton, N.B.
Tel 506/454-5192
Works by local artists are sold in this gallery.

CRAFTS & JEWELRY
Aitkens Pewter
408 Regent St., Fredericton, N.B.
Tel 506/453-9474
Hand-crafted pewter goblets, accessories, and jewelry.
Confederation Centre Gift Shop: The Showcase
145 Richmond St., Charlottetown, P.E.I.
Tel 902/628-6149
Specializes in quality handcrafts from P.E.I. and across Canada, as well as an assortment of books.
Jennifer's of Nova Scotia
5635 Spring Garden Rd., Halifax, N.B.
Tel 902/425-3119

Locally made jewelry, pottery, wool sweaters, and soaps.
Nova Scotian Crystal
Lower Water St., Historic Properties, Halifax, N.S.
Tel 902/492-0416 or 888/977-2797
Canada's only crystal manufacturer producing hand-crafted pieces in the time-honored way. Visitors can watch craftspeople at work and view their products in the showroom.
The Plaid Place
Barrington Pl., Halifax, N.S.
Tel 902/429-6872
This "New Scotland" store specializes in tartans, kilts, highland dress, sweaters, and other accessories, especially the Nova Scotia variety.

MARKETS
Boyce Farmers' Market
Bounded by Regent, Brunswick, & George Sts., Fredericton, N.B.
A great source of local meats and produce, baked goods, crafts, and such seasonal items as holiday wreaths and maple syrup, on Saturday mornings.
Brewery Market
1496 Lower Water St., Halifax, N.S.
An active and attractive farmers' market on Saturdays.
Saint John City Market
47 Charlotte St., Saint John, N.B.
Tel 506/658-2820
One city block's worth of foods and hand-crafted souvenirs. But don't visit on Sunday because it is closed then.

NEWFOUNDLAND

AREAS TO SHOP
Murray Premises
Harbour Dr., St. John's
These restored mercantile premises house some interesting boutiques, as well as a hotel and restaurants.

ARTS & ANTIQUES
Christina Parker Fine Art
7 Plank Rd., St. John's
Tel 709/753-0580
Paintings, sculptures, and drawings by local artists.

Murray's Antiques
414 Blackmarsh Rd., St. John's
Tel 709/579-7344
Top-notch selection of silver, china, and wooden furniture.

CLOTHES & ACCESSORIES
The Cod Jigger
245 Duckworth St., St. John's
Tel 709/726-7422
Newfoundland's own Grenfell coats are sold here, as well as other crafts.
Nonia
286 Water St., St. John's
Tel 709/753-8062
This nonprofit store offers the very best in Newfoundland handknits and weaving.

CRAFTS & JEWELRY
Craft Council Shop & Gallery
59 Duckworth St., St. John's
Tel 709/753-2749
Only juried crafts are carried in this gallery, owned by the Newfoundland and Labrador Crafts Development Association.

GIFTS & MISCELLANEOUS
Wordplay
221 Duckworth Street, St. John's
Tel 709/726-9193
A full selection of books as well as other local products. There's also an art gallery.

QUÉBEC

AREAS TO SHOP
Rue Petit-Champlain
Lower Town, Québec City
Along this charming old street is a fine collection of artisan-owned boutiques, galleries, and cafés specializing in Québec crafts and designs.
**Knowlton
(Ville du Lac-Brome)**
This small community in Québec's Eastern Townships has a fine collection of antique stores and other interesting boutiques housed in original Victorian houses on English Hill, its main street.

ARTS & ANTIQUES
Antiques Row
Rue Notre-Dame Ouest between Guy & Atwater, Montréal
This run-down section of Notre-Dame Street houses a large number of antique and second-hand stores. It is not a glamour-ous and glitzy district, but can be paradise for the person intent on seeking out a bargain. Most stores open about 11 a.m., some not before noon, and they close by 5 or 6 p.m.
Desmarais & Robitaille
60 Notre-Dame Ouest, Montréal
Tel 514/845-3194
Situated close to the Notre-Dame Basilica, this store offers a fine selection of Roman Catholic religious souvenirs. In addition to books and posters, it sells gold and silver objects, stained glass, and vestments fabricated on the upper floors of the building.
Rue du Trésor
Between rue Ste.-Anne & rue Buade, Québec City
Along this narrow street in Old Québec, numerous artists display their works—watercolors, prints, etchings, silkscreens, reproductions, etc.

CLOTHES & ACCESSORIES
Fourrures du Vieux-Port
55 Saint-Pierre, Québec City
Tel 418/692-6686
Fabulous collection of designer items including fur hats, coats and jackets displayed on three floors. Also leather and woollen goods.
McComber/Grosvenor
402 blvd. de Maisonneuve Ouest, Montréal
Tel 514/845-1167
Stylish house designs for mink and other furs at a century-old business.

CRAFTS & JEWELRY
Bonsecours Market
350 St.-Paul E., Old Montréal
This former wholesale market now houses a fascinating collection of craft and design stores on its main floor, and food outlets on the lower level.

Boutique Canadeau
1124 Saint-Jean, Québec City
Tel 418/692-4850
This boutique on Québec City's main shopping street has a superior collection of Canadian-made products, including lovely sweaters, jewelry, and Inuit soapstone sculptures.
Canadian Guild of Crafts
1460 Sherbrooke Ouest, Montréal
Tel 514/849-6091
Wonderful store run by the nonprofit institution that promotes Canadian art and crafts. Superb Inuit art gallery.
Joaillier Louis Perrier
48 rue du Petit-Champlain, Québec City
Tel 418/692-4633
Locally designed gold and silver jewelry.

GIFTS & MISCELLANEOUS
Papeterie St.-Gilles
304 rue F.A. Savard , St.-Joseph-de-la-Rive
Tel 418/635-2430
Wondrous handcrafted stationery, made on antique machines.
Paragraphe
2220 McGill College Ave., Montréal
Tel 514/845-5811
Large and well-stocked English bookstore for anyone interested in books on Canadian or general subjects.
Ulysse Travel Bookshop
4176 Saint-Denis, Montréal
Tel 514/843-9447
Bookstore that specializes in travel books to every part of the globe. There is also a branch in the downtown Infotouriste Centre (1001 Dorchester Sq.), which carries local travel guides.

MARKETS
Les Halles de la Gare
Central Station, 895 rue de la Gauchetière Ouest, Montréal
A fine collection of restaurants and take-out food. Just the place for lunch or to pick up a gourmet picnic. Access from Queen Elizabeth Hotel or Place Ville-Marie.

Marché Atwater
138 Atwater at rue Notre-Dame Ouest, Montréal
The market building houses an amazing collection of traditional butchers and cheese stores. In season, the exterior is alive with flowers and a wide variety of fruit and vegetables.

Marché Jean-Talon
7075 Casgrain, Montréal
In the center of the city's Italian quarter, this market really comes to life in the late summer and fall, when farmers from far and wide bring their produce to sell. It is surrounded by small Italian meat and pasta shops.

Québec Public Market
160 Quai Saint-André, Québec City
Tel 418/692-2517
This public market in the Old Port area offers a wonderful selection of breads, cheeses, and seasonal local fruits and vegetables. (Closed Mon.–Wed. Jan.–March)

ONTARIO

AREAS TO SHOP

Queen's Quay Terminal
207 Queen's Quay W., Toronto
This building at the foot of York Street on the waterfront houses about 50 specialty shops, galleries, and restaurants.

Queen Street West
Between University Ave. & Bathurst, Toronto
Known for its eclectic and eccentric stores selling a wide variety of antiques, books, hip fashions, and other bric-a-brac.

Toronto Eaton Centre
220 Yonge St., Toronto
The Toronto Eaton Centre is like no other shopping complex. The architecture is fabulous. You can sit and admire it or venture into some of the over 300 stores.

ARTS & ANTIQUES

Gallery One Arts
121 Scollard St., Toronto
Tel 416/929-3103
This large gallery in the fashionable Yorkville area promotes many up and coming

young Canadian artists. It displays paintings, drawings, sculpture, and photography.

The Guild Shop
118 Cumberland St., Toronto
Tel 416/921-1721
Aboriginal painters and sculptors are among the many Canadian artists represented.

GIFTS & MISCELLANEOUS

Amethyst Gift Centre
400 Victoria Ave. E., Thunder Bay
Tel 807/622-6908
Wonderful selection of pieces of precious purple amethyst. The area north of Lake Superior is one of the very few places in the world where the stone is found.

Arts-on-Queen
2198 Queen St. E., Toronto
Tel 416/699-6127
Funky store specializing in Canadian arts and crafts, with fine art and unique glass, ceramic, papier mâché, and wood offerings.

Honest Ed's Bargain Store
581 Bloor St., Toronto
Tel 416/537-1574
This is a massive and quite amazing bargain shopping center run by Toronto personality Ed Mirvish. Worth a visit even if you don't buy anything.

Corkin Shopland Gallery
55 Mill St., Toronto
Tel 416/979-1980
This gallery in the newly fashionable Distillery district exhibits contemporary works, notably photographs but also sculpture, ceramics, and paintings.

National Gallery of Canada Gift Store
380 Sussex Dr., Ottawa
Tel 613/990-1985
This world-class art gallery has a magnificent gift store where you can purchase wonderful Canadian souvenirs as well as art books and other collectibles.

Royal Canadian Mint Store
320 Sussex Dr., Ottawa
Tel 613/993-8990
The place to purchase investment coins made in silver, platinum, and gold. The Canadian gold "Maple Leaf" is on sale here

as are a great many other collector coins. You do have to take the tour of the Mint first (30 minutes) and security is very tight.

William Ashley China
55 Bloor St. W., Toronto
Tel 416/964-2900
Considered North America's largest shop devoted to tableware, this store stocks fine china, crystal, silver, and many other items.

MARKETS

Byward Market
Between George & York Sts. just E of Sussex Dr., Ottawa
This colorful market with its fruit and flowers in season has existed since 1846. The main building houses craft stores, and it is surrounded by a myriad of restaurants.

Kensington Market
NW of Dundas St. & Spadina Ave., Toronto
Open-air food market serving the city's newest immigrants from Asia and Africa.

Kitchener Market
Market Square Mall, Kitchener
Tel 519/741-2287
Hundreds of farmers come every Saturday (and Wednesdays in summer months) to sell their produce and crafts.

Kingston Farmers' Market
Behind City Hall, Ontario St., Kingston
In existence since 1801, this market offers agricultural produce and local handmade crafts every Tuesday, Thursday and Saturday. On Sundays, the same area is transformed into an antiques market.

St. Lawrence Market
Front & Jarvis Sts., Toronto
Covered food hall with two levels of butchers, cheese shops, and bakeries (Tues.–Sat.) in a building on the north side of Front Street. A farmers' market is set up every Saturday.

PRAIRIES

AREAS TO SHOP
Osborne Village
Osborne St. near Corydon Ave.
S of the Assiniboine River,
Winnipeg, Man.
Along five blocks of Osborne
Street, you can shop for unique
pieces by local artisans, jewelry,
and clothing. Also offers cafés.

ARTS & ANTIQUES
Exchange District
W & E of Main St; N & S of
McDermot, Winnipeg, Man.
Art galleries and antique stores
line the streets of this architec-
turally interesting area of
Winnipeg. Also restaurants and
bars.
Northern Images
Portage Place Mall, Portage Ave.,
Winnipeg, Man.
Tel 204/942-5501
Inuit and Déné artists belonging
to the North Territories Co-
operative showcase their work.

CLOTHES &
ACCESSORIES
Alberta Boot Manufacturing
614 10th Ave. S.W., Calgary, Alta.
Tel 403/263-4605
You've bought your hat, now for
the cowboy boots. This company
sells thousands of pairs every
year, but they're not cheap—
expect to pay up to $250.
Smithbilt Hats
1235 10th Ave. S.W., Calgary,
Alta.
Tel 403/244-9131
You can buy Western gear all
over Calgary, but this is the place
to purchase that white Stetson
hat that everyone wears during
the Stampede.
Winnipeg Outfitters
250 McPhillips St., Winnipeg,
Man.
Tel 204/775-9653
This hunting outfitter specializes
in gear for extremely cold
weather.

CRAFTS & JEWELRY
**Museum Shop, Manitoba
Museum**
190 Rupert Ave., Winnipeg, Man.

Tel 204/988-0615
This shop sells a great selection
of merchandise made by local
craftsmen and artists reflecting
Manitoba's diverse cultural
heritage and history. Items range
from jewelry to toys.
Trading Post Ltd.
226 2nd Ave. S., Saskatoon, Sask.
Tel 306/653-1769
Vast selection of aboriginal crafts
and Saskatoonberry products.

GIFTS &
MISCELLANEOUS
High Country Colour
1909 10 Ave. SW, Calgary, Alta.
Tel 403/244-3511
Books, calendars and postcards
of Alberta, British Columbia, and
the Rockies; also Canadian
souvenirs of all kinds.

MALLS & DEPARTMENT
STORES
West Edmonton Mall
170th St. at 87th Ave.,
Edmonton, Alta.
Tel 403/444-5200
Covering the equivalent of 48
city blocks, this megamall bills
itself as the world's largest with
800 or more stores, 100 or
more eating establishments, a
huge indoor amusement park, a
water park with submarine
voyages, a replica of Christopher
Columbus' Santa Maria, an 18-
hole miniature golf course, an
NHL-size skating rink, the
Fantasyland Hotel (see p. 367),
and more. You can even rent a
mechanical shopping cart to take
you around.

MARKETS
Forks Market
Winnipeg, Man.
Offers fresh produce including
meat, fish, and bread, as well as
taste sensations from all over
the world reflecting the ethnic
origins of Winnipeg's population.

THE ROCKIES

AREAS TO SHOP
Banff Avenue
Banff
The main street of this mountain

community in the heart of Banff
National Park is lined with
tempting stores selling arts,
crafts, and souvenirs of every
description for almost any
pocket.

GIFTS &
MISCELLANEOUS
Banff Book and Art Den
94 Banff Ave., Banff
Tel 403/762-3919
Extensive collection of guide-
books, maps, and general
information.
Banff Indian Trading Post
Cave Ave., Banff
Tel 403/762-2456
Large selection of Amerindian
arts and crafts, jewelry,
moccasins, and other clothing.

LEISURE
Mountain Magic
224 Bear St., Banff
Tel 403/762-2591
Three floors of hiking, skiing,
running, and biking equipment, as
well as a 30-foot climbing wall to
test some of it.

THE WEST

AREAS TO SHOP
Fan Tan Alley
Chinatown, Victoria
These former opium dens and
gambling parlors house neat
little stores selling bric-a-brac of
every description.
Gastown
Water St., Vancouver
This attractive area of restored
19th-century buildings holds a
wide range of art galleries, craft
stores, and other boutiques.
Government Street
N of Empress Hotel between
Humboldt & Johnson, Victoria
Victoria's main shopping street
(closed to traffic) is lined with
stores selling English bone china,
Scottish woolens, Irish linen, and
no doubt something Welsh.
These imports from the "Olde
Country" are very good value.
Robsonstrasse
Robson St. between Granville &
Jervis Sts., Vancouver
Vancouver's main shopping

street with its trendy boutiques and sidewalk cafés is always lively. Its name comes from the original German occupants of the area.

Yaletown
SE of downtown Vancouver on shores of False Creek Vancouver's newest hip area. Warehouses have been renovated as art galleries, trendy restaurants, and boutiques.

ARTS & ANTIQUES
Antique Row
Fort St. between Government & Cook, Victoria
This strip of Fort Street boasts a large number of antique shops.
The Inuit Gallery of Vancouver
206 Cambie St., Vancouver
Tel 604/688-7323
Coastal native art.

CLOTHES & ACCESSORIES
Hills Indian Crafts
Hwy. 1, 1 mile S of Duncan
Tel 250/746-6731
Large selection of Cowichan wool sweaters and other handicrafts.
Tilley Endurables
2401 Granville St., Vancouver
Tel 604/732-4287
Famous for their hats, this Canadian company also makes practical travel clothing for a wide range of activities and destinations.

CRAFTS & JEWELRY
Cowichan Trading Co. Ltd.
1328 Government St., Victoria
Tel 250/383-0321
Jewelry, moccasins, and sweaters produced by the eponymous native tribe.

FOOD & DRINK
Roger's Chocolates
913 Government St., Victoria
Tel 250/384-7021
Hand-crafted chocolates made without preservatives.

GIFTS & MISCELLANEOUS
Vancouver Aquarium Gift Store

Stanley Park, Vancouver
Tel 604/659-3474
The famous aquarium has a splendid gift store featuring items with a fishy flavor, local crafts, and Amerindian art.
The Landing
375 Water St., Vancouver
Renovated heritage building on the edge of Gastown that houses an interesting collection of specialty shops and restaurants.

MALLS & DEPARTMENT STORES
Market Square
560 Johnson St., Victoria
Tel 250/386-2441
Three levels of funky boutiques and specialty stores selling everything from comic books to incense.

MARKETS
Granville Island Public Market
Johnson St., Granville Island, Vancouver
Tel 604/666-5784
Unique boutiques and a dazzling selection of produce, including smoked salmon packaged for travel.
Lonsdale Quay Market
Seabus Terminus, North Vancouver
Food counters, coffee bars, and bookstores as well as fresh fruit and vegetables in season.

THE NORTH

GIFTS & MISCELLANEOUS
Mac's Fireweed Books
203 Main St., Whitehorse, Yukon
Tel 867/668-2434
Features books and maps about Alaska, the Yukon, and the Klondike Gold Rush.
Midnight Sun Gallery and Gifts
205C Main St., Whitehorse, Yukon
Tel 867/668-4350
Specializes in Yukon-made products, local art, posters, pottery, jewelry, and other souvenirs.

Murdoch's Gem Shop
207 Main St., Whitehorse, Yukon
Tel 867/667-7403
Gold nuggets from the world's biggest manufacturer.
Nunavut
Almost every community in the Arctic has its own cooperative to sell local arts and crafts. For a complete list, contact:
Nunavut Tourism
P.O. Box 1450
Iqaluit, Nunavut X0A 0H0
Tel 866/686-2888 or 867/979-6551
www.nunavuttourism.com
Tgit Geomatics Ltd.
Yellowknife, N.W.T.
Tel 867/873-8448
The place to buy maps of the north as well as aeronautical and hydrographic charts. Agents for the Geological Survey of Canada and the National Air Photo Library.
The Yellowknife Book Cellar
Yellowknife, N.W.T.
Tel 867/920-2220
Good selection of northern and native studies books as well as current titles in hardcover and paperback.
Wolverine Sports Shop
Stanton Plaza, Old Airport Rd., Yellowknife, N.W.T.
Tel 867/873-4350
Specializes in mountain outdoor wear and camping, fishing, and hunting supplies.

ENTERTAINMENT & ACTIVITIES

Canada is a vast and varied country with an amazing array of possibilities for entertainment. The variety of different activities across the country is staggering so only the major and most typical ones are mentioned here. Every city has its own cultural, sporting, and social life, often reflecting the origins of its inhabitants. In addition, cultural centers and nightlife vary enormously from coast to coast.

MARITIMES

FESTIVALS
Scotia Festival of Music
Halifax, N.S.
Tel 902/429-9467
May & June
Master classes and concerts by internationally recognized classical musicians.
Nova Scotia International Tattoo
Metro Centre
Halifax, N.S.
Tel 902/451-1221
First week of July
Every day for a week, two-hour spectacles featuring over 2,000 Canadian and international, military and civilian performers with pipes, drums, military bands, singing, dancing, acrobatics, etc.
Antigonish Highland Games
Antigonish, N.S.
Mid-July
Staged annually since 1863, these games highlight the best in Scottish music, dance, and sports. The caber toss is one of the more popular features.
Festival by the Sea
Saint John, N.B.
Tel 506/632-0086
August
Performances of Canadian music, dance, and culture in this summer festival on the shores of the Bay of Fundy.
Natal Day
Halifax & Dartmouth, N.S.
Tel 902/490-6773
www.natalday.org
First weekend in August
The Halifax and Dartmouth area celebrates the anniversary of its foundation in grand style with parades in both communities and lots of other activities.
Celtic Festivities
South Gut St. Ann's

Cape Breton Island, N.S.
Tel 902/295-3411
www.gaeliccollege.edu
July & August
The Gaelic College of Arts and Culture is the only educational institution devoted to promoting the Gaelic language and culture in North America. During the summer months, there are occasional performances of bagpipe playing, Highland dancing, and other Scottish activities.
Festival Acadien
Caraquet, N.B.
Tel 506/727-2787
www.festivalacadiencaraquet.com
August
Celebration of Acadian culture with lots of joie de vivre. Also the official Blessing of the Fishing Fleet.
Atlantic Film Festival
Halifax, N.S.
Tel 902/422-3456
September
Regional feature films, TV movies, and documentaries are screened at half-a-dozen venues over nine days in September; call for tickets, times, and places.

CULTURAL CENTERS
Confederation Centre for the Arts
145 Richmond St.,
Charlottetown, P.E.1.
Tel 902/628-1864
www.confederationcentre.com
The musical version of *Anne of Green Gables* plays here during the Charlottetown Festival, which runs from June through September. The building houses three theaters, as well as a gift shop, art gallery, and restaurant.
Imperial Theatre
24 King St. S., Saint John, N.B.
Tel 506/674-4100
Beautifully restored vaudeville

theater is the year-round venue for both local and touring theater, opera, ballet, and symphony companies.
The Playhouse
686 Queen St., Fredericton, N.B.
Tel 506/458-8344
Venue for Theatre New Brunswick and Symphony New Brunswick.
Neptune Theatre
1593 Argyle St., Halifax, N.S.
Tel 902/429-7070
Year-round performances of drama classics and contemporary Canadian works.

NIGHTLIFE
Benevolent Irish Society Hall
582 North River Rd.,
Charlottetown, P.E.1.
Tel 902/892-2367
Traditional Celtic ceilidhs, a combination of music, dancing, and comedy, take place here Friday nights from mid-May through October.
Dolan's Pub
Pipers Ln., Fredericton, N.B.
Tel 506/454-7474
Maritime bands play Thursday, Friday, and Saturday nights.
The Lunar Rogue
625 King St., Fredericton, N.B.
Tel 506/450-2065
Old-fashioned pub with Maritime live music on Fridays and Saturdays. Summer patio.
O'Carroll's Pub
1860 Upper Water St.,
Halifax, N.S.
Tel 902/423-4405
Maritime melodies and sea shanties share the bill with traditional Irish and Scottish music at this popular pub nightly.
O'Leary's Pub
46 Princess St., Saint John, N.B.
Tel 506/634-7135
Wednesday is audience participation night at this folksy Maritime pub; bands play Thursday through Sunday evenings.

OTHER ACTIVITIES
Reversing Falls Jet Boat Ride
Falls View Park, Saint John, N.B.
Tel 506/634-8987

A close-up view of this natural phenomenon, which takes place twice daily, from late May through September.

Small Craft Aquatic Center
Woodstock Rd.,
Fredericton, N.B.
Tel 506/460-2260
Late May–Labor Day
Rent canoes and kayaks here to explore the Saint John River on your own or with a guide.

Whale-Watching Cruises
Cape Breton Island, N.S.
For details of cruises from Ingonish, Pleasant Bay, and Chéticamp contact Cape Breton Tourism Tel 800/565-0000
Explore the rugged coast of Cape Breton and search for pilot, minke, fin, and humpback whales as well as seals, bald eagles, cormorants, and other sea birds.
St. Andrews, N.B.
Tel 506/529-3555 or 506/529-3556 (summer months)
Several companies offer whale-watching trips into the wild waters of the Bay of Fundy where whales go up and down with the 50-foot tides.

Lobster Suppers
St. Ann's Church, P.E.I. (off Rte. 224)
Tel 902/621-0635
Mon.–Sat. 12–2 p.m. & 4–8:30 p.m.
There are many places in P.E.I. to enjoy this tradition, which began as an activity to raise money for the church. Today, the lobster supper in the church hall at St. Ann is one of the few which remains a charitable affair. Home-cooked food: salads, rolls, seafood, desserts, and, of course, lobster.

NEWFOUNDLAND

FESTIVALS
Newfoundland and Labrador Folk Festival
St. John's
Tel 709/576-8508
Early in August
Three days of traditional music at Bannerman Park draws 30,000 listeners.

CULTURAL CENTERS
Resource Centre for the Arts
LSPU Hall
3 Victoria St., St. John's
Tel 709/753-4531
Open year-round, experimental theater in the fall and winter, cabarets and outdoor concerts in the summer.

NIGHTLIFE
Bridie Molloy's
5 George St., St. John's
Tel 709/576-5990
This popular pub serves Guinness and traditional "pub grub" with music nightly.
Trapper John's
2 George St., St. John's
Tel 709/579-9630
Good place to undergo that famous (or infamous) Newfoundland activity, the "screech-in."

OTHER ACTIVITIES
Signal Hill Tattoo
St. John's
Tel 709/772-5367
July & August
Military exercises of the 19th century performed high above the city on Signal Hill. A great pageant on a fine day, cancelled in bad weather. Call for exact days and times.
Birds, Whales, and Icebergs
These boat trips offer magnificent experiences, but rough seas and wild weather can lead to cancellations on few hours' notice.
St. John's
Tel 709/726-5000
May–October
Watch icebergs and whales from a two-masted schooner.
Trinity
Tel 709/464-2133
June–September
Whales up close in summer months, seals and sea birds, too.
Twillingate
Tel 709/884-2242
May–September
Exciting trips to see icebergs, whales, birds, dolphins, and seals.
Witless Bay
Tel 709/334-2722
May–September

The largest puffin colony in North America is located just off this community 20 miles south of St. John's. Murres, whales, and icebergs also abound.

QUÉBEC

FESTIVALS
Carnaval d'Hiver (Winter Carnival)
Québec City
Tel 418/626-3716
February
A great winter celebration for the whole family—art, culture, sports, and entertainment, presided over by a huge snowball called Bonhomme Carnival.
Montréal en Lumière (High Lights Festival)
Montréal
Tel 514/288-9955 or 888/477-9955
February
For ten days in February, Montréal is lit up in style with firework displays, theatrical events, and restaurants offering special gourmet menus with visiting celebrity chefs. On one Saturday evening, a *Nuit blanche* occurs when every museum and cultural institution in the city stays open all night, offering special displays, hot chocolate (and things stronger), etc.
Fête nationale
Québec City, Québec
Tel 418/640-0799
June 24
The saint's day of John the Baptist on June 24 is celebrated as the national holiday of the province of Québec. There are festivities all over the province but the most spectacular is held on the Plains of Abraham in the capital when a concert is capped by fireworks at midnight.
International Pyrotechnical Competition
La Ronde, Île Notre-Dame
Montréal
Tel 514/397-2000
June & July
Amazing firework displays in a popular competition with about

ENTERTAINMENT & ACTIVITIES

10 competing countries. The shows take place at La Ronde amusement park, but it is possible to view them for free along the waterfront. Extremely popular, so streets and bridges are closed to vehicles.

International Jazz Festival
Montréal
Tel 514/871-1881
or 888/515-0515
July
One of the continent's great jazz festivals with many free shows on outdoor stages, in addition to the big-name ticketed events.

Juste pour Rire (Just for Laughs)
Montréal
Tel 514/790-4242
July
One of the world's few comedy festivals, with 600 artists from 14 countries in over 1,000 shows.

Festival d'été international (Summer Festival)
Québec City
Tel 418/529-5200
July
The largest Francophone cultural event in North America. Activities take over the streets and squares of the Old City.

Festival de Montgolfières (Hot Air Balloon Festival)
Saint-Jean-sur-Richelieu
Tel 450/347-9555
August
More than 100 brightly colored balloons, some with unusual shapes, fly every evening.

Montréal World Film Festival
Montréal
Tel 514/848-3883
August & September
Competitive festival and great popular event drawing 350,000 viewers.

CULTURAL CENTERS
Centaur Theatre
453 Saint-François-Xavier, Montréal
Tel 514/288-3161
Located in the renovated 1903 Stock Exchange building, Centaur is the city's leading English-language theater. New and especially local playwrights tend to be favored although there are

occasional performances of Broadway hits and more classical works (Sept.–May).

Ex-centris
3536 bvld. Saint-Laurent, Montréal
Tel 514/847-3536
Innovative cinemagraphic center specializing in offbeat, unusual productions from all over the world.

Grand Théâtre de Québec
269 bvld. René Lévesque Est, Québec City
Tel 418/643-8131
Plays (in French), dance, and symphony performances are staged September through April.

Place des Arts
Corner rue Ste.-Catherine Ouest & Jeanne Mance, Montréal
Tel 541/285-4200 (information)
514/842-2112 (box office)
Montréal's showcase for the performing arts comprises five multifaceted halls including the prestigious Salle Wilfrid Pelletier concert hall with nearly 3,000 seats. Home to the symphony orchestra, the Opéra de Montréal, the city's principal ballet company, Les Grands Ballets Canadiens, and several theater companies. There is also an informal Sunday brunch series.

Saidye Bronfman Centre
5170 chemin de la Côte Ste.-Catherine, Montréal
Tel 514/739-2301
or 514/739-7944
English- and Yiddish-language dramas are staged here, along with many free lectures and concerts.

Théâtre Lac Brome
Knowlton
Tel 450/242-2270
Broadway and West End hits come to life in English-language productions running during summer months.

NIGHTLIFE
Angels
3604 blvd. St.-Laurent, Montréal
Tel 514/282-9944
Nightly 8 p.m.–3 a.m.
The two floors of this popular nightspot offer several dance floors and lounges.

Aux Deux Pierrots
104 rue St.-Paul Est, Montréal

Tel 514/861-1270
Traditional Québecois folk music (outdoor terrace performances in summer). Crowded but convivial.

Les Beaux Jeudis (Thursdays)
1449 Crescent, Montréal
Tel 514/288-5656
Located on Montréal's downtown bar and nightclub strip, Thursdays attracts the younger crowd year-round. In summer, the terrace is always popular, things hop at cocktail hour, and the disco swings until the early hours of the morning.

Café Campus
57 rue Prince-Arthur Est, Montréal
Tel 514/844-1010
Alternative music from live bands and DJ's in this small venue. Popular with many young Montréalers.

Casino de Montréal
1 ave. du Casino, Montréal
Tel 514/392-2746
or 800/665-2274
Occupying the former 1967 World's Fair pavilions of France and Québec on Île Notre-Dame, this large casino has 120 gaming tables, more than 3,000 slot machines, a cabaret, and 4 restaurants. Open 24 hours a day to those 18 years and over.

Le Cheval Blanc
809 rue Ontario Est, Montréal
Tel 514/522-0211
Traditional pub with beer brewed on the premises. Cultural chat at the communal tables sometimes drowns out the music.

Club Balattou
4372 Saint-Laurent, Montréal
Tel 514/845-5447
This popular disco offers World Music, especially Caribbean and African performers. It's open until 3 a.m. every night.

L'Emprise at Hôtel Clarendon
57 rue Ste.-Anne, Québec City
Tel 418/692-2480
Art deco bar with live jazz nightly (Thurs.–Sat. in winter months).

Les Foufounes Électriques
87 rue Ste.-Catherine Est,

Montréal
Tel 514/844-5539
Les "Foues" considers itself Montréal's cultural and musical mosaic. Eccentric interior decor attracts a diverse range of customers to this bar and music venue.

Hurley's Irish Pub
1225 rue Crescent, Montréal
Tel 514/861-4111
Celtic music and dancing every night of the week, Guinness for sale, too.

Maison du Jazz
2060 rue Aylmer, Montréal
Tel 514/842-8656
Formerly Biddles, the name of this Montréal institution changed when jazz pianist Charlie Biddle died. It is still the top club in a city devoted to jazz with music nightly and excellent barbecued chicken and ribs.

OTHER ACTIVITIES

Glissades de la Terrasse (Dufferin Terrace Slides)
Québec City
Mid-December–mid-March
In a toboggan, slide down the ice onto the wide terrace beside the Château Frontenac. Also skating.

Mont-Sainte-Anne Ski Centre
25 miles E of Québec City
Tel 418/827-4561
63 trails, a vertical drop of over 2,000 feet, and stunning views of the St. Lawrence and the capital. Also snowboarding, cross-country skiing, and snowshoeing.

Owl's Head Ski Area
Rte. 243 S., Mansonville
Tel 450/292-3342
or 800/363-3342
December–mid-April
Quiet slopes with 44 trails and the area's longest runs.

Mont-Tremblant Ski Hill
Mont-Tremblant
Tel 819/681-3000
or 888/857-8043
Late November–mid-April
More than 90 downhill ski trails and 50 miles of cross-country trails at this resort, a two-hour drive northwest of Montréal.

Ice Hockey at Bell Centre
1260 rue de la Gauchetière

Ouest, Montréal
Tel 514/932-2582
Canada's unofficial national sport fires the passions of most Canadians, but in Montréal hockey is not a sport—it's a religion. The Montréal Canadiens, known as Les Habs (short for les Habitants), have won the National Hockey League's Stanley Cup a record 24 times, twice as many times as any other team.

Canadian Grand Prix
Circuit Gilles Villeneuve, Île Notre-Dame, Montréal
Tel 514/350-0000 or -4731
June
Every year, the Canadian Grand Prix is run in Montréal. For a week in June, the pace reaches fever pitch as Formula One racing takes over the city. Reserve accommodations far in advance.

Harness Racing
Hippodrome Blue Bonnets
7440 blvd. Décarie, Montréal
Tel 514/739-2741
Two-wheel trotting races are held at this hippodrome in northern Montréal.

Cirque du Soleil
Montréal
Tel 514/722-2324
Montréal's circus has achieved international fame with its blend of daredevil acts and state-of-the-art presentation. No animals are used. Trapeze artists, acrobats, jugglers, clowns, and contortionists perform innovative acts choreographed to stunning light shows and original music. It can only be seen in Montréal every two years.

Saute Moutons Jet-boating (Lachine Rapids Tours)
Old Port, Quai de l'Horloge, Montréal
Tel 514/284-9607
May–mid-October
Shoot the Lachine Rapids aboard open hydrofoil-type boats. Wild, wet, and wonderful. Reservations required. No children under 6.

Jacques Cartier Excursions
860 ave. Jacques Cartier Nord, Tewkesbury
Tel 418/848-7238
Summer

Half-day rafting trips on the Jacques Cartier River leaving from Tewkesbury, about 30 minutes northwest of Québec City.

Whitewater Rafting
Grenville-sur-la-rouge, Rivière Rouge
Tel 819/242-7238
or 800/361-5033
April–October
Thrilling expeditions down this wild river and through its swirling rapids. Not for the faint of heart.

Whale-Watching Cruises
Tadoussac and other places on the North Shore of the St. Lawrence
Tel 866/235-4744 (for names of companies and details)
The confluence of the St. Lawrence and Saguenay Rivers is a rich summer feeding place for whales. Small craft sail far out into this deep water to offer close-up views of these huge mammals.

Hull/Chelsea/Wakefield Steam Train
Gatineau
Tel 800/871-7246 or 819/778-7246
www.steamtrain.ca
Summer months
Reservations are essential for excursions aboard one of the last steam trains in operation in Canada.

Snow Geese Migration
Cap-Tourmente
October
During their annual migration south, thousands of snow geese stop in the bulrushes beside the St. Lawrence below Cap-Tourmente. It's amazing to see these huge birds rise off the water like a cloud.

ONTARIO

FESTIVALS

Winterlude
Ottawa
Tel 613/239-5000
Mid-February
In winter, 6 miles of the Rideau Canal are cleared to make a wonderful long skating rink with

great views and numerous events.

Tulip Festival
Ottawa
Mid-May
Since the Dutch Royal family took refuge in Ottawa during World War II, the city has received annual gifts of tulips from Dutch bulb growers. The result is millions of tulips of every shape and color decorating the city, especially the Rideau Canal and the area around Dow's Lake.

Caribana
Toronto
Tel 416/466-0321
July
The city takes on the appearance of a Caribbean Island for two weeks with traditional foods and activities of the Caribbean and Latin America.

Peterborough Summer Festival of Lights
Peterborough
Tel 705/742-7777
www.festivaloflights.ca
July & August
Free outdoor concerts followed by firework displays every Wednesday and Saturday night for two months every summer.

Fergus Scottish Festival and Highland Games
Tel 519/787-0099
www.fergusscottishfestival.com
August
Celebration of Scottish heritage with bagpipes, Highland dancing, a tattoo and Celtic music.

Canadian National Exhibition
CNE Grounds
Toronto
Tel 416/263-3800
August & September
An enormous extravaganza with display pavilions, grandstand performances, and an air show.

Niagara Grape and Wine Festival
Tel 905/688-0212
www.niagarawinefestival.com
September
At the end of September, the Niagara peninsula celebrates their budding industry with visits to wineries, wine-tasting and much more.

Toronto International Film Festival
Tel 416/968-3456
September
Ten days of top-notch cinema in September.

Oktoberfest
Kitchener-Waterloo
Tel 519/570-4267
October
The distinctly Germanic origin of these twin cities is celebrated in their Bavarian festivities with a grand pageant and parade, lederhosen, schnitzel, sauerkraut, strudel, and, of course, beer.

CULTURAL CENTERS
National Arts Centre
Ottawa
Tel 613/947-7000
This cultural complex on the banks of the Rideau Canal offers a wide range of concerts, plays, musicals, and other activities.

Shaw Festival
Niagara-on-the-Lake
Tel 905/468-2172
or 800/511-7429
www.shawfest.com
April–November
Although plays by George Bernard Shaw are still featured, this festival also offers classics, musicals, and comedies old and new.

Stratford Festival
Stratford
Tel 519/271-4040
or 800/567-1600
www.stratford-festival.on.ca
Early May–late October
The works of the Bard, along with contemporary dramas and musicals, play to packed houses.

Hummingbird Centre for the Performing Arts
1 Front St. E., Toronto
Tel 416/393-7474
This is a large venue with a wide variety of shows, concerts, and theater. It's also the home of the National Ballet of Canada.

Roy Thomson Hall
60 Simcoe St., Toronto
Tel 416/872-4255
This is home to the Toronto Symphony Orchestra and the Toronto Mendelssohn Choir. Modern design and outstanding acoustics make it the city's

preeminent concert hall.

Premiere Dance Theatre
Queen's Quay, Toronto
Tel 416/973-4000
Many major dance companies perform at this venue including the Toronto Dance Theatre, a leading contemporary dance company.

Theater in Toronto
Toronto has a very active theater scene and is considered by many to be the world's third great center of English-language production (after London and New York).

Royal Alexandra Theatre
260 King St. W., Toronto
Tel 416/593-4142 or
800/724-6420
Broadway shows in an amazing 1906-07 beaux arts building, which is worth seeing in its own right.

Princess of Wales Theatre
300 King St. W., Toronto
Tel 416/593-4142 or
800/724-6420
A spectacular state-of-the-art theater opened by the late Princess. Popular for large productions such as *Miss Saigon*.

Pantages Theatre
244 Victoria St., Toronto
Tel 416/364-4100
Magnificent theater hosting Broadway shows such as *The Phantom of the Opera*.

Buddies in Bad Times
12 Alexander St., Toronto
Tel 416/975-8555
Not only is this the premier gay theater company in Canada, but it has also nurtured many contemporary straight writers. It is always cutting edge, delivering productions that challenge social boundaries. Home to Tallulah's Cabaret, which is very popular on Friday and Saturday nights.

Lorraine Kimsa Theatre for Young People
165 Front St. E, Toronto
Tel 416/862-2222
Productions from October through May offering adaptations of Dickens, C.S. Lewis, and other popular children's authors.

NIGHTLIFE
Bar Italia
582 College St., Toronto
Tel 416/535-3621
Young and trendy spot in Little Italy. Italian specialties plus live jazz or R&B.

Chick 'N' Deli
744 Mount Pleasant Rd., Toronto
Tel 416/489-3363
Busy and youthful club serving up contemporary pop for the energetic dancer and barbecue dishes for the hungry.

Crocodile Rock
240 Adelaide St. W., Toronto
Tel 416/599-9751
DJ and dancing nightly at this popular spot in the Entertainment district. Restaurant with late night menu, roof top patio.

Horseshoe Tavern
370 Queen St. W., Toronto
Tel 416/598-4753
A venerable institution devoted to live music in existence for half a century, this club features blues, rock and alternative bands from across Canada. Open daily.

El Mocambo
464 Spading Ave., Toronto
Tel 416/968-2001
Grungy rock spot whose stage was once graced by The Rolling Stones. Showcases local talent on Monday evenings.

Second City
56 Blue Jays Way, Toronto
Tel 416/343-0011
Canadian comics like John Candy and Bill Murray performed at this venue before achieving fame south of the border.

Top O' The Senator
253 Victoria St., Toronto
Tel 416/364-7517
Intimate jazz club on the third floor of the Senator restaurant. Supper packages available.

Wayne Gretzky's
99 Blue Jays Way, Toronto
Tel 416/979-7825
A shrine to the Canadians' premier ice hockey player. Not necessarily the best place to eat, but great views from the rooftop patio.

Yukyuk's
224 Richmond St. W., Toronto
Tel 416/967-6425
Inspired by the comedy theaters of New York and Los Angeles, this venue was begun in the 1960s and has subsequently nurtured Canadian comedy stars like Jim Carrey.

OTHER ACTIVITIES
Maple Leafs Ice Hockey
Air Canada Centre, Toronto
Tel 416/872-5000
Witness Canadians succumbing to unbridled passion as they support their local hockey team. Tickets are expensive and difficult to obtain.

Glen Abbey
1333 Dorval Dr., Oakville, Toronto
Tel 905/844-1800
Top-notch, 18-hole golf course about 45 minutes from Toronto. The Canadian Open Championship is played here.

Niagara Wine Tours
92 Picton St., Niagara-on-the-Lake
Tel 905/468-1300
Leisurely tours daily of wineries by bicycle or van, lunch included.

Baseball at Rogers Centre
1 Blue Jays Way, Toronto
Tel 416/341-3663
The Toronto Blue Jays attract 4 million fans every season. Their stadium with its retractable roof is so revolutionary in design that people tour it in its own right.

Changing of the Guard
Parliament Hill, Ottawa
July–August, 10 a.m. daily
A colorful and popular ceremony held on the lawns in front of the Canadian Parliament, with over a hundred soldiers parading in busbies and scarlet tunics.

Agawa Canyon Train Tours
Sault Ste. Marie
Tel 800/242-9287 or 705/946-7300
June–October
Scenic day trips into the rugged wilderness north of Lake Superior. Summer stop-over in Agawa Canyon or the awesome beauty of the fall colors. Reservations essential.

Polar Bear Express
Cochrane (northern Ontario)
Tel 705/472-4500 ext. 489 or 390 or 866/472-3865
www.polarbearexpress.ca
Late June–early September
All-day train trip from Cochrane (northern Ontario) to the Arctic watershed, Moosonee, on the shores of James Bay. Frontier life, muskeg, and scrub bush. A naturalist's delight. Reservations essential.

Playdium
99 Rathburn Rd. W, Mississauga
Tel 416/273-9000
Interactive games, simulators, rock-climbing walls, go-carts, and an IMAX theater make this a paradise for kids.

Niagara Casinos
Niagara
Tel 888/946-3255
There are two casinos in Niagara Falls: Casino Niagara (on Falls Ave.) and Niagara Fallsview Casino Resort (on Fallsview Blvd.). The latter overlooks the falls and occupies a massive 2.5 million square foot complex with more than 3,000 slot machines and 150 gaming tables. Both casinos are open 24 hours; must be 19 years old or over to play.

PRAIRIES

FESTIVALS
Calgary Exhibition and Stampede
Calgary, Alta.
Tel 800/661-1767 (box office) or 403/261-0101
www.calgarystampede.com
July
One of the biggest cowboy events of them all and it's fun. A wonderful spirit overtakes the city and wearing Western gear becomes de rigueur. Even oil company executives, who've never been near a horse in their lives, don white Stetsons and cowboy boots. Offering a huge parade, chuckwagon races, rodeo events such as riding bucking broncos, roping calves, and wrestling steers, a stock show, and much more. The city is packed. Hotel reservations must be made months in advance.

Klondike Days
Edmonton, Alta.
July

ENTERTAINMENT & ACTIVITIES

For ten days, Edmonton recreates the era of the 1890s with a King of the Klondike parade, gold-panning, and other gold rush activities.

The Trial of Louis Riel
Mackenzie Art Gallery
Regina, Sask.
Tel 306/728-3617
July–early August
This play is an historically accurate account of the trial of this figure who still raises controversy a hundred years after his death.

Shakespeare on the Saskatchewan
Saskatoon, Sask.
Tel 306/652-9100
July–mid-August
Award-winning theater with innovative interpretations of the classics held in two brightly colored festival tents on the riverbank.

Folklorama
Winnipeg, Man.
Tel 204/982-6210
August
Multicultural pavilions throughout the city offer entertainment, exotic foods, and cultural displays.

CULTURAL CENTERS
Citadel Theatre
9828 101A Ave., Edmonton, Alta.
Tel 780/426-4811
or 780/425-1820 (box office)
One of the largest and busiest theater complexes in Canada today. There are five auditoriums adapted to different types of productions and audiences, as well as workshops and classrooms.

EPCOR Centre
205 8th Ave. S.E., Calgary, Alta.
Tel 403/294-7455
Home to the Calgary Philharmonic Orchestra and several theater companies.

Globe Theatre
1801 Scarth St., Regina, Sask.
Tel 306/525-6400
Local dramatic works performed on a round stage inside the old Regina City Hall.

Manitoba Theatre Centre
174 Market Ave., Winnipeg, Man.
Tel 204/942-6537

The MTC stages mainline theater at the Mainstage and more experimental productions at the Warehouse. Also home to the Winnipeg Fringe Theatre Festival (summer).

Rainbow Stage
2021 Main St.
(in Kildonan Park),
Winnipeg, Man.
Tel 204/989-5261
July–August
Outdoor summer theater on the banks of the Red River under the stars.

Twenty Fifth Street Theatre Centre
600-245 3rd Ave. S.,
Saskatoon, Sask.
Tel 306/664-2239
Mounts works by Saskatchewan playwrights, and hosts a summer Fringe Festival.

NIGHTLIFE
The Bassment
245 3rd Ave. S., Saskatoon, Sask.
Tel 306/683-2277
Home to the Saskatchewan Jazz Society with performances given mid-September through mid-May.

Casino Regina
1880 Saskatchewan Dr.,
Regina, Sask.
Tel 800/555-3189
or 306/565-3000
Renovated train station with slot machines and table games.

Cowboys
10102-180 St., Edmonton, Alta.
Tel 780-481-8739
This popular nightclub has a dance floor, pool tables, and beer on tap.

Whiskey Pub & Nightclub
341 10th Ave. SW, Calgary, Alta.
Tel 403/770-2323
A popular club that is transformed into a whisky salon during the Calgary Stampede.

OTHER ACTIVITIES
Canadian Olympic Park
88 Canada Olympic Rd. S.W.,
Calgary, Alta.
Tel 403/247-5452
Site of the XV Olympic Winter Games. Open for tours, bobsleigh and luge rides, mountain biking, and more.

Nakiska
Kananaskis Village, Alta.
Tel 403/591-7777 or
800/258-7669
Just west of Calgary, Nakiska was the location for the downhill ski events during the Calgary Winter Olympic Games of 1988. Excellent skiing.

RCMP Sergeant Major's Parade
RCMP Training Academy,
Regina, Sask.
Tel 306/780-5900
Drill parade demonstration Monday through Friday, all year, weather permitting. Also, Sunset Retreat Ceremonies, centered around the lowering of the flag (Tuesdays in July and August).

Prairie Dog Central
Winnipeg, Man.
Tel 204/832-5259
Weekends July & August; Sun. only May, June, & September
Two-hour excursions north of Winnipeg in a 1900 steam train offer vistas of prairie landscape as it was when the first settlers arrived.

ROCKIES

CULTURAL CENTERS
Banff Centre
107 Tunnel Mountain Dr.,
Banff, Alta.
Tel 403/762-6100 or
800/422-2633
Music, theater, and dance performances year-round, culminating in the three-month Banff Festival of the Arts each summer. The Walter Philips Gallery displays contemporary works by Canadian and international artists.

Canada House Gallery
201 Bear St.,
Banff, Alta.
Tel 403/762-3757 or
800/419-1298
www.canadahouse.com
This gallery exhibits exclusively Canadian art and sculpture including Aboriginal and Inuit works. There are regular changing exhibitions.

NIGHTLIFE
Athabasca Hotel
510 Patricia St., Jasper, Alta.
Tel 780/852-3386
Dance to Top 40 music and live bands at the Atha-B nightclub.

OTHER ACTIVITIES
Numerous outfitters provide help for visitors looking to enjoy the natural parks of the Rockies. Several are listed below. Many provide more than one service so ask about other areas of interest.

Biking
Bactrax
Banff, Alta.
Tel 403/762-8177

Fishing
Banff Fishing Unlimited
Banff, Alta.
Tel 403/762-4936
Maligne Tours
Jasper, Alta.
Tel 780/852-3370

Helihiking
Canadian Mountain Holidays
Banff, Alta.
Tel. 403/762-7100
Alpine Helicopters
Canmore, Alta.
Tel 403/609-1714

Horseback Riding
Warner Guiding and Outfitting
Banff, Alta.
Tel 403/762-4551
Brewster Mountain Pack Trains
Banff, Alta.
Tel 403/762-5454
Emerald Lake Lodge
Yoho National Park, B.C.
Tel 250/343-6321

Rail Trips through the Rockies
From Vancouver, Jasper, or Calgary
Tel 800/665-7245
The *Rocky Mountaineer* makes two-day excursions through Banff National Park or Jasper National Park. From the comfort of the train, you can experience the grandeur of these mountains. Both trips either start or finish in Vancouver and overnight in Kamloops.

River Adventures
White Water Rafting
Jasper, Alta.
Tel 780/852-7238
Jasper Raft Tours

Jasper, Alta.
Tel 780/852-2665

Ski Centers
Banff/Mount Norquay
Tel 403/762-4421
Sunshine Village
Tel 403/762-6500
Lake Louise
Tel 403/522-3555
Marmot Basin
Tel 780/852-3816
Mount Norquay and Sunshine Village near Banff, the Lake Louise Ski Centre, and Marmot Basin at Jasper offer wonderful downhill skiing.

For additional recommendations contact the individual national parks:
Banff (Tel 403/762-1550)
Jasper (Tel 780/852-6176)
Yoho (Tel 250/343-6100)
Kootenay (Tel 250/347-9615)

THE WEST

FESTIVALS
Polar Bear Swim
English Bay
Vancouver
Tel 604/665-3424
New Year's Day
Thousands of hardy Vancouverites rush into the icy cold waters of English Bay to celebrate the new year. Visitors can join them or just watch.

Flower Count Week
Victoria
Tel 250/953-2033
February
To emphasize the mildness of its winter when most of the rest of Canada is deep under snow, the British Columbia capital organizes a count of the thousands of flowers that bloom in February.

Nanaimo Championship Bathtub Race
Tel 250/753-7223
July
This famous race across Nanaimo harbour to Departure Bay is part of the city's Marine Festival. Participants really do use bathtubs, but they are powered by outboard motors today rather than muscles as in

the past. There are also barbecues, concerts, fireworks, and a parade.

Squamish Days Logger Sports Festival
Squamish
Tel 604/815-4994
Late July—early August
Demonstrations of all aspects of logging and the lumberjack's life.

International Air Show
Abbotsford, Fraser Valley
Tel 604/852-8511
August
One of Canada's major air shows.

Pacific National Exhibition
PNE Grounds, Vancouver
Tel 604/253-2311
August & September
One of the great agricultural and industrial shows of the Pacific Northwest. Livestock shows and all kinds of other entertainment. The lumberjack competitions are a highlight.

Christmas Carol Ship Parade
English Bay, Vancouver
Tel 604/878-8999 (seasonal)
December
Onboard ship, young carollers parade around the harbor as they sing, followed by dozens of other craft covered with lights.

CULTURAL CENTERS
The Centre in Vancouver for Performing Arts
777 Homer St., Vancouver
Tel 604/602-0616
Contemporary facility for traveling Broadway shows, concerts, and other live performances.

Orpheum Theatre
Smithe at Seymour, Vancouver
Tel 604/665-3050
Many musical events are held in this gracious and elegant venue, built as a vaudeville hall in 1927, including performances by the Vancouver Symphony Orchestra.

Waterfront Theatre
Granville Island, Vancouver
Tel 604/257-0366
Local theater with performances varying from Shakespeare to popular drama and works by local playwrights.

Theatre under the Stars
Stanley Park, Vancouver
Tel 604/257-0366
Popular plays and musicals at the
Malkin Bowl bandstand in Stanley
Park in July and August, weather
permitting. Especially good with
a picnic under a full moon.

Bard on the Beach
Vanier Park, Vancouver
Tel 604/739-0559
June–September
Shakespeare on the sands to
the sounds of the ocean with
mountains as a backdrop.

**University Centre
Auditorium**
Finnerty Rd., University of
Victoria, Victoria
Tel 250/721-6561
Year-round classical music concerts.

McPherson Playhouse
3 Centennial Sq., Victoria
Tel 250/361-0800 or
250/386-6121 (box office)
Baroque Edwardian concert hall
restored in 1962, home to the
Victoria Symphony Orchestra,
the Pacific Opera Victoria, and
many other musical and
theatrical groups.

Royal Theatre
805 Broughton St. at Blanshard,
Victoria
Tel 250/361-0800 or
250/386-6121 (box office)
A variety of theatrical presentations including summer "Pops"
concerts by the Victoria
Symphony Orchestra.

BC Place Stadium
Vancouver
Major Canadian and international music groups entertain in
this huge stadium, which seats
60,000 people. It's also home to
the BC Lions football team.

NIGHTLIFE
O'Doul's Bar
1300 Robson St., Vancouver
Tel 604/661-1400
In the heart of the downtown
action, this popular bar offers
live local jazz every night.

Skybar
670 Smithe St., Vancouver
Tel 604/697-9199
Popular nightclub on three levels
complete with a rooftop
restaurant and bar.

The Yale
1300 Granville St., Vancouver
Tel 604/681-9253
Funky rhythm and blues any
evening. Sunday blues jam: bring
your instrument and join in.

Richard's on Richards
1036 Richards St., Vancouver
Tel 604/688-1099
One of Vancouver's most
popular and lively night clubs.

OTHER ACTIVITIES
Bayshore Bicycles
745 Denman St., Vancouver
Tel 604/688-2453
Bicycle and roller blade rentals
for Stanley Park.

Pacific Spirit Park
4915 W. 16th Ave. on campus of
University of British Columbia,
Vancouver
Tel 604/224-5739
Almost 40 miles of hiking trails
located only 15 minutes from
downtown.

Hiking the West Coast Trail
Pacific Rim National Park
Vancouver Island
Tel 800/663-6000 (info and
reservations)
Considered an adventure of a
lifetime by hikers and backpackers and one of the world's
most challenging treks. It can
take 10 days to complete the
entire 45 miles of this rugged
trail. Reservations required.

Skiing at Whistler
75 miles N of Vancouver
Whistler Visitor Info Centre
Tel 604/932-5528 or
800/766-0449
World-famous, the Whistler-
Blackcomb complex is one of
the largest and most popular ski
resorts in North America. Mile-
high vertical drops, hundreds of
marked runs, opportunities for
snowboarding and helicopter
skiing, glacier skiing in the
summer months, and a full range
of other activities attract crowds
of people.

Train excursions
www.viarail.ca
www.amtrakcascades.com
VIA Rail trains across Canada
(Tel 888/842-7245) and Amtrak
trains to Seattle (Tel 800/872-
7245) leave from 1150 Station

St., Vancouver, as does the Rocky
Mountaineer (see p. 387).

Whale-watching cruises
Great Pacific Adventures
Victoria
Tel 250/386-2277
Whale-watching tours all year
round.
For a list of companies in Tofino
and other places on Vancouver
Island, call 250/953-2033
March–October
It is a magnificent experience to
take one of these cruises to see
gray whales, porpoises, orcas,
seals, sea lions, and sea birds.

**Swan Lake Christmas Hill
Nature Sanctuary**
3873 Swan Lake Rd., Victoria
Tel 250/479-0211
Nature walks and bird watching
just minutes from downtown.

THE NORTH

FESTIVALS
Only major festivals are listed
below but every small Inuit or
Dene community in the North
has celebrations or festivities of
its own, generally in the summer.
For details, contact the tourism
departments of Yukon, the
Northwest Territories, and
Nunavut (addresses on page
346).

Yukon Quest Sled Dog Race
Whitehorse, Yukon
Tel 867/668-4711
February
International 1,000-mile race
between the Yukon capital and
Fairbanks, Alaska. Considered
the toughest dogteam race in
the world.

Caribou Carnival
Yellowknife, N.W.T.
Tel 867/873-4262
March
International sporting
competition and cultural gala.
Harpoon throwing, dog mushing,
ice fishing, drum dancing, etc.
Wear your long johns!

**Midnight Sun Golf
Tournament**
Yellowknife, N.W.T.
Tel 867/873-4326
Summer solstice

Famous golf tournament with teeing off at midnight. The greens are artificial grass and the fairways are sand, but this is a tournament much enjoyed by everyone—including Yellowknife's huge black ravens, which have an unfortunate habit of making off with the golf balls.

Yukon Gold Panning Championships
Dawson, Yukon
Tel 867/993-5575
July 1
In this annual event, prospectors, amateur and professional, compete against each other to see who can find gold first. There are timed trials and then finals. And yes, there still is gold to be found in the Yukon.

Yukon Storytelling Festival
Whitehorse, Yukon
August
There is something about living in the North that sometimes makes people slightly silly. As poet Robert Service wrote: "you wouldn't believe the things done by the Midnight Sun...." This festival celebrates a powerful art form with myths, legends, drama, and song.

Discovery Days Festival
Dawson, Yukon
Tel 867/993-2353
Mid-August
The anniversary of the first great gold find, which sparked the Klondike Gold Rush, is celebrated in style with a jamboree.

NIGHTLIFE
Diamond Tooth Gertie's Gambling Hall
4th Ave. & Queen St.
Dawson, Yukon
Tel 867/993-5575 (Klondike Visitors' Association)
Glimpse of the Gold Rush with cancan dancers and gambling. No minors allowed. Mid-May–mid-September only.

Frantic Follies Vaudeville Revue
Westmark Whitehorse Hotel
Whitehorse, Yukon
Tel 867/668-2042
Zany and popular show recreating the halcyon days of the Gold Rush. May–September.

Palace Grand Theatre
Dawson, Yukon
Tel 867/993-7200
Every evening in the summer months, Parks Canada shows silent films of the Gold Rush era in this beautifully restored pinewood theater of 1899.

OTHER ACTIVITIES
The North is a paradise for people seeking the ultimate outdoors experience. Possibilities are endless for white-water canoe trips, fishing remote lakes, hiking the wilderness, seeing wildlife up close, etc. Outdoor service providers are abundant in the North. Some outfitters that might assist you with planning and transportation are:

Dechenla
Whitehorse, Yukon
Tel 867/667-2639
Naturalist-led outdoor activities from a base lodge located on the Canol Heritage Trail.

Nahanni River Adventures
Whitehorse, Yukon
Tel 867/668-3180
Guided canoe and raft wilderness adventure tours on the wild and turbulent Nahanni River.

Yukon Wide Adventures
Whitehorse, Yukon
Tel 867/393-2111
Canoe and hiking tours in summer; snowshoe, cross-country ski, and snowmobile tours in the winter months.

Arctic Nature Tours
Inuvik, N.W.T.
Tel 867/777-3300
Specializes in natural and cultural tours of the Mackenzie Delta.

Enodah Wilderness Travel
Yellowknife, N.W.T.
Tel 867/873-4334
Caribou and duck-hunting expeditions; fishing.

Great Canadian Ecoventures
Yellowknife, N.W.T.
Tel 867/920-7110
Guides lead trips focused on the native habitat and the creatures that inhabit it.

Sah Naji Kwe Wilderness Spa
Rae-Edzo, N.W.T.
Tel 867/371-3144
Traditional outdoor experience and cross-cultural programs.

Note, exploring the North frequently requires charter flight services. A few of the commercially licensed operations are:

Alkan Air
Whitehorse, Yukon
Tel 867/668-2107

Yukon Wings
Whitehorse, Yukon
Tel 867/668-4716

North-Wright Air
Norman Wells, NWT
Tel 867/587-2288

Canadian North
Yellowknife, N.W.T.
Tel 800/661-1505

Air Tindi
Yellowknife, N.W.T.
Tel 867/669-8200

Wolverine Air
Fort Simpson, N.W.T.
Tel 867/695-2263

Simpson Air
Fort Simpson, N.W.T.
Tel 867/695-2505

As always, the tourism departments of the Yukon, the Northwest Territories, and Nunavut, as well as the national parks of the region, can supply you with longer lists of registered outfitters, suppliers, and other companies specializing in northern travel (addresses on p. 346).

INDEX

Bold page numbers
indicate illustrations.

A

Abbaye de Saint-Benoît-du-
Lac, Que. **130**, 131
Acadia (Acadie) 62–63
Acadian Peninsula 61
Acadians 32, 60–61, 66,
80, 81
Agawa Rock, Ont. 206
Ainsworth Hot Springs,
B.C. 310
Airports and air services
50, 341, 389
Alaska Highway 320–22
Alberta 23, 24, 38, 231–40,
242–61, 320-21, 323–28
Alberta badlands 213,
233–34, **233**
Alert Bay, B.C. 298
Algoma Central Railway
209
Algonquin Island, Ont. 175
Algonquin Provincial Park,
Ont. **156**, 203
Annapolis Royal, N.S. 81
Annapolis Royal Historic
Gardens 81
Fort Anne National
Historic Site 81
Annapolis Valley, N.S. 22,
80–81, **80**
Appalachian range 20, 22
Architecture 40–45
Arctic 336–38
Ash Island, Que. 128
Athabasca Falls, Alta. 255
Athabasca Glacier, Alta.
254, **254–55**
Athabasca Valley, Alta. 255
Athapaskan 304
Aulavik National Park 329
Aurora borealis **219**
Auyuittuq National Park,
Nunavut 338
Avalon Peninsula, Nfld.
94–96
Avalon Wilderness
Reserve, Nfld. 94

B

Baddeck, N.S. 82
Baffin Island, Nunavut
337–38
Auyuittuq National Park
338
Cape Dorset 338
Iqaluit 338
Katannilik Territorial Park
338
Kekerton Island Historic
Park 338
Lake Harbour 338
Mallikjuaq Historic Park
338
Mount Thor 338
Nanisivik 337

Pond Inlet 337, **337**
Qammaarviit Historic
Park 338
Sirmilik National Park 337
Summit Lake 338
Sylvia Grinnell Territorial
Park 338
Baie-Comeau, Que. 149
Baie des Chaleurs, Que.
61, 154
Centre de l'Heritage
Britannique de la
Gaspésie 154
Musée Acadien du
Québec 154
Baie-Sainte-Catherine,
Que. 146
Baie-Saint-Paul, Que. 145,
303, 353
Centre d'Exposition de
Baie-Saint-Paul 145
Centre d'Histoire
Naturelle de Charlevoix
145
Balfour, B.C. 310
Banff National Park, Alta.
242, 244–49, **244–45**, 368
Banff Park Museum
National Historic Site
247
Banff Springs Hotel 43,
245, **246–47**, 367
Banff townsite 246,
367–68
Bow Falls 247
Bow Valley Parkway 248
Castle Junction 248
Cave and Basin National
Historic Site 247
Hoodoos 248
Johnston Canyon 248
Lake Minnewanka Loop
Drive 248
Lower Falls 248
Luxton Museum 247
Mount Norquay 248
Sulphur Mountain 248
Upper Hot Springs 248
Vermilion Lakes Drive
248
Whyte Museum of the
Canadian Rockies 247
Baranof Island, B.C. 301,
304-5
Barkerville, B.C. **306**, 307,
307
Barrington, N.S. 77
Old Meeting House 77
Basilique Sainte-Anne-de-
Beaupré, Que. 142–43,
143
Batoche National Historic
Site, Sask. 227
Battle Harbour, Nfld. **102**
Bay Bulls, Nfld. 94
Bay of Fundy, N.B.-N.S.
56–59
Bears
black bears 250, **250**

polar bears 219, **219**,
318, **318**
Beatton River air strips,
B.C. 321
Beaupré shore, Que. 142–3
Beausoleil, Ont. 202
Beaver Creek, Yukon 322
Beaver Lodge Lake 223
Beechey Island 336
Bell, Alexander Graham
82, 198
Bella Bella, B.C. 301
Bella Coola, B.C. 307
Belle Isle Strait, Que. 102
Bennett Lake **56**
Big Bend, Alta. 254
Big and Little Beehives,
Alta. 251
Bird Rock **95**, 96
Birdlife 94, 198, 319
Bison 24, 27, 212, 240
Black Creek Pioneer
Village, Ont. 184, **184**
Blackcomb Mountain,
B.C. 287
Blockhaus de Lacolle,
Que. 128
Blueberry Control Station,
B.C. 321
Boat Bluff lighthouse, B.C.
301
Boldt Castle, Ont. 169
Bombardier, Joseph-Armand
131
Bonaventure, Musée
Acadien du Québec **62**,
154
Bonaventure Island, Que.
154
Bonavista, Nfld. 97
Mockbeggar Property 97
Ryan Premises National
Historic Site 97
Bonavista Peninsula, Nfld.
97
Borduas, Paul Emile 47
Bouctouche, N.B. 61
Musée de Kent 61
Pays de la Sagouine 61
Bow Lake, Alta. 252
Bow Summit, Alta. 252
Bracebridge, Ont. 201
Brackley Beach 347, 350
Brantford, Ont. 198
Bell Homestead 198
Her Majesty's Chapel of
the Mohawks 198
Bridal Falls, Alta. 251
Bridal Veil Falls, Alta. 254
Bridgetown, N.S. 80
Brigus, Nfld. 95
Brigus South, Nfld. 94
Britannia Beach, B.C. 286
British Columbia Museum
of Mining 286
British Columbia 10,
261–322, 324
British Columbia Wine
Centre, B.C. 312

Broadcasting and film
48–49
Brock, General Sir Isaac
192, **192**
Broken Group Islands, B.C.
298
Bruce Peninsula, Ont. 179,
203
Bruce Peninsula National
Park, Ont. 203
Bruce Trail, Ont. 203
Burin Peninsula, Nfld. 96
Burrard Inlet, B.C. 276
Bylot Island 337

C

Cabot, John 28, 97
Cache Creek, B.C.
308–309
Calgary, Alta. 45, 235–40,
236, 366
Bar U Ranch 239
Calgary Stampede **235**,
238–39, **238**, **239**
Calgary Tower 237
Calgary Zoo, Botanic
Garden and Prehistoric
Park 237, **237**
City Hall 236
Devonian Gardens 236
excursions from 240
Fort Calgary 237
Glenbow Museum 237
Heritage Park Historical
Village 237
Chambly, Que. 129
Cambridge, N.B. 359
Campobello Island 57
Roosevelt Campobello
International Park 57
Canada
architecture 40–45
Canadian people 10, 12,
14
culture 46–9
fishing industry 15, 22,
92–93, 274
French-speaking popu-
lation 12, 39, 120–121
government and politics
14–17
history 26–39
logging 20, 25, 274–75
maritime heritage 78–79
native peoples 18–19
separatism 15, 39
Canada Aviation Museum,
Ont. 167
Canada Science and
Technology Museum,
Ont. 167
Canadian Confederation
14, 38, 66, 68–69
Canadian Museum of
Civilization 166
Canadian Pacific Railway 38,
59, 244, 245, 262–63, **262**,
263, 264, 268, 308
Canadian Shield 20, 178, 200

Canol Heritage Trail, N.W.T. 332
Cantons de l'Est, Que. 130–31
Cap-à-l'Aigle 351
Cap aux Meules, Que. 151
Cap Trou 151
l'Étang-du-Nord 151
Notre-Dame-du-Rosaire 151
Cap-des-Rosiers, Que. 153
Cap Trinité, Que. 146
Cape Bonavista Lighthouse, Nfld. 97, **97**
Cape Breton Highlands National Park, N.S. 82
Cape Breton Island, N.S. 22, 54, 55, 82–83
Alexander Graham Bell National Historic Site 82
Baddeck 82
Black Brook Cove 82
Cabot Trail 82, **82**
Cape North 82
Cape Smokey 83
Chéticamp 82
Gaelic College of Arts and Crafts 83
Keltic Lodge 82
Lone Shieling 82
Middle Head 82
Neil Harbour 82
Pleasant Bay 82
South Gut St. Ann's 83
Cape Broyle, Nfld. 94
Cape Onion 352
Cape Parry 329
Cape St. Mary's Ecological Reserve, Nfld. **95**, 96
Cape Shore, Nfld. 96
Cape Spear National Historic Site, Nfld. **85**, 94
Capilano Canyon, B.C. 285
Car rental 341
Caraquet 61
Acadian Museum **61**
Village Historique Acadien 61
Cardston, Remington-Alberta Carriage Centre 240
Cariboo, B.C. 306–307
Cariboo Road 273, 306
Caribou **316–17**
Carleton, Que. 154
Carmacks, Yukon 325
Carmichael, Franklin 187
Carr, Emily 280, **280**
Cartier, Jacques 28–29, 61, 142, 153, 154
Castle Hill National Historic Site, Nfld. 96
Castlegar, B.C. 310
Cathedrals of the Prairies (grain elevators), Sask. 215
Cavell Lake, Alta. 260
Cavendish, P.E.I.
Green Gables House 70, **71**

Lucy Maud Montgomery Heritage Museum 69
Chambly Canal, Que. 129
Champlain, Samuel de 30, **30**, 80
Channel-Port aux Basques, Nfld. 98
Charlevoix, Que. 144–45, **144**
Charlevoix crater, Que. 144
Charlottetown, P.E.I. 42, 68–69, 350
Beaconsfield 68
Confederation Centre of the Arts 69
Fort Amherst 68
Government House 68
Province House National Historic Site **35**, 68–69, **68**
St. Dunstan's Basilica 68
Victoria Park 68
Chemainus, B.C. 295
Chester, N.S. 75, 347, 350
Chéticamp, N.S. 82
Chicoutimi, Que. 146–47
Chicoutimi Pulp Mill 147
La Pulperie 147
Chuckwagon racing 238, **238**
Churchill, Man. 219
Eskimo Museum 219
Prince of Wales Fort 219
Churchill, Winston 96, **96**
Cirque du Soleil 48
Cirque of the Unclimbables, N.W.T. 333
Cirrus Mountain viewpoint 254
Clare County, N.S. 81
Clayoquot Sound, B.C. 275, 298
Clear Lake, Man. 223, **223**
Climate 52, 340
Clinton, B.C. 306
Coast Mountains, B.C. 302
Cobalt Heritage Silver Trail 205
Collingwood 359
Colony of Avalon Archaeology Site, Nfld. 94
Columbia Icefield, Alta. 25, 254–55
Columbia River 269
Conception Bay, Nfld. 95
Consolation Valley, Alta. 251
Consulates 346
Cormorant Island, B.C. 298
Corner Brook, Nfld. 98, 352
Cornwallis Island 336
Côte Nord, Que. 148–49
Cottonwood House 307
Cranbrook, B.C. 311
Canadian Museum of Rail Travel 311

Credit cards 344–48
Crescent Beach, N.S. 76
Crowfoot Glacier, Alta. 252
Crowsnest Highway, B.C. 273
Crowsnest Pass, Alta. 240
Cullen, Maurice 186
Cultural scene 46–9
Cumberland Sound 337
Cupids, Nfld. 96
Conception Bay Museum 96
Currency 344
Cypress Hills Interprovincial Park, Sask./Alta. 212, 230
Cyprus Lake, Ont. 203

D
Dance 48
Daniel Johnson Dam, Que. 149
Dawson, Yukon 325, 328, **328**, 374
Dänojà zho Cultural Centre 328
Dawson City Museum 328
Diamond Tooth Gerties 328
Jack London's Cabin 328
Palace Grand Theatre 328
Robert Service's Cabin **325**, 328
Dawson Creek, B.C. 321
De Gaulle, Charles 112
Dean Channel, B.C. 301
Deer Island, N.B. 57
Deer Lake, Nfld. 98
Dempster Highway, Yukon-N.W.T. 316
Destruction Bay, Yukon 322
Devon Island 336
Dickens, Charles 74
Digby, N.S. 81, 350
Dinosaur Provincial Park 213, 234
Dinosaur Trail 233
Dionne quintuplets 206, 209, **209**
Disabilities, visitors with 346
Discovery Harbour, Ont. 202
Dougans Lake **21**
Doukhobor Heritage Museum, Ont. 310
Doukhobors 214–15, 311
Drapeau, Jean 109
Driving 341
Drumheller, Royal Tyrrell Museum of Palaeontology 213, 234
Duncan, Alta.-B.C. 295
British Columbia Forest Discovery Centre 295

Quw'utsun' Cultural Centre 295, 307
Dunham, Que. 130

E
Earhart, Amelia 96
Eastern Townships, Que. 130–31
Edmonton, Alta. 43, 45, 231–32, 366
Alberta Legislative Building 231
Citadel Theatre 231
Fort Edmonton Park 232
Muttart Conservatory 231, **231**
Royal Alberta Museum 232
West Edmonton Mall 232, **232**
Edmunston, N.B. 64
Egg Island, B.C. 301
Elora 359-60
Emerald Lake, B.C. 265, **265**
Emergencies 346–47
Emergency telephone numbers 346–47
English-language newspapers 344
Entertainment 380–89
Erie Canal 173, 191

F
Fathom Five National Marine Park, Ont. 203
Ferry services 50
Ferryland, Nfld. 94–95
Festivals 380
Film festivals 49
First Nations peoples 12, 19, 40, 306–307
Fishing industry 15, 22, 92–93, 274
Fitzhugh Sound, B.C. 301
Five Finger Rapids 325
Fort Battleford National Historic Site, Sask. 227
Fort Beauséjour, N.B. 60
Fort Calgary, Alta. 225, **225**
Fort Chambly National Historic Site, Que. 129
Fort Erie 192
Fort Kitwanga, B.C. 303
Fort Langley National Historic Site, B.C. 287
Fort Lennox National Historic Site, Que. 128–29, **129**
Fort Macleod, Alta. 240
Fort Malden, Ont. 199
Fort Nelson, B.C. 321
Fort Smith 336
Fort Steele Heritage Town, B.C. 311
Fortified settlements 41–42
Frank Slide Interpretive Centre, Alta. 240
Franklin, Benjamin 112

Franklin, Sir John 335
Fraser, Simon 35, 308
Fraser River, B.C. 261, 273, 276, 308
Fredericton, N.B. 54, 65, 349
 Beaverbrook Art Gallery 65
 Changing of the Guard 65
 Christ Church Cathedral 65
 Military Compound Provincial Historic Site 65
 Provincial Legislative Assembly Building 65
 York-Sunbury Historical Society Museum 65
Fundy National Park, N.B. 58–59
Fur trade 29, 41, 220–21

G

Gander, Nfld. 86, 98
Ganong Chocolatier Plant, N.B. 57
Gardenton, Man. 215
Garibaldi Provincial Park, B.C. 272, 286
Gaspé, Que. 153–54
 Musée de la Gaspésie 154
Gaspésie (Gaspé Peninsula), Que. 22, 152–54
Geology 20, 256–57
Georgian Bay, Ont. 157, 201–202
Georgian Bay Islands National Park, Ont. 202
Glacier Bay National Park, Alaska 299, 301
Glacier National Park, B.C. 25, 263, 268
 Abandoned Rails Trail 268
 Bear Falls Trail 268
 Hemlock Grove Trail 268
 Illecillewaet campground 268
Goats and Glaciers Viewpoint 255
Goderich, Ont. 199
 Huron County Museum 199
 Huron Historic Gaol 199
Gold Rush 326–27
Goose Bay, Nfld. 102
Graham Island, B.C. 303
 Haida Gwaii Museum 303
 Queen Charlotte City 303
Grand Échouerie, Que. 151
Grand Falls, Nfld. 86, 98
 Beothuk Village 98
 Mary March Regional Museum 98
Grand Falls Park, N.B. 64
Grand-Pré National Historic Site, N.S. 80, 81
Grande-Grave National Historic Site, Que. 153
Grasslands National Park, Sask. 230, 230

Gravenhurst, Ont. 201
Great Bear Rainforest Park 274–75
Great Lakes 22–23, 178–79
Grenville Channel, B.C. 301
Gros Morne National Park, Nfld. 86, 99, 352
 James Callaghan Trail 99
 Western Brook Pond Boat Tours 99
Grosse-Île and the Irish Memorial National Historic Site, Que. 152
Group of Seven 164, 166, 183, 184, 186, 186–87, 209
Gulf of St. Lawrence 22, 70

H

Haida 299, 303, 307
Haines Junction, Yukon 322, 322
Halifax, N.S. 10, 42, 52, 54, 72–74, 72–73, 351
 Art Gallery of Nova Scotia 73
 Bluenose II 73, 79
 Citadel National Historic Site 74
 Historic Properties 72–73, 74
 Maritime Command Museum 79
 Maritime Museum of the Atlantic 73
 Mont Blanc explosion 74
 Privateer's Warehouse 73
 Province House 74
 Town Clock 72, 74
Hamilton, Ont. 197
 Art Gallery of Hamilton 197
 Dundurn Castle 197
 Royal Botanical Gardens 196, 197
Harbour Grace, Nfld. 96
Harris, Lawren 187
Hartland, N.B. 64
Hat Creek House, B.C. 304
Havre-Aubert 151
Havre aux Maisons 151
Havre Saint-Pierre 149
Hawthorne Cottage National Historic Site, Nfld. 95–6
Head-Smashed-In Buffalo Jump, Alta. 240, 240
Health care 347
Heart's Content, Nfld. 96
 Cable Station 96
Hecate Strait, B.C. 299, 303
Hector Lake, Alta. 252
Hell's Gate, B.C. 308
 Airtram 308
Hope, B.C. 308
Hopewell Cape, N.B. 58, 59
Horseshoe Bay, B.C. 286
Horseshoe Canyon, B.C. 233
Hotel chains 348

Hotels and restaurants 348–74
Howe Sound, B.C. 273, 286
Howse Peak, Alta. 253
Hudson, Henry 334
Hudson's Bay Company 31, 35, 38, 220–21
Hull, Que. 161
Hunter Island, Ont. 301
Huntsville, Ont. 201, 360
Huron-Erie Peninsula 196–99
Hydroelectric power 20, 148–49, 192

I

Icefields Parkway, Alta. 252–55, 368
Ignace 204
Île d'Anticosti, Que. 150, 151
 La Patate 150
 Pointe de l'Ouest lighthouse 150
 Port-Menier 150
 Vauréal Canyon 150
Île d'Entrée, Que. 151
Îles de la Madelaine, Que. 151
Inglis, Man. 215
Ingonish 351
Inside Passage 272, 299–301
Interior plains 23–24
Inuit 12, 18–19, 18–19, 315, 317, 329, 330–31, 331
Inuvik, N.W.T. 329, 332
 Our Lady of Victory "igloo" church 329
Iqaluit, Nunavut 374
 Sunakkutaangit Museum, Nunavut 338
Iroquois 30, 40, 128, 158

J

Jackson, A.Y. 187
Jardins de Métis, Que. 153
Jasper Lake, Alta. 261
Jasper National Park, Alta. 258–59, 368
 Disaster Point 261
 Jasper townsite 258
 Jasper Tramway 259
 Maligne Valley 260–61, 260
 Miette Hot Springs 261
 Mount Edith Cavell 259–60
 Parks Canada Information Centre 258
 Tonquin Valley 260
 Yellowhead Museum and Archives 258
Johnston, Frank 187
Juneau, Alaska 301

K

Kamloops, B.C. 273, 309
Kamloops Lake, B.C. 309

Kananaskis Country, Alta. 243
Kane, Paul 165, 186
Kaslo, B.B. 310–11
 S.S. Moyie, B.C. 311
Kawartha Lakes, Ont. 200
Kekerton Island Historic Park 338
Kelowna, B.C. 312, 369
Kent, Rockwell 95
Ketchikan, Alaska 301
Khristianovka 214–15
Kicking Horse Pass, Alta. 262, 264
Killarney Provincial Park, Ont. 206
Kings Landing Historical Settlement, N.B. 64–5
Kingston, Ont. 168–69, 360
 Bellevue House 43, 168
 City Hall 168
 Court House 168
 Fort Henry 168–69, 168
 Marine Museum of the Great Lakes 168
 Murney Tower 168
 Pump House Steam Museum 168
 St. George's Cathedral 168
Kispiox, B.C. 303
Kitchener, Ont. 196–97
 Farmers' Market 196
 Joseph Schneider House 197
 Woodside National Historic Site 197
Kitseguecla, B.C. 303
Kitwancool, B.C. 303
Klondike Highway, Yukon 322, 324–25
Klondike River, Yukon 325
Kluane National Park, Yukon 322
Knowlton, Que. 131, 353
 Brome County Historical Museum 131
Kootenay National Park, B.C. 266–67, 266–67
 Castle Junction 266
 Fireweed Trail 266
 Kootenay Crossing 267
 Kootenay Valley 267
 Marble Canyon 266
 Mount Wardle 267
 Paint Pots 266–67
 Radium Hot Springs 267
 Rockwall 267
 Sinclair Pass 267
 Sinclair Valley 267
 Tokkum Creek 266
 Vermilion Crossing 267
 Vermilion River 266
Kootenays, B.C. 310–11
Kouchibouguac National Park, N.B. 60–61, 60

Krieghoff, Cornelius **107**, 186
Ksan Historical Village Museum, B.C. 303, 305

L

La Grave, Que. 151
La Malbaie-Pointe-au-Pic, Que. 145
Labrador 102
Labrador City, Nfld. 149
Lac des Deux Montagnes, Que. 124, **124**
Lac Saint-Jean, Que. 147
Lachine Rapids, Que. 113, 125
Lake Agnes, Alta. 251
Lake Annette, Alta. 259
Lake Athabasca, Alta. 255, 332
Lake Audy, Man. 223
Lake Brome, Que. 131
Lake Edith, Alta. 259
Lake Erie 157, 178, 179
Lake Hertel, Que. 129
Lake Huron 157, 178–79
Lake Laberge, Yukon 324
Lake Louise, Alta. 250, **251**, 368-69
    Parks Canada visitor center 250
Lake Memphremagog, Que. 131
Lake Michigan 178
Lake Minnewanka Loop Drive, Alta. 248
Lake Nipissing, Ont. 206
Lake O'Hara, B.C. **44–45**, 265
Lake Ontario 178, 179
Lake Ouimet, Que. 127
Lake Superior 157, 178, **178–79**, 179
Lake Superior Provincial Park 206
Lancaster Sound 337
Language 12, 39, 120–21
L'Anse aux Meadows National Historic Site, Nfld. 40, 99, **99**, 100–101, **100, 101**
L'Anse-Saint-Jean, Que. 146
Larch Valley, Alta. 251
Laurentians (Les Laurentides), Que. 126–27, **127**, 353
Lavallée Lake 230
Leitch Collieries, Alta. 240
Les Éboulements 145
Lewisporte 98
Liard Hot Springs 322
L'Île-aux-Coudres, Ont. 145
    Musée les Voitures d'Eau 145
Lismer, Arthur 187
Literature 47, 341
Little Fox Lake 324
Liverpool, N.S. 76–77

1766 Perkin's House 76–77
Queen's County Museum 76
Logging 20, 25, 274–5
London, Jack 323, 325, 328
Long Range Mountains 99
Longhouses 40
Longue-Pointe 149
Louisbourg 42, 54, 84, **84**
Lower Fort Garry National Historic Site 41, 222
Lunenburg 42, 55, 75–76, **75**
    Bluenose 76
    Fisheries Museum of the Atlantic 76
    Old Town Lunenburg 76
    Romkey House 76
    St. John's Church 76
Lynn Canal, B.C. 301
Lytton, B.C. 308

M

Macdonald, J.E.H. 187
McKellar, Ont. 360
Mackenzie, Alexander 35, 301, 332
Mackenzie, William Lyon 36
Mackenzie Mountains 24
Mackenzie Rebellion 36, 173, 199
Mackenzie River 316, 332, **332**
McMichael Canadian Art Collection, Ont. 184
MacMillan Pass, N.W.T. 332
McQuesten, Yukon 325
Magog, Que. 131
Mahone Bay, N.S. 75
Mail services 343
Malbaie River, Que. 145
Maligne Canyon 260, **260**
Maligne Lake, Alta. **241**, **258–59**, 260–61
Maligne Valley 260–61, **260**
Manic-Outardes Complex, Que. 149
Manitoba 12, 23, 216-23
Manitoba Museum of Man and Nature 217, 217
Manitoulin Island, Ont. 179, 206
Manoir Mauvide-Genest, Que. 142
Marconi, Guglielmo 91
Maritime Archaic Funeral Monument National Historic Site 102
Maritimes 10, 22, 54–84
    hotels & restaurants 349–51
    map 54–55
Meares Island, B.C. 298
Medical treatment 347
Medicine Lake 260
Mennonite Heritage Village 222, **222**

Mennonites 196, 214
Métis 38, 213, 214, 227, 228
Midland, Ont. 201–202
    Huron Indian Village 202
    Huronia Museum 202
Miette Hot Springs, B.C. 261
Miguasha Peninsula 154
Milbanke Sound, B.C. 301
Miles Canyon, Yukon 323
Mingan Archipelago, Que. **148**, 149
Mining towns 204–205, 206, 208
Minto, Yukon 325
Mirror Lake, Alta. 251
Miscou Island, N.B. 61
Mistaya Canyon, Alta. 253
Mistaya Valley, Alta. 252
Monashee Mountains, B.C. 269
Moncton 59, 63, 348–49
    Boreview Park, N.B. 59
Mont Jacques-Cartier 153
Mont Sainte-Anne 154
Mont-Saint-Hilaire, Que. 129
Mont Saint-Joseph 154
Mont-Tremblant Provincial Park, Que. 127
Mont-Tremblant Village 127, 353
Montagnais, Que. 148
Montgomery, Lucy Maud 46, 69–70, 71
Montmagny, Que. 152
Montmorency Falls **142**, 143
Montréal, Que. 42, 44, 104, 108–25, 354-57
    Basilique Notre-Dame 43, 111, 114
    Biodôme 122
    Biosphere 123
    BNP/Laurentian Bank Tower 116
    Boulevard Saint-Laurent 124
    Cathédrale Marie-Reine-du-Monde 43, 115
    Centre Canadien d'Architecture 118
    Centre d'Histoire de Montréal 111, 114
    Champ-de-Mars 110
    Chapelle Notre-Dame-de-Bon-Secours 110, 112–13
    Château Ramezay 112
    Christ Church Cathedral 117, **117**
    Complexe Desjardins 117
    Customs House 114
    Downtown Montreal **109**, 115–16
    Fur Trade Warehouse 125
    Gray Nuns' Convent 111

Hôtel de Ville 112, **113**
hotels & restaurants 355–57
Île Notre-Dame 123
Jardin Botanique de Montréal 122, **122**
La Ronde 123
Les Promenades Cathédrale 117
Lieu Historique Sir George Étienne-Cartier 112
McGill University 116–17
Maison du Calvet 110
Maison Papineau 110
Maison del Vecchio 112
Maison Viger 112
map 111
Metro 116, **116**
Mont-Royal 118–19
Musée d'Archéologie et d'Histoire de Montréal 110, 113
Musée d'Art Contemporain de Montréal 117
Musée David M. Stewart 123
Musée des Beaux-Arts de Montréal 118
Musée Ferroviaire Canadien 125
Musée McCord 117
Notman Photographic Archives 117
Old Montréal 108–13, **108, 110**
Olympic Stadium 122, **123**
Oratoire Saint-Joseph 43, 118–19, **119**
Parc des Îles 122–23
Parc des rapides 125
Pavillon Jacques-Cartier 110
Place d'Armes 111
Place des Arts 117
Place du Canada 115
Place de la Cathédrale 45
Place Jacques-Cartier 110, 112
Place Montréal Trust 116
Place Ville-Marie 115–16
Place d'Youville 110–11
Pointe-à-Callière 113–14
Rue Sainte-Catherine 124, **125**
Rue Saint-Denis 124
St. George's Church 115
Salle Wilfrid-Pelletier 117
Shaughnessy House 118
Square-Dorchester 115, **115**
Sun Life Building 115
Underground City 45, 109, 116
Université du Québec à Montréal 117
Vieux-Port 110, **111**, 113

Vieux Séminaire de Saint-Sulpice 114
walk 110–11
Westmount 124
Westmount Square 44
Windsor Station 43, 115
Youville Stables 111
Moose Lake, B.C. 261
Moraine Lake, Alta. 11, 251, 256
Moravian Brethren 102
Moresby Island, B.C. 303, 307
Gwaii Haanas National Park Reserve 303
Ninstints 307
Skedans 307
Mount Assiniboine, Alta. 249
Mount Caubvick 102
Mount Chephren, Alta. 253
Mount Edith Cavell, Alta. 259–60
Mount Logan 24
Mount Norquay, Alta. 248
Mount Orford, Que. 130
Mount Revelstoke National Park, B.C. 268–69, 269
Giant Cedars Trail 268–69
Meadows in the Sky Parkway 269
Meadows in the Sky Trail 269
Revelstoke townsite 269
Mount Robson Provincial Park, B.C. 24, 261
Berg Lake Trail 261
Mount Seymour Provincial Park, B.C. 285
Mount Stephen, B.C. 264
Mount Wilson, Alta. 253
Mountains 24–25
Muncho Lake Provincial Park, B.C. 322
Music 48
Musk oxen 318–19, 319
Muskoka Lakes, Ont. 200–201

N

Nahanni National Park 316, 333
Cirque of the Unclimbables 333
Rabbitkettle Hot Springs 333
Virginia Falls 333, 333
Nain 102
Namu, B.C. 301
Nanaimo, B.C. 369
Nanisivik, Nunavut 337
National flags 120
National Gallery of Canada, Ont. 164
National holidays 344
National and provincial parks 52
Nelson 310

Courthouse 310
New Bergthal 214
New Brunswick 12, 54, 55, 56–65
New France, Que. 30–31, 33, 34, 106–107
New London, P.E.I., Lucy Maud Montgomery Birthplace 69
Newfoundland 10, 22, 86–102
hotels & restaurants 351–52
map 87
Niagara Escarpment, Ont. 179, 203
Niagara Falls, Ont. 157, 179, 188–91, 188, 189, 190–91, 360
American Falls 188
Goat Island 189
Horseshoe Falls 188
Table Rock 188
Whirlpool Aero Car 192
White Water Walk 192
Niagara Glen Nature Reserve, Ont. 192
Niagara-on-the-Lake, Ont. 192–93, 193, 360
Apothecary 193
Fort George National Historic Site 193
St. Andrew's Church 193
Niagara Parks Commission's School of Horticulture 192
Niagara Parkway, Ont. 191, 192
Nordenski River, Yukon 324
Norman Wells, N.W.T. 332
Norsemen 28, 40, 100–101
North 313–38
hotels and restaurants 374
map 314–15
North Bay, Ont. 206
Dionne Homestead Museum 206
North Hatley, Que. 130, 357
North Rustic Harbour 53
Northumberland Strait, P.E.I. 66, 67
Northwest Passage 334–35
Northwest Territories 23, 314, 316, 329, 332, 336
Nova Scotia 54, 55, 72–84
Nunavut 314–15, 317, 336–38

O

Okanagan Lake, B.C. 312
Okanagan Valley, B.C. 312
Old Sow Whirlpool, N.B. 57
Ontario 10, 12, 155–210
hotels and restaurants 359–65
map 156–57

Ontario Science Centre 185, 185
Opening hours 345, 375
Oshawa, Ont. 185
Canadian Automotive Museum 185
Parkwood 185
Ottawa, Ont. 160–67
Bytown Museum 167
Canada Aviation Museum 167
Canada Science and Technology Museum 167
Canadian Museum of Civilization 166, 166
Canadian Museum of Nature 167
Canadian Postal Museum 166
Canadian War Museum 167
Centre Block 162
Château Laurier Hotel 162
Children's Museum 166
Gatineau Park 167
Government Conference Centre 162
hotels and restaurants 360–61
Laurier House National Historic Site 167
Library 162–63
map 161
National Arts Centre 162
National Gallery of Canada 164
National War Memorial 162
Parliament Hill 43, 162–63, 163
Peace Tower 162
Rideau Canal 160, 160
Overlander Falls, B.C. 261

P

Pacific Rim National Park Reserve, B.C. 296
Pain du Sucre, Que. 129
Panther Falls, Alta. 254
Parc de la Gaspésie 153
Parc de Miguasha 154
Parc National de Forillon 153
Parc National de la Mauricie, Que. 133, 133
Parc Régional des Hautes-Gorges-de-la-Rivière-Malbaie, Que. 145
Parker Ridge, Alta. 254
Parlee Beach Provincial Park, N.B. 60
Passamaquoddy Bay, N.B. 57
Passports 340
Patricia Lake, B.C. 259
Peace River Bridge, B.C. 321
Peggys Cove, N.S. 75

Pelly Crossing, Yukon 325
Penetanguishene, Ont. 202
Penticton 312
Percé Rock, Que. 152–53, 154
Peterborough, Ont. 200
Petersburg, B.C. 301
Petitcodiac River, N.B. 59
Petroglyphs Provincial Park 200
Petty Harbour, Nfld. 94
Pickle Lake, Ont. 204
Placentia Bay, Nfld. 96
Plain of Six Glaciers, Alta. 251
Plains tribes 27, 40
Planning the trip 340
Point Pelee 20, 23
Point Pelee National Park, Ont. 198, 198
Pointe-au-Pere, Musée de la Mer, Que. 152–53
Pointe-a-la-Croix 154
Pointe de l'Église, N.S. 81
Pointe de l'Église St. Bernard, N.S. 81
Sainte-Marie, N.S. 81
Pointe-Noire Interpretation and Observation Centre, Que. 146
Police 347
Pond Inlet, Nunavut 337, 337
Port Alberini, B.C. 297
Port au Choix National Historic Site, Nfld. 99
Port au Port Peninsula, Nfld. 98
Port Edward, B.C. 302
North Pacific Cannery Village Museum, B.C. 302
Port Hardy, B.C. 299
Port McNeill, B.C. 298
U'Mista Cultural Centre 298
Port Royal Habitation 41, 62, 80–81, 81
Povungnituk 14
Prairies 10, 211–40
hotels and restaurants 365–67
map 212–13
Prescription medications 347
Prince Albert National Park, Sask. 230
Prince Edward Island 22, 54, 66–71, 69, 70
Acadian Museum at Miscouche 71
Anne of Green Gables 69–70, 71
Basin Head Fisheries Museum 71
"Canada's Only Potato Museum" 71
Cavendish 69, 70
Charlottetown 68–9

Confederation Bridge 66, **67**, 68
Elmira Railway Museum 71
Gateway Village Complex 68
Kings County 70
Mount Carmel **63**
New London 69
Orwell Corner Historic Village 71
Prince County 70
Prince Edward Island National Park 70, **70**
Silverbush 69
Prince Rupert, B.C. 273, 301, 302, 369–70
Museum of Northern British Columbia 302
Princess Royal Island, B.C. 301
Public transport 340
Pukaskwa National Park, Ont. 206
Pyramid Lake, Alta. 259

Q
Quadra Island, B.C. 298
Kwagiulth Museum 298, 306, 307
Québec 10, 12, 15, 16–17, 39, 42, 103–54
hotels and restaurants 353–59
map 104–105
Québec City 42, 43, 52, 104, 134–41, 357–59
Artillery Park 140
Cathédrale de Notre-Dame de Québec 134
Chapelle des Ursulines 135–36
Château Frontenac 43, 134, **135**
Chevalier House 138
Citadel 42, 140–41, **141**
Église Notre-Dame-des-Victoires 136, **139**
Fortifications Interpretation Centre 140
Holy Trinity Anglican Cathedral 135
Hôtel-Dieu Hospital 135
hotels and restaurants 357–59
Maison Estebe 136–37
Maison Jacquet 138
Manoir Montmorency 143
maps 137, 139
Monastère des Ursulines 135
Musée de l'Amérique Française 134–35
Musée des Augustines de l'Hôtel-Dieu de Québec 135
Musée de Cire 134

Musée de la Civilisation 136, 138
Musée du Fort 134
Musée du Québec 141
Musée des Ursulines de Québec 136
National Battlefields Park Interpretation Centre 141
Old Port of Québec Interpretation Centre 137
Parc des Champs-de-Bataille 140–41
Parc de la Chute-Montmorency 143
Place d'Armes 138
Place de l'Hôtel de Ville 138
Place Royale 136, **139**
Price Building 44
Promenade des Gouverneurs 140
Québec Expérience 134
Rue du Petit-Champlain 138
Séminaire de Québec 134–35
Terrasse Dufferin 134
Urban Life Interpretation Centre 138
Vieux-Port 137
walk 138–39
Queen Charlotte Islands, B.C. 40, 273, 303
Queen Charlotte Sound, B.C. 299, 301
Queenston Heights, Ont. 192
Laura Secord Homestead 192
Quesnel, B.C. 305
Quidi Vidi, Nfld. 91

R
Rabbitkettle Hot Springs 333
Radium hot springs 267
Rail services 50, 342
Red Bay National Historic Site 102
Red Deer, Alta. 253
Red River Rebellion 38
Regina, Sask. 43, 224, 366
R.C.M.P. Centennial Museum 224
Royal Saskatchewan Museum 224
Saskatchewan Legislative Building 224
Wascana Centre 224
Reindeer Grazing Reserve, N.W.T. 329
Resolute, Nunavut 336
Richelieu River Valley, Que. 128–29
Rideau Canal, Ont. 160, **160**
Riding Mountain National Park, Man. 223, **223**
Agassiz Ski Hill 223

Beaver Lodge Lake 223
Clear Lake 223, **223**
Lake Audy 223
Riel, Louis 38, 218, 227, 228–29, **228**
Rimouski, Que. 152
Riviere-du-Loup, Que. 152
Roche Miette, B.C. 261
Rockies 10, 24, 241–70
hotels and restaurants 367–69
map 243
Rocky Harbour, Nfld. 99
Roman Catholic Church 42–43
Roosevelt, Franklin D. 57, 96, **96**
Roosevelt International Suspension Bridge 57
Royal Canadian Mounted Police 213, 224–45
Royal Ontario Museum, Ont. 180

S
Saanich Inlet, B.C. **290**
Saguenay Fjord, Que. 146, **147**
Sainte-Adèle 126, 355
Sainte-Agathe-des-Monts, Que. 126–27
St. Andrews, N.B. 57, 349
Ross Memorial Museum 57
Sheriff Andrew's House Provincial Historic Site, N.B. 57
St. Anthony, Nfld. 99
St. Barbe, Nfld. 99, 102
St. Croix Island, N.B. 56
Sainte-Famille, Que. 142
Maison Drouin 142
Saint-François, Que. 142
Saint-Irénée, Que. 145
St. Jacobs, Ont. 196, 361
Saint-Jean-des-Piles, Ont. 133
Saint-Jean-sur-Richelieu, Que. **128**, 129
Saint-Jérome, Que. 126
Saint John, N.B. 57–58, 349–50
Barbour's General Store 58
Loyalist Burial Ground 58
Loyalist House 58
New Brunswick Museum 58
Reversing Falls Rapids 58
Saint John River Valley, N.B. 64–65
St. John's, Nfld. 86, 88–91, **88–89, 91,** 352
Cabot Tower 91
Cathedral of St. John the Baptist 90
Colonial Building 90
Commissariat House 90
Courthouse 89

Duckworth Street 88–9
Fluvarium 90–91
Government House 90
Hotel Newfoundland 88
Murray Premises 89
Newfoundland Freshwater Resource Centre 90
Newfoundland Museum 90
Pleasantville 91
Quidi Vidi 91
Roman Catholic Basilica of St. John the Baptist 90
Signal Hill National Historic Site **88–89, 90,** 91
Water Street 88
Saint-Joseph, Que. 145
Manoir Richelieu 145
Musée de Charlevoix 145
Saint-Jovite, Que. 127
Saint-Laurent, Que. 142
Parc Maritime de Saint-Laurent 142
St. Lawrence River 169, **169**
St. Lawrence Seaway 179
St. Margaret's Bay, N.S. 75
St. Martins, N.B. 58
St. Mary's Bay, N.B. 81
St. Mary's Point, N.B. 59
Sainte-Marie among the Hurons, Ont. 40, 158, 202
Martyrs' Shrine 202
Saint-Matthieu, Que. 133
Sainte-Pétronille, Que. 142
St.-Pierre, Nfld. 96
Sainte-Rose-du-Nord, Que. 146
Saint-Sauveur-des-Monts, Que. 126
Pavillon Soixante-Dix 126
Sales tax 375
Samson Narrows, Alta. 260
Saskatchewan 23, 38, 224–30
Saskatchewan River Crossing 253
Saskatoon, Sask. 226–27, 366
Diefenbaker Canada Centre 226–27
Farmers' Market **226**
Meewasin Trail 226
Meewasin Valley Centre 226
Mendel Art Gallery 226
Ukrainian Museum of Canada 226
Wanuskewin Heritage Park 227
Western Development Museum 227
Sault Ste.-Marie 179, 208–209
Algoma Central Railway 209
Ermatinger House 209

Sault Canal National Historic Site 209
Science North 208, **208**
Sea to Sky Highway 286
Sentinel Pass, Alta. 251
Sept-Îles, Que. 149
    Musée Régional de la Côte-Nord 149
    Vieux-Poste 149
Shakespeare Festival 197–98
Shediac, N.B. 60
Shefferville, Que. 149
Shelburne, N.S. 77
    Dory Shop 77
Sherbrooke, Que. 131
    Centre d'Interpretation de l'Histoire de Sherbrooke 131
    Musée des Beaux-Arts de Sherbrooke 131
    Old Quartier du Vieux-Nord 131
Shopping 375–79
Silverbush, Anne of Green Gables Museum 69
Skagway, B.C. 301
Skaha Lake 312
Skeena Valley, B.C. 302–303
Skiing 52, 126, 130, 223, 242, 286–87
Sleeping Giant Provincial Park, Ont. 206
Snowmobiles 131, 131
Soda Creek, B.C. 304
Soldiers' Summit, B.C. 320
Somerset Island, Nunavut 336
Sooke 370
Spiral Tunnel viewpoint 265
Spirit Island 260–61
Squamish, B.C. 286
    West Coast Railway Heritage Park 286
Stamps 343
Stewart Crossing, Yukon 325
Stone Mountain Provincial Park, B.C. 321–22
Stony Lake, Ont. 200
Stratford, Ont. 197–98, 361
Strathcona Provincial Park, B.C. 298
Sudbury, Ont. 204, 206, 208
    Dynamic Earth 208
    Science North 208, **208**
Sudbury Basin, Ont. 204
Sulphur Mountain, Alta. 248
Sunwapta Falls, Alta. 255
Sunwapta Pass, Alta. 254
Sutton, Que. 130

T

Tablelands, Nfld. 99
Tadoussac, Que. 146
    Marine Mammal Interpretation Centre 146
Takakkaw Falls, B.C. 265

Tangle Falls **24**
Television and radio network 344
Tern Rock, N.S. 82
Terra Nova National Park, Nfld. 98, **98**
    Marine Interpretation Centre 98
Teslin, Yukon 322
Theater 47–8
Thomson, Tom 187, **187**
Thousand Islands, Ont. 169, **169**
Thousand Islands Parkway 169
Thunder Bay, Ont. 209–210
    Old Fort William 210, **210**
Time zones 345
Timmins, Ont. 204–205
    Hollinger Mine 205
Tipping 345
Tlingit, B.C. 306–307
Toad Mountain 310
Tobermory, Ont. 203
Tofino, B.C. 298, 369
Toronto, Ont. 10, 12, 43, **43**, **46–7**, 156, 170–77, **170–71**, 180–85
    Algonquin Island 175
    Art Gallery of Ontario 181, **181**
    Bank of Commerce 177
    Bata Shoe Museum 182
    BCE Place **13**, 176
    Black Creek Pioneer Village 184
    Canadian Pacific Building 177
    Casa Loma 182
    Chinatown 173
    City Hall 182
    CN Tower 174–75, **174**
    Corso Italia 173
    Dominion Centre 44
    Eaton Centre 177
    excursions from 184–85
    Flatiron Building **176**
    Fort York 182
    Gardiner Museum of Ceramic Art 182
    The Grange 43, 182–83
    Hockey Hall of Fame 176
    hotels & restaurants 362–65
    Hydro Place **155**
    Kensington Market 173
    McMichael Canadian Art Collection 184
    map 177
    Metro Toronto Zoo 185
    Nathan Philips Square **40–41**, 182
    Old City Hall 177, **177**
    Ontario Parliament 183
    Ontario Place 183
    Ontario Science Centre 185, **185**
    Queen's Quay Wharf **173**
    Rogers Centre 175, **175**

Royal Bank Plaza 45
Royal Ontario Museum 180, **180**
Royal York Hotel **172**, 176
St. James' Cathedral 176–77
St. James' Park 176
St. Lawrence Hall 176
St. Lawrence Market 176
Spadina House 183
Toronto Dominion Centre 177
Union Station 43, 176
    walk 176–77
Ward's Island 175
Yorkville 173
Toronto Power Generating Station 192
Totem-carving 306–307
Touring 50
Tourist offices 346
Tower of Babel, Alta. 251
Trans-Canada Highway 89, **207**
Trent-Severn Canal 200
Trinity, Nfld. 97
    Green Family Forge 97
    Trinity Historical Society Museum and Archives 97
    Trinity Interpretation Centre 97
Trinity Bay **86**
Trois-Pistoles, Que. 152
Trois-Rivières, Que. 42, 132–33
    Centre d'Exposition sur l'Industrie des Pâtes et Papiers 132
    Cité de l'Énergie 133
    Forges-du-Saint-Maurice National Historic Site 132–33
    Le Platon 132
    Manoir Boucher-de-Niverville 132
    Manoir de Tonnancour 132
    Monastère des Ursulines 132
    Musée Québécois de culture populaire 132
    Musée des Ursulines 132
    Parc Portuaire 132
    Sanctuaire Notre-Dame du Cap 133
Trudeau, Pierre 15–16
Tuktoyaktuk, N.W.T. 329
Tuktut Nogait National Park, N.W.T. 329
Tyne Valley 350

U

Ukrainian prairie churches 215
Upper Canada, Ont. 156, 158–9
Upper Canada Village, Ont. 169

Upper Waterfowl Lake, Alta. 252–53

V

Val Marie, Sask. 230
Valcourt, Que. 131
    Musée J.-Armand Bombardier 131
Vancouver, B.C. 10, 272, 276–87, **276–77**
    Aquarium 281
    Art Gallery 280
    Bloedel Floral Conservatory 284
    Canada Place 277, 278, **281**
    Cathedral Place 45, 280
    Chinatown 280
    Christ Church Cathedral 280
    Coal Harbour 281
    Dr. Sun Yat-Sen Garden 280
    Emily Carr College of Art and Design 282
    excursions from 286–87
    False Creek 282
    Gastown 278–80
    Granville Island 282, **282–83**
    Granville Square 278
    Grouse Mountain 284–85, **285**
    Hallelujah Point 281
    hotels and restaurants 370–72
    H.R. Macmillan Space Centre 283
    Lions Gate Bridge 281
    Lost Lagoon 281
    map 278–79
    Marine Building 44, 277
    Maritime Museum 283–84
    Museum of Anthropology **283**, 284
    Narrows 281
    Nitobe Japanese Garden 284
    North Shore 284–85
    Pacific Space Centre 283
    Prospect Point 281
    Queen Elizabeth Park 284
    Robson Square 280
    Simon Fraser University 284
    Stanley Park **278**, 280–81
    Steam Clock 279
    University of British Columbia 277–78, 284
    University of British Columbia Botanical Garden 284
    Vancouver Museum 282–83
    West Coast Trail 296
Vancouver Island, B.C. 272, 288–98, **288–89**
    Bamfield 297

Butchart Gardens
294–95, **294**
Campbell River 298
Cathedral Grove 297
Chemainus 295
Clayoquot Sound 275, 298
Craigdarroch Castle 294
Duncan 295
Englishman River & Falls
Provincial Park 296
Lismer Beach 298
Little Qualicum Falls
Provincial Park 296–97
Long Beach 298
McLean Mill 297
Pacific Rim National Park
Reserve 272, 296
Port Alberini 297
Port McNeill 298
Radar Hill 298
Sea Lion Rocks 298
Strathcona Provincial Park
298
Telegraph Cove 298
Tofino 298
Ucluelet 297
West Coast Trail 298
Wickanninish Interpretive
Centre 298
Varley, Fred 187
Vernon 312
Historic O'Keefe Ranch
312
Victoria, B.C. 272, 288–93,
366–7
Art Gallery of Greater
Victoria 294
Bastion Square 292–93
Beacon Hill Park 294
Butchart Gardens
294–95, **294**
Craigdarroch Castle 43,
294
Crystal Garden 292
Empress Hotel 292, 293,
293

excursions from 294
Fort Rodd Hill 290
Government House 294
Government Street 292
Johnson Street Lifting
Bridge 293
Maritime Museum 293
Parliament Buildings **288**,
292
Royal British Columbia
Museum 272, 291
St. Anne's Schoolhouse
292
Thunderbird Park 292
Victoria Conference
Center 292
walk 292–93
Victoria Glacier, Alta. 251
Vineyards and wineries
194–95
Virginia Falls 333, **333**
Visual arts 47, 186–87

W

Wapta Falls, B.C. 265
Waputik Icefield, Alta.
252
Ward's Island, Que. 175
Waskesiu Lake, Sask. 230
Waterloo, Ont. 196
Waterton Lakes National
Park 270, **270**
Crypt Lake 270
Prince of Wales Hotel
270
Red Rock Canyon Trail
270
Waterton townsite 270
Watson Lake, Yukon 322
Wedge Mountain, B.C.
286
Weeping Wall, Alta. 254
Welland Canal 191, 192
The West 271–312
hotels and restaurants
369–74

map 272–73
West Coast Railway
Heritage Park, B.C. 286
Western Brook Pond Boat
Tours 99
Whale Channel 301
Whale-watching 82, 146,
147, 298, 301
Whistler, B.C. 286–77,
373–74
Whistler Mountain 259,
287, **287**
Whitehorse, Yukon 322,
323, 374
Log Church **322**, 323
MacBride Museum 323
S.S. *Klondike* 323, **323**
Wildlife 25, 318–19
see also Bears; Birdlife;
Whale-watching
Williams Lake, B.C.
304–305
Windsor, Ont. **199**
Windsor Community
Museum 199
Wine Routes 194, 312
Wines 194–95
Winnipeg, Man. 43, 45, 52,
216–18, 365–66
Forks National Historic
Site 216, 218
Manitoba Legislative
Building **216**, 218
Manitoba Museum
217, **217**
North End 216
Riel House National
Historic Site 218
Roman Catholic
Cathedral of St Boniface
229
St. Boniface 216
St. Boniface Museum
218
Winnipeg Art Gallery
218

Witless Bay, Nfld. 94
Witless Bay Ecological
Reserve, Nfld. 94
Wolfe, General James
33–34, 84, 140
Wolfville, N.S. 80
Acadia University, N.S.
80
Wood Buffalo National
Park, Northwest
Territories 336
Woodland tribes 27

Y

Yale, B.C. 308
Historic Yale Museum
308
Yarmouth, N.S. 81
Yellowhead Lake, B.C.
261
Yellowhead Pass 261,
0262
Yellowknife, N.W.T. 316,
332, 336, 374
Caribou Carnival 336
Festival of the Midnight
Sun 336
Prince of Wales Northern
Heritage Centre 336
Yoho National Park, B.C.
264–65, **264**, 369
Burgess Shale 265
Cataract Brook 264–65
Emerald Lake 265, **265**
Kicking Horse Pass 262,
264
Spiral Tunnels 263, 265
Takakkaw Falls 265
Wapta Falls 265
York 42
Yukon 314–16, 323-28

Z

Zoo sauvage de Saint-
Félicien, Que. 147
Zuckerberg Island 310

ILLUSTRATIONS CREDITS

Cover: (l), Tony Stone Images. (c), Ron Atkins/Getty Images. (r), Photographers Library. 9, AA Photo Library. 11, Graeme Wallace. 13, Gerd Ludwig. 14, Telegraph Colour Library. 15, Rex/Sipa Press. 16/17, Maggie Steber. 18/19, Bryan and Cherry Alexander. 21, Telegraph Colour Library. 22/23, Gunter Marx Photography/ CORBIS. 24, Graeme Wallace. 26/27 Bridgeman Art Library. 30, CORBIS. 31, Giraudon. 32/33, E T Archive. 34, Hulton Getty. 35,Winston Fraser. 36/37, Christopher J. Morris/CORBIS. 38, Sally A. Morgan; Ecoscene/CORBIS. 39, Winston Fraser. 40/41, Gerd Ludwig. 42, AA Photo Library/Chris Coe. 43, Masterfile. 44/45, Michael Melford/ National Geographic Society. 46/47, Winston Fraser. 48a, Hillstrom /Winston Fraser. 48b, Rex. 49a, AP Images/Wide World Photos. 49b, Rex/Sipa. 50/51, Chris Noble. 52, Royalty-Free/CORBIS. 53, Masterfile. 56, Nik Wheeler/CORBIS. 57, Hulton Getty. 58, Winston Fraser. 58/59, Winston Fraser. 60, Winston Fraser. 61, John Neubauer/Lonely Planet. 62(t),Winston Fraser. 62(b), Winston Fraser. 63, Winston Fraser. 64, Andre Jenny/Alamy Ltd. 65, Carl & Ann Purcell/CORBIS. 66, AA Photo Library/ Chris Coe. 67, Winston Fraser. 68, Masterfile. 69, Peter Finger/CORBIS. 70, Masterfile. 71, Buddy Mays/CORBIS. 72, Carl & Ann Purcell/CORBIS. 72/73, Andre Gallant/The Image Bank/Getty Images. 74, Will & Deni McIntyre/ CORBIS. 75, Wolfgang Kaehler/CORBIS. 78(t), Winston Fraser. 78(b), AA Photo Library/Jean Francois Pin. 79, Winston Fraser. 80, Masterfile. 81(t), Masterfile. 81(b), Winston Fraser. 82, Masterfile. 84, Wolfgang Kaehler/CORBIS. 85, Paul A. Souders/CORBIS. 86, Masterfile. 88/89, David Noton/The Image Bank/Getty Images. 90, AA Photo Library/Jean Francois Pin. 91, Nik Wheeler/CORBIS. 92, AA Photo Library/Jean Francois Pin. 93(t), Ann Ronan Picture Library/ Heritage-Images. 93(b), Nathan Benn/CORBIS. 94, Royalty-Free/ CORBIS. 95, AA Photo Library/Jean Francois Pin. 96, CORBIS. 97, Tom Bean/CORBIS. 98, Winston Fraser. 99(t), Winston Fraser. 99(b), AA Photo Library/Jean Francois Pin. 100, AA Photo Library/Jean Francois Pin. 101(t), Winston Fraser. 101(b), AA Photo Library/Jean Francois Pin. 102, Wolfgang Kaehler/CORBIS. 103, Jean François Pin. 106, Roger Viollet Collection/Getty Images. 107(t), Bridgeman Art Library. 107(b), North Wind Picture Archives. 108, Masterfile. 109, Masterfile. 110, (no copy) FPG. 111, Masterfile. 113, Carl & Ann Purcell/CORBIS. 114, Wolfgang Kaehler/CORBIS. 115, Winston Fraser. 116, imagebroker /Alamy Ltd. 117, Winston Fraser. 119, SIME/CORBIS. 120,

Winston Fraser. 121, Richard Wareham Fotografie /Alamy Ltd. 122, AA Photo Library/Jean Francois Pin. 123,Winston Fraser. 124, Publiphoto Diffusion Inc/ Alamy Ltd. 125, AA Photo Library/ Jean Francois Pin. 127, Wolfgang Kaehler/CORBIS. 128, Winston Fraser. 129, Winston Fraser. 130, Gilles Rivest/ Tourisme Québec. 131, Masterfile. 133, Publiphoto Diffusion Inc/Alamy Ltd. 135, Dave G. Houser/Post-Houserstock/ CORBIS. 136, AA Photo Library/Jean Francois Pin. 138, Jose Azel/Aurora/Getty Images. 139, Nik Wheeler/CORBIS. 140, Winston Fraser. 141, Masterfile. 144, Masterfile. 145,Winston Fraser. 147, Winston Fraser. 148, Winston Fraser. 149, Winston Fraser. 150, Winston Fraser. 151, Winston Fraser. 152/3, Wolfgang Kaehler/ CORBIS. 154, Andre Jenny/Alamy Ltd. 155, Jason Horowitz/zefa/CORBIS. 158(t), Mary Evans Picture Library. 158(b), Mary Evans Picture Library. 159, Masterfile. 160(t), AA Photo Library/ Chris Coe. 160(b), Masterfile. 162, Wolfgang Kaehler/CORBIS. 163, Ron Watts/CORBIS. 165, AA Photo Library/Jean Francois Pin. 166, Ron Watts/CORBIS. 168, Winston Fraser Photos. 169, Michael S. Yamashita/ CORBIS. 170/1, FPG. 172, Masterfile. 173, AA Photo Library/Jon Davison. 174, Chris Fairclough Worldwide Ltd. 175, AA Photo Library/Jean Francois Pin. 176, Royalty-Free/CORBIS. 178/9, Paul A. Souders/CORBIS. 180, AA Photo Library/Jon Davison. 181, AA Photo Library/Jon Davison. 183, AA Photo Library/Jon Davison. 184, Winston Fraser. 185, AA Photo Library. 186, Members of the Group of Seven, from left to right: F.H. Varley, A.Y. Jackson, Lawren Harris, Barker Fairley (not a Group member), Frank Johnston, Arthur Lismer, and J.E.H. MacDonald/Photo by Arthur Goss/Arts & Letters Club/ McMichael Canadian Art Collection Archives. 187, McMichael Canadian Art Collection, Gift of the Founders, Robert and Signe McMichael. In Memory of Norman and Evelyn McMichael. 1966.16.76. 188, James Nazz/CORBIS. 189, Hubert Stadler/CORBIS. 190/1, Toyohiro Yamada/Taxi/Getty Images. 192, Hulton Getty. 193, Masterfile. 194, Winston Fraser. 195, Winston Fraser. 196, Masterfile. 197, Winston Fraser. 198(t), Winston Fraser/National Archives of Canada. 198(b), Michael S. Lewis/ CORBIS. 199, Masterfile. 200/1, Robert Estall/CORBIS. 203, Winston Fraser. 204, Phil Jason/Getty Images. 205, Masterfile. 207, Masterfile. 208, Winston Fraser. 209, Winston Fraser. 210, Winston Fraser. 211, Momatiuk - Eastcott/CORBIS. 214/5, Winston Fraser. 216, Cosmo Condina/ Stone/Getty Images. 217, Winston Fraser. 219(t), Bryan &Cherry Alexander. 219(b), Masterfile. 220, Ann Ronan Picture Library/Heritage-Images. 221(t), AA Photo Library/Chris Coe. 221(b),

Bridgeman Art Library. 222, Masterfile. 223, Masterfile. 224, AA Photo Library/Chris Coe. 225(t), Richard Hamilton Smith/CORBIS. 225(b), Winston Fraser. 226, Winston Fraser. 227, Winston Fraser. 228, National Archives of Canada. 229(a), Mary Evans Picture Library. 229(b), Winston Fraser. 230, Todd Korol/Getty Images. 231, Jack Fields/CORBIS. 232, AA Photo Library/ Chris Coe. 233, Paul A. Souders/CORBIS. 234, Paul A. Souders/CORBIS. 235, Winston Fraser. 236, Walter Bibikow/The Image Bank/Getty Images. 237, Winston Fraser Photos. 238, Lindsay Hebberd/ CORBIS. 239, Gunter Marx Photogra-phy/CORBIS. 240, Winston Fraser. 241, Third Eye Images/CORBIS. 242, Graeme Wallace. 244/5, Masterfile. 246/7, Graeme Wallace. 249, Graeme Wallace. 250, Ric Ergenbright/CORBIS. 251, Lester Lefkowitz/CORBIS. 252, Graeme Wallace. 254, Graeme Wallace. 255, Philip & Karen Smith/Getty Images. 256, Graeme Wallace. 256/7, Maltings. 258/9, Raymond Gehman/CORBIS. 260, Chris Fairclough Worldwide Ltd. 261, Chris Coe. 262(t), AA Photo Library/Chris Coe. 262(b), National Archives of Canada. 263, Vince Streano/CORBIS. 264, Royalty-Free/CORBIS. 265, AA Photo Library/Chris Coe. 266/7, Royalty-Free/CORBIS. 268, Winston Fraser Photos. 269, AA Photo Library/Chris Coe. 270, Andrea Pistolesi/The Image Bank/Getty Images. 271, Chris Fairclough Worldwide Ltd. 275(t), Gunter Marx Photography/CORBIS. 275(b), Ann Ronan Picture Library/ Heritage-Images. 276/7, Joe McNally/ Getty Images. 278, AA Photo Library/ Michael Diggin. 280, Winston Fraser. 281, Richard T. Nowitz/CORBIS. 282/3, AA Photo Library/Chris Coe. 283, Gunter Marx Photography/CORBIS. 285, AA Photo Library/Harold Harris. 286, Cliff LeSergent/Alamy Ltd. 287, Gunter Marx Photography/CORBIS. 288, Richard T. Nowitz/CORBIS. 288/9, Gunter Marx Photography/CORBIS. 290, AA Photo Library. 293, Jan Butchofsky-Houser/CORBIS. 294, Richard T. Nowitz/CORBIS. 295, AA Photo Library/ Peter Timmer mons. 296/7, Gunter Marx Photography/CORBIS. 299, Wolfgang Kaehler/CORBIS. 303, Masterfile. 304, Edward Curtis/Stapleton Collection/ CORBIS. 305, Spectrum. 306, Winston Fraser. 307(t), AA Photo Library/Chris Coe. 307(b), Bridgeman Art Library. 309(b), Tracy Ferrero/Alamy Ltd. 311, Philip & Karen Smith/Getty Images. 312, Masterfile. 313, Alison Wright/Getty Images. 316/7, Bryan & Cherry Alexander. 318, Bryan & Cherry Alexander. 318/9, Bryan & Cherry Alexander. 321, Winston Fraser. 322(t), AA Photo Library/Chris Coe 322(b), Winston Fraser. 323, Winston Fraser. 324, AA Photo Library/Chris Coe. 325(t), J Allan Cash. 325(b), Gary Cook/Alamy

The world's largest nonprofit scientific and educational organization, the National Geographic Society was founded in 1888 "for the increase and diffusion of geographic knowledge." Since then it has supported scientific exploration and spread information to its more than nine million members worldwide.

The National Geographic Society educates and inspires millions every day through magazines, books, television programs, videos, maps and atlases, research grants, the National Geography Bee, teacher workshops, and innovative classroom materials.

The Society is supported through membership dues, charitable gifts, and income from the sale of its educational products. Members receive NATIONAL GEOGRAPHIC magazine—the Society's official journal—discounts on Society products, and other benefits.

For more information about the National Geographic Society, its educational programs, publications, or how to support its work, call 1-800-NGS-LINE (647-5463), or write to: National Geographic Society, 1145 17th Street, N.W., Washington, D.C. 20036 U.S.A. Visit the Society's Web site at www.nationalgeographic.com.

For information about special discounts for bulk purchases, please contact National Geographic Books Special Sales: ngspecsales@ngs.org

Printed and bound by Cayfosa Quebecor, Barcelona, Spain
Color separations by Quad Graphics, Alexandria, Virginia

Published by the National Geographic Society

John M. Fahey, Jr., *President and Chief Executive Officer*
Gilbert M. Grosvenor, *Chairman of the Board*
Nina D. Hoffman, *Executive Vice President*
  President, Book Publishing Group
Kevin Mulroy, *Senior Vice President and Publisher*
Marianne Koszorus, *Design Director*
Elizabeth L. Newhouse, *Director of Travel Publishing*
Barbara A. Noe, *Senior Editor and Series Editor*
Cinda Rose, *Art Director*
Carl Mehler, *Director of Maps*
Richard S. Wain, *Production Manager*
Caroline Hickey, *Project Manager 2006 edition*
Fiona Malins, *Writer 2006 edition*
Jane Sunderland, *Editor 2006 edition*
Ruth Thompson, *Designer 2006 edition*
Jennifer Davis, Steven D. Gardner, Teresa Neva Tate, and
  Mapping Specialists, *Contributors to 2006 edition*
R. Gary Colbert, *Production Director*
Rebecca Hinds, *Managing Editor*

Edited and designed by AA Publishing (a trading name of Automobile Association Developments Limited, whose registered office is Norfolk House, Priestley Road, Basingstoke, Hampshire, England RG24 9NY. Registered number: 1878835).

Betty Sheldrick, *Project Manager*
David Austin, *Senior Art Editor*
Ian Morgan, *Editor*
Tom Reynolds, Keith Russell, *Designers*
Simon Mumford, *Cartographic Editor*
Nicky Barker-Dix, Helen Beever, *Cartographers*
Richard Firth, *Production Director*
Picture Research by Letty Savonitto at I.S.I.
Drive maps drawn by Chris Orr Associates, Southampton, England
Cutaway illustrations drawn by Maltings Partnership, Derby, England

Second Edition 2006
ISBN-10: 0-7922-6201-8; ISBN-13: 978-0-7922-6201-5
First Edition ISBN 0-7922-7427-X

Library of Congress Cataloging-in-Publication Data (1st Ed.)
    National Geographic traveler. Canada.
        p. cm.
        Includes index.
        ISBN 0-7922-7427-X (alk. paper)
        1. Canada—Tours.   2. Canada—Description and travel.
    I. National Geographic Society (U.S.)   II. Title: Canada.
    F1009.N38 1999
    917.104'648—dc21   99-10549
                                                   CIP

NATIONAL GEOGRAPHIC
TRAVELER

A Century of Travel Expertise in Every Guide

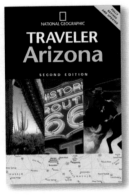

- **Alaska** 0-7922-5371-X
- **Amsterdam** ISBN: 0-7922-7900-X
- **Arizona** (2nd Edition) ISBN: 0-7922-3888-5
- **Australia** (2nd Edition) ISBN: 0-7922-3893-1
- **Barcelona** (2nd Edition) ISBN: 0-7922-5365-5
- **Berlin** ISBN: 0-7922-6212-3
- **Boston & environs** ISBN: 0-7922-7926-3
- **California** (2nd Edition) ISBN: 0-7922-3885-0
- **Canada** (2nd Edition) ISBN: 0-7922-6201-8
- **The Caribbean** ISBN: 0-7922-7434-2
- **China** ISBN: 0-7922-7921-2
- **Costa Rica** (2nd Edition) ISBN: 0-7922-5368-X
- **Cuba** ISBN: 0-7922-6931-4
- **Egypt** ISBN: 0-7922-7896-8
- **Florence & Tuscany**
  (2nd Ed.) ISBN: 0-7922-5318-3
- **Florida** ISBN: 0-7922-7432-6
- **France** ISBN: 0-7922-7426-1
- **Germany** ISBN: 0-7922-4146-0
- **Great Britain** ISBN: 0-7922-7425-3
- **Greece** ISBN: 0-7922-7923-9
- **Hawaii** (2nd Edition) ISBN: 0-7922-5568-2
- **Hong Kong**
  (2nd Edition) ISBN: 0-7922-5369-8
- **India** ISBN: 0-7922-7898-4
- **Ireland** ISBN: 0-7922-4145-20
- **Italy** (2nd Edition) ISBN: 0-7922-3889-3

- **Japan** (2nd Edition) ISBN: 0-7922-3894-X
- **London** ISBN: 0-7922-7428-8
- **Los Angeles** ISBN: 0-7922-7947-6
- **Madrid** 0-7922-5372-8
- **Mexico** (2nd Edition) ISBN: 0-7922-5319-1
- **Miami & the Keys**
  (2nd Edition) ISBN: 0-7922-3886-9
- **New York** (2nd Edition) ISBN: 0-7922-5370-1
- **Paris** ISBN: 0-7922-7429-6
- **Piedmont & Northwest Italy**
  ISBN: 0-7922-4198-3
- **Portugal** ISBN: 0-7922-4199-1
- **Prague & the Czech Republic**
  ISBN: 0-7922-4147-9
- **Provence & the Côte d'Azur**
  ISBN: 0-7922-9542-0
- **Rome** (2nd Edition) ISBN: 0-7922-5572-0
- **San Diego** (2nd Edition) ISBN: 0-7922-6202-6
- **San Francisco** (2nd Edition) ISBN: 0-7922-3883-4
- **Sicily** ISBN: 0-7922-9541-2
- **Spain** (2nd Edition) ISBN: 0-7922-3884-2
- **Sydney** ISBN: 0-7922-7435-0
- **Taiwan** ISBN: 0-7922-6555-6
- **Thailand** (2nd Edition) ISBN: 0-7922-5321-3
- **Venice** ISBN: 0-7922-7917-4
- **Vietnam** ISBN: 0-7922-6203-4
- **Washington, D.C.**
  (2nd Edition) ISBN: 0-7922-3887-7

AVAILABLE WHEREVER BOOKS ARE SOLD